PENGUIN BOOKS

MEDIA LAW

'T... ... ...
wh... ... ... who has power to impose restrictions on free
spe... and how best to evade them . . . A powerful indictment of
those legislators and judges who have inflicted on us laws of contempt,
obscenity, blasphemy, confidence and libel which inhibit the free
flow of information.'   David Pannick in the *Listener*

'An excellent book. It is written in a lively and lucid manner, and the
authors frequently draw on unreported cases and other incidents to
illustrate their points . . . The scope of the book is enormous . . . The
student and the general practitioner, as well as the media professionals
. . . will find it an invaluable guide.'   Eric Barendt, Goodman
Professor of Media Law, University of London

'Gives an excellent and concise explanation of the new legislation . . .
[and] covers other recent developments: the ban on the broadcasting
of the views of IRA members; the loathsome attempt of *Sunday
Sport* to "interview" a semi-comatose Gorden Kaye on his hospital
bed; the Press Council fiascos . . . These, and the other matters in the
book, are dealt with with admirable clarity. But what chiefly
distinguishes this work is the determination of the authors to uphold
freedom of speech, thought and deed at a time when they seem most
under attack.'   Daphne Romney in *International Media Law*

'If only more law books could combine legal authority with the
deftness of touch and literary qualities achieved by *Media Law* . . . a
unique work. It should be read by media lawyers as well as lawyers
with an interest in the media, journalists and publishers, and, above
all, by those who doubt the extent of media regulation in the
UK.'   David Newell, Head of Government and Legal Affairs,
Newspaper Society, in the *New Law Journal*

About the authors

Geoffrey Robertson QC has appeared as counsel in many landmark cases concerning media law and has conducted human rights litigation in Commonwealth courts and in the European Court of Human Rights. A Rhodes scholar, he is the author of *Reluctant Judas* (1976), *Obscenity* (1979), *People Against the Press* (1983), *Does Dracula Have Aids?* (1986), *Freedom, the Individual and the Law* (Penguin 1989) and *Geoffrey Robertson's Hypotheticals* (1986 and 1991). He has made many television programmes in Britain and Australasia and his television play *The Trials of Oz* received a BAFTA 'Best Single Drama' nomination in 1992. He has conducted missions for Amnesty International to South Africa and Vietnam, and in 1990 served as counsel to the Royal Commission investigating gun-running to the Colombian drug cartels. Geoffrey Robertson lives in London, where he is head of Doughty Street Chambers and a member of the executive councils of 'Charter 88', 'Justice', the Freedom of Information Campaign and the Institute of Contemporary Arts.

Andrew Nicol was educated at Cambridge and was awarded a Harkness Fellowship for study at Harvard and Berkeley. He worked briefly for the State of California and then for a firm of solicitors in Sydney, Australia, after which he taught law at the London School of Economics for ten years. At the same time he qualified for and began practice at the Bar, and has been practising full-time for the last five years. Specializations include media law and immigration. He is co-author of *Subjects, Citizens, Aliens and Others* (1990), a book on the history of UK immigration and nationality law and policy. He was Secretary to the Hodgson Committee, whose report *Profits of Crime* was published by Sage. He has two children and lives in London.

MEDIA LAW

Second edition (revised)

Geoffrey Robertson BA, LLB, BCL,
one of Her Majesty's Counsel and
Andrew G. L. Nicol BA, LLB, LLM,
of the Middle Temple, Barrister

Penguin Books

PENGUIN BOOKS

Published by the Penguin Group
Penguin Books Ltd, 27 Wrights Lane, London W8 5TZ, England
Penguin Books USA Inc., 375 Hudson Street, New York, New York 10014, USA
Penguin Books Australia Ltd, Ringwood, Victoria, Australia
Penguin Books Canada Ltd, 10 Alcorn Avenue, Toronto, Ontario, Canada M4V 3B2
Penguin Books (NZ) Ltd, 182–190 Wairau Road, Auckland 10, New Zealand

Penguin Books Ltd, Registered Offices: Harmondsworth, Middlesex, England

First published by Longman Group UK Ltd 1984
Second edition 1990
Third edition Penguin Books 1992
    3 5 7 9 10 8 6 4

Printed in England by Clays Ltd, St Ives plc

Contents

Preface		xv
Table of Cases		xxi
Table of Statutes		xlix
Table of Statutory Instruments		lxii

1 Freedom to Communicate — 1

The European Convention on Human Rights — 3
Article 10: Freedom of expression — 4
The importance of Article 10 — 6

Trial by Jury — 10
Media offences with a right to trial by jury — 12

The Open-justice Principle — 14
Journalists' special rights — 17

The Rule against Prior Restraint — 19
Contemporary position in the United Kingdom — 20

Freedom from Government Interference — 25
Broadcastings bans — 26
Patronage — 28
The ITC — 29
Theatre an film censorship — 32

Prosecution Policy and the Public Interest — 33

Conclusion — 35

2 Defamation — 38

Press Advantages — 39
Absence of legal aid — 39
False statements not necessarily libellous — 40
Truth: an absolute defence — 40

Press Disadvantages — 41
Burden of proof on media defendant — 41
Technicality — 41
Uncertainty — 42
Costs and damages — 43

Defamation Defined — 46
The test — 46
Malicious falsehood and conspiracy to injure — 46
Importance of context — 48
The 'ordinary reader' test — 49
Defamatory innuendo — 53

Libel and Slander Distinguished 53
Who Can Sue? 54
  The dead 55
  Companies 56
  Local authorities 56
  Trade unions 56
  Groups 57
  Identification 57
  Those unintentionally defamed 58
Who Can Be Sued? 61
  Avoiding responsibility 61
  Foreign publications 65
  Innocent dissemination 66
The Rule against Prior Restraint 67
Defences Generally 70
  Burden of proof 70
  The meaning of 'malice' 71
Truth as a Defence 73
  The defence of justification 73
  Practical problems 76
  Reporting old criminal convictions 77
'Opinion' as a Defence 79
  Distinction between fact and opinion 80
  The opinion must have some factual basis 81
  Absence of malice 83
  Public interest 85
  Whose comment is it? 85
Absolute Privilege 86
Qualified Privilege 86
  A general privilege for investigative journalists? 87
  Reply to an attack 90
  Parliamentary and court reports 91
  Other public occasions 91
Other Defences 94
  Consent 94
  Apology 94
Limitation 95
Damages 96
  Trial by jury 98
Criminal Libel 99
Conclusion 102

3 Obscenity, Blasphemy and Race Hatred 105
Obscenity 106
  History 106

The test of obscenity 110
Prohibited acts 119
The public-good defence 120
Expert evidence 123
Prosecution practice 125
Drugs 126
Violence 128
Horror publications 129
Child involvement 129
Procedures and penalties 133
The cinema and film censorship 135
Television and radio 137

Theatre Censorship 138
Plays defined 139
Public-good defence 141
Limits on police powers 141
Liability for prosecution 142
Evidence 143
The Romans in Britain *prosecution* 144

Indecency Laws 147
The test of indecency 148
Indecency offences 150

The Common Law 155
Corrupting public morals 155
Outraging public decency 157
Exposure to the common law 158

Blasphemy 160

Reform of Obscenity and Indecency Laws 165

Race Hatred 167

4 Confidence and Privacy 172

The Obligation of Confidence 174
Contractual relationships 176
Domestic relationships 179
Government confidences 181
Documents subject to discovery 183

Public-interest Defence 183

Public Domain 188

Procedure 190
Who can sue? 190
Interim injunctions 190

Confidential Ideas 194

Protection of Sources 196
The police and other investigators 196
Plaintiffs in libel actions 197

The courts	198
Police powers of search and seizure	205
Private Photographs	208
Data Protection Obligations	209
Privacy	210

5   Copyright   213

Existence of Copyright	216
Original literary, dramatic or musical works	216
News stories and programme formats	219
Published editions	221
Artistic works	222
Sound recordings	223
Films	223
Broadcasts and cable programmes	224
Territorial connection	225
Period of copyright	225

Infringement of Copyright	226
Copying	226
Other types of infringement	233

Defences	235
Fair dealing	235
Public interest	239
Immorality	241
Licences	242
Copyright Tribunal	245
Other defences	247

Moral Rights	250
Right to be identified as author or director	251
Derogatory treatment	251

Rights in Performances	253

Remedies	255
Injunctions	255
Private search warrants and compulsory disclosure	255
Damages	257
Account of profits	258
Delivery up of copies	258
Criminal offences	258

6   Contempt of Court   261

Types of Contempt	264

Strict-liability contempt	265
Which court?	268
Contempt risks	271
The sub judice *period*	278

Defences	281
Gagging writs	284
Deliberate Contempt	285
Intentionally prejudicing potential criminal proceedings and civil jury trials	286
Frustrating court orders against others	293
Scandalizing the Court	296
Publishing Details of Jury Deliberations	299
Procedure and Punishment	301
7 Reporting the Courts	305
Public Access to the Courts	309
Exclusion in the public interest	311
Committal proceedings	315
Voluntary bills of indictment	315
Official secrets	316
Private secrets	317
Family cases	317
Possession actions	319
Appeals	320
'In chambers' hearings	320
Disorder in court	323
Reporting Restrictions	323
Remands and committal hearings	324
Serious fraud	326
Juveniles	327
Family cases	329
Wards of court	332
Rape	336
Attorney-General's reference to the Court of Appeal	338
Indecent evidence	338
Secrecy Orders	338
Section 11 orders	338
Postponement orders	341
Challenging postponement and partial secrecy orders	345
Gathering Information	350
Tape-recording	351
Transcripts and skeleton arguments	352
Court records	353
Writs, pleadings and affidavits	354
Discovered documents	355
Documents in criminal proceedings	358
Photographs and sketches	359
Television and the courts	360
Protection from Libel	362
Absolute privilege	363
Qualified privilege	365

8 Reporting Lesser Courts and Tribunals 367

Inquests 368
Courts Martial 372
Church Courts 373
Industrial Tribunals 374
Immigration Appeals 374
Mental Health Review Tribunals 375
Licensing 377
Planning Inquiries 377
Disciplinary Hearings 378
Public Inquiries 379
Other Inquiries 380
Televising Tribunals 381
Contempt 382
Libel 387
    Absolute privilege 387
    Qualified privilege 387

9 Reporting Parliament and Elections 390

The Privileges for Reporting Parliamentary Debates 393

Contempt of Parliament 395

MPs' Conflicts of Interest 401

Election Reporting 403
    Injunctions 403
    Advertisements 404
    Broadcasting coverage of the campaign 405
    Access to meetings 410
    Access to register and candidates' returns 410

10 Reporting Whitehall 412

The Official Secrets Act 414
    Offences by 'insiders' 418
    Offences by 'outsiders' 423
    1911 Act, section 1: 'penalties for spying' 428
    Police powers and compulsory questioning 430

Specific Secrecy Legislation 432
    Nuclear secrets 432
    Other statutes 433
    Radio eavesdropping and telephone tapping 434

D-notices 435

Ministerial and Civil Servant Memoirs 438
    Ministers 438
    Civil servants 439

Public Records   440
European Communities   442
Reporting Northern Ireland   443
  Information of use to terrorists   443
  Reporting demonstrations   444
  Prevention of terrorism   444
  Broadcasting censorship   445

Other Political Offences   446
  Treason   446
  Sedition   447
  Incitement to mutiny and disaffection   448
  Reform   450

War Reporting   450
  Protection of war correspondents   450
  Military censorship   452

Negotiating Civil Service Disclosure   456
  The Croham Directive   457
  ESTACODE   458

Using the US Freedom of Information Acts   459

11   Reporting Local Government   461

Rights of Admission   462
  Council meetings   462
  Committees, subcommittees and caucuses   463
  'Secrecy motions' and other limitations on access 464
  Agendas   467
  Reporting   468

Inspection of Documents   469
  Accounts and supporting documents   469
  Audit   471
  Minutes, reports and rating records   471
  Councillors' conflicts of interest   472
  Rates and poll tax   473
  Planning   474
  Local ombudsmen   475
  Local parliamentary bills   475
  Pollution control   476
  Housing   477
  Education and social services   477
  Annual reports   478
  Land ownership   479
  Leaks   480

Libel   480

Local Authority Sponsored Publications   482
  Clause 28   483

12   Reporting Business   485

Companies   487
   A beginner's lexicon   487
   Ownership and control   489
   Major shareholdings by companies   492
   Directors' dealings   492
   Economic performance   494
   Inspecting public documents   498
   Meetings   500
   Take-overs   501

Press Monopolies   502

Broadcasting and Press Conglomerates   506

DTI Investigations   507

Other Businesses   509
   Partnerships   509
   Co-ops and housing associations   509
   Building societies   510
   Nationalized industries   510

Special Privileges   511
   Charities   511
   Investment business   513
   Consumer credit   515
   Restrictive practices   515
   Other registers   516

Insolvency   516

13   Public Complaints   519

The Press Complaints Commission   521
   History of the Press Council   521
   The Calcutt Report   524
   Structure of the Commission   527
   The complaints procedure   528
   The Code of Practice   529
   Will the PCC work?   542

The Broadcasting Complaints Commission   545
   Structure   546
   Jurisdiction   547
   Unjust or unfair treatment   548
   Unwarranted invasion of privacy   553
   Who may complain?   554
   Procedure   556
   Publication of adjudications   558

The Advertising Standards Authority   559

ICSTIS   561

NUJ Code of Conduct   563

14 Censorship of Films and Video   564

Film Censorship   566
  History   566
  Local council licensing   569

The Advent of Video   572
  The Video Recordings Act 1984   575

The British Board of Film Classification   583
  What will be censored?   584
  The Video Appeals Committee   590
  In the realm of the censors   592

15 Broadcasting Law   594

Programme Standards   599
  The law of obscenity   599
  The statutory duties   600
  The Broadcasting Standards Council   606

The Codes of Practice   612
  The watershed hour   612
  'Offending against good taste or decency'   613
  'Likely to encourage crime or lead to disorder'   615
  Violence   618
  Drink and drugs   619
  Privacy   619
  'Due accuracy and impartiality'   620

Enforcing the Codes   624
  The BBC   625
  Government controls   629
  ITC licences   632
  Editorializing   638
  Religion   638
  Advertising   639
  The European Convention on Transfrontier Television   641
  The Radio Authority   644
  Cable television   646
  Satellite broadcasting   648

Select Bibliography   653
Index   657

Preface

This is a book about the legal rights of journalists, broadcasters, authors, editors, dramatists, film makers, photographers, producers and others who publish news or views through the communications media. The introductory chapter examines the procedural pillars of freedom of expression in Britain: the generalized rights that may be claimed by all who venture into print or picture. The next section states the basic laws that apply to all publishing enterprises – libel, contempt, confidence, copyright and obscenity. There follows an examination of the laws applicable to particular areas of reporting: the ground rules that open or close the doors of the courts, Whitehall, Parliament, local government and commercial enterprises. Finally, there is an account of the practices and procedures of regulatory bodies – the British Broadcasting Corporation (BBC) and Independent Television Commission (ITC), the British Board of Film Censors (BBFC), the Press Complaints Commission, the Broadcasting Complaints Commission (BCC) and the Broadcasting Standards Council (BSC).

Journalism is not just a profession. It is the exercise by occupation of the right to free expression available to every citizen. That right, being available to all, cannot in principle be withdrawn from a few by any system of licensing or professional registration, but it can be restricted and confined by rules of law that apply to all who take or are afforded the opportunity to exercise the right by speaking or writing in public. There are, as the length of this book attests, a myriad of rules that impinge upon the right to present facts and opinions and pictures to the public: we have made an attempt to state and to analyse them as a comprehensive and inter-related body of doctrine.

The first edition of this work was published in 1984. The very fact that the phrase 'media law' was available to us for a title was evidence of the failure of academics and practitioners to perceive the disparate laws that impinge upon the right to publish as being worthy of coherent study. There were a few elementary primers for trainee journalists, and a few weighty tomes for practitioners on defamation and contempt and copyright, but no serious treatment of the subject in its entirety. The wood – or at least the overgrown jungle – that comprises media law could not be seen for the trees of tort and property and criminal law. It took only a few years for our title phrase to enter fashionable legal parlance, from the glossy brochures of barristers' chambers and upmarket solicitors to the latest Chair at London University. Media law is lucrative (publishers and their opponents rarely qualify for legal aid), high in profile (the media, not unnaturally, regards itself as highly newsworthy) and in a state of exponential growth. More significantly, the English courts are beginning to pay attention to the 'freedom of expression' guarantee of the European Convention on Human Rights, and there is hope that it will emerge (whether or not the Convention is incorporated in British law) as the bedrock for media law, a common standard by which all restraints on publication may be judged.

Most European countries have a statutory 'press law' which comprehensively enshrines the privileges and responsibilities of news enterprises. In Britain the tradition that journalists should have no greater rights, and no heavier duties, than those that attach to any other citizen has tended to obscure the development by Parliament and the courts of special rules for circumscribing the freedom of the press. The principles that can be derived from these disparate rules lack consistency and coherence because they have been imposed haphazardly, by different bodies and from different perspectives. Laws widely drafted or declared to catch criminals and commercial pirates have been pressed into service to stop public interest reporting, and regulatory enterprises have been established with broad powers to censor films and broadcasting without thought for the safeguards necessary to secure freedom of speech.

At first blush, the array of media laws and regulations appears formidable. There are criminal laws – of contempt, official secrecy, sedition, obscenity and the like – which can be enforced by fines and even by prison sentences. There are civil laws, relating to libel and breaches of copyright and confidence, which can be used to injunct public-interest stories and programmes before publication, or to extract heavy damages afterwards. And there are laws that permit regulatory bodies, like the BSC and the BBFC, to censor films and television programmes and video-cassettes. These laws have emanated from different sources at different times: statutory laws, imposed by Parliament and interpreted by the courts; common law, built up by judges with reference to precedents from centuries of case law; decisions of regulatory bodies based on broad duties to ensure 'good taste' and 'due impartiality' and informal 'arrangements' like the lobby and the D-notice systems, which exert secret pressures and persuasions.

Newspapers and broadcasting organizations employ teams of lawyers to advise on stories that might otherwise court reprisals. Press lawyers are inevitably more repressive than press laws, because they will generally prefer to err on the safe side, where they cannot be proved wrong. The lawyer's advice provides a broad penumbra of restraint, confining the investigative journalist not merely to the letter of the law but to an outer rim bounded by the mere possibility of legal action. Since most laws pertaining to the media are of vague or elastic definition, the working test of 'potential actionability' for critical comment is exceptionally wide. Journalists are often placed on the defensive: they are obliged to ask, not 'what *should* I write' but 'what *can* I write that will get past the lawyers?' The lawyers' caution is understandable if they are instructed by proprietors who want to avoid the high legal costs of defending, even successfully, actions brought by the government or by wealthy private plaintiffs.

For all these obstacles, however, media law is not as oppressive as it may at first appear. When there is a genuine public interest in publishing, legal snares can usually be side-stepped. We have been anxious, in writing this book, to emphasize ways in which legal problems can be avoided in practice. Many laws that are restrictive in their letter are enforced in a liberal spirit, or simply not enforced at all. Editors and broadcasters will be familiar with the solicitor's 'letter before action', threatening proceedings in the event that investigations unflattering to clients are published. Often such letters are bluff, and it is important to know how and when that legal bluff can be called. In addition, it must be remembered that the law can give as well as take away: there are many little-known publicity provisions that can be exploited by inquisitive reporters. Although the law creates duties, it also provides rights that assist those who know what to look for and where to find it. In the chapters on reporting significant areas of power and influence – the courts, Whitehall, local government, Parliament and business – we have endeavoured to highlight sections of the law that help, rather than hinder, the investigative journalist. Our hope is that journalists will regard the book not merely as a manual for self-defence, but as a guide to a complicated armoury of legal weapons for battering down doors unnecessarily shut in their faces.

It is, none the less, regrettable that so much of media law should impinge upon public-interest reporting, and so little of it work to eradicate discreditable press practices. The blind Goddess of Justice seems to raise her sword against investigative journalism while her other hand fondles the Sunday muckraker. Although the scales of justice balance badly, they can always be tipped, and we have indicated at appropriate points in the text the reforms that would permit the media to fulfil its responsibility to the public. Freedom-of-information legislation, for example, would give statutory support to the principle that, in a democracy, the public have a right to know that basis upon which decisions affecting the common good are made. The dangers of suppressing important stories on the pretext of confidence or copyright could be minimized by a public-interest exception to the rules that regulate the grant of injunctive relief. Where actions or reputations are mishandled by the media, individuals should have equal access to a speedy system of redress for misstatements of fact, without the delays, uncertainties and expense of libel proceedings or inadequate Press Complaints Commission adjudications. The right to enjoy a private life free from media harassment and embarrassment might also receive some effective guarantee. Developments of this sort would promote accurate and responsible journalism, while at the same time opening up new areas of public importance for investigation and criticism. The worst aspects of defamation, breach of confidence and official secrecy should die unlamented, replaced by a proper concern for public disclosure and protection of human rights.

The prospects for reform of media law are rather better than they were when one Home Secretary, taxed by an MP with his failure to implement an election promise to introduce a Freedom of Information Act, could sneer 'only two or three of your constituents would be interested'. The list of 'cover-ups' by officials in various government establishments, ranging from the Stalker and Wallace affairs to food contamination and environmental hazards, have made the public more aware of the need to legislate for a 'right to know'. Massive libel awards to unprepossessing plaintiffs contrast too starkly with the inability of the average citizen to obtain a right of reply or to be protected against media intrusions into private joys and griefs. The futility of sending journalists to prison for refusing to reveal their sources of news about the activities of private companies was emphasized in the course of proceedings against trainee reporter Bill Goodwin, while the *Spycatcher* saga demonstrated how laws that require the suppression in Britain of a book available in other countries will be treated with derision. There have been a good many recent developments in case law, and 'the balance of public interest' is emerging as the favoured basis for judges to decide whether a story should be liable to legal suppression. Supporters of this test would do well to observe how haphazardly and unpredictably it has worked in those areas of media law where it is currently applied: it is a phrase that inevitably cloaks subjective value-judgements by judges who generally dislike the media. Unless it is controlled by a presumption in favour of freedom of expression, of the sort applied by Article 10 of the European Convention (by which any restrictions on publication must be reasonable, clear and justified by a pressing social need), judges will continue to find that rights of property and confidentiality outweigh the public right to know.

There are other forces working to reshape media law in the United Kingdom. The revolution in information technology has produced international newspapers, instantaneous satellite communication and contemporaneous book publishing. Commercial freedom in Europe requires some degree of uniformity, and the European Parliament and courts are beginning to issue directions and rulings that affect media law in Britain. Decisions of the European Court of Human Rights have required a liberalization in the English law of contempt of court, and a statutory right of appeal for journalists against suppression orders imposed at criminal trials, while an EEC directive on broadcasting will provide a basic law for television advertising across the continent. It is likely that the human rights dimension of media law will become increasingly important, and that more international attention will focus on the various ways in which the existing law fails to comply with the principle expressed in Article 19 of the Universal Declaration of Human Rights: 'Everyone has the right to freedom of opinion and expression; this right includes the freedom to hold opinions without interference and to seek, receive and impart information and ideas through any media and regardless of frontiers.'

The views expressed in this book have been formed in the course of defending individual writers, editors and artists, and it is to them that we owe the greatest debt of thanks. We are grateful to Barbara Horn, Jon Riley and Helen Bramford for their work on the manuscript and to David Bowron for preparing the index and list of cases. Kathy Lette and Camilla Palmer deserve the first of a thousand footnotes.

Geoffrey Robertson, QC
Andrew Nicol

Doughty Street Chambers
March 1992

Table of Cases

A & M Records *v* Audio Magnetics (UK) [1979] FSR
  1, DC   234
Abrahams *v* Cavey [1968] 1 QB 479; [1967] 3 WLR
  1229; 111 SJ 654; [1967] 3 All ER 179   147
Adam *v* Ward [1917] AC 309   90
Agricultural Industries, *Re* [1952] WN 209; [1952] 1
  All ER 1188   320
Albutt *v* General Council of Medical Education and
  Registration (1889) 23 QBD 400   388
Allen *v* Jambo Holdings [1980] 1 WLR 1252; (1979)
  124 SJ 742; [1980] 2 All ER 502, CA   192
Ambard *v* A-G for Trinidad and Tobago [1936] AC
  322   296
American Cyanamid Co *v* Ethicon [1975] AC 396;
  [1975] 2 WLR 316; 119 SJ 136; [1975] 1 All ER
  504; [1975] FSR 101; [1975] RPC 513, HL;
  reversing [1974] FSR 312, CA   192–4
Antocks Lairn *v* Bloohn [1971] FSR 490; [1972] RPC
  219   244
Anton Piller KG *v* Manufacturing Processes [1976]
  Ch 55   256
Application under s 9 of Police and Criminal Evidence
  Act 1984, *Re* (1988), *The Independent*, 27 May   323
Argent *v* Donigan (1892) 8 TLR 432   54
Argyll (Duchess of) *v* Argyll (Duke of) [1967] Ch
  302; [1965] 2 WLR 790; [1965] 1 All ER 611   180, 331
Arkell *v* Pressdram   104
Arrowsmith *v* United Kingdom; *see* R *v* Arrowsmith
Ashburton (Lord) *v* Pape [1913] 2 Ch 469   175
Associated Newspapers, *ex p* (Practice Note) [1959] 1
  WLR 993; 103 SJ 797; [1959] 3 All ER 878   355
Associated Newspapers *v* Insert Media [1990] 2 All
  ER 803   216
Associated Newspapers Group *v* News Group
  Newspapers [1986] RPC 515   236, 238
A-G *v* Able [1984] QB 795; 127 SJ 731; [1984] 1 All
  ER 277; (1984) 78 Cr App R 197; [1984] Crim LR 35   14, 354
A-G *v* Barker [1990] 3 All ER 257   24, 177

A-G v Brandon Book Publishers [1989] FSR 37   189
A-G v British Broadcasting Corporation [1981] AC
    303; 3 WLR 109; (1980) 124 SJ 444; (1980) 3 All
    ER 161; 78 LGR 529, HL   7, 191, 383
A-G v British Broadcasting Corporation (1987) *The
    Times*, 18 December; *The Independent*, 18 December   35, 192
A-G v Cape (Jonathan); A-G v Times Newspapers
    [1976] QB 752; [1975] 3 WLR 606; 119 SJ 696;
    [1975] 3 All ER 484   181, 187, 438
A-G v Channel Four Television Co (1987) *The
    Independent*, 3 December; (1987) *The Times*, 18
    December, CA   270
A-G v Clough [1963] 1 QB 773; [1963] 2 WLR 343;
    107 SJ 96; [1963] 1 All ER 420   386, 432
A-G v English [1983] AC 116; [1982] 3 WLR 278;
    (1982) 126 SJ 511; [1982] 2 All ER 903; [1982]
    Crim LR 743; (1982) 79 LS Gaz 1175; (1982) 75 Cr
    App R 302, HL   266, 281, 282
A-G v Guardian Newspapers [1987] 1 WLR 1248;
    (1987) 131 SJ 1122; [1987] 3 All ER 316; (1987) 84
    LS Gaz 2689; (1987) 137 New LJ 785, HL   22, 192
A-G v Guardian Newspapers (No 2) [1988] 3 WLR
    776; (1988) 132 SJ 1496; [1988] 3 All ER 545;
    (1988) 138 New LJ 296; LS Gaz November 16, 45,
    HL   7, 177, 180, 182, 185, 186, 188, 241, 244, 307
A-G v Guardian Newspapers (1992) *The Times*,
    28 February   267, 346
A-G v Hislop [1991] 1 All ER 911   274, 291
A-G v Leveller Magazine [1979] AC 440; [1979] 2
    WLR 247; (1979) 123 SJ 129; [1979] (1979) 68 Cr
    App R 343; [1979] Crim LR 247, HL; *reversing*
    [1978] 3 All ER 731   312, 340
A-G v Lundin (1982) 75 Cr App R 90; [1982] Crim
    LR 296, DC   199, 302
A-G v Mulholland; A-G v Foster [1963] 2 QB 477;
    [1963] 2 WLR 658; 107 SJ 154; [1963] 1 All ER
    767   203, 386, 432
A-G v New Statesman and Nation Publishing Co
    [1981] QB 1   300
A-G v News Group Newspapers (1982) 4 Cr App
    R(s) 182, DC   280
A-G v News Group Newspapers [1987] QB 1; [1986]
    3 WLR 365; (1986) 130 SJ 408; [1986] 2 All ER
    833; (1986) 83 LS Gaz 1719; (1986) 135 New LJ
    584, CA   263, 284
A-G v News Group Newspapers [1988] 3 WLR 163;

132 SJ 934; [1988] 2 All ER 906; (1988) New LJ
55, DC   287, 291
A-G *v* Newspaper Publishing [1988] Ch 33; [1987] 3
WLR 942; (1987) 131 SJ 1454; [1987] 3 All ER
276; (1987) 137 New LJ 686, CA   23, 291
A-G *v* Newspaper Publishing (1989) *The Independent*,
9 May   291
A-G *v* Observer, The; A-G *v* Guardian Newspapers,
Re An Application by Derbyshire County Council
[1988] 1 All ER 385   295
A-G *v* Sport Newspapers [1992] 1 All ER 503   287–8
A-G *v* Times Newspapers [1974] AC 273; [1973] 3
WLR 298; 117 SJ 617; [1973] 3 All ER 54, HL;
reversing [1973] 1 All ER 815, CA   264, 290, 393
A-G *v* Times Newspapers (1983) *The Times*,
12 February   267, 270
A-G *v* Times Newspapers [1991] 2 All ER 398   23, 194, 293
A-G *v* Turnaround Distribution [1989] FSR 169,
QBD   189
A-G *v* TVS Television; A-G *v* Southey (HW) & Sons
(1989) *The Independent*, 7 July   282
A-G's Reference No 2 of 1975 [1976] 1 WLR 710;
120 SJ 315; [1976] 2 All ER 753; (1976) 62 Cr App
R 255; [1976] Crim LR 444, CA   114, 119, 569
A-G's Reference No 3 of 1977 [1978] 1 WLR 1123;
(1978) 122 SJ 641; [1978] 3 All ER 1166; (1978) 67
Cr App R 393, CA   121
A-G's Reference No 5 of 1980 1 WLR 88; (1980) 124
SJ 827; [1980] 3 All ER 816; (1980) 72 Cr App R
71; [1981] Crim LR 45, CA   119, 136, 572
A-G (NSW) *v* John Fairfax & Sons (1986) 6 NSWLR
695   394
A-G (*ex rel* McWhirter) *v* Independent Broadcasting
Authority [1973] 1 QB 629; [1973] 2 WLR 344;
[1973] 1 All ER 689; *sub nom* McWhirter *v* IBA,
117 SJ 126   30, 148–9, 603
A-G for England and Wales *v* Heinemann Publishers
Pty (1988) 78 ALR 449 HCA   189 .
Australian Broadcasting Commission *v* Comalco Ltd
(1968) 68 ALR 259   89
Australian Broadcasting Tribunal *v* Bond (Alan)
(1990) 64 ALJR 462   635–6
Autronic *v* Switzerland (1990) European Court of
Human Rights, 22 May, Series A No 178   596–7

B (P) *v* A-G [1965] 3 All ER 253   318

Badry v DPP of Mauritius [1983] 2 WLR 161; (1982)
126 SJ 819; [1982] 3 All ER 973   296, 298
Bahama Islands, *In re* Special Reference from [1893]
AC 138   198, 296
Balaghat Gold Mining Co, Re [1901] 2 KB 665, CA   499
Barber v Time Inc (1942) 159 SW 2nd 291   211
Barnet v Crozier [1987] 1 WLR 272; (1987) 131 SJ
298; [1987] 1 All ER 1041; (1987) 84 LS Gaz 658, CA   62–3
Barritt v A-G [1971] 1 WLR 1713; 115 SJ 889; [1971]
3 All ER 1183   318
Baylis & Co (The Maidenhead Advertiser) v Derlenko
[1974] FSR 284   229
BBC Enterprises Ltd v Hi Tech Xtravision Ltd [1991]
3 All ER 257   224
Beach v Freeson [1972] 1 QB 14; [1971] 2 WLR 805;
115 SJ 145; [1971] 2 All ER 854   87
Beal v Kelley [1951] WN 505; [1951] 2 TLR 865; 115
JP 566; 95 SJ 685; [1951] 2 All ER 763; 35 Cr
App R 128; 49 LGR 833   147
Bebage v Times Newspapers (1981) *The Times*, 1 May   191
Beloff v Pressdram [1973] 1 All ER 241; [1973] FSR
33B   196, 240
Bernstein of Leigh (Baron) v Skyways & General
[1977] 3 WLR 136   210
Bestobell Paints v Bigg [1975] FSR 421; (1975) 119 SJ
678   191
Beta Construction Ltd v Channel 4 [1990] 1 WLR
1042   99
Bibby Bulk Carriers v Cansulex [1988] 2 All ER 532;
(1988) 132 SJ 1640; [1988] 1 Lloyd's Rep 565;
[1988] 1 FTLR 13   357
Blackburn v British Broadcasting Corporation (1976)
The Times, 15 December   266
Blackshaw v Lord [1984] QB 1; [1983] 3 WLR 283; 2
All ER 311   88–9, 93, 99
Bognor Regis UDC v Campion [1972] QB 169; [1972]
2 WLR 983; 116 SJ 354; [1972] 2 All ER 61; 12
KIR 313   481
Bond van Adverteers v Netherlands, Case No 352/85,
Judgment, 16 April 1988   643
Bonnard v Perryman [1891] 2 Ch 269   68, 191
Borough of Sunderland Case (1896) 50 M & H 62   404
Boston v Bagshaw (WS) & Sons [1966] 1 WLR 1126;
110 SJ 350, 352; [1966] 2 All ER 906   42
Boucher v R [1951] 2 DLR 369   447
Boulter v Kent Justices [1897] AC 556   377

Braddock *v* Bevins [1948] 1 KB 580; [1948] LJR 1278;
  64 TLR 279; [1948] 1 All ER 450, CA   405
Brent Walker Group and George Walker *v* Time Out
  Ltd [1991] 2 All ER 753   83
Bridges *v* California 314 US 252 (1941)   299
Brind *v* Secretary of State for the Home Department
  [1991] 1 All ER 720   7, 630
British Amusement Catering Trades Association *v*
  Westminster City Council [1988] 2 WLR 485;
  (1988) 132 SJ 374; [1988] 1 All ER 740; (1988) 86
  LGR 312; [1988] LS Gaz, April 13, HL   572
British and Commonwealth Holdings *v* Quadrex
  Holdings (1988) *The Independent*, 13 December   317, 323
British Broadcasting Corporation *v* British Satellite
  Broadcasting [1991] 3 All ER 833   239
British Broadcasting Corporation *v* Wireless League
  Gazette Publishing [1926] Ch 433   231
British Leyland Motor Corporation *v* Armstrong
  Patents Co [1986] AC 577; [1986] 2 WLR 400;
  (1986) SJ 203; [1986] 1 All ER 850; [1986] RPC
  279; [1986] FSR 221; (1986) 5 TLR 97; [1986]
  ECC 534; (1986) 136 New LJ 211; (1986) 83 LS
  Gaz 974, HL   230, 247
British Oxygen Co *v* Liquid Air [1925] Ch 383   237
British Steel Corporation *v* Granada Television [1982]
  AC 1096; [1980] 3 WLR 774; (1980) 124 SJ 812;
  [1981] 1 All ER 417, HL   178, 179, 185, 199, 511
Broadway Approvals Ltd *v* Odhams Press Ltd [1965]
  1 WLR 805; 109 SJ 294; [1965] 2 All ER 523, CA   73
Brookman *v* Green (1983) 147 JP 555; [1984] LGR 228   470
Brooks *v* Muldoon (1973) NZLR 1   73
Brown *v* Crome (1817) 2 Stark 297   87
Brych *v* Herald and Weekly Times [1978] VR 727   281
Buckingham *v* Daily News [1956] 2 QB 534; [1956] 3
  WLR 375; 100 SJ 528; [1956] 2 All ER 904, CA   144
Buckingham *v* Shackleton [1981] 79 LGR 484, DC   470
Buenos Aires Gas Co *v* Wilde (1880) 42 LT 657   341
Burns *v* Associated Newspapers (1925) 42 TLR 37   404
Byrne *v* Deane [1937] 1 KB 818   40
Byrne *v* Statist Co [1914] 1 KB 622   233, 245
Byron *v* Johnston (1816) 2 Mer 29   212

C (A Minor) (Wardship: Medical Treatment) (No 2),
  Re [1989] 3 WLR 252; [1989] 2 All ER 791; (1989)
  139 New LJ 613; (1990) 154 JPN 11, CA   334
Calder (John) Publications *v* Powell [1965] 1 QB 509;

[1965] 2 WLR 138; 129 SJ 71; [1965] 1 All ER 159,
DC   127, 128
Camporese v Parton (1983) 150 DLR (3d) 208   89
Cantrell v Forest City Publishing 419 US 245 (1974)   211
Cantwell v Connecticut 310 US 296 (1940)   165
Carson v Here's Johnny Portable Toilets Inc (1983)
698 F (2d) 831   212
Cassell & Co v Broome [1972] AC 1027; [1972] 2
WLR 645; 116 SJ 199; [1972] 1 All ER 801, HL   97
Cassidy v Daily Mirror [1929] 2 KB 331   60
CBS Songs v Amstrad Consumer Electronics [1988]
AC 1013; [1988] 2 WLR 1191; (1988) 132 SJ 789;
[1988] 2 All ER 484; [1988] 2 FTLR 168, HL   235
Central Television, Re [1991] 1 All ER 347   266, 343, 348
Chandler v DPP [1965] AC 763; [1962] 3 WLR 694;
106 SJ 588; [1962] 3 All ER 142; 46 Cr App R 347,
HL   429
Channel 4 v United Kingdom (No 11658/85) Decision
on admissibility, 9 March 1987   7–8
Chaplin v Boys [1971] AC 356; [1969] 3 WLR 322;
113 SJ 608; [1969] 2 All ER 1085, HL   651
Chappell & Co v Thompson (DC) & Co (1928–35)
MCC 467   230
Cheeseman v DPP [1991] 3 All ER 54   152
Chernesky v Armadale Publishers (1978) 90 DLR (3d)
371   85
Chief Constable of Avon and Somerset v Bristol
United Press (1986) (Unreported) The Independent,
4 November, Bristol Crown Court   206, 323
Chokolingo v A-G for Trinidad and Tobago [1981] 1
All ER 244   297
Church of Scientology v North News Ltd (1973) 117
SJ 566   63
Church of Scientology v Transmedia Production Pty
(1987) Aust Torts Reports 80–101   211
Church of Scientology of California v Johnson-Smith
[1972] 1 All ER 294   393
Church of the New Faith v Commissioner for Pay-
Roll Tax (1983) ALJR 785   162
Clement & Johnson v Associated Newspapers (1924)
The Times, 30 July   191
Cleveland County Council v W (1988) The
Independent, 29 April   336
Clyde Cablevision v Cable Authority (1990) SCLR 28   633
Coco v Clark (AN) Engineers [1986] FSR 415;
[1969] RPC 41   177

Columbia Picture Industries v Robinson [1987] Ch
38; [1986] 3 WLR 542; (1986) 130 SJ 766; [1986] 3
All ER 338; [1986] FSR 367; (1986) 83 LS Gaz 3424   257
Commercial Bank of Australia v Preston [1981] 2
NSWLR 554   290
Commissioners of Customs and Excise v Sun &
Health (Unreported) 29 March 1973   131
Commonwealth of Australia v John Fairfax (1981) 32
ALR 485   182, 187, 191, 228, 238, 438
Conegate v Commissioners of Customs and Excise
[1987] QB 254; [1986] 2 All ER 688   153–4
Cook v Alexander [1974] 1 QB 279; [1973] 3 WLR
617; 117 SJ 618; [1973] 3 All ER 1037, CA   366, 394
Cork v McVicar (1985) *The Times*, 31 October   184
Crook (Tim), *Re* (1989) 133 SJ 1577; (1989) 139 New
LJ 1633; [1991] 93 Cr App R 17, CA   320, 350
Crowe v Graham (1968) 41 ALJR 402   149
Crown Bank, *In re*; *In re* O'Mally (1890) 44 Ch D 649   288
Curtis Publishing Co v Butts 388 US 130 (1967)   71

Darbo (David John) v DPP (1991) *The Times*, 11 July,
Divisional Court 28 June 1991   112
Davies v Eli Lilley and Co (1987) [1987] 1 WLR 428;
1 All ER 801; (1987) 131 SJ 360; [1987] ECC 340;
84 LS Gaz 826; *The Independent*, 23 July   290
De Geillustreede Pers NV v Netherlands, The [1979]
FSR 173, European Commission of Human Rights   231
De Libellis Famosis (1606) 5 Co Rep 125(a),(b)   100
De L'Isle v Times Newspapers [1988] 1 WLR 49;
(1988) 132 SJ 54; [1987] 3 All ER 499; (1988) 85
LS Gaz 38, CA   98
Debi Prasad Sharma v Emporer [1943] AIR 2020   296
Derby and Co v Weldon (1988) *The Independent*, 20
October, Ch D   357, 358
Derbyshire County Council v Times Newspapers
[1992] 2 NLJ Law Reports 275; (1991) *The Times*,
8 April   56, 481
Derrick v Commissioners of Customs and Excise
[1972] QB 28; [1972] 2 WLR 359; [1971] 116 SJ
97; [1972] 2 All ER 993; [1972] Crim LR 112, DC   153
Desmond v Thorne [1983] 1 WLR 163; (1982) 126 SJ
783; [1982] 3 All ER 268   101
Dicks v Yates (1881) 18 Ch D 76   228
Director General of Fair Trading v Tobyward [1989]
1 WLR 517; (1989) 133 SJ 184; [1989] 2 All ER 266   560
Director of Public Prosecutions v A & B Chewing

Gum [1968] 1 QB 159; 3 WLR 493; 131 JP 373;
    [1967] 2 All ER 504, DC   124, 128
Director of Public Prosecutions v Beate Uhse (UK)
    [1974] QB 158; [1974] 2 WLR 50; (1973) 118
    SJ 34; [1974] 1 All ER 753; [1974] Crim LR 106,
    DC   151
Director of Public Prosecutions v Jordan [1976] 3
    WLR 887; [1976] 3 All ER 775; (1976) 64 Cr App
    R 33; [1977] Crim LR 109; *sub nom* R. v Staniforth;
    R. v Jordan [1977] AC 699   123
Director of Public Prosecutions v Luft; Same v
    Duffield [1977] AC 962; *sub nom* DPP v Luft;
    Duffield v DPP [1977] Crim LR 348, HL   405
Director of Public Prosecutions v Verrier [1991] 4 All
    ER 18   140
Director of Public Prosecutions v Whyte [1972] AC
    849; [1972] 3 WLR 410; 116 SJ 583; [1972] 3 All
    ER 12; 57 Cr App R 74; Crim LR 556, HL   114, 115, 125
Distillers Co (Biochemicals) v Times Newspapers;
    Same v Phillips [1975] QB 613; [1974] 3 WLR 728;
    118 SJ 864; [1975] 1 All ER 41   183, 186, 238, 356
Dobson v Hastings (1991) *The Independent*,
    12 November   292, 353
Donoghue v Allied Newspapers [1938] Ch 106   217
Duncombe v Daniell (1837) 2 Jur 32   87
Dunn, *In re* Andrew and the Morning Bulletin [1932]
    St R Qd 1   18
Dunsford and Elliott v Johnson & Firth Brown [1976]
    121 SJ 53; [1977] 1 Lloyd's Rep 505; [1978] FSR
    143, CA   178

EETPU v The Times Newspapers [1980] 3 WLR 98   56
Eastwood v Ryder (1990) *The Times*, 31 July   64
Edmonton Journal v A-G for Alberta (1989) 64
    DLR(4th) 577   306
Egger v Chelmsford (Viscount) [1965] 1 QB 248; 3
    WLR 714; [1964] 3 All ER 406; *sub nom* Egger v
    Davies 108 SJ 619   73
Elanco Products v Mandops (Agrochemicals)
    Specialists [1980] RPC 213; [1979] FSR 46, CA   228
Ellis v National Union of Conservative and
    Constitutional Associations, Middleton and
    Southall (1900) 44 SJ 750   404
EMI Records v Kudhail [1983] Com LR 280; (1984)
    134 New LJ 408; (1983) *The Times*, 28 June, CA   320
Emmens v Pottle (1885) 16 QBD 354   117

English and Scottish Co-operative Properties
Mortgage & Investment Society *v* Odhams Press
[1940] 1 KB 440   49
Esterhuysen *v* Lonrho (1989) *The Times*, 29 May, CA   355
Evans *v* Hulton (E) and Co (1924) *The Times*, 20 March   217
Evans *v* Lloyd [1962] 2 QB 471; [1962] 2 WLR 541;
126 JP 96; 106 SJ 196; [1962] 1 All ER 239; 60
LGR 98, DC   470
Express Newspapers *v* News (UK) [1990] 3 All ER
376   220, 227, 240
Exxon Corporation *v* Exxon Insurance Consultants
International [1982] Ch 119; (1981) 125 SJ 527;
[1981] 3 All ER 241; [1982] RPC 81, CA   228

F (A Minor) (Publication of Information), *Re* [1976] 3
WLR 813; [1977] 1 All ER 114; *sub nom* A (A
Minor), *Re*, 120 SJ 753, CA   317, 322, 332, 333, 355
Faccenda Chicken *v* Fowler; Fowler *v* Faccenda
Chicken [1987] Ch 111; [1986] 3 WLR 288; (1986)
130 SJ 573; [1986] All ER 617; [1986] ICR 297;
[1986] IRLR 69; [1986] FSR 291; (1986) 136 New
LJ 71; (1986) 83 LS Gaz 288, CA   177
Fairfax (John) & Sons *v* Police Tribunal of NSW
(1986) 5 NSWLR 465   339
Farmer *v* Hyde [1937] 1 KB 728   363
Felkin *v* Herbert (1861) 30 LJ Ch 798   386
Femis-Bank (Anguilla) *v* Lazar [1991] 2 All ER 865   48
Francome *v* Mirror Group Newspapers [1984] 1 WLR
892; (1984) 128 SJ 484; [1984] 2 All ER 408; (1984)
81 LS Gaz 2225, CA   175, 186–7, 204
Franklin *v* Giddins [1978] Qd R 72   175
Franks *v* Westminster Press (1990) *The Times*, 4 April   528
Fraser *v* Evans [1969] 1 QB 349; [1968] 3 WLR 1172;
112 SJ 805; [1969] 1 All ER 8   68, 190, 191, 237
Fraser *v* Thames Television [1984] QB 44; [1983] 2
WLR 917; (1983) 127 SJ 379; [1983] 2 All ER 101;
(1983) 133 New LJ 281   195
Furniss *v* Cambridge Daily News (1907) 23 TLR 705,
CA   363

Galletly *v* Laird (1953) SC(J) 16   149
Gardiner *v* John Fairfax & Sons (1942) 42 SR (NSW)
171   79
Garnett *v* Ferrand (1827) 6 B & C 611   371
Garrison *v* Louisiana 379 US 64 (1964)   99
Gartside *v* Outram (1856) 26 LJ Ch 113   183

Gaskell and Chambers *v* Hudson and Dodsworth and
Co [1936] 2 KB 595   355
Gay News and Lemon *v* United Kingdom [1983] 5
EHRR 123   164
Gee *v* British Broadcasting Corporation (1986) 136
New LJ 515, CA   263, 268
Geers Gross, *Re* [1987] 1WLR 1649; (1987) 131 SJ
1624; [1988] 1 All ER 224; [1988] BCLC 140;
[1988] PCC 126; (1987) 3 BCC 528; (1987) 2 FTLR
498, CA   491
Gleaves *v* Deakin (1979) 123 SJ 320; 2 All ER 497;
(1979) 69 Cr App R 59; [1979] Crim LR 458, [1980]
AC 477, HL; *see also* R. *v* Wells Street Stipendiary
Magistrate   99
Glyn *v* Weston Feature Film Co [1916] 1 Ch 261   241
Gold Star Publications *v* DPP [1981] 1 WLR 732;
(1981) 125 SJ 376; [1981] 2 All ER 257; (1981) 73
Cr App R 141; [1981] Crim LR 634, HL   120
Goldsmith *v* Pressdram [1976] 3 WLR 191   101, 161
Goldsmith *v* Pressdram [1988] 1 WLR 64   99
Goldsmith *v* Sperrings; Goldsmith *v* Various
Distributors [1977] 1 WLR 478; [1977] 121 SJ 304;
[1977] 2 All ER 566, CA   66
Goodwin, *Re* [1990] 1 All ER 608, Ch D   175
Goody *v* Odhams Press [1967] 1 QB 333; [1966] 3
WLR 460; 110 SJ 793; [1966] 3 All ER 1369; (1967)
Daily Telegraph, 22 June, CA   77
Gorton *v* Australian Broadcasting Corporation (1973)
22 FLR 181   90, 651
Gould *v* Evans & Co [1951] 2 TLR 1189   144
Gouriet *v* Union of Post Office Workers [1978] AC
435; [1977] 3 WLR 300; [1977] 3 All ER 70; *sub
nom* A-G *v* Gouriet; Post Office Engineering Union
v Gouriet; Union of Post Office Workers *v* Gouriet
(1977) 121 SJ 543, HL; *reversing* [1977] 1 All ER
696, CA   24, 330
Grade *v* Director of Public Prosecutions [1942] 2 All
ER 118; 86 SJ 321, DC   142
Grapelli *v* Block (Derek) Holdings [1981] 1 WLR
822; 125 SJ 169; [1981] 2 All ER 272, CA   47
Grech *v* Odhams Press; Addis *v* Same [1958] 2 QB
276; [1958] 3 WLR 16; 102 SJ 453; [1958] 2 All ER
462, CA   83, 395
Green *v* Broadcasting Corporation of New Zealand
[1989] 2 All ER 1056; *The Times*, 24 July   221
Grieve *v* Douglas-Home [1965] SLT 186í   405

Groppera Radio *v* Switzerland (1990) European Court
  of Human Rights, 28 March, Series A No 173   596
Gross *v* Seligman (1914) 212f 930; (1911–16) MCC 219   232
Grubb *v* Bristol United Press [1963] 1 QB 309; 3
  WLR 25; 106 SJ 262; [1962] 2 All ER 380   49
Gulf Oil (Great Britain) *v* Page [1987] Ch 327   47

Haldie and Lane *v* Chiltern (1927) 43 TLR 477   322
Hall-Brown *v* Iliffe and Sons (1928–35) MCC 88   244
Handelskwekerij GK Bier BV *v* Mines de Potasse
  d'Alsace SA [1978] QB 708   651
Handmade Films (Productions) *v* Express
  Newspapers [1986] FSR 463   200, 204
Handyside *v* United Kingdom [1976] EHRR 737   4, 5, 134
Harakas *v* Baltic Mercantile and Shipping Exchange
  [1982] 1 WLR 958; (1982) 126 SJ 414; [1982] 2 All
  ER 701, CA   68
Harman Pictures NV *v* Osborne [1967] 1 WLR 723;
  111 SJ 434; [1967] 2 All ER 324   228
Harper *v* Provincial Newspapers (1937) SLT 462   363
Harrison and Starkey *v* Polydor [1977] 1 FSR 1   253
Hawkes and Son (London) *v* Paramount Film
  Services [1934] Ch 593   238
Hayward *v* Thompson [1982] QB 47; 3 WLR 470;
  125 SJ 625; [1981] 3 All ER 450, CA   51, 58, 63, 96
Hearts of Oak Assurance Co *v* A-G [1932] AC 392;
  [1931] 2 Ch 370   508
Hector *v* A-G of Antigua and Barbuda [1990] 2 All
  ER 103H   10, 102
Henderson *v* Radio Corp'n Pty [1969] RPC 218   253
Henn & Darby *v* DPP [1980] AC 850; [1980] 2 WLR
  597; 124 SJ 290; (1980) 71 Cr App R 44; *sub nom* R.
  v Henn & Darby [1980] 2 All ER 166; *sub nom* DPP
  v Henn & Darby [1980] 21 QBD 509   154
Hennessy *v* Wright (1888) 21 QBD 509   198
Hensher (George) *v* Restawile Upholstery (Lancs)
  [1976] AC 64; [1974] 2 WLR 700; 118 SJ 329;
  [1974] 2 All ER 420; [1974] FSR 173; 1975 RPC 31,
  HL   122
Herbage *v* Pressdram [1984] 1 WLR 1160; 128 SJ
  615; [1984] 2 All ER 769; (1984) 81 LS Gaz 1844,
  CA   68
Herbage *v* Times Newspapers (1981) *The Times*, 1 May   191
Hillfinch Properties *v* Newark Investments (1981) *The
  Times*, 1 July   289
Hilliard *v* Penfield Enterprises [1990] IR 38   101

Hillingdon London Borough *v* Paullson [1977] JPL
    518, Middlesex Crown Court   469
Hinch *v* A-G (Vic) (1987) 74 ALR 353   286, 394
Hinds *v* Sparks (No 2) (1964) *The Times*, 20 October   77
Hoare *v* Silverlock (1848) 12 QB 630   48
Hodgson and Others *v* United Kingdom (No 11553/85)   7–8
Hoffman La Roche (F) & Co AG *v* Secretary of State
    for Trade and Industry [1975] AC 295; [1974] 3
    WLR 104; 118 SJ 500; [1974] 2 All ER 1128, HL   192
Home Office *v* Harman [1983] AC 280; [1982] 2
    WLR 338; (1982) 126 SJ 136; [1982] 1 All ER
    532, HL   15, 186, 304, 356–8
Hope *v* Leng (1907) 23 TLR 243   365
Horrocks *v* Lowe [1975] AC 135; [1974] 2 WLR 282;
    118 SJ 149; [1974] 1 All ER 662; 72 LGR 251,
    HL   71
Hubbard *v* Vosper [1972] 2 QB 84; [1972] 2 WLR
    389; (1971) 116 SJ 95; [1972] 1 All ER 1023,
    CA   184, 191, 236, 237
Hulton *v* Jones [1910] AC 20   59
Hunt *v* Clarke (1889) 58 LJQB 490   272
Hunt *v* Star Newspapers (1908) 2 KB 309   82
Hutchinson *v* AEU (1932) *The Times*, 25 August   276, 289

Independent Television Companies Association *v*
    Performing Rights Society (1982) *The Times*, 23
    November   233
Independent Television Publications *v* Time Out;
    British Broadcasting Corporation *v* Time Out
    [1984] FSR 64   228, 231
Initial Services *v* Putterill [1968] 1 QB 396; 3 WLR
    1032; 111 SJ 541; [1967] 3 All ER 145; 2 KIR 863,
    CA   184
Inquiry under the Company Securities (Insider
    Dealing) Act 1985, *In re* [1988] 1 All ER 203; (1988)
    The Independent, 27 January   197
International News Service *v* Associated Press 248
    US 215 (1918)   227

James *v* Commonwealth of Australia [1936] AC 578   2
James *v* Robinson (1963) 109 CLR 593   288
Jenkins *v* Socialist Worker (1977) *The Times*, 28
    February   217
Jenner *v* Sea Oil [1952] DLR 526   651
Johnson (PS) and Associates *v* Bucko Enterprises
    [1975] 1 NZLR 311   122

Johnstone *v* Jones (Bernard) Publications [1938] 1 Ch
  599   236
Jones *v* Skelton [1963] 1 WLR 1362; 107 SJ 870; 3
  All ER 952   52
Joy Music *v* Sunday Pictorial Newspapers (1920)
  [1960] 2 QB 60; [1960] 2 WLR 645; 104 SJ 289;
  [1960] 1 All ER 703   230

K, *Re* [1965] AC 201   312
Kashoggi *v* IPC Magazines [1986] 3 All ER 577   69
Kaye (Gorden) *v* Andrew Robertson & Sport
  Newspapers [1991] FSR 62, CA   47, 211
Keays *v* Murdoch Magazines (UK) [1991] 4 All ER
  491   53
Kemsley *v* Foot [1952] AC 345; [1952] TLR 532; 96
  SJ 165; [1952] 1 All ER 501, HL   82
Kennard *v* Lewis [1983] FSR 346   230
Kenrick & Co *v* Lawrence & Co (1890) 25 QBD 99   222, 229
Kerr *v* Kennedy [1942] 1 All ER 412   54
Khan *v* Ahmed [1957] 2 QB 149; [1957] 2 WLR
  1060; 101 SJ 447; [1957] 2 All ER 385   93, 389
Kimber *v* Press Association [1893] 1 QB 65   363
King Features Syndicate *v* Kleeman (O & M) [1941]
  AC 417, HL   222, 232
Kingshott *v* Associated Kent Newspapers [1991] 2
  All ER 99   93
Knuller (Publishing, Printing and Promotions) *v* DPP
  [1973] AC 435; [1972] 3 WLR 143; 116 SJ 545; 56
  Cr App R 633; [1975] Crim LR 704,
  HL   111, 148, 156, 157, 338
Kroch *v* Russell et cie [1937] 1 All ER 725   651

L, *In re* (1990) *Guardian*, 5 December   319
L (A Minor), *Re* (Wardship: Freedom of Publication)
  [1988] 1 All ER 418; [1988] 1 FLR 255; (1987) 137
  New LJ 760   333, 335, 336
Ladbroke (Football) *v* Hill (William) (Football) [1964]
  1 WLR 273; 108 SJ 135; [1964] 1 All ER 465, HL   228
Lambeth London Borough Council *v* Grewal (1985)
  150 JP 138; (1985) 82 Cr App R 301; [1986] Crim
  LR 260; (1985) 150 JPN 111; (1985) *The Times*, 26
  November   166
Langrish *v* Archer (1882) 10 QBD 44   140
Laughton *v* Bishop of Sodor and Man (1872) LR&PC
  495   90
Le Fanu *v* Malcomson (1848) 1 HL Cas 637   58

Lennon *v* News Group Newspapers and Twist [1978]
FSR 573   181
Lewis *v* British Broadcasting Corporation [1979]
Court of Appeal Transcript 193   385
Lewis *v* Cattle [1938] 2 All ER 368   431
Lewis *v* Daily Telegraph [1964] AC 234   38, 49, 50–51, 75
Lincoln Hunt (Aust) Pty *v* Willesee (1986) 4 NSWR
457   211
Lingens *v* Austria (1986) 8 EHRR 425   89–90, 101
Lion Laboratories *v* Evans [1985] QB 526; 3 WLR
539; (1984) 128 SJ 533; [1984] 2 All ER 417; (1984)
81 LS Gaz 2000; (1984) 82 LS Gaz 1233, CA   173, 185, 317
Lloyd (FH) Holdings, *Re* [1985] BCLC 293; PCC 268   491
Lloyd *v* Syme (David) & Co [1986] AC 350; [1986] 2
WLR 69; (1986) 130 SJ 14, PC   58
Loat *v* Andrews [1985] ICR 679   419
Lombard North Central *v* Pratt (1989) New LJ 1709,
CA   353
London and Norwich Investment Services, *Re* [1988]
BCLC 226; (1987) *The Times*, 16 December   317
London Artists *v* Littler; Grade Organisation *v* Same;
Associated Television *v* Same; Grade *v* Same [1969]
2 QB 375; [1969] 2 WLR 409; *sub nom* London
Artists *v* Littler (and Associated Actions) [1969] 1
All ER 1075   80, 83, 88
London Borough of Hillingdon *v* Paullson; *see*
Hillingdon London Borough *v* Paullson
London Borough of Southwark *v* Peters (1972) LGR 41   464
Lonrho and Observer, *Re* (1989) *The Independent*, 28
July; [1989] 2 All ER 1100, HL   269, 304
Lord Advocate *v* Scotsman Publications [1989] 3
WLR 358; [1989] 2 All ER 852, HL   7, 189, 193, 424
Loveday *v* Sun Newspapers (1938) 59 CLR 503   90
Lynam *v* Gowring (1880) 6 LR Ir 259   264
Lynch *v* British Broadcasting Corporation [1983] 6
Northern Ireland Judgments Bulletin   407, 601
Lynch *v* Knight (1861) 9 HL Cas 592   54
Lyngstad *v* Anabas [1977] FSR 62   253
Lyon *v* Daily Telegraph [1943] 2 All ER 316   85

M, *Re* [1990] 1 All ER 205   306
M (A Minor), *Re*; N (A Minor), *Re* [1989] 3 WLR 1136   335
McAliskey *v* British Broadcasting Corporation [1980]
NI 44   406, 601
McCarey *v* Associated Newspapers [1965] 2 QB 86; 2
WLR 43; 108 SJ 916; [1964] 3 All ER 947, CA   387

McCrum *v* Eisner (1917) 117 LT 536; (1917–23)
MCC 14   229
McCulloch *v* May (1947) 65 PRC 58   253
McGovern *v* A-G [1982] Ch 321; [1982] 2 WLR 222;
(1981) 125 SJ 255; [1981] All ER 493; [1982] TR 157   513
McLeod *v* St Aubyn [1899] AC 549   296
McPherson *v* McPherson [1936] AC 177   310
Magill TV Guide *v* Independent Television
Publications [1990] FSR 71, EC Comm.   231
Malone *v* Metropolitan Police Commissioner (No 2)
[1979] Ch 344; [1979] 2 WLR 700; (1979) 69 Cr
App R 168; *sub nom* Malone *v* Commissioner of
Police of the Metropolis (No 2) [1979] 2 All ER 620   175
Mandla *v* Dowell Lee [1983] 2 AC 548; [1983] 2
WLR 620; [1983] ICR 385; (1983) 127 SJ 242;
[1983] 1 All ER 1062; [1983] IRLR 209, HL   168
Mangena *v* Wright [1909] 2 KB 958   83, 395
Marsh, *In the Appeal of* (1973) 3 DCR (NSW) 115   148
Marshall *v* British Broadcasting Corporation [1979] 1
WLR 1071; (1979) 123 SJ 336; [1979] 3 All ER 80,
CA
Masterman's Application, *Re* (1990) *The Times*, 19
December   242
Mawe *v* Pigott (1869) IR 4 CL 54   40
Maxwell *v* Pressdram [1987] 1 WLR 298; (1987) 131
SJ 327; [1987] 1 All ER 656; (1987) 84 LS Gaz
1148, CA   69
Meek *v* Lothian Regional Council (1983) SLT 494   405
Merivale *v* Carson (1887) 20 QBD 275   79
Mills *v* London County Council [1925] 1 KB 213   567, 569
Moore *v* News of the World [1972] 1 QB 441; [1972] 2
WLR 419; (1971) 116 SJ 137; [1972] 1 All ER 915,
CA   217
Moores *v* DPP [1991] 4 All ER 521   160
Morgan *v* Odhams Press [1971] 1 WLR 1239; 115 SJ
587; [1971] 2 All ER 1156, HL   59
Morrell *v* International Thomson Publishing [1989] 3
All ER 733; (1989) 139 New LJ 1007, CA   42
Mueller *v* Switzerland (1988) 24 May 1988 Series A,
No 33   135
Mustad (O) & Son *v* Dosen [1964] 1 WLR 109; [1963]
RPC 41; *sub nom* Mustad (O) & Son *v* Allcock (S)
& Co and Dosen [1963] 3 All ER 416, HL   188
Mycroft *v* Sleight (1921) 90 LJKB 883   48

Nambooripad *v* Mambiar [1970] All India Reps 1318   297

National Broadcasting Company *v* Meyers 635 F2d
   945 (1980)   351
New York Times *v* Sullivan 401 US 265 (1964)   103
New York Times *v* US 403 US 713 (1971)   20, 182
Newstead *v* London Express [1940] 1 KB 377   60
Norwich Pharmacal Co *v* Customs and Excise
   Commissioners [1974] Ac 133; [1973] 3 WLR 164;
   117 SJ 567; *sub nom* Norwich Pharmacal Co *v*
   Commissioners of Customs and Excise [1973] 2 All
   ER 943; [1973] FSR 365; [1974] RPC 101, HL   256

Oberschlick *v* Austria, European Court, 23 May 1991   90
Observer and Guardian *v* United Kingdom (51/1990/
   242/313) ECHR, 1991   5, 22, 183
Oliver *v* Northampton Borough Council (1986) 151
   JP 44; (1986) *The Times*, 8 May, DC   469
Olivier *v* Buttigieg [1966] 2 All ER 459   9–10
Ormerod Grierson and Co *v* St George's Ironworks
   [1905] 1 Ch 505, CA   499
Oxford *v* Moss (1978) 68 Cr App R 183; [1979] Crim
   LR 119, DC   175

Paterson Zochonis and Co *v* Merfaken Packaging
   [1986] 3 All ER 522; [1982] Com LR 260; [1983]
   FSR 273, CA   235
Paul *v* Ministry of Posts and Telecommunications
   [1973] RTR 245; [1973] Crim LR 322, DC   434
Paul *v* National and Local Government Officers
   Association [1987] IRLR 413   405
Peacock *v* London Weekend Television (1985) 150
   JP 71; (1986) 150 JPN 47; (1985) *The Times*,
   27 November   302, 372, 384
Perera *v* Peiris [1949] AC 1; [1949] LJR 426; 64 TLR
   590; 92 SJ 688   388
Philadelphia Newspapers *v* Hepps 475 US 767 (1986)   71
Phillips (1977) 6 Anglo-Am LR 138   241
Pickering *v* Liverpool Daily Post and Echo
   Newspapers [1991] 1 All ER 622; (1991) New LJ
   166, HL   302, 376
Pinkus *v* USA 434 US 919   114
Pinniger *v* John Fairfax (1979) 53 ALJR 691   73
Plating Co *v* Farquharson (1881) 17 Ch D 49   276
Polly Peck International *v* Nadir (1991) *The Times*, 11
   November, CA   313
Popow *v* Samuela [1973] 4 SASR 594   112
Price *v* Humphries [1958] 2 QB 353; [1958] 3 WLR

304; 122 JP 423; 102 SJ 583; [1958] 2 All ER 725,
    DC   137
Prior *v* Prior (By his Guardian) (1970) 114 SJ 72,
    PDA Div   318
Procureur du Roi *v* Debauve [1980] ECR 833   597, 643
Proetta *v* Times Newspapers [1991] 4 All ER 46   45
Prudential Assurance Co *v* Fountain Page [1991] 3
    All ER 878   358
Purcell (Betty) *v* Ireland (1991) European
    Commission of Human Rights, 16 April   630

R (MJ) (A Minor) (Publication of Transcripts), *Re*
    [1975] Fam 89; [1975] 2 WLR 978; 119 SJ 338; *sub*
    nom R (MJ) (An Infant) (Proceedings Transcripts:
    Publication), *Re* [1975] 2 All ER 749; *sub nom* R
    (MJ) (A Minor) 5 Fam Law 154   322
R *v* Aitken and Others [1966] 1 WLR 1076; 110 SJ
    526; [1966] 2 All ER 453; 50 Cr App R 204, CCA   416
R *v* Aldred (1909) 22 Cox CC 1   447
R *v* Almon (1765) Wilm 243; 97 ER 94   296, 299
R *v* Ameer and Lucas [1977] Crim LR 104   277, 537
R *v* Anderson; R *v* Neville; R *v* Dennis; R *v* Oz
    Publications Ink [1972] 1 QB 304; [1971] 3 WLR
    939; 115 SJ 847; *sub nom* R. *v* Anderson [1971] 3
    All ER 1152; 59 Cr App R 115; [1972] Crim LR
    40, CA   111, 112, 116
R *v* Angel [1968] 1 WLR 669; (1968) 112 SJ 310;
    [1968] 2 All ER 607; 52 Cr App R 280, CA   137
R *v* Armstrong (1885) 49 JP 745   147
R *v* Arrowsmith [1975] QB 678; [1975] 2 WLR 484;
    (1974) 119 SJ 165; [1975] 1 All ER 463; [1975]
    Crim LR 161; *sub nom* R *v* Arrowsmith (Pat) (1974)
    60 Cr App R 211, CA   449
R *v* Arundel Justices, *ex p* Westminster Press [1985] 1
    WLR 676; (1985) 149 JP 299; (1985) 129 SJ 274;
    [1985] 2 All ER 390; (1985) 82 LS Gaz 178, DC   340
R *v* ASA, *ex p* The Insurance Service (1989) *The*
    Times, 14 July   561
R *v* Bedwellty UDC, *ex p* Price [1934] 1 KB 333   470
R *v* Blackpool Justices, *ex p* Beaverbrook Newspapers
    [1972] 1 WLR 95; (1971) 115 SJ 928; [1972] 1 All
    ER 388, DC   325
R *v* Blake [1962] 2 QB 377; [1961] 3 WLR 744; 125
    JP 571; [1961] 3 All ER 125; 45 Cr App R 292, CCA   428
R *v* Bogdanov, Horseferry Road Magistrates' Court   146
R *v* Bolam, *ex p* Haigh (1949) 93 SJ 220   261

R *v* Boulter (1908) 72 JP 188   161
R *v* Bow Street Magistrates, *ex p* Kray (Reginald)
    [1969] 1 QB 473; [1968] 3 WLR 1111; 133 JP 54;
    (1968) 112 SJ 820; [1968] 3 All ER 872; (1969) 53
    Cr App R 412   325
R *v* Bow Street Magistrates, *ex p* Noncyp [1990] 1
    QB 123; (1989) 133 SJ 1031; (1989) 89 Cr App R
    121; [1989] COD 357, CA   154
R *v* Bow Street Magistrates' Court, *ex p* Choudhury
    [1991] 1 All ER 306   164, 171, 448
R *v* Brent Health Authority, *ex p* Francis [1985] QB
    869; 3 WLR 1317; (1984) 128 SJ 815; [1985] 1 All
    ER 74; (1985) 82 LS Gaz 36   464
R *v* Bristol Crown Court, *ex p* Bristol Press and
    Picture Agency (1987) 85 Cr App R 190; [1987]
    Crim LR 329   206
R *v* Broadcasting Complaints Commission, *ex p* BBC
    (1984) 128 SJ 384; (1984) 81 LS Gaz 1992; (1984)
    The Times, 17 May   556
R *v* Broadcasting Complaints Commission, *ex p*
    Owen [1985] QB 1153; 2 WLR 1025; (1985) 129 SJ
    349; [1985] 2 All ER 522; (1985) 82 LS Gaz 2161,
    DC   408
R *v* Broadcasting Complaints Commission, *ex p*
    Thames Television (1982) *The Times*, 8 October   556
R *v* Brownson [1971] Crim LR 551   142
R *v* Bulgin, *ex p* British Broadcasting Corporation
    (1977) *The Times*, 14 July, DC   269
R *v* Burns (1886) 16 Cox 355   447
R *v* Calder & Boyars [1969] 1 QB 151; [1968] 3 WLR
    974; 133 JP 20; 112 SJ 688; 3 All ER 644; 52 Cr
    App R 706, CA   112, 115, 118, 123, 617
R *v* Carr-Briant [1943] KB 607   283
R *v* Caunt (1948) LQR 203   447
R *v* Central Criminal Court, *ex p* Crook (1985) LS
    Gaz 1408; *The Times*, 8 November, QBD   16, 340
R *v* Central Criminal Court, *ex p* DPP (1988) *The
    Independent*, 31 March; *The Times*, 1 April, DC *   323
R *v* Central Criminal Court, *ex p* Randle and Pottle
    (1990) 92 Cr App R 323; (1990) *The Independent*,
    16 November   347, 540
R *v* Chancellor of the Chichester Consistory Court,
    ex p News Group Newspapers (1991) *The Times*,
    15 July   374
R *v* Chief Registrar of Friendly Societies, *ex p* New
    Cross Building Society [1984] QB 227; [1984] 2

WLR 370; (1984) 2 All ER 27; (1984) 81 LS Gaz
509; (1984) *The Times*, 14 January, DC — 312
R *v* Christian (1913) 78 JP 112 — 146
R *v* Cinecentre (1976) Birmingham Crown Court — 159
R *v* Clayton & Halsey [1963] 1 QB 163; [1962] 3
WLR 815; 127 JP 7; 106 SJ 652; [1962] 3 All ER
500; 46 Cr App R 450, CCA — 114
R *v* Clement (1821) 4 B & Ald 218; 106 ER 918 — 342
R *v* Commissioner of Police for the Metropolis, *ex p*
Blackburn (No 2) [1968] 2 QB 150; [1968] 2 WLR
1204; *sub nom* R *v* Metropolitan Police
Commissioner, *ex p* Blackburn (No 2) — 297
R *v* Creevey (1813) 1 M and S 273; 105 ER 102 — 393
R *v* Crisp and Homewood (1919) 83 JP 121 — 419
R *v* Cullen, McCann and Shanahan (1990) 92 Cr App
R 239 — 263
R *v* Daily Herald, *ex p* Bishop of Norwich [1932]
2 KB 402 — 384
R *v* Daily Mirror, *ex p* Smith [1927] 1 KB 845 — 275
R *v* Denbigh Justices, *ex p* Williams and Evans [1974]
QB 759; [1974] 3 WLR 45; 118 SJ 478; [1974] 2 All
ER 1052; [1974] Crim LR 442, DC — 323
R *v* Derbyshire County Council, *ex p* Times
Supplements (1991) 3 Admin LR 241 — 561
R *v* Dover Justices, *ex p* Dover District Council (1991)
Divisional Court, 14 October — 339
R *v* Dover Justices, *ex p* Dover District Council (1991)
The Times, 21 October — 313
R *v* Duffy, *ex p* Nash [1960] QB 188; [1960] 3 WLR
320; 104 SJ 585; [1960] 2 All ER 891, DC — 269, 270, 289
R *v* Ealing Justices, *ex p* Weaver (1982) 74 Cr App R
204; [1982] Crim LR 182, DC — 312
R *v* Ealing London Borough Council, *ex p* Times
Newspapers (1987) 85 LGR 316; [1987] IRLR 129;
(1987) 151 Rev 530, DC — 487
R *v* Eden District Council, *ex p* Moffat (1988) *The
Independent*, 16 December, CA — 464
R *v* Edwards (RH) (1983) 5 Cr App R(S) 145, CA — 170
R *v* Epping and Ongar Justices, *ex p* Breach; R *v*
Same, *ex p* Shippam (C); *see* R *v* Epping and Ongar
Justices, *ex p* Shippam (C); R *v* Same, *ex p* Breach
R *v* Epping and Ongar Justices, *ex p* Shippam (C); R
v Same, *ex p* Breach [1986] Crim LR 810; (1986)
150 JPN 542 — 314
R *v* Evening Standard, *ex p* A-G (1976) *The Times*,
3 November — 275

R v Evening Standard, *ex p* Director of Public
    Prosecutions (1924) 40 TLR 833   277
R v Evesham Justices, *ex p* McDonagh and Berrows
    Newspapers; *see* R v Malvern Justices, *ex p* Evans
R v Farmer, *ex p* Hargrave [1981] 79 LGR 676, DC   471
R v Felixstowe Justices, *ex p* Leigh [1987] QB 582;
    [1987] 2 WLR 380; (1987) 151 JP 65; [1987] 1 All
    ER 551; (1987) 84 Cr App R 327; [1987] Crim LR
    125; (1987) 84 LS Gaz 901; (1986) 130 SJ 767;
    (1986) 136 New LJ 988; 151 JPN 31, DC   15, 311
R v Fox, *ex p* Mosley (1966) *The Times*, 17 February;
    Guardian, 17 February   284
R v Galvin [1987] QB 862; 3 WLR 93; (1987) 131
    SJ 657; [1987] 2 All ER 851; (1988) 86 Cr App R
    85; [1987] Crim LR 700; (1987) 84 LS Gaz 1651,
    CA   419, 422
R v Gaming Board, *ex p* Benaim [1970] 2 QB 417   634
R v Gay News; *see* R v Lemon
R v George [1956] Crim LR 503   147
R v Gibson [1991] 1 All ER 439   157-8
R v Gilligan [1987] Crim LR 501   337, 346
R v Glamorganshire County Council, *ex p* Collier
    [1936] 2 All ER 168   470
R v Gold; R v Schifreen [1988] AC 1063; [1988] 2
    WLR 984; 152 JP 445; (1988) 132 SJ 624; [1988] 2
    All ER 186; (1988) 87 Cr App R 257; [1988] Crim
    LR 437; (1988) 152 JPN 478; (1988) 138 New LJ
    117; [1988] LS Gaz May 18, 38, HL   175
R v Graham-Kerr (1989) 88 Cr App R 302; (1989)
    153 JP 171; (1989) 153 JPN 170, CA   131, 132
R v Gray [1900] 2 QB 36   296, 297
R v Greater London Council, *ex p* Blackburn [1976] 1
    WLR 550; 120 SJ 421; [1976] 3 All ER 184; (1976)
    74 LGR 464, CA   567
R v Greater London Council, *ex p* Westminster City
    Council (1985) *The Times*, 22 January   482
R v Gunn, *ex p* A-G (No 2) (1953) *The Times*, 14
    November; [1954] Crim LR 53   384
R v Halkin 598 F2d 176 (DC CA 1979)   356
R v Hammersmith Coroner, *ex p* Peach [1980] All ER
    7, CA   369, 370
R v Henn & Darby; *see* Henn & Darby v DPP
R v Hicklin (1868) LR 3 QB 360   107
R v Hochhauser (1964) 47 WWR 350   140
R v Holbrook (No 1) (1877) 3 QBD 60   161
R v Holbrook (No 2) (1878) 4 QBD 42   161

R v Holloway (1982) 4 Cr App R (s) 128 — 135

R v Holmes (1853) Dears CC 207 — 140

R v Horseferry Road Justices, *ex p* Siadatan [1991] 1
All ER 324 — 171

R v Horsham Magistrates, *ex p* Farquharson and West
Sussex County Times [1982] QB 762; [1982] 2
WLR 430; (1982) 126 SJ 98; [1982] 2 All ER 269;
(1983) 76 Cr App R 87, CA — 326, 342–4

R v Hutchison, *ex p* McMahon [1936] 2 All ER 1514 — 274

R v ILEA, *ex p* Westminster City Council (1984) *The
Times*, 31 December — 482

R v Independent Broadcasting Authority, *ex p*
Whitehouse (1985) *The Times*, 4 April, CA — 30–31, 604

R v Ingrams, *ex p* Goldsmith [1977] Crim LR 240 — 289

R v Kopyto (1987) 47 DLR 213 — 299

R v Kray (1969) 53 Cr App R 412 — 342

R v Leeds Justices, *ex p* Sykes [1983] 1 WLR 132;
(1983) 147 JP 129; (1982) 126 SJ 855; [1983] 1 All
ER 460; (1983) 76 Cr App R 129; [1983] Crim LR
180; (1983) LS Gaz 154, DC — 326

R v Leicester Crown Court, *ex p* S (1990) *The
Independent*, 12 December, QBD — 328, 347

R v Lemon; R v Gay News [1979] AC 617; [1979] 2
WLR 281; (1979) 123 SJ 163; [1979] 1 All ER 898;
[1979] Crim LR 311; *sub nom* Whitehouse v Gay
News — 160, 447

R v Lewes Prison (Governor), *ex p* Doyle [1917] 2
KB 254 — 312

R v Liverpool City Council, *ex p* Liverpool Taxi Fleet
Operators Association [1975] 1 All ER 379; [1975] 1
All ER 379 — 464, 466

R v Local Commissioner for Administration for the
North & East Area of England, *ex p* Bradford MDC
[1979] QB 287; [1979] 2 WLR 1; (1978) 122 SJ
573; [1979] 2 All ER 881; (1978) LGR 305; [1978]
JPL 767, CA — 475

R v Love (1955) 39 Cr App R 30 — 117

R v Malik [1968] 1 WLR 353; (1968) 132 JP 169; 112
SJ 91; [1968] 1 All ER 582; 52 Cr App R 140, CA — 169

R v Malvern Justices, *ex p* Evans; R v Evesham
Justices, *ex p* McDonagh [1988] QB 553; [1988] 2
WLR 218, 227; (1987) 131 SJ 1698; (1988) 152 JP
65; [1988] 1 All ER 371; (1988) 87 Cr App R 19,
28; [1988] Crim LR 120; (1988) 152 JPN 30; (1987)
137 NLJ 757, DC — 16, 311, 314, 339, 363, 386

R v Manchester Crown Court, *ex p* Taylor [1988] 1

WLR 705; (1988) 132 SJ 899; [1988] 2 All ER 769;
[1988] Crim LR 386, DC   206
R *v* Martin Secker & Warburg [1954] 1 WLR 1138;
118 JP 438; 98 SJ 577; [1954] 2 All ER 683; 38 Cr
App R 124   111
R *v* Mason (1932) *The Times*, 7 December   272
R *v* Mayling [1963] 2 QB 717; [1963] 2 WLR 709;
127 JP 269; 107 SJ 177; [1963] 1 All ER 687; 47 Cr
App R 102, CA   140
R *v* Metropolitan Commissioner, *ex p* Blackburn (No
2); *see* R *v* Commissioner of Police for the
Metropolis. *ex p* Blackburn (No 2)
R *v* Middlesex Crown Court, *ex p* Godwin [1991] 3
All ER 818; (1990) *The Independent*, 15 October   329, 349
R *v* Monmouthshire County Council (1935) 153 LT
338   469
R *v* Murray & Others (1990) *The Times*, 22 March   646
R *v* Nat West Investment Bank (1991) (Unreported)
11 January (Central Criminal Court)   344, 345
R *v* New Statesman, *ex p* DPP (1928) 44 TLR 301   297
R *v* Newcastle upon Tyne Justices, *ex p* Vickers (1981)
The Times, 18 April   342
R *v* Newham, *ex p* Haggerty (1986) 85 LGR 48   473
R *v* Nield (1909) *The Times*, 27 January   272
R *v* Nooy & Schyff (1982) 4 Cr App R (S) 308   135
R *v* Ouillet (1977) 36 Crim Reps (Nova Scotia) 296   297
R *v* Owen (Charles) [1988] 1 WLR 134; (1987) 131 SJ
1696; (1988) 86 Cr App R 291; [1988] Crim LR
120, CA   132
R *v* Panel on Take-Overs and Mergers, *ex p* Datafin
(Norton-Opax Intervening) [1987] QB 815; [1987]
2 WLR 699; (1987) 131 SJ 23; [1987] 1 All ER 564;
[1987] PCC 120; [1987] BCLC 104; [1987] 1 FTLR
181; (1987) 84 LS Gaz 264; (1986) 136 New LJ
1207, CA   561
R *v* Parrott (1913) 8 Cr App Rep 186   429
R *v* Payne [1896] 1 QB 577   386
R *v* Penguin Books [1961] Crim LR 176   143
R *v* People, The (1925) *The Times*, 5 April   270
R *v* Perryman (1892) *The Times*, 19 January–9 February   100
R *v* Ponting [1985] Crim LR 318   422
R *v* Quinn; R. *v* Bloom [1962] 2 QB 245; [1961] 3
WLR 611; 125 JP 565; 105 SJ 590; [1961] 3 All ER
88; 45 Cr App R 279, CCA   143, 159
R *v* Raymond [1981] QB 910; (1981) 125 SJ 693;
[1981] 2 All ER 246; (1980) 72 Cr App R 151, CA   316

R *v* Redditch Justices (1885) 2 TLR 193 — 377

R *v* Registrar of Building Societies, *ex p* A Building
Society [1960] 1 WLR 669; 104 SJ 544; [1960] 2
All ER 549, CA — 320

R *v* Reigate Justices, *ex p* Argus Newspapers (1983)
147 JP 385; (1983) 5 Cr App R(S) 101; [1983] Crim
LR 564, DC — 308, 313

R *v* Reiter [1954] 2 QB 16; [1954] 2 WLR 638; 118 JP
262; 98 SJ 235; [1954] 1 All ER 741; 38 Cr App R
62, CCA — 118

R *v* Rhuddlan Justices, *ex p* HTV [1986] Crim LR
329 — 344

R *v* Richards, *ex p* Fitzpatrick and Browne (1955) 92
CLR 157 — 401

R *v* Rose; R *v* Clarke; R *v* Henry [1982] AC 822; 3
WLR 192; (1982) 126 SJ 479; [1982] 2 All ER 731;
(1982) 75 Cr App R 322; [1982] Crim LR 696, HL — 301

R *v* Runting [1989] Crim LR 282, CA — 359

R *v* Russell, *ex p* Beaverbrook Newspapers [1969] 1
QB 342; [1968] 3 WLR 999; (1968) 133 JP 27; 112
SJ 800; [1968] 3 All ER 695, DC — 325

R *v* Salter & Barton [1976] Crim LR 514 — 120

R *v* Saunders (1990) *The Independent*, 8 February;
[1990] Crim LR 597 — 327, 343

R *v* Savundranayagan and Walker [1968] 1 WLR
1761; 3 All ER 438; *sub nom* R *v* Savundra-Nayagan;
R *v* Walker, 112 SJ 621; *sub nom* R *v* Savundra
(Emil); R *v* Walker (Stewart de Quincy Walker), 52
Cr App R 637, CA — 293

R *v* Secretary of State, *ex p* London Borough of
Greenwich (1989) *The Independent*, 17 May — 482

R *v* Secretary of State for Home Affairs, *ex p*
Hosenball [1977] 3 All ER 452 — 430

R *v* Secretary of State for the Home Department, *ex p*
Brind [1990] 1 All ER 469 — 629

R *v* Secretary of State for the Home Department, *ex p*
Cheblak [1991] 2 All ER 319 — 419

R *v* Secretary of State for Trade and Industry, *ex p*
Lonrho [1989] 1 WLR 525; (1989) 133 SJ 724;
[1989] 2 All ER 609; 5 BCC 633; (1989) 139 New
LJ 717, HL — 509

R *v* Sheffield City Council, *ex p* Chadwick (1986) 84
LGR 563 — 464

R *v* Skirving; R *v* Grossman [1985] QB 819; [1985] 2
WLR 1001; (1985) 129 SJ 299; (1985) 81 Cr App R
9; [1985] Crim LR 317; (1985) 82 LS Gaz 1409, CA — 124, 127

R v Socialist Worker Printers and Publishers, *ex p*
A-G [1975] QB 637; [1974] 3 WLR 801; 118 SJ 791;
[1975] 1 All ER 142; Crim LR 711, DC   338
R v Stanley [1965] 2 QB 327; 2 WLR 917; 129 JP
279; 109 SJ 193; [1965] 1 All ER 1035; 49 Cr App
R 175, CCA   148
R v Sutton [1977] 1 WLR 1086; (1977) 121 SJ 676;
[1977] 3 All ER 476; [1977] Crim LR 569, CA   130
R v Thomson (1906) 64 JP 456   108
R v Thomson Newspapers, *ex p* A-G [1968] 1 WLR
1; (1967) 111 SJ 943; [1968] 1 All ER 268, DC   274, 283
R v Tower Bridge Magistrates' Court, *ex p* Osborne
(1989) 88 Cr App R 28; [1988] Crim LR 382, DC   312, 314
R v Townsend [1982] 1 All ER 509; (1982) 74 Cr App
R 218; [1982] Crim LR 186, CA   301
R v Tronoh Mines and Times Publishing Co [1952]
TLR 461; 116 JP 180; 96 SJ 183; [1952] 1 All ER
697; 35 Cr App R 196; 50 LGR 461   405
R v Waterfield [1975] 1 WLR 711; 119 SJ 300; [1975]
2 All ER 40; 60 Cr App R 296; [1975] Crim LR
298, CA   17
R v Wealdstone and Harrow News; Harley v Sholl
[1925] WN 153   277
R v Wells Street Stipendiary Magistrate, *ex p* Deakin
[1980] AC 477; [1979] 2 WLR 665; *see also* Gleaves
v Deakin   99
R v West Yorkshire Coroner, *ex p* Smith [1985] QB
1096; [1985] 2 WLR 332; (1985) 149 JP 97; (1985)
129 SJ 131; [1985] 1 All ER 100, DC   384
R v Wilkinson (1930) *The Times*, 16 July   297
R v Williams (1822) 5 B & Ald 595   101
Radio Telefis Eirann v Commission of the European
Community and Magill TV Guide, Luxembourg,
10 July 1991   246
Randle and Potter, *Re: see* R v Central Criminal
Court, *ex p* Randle and Potter
Raybos Australia Pty v Jones (1985) 2 NSWLR 47   339
RCA Corp v Pollard [1983] Ch 135; [1982] 3 WLR
1007; [1982] 3 All ER 771; [1983] FSR 9, CA   253
RCA Corporation v John Fairfax & Sons [1982] RPC
91, Sup Ct of NSW   234
Ricci v Chow [1987] 1 WLR 1658; (1987) 131 SJ
1156; [1987] 3 All ER 534, CA   198
Richard Newspapers v Virginia (1980) 448 US 555   306
Richardson v Wilson (1879) 7 R 237   323
Riches v News Group Newspapers [1986] QB 256;

[1985] 3 WLR 43; (1985) 129 SJ 401; [1985] 2 All
    ER 845; (1985) 135 New LJ 391; (1985) 82 LS Gaz
    2088, CA   52, 57, 97
Richmond Newspapers Inc v Commonwealth of
    Virginia 448 US 555 (1980)   18, 306
Rickless v United Artists Corporation [1988] QB 40;
    [1987] 2 WLR 945; (1987) 131 SJ 362; [1987] 1 All
    ER 679; [1987] FSR 362; (1987) 84 LS Gaz 654, CA   253
Roberts v Candiware [1980] FSR 352   244
Ross v Hopkinson (1956) *The Times*, 17 October   94
Rost v Edwards and Others [1990] 2 All ER 641   393
Rothermere (Lord) v Levin (Bernard) & Times
    Newspapers [1973] (Unreported)   99
Royal Aquarium v Parkinson [1892] 1 QB 431   73

St Andrews, Heddington, *Re* [1978] Fam 121; [1977]
    3 WLR 286; (1976) 121 SJ 286, Salisbury
    Consistory Court   360
St Mary's, Barnes, *Re* [1982] 1 WLR 531; [1982] 1
    All ER 456, Const Ct   373
Saltman Engineering Co, Ferotel and Monarch
    Engineering Co (Mitcham) v Campbell Engineering
    [1963] 3 All ER 413; (1963) 65 RPC 203, CA   188
Savoy Hotel PLC v British Broadcasting Corporation
    (1983) New LJ 1100; *reversing* (1982) 133 New LJ
    105   176
Schering Chemicals v Falkman [1982] QB 1; [1981] 2
    WLR 848; (1981) 125 SJ 342; [1981] 2 All ER
    321, CA   21, 179, 188, 269, 277
Schild v Express Newspapers (1982) *The Times*,
    5 October   50
Schweppes v Wellingtons [1984] FSR 210   230
Scott v Scott [1913] AC 417   14, 305, 311, 319
Searle (GD) & Co v Celltech [1982] FSR 92, CA   177
Secretary of State for Defence v Guardian
    Newspapers [1985] AC 339; [1984] 3 WLR 986;
    (1984) 128 SJ 571; [1984] 3 All ER 601; (1984) 81
    LS Gaz 3426, HL   202, 297
Senior v Holdsworth, *ex p* Independent Television
    News [1976] QB 23; [1975] 2 WLR 987; 119 SJ
    393; [1975] 2 All ER 1009, CA   198
Shaw v DPP [1962] AC 220; [1961] 2 WLR 897; 125
    JP 437; 105 SJ 421; [1961] 2 All ER 446; 45 Cr
    App R 113, HL   155-7
Sheen v Clegg (1967) *Daily Telegraph*, 22 June   210
Shevill v Presse Alliance [1992] 1 All ER 404, CA   651

Silkin *v* Beaverbrook Newspapers [1958] 1 WLR 743;
102 SJ 491; [1958] 2 All ER 516   80
Singh *v* Gillard (1988) 138 New LJ 444; *The*
Independent, 5 May   42
Singh *v* Observer [1989] 3 All ER 777, CA; [1989] 1
All ER 751   55
Slim *v* Daily Telegraph (1968) 2 QB 157; [1968] 2
WLR 599; 112 SJ 97; [1968] 1 All ER 497, CA   80
Slipper *v* British Broadcasting Corporation [1991] 1
All ER 165   96
Snepp *v* US 444 US 507 (1980)   177
Sports & General Press Agency *v* Our Dogs
Publishing Co [1916] 2 KB 880   208
Springfield *v* Thame (1903) 89 LT 242   219, 244
Stephens *v* Avery [1988] Ch 449; [1988] 2 WLR 1280;
(1988) 132 SJ 822; [1988] 2 All ER 477; [1988]
FSR 510; [1988] LS Gaz June 29, 45, Ch D   180, 241
Stirling *v* Associated Newspapers (1960) SLT 5   288
Sun Life Assurance Co of Canada *v* Smith (WH)
(1934) 150 LT 211   117
Sun Printers *v* Westminster Press (1982) 126 SJ 260;
[1982] 1 IRLR 292, CA   237
Sunday Times *v* United Kingdom [1979] 2 EHRR
245, European Court of Human Rights   5, 6–7, 264
Sunday Times *v* United Kingdom, European Court
of Human Rights, 26 November 1991   6
Sutcliffe *v* Pressdram [1990] 1 All ER 269   44

Tate *v* Thomas (1924) 1 Ch 503   217
Taverner Rutledge *v* Trexapalm (1975) 119 SJ 792;
[1975] FSR 479   228
Taylor (S.H.) and Co *v* Director-General of the
Office of Fair Trading (Unreported) 4 July 1980,
but see (1980) *The Times*, 15 February   434
Taylor *v* Topping (1990) *The Times*, 15 February   302
Telnikoff *v* Matusevitch [1990] 3 All ER 865; [1991]
4 All ER 817, HL   43, 80–81, 84, 85
Tennant (Lady Anne) *v* Associated Newspapers
[1979] FRS 298   209
Thomson *v* Times Newspapers [1969] 1 WLR 1236;
113 SJ 549; [1969] 3 All ER 648, CA   285
Thorpe *v* Waugh 1979 (Unreported) Court of Appeal
Transcript No 282   70
Tracy *v* Kemsley Newspapers (1954) *The Times*,
9 April   62
Trevor & Sons *v* Solomon (1978) 248 EG 779   191

'Truth & Sportsmen', *Re*, *ex p* Bread Manufacturers
 (1937) 37 SRNSW 249 — 281
Turner *v* MGM [1950] WN 83; 66 TLR (Pt 1) 342;
 94 SJ 145; [1950] 1 All ER 449, HL — 83
Turner *v* Robinson (1860) 101 Ch R 121 — 232
Turner *v* Sullivan (1862) 6 LT 130 — 364

Union of Construction, Allied Trades and
 Technicians (UCATT) *v* Brain [1981] ICR 542;
 [1981] IRLR 224, CA — 61
United States *v* Mitchell, Appeal of Warner
 Communications 551 F2d 1252 (1976) — 351
Universal City Studios *v* Hubbard [1984] Ch 225;
 [1984] 2 WLR 492; (1984) 128 SJ 247; [1983] 2 All
 ER 596; (1984) 81 LS Gaz 1291, CA — 256
University of London Press *v* University Tutorial
 Press [1916] 2 Ch 601 — 216, 229
University of Oxford *v* Pergamon Press (1977) *The
 Times*, 19 October, CA — 229

Victoria Park Racing Co *v* Taylor (1937) 58 CLR 479 — 210
Victoria *v* Australian Building Construction
 Employees and Building Labourers Federation
 (1982) 152 CLR 25 — 381

W, *Re* (1991) *Guardian*, 7 August — 335
W *v* Edgell (1989) *The Independent*, 10 November,
 CA; *affirming* [1989] 1 All ER 1089 — 377
Wakeley *v* Cooke (1849) 4 Exch 511 — 74
Wallersteiner *v* Moir [1974] 1 WLR 991; 118 SJ 464;
 [1974] 3 All ER 217, CA — 284
Walter *v* Lane [1900] AC 539 — 218–19
Walter *v* Steinkopf [1892] 3 Ch 489 — 220–21, 227
Warner *v* Gestetner [1988] EIPR D-89 — 244
Warwick Film Productions *v* Eisinger [1969] 1 Ch
 508; [1967] 3 WLR 1599; 111 SJ 961; [1967] 3 All
 ER 367 — 229
Wason *v* Walter (1868) LR 4 QB 74 — 394
Waterlows *v* Butterworths (1990) (Unreported, *but
 see The Independent*, 5 October) — 229
Webb *v* Times Publishing Co [1960] 2 QB 535; 3
 WLR 352; 104 SJ 605; [1960] 2 All ER 789 — 88
Weber case (10/1989/170/226) European Court of
 Human Rights, 22 May 1990, Series A No 177 — 357
Westminster City Council *v* Croyolgrange [1986] 2
 All ER 353 — 167

Whitehouse v Lemon (1978) 67 Cr App 70; *see also* R
  v Lemon; R v Gay News   160, 162
Wigan v Strange (1865) LR 1 CP 175   139–40
Wiggins v Field (1968) 112 SJ 656; (1968) LGR 635;
  [1968] Crim LR 503, DC   147, 148
Williams v Settle [1960] 1 WLR 1072; 104 SJ 847;
  [1960] 2 All ER 806, CA   208, 257
Williamson Music v The Pearson Partnership [1987]
  FSR 97   230
Wilson v IBA (No 2) [1988] SLT 276   408
Wombles v Wombles Skips [1975] FSR 488   228
Woodward v Hutchins [1977] 1 WLR 760; (1977) 121
  SJ 409; [1977] 2 All ER 751, CA   185, 191
Wright v Outram (1890) 17 R 596   364
Wyrko v Newspaper Publishing Co (1988) *The
  Independent*, 27 May   206

X (A Minor), *Re* [1984] 1 WLR 1422; 1 All ER 53;
  (1985) 15 Fam Law 59; (1984) 81 LS Gaz 3259   334
X (A Minor), (Wardship: Jurisdiction), *Re* [1975]
  Fam 47; [1975] 2 WLR 335; *sub nom* X (A Minor)
  (Wardship: Restriction on Publication), *Re* [1975] 1
  All ER 697, CA   25, 334
X v Morgan Grampian Publishers & Others [1990] 2
  All ER 1   200
X v Y [1988] 2 All ER 648   187, 203
X and Association of Z v United Kingdom 38 Coll
  Dec 86, 4515/70   4
X County Council v A; *see* X (A Minor), *Re*
X, Y and Z (Minors), *In re* (1991) *The Times*, 20 March   333

Yousoupoff v MGM Pictures (1939) 50 TLR 581   49

Table of Statutes

Administration of Justice
  Act 1960
  s 12   304
    (1)   332
    (2)   321
Administration of Justice
  Act 1982
  s 62   369
Administration of Justice
  (Miscellaneous
  Provisions) Act 1933
  s 2(2)   315–16
Admission of Press to
  Meetings Act 1908   462
Air Force Act 1955
  s 94(2)   373
  s 193   449
Aliens Restriction
  (Amendment) Act 1919
  s 3   449
Army Act 1955
  s 94(2)   373
  s 97   449
  s 193   449
Atomic Energy Act 1946
  s 11   433
Atomic Energy Act 1954
  s 6(3)   433
Atomic Energy Act 1965
  Sched 1 para 3   433

Backing of Warrants
  (Republic of Ireland)
  Act 1965
  Sched 2 para 2   310
Betting, Gaming and
  Lotteries Act 1963
  s 1   377

Bill of Rights 1688
  Art 9   391–2
British
  Telecommunications
  Act 1984
  s 43   101
Broadcasting Act 1981   546
  s 2   605
  s 4   624
  s 5(1)   624
  s 29(3)   629, 630
Broadcasting Act 1990   31,
              137, 516, 594, 597, 598
  s 2   605–6
    (2)   632
  s 3(3)   635
  s 6   601–2, 611
    (1)   29, 30, 407, 445
    (2)   407, 621
    (6)   597
    (8)   647
  s 7   611
    (b)   469
  s 8   639
    (2)   640
  s 9   639, 641
  s 10   26–7, 409, 630
    (3)   629
  s 11(2)   624
  s 15(5)(1)   600
  s 16   632
  s 17   632–4
    (3)–(6)   632
    (12)   633
  s 20   168
    (1)   633
  s 23   168–9
    (4)   631

s 25	635	Sched 11 Part 2, para	
s 36	408	1(3)	624
ss 40–42	636	Sched 15	119, 599
s 44	649	para 6	159
s 45(2)	649	Sched 16	645
s 47	644	Sched 17	232
s 49(2)	647	Sched 20	395
s 74(*c*)	646	para 26	337
s 85	644	para 29	331
ss 86–9	644	**Building Societies Act**	
s 90	644	**1986**	
ss 91–2	611	s 73	510
s 92(2)	647	s 81	510
s 94	644	Sched 12 para 9	510
s 143(3)	547	**Business Names Act 1985**	
s 144		s 4	509
(4)(*c*)	556		
(4)(*d*)	555, 556	**Cable and Broadcasting**	
(5)	555	**Act 1984**	633, 648
s 145	557	Sched 3 para 31	336
(2)	557	**Charities Act 1960**	
s 146	558	s 4	
s 147(2)	546	(4)(*c*)	512
s 150	548	(7)	512
ss 151–61	606	ss 6–8	512
s 152(3)	612	**Children Act 1989**	
s 153	611	ss 17, 18, 20, 24, Sched	
s 154(7)	607	2	478
s 155(4)	610	s 97	331
s 157	611	**Children and Young**	
s 162	119, 599	**Persons Act 1933**	
s 164	168	s 37	
s 166	54, 388	(1)	319
(1)	101	(2)	17
(3)	91–2	s 39	328, 329, 347
s 167	599	s 47	319
ss 168–74	645	(2)	17
s 175	247	s 49	
s 176	246	(1)	328
s 177	650	(2)	329
s 178	650	**Children and Young**	
s 182	631	**Persons Act 1963**	
s 188	632	s 57	328
Sched 2	639	(4)	329
Part IV	649	**Children and Young**	
Sched 5	647	**Persons Act 1969**	

s 10   328

Chronically Sick and
  Disabled Persons Act
  1970
 s 1(2)(*a*)   478

Cinemas Act 1985   69–70
 s 1(3)   567, 571
 ss 5–7   571

Cinematograph Act
  1909   566, 571

Cinematograph Act
  1952
 s 3   567

Cinematograph Films
  (Animals) Act 1937   126, 584

Civil Evidence Act 1968
 s 13(1)   77

Civil Jurisdiction and
  Judgments Act 1982   651

Civil Liability
  (Contribution) Act 1978
 s 1   64

Civil Service Reform Act
  1978   414

Community Health
  Councils (Access to
  Information) Act 1988   462
 s 1   463
  (1)(*c*)   472
 s 2   472
  (6)   466

Companies Act 1976
 s 1   495

Companies Act 1980
 s 4   488

Companies Act 1985
 s 10   498
 s 18   498
 ss 56–65   497
 s 190   490, 498
 s 191   490, 498, 499
 ss 198–200   490
 s 202   491
 s 203   490
 ss 204–5   490
 s 210   490

s 211(8)   498
s 213   491
s 214   491
s 217   491
s 219   499
 (2)   499
s 226(2)   494
s 232   494
s 233   494
s 235   496
s 237   496
s 239   496, 498
s 241   498
s 242   496
s 242A   497
s 247   495
s 248   495
s 249   495
s 250   495
s 254   495
s 255   495
s 255A   495
s 257   492
s 287   498
s 288   498
s 289   494
s 303   500
s 318   493
s 323   493
s 324   493
s 325   493
s 327   493
s 330   494
s 352   489, 498
s 353   498
s 356   489, 499
s 363   498
s 369   493
s 386   496
s 387   496
s 390   496
s 401   498
s 432   507
s 432(2A)   508
s 434   197
s 436   197

s 437
  (3)(*a*)   508
  (3)(*c*)   508
s 442   508
s 444   508
s 446   508
s 447   508
  (5)(*a*)   508
s 449   508
s 709   496, 499, 517
s 713   496
s 715   499
Sched 5
  paras 7–13
  para 24(2)   493
  para 25(3)–(5)   493
Sched 7   496, 497
  para 2   493
Sched 8   495
Sched 13   493
  para 17(2)   493
  para 25   498, 499
  para 26   499
  para 29   498
  Part IV   493
Companies Act 1989
s 4   494
s 7   495
s 9   496
s 11   496, 497
s 13   495
s 18   495
s 55   508
s 63   508
s 134
  (2)   490
  (3)   491
s 211   491
  (9)   491
s 212   491
s 219   491
Company Directors
  Disqualification Act
  1986
  ss 1–6, 11, 14, 18   518
Company Securities

(Insider Dealing) Act
  1985   197
Competition Act 1980   246
Computer Misuse Act
  1990   175
Conspiracy and
  Protection of Property
  Act 1875
s 7   212
Consumer Credit Act 1974
Part III   515
Contempt of Court Act
  1981   6, 18, 382–6
s 2
  (1)   283, 285
  (3)   278
s 3
  (1)   283
  (2)   283
  (3)   283
s 4   341–5, 365
s 5   281–3, 386
s 6
  (1)   286
  (2)   386
s 7   302, 304
s 8(3)   301
s 9   351–2
s 10   197, 198, 199–204, 431
s 11   338–41
s 12   302
s 13   302
s 14(1)   304
s 19   382
Sched 1
  para 4   278
  para 5   280
  para 6   280
  para 11   279
  para 12   279, 280
  para 13   279
  para 15   280
  para 16   281
Control of Pollution Act
  1974
s 6   476

s 41	476	(2)	227
s 42	476	(3)	232
s 64	476	(4)	233
s 82 (3)(*d*)	476	(5)	233
Copyright Act 1956	213	(6)	233
s 4(2)	243	s 18	234
s 18	257	s 19	234
s 43	217	s 20	233
(1)	217	s 21	234
(5)	217	s 23	235
Copyright, Designs and		s 24	235
Patents Act 1988	213	s 25	235
s 1(3)	225	s 26	235
s 3	216	s 29	235
(1)(*b*)	218	s 30	235
(2)	216	s 31	247
(3)	217	s 45	248
s 4	222	s 46	248
(2)	223	s 47	248
s 5	222, 223	s 49	248
s 6	224	s 50	248, 249
(3)	233, 242	s 58	248
s 7	224	s 60	249
(1)	224	s 62	249
s 8	221	s 63	249
s 9		s 64	249
(1)(*b*)	242	s 66	246
(1)(*c*)	243	s 68	249
(1)(*d*)	243	s 69	249
(2)(*a*)	242	s 70	249
(3)	242	s 71	249
s 10	243	s 72	250
s 11(2)	243	s 73	245
s 12		s 77	251
(2)	226	(1)	251
(3)	225	s 78	251
s 13	226	(5)	258
s 14	226	s 79(2)–(6)	251
s 15	221, 226	s 80	253
s 16		(1)	253
(1)(*a*)	227	(2)(*b*)	253
(2)	234	s 81	253
(3)	227	s 82	253
(3)(*b*)	232	s 83	253
s 17		s 84	218
(1)	240	s 85	208

(2)	208
s 86	250
(2)	217
s 87	208, 250
s 89	
(1)	251
(2)	218, 253
s 90(3)	244
s 91	244
s 92	244
s 94	250
s 95	250
s 96(2)	257
s 97	
(1)	257
(2)	257
s 99	258
s 103	
(1)	257
(2)	255
s 107	259
s 108	259
s 109	259
(2)	259
s 111	259
s 113	258
ss 116–35	245
s 129	246
s 135A–G	247
s 141	246
s 144	247, 258
s 153	225
s 154	225
s 155	225
s 163(3)	226
s 165(3)	226
s 178	216, 224, 236, 248, 255
s 180	
(2)	254
(4)(a)	155
s 182(1)	254
s 183	254
s 184	254
ss 185–8	255
s 190	255
s 191	255

s 192	255
ss 194–200	255
s 206	254
s 298	224
Sched 1	226
Sched 2	255
Copyright (Works of Art) Act 1862	222
Coroners Act 1988	
s 8(3)(d)	369
County Courts (Penalties for Contempt) Act 1983	304
Courts and Legal Services Act 1991	
s 8	44, 98
Criminal Justice Act 1925	
s 41	381
Criminal Justice Act 1961	
s 22	617
Criminal Justice Act 1972	
s 36	338
Criminal Justice Act 1987	
s 2	197
s 8	327
s 11	327
Criminal Justice Act 1988	
s 35	338
s 36	338
s 71	540, 581
s 158	535
s 159	8, 18, 347
s 160	133
Criminal Justice Act 1991	
s 68	327
Criminal Justice (Amendment) Act 1981	
s 1	326
Criminal Law Act 1967	
s 4(1)	617
Criminal Law Act 1977	
s 6	212
s 53	136–7
Customs and Excise Act 1952	154

ss 44(b) and 275, and
   Sched 7   155
Customs Consolidation
   Act 1876   153

Data Protection Act 1984
   s 1   209
   s 9   209
   s 10   209
   s 13   209
   s 34(1)   310
   Sched 1   209
Defamation Act 1952   388–9
   s 1   54
   s 4   94
   s 5   74
   s 7   91, 93, 481, 500
     (3)
     (5)   388
   s 9   500
     (1)   395
     (2)   363
   s 10   405
   s 16(3)   54
   s 17(2)   101
   Sched
     para 6   481
     para 8   388, 481
     para 10   388, 481
     Part II para 11   500
Defence Contracts Act
   1958
   s 4(3)   316–17
Dentists Act 1984
   s 22   516
Domestic and Appellate
   Proceedings
   (Restrictions of
   Publicity) Act 1968
   s 1   320
   s 2   318
     (3)   330

Ecclesiastical Jurisdiction
   Measure 1963
   s 81(2)   384

Education Act 1980
   s 8   478
Emergency Provisions
   (Northern Ireland) Act
   1978
   s 18   445
   s 22   443
Employment Act 1982
   s 15   61
European Assembly
   Elections Act 1978
   s 3   403
   Sched 1 para 2(3)   403
European Communities
   Act 1972
   s 11(2)   443

Fair Trading Act 1973
   s 58(3)(*a*)–(*b*)   505
   s 59(3)   503, 505
   s 61(1)(*b*)   506
   Sched 3 para 22   506
Family Law Reform Act
   1986   330
   ss 55–60   318
Family Law Reform Act
   1987   330
   s 22   318
Financial Services Act
   1986   495
   s 59   514
   s 102   513
   s 103   513
     (2)–(4)   514
   s 177   197, 509
   Sched 1
     para 15   514
     para 25   514
Food Safety Act 1990
   s 19   475

Gaming Act 1968
   s 2   377
Gas Act 1986
   s 36   511

General Rate Act 1967
s 108   473

Health Service Joint
  Consultative
  Committees (Access to
  Information) Act 1986   462
s 2(4)   466
s 3   472
Housing Act 1961
s 22   477
Housing Act 1985
s 106   477
Housing Associations Act
  1985
s 3   510
s 24   510
s 78   510

Immigration Act 1971
s 22(4)   375
Incitement to
  Disaffection Act 1934   448
s 2(1)–(2)   448
Incitement to Mutiny
  Act 1797   447
Indecency with Children
  Act 1960
s 1(1)   130
Indecent Displays
  (Control) Act 1981   151, 166
Industrial and Provident
  Societies Act 1965
s 39   510
s 40   510
Industry Act 1975
s 27   456
Sched 5   456
Inner Urban Areas Act
  1978
Sched para 1(3)(*a*)   475
Insolvency Act 1986
s 47   517
s 48   517
s 131   517
s 133   517

s 236   517
s 290   518
s 366   518
Interception of
  Communications Act 1985
s 1   175, 434

Judicial Proceedings
  (Regulation of
  Reports) Act 1926
s 1
  (1)(*a*)   338
  (1)(*b*)   330
  (3)   330

Land Registration Act
  1988
s 1(1)   480
Law of Libel
  Amendment Act 1888
s 3   86, 387
s 8   101, 161
Legal Aid Act 1974
s 7   39
Sched 1 Part II para 1   39
Libel Act 1843
s 7   161
Licensing Act 1964
ss 30–34   516
Licensing Act 1981
s 2(3)   475
Limitation Act 1980
s 4A   42, 95
s 32A   95
Local Government
  (Access to
  Information) Act
  1985   462, 472
Local Government Act
  1972
ss 23–4   475
s 30   475
s 94   473
s 95(3)   473
s 96   473
s 97   473

s 100	463
s 100A	463
(2) and (3)	465
(4)	466
(5)	466
(6)(*a*)	467
(7)	468
s 100B	
(1)–(6)	468
(7)	467
s 100C	472
s 100D	468
(2)	472
s 100E	463, 468
s 100G	472
s 100H	468
(1)–(3)	472
(3)	472
s 100I	464
s 100J	462
s 101(9)	463
s 102	463
s 105	473
s 159	469
s 225	476
s 228	
(1)	471
(2)	470
(5)	476
s 270(1)	462, 463
Sched 12A	465
Local Government Act 1986	
ss 2–6	482
s 2A	483
Local Government Act 1988	
s 2	479
s 12	479
s 27	482
s 28	483
Local Government and Housing Act 1989	
s 11	469
s 19	473

Local Government Finance Act 1982	
s 12(2)	469
s 15	471
s 17	469–70
(1)	470
(3)	471
s 18(5)	471
s 18A	471
s 24	470
(1)(*a*) and (*b*)	471
s 228(2)	471
Local Government Finance Act 1988	
Sched 2 para 7	474
Sched 10 para 8	474
Local Government Finance (Publicity for Auditors' Reports) Act 1991	471
Local Government (Miscellaneous Provisions) Act 1982	152, 570
s 2	166
Sched 3	
para 3(1)	571
paras (7)–(13)	475
Local Government Planning and Land Act 1980	
s 2	478
s 3(1)	479
s 18	479
ss 95–6	479
Sched 16	479
Local Government (Scotland) Act 1973	
s 40	473
Magistrates' Courts Act 1980	
s 4(2)	315
s 6(2)	315
s 8	324
(3)	324

(6)	325
(9)	365
s 69	
(2)	17
(4)	319
s 71	331
s 121(3),(4)	310
s 147	310
Sched 11	332
Malicious Communications Act 1988	170
Marine Broadcasting (Offences) Act 1967	645–6
Matrimonial Causes Act 1973	
s 45	330
s 48(2)	318
Medical Act 1976	
s 35	516
Ministry of Defence Police Act 1987	
s 6	449
Naval Discipline Act 1957	
s 61(2)	373
s 94	449
Newspaper Libel and Registration Act 1881	161
Newspapers, Printers and Reading Rooms Repeal Act 1869	
Sched 2	198
Obscene Publications Act 1857	107
Obscene Publications Act 1959	105–6, 108–10, 119, 569, 572, 579, 617
s 1	109, 110–11, 116, 133, 138, 154
(2)	143
(3)(*b*)	119
s 2	115
(4)	158–9
(5)	117, 118
(6)	114
s 3	124, 125, 134
s 4	116, 120–24, 143, 154, 159
s 7	132–3
Obscene Publications Act 1964	119
Official Secrets Act 1911	414–15
s 1	196, 415, 417
(2)	429, 430
s 2	12, 413–16, 418
s 6	431
s 8	415
s 9	432
(1)	430
(2)	431
Official Secrets Act 1920	
s 6	196, 431
s 8(4)	316
Official Secrets Act 1939	197, 431
Official Secrets Act 1989	12, 196, 204, 415, 418
s 1	
(1)	419
(3)	419
(4)(*a*)	419
(5)	423
(6)	419
(8)	419
s 2	421, 457
(3)	423
s 3	421
(3)	421
(4)	423
(5)	421
s 4	422
(3)	422
(4)	423
(5)	423
s 5	423–6
s 6	427
s 7	422
s 8	423, 427–8
s 10(1)	432

s 11
  (1)   431
  (4)   316
s 12   419
  (1)(*a*)   420
  (2)   421
  (*f*) and (*g*)   420
s 15(3)   420

Parliamentary Papers Act
  1840
s 3   395
Planning (Hazardous
  Substances) Act 1990
s 28   476
Planning Inquiries
  (Attendance of Public)
  Act 1982
s 1   378
Planning (Listed
  Buildings and
  Conservation Areas)
  Act 1990
s 2   475
Police Act 1964
s 32(2)   379
s 51(3)   196
s 53   449
Police and Criminal
  Evidence Act 1984   445
s 9
  (1)   430
  (2)   259, 430
s 11(2)(*b*)   430
s 13   205
s 14   205
s 19   207
s 24(2)(*b*)   431
Sched 1
  para 2   206
  para 3   205
    (*b*)   430
  para 11   206
  para 12   430
  para 14(*c*)(i)   430
Post Office Act 1953

s 11   101, 150
Prevention of Corruption
  Act 1906   176
Prevention of Terrorism
  (Temporary
  Provisions) Act 1989
s 18   444, 617
s 19   444
Protection of Children
  Act 1978   586
s 1   130
Public Bodies
  (Admission to
  Meetings) Act 1960   462
s 1
  (2)   464
  (4)(*a*)   467
  (4)(*b*)   467
  (4)(*c*)   468
  (7)   467, 468
  (8)   464
s 2(1)   463
Sched   463
Public Order Act 1936
s 9   140
Public Order Act
  1986   101, 167, 447
s 4   170–71
s 5   212
s 18   168
s 19   168
s 22   168
s 25   169
s 26   169
Public Records Act 1958   440
s 5(1)   456
Public Records Act
  1967   440, 456

Rates Act 1984
  Sched 1 para 20   473
Registered Homes Act 1984
s 7   478
Regulation of Railways
  Act 1871
s 7   379

Rehabilitation of
  Offenders Act
  1974   68, 77–8
  ss 8, 9   78
Rent Act 1977
    Sched 15, Part II   319
  ss 64, 66(1)   477
Representation of the
  People Act 1983
  s 63   405
  s 75
    (1)   405–6
    (5)   405
  s 81   411
  s 88   411
  s 89   411
  s 90(1)(*b*)   411
  s 92   410
  s 93
    (1)(*b*)   406
    (2)   404
  s 95   410
  s 106   403
    (5)   404
  s 168(7)   516
    Sched 4, para 8(1) 411
Restrictive Trade
  Practices Act 1976
  ss 6–14   515
  s 23   515
    (3)   515
  s 35   516
Restrictive Trade
  Practices Court Act
  1977   515

Sexual Offences Act 1956 126
  s 13   144–7
Sexual Offences
  (Amendment) Act
  1967
  s 1   336
  s 4   336–7
  s 7   336
Slander of Women Act
  1891   54

Social Security and
  Housing Benefit Act
  1982
  s 31(1)   477
Supreme Court Act
  1981
  s 29(3)   347
  s 69   98
  s 72   204, 256
    (6)   256

Telecommunications Act
  1984
  s 6   647
  s 19   511
  s 43   152
Theatres Act 1843   138
Theatres Act
  1968   138–41, 168
  s 2
    (2)   142
    (4)   141, 146
  s 3   141
    (1)   120–21
  s 4(1)   54
  s 7   140–41
  s 8   145
  s 9   141
    (2)   143
  s 10   143–4
  s 15   141
  s 16   142
  s 18   140
    (2)   142
Theft Act 1968
  s 20   179, 205
Town and Country
  Planning Act 1990
  s 69   474
  s 188   474
  s 214   475
Trade Descriptions Act
  1968   560, 581
Trade Union and Labour
  Relations Act 1974
  s 2(1)   56

Tribunals of Inquiry
  (Evidence) Act 1921
  s 1(2)(*c*)   386
  s 2   379

Unsolicited Goods and
  Services Act
  s 4   150–51

Video Recordings Act
  1984   32, 128, 575–83
  s 2   576–7
  (1)   577
  (2)   576–8
  (11)   575
  s 3   577–8
  (2)   577

  (4)   578
  (5)   578
  (8)   578
  (9)   578
  s 4   578–9, 590
  s 7   579–80

Water Act 1989
  s 31   511
  s 117   511
Wireless Telegraphy Act
  1949
  s 1   644
  s 5   617
  (*b*)(i)   434

Zoo Licensing Act 1981
  s 2(3)   475

Table of Statutory Instruments

Accounts and Audit
  Regulations 1983 (SI
  1983 No 1761)
reg 9   470
reg 11   470, 471
Agricultural Lands
  Tribunal (Rules)
  Order 1978 (SI 1978
  No 259)
r 24   380

Civil Aviation
  (Investigation of
  Accidents) Regulations
  1969 (SI 1969 No 752)   379
Community Charges
  (Administration and
  Enforcement)
  Regulations 1989 (SI
  1989 No 438)
reg 11   474
Companies (Fees)
  Regulations 1991 (SI
  1991 No 1206)   499
Control of Atmospheric
  Pollution (Research
  and Publicity)
  Regulations 1977 (SI
  1977 No 19)
reg 6   476
Control of Pollution
  (Radioactive Waste)
  Regulations 1985 (SI
  1985 No 708)   476

Control of Pollution
  (Registers) Regulations
  1985 (SI 1985 No 813)
reg 6476   476
Copyright (International
  Conventions)
  (Amendment No 3)
  Order 1973 (SI 1973
  No 963)   225
Copyright (Material
  Open to Public
  Inspection) (Making of
  Copies) Order 1990 (SI
  1990 No 1427)   248
Coroners Rules 1984
  (1984 SI No 552)   370
r 37   372
r 36(2)   371
Criminal Appeal
  (Amendment) Rules
  1989 (SI 1989 No
  1102)   348
Criminal Appeal
  (Reference of Points of
  Law) Rules 1973 (SI
  1973 No 1115)
r 6   338
Criminal Appeal Rules
  1968 (SI 1968 No 1262)
r 16A   348
r 16B   349
Crown Court
  (Amendment No 2)
  Rules 1989 (SI 1989
  No 1103)   316

Crown Court Rules 1982
(SI 1982 No 1109)
r 24A   316, 349

Education (School
Government)
Regulations 1989 (SI
1989 No 1503)
regs 21 and 24   478
Education (School
Information)
Regulations 1989 (SI
1989 No 1503)   478
Education (Schools
Curriculum and
Related Information)
Regulations 1989 (SI
1989 No 954)   478
European Assembly
Elections Regulations
1984 (SI 1984 No
137)   403, 411

Financial Services Act
1986 (Restriction of
Scope) Order 1988 (SI
1988 No 318)   514

Gas (Underground
Storage) (Inquiries
Procedure) Rules 1966
(SI 1966 No 1375)
r 8(4)   380
General Development
Order 1988 (SI 1988
No 1813)
Art 27   474
Art 28   474
General Medical Council
Preliminary
Proceedings
Committee and
Professional Conduct
Committee
(Procedure) Rules 1988

(SI 1988 No 2255)   378
General Optical Council
(Disciplinary
Committee)
(Procedure) Rules 1985
(SI 1985 No 1580)
r 11   378

Immigration Appeals
(Procedure) Rules 1984
(SI 1984 No 2041)
r 32(2),(3)   375
Independent Schools
Tribunal Rules 1958
(SI 1958 No 519)
r 8   380
Indictments (Procedure)
Rules 1971 (SI 1971
No 2084)
r 10   316
Industrial Tribunal
(Rules of Procedure)
Regulations 1985 (SI
1985 No 16)
r 17   374
r 9(8)   374
Insolvency Rules 1986
(SI 1986 No 1925)
r 4.11   517
r 4.35   517
r 6.34(3)   518
r 7   353
Insolvent Companies
(Disqualification of
Unfit Directors)
Proceedings Rules
1987 (SI 1987
No 2023)
r 7(2)   518

Land Registration Fees
(No 2) Order 1990 (SI
1990 No 2029)   480
Land Registration (Open
Register) Rules 1990
(SI 1990 No 1362)   480

Lands Tribunal
(Amendment) Rules
1977 (SI 1977 No 1820)
r 33A   380
Local Authorities
(Publication of
Manpower
Information)
(England) Regulations
1983 (SI 1983 No 8)   479
Local Government
(Allowances)
Regulations 1974 (SI
1974 No 447)
reg 5   470
Local Government
(Inspection of
Documents) Order
1986 (SI 1986 No 854)   469
Local Government
(Inspection of
Documents)
(Summary of Rights)
Order 1986 (SI 1986
No 854)   472

Magistrates' Courts
Rules 1981 (SI 1981
No 552)
r 5(1),(3)   325
r 70(6)   315
r 66(12)   354
Matrimonial Causes
Rules 1977 (SI 1977
No 344)
r 37   318
r 48   318
Mental Health Review
Tribunal Rules 1983
(SI 1983 No 942)
r 21   376

National Health Service
(Service Committees
and Tribunal)
Regulations 1974 (SI

1974 No 455)
r 38   380
Nurses, Midwives and
Health Visitors
(Professional Conduct)
Rules 1983 (SI 1983
No 887)
r 16   378

Official Secrets
(Prohibited Places)
Order 1955 (SI 1955
No 1497)   433
Official Secrets
(Prohibited Places)
Order 1975 (SI 1975
No 182)   433

Pharmaceutical Society
(Statutory Committee)
Order of Council 1978
(SI 1978 No 20)
reg 16   378
Police (Discipline)
Regulations 1985 (SI
1985 No 518)
r 18(2)   379
Police (Discipline)
(Senior Officers)
Regulations 1985 (SI
1985 No 519)
r 13   379
Prison Rules 1964 (SI No
1964 No 388)
r 5   304
r 20   304
r 34   304
r 63   304
Public Order (Northern
Ireland) Order 1981
(SI 1981 No 609)
Art 3   444

Register of County Court
Judgments

Regulations 1985 (SI 1985 No 1807) 354
Registration of Restrictive Trading Agreements Regulations 1976 (SI 1976 No 183)
reg 9 515
reg 10 515
Rent Act (County Court Proceedings for Possession) Rules 1981 (SI 1981 No 139)
r 6(2) 319
Rent Assessment Committees (England and Wales) Regulations 1971 (SI 1971 No 1065)
reg 3 380
(1) 380, 381
Representation of the People Regulations 1983 (SI 1983 No 435)
reg 18 410
Rules of the Supreme Court 1965 (SI 1965 No 1776)
Ord 11, r1(1) 651
Ord 24, r 14A 357
Ord 32, r 13 322
Ord 52 302
r 1(2)(a) 382
r 2 303
r 8(ii) 304
Ord 63, r 4 353, 355
1(c) 355
Ord 68, r 1(2) 353
Ord 90, r 7 318
Ord 113 319

Shipping Casualties and Appeals and Rehearing Rules 1923 (SR & O 1923 No 752)

r 11 379
Social Security (Adjudication) Regulations 1986 (SI 1986 No 2218)
reg 4(4) 380
Solicitors (Disciplinary Proceedings) Rules 1985 (SI 1985 No 226)
r 24 379

Town and Country Planning (Local Plans for Greater London) Regulations 1974 (SI 1974 No 1481)
regs 25–8 475
Town and Country Planning (Structure and Local Plans) Regulations 1982 (SI 1982 No 555)
regs 36–9 475

Valuation and Community Charge Tribunals Regulations 1989 (SI 1989 No 439) 380
Veterinary Surgeons and Veterinary Practitioners (Disciplinary Committee) (Procedure and Evidence) Rules 1967 (SI 1967 No 659)
r 15(1) 378
Video Recordings (Labelling) Regulations 1985 (SI 1985 No 911)
reg 2(5)(b) 581

Chapter 1

Freedom to Communicate

We define freedom of the press as that degree of freedom from restraint which is essential to enable proprietors, editors and journalists to advance the public interest by publishing the facts and opinions without which a democratic electorate cannot make responsible judgments.

Third Royal Commission on the Press[1]

The phrase 'freedom of the press' was the chant of the mob that carried courageous publishers in triumph through the streets of London after they had been acquitted by juries for seditious attacks on George III and his ministers. It is a slogan that, for all its rhetorical flourish and historic associations, has never become part of the law of Britain. In the United States, by contrast, it was embodied in the First Amendment to the constitution:

> Congress shall make no law respecting an establishment of religion, or prohibiting the free exercise thereof; or abridging the freedom of speech, or of the press; or the right of the people peaceably to assemble and to petition the government for a redress of grievances.

Britain has no written constitution. Its laws are made piecemeal by Parliament and by judges, who are placed under no overriding constitutional obligation to preserve or protect the media's right to report matters of public interest. British law comprises thousands of separate statutes and decided cases: none of them gives unqualified support to freedom of expression. By and large, Parliament and the judiciary have taken the view that free speech is a very good thing so long as it does not cause trouble. Then, it may become expensive speech – speech visited with costly court actions, fines and damages, and occasionally imprisonment. 'Free speech', in fact, means no more than speech from which illegal utterances are subtracted. If that sounds a circuitous definition compared to

---

[1] Royal Commission on the Press, *Final Report*, HMSO, 1977, Cmnd 6810, Ch 2, para 3.

the sweeping prose of the First Amendment, it none the less reflects
the pragmatic approach of British Law Lords:

> 'Free' in itself is vague and indeterminate. It must take its
> colour from the context. Compare, for instance, its use in free
> speech, free love, free dinner and free trade. Free speech does
> not mean free speech: it means speech hedged in by all the
> laws against defamation, blasphemy, sedition and so forth. It
> means freedom governed by law . . .[2]

In practice, the free press is not a 'free' press: it is what is left of
the copy by laws and by lawyers. Defamation, blasphemy and
sedition have been with us for centuries, but in recent years new
rods have been fashioned and old ones polished for editorial backs:
breach of confidence, contempt of court, official secrecy, D-notices,
incitement to disaffection, prevention of terrorism, copyright – the
grounds for censorship are legion.

There are many reasons for this increase. When Wilkes and
Cobbett were radical journalists, facts belonged to everyone. But
today information is property, which can be bought and sold,
exploited and embargoed. The courts can order presses to be
stopped for the same reasons as they can order assets to be frozen
or property to be returned. In the days when pamphleteers
demanded democracy, they were fighting a ruling class whose
power and position was obvious to all. It had few civil servants
and therefore few official secrets. But for today's public servant,
secrecy is a form of power: actions and advice, of the most routine
nature, must not be shared with the people. We have become more
civilized and more sensitive to the needs of individuals, and more
reluctant to pander to prurience: hence our law against naming
rape or blackmail victims, the limits on reporting evidence in
divorce cases, and the rules against revealing old criminal convictions. We have also become concerned – in a confused and
unscientific way – about the psychological power of new forms of
communication. They need 'control' and 'regulation' and 'licensing', words that are sometimes used as euphemisms for censorship.
Wilkes and Cobbett wrote for a society that still shuddered at the
memory of the puritans and their censors, the good people appointed by Cromwell to license and to regulate the press. Today
that sort of licensing is accepted for much of the media. Television,
radio, cable and video are all 'regulated' by boards and commissions, mostly made up of Government appointees.

The expression of facts and ideas and opinions never can be
absolutely free. Words can do damage, even if they are true – by
betraying a military position or by prejudicing a trial, or by inciting

---

[2] *James v Commonwealth of Australia* [1936] AC 578.

racial hatred. Even the Americans have come to agree that Congress can, despite the First Amendment, make laws stopping people from shouting 'fire' in crowded theatres. It behoves all who wish journalists and broadcasters to enjoy 'rights' to acknowledge that others have valid claims to legal protection as well – to lead a private life, to undergo a trial free from sensational prejudice, and to have false accusations corrected with the same prominence as they are made. These 'rights' are in some cases much more poorly protected than the media rights that form the principal subject of this book. If those who work in the media wish to enjoy the freedom desired for them by the Royal Commission – the freedom to publish facts and opinions that are in the public interest – they may have to forgo some of the comparative freedom they enjoy to publish facts and opinions that are not.

Free speech is what is left of speech after the law has had its say. But even after that long-winded exercise, a considerable amount remains, an amount that still is a matter for pride, if tinged with apprehension at the increasing number of unnecessary restrictions. Despite these restrictions, there are six rules of fundamental importance in the day-to-day defence of public-interest reporting. They form the procedural pillars for freedom of expression in Britain.

The European Convention on Human Rights

The European Convention on Human Rights was drawn up in 1951. Politically, it was the product of a desire for Western European unity, and its ideals were shaped by the need to have some legal bulwark against a resurgence of fascism, and by a wish to articulate those civil rights that seemed threatened by Communist regimes in Eastern Europe. Britain ratified the Convention in 1951 but did not accept its enforcement machinery until 1966, and its impact on English law was not apparent until the next decade, when the European Court of Human Rights in Strasbourg began to hand down decisions holding the United Kingdom in breach of the Convention for failures to guarantee certain basic rights to its citizens.

Any person who believes that his or her rights under the Convention have been infringed by a court ruling or an administrative act, and who has exhausted all the possibilities of redress in the British courts may complain to Strasbourg. If the complaint is upheld, the British Government is required by the Convention to change the law that permitted the original infringement. The Convention is not directly enforceable in British courts. British judges are not 'bound' by the Convention – they are obliged to follow British law.

But where local law is absent or ambiguous, and British courts have the opportunity to shape the law according to their notion of an appropriate public policy, they should give effect to the policy laid down by the Convention. In cases involving media rights heard in British courts today the Convention and the cases on it decided by the European Court are usually cited in argument on behalf of the media. They are not binding on the judges, but they have a persuasive authority where judicial choice is possible.

Article 10: Freedom of expression

Article 10(1) of the European Convention sets out the basic principle that the makers of common and statute law in Britain have never quite mustered the courage to adopt:

> Everyone has the right to freedom of expression. This right shall include freedom to hold opinions and to receive and impart information and ideas without interference by public authority and regardless of frontiers.

The European Court of Human Rights has not hesitated to give prominence to Article 10. It has observed:

> Freedom of expression constitutes one of the essential foundations of a society, one of the basic conditions for its progress and for the development of every man. Subject to paragraph 2 of Article 10, it is applicable not only to 'information' or 'ideas' that are favourably received, but also to those that offend, shock or disturb the state or any sector of the population. Such are the demands of that pluralism, tolerance and broadmindedness without which there is no democratic society.[3]

There are, of course, exceptions. Article 10 does not prevent states from licensing radio, television or the cinema. Nor does it guarantee a right of access to the electronic media – e.g., for extremist political advertising on television.[4] Article 10(2) sets out the qualifications in detail:

> The exercise of these freedoms, since it carries with it duties and responsibilities, may be subject to such formalities, conditions, restrictions or penalties as are prescribed by law and are necessary in a democratic society, in the interests of national security, territorial integrity or public safety, for the prevention of disorder or crime, for the protection of health or morals, for the protection of the reputation or rights of others, for

---

[3] *Handyside* v *United Kingdom* [1976] EHRR 737.
[4] *X and Association of Z* v *UK* 38 Coll Dec 86, 4515/70.

preventing the disclosure of information received in confidence or for maintaining the authority and impartiality of the judiciary.

At first blush Article 10(2) seems to take away most of the freedom guaranteed by Article 10(1). In fact, it marks an improvement on English law in four ways:

- Any infringement of free speech must be 'prescribed by law'. That means that the restriction must be clear, certain and predictable. Law, to be 'prescribed', must be adequately accessible and formulated with sufficient precision to enable citizens to regulate their conduct.[5] A judge who exercised some common-law power in an entirely novel way would be in breach of the Convention, even if he claimed to act 'in the interests' of one of the excepted values.

- The requirement that any infringement must be 'necessary in a democratic society' is even more helpful to the media, thanks to the interpretation of that phrase by the European Court. The Court has held that it means something more than 'useful', 'reasonable' or 'desirable'. Any restriction on the media, to be valid, must in the first place be justified by a *'pressing social need'*, and then, even if the social need *is* pressing, the restriction must be reasonably proportionate to the aim of responding to that need.[6]

- The Court has adopted a general approach to the interpretation of Article 10 that is favourable to the media. It has said that Article 10 should not be seen as requiring a 'balance' between, on the one hand, the value of freedom of expression and, on the other, the value of national security, crime prevention and the other exceptions in Article 10(2). These are not competing principles of equal weight: the values listed in Article 10(2) are simply 'a number of exceptions which must be strictly interpreted'.[7]

- Even when the media restrictions have been imposed by a government acting carefully and in good faith, in pursuance of a legitimate aim to advance an excepted value, the European Court will strike it down under Article 10 if it is not 'proportionate to the legitimate aim pursued' – i.e., if, in all circumstances of the case, the restriction was ineffectual to advance the aim, or irrelevant to it, or insufficiently justified.[8]

---

[5] *The Sunday Times* v *United Kingdom* [1979] 2 EHRR 245 at p. 271, para 49.

[6] *Handyside*, note 3 above, at paras 48 and 49; *The Sunday Times*, note 5 above, at paras 62 and 67.

[7] *The Sunday Times*, note 5 above, at para 65.

[8] On this basis the Court held that the United Kingdom had breached Article 10 by the ban on publication of *Spycatcher* after it had been published in the United States. Once the secrets were out, the injunction could not rationally support the interests of national security: *Observer and Guardian* v *UK* and *The Sunday Times* v *UK*, Strasbourg 26 November 1991.

The importance of Article 10

It is a sad comment on English law that the firmest legal guarantee of freedom of expression should be found in a Convention drafted and developed in the main by lawyers of other European countries. The importance of the Convention for the securing of media rights in Britain was first demonstrated by the decision of the European Court in the *Sunday Times* case.

> *The Sunday Times* proposed to publish an article about the history of the manufacture and marketing of thalidomide, a pregnancy drug that caused birth deformities. These issues were in dispute in long-running legal actions for negligence between parents and the drug manufacturers, and might ultimately have been tried by a judge. The English courts ruled that the article could not be published, because it 'prejudged' issues in litigation, and was therefore a contempt of court. The newspaper and its journalists applied to the European Court, claiming that the ban was an infringement of their right to freedom of expression. The British Government argued that the contempt law, as applied in this case, was necessary to uphold 'the authority of the judiciary' and the legal rights of the drug manufacturers. The Court held for *The Sunday Times*. It said that the thalidomide disaster was a matter of public concern, and the mere fact that litigation was in progress did not alter the right and, indeed, responsibility of the mass media to impart information of public interest. The public had a right to be properly informed, which could be denied them only if it appeared *absolutely certain* that the article would have presented a threat to judicial authority. In the circumstances, the article was moderate in tone and presented both sides of the case; it would not have impaired judicial authority or added much to the growing moral pressure on the manufacturers to settle the claim. It followed that the interference by the English courts did not correspond to a social need sufficiently pressing to outweigh the public interest in freedom of expression. It was both out of proportion to any social need to protect the impartiality of the courts and the rights of litigants, and it was not a restriction necessary in a democratic society to uphold these values.

The *Sunday Times* case had two important consequences. Firstly, because of its treaty obligations, the British Government was obliged to change the law on contempt of court. This it did by the 1981 Contempt of Court Act. No longer can investigative stories be stopped merely because they might 'prejudge' a matter that may have to be decided in litigation at some future time. Secondly, the European Court judgment provided a method of approach to media rights that can be adopted by British judges. The extent to which they will do so, of course, depends on their personal attraction to the ideals of the Convention and the jurisprudence of its court. Lord Scarman has been its most enthusiastic advocate, urging that British media law should be interpreted, as far as possible, in conformity with Article 10: 'If the issue should ultimately be a question of legal policy, we must have regard to the country's international obligation to observe the European Convention as interpreted by the European Court of Human Rights'.[9] Lord Scarman's approach seems now to be accepted by the House of Lords. Its two most recent decisions on the Government's power to restrain publications by former Crown servants – *Spycatcher* and the *Cavendish Memoirs* – were marked by references to the Convention and by an obvious desire manifested by most of the judges to ensure that both the law they were declaring and the decision they were taking in accordance with it would be seen to comply with Article 10.[10]

For all their approval of the Convention's principles, however, English judges have been careful to avoid using Article 10 as a basis for nullifying local laws or administrative practices. When the National Union of Journalists (NUJ) challenged the Home Secretary's ban on broadcasting the voices of members of terrorist organizations, on the grounds that it was an unnecessary interference with editorial freedom, the House of Lords declined to require ministers to take the Convention into account when exercising powers that impinge on freedom of speech.[11] All that the courts can offer in these circumstances is a rule that the Government must be able to justify any restriction on the right to freedom of expression by reference to some important competing public interest. 'The prevention of terrorism' was an interest of sufficient importance to justify the interference, at least in theory, and the courts would not enter into any argument on the merits, in the absence of a bill of rights or of incorporation of the European Convention into domestic law. Victims of such interference must go to Strasbourg in order to have the merits of the executive action examined.

Complaints to Strasbourg under the Convention can be used to force the Government to change administrative practices that shut out the media, and even to oblige it to legislate to give the media specific legal rights necessary to obtain access to information. The leading example is *Hodgson and Channel 4* v *UK*:[12]

---

[9] *A-G* v *BBC* [1981] AC 303 at p. 354.
[10] *A-G* v *Guardian Newspapers Ltd (No 2)* [1988] 3 All ER 545; *Lord Advocate* v *Scotsman Publications Ltd* [1989] 2 All ER 852, HL.
[11] *Brind* v *Secretary of State for the Home Department* [1991] 1 All ER 720.
[12] *Hodgson and Others* v *UK* (No 11553/85) and *Channel 4* v *UK* (No 11658/85) Decision on admissibility, 9 March 1987.

Until 1989 the media had no right to challenge a gag order imposed by a judge at a criminal trial. Newspapers and television stations had no standing to apply to the trial judge to lift the order, and there was no avenue open for them to appeal to any other court. This situation was in blatant breach of Article 13 of the European Convention, which requires that anyone whose rights (e.g. to freedom of expression) are violated should have an 'effective remedy'. Channel 4 had no remedy at all when the judge at the Official Secrets trial of Clive Ponting issued an order banning the television station from using actors to read each evening from the day's transcripts of this controversial trial. So both Channel 4 and Godfrey Hodgson (the programme's presenter) filed a complaint with the European Commission at Strasbourg, alleging that the order was in breach both of Article 10 and Article 13. The Commission upheld the complaint under Article 13. The United Kingdom Government accepted the ruling, and negotiated a 'friendly settlement' with the complainants, which took the form of drafting a new law (now s 159 of the Criminal Justice Act 1988), which gives the media a special right to appeal to the Court of Appeal against gag orders or decisions to exclude the press and public from any part of a trial (see further p. 347).

The *Hodgson* case shows how individual journalists who are aware of the Convention can use it to enhance the rights of the media generally. The initiative in the case came from Tim Crook, an Old Bailey reporter who (with the support of his union, the NUJ) challenged a secrecy order in the Divisional Court, in a case that established that the media had no effective remedy under British law. (It is a prerequisite of a complaint to Strasbourg that any possible domestic remedy should first be explored.) He then filed his application with the European Commission, which was favourably settled by the British Government after the ruling in the *Hodgson* case. Both Crook and NUJ officials were able to participate in the settlement negotiations, conducted with the help of the European Commission, which led to the drafting of s 159.

The practical importance of the European Convention for the British media is lessened by its odd status. It is not binding on the courts, although it remains a treaty obligation for the Government to ensure that the law conforms with it. The English courts can go no further, in the absence of a Bill of Rights 'incorporating' the Convention into English law, than to apply it when interpreting ambiguous statutes, on the presumption that Parliament must intend to legislate in a manner consistent with the United Kingdom's treaty obligations. The Convention cannot be invoked in the English courts to strike down ministerial or bureaucratic actions that imperil free speech: such actions can be attacked only on the very limited 'judicial review' basis offered by domestic law, i.e. if they are unreasonable, irrational or perverse. In 1991 the House of Lords declined to apply any of these adjectives to the Home Secretary's decision to prohibit radio and television broadcasts that included statements by representatives (even democratically elected representatives) of Sinn Fein, and refused even to consider arguments that this broadcasting ban breached Article 10 of the Convention. This case demonstrates the desirability of incorporating the Convention into British law – a step that is urged by the many authors and broadcasters who support this aim through the organization Charter 88. For the present, however, there is no alternative for the media in many cases other than to exhaust their limited remedies in local courts, and then file a complaint with the European Commission of Human Rights in Strasbourg. Certainly, no media organization worth its salt should supinely accept the ruling of a British court that curtails the right of the press to report matters of public interest, where there is a real prospect that the ruling might be condemned in Strasbourg. The nature of British law is such that an adverse ruling becomes a 'precedent' for later cases and the basis for cautious legal advice in the future. The publisher who suffers an adverse judgment is not the only victim: the decision echoes down the corridors of the common law, until shouted down by the European Court or the British Parliament.

It has to be said that in recent years the European Court of Human Rights, which now comprises twenty-four judges (one nominated by each signatory country), has become increasingly pro-government in its decisions. This is partly because other countries have followed the British practice of nominating government lawyers, rather than distinguished and independent jurists, to its bench. The Court has recently produced some confused majority opinions on freedom of expression (especially in the context of national security) and it is possible that British judges, if given the opportunity to interpret a freedom of expression guarantee in a constitutional court, would do better.

British Law Lords have acquired some experience in giving force to constitutional protections for freedom of expression by dint of their service on the Privy Council, which still hears final appeals from a number of Commonwealth countries whose constitutions embody human rights guarantees. In 1967, for example, the Privy Council struck down a Maltese law prohibiting civil servants from bringing into their place of work any newspaper that had been condemned by the Catholic Church.[13] In 1990 it stopped the

---

[13] *Olivier* v *Buttigieg* [1966] 2 All ER 459.

prosecution of the internationally renowned Antiguan journalist, Tim Hector, who faced imprisonment for publishing 'a false statement . . . likely to undermine public confidence in the conduct of public affairs'. The Board held that this law could not be justified as a necessary interference with free speech in a democratic society: since the very purpose of criticizing public officials was to undermine public confidence in their stewardship, the law was by its own definition a cloak for political censorship. The law was not saved by the requirement that the statement should be 'false': freedom of speech would be gravely impeded if would-be critics had to verify all their facts before they could speak without fear of criminal charges.[14]

The European Convention does have its drawbacks. The most crippling is the delay at every stage of the appeal proceedings. The European Commission on Human Rights (which acts as a filter for the Court) first considers applications and, unless they are hopeless, invites the government to respond. Extensions of time are given relatively freely. The publisher is offered an opportunity to respond to the government's response. A date is then arranged when the part-time Commissioners can meet to consider whether the case is 'admissible' (i.e. whether there is a prima facie case). If it is admissible, the parties are invited to consider friendly settlement. If that proves impossible the Commission prepares a report for the European Court, which will usually hear oral argument from the parties before considering its judgment. All this takes far too much time. The House of Lords gave its decision against *The Sunday Times* in July 1973, and the European Court did not declare that decision a breach of the Convention until April 1979 – a delay of almost six years. It follows that the Convention is not a direct protection for freedom of speech in Britain: it is a persuasive and educative force, which, if media interests have the patience and determination to seek rulings from Strasbourg, may slowly shape the operation of British law in favour of public interest reporting.

Trial by Jury

'Freedom of the press' was the chant that greeted jury acquittals of courageous publishers. Today jury trials are out of fashion, because censorship of the media is more easily achieved by an injunction, granted by a judge sitting in secret, or by a directive from a regulatory body. None the less, the right of journalists and broadcasters to demand trial by jury, in those areas of criminal law where it still

---

[14] *Hector v A-G of Antigua and Barbuda* [1990] 2 All ER 103.

exists, is an important security against interference with media freedoms – for reasons explained in 1885 by Dicey, the leading writer on our unwritten constitution:

> Freedom of discussion, is, then, in England little else than the right to write or say anything which a jury, consisting of 12 shopkeepers, think it expedient should be said or written ... Yet nothing has in reality contributed so much to free the press from any control. If a man may publish anything which 12 of his countrymen think is not blameable, it is impossible that the Crown or the Ministry should exert any stringent control over writings in the press ... The times when persons in power wish to check the excesses of public writers are times at which a large body of opinion or sentiment is hostile to the executive. But under these circumstances it must, from the nature of things, be at least an even chance that the jury called upon to find a publisher guilty may sympathize with his language ... as fair and laudable criticism of official errors. What is certain is that the practical freedom of the English press arose in great measure from the trial of 'press offences' by a jury.[15]

Dicey's description of jurors as shopkeepers reflected the former property-owning qualification for jury service. This was abolished in 1972 and consequently the prosecution must now convince a more representative sample of the population that a publisher ought to be punished; a sample, moreover, that has a constitutional right to acquit irrespective of the letter of the law. As Lord Devlin puts it, 'A jury can do justice, whereas the judge, who has to follow the law, may not.'[16]

Juries have freed journalists irrespective of the evidence where the defendant has acted in the public interest or the charge was oppressive. In the mid-1970s, for example, the police fell out with a number of crime reporters and charged them in separate proceedings with a variety of criminal offences. The cases against them were strong in law, but juries, after hearing that the reporters had acted in accordance with a professional duty to inform the public, acquitted. In 1987 an Old Bailey jury acquitted the *Observer* of corruptly offering money to a Crown servant in return for information on waste and mismanagement in the Ministry of Defence – notwithstanding that the Crown servant had already been convicted of corruptly accepting money from the *Observer*! In the same year

---

[15] A. V. Dicey, *An Introduction to the Study of Law of the Constitution*, 10th edn, Macmillan, pp. 246–51.
[16] Lord Devlin, *Trial by Jury: The Hamlyn Lecture, 1956*, rev. edn, Stevens, 1966.

the artist Stephen Boggs was charged with 'reproducing the currency' by painting amusing pastiches of banknotes, which he then
traded as an example of performance art. There was little danger
that his pictures (which were valued at hundreds of pounds) would
devalue the currency or be torn out of their frames and passed off
as real banknotes: his jury acquitted after retiring for only ten
minutes. Government law officers are generally reluctant to put
journalists and publishers in the dock of a criminal court, for fear
that a jury will live up to its historic role and acquit.

Thus the availability of jury trial can have an important effect in
securing a liberal operation of apparently draconian press laws.
Section 2 of the Official Secrets Act 1911 was discredited by the
jury acquittal of the editor of the *Sunday Telegraph* for publishing
a confidential army report about the Biafran War that indicated
that ministerial statements in Parliament were false. The case was
strong in law (so much so that the defendants had contemplated
pleading guilty in return for a fine), but so was the public merit of
the 'illegal action'.[17] Section 2 was further discredited by the jury
acquittal of Clive Ponting, and it remains to be seen whether the
1989 Official Secrets Act fares any better at the hands of twelve
good men and women and true. Jury acquittals in obscenity cases,
beginning with *Lady Chatterley's Lover*, have effectively secured
freedom for art and saved literature from the application of that
controversial law.

Media offences with a right to trial by jury

Any journalist confronted with a legal opinion that a story, or the
conduct necessary to obtain it, might be against the law should
first establish whether that law permits trial by jury. Criminal
offences that are triable by jury include most breaches of the Official Secrets Act, the Prevention of Terrorism Act, criminal libel,
obscenity, blasphemy, sedition and incitement to disaffection.

This is not a very long list of 'media offences'. There are many
ways for the authorities to avoid the embarrassment and
inconvenience of a jury trial when press freedom is involved. There
are four principal exceptions.

Contempt of court
Contempt carries a maximum penalty of two years' imprisonment,
and is the only serious crime in English law that is triable by
judges alone. Judges in contempt cases can be judges in their own
cause; it is doubtful whether juries would have convicted Granada

---

[17] See Jonathan Aitken, *Officially Secret*, Weidenfeld & Nicolson, 1971, p. 147.

Television for refusing to name its 'mole' within British Steel, or solicitor Harriet Harman for giving a journalist access to documents read out in open court, or *The Independent* for publishing excerpts from *Spycatcher* at a time when the Government was trying to stop the British public from reading a book on open sale in other countries.

Breach of confidence and copyright
These civil laws allow judges to grant an 'interim injunction' to stop publication until the trial of the action – which is usually at least a year afterwards. The Government has preferred to rely upon injunctions granted by judges, rather than prosecutions decided by juries, to deter 'leaks' from the security services.

Media offences that are triable only in magistrates' courts
Breaches of restrictions on court reporting, for example, which carry fines of up to £2,000, are not triable by jury. In these cases, magistrates are much more likely to convict for technical breaches of highly technical rules.

Regulatory bodies
These organizations can pre-censor material whenever there is a possibility that transmission might infringe the law. The Independent Broadcasting Authority was an example of a licensing body that on occasion used its powers to stop the broadcasting of items of borderline legality. Those items would not in the event have been proceeded against, because prosecuting authorities would fear a jury acquittal. The British Board of Film Classification is consistently censoring scenes from films and videos that would not disturb an average jury.

The increasing tendency of governments to avoid the right of jury trial by creating 'media offences' punishable only by judges or magistrates is disturbing. The most blatant example came in 1981 when it was made a criminal contempt punishable with two years' imprisonment for journalists, after a trial was over, to interview jurors about their deliberations. The crime was necessary, said the lawyer-MPs who supported the legislation, to preserve the integrity of the jury system. This integrity was hardly preserved by stripping jurors of their right to free speech by a new criminal offence that itself carried no right to trial by jury.

At least where a right to trial by jury exists, the courts are reluctant (in cases where national security is not involved) to allow the Attorney-General to side-step it by approaching the High Court for an injunction to stop the publication or for a declaration that the publication is unlawful:

The Voluntary Euthanasia Society published a booklet entitled *A Guide to Self-Deliverance*, which discussed the pros and cons of committing suicide and described in detail a number of efficacious methods for so doing. After evidence came to light that some members of the Society had committed suicide by following methods described in the booklet, the Attorney-General sought to dissuade the Society from further dissemination of the *Guide* by applying to the High Court for a declaration that its publication amounted to the crime of aiding and abetting suicide. This offence carries the right to jury trial, and the judge declined to usurp the jury's role by declaring that future conduct by the Society would necessarily amount to an offence.[18]

The Open-justice Principle

For a nation whose government workings are swathed in secrecy, British judicial processes are, by comparison, relatively open. 'Every court in the land is open to every subject of the King' is a statement of principle that has been endorsed by the courts on countless occasions.[19] It is now reinforced by Article 6 of the European Convention on Human Rights, which guarantees to every defendant a 'public hearing' whenever legal rights are determined.

One reason for the open-justice principle is to keep the judges themselves up to the mark. As Jeremy Bentham put it, in a passage that has been approved in leading cases:

> Publicity is the very soul of justice. It is the keenest spur to exertion and the surest of all guards against improbity. It keeps the judge himself, while trying, under trial. . . .[20]

Lords Scarman and Simon added a broader objective:

> Whether or not judicial virtue needs such a spur, there is also another important interest involved in justice done openly, namely that the evidence and argument should be publicly known, so that society may judge for itself the quality of justice administered in its name, and whether the law requires modification . . . the common law by its recognition of the principle of open justice ensures that the public administration of justice will be subject to public scrutiny. Such scrutiny serves no purpose unless it is accompanied by the rights of free speech, i.e. the right publicly to report, to discuss, to

---

[18] *A-G v Able* [1984] 1 All ER 277; and see *Gouriet v Union of Post Office Workers* [1978] AC 435.

[19] See *Scott v Scott* [1913] AC 417; *A-G v Leveller Magazine Ltd* [1979] AC 440.

[20] *Scott v Scott*, note 19 above, at p. 447.

comment, to criticise, to impart and to receive ideas and information on the matters subjected to scrutiny. Justice is done in public so it may be discussed and criticised in public.[21]

Open justice has other important virtues. The prospect of publicity deters perjury: witnesses are more likely to tell the truth if they know that any lie they tell might be reported, and provoke others to come forward to discredit them. Press reporting of court cases enhances public knowledge and appreciation of the workings of the law, and it assists the deterrent effect of heavy sentences in criminal cases. Above all, fidelity to the open-justice principle keeps Britain free from the reproach that it permits 'secret courts' of the kind that have been instruments of repression in so many other countries.

The case that comes closest to accepting the principle as a rule of law enforceable by journalists is *R* v *Felixstowe Justices ex parte Leigh*:[22]

> David Leigh, an experienced reporter on the *Observer* was writing an article about a controversial case that had been heard in Felixstowe Magistrates' Court. The clerk of the court refused to supply him with the names of the lay justices who had decided it, pursuant to a policy that was being adopted by an increasing number of magistrates' courts of declining to identify justices to the public or the press. Leigh, with the backing of his newspaper and the NUJ, brought an action against the justices in the High Court, which granted him a declaration that the policy of anonymity was 'inimical to the proper administration of justice and an unwarranted and unlawful obstruction to the right to know who sits in judgment.' The judgment endorsed the importance of the court reporter as 'the watchdog of justice', and the vital significance of press comment and criticism of the behaviour of judges and magistrates. Although there was no specific statutory requirement that justices should be named, the court deduced such a requirement from the fundamental nature of the open-justice principle.

The importance of *Leigh* is that the court was prepared to treat the open-justice principle as a rule of law that could be asserted by a journalist against a discretionary policy, rather than as a desirable state of affairs that could none the less give way to judicial convenience. This was a welcome change from the approach of the House of Lords majority in *Home Office* v *Harman*, decided a few years earlier, which held that a solicitor committed contempt by showing the other side's private documents to a journalist after they

---

[21] *Home Office* v *Harman* [1982] 1 All ER 532 at pp. 546–7.
[22] *R* v *Felixstowe Justices ex parte Leigh* [1987] 1 All ER 551.

had been read out in open court.[23] In that case, the open-justice principle did not prevail over property rights in the documents and the rule that limited their use to the action itself. Harriet Harman, MP, the solicitor in question, took her case to Strasbourg, where the British Government was forced to concede that the decision against her was a breach of the open-justice principle guaranteed by Article 6 of the Convention. The Rules of the Supreme Court were in consequence changed to allow general use of documents read in open court – an ironic example of how the European Convention can still be necessary to enforce a principle that derives from, and should be fundamental to, British domestic law.

There are a number of quite reasonable exceptions to the open-justice principle, settled by Parliament after sometimes anxious debate. Rape victims are entitled to anonymity, to mitigate their humiliation and to encourage other victims to come forward. In youth courts offenders may not be identified; the public and press may be excluded from Official Secrets Act trials where the evidence relates to national security secrets, and the testimony given at committal proceedings usually cannot be published until the trial is over, to avoid prejudicing the jury. Other restrictions are less justifiable: the routine exclusion of the media from in-chambers hearings relating to property in divorce cases, to bail applications in Crown Courts, and to applications for injunctions and eviction orders in the Queen's Bench Division of the High Court are breaches of the open-justice principle that may in due course be struck down by the European Court of Human Rights. The media needs to be constantly on guard against secrecy applications made by lawyers who strive to protect clients and witnesses from the humiliation and embarrassment that frequently follows from reports of their appearances in court. In recent years the press has had to challenge such diverse rulings as an order not to name a witness from a famous family lest publicity might interfere with her cure for heroin addiction;[24] an order not to publish the address of a former Tory MP lest his estranged wife should discover his whereabouts and harass him,[25] and an order that reporters should leave the court so that a distressed defendant could explain in privacy the matrimonial problems that drove her to drink before she drove her car.[26] In all these cases trial courts had been moved by personal plight to overlook the fundamental principle that trials must be open in every respect.

---

[23] See note 21 above.
[24] *R* v *Central Criminal Court ex parte Crook* (1984) *The Times*, 8 November.
[25] *R* v *Evesham Justices ex parte McDonagh* [1988] 1 All ER 371.
[26] *R* v *Malvern Justices ex parte Evans* [1988] 1 All ER 371.

Journalists' special rights

One important application of the open-justice principle that has increased the rights of the press is found in recent cases in which reporters have been accorded special status as 'representatives of the public'. They have been invited to join judges and lawyers in circumstances where it was inconvenient that the public should be admitted as well. In one case, *R* v *Waterfield*, the trial judge had cleared the court while the jury was shown allegedly obscene films.[27] He feared that 'gasps, giggling and comment' from the press bench and the public gallery might distract the jurors from their solemn duty. The Court of Appeal said that the press should have been allowed to remain:

> ... the public generally are interested in cases of this kind, and for not unworthy reasons. Concepts of sexual morality are changing. Whenever a jury in this class of case returns a verdict, whether of guilty or not guilty, intelligent readers of newspapers and weekly journals may want to know what kind of film was under consideration. Experience during the past decades has shown that every acquittal tends to lead to the greater exposure to public gaze of what previous generations thought seemly only in private, if seemly anywhere. Members of the public have to depend on the press for information on which to base their opinions; but if allegedly indecent films are always shown in closed courtrooms the press cannot give the public the information which it may want and which is necessary for the formation of public opinion. ... It follows, so it seems to us, that normally, when a film is being shown to a jury and the judge, in the exercise of his discretion, decides that it should be done in a closed courtroom or in a cinema, he should allow representatives of the press to be present. No harm can be done by doing so: some good may result.

Parliament has given journalists the right to be present, even though the rest of the public is excluded, in the case of youth courts[28] and family proceedings in magistrates' courts.[29] Similarly, the public but not the press can be kept out of an adult court while a child or young person gives evidence in relation to a sex offence.[30] The principle that the press may 'represent the public' should be considered in all cases where the court is cleared, except perhaps

---

[27] [1975] 2 All ER 40.
[28] Children and Young Persons Act 1933 s 47 (2).
[29] Magistrates' Courts Act 1980 s 69(2).
[30] Children and Young Persons Act 1933 s 37(1).

when national security is being discussed. Judges can order reporting to be postponed until the end of the trial, and should, where
necessary, use this power rather than exclude the press. There
have been cases where matters of considerable public interest have
been discussed after the press has been ordered to leave the court.
Such 'secret hearings' are wrong in principle and now, with the
availability of postponement orders under the Contempt of Court
Act 1981, are unnecessary in practice. Journalists should be fully
conversant with their rights to appeal against any exclusion from
the courtroom or any secrecy order made under the Contempt of
Court Act. These rights are contained in s 159 of the Criminal
Justice Act 1988 and the rules made thereunder, and are set out in
detail in Chapter 7.

The principle of open justice has its physical symbol in almost
every courtroom – the press bench. This piece of furniture has
become something of a shibboleth: both the Magistrates' Association and the NUJ have said that it should be regarded as sacrosanct.
This attitude may have the effect of blunting the critical edge of
press coverage, by encouraging court reporters to perceive themselves as part and parcel of the court process, rather than as objective
critics of its workings. However, the press should jealously protect its
right to sit centre-stage in the interests of audibility and accuracy.

> As the United States Supreme Court has put it, while media
> representatives enjoy the same right of access as the public,
> they often are provided special seating and priority of entry so
> that they may report what people in attendance have seen and
> heard. This contributes to the public understanding of the
> rule of law and to comprehension of the functioning of the
> entire criminal justice system.[31]

The media might successfully challenge any decision to deny press
representatives special seats in a courtroom. The Supreme Court
of Queensland has commented that the tradition of the press bench
'implies that the King desires that the representatives of the press
should be afforded special facilities for reporting the proceedings
in his courts, and custom sanctions this and common sense
demands that it should be so.'[32] In 1974 the Lord Chancellor made
a public apology to the NUJ over an incident at the Winchester
Crown Court, where the press bench was commandeered by
counsel for the duration of a drugs conspiracy trial. The NUJ had
complained that reporters were relegated to the public gallery,
where they had difficulty in taking accurate notes of evidence.

---

[31] *Richmond Newspapers Inc* v *Commonwealth of Virginia* 448 US 555 (1980) at
p. 587.
[32] In *Re Andrew Dunn and the Morning Bulletin Ltd* [1932] St R Qd 1 at p. 15.

The Rule against Prior Restraint

The British contribution to the philosophy of free speech might be summed up in the Duke of Wellington's phrase, 'publish and be damned'. The media is free to publish and be damned, so long as damnation comes after, and not before, the word gets out. Journalists cannot claim to be above the law, but what they can claim, in every country that takes free speech seriously, is a right to publish first, and take the risk of conviction afterwards.

When that right was withdrawn by Cromwell, who set up a licensing system for books and newspapers, the poet Milton uttered his immortal cry for press freedom, the *Areopagitica*:

> Promiscuous reading is necessary to the constituting of human nature. The attempt to keep out evil doctrine by licensing is like the exploit of that gallant man who thought to keep out the crows by shutting his park gate ... Lord and Commons of England, consider what nation it is whereof ye are: a nation not slow and dull, but of a quick, ingenious and piercing spirit. It must not be shackled or restricted. Give me the liberty to know, to utter and to argue freely according to conscience, above all liberties.

Cromwell destroyed that liberty: he appointed twenty-seven fit and proper persons – schoolmasters, lawyers, ministers of religion, doctors (the sort of people found nowadays on the regulatory bodies for broadcasting and video) – to censor public reading. They were obliged to reject any book that was 'contrary to good life or good manners'. (Their modern counterparts are obliged to reject any television programme that is offensive to public feeling, good taste or decency.) Milton was among the first to suffer from Cromwell's censors: one of his books was solemnly burned by the public hangman, and two lines were cut from *Paradise Lost*. The public grew to hate the licensors, and Parliament eventually uncovered widespread corruption in their operation – fraud, extortion and intimidation had made the whole system a scandal. In 1695 the licensing system was abolished, and in the following century the rule against prior restraint was given definitive shape by the venerated legal writer Blackstone:

> The liberty of the press is indeed essential to the nature of a free state; but this consists in laying no *previous* restraints on publications, and not in freedom from censure for criminal matter when published. Every free man has an undoubted right to lay what sentiments he pleases before the public; to forbid this is to destroy the freedom of the press; but if he

publishes what is improper, mischievous or illegal, he must take the consequences of his own temerity.[33]

It was this message that went out in the eighteenth century, and became enshrined in the First Amendment to the American Constitution. It was endorsed by the Supreme Court, in its historic *Pentagon Papers* decision. The United States government learnt of the *New York Times*' plan to publish a set of army research papers on the history of American involvement in Vietnam. It tried to injunct the newspaper, on the ground that the papers contained military and diplomatic secrets, the disclosure of which would substantially damage the national interest. The Supreme Court refused:

> Any system of prior restraint on expression comes to this court bearing a heavy presumption against its constitutional validity. The only effective restraint upon executive policy and power in the areas of national defence and international affairs may be an enlightened citizenry – an informed and critical public opinion which alone can here protect the values of democratic government. For without an informed and free press there cannot be an enlightened people.[34]

The justices accepted that publication of those documents would harm the national interest and might even make the newspaper guilty of a criminal offence. But it was entitled to publish and be damned. Only when the government could prove that disclosure would cause 'grave and irreparable injury to the public interest' – details, for example, of troop deployment in wartime or information that might trigger a nuclear war – was a court entitled to stop the presses.

Contemporary position in the United Kingdom

In Britain, which lacks a written constitution, the rule against prior restraint has been badly eroded. Almost every week, at secret hearings in the High Court, judges are asked to issue injunctions against the media. An injunction imposes prior restraint, by stopping presses from rolling and film from running. Most applications for injunctions are based on a complaint that the information about to be revealed has been ordained in breach of confidence. Where that information relates to national security, all that the government has to show is that publication might cause *some* injury to the national

---

[33] William Blackstone, *Commentaries on the Laws of England*, 1765, Book IV, pp. 151–2.
[34] *New York Times* v *US*, 403 US 713 (1971) at p. 729.

interest – a test that would ensure that the British equivalent of the *Pentagon Papers* would never see the light of day.

The inroad upon the rule against prior restraint made by interim injunctions granted for alleged breaches of confidence derives from the 'balance of convenience' test that is applied by the courts. All that the plaintiff need do to obtain a restraining order is to show a prima facie (i.e. arguable) case, and that the public interest in protecting the confidence is not, on the 'balance of convenience' test, outweighed by some urgent public interest in publication. In recent cases the courts have virtually applied a presumption in favour of granting the injunction until trial, on the basis that if the information is allowed into the public domain the plaintiff will be unable to repair the damage. Although in every case the judge must balance the commercial or property rights of the plaintiff in controlling the information against the value of the defendant's right of free speech, for many judges brought up in a world that accords pre-eminent value to rights of property, this may seem like balancing hard cash against hot air.

One example of prior restraint was the injunction that stopped the scheduled screening of a Thames Television documentary on the pregnancy drug Primodos. Lord Denning thought it should be shown:

> . . . the *public* interest in receiving information about the drug Primodos and its effects far outweighs the *private* interest of the makers in preventing discussion of it.[35]

He was outvoted by his brethren. One said:

> The law of England is indeed, as Blackstone declared, a law of liberty; but the freedoms it recognises do not include a licence for the mercenary betrayal of business confidences.[36]

This misses Blackstone's point. The rule against prior restraint is designed to allow publishers to publish even if this means betraying a confidence – a betrayal that as Lord Denning points out, may be very much in the public interest – so long as they pay any damages that may be appropriate.

In this case the majority decision was critized as being wrong in law by the Law Commission, and would almost certainly have been found contrary to the European Convention had Thames Television possessed the spirit to appeal to Strasbourg. None the less, the decision reflects a dangerous tendency among many judges to give property values more weight than media freedom. This

---

[35]   *Schering Chemicals Ltd v Falkman Ltd* [1981] 2 All ER 321, 334.
[36]   ibid. p. 338.

tendency reached a quite ludicrous result in the course of the *Spycatcher* litigation, when the House of Lords at one point narrowly upheld an interim injunction on newspapers publishing details from a book that was on open sale throughout the rest of the world, and numerous copies of which were circulating in Britain.[37] This decision was plainly absurd: all confidentiality in the information had evaporated with overseas publication, and no additional damage to the national interest could possibly have been done by re-publication of the contents of the book in the British press. The House of Lords in two subsequent cases has retreated from the position it adopted in the original litigation, by making plain that the Government must prove some damage to the national interest and that no such damage can be established where the information has already been placed in the public domain by being published abroad.[38]

The European Court of Human Rights in 1991 held that the continuing injunction on publishing *Spycatcher* in Britain long after it had become a best-seller in other countries was an infringement of the Article 10 guarantee of freedom of expression. A narrow majority of the judges was not persuaded, however, that Article 10 prohibited prior restraint in all circumstances, especially when governments were concerned to protect security information that had not yet seen the light of day. The Court did acknowledge that:

> the dangers inherent in prior restraints are such that they call for the most careful scrutiny on the part of the Court. This is especially so as far as the press is concerned, for news is a perishable commodity and to delay its publication, even for a short period, may well deprive it of its value and interest.[39]

It follows that courts in Britain, if they wish henceforth to comply with the Convention, must accept 'newsworthiness' as a public-interest value that weighs heavily against the grant of an interim injunction sought against newspapers and broadcast organizations. Regrettably, however, the majority of European Court judges did not understand how the balance of convenience test operates routinely in breach of confidence actions to produce the very dangers about which they were warning, and declined an invitation to declare the test itself to be an infringement of Article 10 in free speech cases.

The most enduring damage done by the *Spycatcher* litigation to the rule against prior restraint was the emergence of a legal doctrine

---

[37] *A-G* v *Guardian Newspapers Ltd* [1987] 3 All ER 316.
[38] See note 10 above.
[39] *The Observer and Guardian* v *United Kingdom* (51/1990/242/313) ECHR, Strasbourg, 26 November 1991, para 60.

that once a secrecy injunction has been granted against one newspaper, every other section of the media becomes effectively bound by its terms, on pain of punishment for contempt:

> The *Guardian* ran a news story that briefly referred to certain allegations made by Peter Wright in *Spycatcher*. The Government sued for breach of confidence and obtained an 'interim injunction' against it repeating the story prior to the trial. Before his trial took place, *The Independent* came into possession of the manuscript of *Spycatcher* and published a much more detailed account of the book's contents. Instead of proceeding against *The Independent* for breach of confidence, the Government prosecuted it for contempt of court, committed by flouting the spirit of the injunction imposed on the *Guardian*. *The Independent* argued that it could not in natural justice be bound by order made against another newspaper, on different facts, and which it had been given no opportunity to oppose. The Court of Appeal, however, ruled that every newspaper that had notice of the original injunction against the *Guardian* was under an obligation to comply with its terms until it was discharged.[40] In later proceedings *The Independent* and several other newspapers were held to have been in contempt of the court that had made the order against the *Guardian* and were fined, notwithstanding that by this time the Government had lost its original action against the *Guardian*. The House of Lords subsequently confirmed that a third party, although not bound by an injunction restraining another newspaper from publishing confidential information, was guilty of contempt if it nullified the purpose of the original proceedings by destroying the confidentiality of the information by publishing it.[41]

The doctrine that an injunction against one publication binds all who know (or should know) of it is seriously subversive of the rule against prior restraint. It means that a plaintiff with no more than an arguable case for suppressing a story on breach of confidence grounds can obtain, at a secret High Court hearing, an injunction against one defendant (perhaps a journal whose financial position does not permit a legal contest) and thereafter enforce it against every media outlet in the country. Although the doctrine was created in the course of a somewhat panicked reaction by the courts to bogus claims of a national security peril asserted by the Government, it has subsequently been exploited by private corporations wishing to keep their secrets under wraps. It requires newspapers who wish to publish stories about a matter, some aspect of which is affected by an injunction against another publication, to apply to the court for guidance on whether their story trespasses upon the order in existence – a procedure calculated to give High Court judges a good deal of experience in editing newspapers.

---

[40] *A-G v Newspaper Publishing plc* [1987] 3 All ER 276, CA.
[41] *A-G v Times Newspapers* [1991] 2 All ER 398.

The erosion of the rule against prior restraint by judges in granting 'interim injunctions' to restrain alleged breaches of confidence and copyright is the most noticeable example of the law's failure to develop a coherent and principled approach to media freedom. The absurdity of the *Sypcatcher* ban was the result of a dogged insistence on viewing the memoirs of a former MI5 employee as the 'property' of government, and conducting the litigation as if he had stolen the office furniture. The 'balance of convenience' approach in such cases is not a test that applies in libel actions, where the rule against prior restraint still operates. No injunction will be granted to restrain the repetition of an allegedly libellous statement if the publishers indicate an intention to call evidence at the trial to prove the truth of their statement, or to defend it as honest comment. This *is* a firm rule, and it means that the courts will not force publishers to withdraw or recall books and magazines from distribution if they are prepared to swear an affidavit verifying their intention to justify the allegation that is the subject matter of the libel. Another example of the rule against prior restraint is the *Voluntary Euthanasia Society* case (see p. 14), where the Attorney-General was refused an injunction against a publication whose authors were entitled to have the legality of their actions decided at a trial before a jury. On this principle it has been authoritatively stated that no injunction should be granted by the civil courts to restrain the dissemination of allegedly obscene books, as such a step would pre-empt the ultimate decision of a jury.[42]

The rule against prior restraint has not prevailed over the sanctity of contract, and individuals who voluntarily agree to give up freedom of speech in return for money will normally be held to their bargain, if necessary by the court granting injunctive relief against publication. In 1990 the Court of Appeal had no hesitation at all in granting an injunction against a former royal servant and his publisher, ordering that his memoirs of life with the royal family should not be published anywhere in the world. It dismissed the notion that a defence to the breach might be mounted on the basis that the secrecy clause was void as contrary to public policy, because it would deny to foreigners their rights to receive information.[43] The British courts are traditionally over-protective of royal privacy, and it is possible that in other cases, where the public interest in the information is genuine, plaintiffs will be refused an injunction and left to their remedy (if any) in damages.[44]

In deciding whether to grant an injunction in 'balance of convenience' cases, the court must at least weigh in the balance the

---

[42] Viscount Dilhorne in *Gouriet* v *Union of Post Office Workers*, note 18 above.
[43] *A-G* v *Barker* [1990] 3 All ER 257.

claim that free speech should not be restrained before trial of the action. Exactly how much weight it is given will depend on the personal values of the judge and the interest value of the story. However, this balance should be attempted only in cases where there is the clearest precedent for the court to contemplate the exercise of a restraining power. No matter how damaging to individuals may be the consequences of a publication, the right to free speech must prevail unless the individuals possess an established legal right that the publication would infringe:

> In the case of *Re X (a minor)* the mother and stepfather of a sensitive fourteen-year-old girl sought to stop publication of a book that ascribed depraved and immoral behaviour to her deceased father. There was evidence that the book, if published, would almost certainly come to her attention, and would cause her gross psychological damage. The judge at first instance invoked the wardship powers of the court to protect the girl: he weighed her interests against that of the publishers, and concluded that the balance came down in favour of restraining publication, since the book could be rendered harmless by excising a few paragraphs. The Court of Appeal held that this was an incorrect approach. Even if there were no public interest in publication, the right to free speech could not in principle be subordinated to the welfare of an individual whose established legal rights were not infringed. The court had a duty to protect the liberty to publish, by ensuring that the existing ambit of restraints was not extended.[45]

Freedom from Government Interference

The Cromwellian licensors were the last government controllers of the press in peacetime. Today newspapers are entirely free from direct government control over what they can print. If ministers wish to stop a news story, they must ask the courts for an injunction – they have no power to make a direct order. They can, of course, exert political pressure in other ways – by manipulating the lobby system and by withholding information, or simply by threatening legal action. During the Falklands War, for example, the Ministry of Defence quite blatantly manipulated press coverage in what it regarded as the national interest. When the MoD was the sole source of information, the press could only speculate as to the veracity of its statements. Reporters with the Task Force had their

---

[44] See, for example, the decision of Kerr LJ in *Cambridge Nutrition Ltd* v *BBC* [1990] 3 All ER 523, CA, where a company marketing a controversial diet was refused an injunction to stop a BBC programme notwithstanding a claim that the makers were in breach of contract.

[45] *Re X (a minor)* [1975] 1 All ER 697, CA.

stories heavily censored: the army relied, not on the law, but on its control of transmission facilities. In more normal times the government may exert pressure behind the scenes through the operation of the D-notice committee. A D-notice has no legal force: it is merely 'advice' to the media, drawn up by a joint committee of representatives of the press and the armed forces. It is not a crime to break a D-notice – many newspapers have done so without prosecution. It is difficult to understand why so many media interests voluntarily accept D-notices: the system would not work without their support.

Broadcasting bans

In extreme circumstances the Government does have certain direct legal powers over radio and television. In the case of the BBC, these are contained in the Licence Agreement that forms part of the Corporation's charter. Section 19 enables the Home Secretary, when in his opinion there is an emergency and it is 'expedient' so to act, to send troops in to 'take possession of the BBC in the name and on behalf of Her Majesty'. This clause was framed during the General Strike, when Winston Churchill and other members of the Government wanted to commandeer the Corporation. It has never been used for that purpose, although Sir Anthony Eden contemplated invoking it for government propaganda during the Suez crisis, and during the Falklands recapture it provided the legal basis for the Government's use of BBC transmitters on Ascension Island to beam propaganda broadcasts at Argentina.

A more dangerous power is contained in s 13(4) of the Licence Agreement, which gives the Home Secretary the right to prohibit the BBC from transmitting any item or programme, at any time. The power is not limited, like s 19, to periods of emergency. The only safeguard against political censorship is that the BBC 'may' (not 'must') tell the public that it has received an s 13(4) order from the Home Secretary. This safeguard was invoked in 1972 by the Director-General, Lord Hill, when Home Secretary Reginald Maudling threatened an s 13(4) order to stop transmission of a debate about Government actions in Ulster. Lord Hill called his bluff by threatening to make public the reason why the programme could not be shown. Of course, a less courageous Director-General could simply cancel the programme without revealing the existence of a Government order. A parallel power in s 10 of the 1990 Broadcasting Act entitles the Home Secretary to order the Independent Television Commission (ITC) to 'refrain from broadcasting any matter or classes of matter' on commercial television. The exercise of these powers cannot be successfully challenged in the courts unless it can be shown that the Home Secretary has acted unreasonably or perversely.

These powers were invoked in 1988 for the purpose of direct political censorship when the BBC and the IBA (the predecessor of ITC) were ordered not to transmit any interviews with representatives of Sinn Fein, the Ulster Defence Association, the IRA or certain other extremist groups, or to broadcast any statement that incited support for such groups. The ban is a plain infringement on the right to receive and impart information: it prevents representatives of lawful political organizations (Sinn Fein has an MP as well as dozens of local councillors) from stating their case on matters that have no connection with terrorism, and it denies to the public the opportunity to hear those who support violent action being questioned and exposed. The Government believes that terrorists survive by 'the oxygen of publicity', but television confrontations generally demonstrate the moral unattractiveness of those who believe that the end justifies the means. The ban prevents the re-screening of such excellent programmes as Robert Kee's *Ireland: a Television History* or Thames Television's *The Troubles*, which contain interviews with IRA veterans. The BBC and IBA meekly complied with the ban, which further underlines the lack of constitutional protection for freedom of speech in British law. In theory, the Home Secretary's unrestricted powers under s 29(3) and clause 13(4) could permit a directive against transmitting attacks on the Government made by members of the opposition party.

On the other hand it must be conceded that the ban is far less extensive than the total broadcasting ban imposed on terrorist supporters by the Government of Ireland.[46] Moreover, since it prohibits only the actual voices of these people, broadcasters can minimize its impact by the simple expedient of using actors with Irish accents whose voices are dubbed over the voices of terrorists on the film or tape. This device for negativing the ban should have been obvious from the moment it was imposed, in November 1988, but it was not until two years later that Channel 4, in what was perceived as a 'courageous' decision, used dubbing. In 1991 the House of Lords, in refusing to strike down the ban as 'unreasonable', drew attention to its limited effect, which, in view of the dubbing option, they regarded more as an irritant than an infringement.[47] The conclusion is inescapable that both the BBC and the

---

[46] In 1991 the European Commission decided that security interests justified the Irish Government's ban on Sinn Fein interviews. *Purcell and Others* v *Ireland*.

[47] See note 11 above.

IBA interpreted the ban far more broadly than was legally necessary.

One of the most absurd casualties of the ban was a song recorded by an Irish group with lyrics claiming that the 'Guildford 4' were innocent. The Home Secretary shortly afterwards accepted that the 'Guildford 4' were innocent and released them, but the IBA still refused to allow the record to be played on radio or television.

Patronage

The 1988 broadcasting bans are the only examples of direct political censorship of a section of the media by Government ministers. A more subtle form of political influence on the content of television programmes is provided by the Government's power of appointment of controlling bodies (the BBC Board of Governors and the ITC) and to statutory commissions set up to supervise complaints about unfair treatment (the Broadcasting Complaints Commission) and programme standards (the Broadcasting Standards Council). Both Harold Wilson and Margaret Thatcher have appointed BBC chairmen for personal reasons rather than suitable qualifications, and in 1988 the Conservative Government was strongly condemned for appointing its political partisans Lord Rees-Mogg (to the Chairmanship of the BSC) and Lord Chalfont (to the Chairmanship of the Radio Authority). The make-up of these bodies can be particularly important when Governments exert pressure over a particular programme, as happened to the BBC in the case of *Real Lives* (an examination of the life of an IRA sympathizer in Belfast) and to the IBA in the case of *Death on the Rock* (a *This Week* programme about the SAS shooting of three IRA members in Gibraltar). The *Real Lives* episode in 1985 severely damaged the BBC's reputation for independence when its Board of Governors (at the especial urging of its then Deputy Chairman, Lord Rees-Mogg) cravenly banned the scheduled programme after Mrs Thatcher had condemned it, unseen, as likely to encourage support for terrorists. BBC journalists took strike action in protest, and the programme was eventually screened with a few face-saving deletions, but the episode called into question the Board of Governors' commitment to freedom of expression. The IBA was made of sterner stuff when the Foreign Secretary called for the banning of *Death on the Rock*. It supported Thames Television's decision to screen the programme, which gave viewers a much fuller appreciation of the shootings than had been possible from Government statements and MoD briefings. The public importance of the issue, and the high journalistic standards deployed in putting the programme together, were subsequently emphasized by an independent inquiry chaired by Lord Windlesham, which conclusively refuted the Government's allegations that the programme had been deliberately biased and had prejudiced the inquest in Gibraltar.[48]

The ITC

The ITC will, until 1993, possess all the powers of its predecessor (the IBA) to interfere with the content of commercial radio and television programmes. These powers date from 1954, and reflect the exaggerated fears of that period about untried and untrusted commercial exploitation of the medium. Lord Reith described the introduction of commercial television as 'a betrayal and a surrender . . . somebody introduced smallpox, bubonic plague and the Black Death. Somebody is minded now to introduce sponsored broadcasting in this country.'[49] One eminent Law Lord confessed to a 'sense of sacrilege' at the very prospect of an advertisement broadcast on the Sabbath. In this atmosphere it was understandable that commercial television should be placed under the close scrutiny of a licensing body, empowered by what is now s 6(1) of the Broadcasting Act 1990 to ensure:

> (*a*) that nothing is included in its programmes which offends against good taste or decency or is likely to encourage or incite to crime or to lead to disorder or to be offensive to public feeling . . .;
> (*b*) that due impartiality is preserved on the part of the person providing the service as respects matters of political or industrial controversy or relating to current public policy.

There are fourteen commercial television companies, and a host of commercial radio stations. They owe their commercial existence to a contract with the ITC which must be renewed every eight (or in the case of local radio, every ten) years. The ITC comprises a board of eighteen Government appointees, with a staff of several hundred and one subsidiary company responsible for running Channel 4. Under these contracts, the ITC has the right – as it has, indeed, the statutory duty – to vet programmes to ensure that they are neither offensive nor biased. Programme makers often criticized IBA pre-censorship, which is, after all, a direct interference with freedom of expression by way of prior restraint, imposed by Government appointees. The IBA was particularly active in relation to

[48] The Windlesham Rampton Report on *Death on the Rock*, Faber, 1989.
[49] Hansard, House of Lords, 22 May 1952, col 1297.

programmes about Northern Ireland and its interference has ranged from banning entire programmes (e.g. a *This Week* report about RUC brutality) to cutting provocative scenes lasting a few seconds (such as pictures of flowers on an IRA grave).

On two occasions the IBA delayed transmission of programmes involving former security service personnel, fearing that the Authority might be joined in a prosecution under the Official Secrets Act. Its worst loss of nerve was over a Channel 4 programme *MI5's Official Secrets*, in which Cathy Massiter, a former MI5 case officer responsible for surveillance of the peace movement, alleged that her investigations into CND had been passed on to Government ministers for party-political use. Only after the transcript of the programme had been widely published, and Virgin Records had issued a copy for public sale on video-cassette did the IBA agree to allow the programme to be transmitted on Channel 4. It is much more satisfactory, as the Annan Committee on the Future of Television pointed out, for the regulatory authority to leave television stations to make their own decisions about transmission, and to criticize them subsequently if their decisions are mistaken.[50] A further level of pre-censorship, imposed by a bureaucracy headed by government appointees, is an unnecessary institutional restriction on programme-makers.

None the less, the terms of the Broadcasting Acts have imposed duties on the IBA and then the ITC to ensure that this medium, unlike the press, is free from bias and public offence. For many years this duty was thought to require the appointed members of the Authority to approve personally the transmission of programmes that might contravene the duties set out in s 6.[51] However, in 1986 the Court of Appeal gave its approval to a much less interventionist approach:

> *Scum* was a powerful drama about the treatment of young offenders, which depicted the Borstal system as encouraging rather than deterring violent behaviour. It had originally been made by the BBC, which declined to show it after pressure from the Home Office. Subsequently the play was made into a film, which was screened on Channel 4 late at night with the approval of the Director-General of the IBA. Only three viewers complained – two to Channel 4 and one (Mrs Mary Whitehouse) to the courts. She argued that the history of *Scum* should have alerted the IBA to its controversial nature, and that any decision to screen it should have been made by the appointed members

---

[50] *Report of the Committee on the Future of Broadcasting*, HMSO, 1977, Cmnd 6753, Chs 4 and 13.
[51] As a result of *A-G(ex rel McWhirter)* v *Independent Broadcasting Authority* [1973] 1 QB 629.

of the Authority, and not by their executive staff. The Court of Appeal rejected her arguments, pointing out that the statutory duties to ensure 'good taste' and 'due impartiality' are imprecise, and that the Broadcasting Act required only that the IBA should approve a satisfactory system for monitoring standards and public reactions. There was no need for Authority members to preview controversial programmes themselves: the court would only interfere if no reasonable person could believe that the system established by the IBA would maintain programme standards at the general level required by the Act.[52]

The IBA has been replaced by the ITC, which inherits the IBA's duties to ensure due impartiality and decency in the medium. After the new television system is in place in 1993, however, the ITC (unlike the IBA) will not be responsible for broadcasting television programmes, and it will be expected to enforce the statutory duties by financial penalties imposed on offending television companies. In some respects this change (which is part of the 'deregulation' of television provided for in the 1990 Broadcasting Act) will be welcome: no longer will television companies be obliged to submit their controversial programmes to an outside body for preview and pre-censorship. Nor will plans to tackle controversial subjects such as terrorism have to be notified to the licensing body in advance of filming. Whether this change in the law will effect much liberalization, however, will depend on how the ITC wields its powers to impose sanctions. These range from a power to force a television company to broadcast an apology for lapses in taste or impartiality, to a power to revoke a licence in the case of a persistent offender. The financial penalties include a power to fine a company a maximum 3 per cent of its advertising revenue for a first offence and 5 per cent of advertising revenue for further offences – a formula that allows the ITC to impose penalties of millions of pounds. Television companies may prefer to err on the safe side rather than to put their profits at risk by incurring sanctions of this order of magnitude. It remains to be seen how the ITC will go about monitoring compliance with the statutory duties – it will certainly come under pressure to punish television stations that infringe the more detailed codes issued by the Broadcasting Standards Council and that suffer regular adverse adjudications from the Broadcasting Complaints Commission. Although the 1990 legislation was promoted as regulation with 'a lighter touch', it provides a panoply of new punishments for breaches of more complex duties that may lead to regulation with an even heavier hand.

---

[52] *R* v *IBA ex parte Whitehouse* (1985) *The Times*, 4 April, CA.

The best antidote to censorship is publicity. Reporters and producers have a public duty to speak out if their vision of truth is suppressed by government appointees. When the IBA banned a programme about RUC brutality, the producers protested by making a copy available to the BBC, which had no hesitation in showing it as part of a news feature about the IBA decision. Most censorship decisions appear faintly ridiculous in the light of day. None more than the BBC's heavy-handed interference with *Willie – the Legion Hall Bombing*, a play by Caryl Churchill. The prologue criticized Ulster non-jury courts in a manner that BBC executives found unacceptable. So they rewrote and rerecorded the text. In protest, both Ms Churchill and her director succeeded in legal action to have their names removed from the credits. Then they held a press conference to release the original text, which most newspapers juxtaposed with the sanitized version prepared by the Corporation in major news stories on the day of transmission. This ensured the play – and its intended message – a very much wider audience than it would otherwise have obtained.

Theatre and film censorship

The theatre has been free from political censorship since 1967, when the Lord Chamberlain's power to licence stage plays was abolished. The cinema, however, is subject to the British Board of Film Classification (BBFC), a private body, which none the less exercises considerable influence over the way the law is enforced. It is financed by the film industry, and will grant certificates only to movies that it considers are within the limits of public accept-ability. In practice, the Director of Public Prosecutions does not prosecute films with BBFC certificates for cinema showing, so distributors prepared to pay the certification fee and to carry out the 'cuts' insisted upon by the Board are in effect guaranteed freedom from police harassment. This arrangement secures a quiet legal life for the film industry in general, although it is resented by some film makers who are obliged to tailor their product to BBFC standards in order to secure distribution outlets. The Video Record-ings Act gives the BBFC statutory recognition as the body charged with licensing films for sale or rent on video cassettes – a develop-ment that may legally oblige distributors to censor cinema films before transferring them to cassettes for home viewing. In relation to videos, the BBFC has become a fully fledged state censorship board, charged by law with determining whether material on video is 'suitable for viewing in the home' and with determining whether particular cassettes can be sold or hired to children. Its decisions are enforced by police and by trading standards officers, and heavy fines are imposed for non-compliance with its directives.

Prosecution Policy and the Public Interest

The last general safeguard for press freedom is the Attorney-General's 'public interest' discretion. Many of the criminal laws that affect the media – official secrets and prevention of terrorism, and most of the laws relating to contempt, reporting restrictions and obscenity – cannot be invoked in the criminal courts by anyone except the Attorney-General or the Director of Public Prosecutions (who works under the Attorney's superintendence). Likewise, the Attorney alone may enforce the ITC's statutory duties in cases where no individual can show that a breach will involve a personal injury. In all these cases the Attorney-General is not *bound* to take legal action, even if the law has clearly been broken. He has a *discretion* – to prosecute or not to prosecute – depending on his view of the public interest. In exercising his discretion he is entitled to take into account any consideration of public policy that bears on the issue – and the public policy in favour of free speech is important in deciding whether to launch official secrets or contempt or obscenity prosecutions. Actions that appear to compromise free speech are likely to be criticized in Parliament, where the Attorney must answer both his and the DPP's prosecution policy.

There have been cases where the Attorney has refused to act even after judges have called for prosecution. Sometimes his decisions are made on grounds of convenience: after most newspapers in Britain committed contempt of court over the arrest of 'Yorkshire Ripper' Peter Sutcliffe, the Attorney decided against prosecuting on the ground that he would have to put dozens of editors in the dock.[53] On other occasions the public interest of an 'illegal' revelation has tipped the balance against invoking legal discipline against the journalist who revealed it. For example, it is usually contempt to publish a story that causes the discharge of a jury in mid-trial. This consequence was caused by London Weekend Television when it revealed that a juror in an official secrets case was a former member of the SAS, and by the *Guardian* when it published details of information discovered by police when they 'vetted' a jury that was trying some anarchists.[54] In both cases the trial judges complained to the Attorney-General, who decided that prosecution would not be in the public interest. No doubt the decision was heavily influenced by the fact that both stories were correct and had revealed controversial practices in the administration of justice.

There is a danger in placing over-much reliance on the

---

[53] *Press Conduct in the Sutcliffe Case*, Press Council booklet No 7, 1983, pp. 50–2.
[54] David Leigh, *The Frontiers of Secrecy*, Junction Books, 1980, Ch 4.

Attorney's discretion. He is, after all, a Government minister, as well as the leader of the legal profession. In deciding 'public policy', he will obviously be influenced by the outlook of the political party of which he is a member and by the values of the profession that he leads. These influences will not always incline him to the view that revelation of particular legal or political material is necessarily in the public interest.

There are, of course, cases where a newspaper wishes to publish material that is unlawful as the law at present stands, although there is some prospect that if the Attorney-General takes action, no appeal court will overturn an earlier decision and decide in the newspaper's favour. There may be value in provoking a test case, in a way that avoids the danger of a heavy fine if the newspaper is mistaken. The solution sometimes adopted is to send the article to the Attorney-General a few days prior to its intended publication. If he takes no action, well and good. If he seeks an injunction, the issue can be litigated and appealed as a matter of principle, without the danger of suffering a heavy penalty for an offence – e.g. of contempt of court – which would have been committed if the article had actually been published. More common, of course, is the situation where the media is in possession of material that they know the Attorney-General would be able to injunct (normally on grounds of beach of confidence) but would be unlikely to pursue once it had been published. The problem then becomes one of keeping the intention to publish secret, so that the Attorney-General has no forewarning. *The Sunday Times* went to the extreme of publishing a 'dummy' first edition to mislead the authorities on the night it broke the *Spycatcher* revelations in Britain, but such devices are unavailable to television and radio programmes, the advance publicity for which will generally put the Attorney-General's office on notice of a potentially embarrassing 'leak'. The Attorney-General has no statutory right to preview programmes or to see transcripts or articles in draft, and if the rule against prior restraint were honoured in breach of confidence cases he would have to await publication before deciding whether the public interest required action. Regrettably, the courts have been prepared to allow their procedures to be exploited by Governments keen to obtain a glimpse of potentially embarrassing material prior to publication.

In 1987 BBC Radio 4 made a somewhat academic series about the security services entitled *My Country Right or Wrong*, and advertised it in the *Radio Times*. On the strength of this advertisement, the Government persuaded a High Court judge to grant an 'interim injunction' against the broadcast, because it feared that ex-employees of the security services might have breached confidence in the course of their interviews. It had no evidence of this: the BBC had on principle refused an invitation to submit the programme to the Government for 'vetting' in advance, and its own lawyers were satisfied that no breach of confidence had taken place. The interim injunction stopped the broadcast until the matter could be tried, and in due course the court ordered the BBC to 'give discovery' to the plantiff, i.e., to disclose the tapes of the programmes to the Attorney-General, who brought the action on behalf of the Government. After hearing the tapes, and being satisfied that they contained no breach of confidence, the Government discontinued the action and the BBC was finally able to broadcast *My Country Right or Wrong* six months after it had originally been scheduled, and after being forced in this fashion to submit it for state 'vetting'. The High Court had allowed its interlocutory procedures to be used as devices for enabling the Government to postpone and to preview an entirely innocuous public-interest programme, in the absence of any concrete evidence that the broadcast would contravene the civil or criminal law.[55]

There is another danger. The decision to publish often hinges on the question: 'Will the Attorney prosecute if we do?' There is a natural temptation to seek an answer from the horse's mouth, so to speak, by submitting the controversial material to the Attorney for an indication of his attitude. This has been done by the BBC (which is notoriously craven in legal matters) and by several newspapers. It comes perilously close to making the Attorney, in effect, a political censor, an official to whom the media can go, cap in hand, with the question 'please, sir, may we publish this?' The danger, of course, is that if the Attorney's answer is 'no', the material will then not be published. This would be a pity if the Attorney were bluffing. The prospect of scaring off awkward media revelations will always provide a great temptation for Attorneys to bluff.

Conclusion

The European Convention, trial by jury, the openness of courts, the remnants of the rule against prior restraint, the absence of laws permitting direct government interference and the public-interest role of the Attorney-General at least ensure that the British media enjoy relative freedom from censorship by comparison with most Third World countries. When British media law is compared with the jurisprudence of America, Canada, France, Scandinavia and Australia, however, it is seen to lack a number of features that are regarded as fundamental to press freedom in a democracy. When Richard Crossman described secrecy as the British disease, he was

---

[55] *A-G* v *BBC* (1987) *The Times*, 5, 18 December.

not merely referring to the terms of the Official Secrets Act. He was condemning the reluctance of government, national and local, and public employees throughout the civil service, to share information with the public. International studies confirm Crossman's criticism: they place Britain no higher than sixteenth in the league table of countries that most enjoy freedom to publish. The revolutions in Eastern Europe in 1989 have secured freedom of speech and have caused the United Kingdom to slip further down the league table. Britain's low rating is mainly due to the refusal of successive Governments to contemplate a Freedom of Information Act, which would give journalists and others a legal right of access to documents prepared by state officials.

'Freedom of the press' is still, of course, a potent phrase. But the fact that it is protected by unwritten convention rather than by a legal constitution means that there is no external brake upon Parliament or the courts moving to restrict it in particular ways, as the mood of the times takes them. Britain may still be a country where 'everything is permitted, which is not specifically prohibited', but the specific prohibitions have become more numerous, without having to justify themselves against the overriding principle of public interest suggested by the Royal Commission on the Press. However, those who operate the law are well aware that it will only be respected to the extent that it conforms with public opinion; the reason journalists and broadcasters are not prosecuted much more often for undoubted infringements of the letter of the laws of contempt and official secrecy is simply that the authorities are well aware that up-to-the-hilt enforcement of these vague laws would bring the law into further disrepute and precipitate precisely the sort of clash between Government and the press that it has been the British genius to avoid, whenever possible, by cosy arrangements.

Moreover, the law is only one method of control over what is placed in the public arena. Communicators are restrained by other forces: by shared ethical assumptions, by non-legal rules that find favour with the Press Complaints Commission and the Broadcasting Complaints Commission, by pressure from advertisers, by the political predilections of proprietors, and by the host of subjective considerations that go to make up 'editorial discretion'. Press monopolies inhibit those with different views from launching out on their own. The law is often invoked by editors, executives or lawyers to support decisions to censor that are taken on other grounds, or instinctively: legal advice of this sort is usually convenient rather than correct. The decision to publish will involve a calculation of many risks – it is only when the apparition of a successful legal action tips the balance against publishing a story of genuine public interest that 'freedom of expression' has been meaningfully curtailed by law.

That happens often enough to be a matter for public concern. Whether it *should* happen as often as it does is open to doubt. If editors and programme makers and journalists were more aware of their legal rights, and more courageous in calling the lawyers' bluff, they might find that the law is not quite the ass it sometimes appears. Those journalists who recklessly write false stories deserve to be made to grovel in apology. Those prepared to fight for the principle that stories that advance the public interest should be published are usually vindicated. At every stage, the media must insist upon their right to investigate and to publish such stories: if they are right in their identification of the public interest, they are unlikely to come to harm in the long run.

Chapter 2

Defamation

A man who wants to talk at large about smoke may have to pick his words very carefully if he wants to exclude the suggestion that there is also a fire: but it can be done.

Lord Devlin, *Lewis* v *Daily Telegraph* [1]

London is the libel capital of the world. No other legal system offers such advantages to the wealthy maligned celebrity: procedures that tilt the odds in favour of plaintiffs; a law that gives little weight to the principles of freedom of expression; and tax-free damages awarded unrestrainedly by star-struck juries who dislike newspapers. As a result, international politicians, businessmen and socialites such as Bianca Jagger, Sylvester Stallone, Dr Armand Hammer, Andreas Papandreou, Erica Jong, Princess Elizabeth of Toro and the Sheikh of Dubai have chosen to bring or to threaten actions in London against American books and newspapers that cannot be sued – or sued so easily – under American and European laws. [2] The result is that Britain reads less than other countries, as nervous publishers cut passages critical of the wealthy and powerful from books published locally. Even

---

The best textbook on the law of libel is the admirably clear and straightforward account given by Duncan and Neill, *Defamation*, 2nd edn, Butterworths, 1983. A more detailed study is *Gatley on Libel and Slander*, 8th edn, Sweet & Maxwell, 1981. Important reform recommendations were made by the Committee on Defamation chaired by Mr Justice Faulks, which were reported in 1975 (HMSO, Cmnd 5909) and more radically and with characteristic vigour by Lord Denning, in *What Next in the Law*, Butterworths, 1982. The most impressive blueprint for reform, however, is the work of the Australian Law Reform Commission, *Unfair Publication*, 1979. The best account of American law is Robert Stack, *Libel, Slander and Related Problems*, Practicing Law Institute, 1980. *My Learned Friends* by Adam Raphael, W. H. Allen, 1989; and *Public Scandal, Odium and Contempt* by David Hooper, Secker & Warburg, 1984, further illustrate the tortuous path that libel litigation can take. In 1991 the Supreme Court Procedure Committee, chaired by Lord Justice Neill, made wide-ranging suggestions for reform in its *Report on Practice and Procedure in Defamation*.

[1] [1964] AC 234 at p. 285.
[2] See Robin Pogrebin, 'Libel Gripes Go Offshore – London A Town Named Sue', *The New York Observer*, 23 September 1991.

Daniel Moynihan's famous aphorism about Henry Kissinger – 'Henry doesn't lie because it's in his interest. He lies because it's in his nature' – was solemnly edited out of books on American politics before they were published here. In a global village does it make any sense for people to have different reputations in different parts of town?

There is nothing objectionable in the principle that a person's reputation should be protected from falsehoods: problems arise because the practices and procedures of the libel law can also work to prevent the exposure of wrongdoing. The heavy damages awarded in important cases are merely the tip of a legal iceberg that deep-freezes large chunks of interesting news and comment. In newsrooms libel is the greatest inhibition upon freedom of speech, although it also serves as a spur to accuracy and professionalism. The task for the journalist and broadcaster is to recognize and conform to the valuable discipline of the law, while at the same time understanding it sufficiently to be able to call the bluff of those who seek to exploit it to suppress important truths. That the bluff succeeds more often than it should may be the fault of the unconscionably heavy legal costs that can attend even a successful defence, or the business caution of insurance companies that increasingly influences how, or whether, libel writs should be resisted. Journalists can do little about legal costs and insurance, but they should be well versed in the legal defences that give them more latitude than is commonly thought. When the destination is important, the writer's craft can often steer around the libel minefield.

Press Advantages

For all its dangers, there are three features of the present libel law that protect careless or incompetent journalists.

Absence of legal aid

A libel action is the only important civil right for which legal aid is not available.[3] Writers can excoriate poor persons secure in the knowledge that unless a trade union or well-wisher finances the action, it is unlikely to be pursued: even a journalist as senior as Adam Raphael has quailed when told that the legal cost of suing another newspaper to vindicate his reputation could be as high as

---

[3] Legal Aid Act 1974 s 7 Sched 1 Part II para 1.

£250,000 if the case went to trial.[4] He was turned down by the Goldsmith Libel Fund, an eccentric exercise in philanthropy that bankrolls plaintiffs of Conservative persuasion (notably Tory MPs) who bring libel actions against media organizations perceived as left-wing (e.g. the BBC). The very existence of such a fund serves to emphasize the inequity of the present law. There is the possibility of a complaint being upheld by the Press Complaints Commission, which functions in such cases as a poor person's libel court. But an adverse ruling from a private body is much less daunting and much less publicized than a heavy award of damages by judge or jury. The unavailability of legal aid for libel has been defended on the basis that it would bring 'over the fence' disputes to court (the poor being assumed to quarrel in crowded tenements rather more often than the rich accuse one another of cheating at cards), but the inequity is so glaring that the argument for extending legal aid to defamation actions is difficult to resist. If libel is too much of a threat to press freedom already, the answer is to reform the law, not to deny its benefits to disadvantaged sections of society.

False statements not necessarily libellous

The law of libel will not correct all, or even most, false statements. It can be activated only when a false statement actually damages a reputation. An assertion is not defamatory simply because it is untrue – it must lower the victim in the eyes of right-thinking citizens. However irksome it may be to have inaccuracies published about one's life or behaviour – dates misstated, non-existent meetings described, and qualifications misattributed – there must be a 'sting' in the falsehood that reflects discredit in the eyes of society. To publish falsely of an Irish priest that he informed on members of the IRA is not defamatory: it may cause him to be executed by terrorists, but the law offers him no way of securing a correction. 'The very circumstances which will make a person be regarded with disfavour by the criminal classes will raise his character in the estimation of right-thinking men. We can only regard the estimation in which a man is held by society generally.'[5]

Truth: an absolute defence

The third debatable advantage enjoyed by the British press is that truth is an absolute defence to libel, no matter how unnecessary or unfair its revelation. The publication of intimate details of private

---

[4] Adam Raphael, *My Learned Friends*, W. H. Allen, 1989, Ch 3.
[5] *Mawe* v *Pigott* (1869) IR 4 CL 54. And see *Byrne* v *Deane* [1937] 1 KB 818.

lives without the slightest public-interest justification cannot be the subject of legal action, unless they have stemmed from a breach of confidence or some other legal wrong. There is no substantive protection for privacy in British law. Truth, however tawdry or trivial, may be told without let or hindrance from libel laws.

Press Disadvantages

In practice, then, journalists have the 'power' – in the sense that they are unlikely to be stopped – to defame the poor, to publish falsehoods that do not injure reputations, and to invade personal privacy. But there is no doubt that libel law does in other respects impinge upon the justifiable freedom of the press. Its very basis has an anachronistic flavour. The idea that large sums of money must be awarded to compensate people for words that 'tend to lower them in the estimation of right-thinking members of society' smacks of an age when social and political life was lived in gentlemen's clubs, when escutcheons could be blotted and society scandals resolved by writs for slander. Libel damages call for a metaphysical evaluation of dignity, a compensation, in many cases, for loss of *amour propre* that may be higher than the courts would award for the loss of an arm or a leg. An ideal law would ensure both the speedy correction of false statements and the protection of the expression of honest opinion. There are cases where British law secures neither goal. For the media, the present law of libel induces a number of major headaches.

Burden of proof on media defendant

A published allegation may be true, but the defendant carries in law the burden of *proving* its truth, upon evidence admissible in court. Statements made out of court and assurances recorded by reporters at the time are likely to be inadmissible or of less value because they are 'hearsay': real witnesses must be enticed or subpoenaed to give evidence before the jury. Where the 'source' for a story dies, or is out of the country, or has been promised confidentiality, or goes back on what he said, the difficulties of proving the truth of a true statement may be too great.

Technicality

Libel law has been allowed to become extremely complex. One straightforward case – involving a *Police 5* message about a confidence trickster who had used a name belonging to an innocent plaintiff – had consequences devastatingly described by Lord Diplock:

This is an ordinary simple case of libel. It took fifteen days to try: the summing-up lasted for a day: the jury returned thirteen special verdicts. The notice of appeal sets out seven separate grounds why the appeal should be allowed and ten more why a new trial should be granted, the latter being split up into over forty sub-grounds. The respondents' notice contained fifteen separate grounds. The costs must be enormous. Lawyers should be ashamed that they have allowed the law of defamation to have become bogged down in such a mass of technicalities that this should be possible.[6]

That case was heard in 1966, since when the 'mass of technicalities' has been piled much higher. In the late 1980s a number of libel cases were taken to the Court of Appeal on pre-trial issues concerning technical points of pleading, and much criticism was levelled at the complexity, expense and delay that have become associated with libel actions.[7] A plaintiff can sue within three years of the date of publication of the libel,[8] and actions often take two years to come to trial after the writ has been issued. Such delays do not help the plaintiff who wants to set the record straight, but they are equally unpleasant for defendants, who face escalating costs and witness difficulties.

Uncertainty

Perhaps the most crippling feature of libel actions is their uncertainty. Some civil litigation may be finely balanced, but the decisions made by judges are reasoned on predictable lines. There is no case more difficult to predict than that decided by a libel jury – and plaintiffs nowadays usually insist on their 'right' to have the case tried by a jury rather than a judge. Jury decisions on damages are entirely unpredictable, and jury decisions on liability are often difficult to predict by relation to the merits of the case: juries normally find for the plaintiff, sometimes irrationally, but on occasions find irrationally for the defendant. Many defences that should protect media defendants, such as fair comment and qualified privilege, are contingent upon findings of fact by juries, and are therefore fragile, since juries can strain the facts to find against newspapers. In 1991 the appeal courts damaged these defences by restricting the power of the trial judge to stop an action in circum-

---

[6] *Boston* v *Bagshaw & Sons* [1966] 1 WLR 1126.
[7] *Singh* v *Gillard* (1988) *The Independent*, 5 May; 138 NLJ 444 and *Morrell* v *International Thomson Publishing Ltd* [1989] 3 All ER 733, where libel pleadings were called an archaic 'saraband' (according to the OED, 'a slow and stately Spanish dance in triple time').
[8] Limitation Act 1980 s 4A.

stances where he or she thought (and any other reasonable judge would think) that the defence was made out on the facts.[9] The result is further unpredictability in relation to legal rules, which should be capable of confident application. For example, it cannot now be predicted that a report of a planning inquiry that is, on balance, fair and accurate will attract qualified privilege: since the jury has a right to decide for itself, without giving reasons, whether the report is, in fact, fair and accurate, the trial must proceed if this question is at all capable of argument, even if reasonable judges would have little doubt about the outcome of that argument. It follows that the protections afforded to media defendants in libel actions can be stated only theoretically: if plaintiffs have more lovable characters, more star-studded witnesses or more eloquent lawyers than their journalist opponents, defences of fair comment and qualified privilege may not work in practice as effectively as textbooks suggest they should.

Costs and damages

Libel actions launched by wealthy and determined plaintiffs can be enormously expensive to combat. Even if successful, the defendant is unlikely to recoup more than 70 per cent of the costs. When the *Daily Mail* was sued by the head of the 'Moonies' over allegations that the sect brainwashed converts and broke up families, the editor was warned by his lawyers that an adverse verdict might cost him £1 million. The case lasted 100 days, required the attendance of many witnesses from abroad, and the defendant's legal costs alone amounted to some £400,000.

Damages for libel are notoriously unpredictable. Women who are raped receive about £5,000 compensation, and in recent civil actions for negligence heard by judges plaintiffs have been awarded £50,000 for loss of a leg, £20,000 for loss of an eye and £5,000 for loss of a finger. A worker who contracted asbestosis as a result of his employer's carelessness received £25,000. But when film star Telly Savalas sued over a gossip columnist's unjustifiable remarks about hang-overs interfering with his work, he was awarded £34,000. The foreman of his jury wrote a letter to *The Times*:

> Where a jury has to decide, as men and women of the world, 'how much', the degree of uncertainty is so great that a random answer, consistent only with a total lack of any sort of yard-stick, can be expected. Their lordships would do as well to use an Electronic Random Number Indicating Machine.[10]

---

[9] See *Telnikoff* v *Matusevitch* House of Lords, [1991] 4 All ER 817.
[10] (1976) *The Times*, 22 June.

Those who throw sticks and stones that break bones can be better off in law than those who project hurtful words that leave no permanent mark. In 1987 libel damages of £450,000 were awarded against a Greek newspaper, although only fifty copies of it were circulated in Britain. This was followed by a £500,000 award to Jeffrey Archer against a newspaper that wrongly suggested (albeit on considerable circumstantial evidence) that he had sex with a prostitute, and by an award of £300,000 against a small trade journal. Koo Stark was awarded £300,000 by a jury the following year, and Elton John set a short-lived record with his £1 million settlement against the *Sun*. In 1989, the wife of the 'Yorkshire Ripper' was awarded £600,000 by a jury to compensate her for a false story in *Private Eye*, published eight years previously, to the effect that she had been prepared to sell her story to newspapers. This last award was too much even for the Court of Appeal (which has an aversion to interfering with jury awards) to countenance. It was a sum 'so unreasonable as to be divorced from reality'.[11] The Court of Appeal expressed hope that judges might give some help to juries in future about the real value of money.

In the first case in which such guidance was received, the jury returned with a new British and Commonwealth record of £1.5 million, against an author who had attacked Lord Aldington as a 'war criminal' over his role in the forcible repatriation of Cossacks to their deaths at the end of the Second World War. The judge had warned the jury not to award 'Mickey Mouse money', by which he apparently intended to refer to a sum so large as to be unrealistic (such as £1.5 million). The jury may have understood the phrase to refer to small or trifling amounts, and followed his direction by awarding the sort of sum they imagined in the coffers of Scrooge McDuck. The episode further emphasized the unsatisfactory state of the libel law, and how the prospect of massive awards of damages may serve as a real threat to freedom of expression.

Two further examples of absurdly high awards *after* the Court of Appeal decision in the *Private Eye* case were £100,000 to explorer Ranulph Fiennes against *Macleans*, a Canadian magazine that sold only 400 copies in the United Kingdom, and £150,000 to Teresa Gorman MP for a spoof press release circulated to only 91 people. Plainly the present rules are incapable of producing rational and consistent jury awards. In 1991 the Court of Appeal was empowered (by section 8 of the Courts and Legal Services Act) to substitute its own award in place of damages that it regards as excessive, without having to put the parties to the inconvenience of a new trial. This provides some safeguard against arbitrary

---

[11]   *Sutcliffe* v *Pressdram Ltd* [1990] 1 All ER 269, CA.

awards, but so far it has meant that most appeals are secretly 'compromised' by the parties reaching agreement on a sum before the appeal is heard. The large damages remain on the public record, and for the plaintiff to boast about, but the real sum received is much less.

Each case that goes to trial is an elaborate gamble. How much should be paid into court, and when? If the defendant makes a payment into court, the plaintiff may seize it and call quits. If the plaintiff presses on and wins, but is awarded no more in damages than the amount of the 'payment in', the plaintiff must foot the entire legal bill incurred by both the sides since the day of the payment.[12] In one celebrated case in 1975 a colonel with a penchant for spanking unsuspecting women sued the *Sunday People* for exposing his activities: he was awarded a derisory halfpenny. But the newspaper was saddled with the legal costs of the trial, which it could have avoided by 'paying in' the lowest denomination coin of the realm before the trial began. The publishers of *Exodus* had greater foresight. When sued for libel by Dr Dering, an Auschwitz prison doctor criticized in the book, they 'paid in' the derisory sum of £2 before the trial. Dr Dering declined this contemptible compensation, and risked crippling legal costs on a trial that he hoped would win him heavy damages. The jury awarded him the libel raspberry – a halfpenny – so he was forced to pay for the whole action. When *Coronation Street* actor Bill Roach sued the *Sun* for suggesting that everybody thought he was as boring in real life as the character he played, the newspaper had the foresight to 'pay in' £50,000, which Roach thought far too small a sum to compensate him for the libel. The case went to trial, and the jury (who are kept in the dark, in true game-show tradition, about 'payments in') awarded him precisely £50,000. Had it also undertaken not to repeat the libel, the *Sun* would not have been liable for Roach's legal costs, estimated at over £100,000. In circumstances like these the temple of law becomes a casino.

Given the expense and uncertainty of defending libel actions, it is not surprising that media organizations, in consultation with their libel insurers, often prefer to pay up and apologize. But these difficulties should not be exaggerated: some of them are, after all, suffered by the plaintiff as well. A newspaper or television station that gains the reputation, amongst the legal fraternity who specialize in libel, of being a 'soft touch', will soon find itself being touched very often for damages and apologies. The *Daily Mail*

---

[12] The plaintiff has twenty-one days to accept the 'payment in'. After that time the plaintiff may still accept the offer, but only with leave of the court, which should not be granted if the risks have changed (e.g., by a new plea of justification): *Proetta* v *Times Newspapers* [1991] 4 All ER 46.

may have lost money in taking on the 'Moonies', but it gained both in reputation and by discouraging similar actions against itself. It is ironic to record that the media's greatest recent libel triumph – the jury's rejection of Sonia Sutcliffe's case for damages against *News of the World* – came only after the newspaper had 'paid in' £50,000 in the hope of settling the case. The newspaper had little alternative but to fight when Sutcliffe rejected the offer in the hope that a jury would award her more money, and its victory was largely due to the journalist (from another newspaper) who had written the story, and who defended her freedom to tell it personally in the courtroom.

Defamation Defined

The test

Whether a statement is capable of bearing a defamatory meaning is a question of law, to be decided by the judge at the outset of a trial. A defamatory meaning is one that, in the circumstances of publication, would be likely to make reasonable and respectable people think less of the plaintiff. The test is variously described as 'lowering the plaintiff in the estimation of right-thinking people generally'; 'injuring the plaintiff's reputation by exposing him to hatred, contempt or ridicule' and 'tending to make the plaintiff be shunned and avoided'. It is all a question of respect and reputation – not just of the plaintiff as a human being, but as a worker – a public official, business executive, professional or performer. To allege incompetence at playing the tuba would not lower most people in the eyes of their fellow citizens – unless they happened to be professional tubists. To say that someone votes Conservative is not a libel – unless it be said of a Labour MP, and, in consequence, would be defamatory in its implication of personal and political hypocrisy.

Malicious falsehood and conspiracy to injure

A statement may be entirely false and deeply upsetting to the person about whom it is made. But unless it tends to lessen respect for that person, it will not be defamatory. The victim may have an action for *malicious falsehood*, however, if it can be proved that the untrue statement was made spitefully, dishonestly or recklessly, and that it has in fact caused financial loss.

> Stephane Grappelli, the renowned jazz violinist, employed English agents, who booked him for certain concerts. Grappelli claimed they

acted without reference to him, and the concerts had to be cancelled. The reason given by the agents for the cancellation was: 'Stephane Grappelli is very seriously ill in Paris and is unlikely ever to tour again.' This was an entirely false statement, obviously damaging to a thriving professional musician. However, the statement was not defamatory: to say that someone is seriously ill might excite pity, but not ridicule or disrespect. Grappelli had to be content with an action for malicious falsehood.[13]

The action for malicious falsehood is much less favourable to plaintiffs than defamation. They have no right to jury trial, and they have to prove that the words were false (in libel, the burden of proving that the words are true is on the defendant), that the words were published maliciously and that they were likely to cause financial loss. 'Conspiracy to injure' is another civil wrong that can be invoked against media falsehoods although it requires proof of an agreement where the sole or dominant purpose is to injure the plaintiff.

Although actions against the media for these civil wrongs have been rare in the past, they have two practical advantages for plaintiffs. Firstly, legal aid is not available for libel, but it may be granted for malicious falsehood. Secondly, plaintiffs cannot obtain an injunction against a libellous publication, where the defendant indicates an intention to justify or to plead fair comment. In either civil case, however, injunctions may be granted on the 'balance of convenience' test, which is usually unfavourable to the media. The following case provides a recent example of a 'malicious falsehood' injunction where a libel injunction could not have been granted:

> Gorden Kaye, star of the television comedy *'Allo 'Allo!*, was taken to hospital after sustaining serious head injuries. As he was coming out of the anaesthetic following brain surgery, a reporter from the *Sunday Sport* gained access to his hospital room and purported to interview him. The newspaper planned to publish the story as a 'world exclusive' voluntary interview. The Court of Appeal granted a limited injunction against the newspaper on the basis that Mr Kaye had an arguable case that it amounted to 'malicious falsehood' to claim that he had voluntarily surrendered a valuable property right (i.e. in his 'exclusive' story) in these circumstances.[14]

The power to award these injunctions is still discretionary, and

---

[13] *Grappelli* v *Derek Block Holdings Ltd* [1981] 2 All ER 272.
[14] *Kaye* v *Robertson* [1991] FSR 62, CA. In cases where the defendant's behaviour is less outrageous, the court will look carefully at claims for malicious falsehood and conspiracy to injure that have been 'tacked on' to libel claims in the hope of more readily obtaining an interim injunction: see *Gulf Oil (Great Britain) Ltd* v *Page* [1987] Ch 327.

the Vice-Chancellor has recently said that for judges weighing the pros and cons the public interest in freedom of speech is one of the most important factors to be taken into account.[15] In a conspiracy to injure case he decided that in exercising discretion 'the important questions are questions of public interest, not of private rights'. The public interest of freedom of speech, and the narrower public interest of allowing allegations of financial misconduct to come to the attention of investors and regulatory authorities, defeated the plaintiff's claim for an injunction until trial.

Importance of context

Whether statements are capable in law of being defamatory depends on the content and context of the whole article or programme, and the impression it would convey to the average viewer. It is not helpful to lay down hard and fast rules: judges and juries place themselves (without very much difficulty) in the position of 'right-thinking members of society', and ask themselves whether they think the statement would injure the plaintiff's reputation. A statement that the plaintiff has supplied information to the police about crime would not, as we have seen, be defamatory. Nor would a suggestion that plaintiffs are poor – unless they are in business and the implication is that they are unable to pay their debts. The court must bear contemporary social standards in mind in making what will in some cases necessarily be a value judgement. The values of judges in the deep south of the United States of America, who have held it defamatory to suggest that a white person has 'coloured' blood, would not be shared in Britain. Not, one hopes, for the reason given in 1848 by the Chief Justice, who argued that being black was 'a great misfortune, but no crime'.[16]

Clearly, there is an element of political value judgement in such decisions: in 1921 a judge held that reasonable citizens would not think less of a trade unionist if it were claimed that he had worked during a strike:[17] some juries might reach a different decision today. Ideas about immorality and what constitutes dishonourable conduct change over time, but the views of judges change more slowly than most. Would it still be defamatory to describe a heterosexual as 'gay'? Damages of £18,000 were awarded by a jury against the *Daily Mirror* for that very imputation about Liberace in 1959. It would be open to a jury to decide that a false imputation that a plaintiff had contracted the AIDS virus (as Liberace did almost thirty years after his libel win) is defamatory in so far as it

---

[15] *Femis-Bank (Anguilla)* v *Lazar* [1991] 2 All ER 865.
[16] *Hoare* v *Silverlock* (1848) 12 QB 630 at p. 632 per Lord Denman CJ.
[17] *Mycroft* v *Sleight* (1921) 90 LJKB 883 per Mr Justice McCardie.

might suggest promiscuous or unsafe sexual conduct. In 1934 the Court of Appeal somewhat emotionally rejected the argument that it did not lower Princess Yousoupoff in reputation to suggest that she had been raped by Rasputin;[18] by today's standards it could hardly be said that the innocent victim of a sex (or any other) crime would be diminished in the eyes of 'right-thinking' members of the community.

It is not defamatory to predict, incorrectly, take-overs or cessations of business, which might have the effect of injuring trade but which do not reduce esteem for the trader. It is possible to criticize a merchant's goods without reflecting on the competence or the probity of their producer. The question, always, is whether the words, in their published context, would be likely to lower the plaintiff in the minds of ordinary, decent readers. That depends, of course, on how the ordinary decent reader interprets the words, 'reading between the lines in the light of his general knowledge and experience of worldly affairs'.[19]

The 'ordinary reader' test

In deciding what words mean for the purpose of defamation, the intention of the writer or speaker is largely irrelevant. The test is the effect on the ordinary reader, who is endowed for this purpose with considerable wisdom and knowledge of the way of the world. The literal meaning is not conclusive: the ordinary reader knows all about irony. To say of John Smith 'His name is certainly not George Washington' is capable of being defamatory of Smith: the ordinary reader knows that George Washington could never tell a lie, and is likely to infer that Smith is therefore untruthful.[20] The ordinary reader is impressed by the tone and manner of publication, and the words chosen to headline a story. In a popular paper the headline 'False profit return charge against Investment Society' suggests fraud and not an arguable error by accountants in attributing profit to capital rather than income.[21]

The courts accept that ordinary readers are not literal-minded simpletons. They are capable of divining the real thrust of a comment, and able to respond to a joke, even a joke in bad taste, in the spirit intended by the commentator. In this sense, the author's intention does play an indirect part in determining the meaning of the words in question, because that meaning is decided by the

[18] *Yousoupoff* v *MGM Pictures Ltd* (1934) 50 TLR 581.
[19] *Lewis* v *Daily Telegraph*, note 1 above, at p. 258 per Lord Reid.
[20] *Grubb* v *Bristol United Press Ltd* [1963] 1 QB 309 per Holroyd Pearce LJ.
[21] *English & Scottish Co-operative Properties Mortgage & Investment Society Ltd* v *Odhams Press Ltd* [1940] 1 KB 440 at p. 452 per Slesser LJ.

ordinary reader's response to the question: 'What on earth is the author getting at?' An example is provided by *Schild* v *Express Newspapers*:[22]

> The plaintiff, a leading businessman, and his family were kidnapped in Sardinia by bandits who demanded a £3 million ransom. This incident was the cue for an unkind comment in a column by Sir John Junor:
>
>> Isn't it an extraordinary coincidence that the reported ransom of £3 million ... is exactly the amount, including interest, which Mr Schild is said to owe the London merchant bank of Keyser Ullman? It could not possibly be, could it, that the man responsible for taking on the loan, the then chairman of Keyser Ullman, Mr Edward du Cann MP, is spending the parliamentary recess leading a debt-collecting bandit gang in Sardinia?
>
> Schild claimed that these words meant that the kidnapping was a sham arranged by him to avoid his debts, and implied that he was a dishonest hypocrite prepared to exploit his family. Had the words been capable of bearing this defamatory meaning, Schild might have been awarded enormous damages. But the Court of Appeal ruled that no reasonable reader, asking 'what on earth was Sir John Junor getting at?' could have thought he was seriously accusing Schild. The comment was pointed at du Cann.

How the minds of ordinary readers receive and interpret newspaper stories is an interesting question of psychology: in law, the answer depends upon the assumptions of lawyers. What do ordinary readers think when their eyes catch the fact that someone they know is concerned with a police inquiry into crime?

> In *Lewis* v *Daily Telegraph* the newspaper announced:
>
>> 'INQUIRY ON FIRM BY CITY POLICE. Officers of the City of London Fraud Squad are inquiring into the affairs of Rubber Improvement Ltd. The investigation was requested after criticisms of the chairman's statement and the accounts by a shareholder at a recent company meeting. The chairman is Mr John Lewis, former Socialist MP.'
>
> The inquiry subsequently exonerated Lewis and his company. They sued, claiming that the news story implied, to the ordinary reader, that they were involved in fraud. The newspaper argued that the ordinary reader, possessed of a fairer and less suspicious mind, would

---

[22] *Schild* v *Express Newspapers Ltd* (1982) *The Times*, 5 October, CA.

presume innocence. The jury awarded £100,000 damages against the paper. But the House of Lords held that the statement was not capable of meaning that the plaintiffs were guilty of fraud. 'The ordinary man, not avid for scandal', would not infer guilt merely because an inquiry was under way.[23]

So suspects, innocent until proven guilty, may be described as 'assisting police with their inquiries' and have no remedy in libel. Unless, of course, the story is written in a way that suggests that police have every reason to suspect them. Much – very much, in financial terms – depends upon the care with which the story is written, as the same newspaper once again discovered in *Hayward* v *Thompson*.[24]

During preliminary police investigations into Norman Scott's allegations that he had been the victim of a conspiracy to murder in order to protect a former lover, Liberal leader Jeremy Thorpe MP, the *Daily Telegraph* obtained a scoop from a police source. It published:

TWO MORE IN SCOTT AFFAIR

The names of two more people connected with the Norman Scott affair have been given to the police. One is a wealthy benefactor of the Liberal Party ... Both men, police have been told, arranged for a leading Liberal supporter to be 'reimbursed' £5,000, the same amount Mr Andrew Newton alleges he was paid to murder Mr Scott.

Mr Jack Hayward, the wealthy benefactor, claimed that the article meant that he was guilty of participating in or condoning a murder plot. The newspaper, relying on the *Lewis* case, said that the words would mean to the ordinary reader no more than that an inquiry was under way, and that Hayward would be able to assist it. The jury awarded Hayward £50,000, and the Court of Appeal upheld the verdict because the article *was* capable of implying guilt. Its headline put the wealthy benefactor 'in' the Scott affair, and the copy never got him out of it. 'IN' means 'in', and that implication of involvement with a conspiracy was reinforced by the phrase 'connected with' and the inverted commas around 'reimbursed'. These stylistic features of the story as published would give the ordinary reader the impression that Hayward was an accomplice in the plot – 'the paymaster of blood money', as his counsel put it.

The *Hayward* case underlines the importance of the way in which the story is presented to the public. The art is to put across important information without using a language or style that carries

---

[23] [1964] AC 234.
[24] *Hayward* v *Thompson* [1981] 3 All ER 450.

a defamatory implication. That art was demonstrated with conspicu-
ously different talents by British editors and journalists in the
aftermath of the revelation that Jeffrey Archer, best-selling novelist
and deputy chairman of the Conservative party, had paid a
Shepherd Market streetwalker £2,000 to leave the country.
Certain newspapers that jumped to the wrong conclusion that he had
engaged in sex with the woman were sued for libel, but were
unable to discharge the burden of proving a case that hinged upon
the word of a prostitute against the word of the plaintiff and his
'fragrant' wife. The *Star* was ordered to pay £500,000 damages
after a trial that amassed an estimated £750,000 in legal costs.
Newspapers that confined themselves to demonstrable facts, and
left readers to draw their own conclusions, were not sued.

However, there is a distinction between their own conclusions
and inviting them to draw a particular conclusion by inflaming
their suspicions. The author who is anxious to wound but fearful
to strike too obviously will not escape. If the reader is invited to be
suspicious and is nudged towards a defamatory explanation that
the writer 'did not care or did not dare to express in direct terms',
the publication will be capable of carrying a defamatory imputation.[25]

The 'ordinary reader' may vary in discernment according to the
newspaper that he reads and the way in which the article is
presented:

> Ten of the twelve CID officers stationed at Banbury sued the *News
> of the World*. At a time when a deranged man was holding hostages at
> gunpoint, the newspaper splashed on its front page:
> 'EXCLUSIVE. SIEGE MAN TELLS US WHY HE DID IT.'
> The story contained an edited version of a letter the man had written
> to the newspaper accusing Banbury CID officers of raping and beat-
> ing his wife. There was nothing in the presentation of the story to
> suggest that the allegations were untrue. The jury rejected the news-
> paper's defence that the ordinary reasonable reader of the *News of the
> World* would not take the allegations of such a person seriously.
> (Perhaps an ordinary reader of *The Times* would have been deemed
> more discerning.) Had the newspaper been less callous and opportun-
> istic in its presentation, it could have avoided a successful libel action
> by publishing its exclusive insight into the mind of the hostage-taker
> with sufficient background material to remove any suggestion that his
> allegation was other than paranoid fantasy.[26]

It will be for the jury to decide whether the words have the

---

[25] See *Jones* v *Skelton* [1963] 1 WLR 1362.
[26] 'Rapist CID Libel Costs Paper Record £250,000', *Guardian*, 10 February 1984.
The damages were subsequently reduced on appeal: *Riches* v *News Group
Newspapers Ltd* [1985] 2 All ER 845.

defamatory meaning alleged by the plaintiff, unless the judge rules at the outset that no sensible argument can be addressed to a jury to suggest this meaning – in which case the plaintiff's case will collapse. There is now a speedy avenue available to put an end to misconceived libel actions, by having the question of 'meaning' tried as a preliminary issue.[27] Regrettably, judges are rarely robust enough to withdraw the issue from a jury, even where they think the plaintiff's pleaded 'meaning' is grossly exaggerated, and *Schild* v *Express Newspapers* (see p. 50) is one of the few examples of a libel action being struck out on this basis.

Defamatory innuendo

The test of the ordinary reader is subject to qualification in the case of statements that are not defamatory on their face, but that carry discreditable implications to those with special knowledge. To say that a man frequents a particular address has no defamatory meaning to ordinary readers – unless they know that the address is a brothel. Here, libel is by *innuendo*, i.e., the statement is defamatory to those with knowledge of facts not stated in the article. If it is said of a barrister that he has refused to appear for an unsavoury criminal, the ordinary reader may applaud, but his professional reputation is lowered amongst colleagues who understand the story to mean that he has betrayed his ethical duty to appear for all who seek his services. Where the sting is not a matter of general knowledge, its defamatory capacity is judged by its impact upon ordinary readers who have such knowledge – if the plaintiff can first prove that such persons were amongst the actual readership.

Libel and Slander Distinguished

There are irritating, complicated and unnecessary distinctions in law between two types of defamation – libel and slander. Libel is a defamatory statement made in writing or – in the case of films and video-tapes – at least in some permanent form. Slander is a defamatory statement made by word of mouth or by gesture. Plaintiffs may sue for libel even though they have suffered no financial loss, but for slander (with certain exceptions) they must be able to prove actual damage and not mere injury to feelings. Historically, the distinction is explained by the view that writing was a premeditated and calculated act, which affected reputation much more drastically

---

[27] See Rules of the Supreme Court (RSC) Order 33 Rule 3. *Keays* v *Murdoch Magazines (UK) Ltd* [1991] 4 All ER 491 is a good example both of the jurisdiction and of the judicial nervousness about using it, even in a strong case.

and permanently than off-the-cuff comments. With the advent of radio, television and satellite broadcasting, this reasoning is anachronistic, and Parliament has enacted that words spoken in theatres, and in broadcasts for general reception, shall be deemed libels and not slanders.[28] The same provision is made for words spoken on television programmes.[29] However, the distinction still remains in certain areas, notably criminal libel (see p. 99), *extempore* statements at public meetings and noises of disapproval. Dramatists or actors whose work is maliciously booed or hissed off the stage would sue their tormentors for slander rather than libel.

The importance of the distinction is that there can be no action for slander unless the plaintiff has suffered damage that can be calculated in monetary terms. Victims of verbal assaults who suffer hurt feelings, sleepless nights, physical illness, or ostracism by friends and neighbours cannot bring an action.[30] There are only five exceptions: accusations of a crime punishable by imprisonment, suggestions that the plaintiff carries a contagious disease; adverse reflections on a person's ability to carry out an office, business or profession; slanders on the reputation or credit of tradespeople; and words imputing unchastity or adultery to a woman or girl.[31] Only in these five cases may the plaintiff sue for slander without having to prove financial loss.

Who Can Sue?

Any living individual, if made the identifiable subject of a defamatory attack, may take legal action. This includes infants (who sue 'by their next friend'), lunatics, bankrupts and foreigners. Animals, however, are fair game.

The question of who *can* sue is less important than the question of who *will* sue. The enormous cost of contested libel actions means that most plaintiffs will need financial support from unions or employers. Some organizations find that supporting libel actions on behalf of their members is politically convenient because it assures them a better or more polite press; the Police Federation is one example. There is nothing to stop such organizations offering

---

[28] See Theatres Act 1968 s 4(1) and Defamation Act 1952 ss 1, 16(3).
[29] Broadcasting Act 1990 s 166.
[30] *Argent* v *Donigan* (1892) 8 TLR 432; *Lynch* v *Knight* (1861) 9 HL Cas 592.
[31] Slander of Women Act 1891. In one of the last reported cases under this category, the plaintiff was awarded £300 for being called a lesbian. The judge observed that compared with a charge of heterosexual immorality this was 'more wounding, more likely to excite abhorrence on the part of reasonable people, and more likely to spoil the victim's prospects of marriage'. *Kerr* v *Kennedy* [1942] 1 All ER 412 at p. 414 per Asquith J.

to pay the costs of libel actions, and editors deciding whether to settle will bear in mind the strength of the organization behind the plaintiff. In recent years the use of *public* funds for individual libel actions has been heavily criticized. Local councils have voted their ratepayers' money to help executives defend their reputations, the BBC hazarded licence-money in backing Desmond Wilcox's claim against *Private Eye,* and the Foreign Office footed the legal bill for diplomats accused of 'covering up' the truth about the death of nurse Helen Smith. There is nothing to stop a private benefactor from bankrolling libel victims, and Sir James Goldsmith has sponsored a fund to assist like-minded litigants. However, the benefactor may have to pay the newspaper's costs if the latter is successful.[32]

The dead

The dead cannot sue or be sued for libel. Indeed, if a plaintiff dies on the day before the trial, the action dies as well. Neither the trustees of the estate nor the outraged relatives have any form of legal redress. This right to speak ill of the dead is justified in the interests of historians and biographers, and by the practical difficulties of subjecting deceased persons to cross-examination. The freedom, has, of course, been criticized – especially after the ferocious attack on Lord Goddard made by Mr Bernard Levin in *The Times* a few days after Goddard's death.

In 1975 the Faulks Committee on libel expressed great concern about stories that added to the grief of a widow, and recommended that relatives should be allowed to sue within five years of death (a cynical estimate, critics suggested, of the length of a widow's solicitude). There may be some unseemliness about the opportunism of assassinating characters still warm in their graves, but at least they cannot feel the stings and arrows of outrageous libels. The impossibility of shaking them in cross-examination would make such a reform grossly unfair to the media.

The Faulks Committee would have done better to concentrate on methods for speeding up libel hearings. The delays are always measured in years, and some plaintiffs die in the interim. In 1991 the death of Armand Hammer aborted one of the largest actions yet to be tried, although wailing at the libel bar was loudest over the fate of Robert Maxwell, a hypocrite who made his fortune by the exercise of a freedom of expression that he anxiously denied to anyone who wrote in less than hagiographic terms about himself. When Reginald Maudling brought actions against Granada

---

[32] *Singh* v *The Observer Ltd* [1989] 1 All ER 751; [1989] 3 All ER 777, CA.

Television and the *Observer* for similar libels, the *Observer* settled for £15,000. Granada held out, and the action was aborted by Maudling's death before it could come to trial. Although the death of the plaintiff ends the action, it does not pay the defendant's costs. The Faulks Committee failed to consider this unfair burden on the media, or to recommend the obvious reform that it should be borne by the plaintiff's estate.

Companies

A company may sue for defamation, but only in respect of statements that damage its business reputation. In legal theory a company has no feelings capable of injury, although adverse reports may lower the value of its 'goodwill' asset. Normally, individual officers or employees singled out by the criticism will additionally have an action: in *Lewis* v *Daily Telegraph*, for example, both the company and its managing director were plaintiffs.

Local authorities

In 1992 the Court of Appeal held that a local authority could not bring an action in defamation for words that reflected upon its governmental or administrative conduct. There was a danger that local authorities would use such a power to stifle legitimate public criticism of their activities, and the power was 'unnecessary in a democratic society' since an authority could sue for malicious falsehood if the attack had been improper and untrue, and its officers could sue for libel if they were personally identified by the attack.[33]

Trade unions

Trade unions and most other unincorporated associations cannot sue for libel. An unincorporated association has no legal personality of its own to protect, and it cannot bring a 'representative action' on behalf of all its members. This was decided in 1979 by *EETPU* v *Times Newspapers*, which held that the capacity of trade unions to sue had been removed by s 2(1) of the Trade Union and Labour Relations Act 1974.[34] The practical significance of this change is mainly to reduce the damages by removing one possible plaintiff, rather than by removing the prospect of an action. Most criticisms of trade unions will reflect upon individual officers, who will usually be financially supported by their union in vindicating their own reputations.

---

[33] *Derbyshire County Council* v *Times Newspapers Ltd* (1992) NLJ Law Report, p. 275.
[34] *EETPU* v *Times Newspapers Ltd* [1980] 3 WLR 98.

Groups

There is, in defamation law, a certain safety in numbers. Defamatory comment may not be actionable if it refers to people by class rather than by name. Whether an individual member of the class can sue depends upon the size of the class and the nature of the comment: there must be something in the circumstances to make the ordinary reader feel that the plaintiff personally is the target of the criticism. To say 'All barristers are thieves' does not entitle any one of 4,000 barristers to sue – the class is too large to argue that the comment singles out individuals. But to say 'All barristers in chambers at 11 Doughty Street are thieves' would be sufficiently specific to allow the thirty or so barristers in those chambers to take action. In 1971 the small group of regular journalists at the Old Bailey received £150 damages each for the intolerable insult of being collectively described in the *Spectator* as 'beer-sodden hacks'. The question always is whether the defamation is of the class itself (in which case no action arises) or whether ordinary readers would believe that it reflected directly on the individual plaintiff. In the case of the *News of the World* and Banbury CID mentioned above, the allegation was simply that unnamed CID officers from that particular police station had committed the rape. That allegation reflected on each officer at Banbury because that CID office had only twelve members. Had the allegation been less specific – had it referred only to 'certain police officers in Oxfordshire', for example – the Banbury officers would not have been able to prove that what was published related to them.

Identification

The test, in every case, is whether reasonable people would understand the words to point to the plaintiff personally, and the journalist cannot escape simply by widening the net of suspects. The statement 'Either A or B is the murderer' entitles *both* A and B to sue over a statement that carries the defamatory meaning that there is a substantial prospect that each is guilty. The distinction is not always easy to keep in mind:

> Lord Denning, Britain's most experienced judge in defamation cases, published a book in which he criticized a jury in Bristol for acquitting defendants who had been charged with rioting. Two members of the jury threatened to sue, because the comments (which were based upon misstatements of fact) suggested they had been false to their oaths by acquitting black defendants because they (the jurors) were black. The publishers withdrew all 10,000 copies of the book from sale.

A writer will not necessarily escape by criticizing 'some' members of a class if other evidence serves to identify the plaintiff as a member of the criticized section. An article stating that 'some Irish factory-owners' were cruel to employees enabled one particular owner to obtain damages, because other references in the article pointed to his factory. 'If those who look on know well who is aimed at', the target may sue.[35] Where the knowledge depends upon special circumstances of which not everyone is aware, the plaintiff has to prove that the article was published to persons who were able to make the identifying connection.

> In the Jack Hayward case, the *Daily Telegraph* argued that the plaintiff could not be identified from the description 'a wealthy benefactor of the Liberal party'. Unfortunately for the newspaper, that party did not have many wealthy benefactors, and evidence was admitted to show that others immediately made the connection. His friends put two and two together, and so did the media, which besieged his home by telephone and helicopter. In a national news-paper with a wide circulation the inference was that some readers would know the special facts which identified him.[36]

The moral of these cases is that journalists cannot avoid liability for defamation merely by avoiding the naming of names. Any story that carries the imputation of discreditable conduct by somebody will be actionable by a plaintiff who can show that at least some readers would recognize him as the person being criticized, or that the facts in the story necessarily imply such an allegation against him. An allegation that drugs are being supplied as a 'liquid cosh' to modify behaviour at a particular prison may point a sufficient finger at the medical officers working at that prison, even though they are not referred to by name. When an Australian newspaper alleged that Kerry Packer had 'fixed' the result of a cricket match involving the West Indian team, its captain (Clive Lloyd) was entitled to damages even though he was not named in the article and had not been playing in the particular match. The 'ordinary reader' would infer that the 'fixing' had involved the team as well as Packer, and that the captain of the team would have been party to the plot even though he had not played in the match.[37]

Those unintentionally defamed

Where a journalist *intends* to refer to an unnamed individual, it is reasonable that the individual should have an action for libel if others have correctly identified him or her as the target, whatever

---

[35] *Le Fanu* v *Malcomson* (1848) 1 HL Cas 637.
[36] See *Hayward* v *Thompson*, note 24 above.
[37] *Lloyd* v *David Syme & Co Ltd* [1986] AC 350.

literary devices have been used as camouflage. Asterisks, blanks, initials and general descriptions will not avail if evidence proves that readers have solved the puzzle correctly. Much less satisfactory, however, is the harsh rule that holds a writer responsible for *unintentional* defamation, where readers have jumped to a conclusion that was never intended. This rule is the bane of fiction writers, who must take special care to ensure that the more villainous characters in their plots cannot be mistaken for living persons. The leading case is *Hulton v Jones*.[38]

> In 1909 the *Sunday Chronicle* published a lighthearted sketch about a festival in Dieppe, dwelling upon the tendency of sober Englishmen to lead a 'gay' life (in the 1909 sense of the word) when safely across the Channel. 'Whist! There is Artemus Jones with a woman who is not his wife, who must be, you know – the other thing . . .' Whist! There were very heavy libel damages awarded to one Artemus Jones, a dour barrister practising on the Welsh circuit. Five of his friends thought the article referred to him – an identification made all the more far-fetched by the fact that the fictitious character was described as a Peckham Church Warden. The House of Lords upheld the award, ruling that the writers' intention was immaterial; what mattered was whether reasonable readers would think that the words used applied to the plaintiff.

The principle of this case lingers on, although Parliament sought to mitigate its harshness by a special provision that enables publishers of unintentional defamation to make amends without incurring heavy damages. The provision is so cumbersome it is rarely used (see p. 94), and in any event it can be availed of only where 'all reasonable care' had been taken to avoid such misunderstandings. Authors who employ fictional characters with realistic status or occupations should check available sources to ensure their characters could not be confused with persons of the same name and position. The entire print-run of one major novel had to be pulped because the author had chosen the actual name of a noble family to describe a fictional unsavoury aristocrat. A check with *Debrett* or *Who's Who* would have revealed the danger.

The rule that imposes liability for unintentional defamation has had absurd results. The House of Lords has solemnly decided that 'ordinary readers' do not read very carefully – at least when they are skimming through the *Sun*. They might jump to a conclusion from certain comments in that newspaper, and ignore others that point away from the plaintiff in question.[39] The height of absurdity was reached in a case where the wife of a race-horse owner pictured

---

[38] *Hulton v Jones* [1910] AC 20.
[39] *Morgan v Odhams Press Ltd* [1971] 1 WLR 1239.

with a woman he had described to the photographer as his fiancée was allowed to recover damages on the basis that her neighbours would think she was living in sin.[40] Equally unsatisfactory is the decision that Harold Newstead, a bachelor hairdresser living in Camberwell, was libelled by a perfectly accurate court report that another Harold Newstead, also a Camberwell resident, had been gaoled for bigamy ('I kept them both till the police interfered').[41] The *Newstead* case is used to warn young journalists of the importance, in court reporting, of giving occupations and addresses of defendants and witnesses, so that confusion can be avoided. Journalists should insist on receiving these details from the court clerk by citing the case of *R* v *Evesham Justices ex parte McDonagh*:[42]

> A former Tory MP was charged with driving without a tax disc. He begged the court not to disclose his home address lest his ex-wife discovered it and harass him. The court allowed him to write the address on a piece of paper rather than state it publicly. The Divisional Court held that there was an unlawful departure from the open-justice principle, which required defendants' addresses to be given publicly in court. The well-established practice, which helped to avoid wrongful identification and risks of libel action, should not be departed from for the benefit of the comfort and feelings of defendants.

The problems of 'unintentional defamation' underline the general unsuitability of libel law as a method of correcting factual errors and innocent confusion. The wife and the bachelor in the above cases should have been entitled to insist that the confusion be cleared up by a published clarification, but they should not have been able to obtain an award of damages against a newspaper that was not at fault. This is a problem that a 'legal right of reply' – requiring a correction without compensation – could resolve more effectively.

Not all unintentional defamations come cheaply. Damages of £20,000 were awarded against Granada Television in 1983 for unintentionally defaming a police officer in a *World in Action* programme about police corruption. A shot of a police station was used to accompany a voice-over commentary that 'some CID men take bribes'; for two and a half seconds, the officer could be identified in the film as he walked down the station steps. Granada's defence that the words were not intended to refer to the plaintiff and would not have been so regarded by reasonable viewers was rejected by the jury, after hearing that the officer had received 'unpleasant and damaging' comments afterwards.

---

[40] *Cassidy* v *Daily Mirror* [1929] 2 KB 331.
[41] *Newstead* v *London Express* [1940] 1 KB 377.
[42] [1988] 1 All ER 371.

Who Can Be Sued?

As a general rule, everyone who can sue for libel can also be sued for libel if responsible for a defamatory publication. There seems to be an exception in the case of trade unions, which cannot sue for libel (see above) but can nevertheless be made defendants as a result of the abolition of their immunity in tort by s 15 of the 1982 Employment Act. Unincorporated associations are exempt from suit, but their officials and employees have no such immunity. Editors and journalists employed on journals published by these organizations are therefore at great financial risk, and should ensure that their contracts of employment indemnify them against costs and damages that may accrue from libel actions, which are often brought by opponents of their employer's policies.

Every person who is responsible for a defamatory publication is a candidate for a writ: author, editor, informant, printer, proprietor and distributor.

Avoiding responsibility

Journalists whose bylines are on defamatory stories can exculpate themselves by proving that the defamation was added to their copy without their consent (a common occurrence where the sting emanates from clumsy sub-editing). In such cases they should seek independent advice and think carefully before allowing their reputation to be sacrificed by a 'tactical apology' prepared by lawyers acting in the interests of their employers. An important case that casts helpful light on a journalist's rights in this situation is *UCATT* v *Brain*.[43]

> A trade union employed a journalist to edit its newspaper. He was subject to the direction of the General Secretary, who sometimes insisted on the publication of articles seen as politically important for the union. One such article, written by the General Secretary, was ordered to be printed and the editor had no option other than to deliver it to the printers. It libelled the plaintiff, who issued a writ against the editor. The union's lawyers decided to apologize, and the editor was directed to approve the apology, which was to be made in open court. The editor, fearing that this would reflect on his credit as a journalist, declined. He was sacked. The Court of Appeal upheld his claim for damages for wrongful dismissal. It pointed out that he had a good defence to the action, namely that he was not responsible for publication. The solicitors had a conflict of interests, and should have arranged for him to receive independent legal advice. The union acted wrongfully in dismissing him for insisting on his legal rights.

---

[43] *UCATT* v *Brain* [1981] ICR 542.

Employers have no right to bargain away journalists' reputations without their consent merely because some sacrifice of those reputations would be in the interests of management. A public apology is a reflection on all associated with it, and journalists should take independent advice before they agree to fall on their pens.

A public apology defames the author of the article apologized for by suggesting that the author has written carelessly. An author who has not approved the apology is entitled to sue the person who has issued it.[44] Unapologetic authors could not sue if the retraction was made in open court: the statement would then be privileged and so too would any report of it. However, they can still disassociate themselves from the apology. They will either have been named as co-defendants, along with their employers, or they can apply to the court to be joined as such. Normally, all defendants in libel cases use the same solicitors and barristers, but where, as here, there is a conflict of interest, each would be entitled to separate representation and the authors who stood by their story would thus be able to disown the apology. Alternatively, writers might approach the judge before whom the apology is to be made and ask him to refuse to sanction it because of the reflection that it would cast on their reputations. However, courts are predisposed in favour of settlements, and are reluctant to prevent statements being made that dispose of libel actions, even when such statements imply criticisms of others:

> The historian Richard Barnet wrote a book about foreign policy, which was reviewed in the *Spectator*. The review elicited a letter from Brian Crozier, a right-wing journalist, which alleged that Barnet was associated with KGB-influenced institutions. Barnet sued both Crozier and the *Spectator*. The magazine found that it could not justify the Crozier allegations that it had published, and agreed to apologize, pay damages and make a statement in open court publicly retracting the libel. Crozier sought to delay the making of the statement on the ground that it defamed him and might prejudice the jury in Barnet's action against him, which would come on for trial some six months later. The Court of Appeal held that although 'the court should be vigilant to see that the benefit of the procedure of making a statement in open court is not used to the unfair disadvantage of a third party', the public interest in allowing libel actions to be settled outweighed the damage that Crozier apprehended. The statement would certainly have no effect on a jury trial taking place six months later, and the court was not convinced that the statement carried the defamatory implication that Crozier was dishonest or incompetent. But had the statement been plainly defamatory of Crozier, the court would have ordered the settlement to be postponed until after his

---

[44] *Tracy* v *Kemsley Newspapers* (1954) *The Times*, 9 April.

trial, and may not have allowed it to be made at all under the cloak of absolute privilege.[45]

The 'statement in open court' is a procedural device used in most libel settlements, often after the plaintiff has 'taken out' money that has been paid into court by the defendant. It is valuable as a means of helping the plaintiff to restore his reputation (at least when it is reported) but it can be exploited to present a false picture under the pressure to avoid trial. Although judges should approve it before it is made, they normally make no inquiries and allow the parties to say whatever they like. It seems quite wrong, for example, that they should not be required to state explicitly the amount of damages that have been paid in settlement of the action. Judicial complaisance may change as a result of the *Elton John* case, where the statement was published by the *Sun* as a 'world exclusive' before it had even been made in court. The court gave a stern warning against future attempts to scoop it. Plaintiffs should not assume that they are entitled to be 'whitewashed' by a defendant who has paid them merely nominal damages, and it would be more satisfactory if judges made some inquiries of the parties before they approve statements that are made as matters of public record.[46]

Writers and speakers cannot be held responsible unless they authorize, or at least foresee, the publication that causes complaint. Participants in a television programme, for example, who are told that it is a 'pilot' that will not be transmitted, cannot be held responsible for defamatory statements they have made if it is subsequently screened at prime time. If the defamatory material has been supplied 'off the record' by a third party, a difficult question arises. The informant is responsible in law (unless the information was provided solely for the journalist's background reference and not for use even on an unattributed basis) but the media, having promised confidentiality, will be under an ethical duty not to reveal the name of the informant. The plaintiff may want, even more than damages, to discover the identity of the source. In those defamation cases where journalists can keep the identity of informants a secret (see p. 197) they are likely to find that their refusal to answer such questions is a ground for increasing the sum total of damages.[47] It may also, of course, be the reason why the action is lost in the first place, because evidence for the truth of the statement is unavailable from the person who originally made it.

---

[45] *Barnet* v *Crozier* [1987] 1 All ER 1041.
[46] See *Church of Scientology* v *North News Ltd* (1973) 117 SJ 566.
[47] *Hayward* v *Thompson*, note 24 above per Lord Denning at p. 459.

Book publishers usually insist on contracts whereby the author indemnifies them against defamation liability or warrants that the manuscript is libel-free. This practice reflects the superior bargaining power of the publisher in negotiating the agreement rather than a custom appropriate to the book trade, so where an indemnity clause is overlooked, the courts will not imply one into the contract by reference to custom and usage.[48] Freelancers who submit articles to newspapers and magazines cannot in consequence be made automatically liable for all the publisher's legal costs of defending a libel action, in the absence of express agreement. However, even in the absence of a contractual agreement the courts can apportion liability between defendants responsible for the same publications.[49] In practice most publishers will be insured against libel and may pay for the defence of the author under their policy, until such point as interests in the litigation begin to diverge – usually by the insurers wishing to settle and the author wishing to fight. Legal aid is unavailable for libel defendants, as it is for plaintiffs, and some authors in this position must confront the agonizing choice between standing by their story and possible bankruptcy. Most yield to their insurance-company-controlled publisher's request to join in a settlement by making a public apology: if they refuse, the plaintiff will sometimes be satisfied with the publisher's apology and damages, and withdraw the action against them in any event.

If a newspaper publishes a defamatory statement, it cannot shift all the blame to the person who uttered it in the first place. The first trap for young reporters is to assume that responsibility for a libel can be avoided if it is made in an attributed quotation. Every repetition of a libel gives a fresh cause of action against the persons responsible for the repetition. For example, a defamatory placard held in front of a television camera during a demonstration may attract a writ against the television company that broadcasts the picture on a news programme. When the press is sued over a reported quotation, it may obtain some relief by joining the speaker as co-defendant and thereby make the real libeller liable to contribute to costs and damages. The status and availability of the original speaker is therefore of great importance in deciding whether to publish the remark. Where the criticism is uttered on an unprivileged occasion by the Prime Minister, the risk would be worth taking, but not when it is uttered by the likes of General Amin. His false allegations about promiscuous behaviour by his former Minister for Foreign Affairs, Princess Elizabeth of Toro,

---

[48] *Eastwood* v *Ryder* (1990) *The Times*, 31 July.
[49] Civil Liability (Contribution) Act 1978 s 1.

won that worthy woman large damages from British newspapers that published them. By the time the case came to court General Amin was neither available as a witness nor regarded as a person worthy of belief.

Foreign publications

Many journalists resident in Britain write for overseas publications. Although the British law of libel has largely been adopted in Commonwealth countries, it is very different – and very much more onerous – than that which obtains in Europe and in America. This frees journalists from some restraints when they write for foreign publications but has awkward consequences for those who distribute foreign papers in this country. The legal rules are unsettled and are causing some confusion with the advent of satellite television. American law, for example, provides a special 'public figure' defence: however inaccurate a speculation about the conduct of a person in the public eye, the journalists who make it will not be liable unless they have acted maliciously. The better view is that no action can be brought in Britain against the author of an article circulated only in America unless the article is also actionable under the law of the country where publication took place.[50] It would follow that journalists writing for American publications have considerably more latitude in criticizing public figures so long as their articles are not reprinted in Britain.

Many American and other foreign magazines have a small circulation in Britain, often only to specialists or to libraries. It would seem that a tort is committed by deliberate circulation in this country irrespective of the number of copies, and judges have failed to develop what might be regarded as obviously just rules to limit damages by reference to minimal circulation. (In 1987 £450,000 was awarded against a Greek newspaper, fifty copies of which circulated in Britain.) British libel law is so notoriously favourable to plaintiffs that an increasing number of forum-shopping foreigners are taking action in London against newspapers and books that are printed, and mainly circulated, abroad. English law offers no ready solution to these anomalies. While there can be no objection to allowing foreigners access to British courts, it should at least be incumbent on them to show a more than *de minimis* circulation of the libel in this country, and that the criticism alleged to be defamatory in England would not be permitted to circulate in the country where the plaintiff's reputation would be most affected, at least without attracting more than nominal

---

[50] See Duncan and Neill, *Defamation*, Ch 8, paras 10 and 11.

damages. This second rule would have required the Greek Prime Minister, when accused of corruption in *Time* magazine, to issue his writ in Athens, where the real damage to his reputation had been done, and not in London.

Innocent dissemination

Distributors of newspapers, books and magazines have a special defence of 'innocent dissemination'. Obviously they cannot be expected to vet all the publications they sell, and it would be grossly unfair to hold them responsible for libels of which they could have no knowledge. In such cases they will escape, unless they have been negligent or at least ought to have known that the publication 'was of such a character that it was likely to contain libellous matter'.[51] The strictness of the defence has unfortunate consequences for some controversial publications: distributors are prone to equate political radicalism with a propensity to libel, and are thus provided with a ready-made legal excuse for a decision not to stock them.

One way to avoid such discrimination – or at least the legal grounds for it – is to supply a lawyer's opinion to the effect each edition is libel-free. This is an expensive expedient, but it should be sufficient in many cases to enable the distributor to raise the defence of innocent dissemination.

A plaintiff determined to damage a journal that torments him can, at least if that journal has a poor track record in libel actions, sue the distributors and settle on terms that they will not stock the publication in the future. For most small newsagents the prospect of defending a major libel case is frightening, and when Sir James Goldsmith threatened *Private Eye*'s distributors in this fashion, many of them caved in. The magazine's loss of circulation was dramatic, and Lord Denning thought that Goldsmith's tactics were oppressive: 'The freedom of the press' he stated 'depends on the channels of distribution being kept open.' He held that Goldsmith's flurry of 'frightening writs' was an abuse of legal process. His fellow judges, however, pointed out that Goldsmith had merely *used* the legal process according to his rights. Any threat to press freedom came, not from Goldsmith, but from the law that allowed him to sue distributors of libel-prone magazines. If the law threatened press freedom, it was for Parliament, not the courts, to change it.[52]

Since this judgment in 1977, Parliament has shown little inter-

---

[51] See *Gatley on Libel*, paras 241–50.
[52] *Goldsmith* v *Sperrings* [1977] 1 WLR 478.

est, although the Labour Party has endorsed a proposal that those in the distribution business should be under a legal obligation to supply any publication requested by their customers – a reform that would require abolition of the rule that distributors can be held responsible for particular defamations of which they have no knowledge but that are none the less contained in libel-prone publications. Of course, a well-heeled litigant would still be able to frighten booksellers and newsagents by notifying them of the alleged libel and threatening to join them in the action unless they withdrew the offending publication from sale. Robert Maxwell deployed this tactic with considerable success to limit the circulation of several books about him to which he took exception. This is yet another example of how the present libel law favours the very rich, and will continue to do so in this respect unless damages are restricted to those primarily responsible for publication.

A routine unfairness in defamation has been the legal liability placed on printers, who will normally be unaware of any libels contained in the newspapers or magazines they print on tight time-schedules. In 1991 the Lord Chancellor announced the Government's decision to extend the defence of innocent dissemination to printers as soon as a convenient legislative vehicle became available.

The Rule against Prior Restraint

The media have a right to publish defamatory remarks at the risk of paying heavy damages if they cannot subsequently be justified. The courts will not stop publication of defamatory statements in any case where the person who wants to make them is prepared to defend. Threats by angry complainants and their solicitors to stop the presses with eleventh-hour injunctions are largely bluff. The rule has been stated often enough, because plaintiffs willing to 'try it on' sometimes try it as far as the Court of Appeal. In one leading case Lord Denning said:

> The court will not restrain the publication of an article, even though it is defamatory, when the defendant says he intends to justify it or to make fair comment on a matter of public interest. The reason sometimes given is that the defences of justification and fair comment are for the jury, which is the constitutional tribunal, and not for the judge. But a better reason is the importance in the public interest that the truth should out. ... The right of free speech is one which it is for the public interest that individuals should possess, and, indeed, that they should exercise without impediment, so long as no wrongful

act is done. There is no wrong done if it is true, or if it is fair comment on a matter of public interest. The court will not prejudice the issue by granting an injunction in advance of publication.[53]

If the plaintiff can prove immediately and convincingly that the defendant is intending to publish palpable untruths, an injunction could be granted. Otherwise, the rule against prior restraint must prevail in libel actions. But it is surprising how often High Court judges, pressed for time and hearing only the plaintiff's side, overlook the principle and grant an 'interim injunction' without inquiring whether the defendant intends to defend. Such injunctions are normally immediately set aside on the publisher's application or lifted by the Court of Appeal. In 1982 two experienced High Court judges were prevailed upon to grant an injunction against the circulation of information by a shipping exchange accusing the plaintiff of connection with fraud. The Court of Appeal lifted it as a matter of principle, even though a hearing on the merits was set for the following day. 'The only safe and correct approach is not to allow an injunction to remain, even for a single day, if it was clearly wrong for it to have been granted.'[54]

The rule against prior restraint is secure in libel cases 'because of the value the court has placed on freedom of speech and freedom of the press when balancing it against the reputation of a single individual who, if wronged, can be compensated in damages'.[55] It applies whenever the defendant raises the defences of justification and fair comment, and will apply if the defence is to be qualified privilege unless the evidence of malice is so overwhelming that no reasonable jury would sustain the privilege. The Court of Appeal has on this basis refused an interim injunction against *Private Eye* when it published details of convictions that had been 'spent' under the Rehabilitation of Offenders Act (see p. 77). It has even refused to injunct a magazine that had published an allegation it could not justify, where it might succeed at trial for other reasons:

> Soraya Kashoggi sought an injunction to withdraw *Woman's Own* from circulation when it published a statement that she was having an extra-marital affair with a Head of State. The magazine could not prove the truth of this statement, which it had sourced to an MI5 report, but it claimed to be able to justify the 'sting' of the libel, namely that the plaintiff was a person given to extra-marital affairs, a

---

[53] *Fraser* v *Evans* [1969] 1 QB 349, per Lord Denning at p. 360. The rule derives from the case of *Bonnard* v *Perryman* [1891] 2 Ch 269.
[54] *Harakas* v *Baltic Mercantile and Shipping Exchange* [1982] 2 All ER 701 at p. 703 per Kerr LJ.
[55] *Herbage* v *Pressdram Ltd* [1984] 2 All ER 769 per Griffiths LJ.

number of which had been referred to in the article without attracting complaint. The Court of Appeal held that the rule against prior restraint would still operate, given that this defence of justifying the 'common sting' of the allegations might succeed at the trial. If it did not, the plaintiff would be adequately compensated by damages.[56]

One important practical benefit of this rule is that journalists can approach the subject of their investigation for a response to an article in draft without fear that they will receive a pre-publication injunction instead of a quote. However, editors and their advisers must be conscious of one trap for unwary players that can be sprung by a determined litigant who seeks an interim injunction at the outset of his action. In order to invoke the rule against prior restraint the defendant must state on affidavit his intention to justify the allegation. If, contrary to this sworn determination, the defence of justification is not proceeded with when the matter comes to trial, his conduct in recklessly signalling a defence that does not materialize can inflate the damages alarmingly. This will be the case especially where the actual affidavit boasts of 'highly placed sources' who can be summoned to verify the allegation. *Private Eye* fell into this trap when it beat off an interim injunction from Robert Maxwell by promising to prove at trial that he had financed Neil Kinnock's foreign travel in the hope of being awarded a peerage. Its defence of justification was withdrawn at the trial when its alleged 'highly-placed sources' went to ground. It narrowly escaped being called upon to name them, but its conduct in promising a plea of justification and persisting in such a plea until the last moment was punished by damages of £50,000. The jury found the libel itself to be worth only £5,000.[57]

The difficulty encountered by plaintiffs in obtaining injunctions to stop libels has led to a growth in applications for injunctions on the grounds of breach of confidence, i.e., that the information has been obtained from someone who is under a duty not to reveal it. In breach of confidence cases the rule against prior restraint does not apply: even if the newspaper has a strong defence, the story may be injuncted until trial of the action if the 'balance of convenience' so dictates. Where freedom of speech is at stake, it is unsatisfactory to make the grant of an injunction hinge upon whether the plaintiff happens to sue for libel or breach of confidence.

When the principle of free speech collides with the principle of fair trial, the former may have to give way. Courts may grant injunctions to stop defamatory publications that would prejudice

---

[56] *Kashoggi v IPC Magazines Ltd* [1986] 3 All ER 577.
[57] See *Maxwell v Pressdram Ltd* [1987] 1 All ER 656.

pending criminal trials. This jurisdiction is not often used – the normal procedure is for the Attorney-General to bring proceedings for contempt once the trial has concluded. It may, however, present a defendant in a criminal trial with a way of side-stepping the requirement that only the Attorney may bring actions for unintentional contempt. In 1979 the Court of Appeal, at the behest of Mr Jeremy Thorpe, stopped the *Spectator* from publishing an election address by Auberon Waugh, 'Dog Lovers Candidate' for North Devon, on the grounds that it contained matter that would prejudice Thorpe's impending trial for conspiracy to murder.[58] However, the scope for publishing a defendant's side of the story prior to trial is wider than is commonly believed. Both John Stonehouse and Ernest Saunders published their life stories in the period between their arrest and trial, although the publishers carefully curbed their comments on the charges and the prosecution witnesses to avoid charges of contempt of court.

Defences Generally

Burden of proof

Plaintiffs must prove that the words of which they complain have a defamatory meaning, that the words refer to them, and that the defendant was responsible for publishing them. Once these matters are established the burden shifts to the defendants. They must convince the jury, or a judge sitting without a jury, that the words were true, or the comment was honest, or that the report was 'privileged'. The burden of proving these defences rests squarely on the media, although proof does not have to be 'beyond reasonable doubt', but rather 'on the balance of probabilities': 51 per cent proof will suffice. This can still be a heavy burden where witnesses have died, or are overseas, or have been promised confidentiality. A simple but far-reaching reform in libel law, which would enhance freedom of expression, would be to reverse this burden: to oblige the plaintiff to prove, on balance, the falsity or unfairness of the criticism. This modest proposal was made to the Faulks Committee, which described it as 'the most radical' it had received. But the Committee was 'firmly opposed' to any alteration in the 'sound principle' that publishers of defamatory words must prove truth.[59] 'It tends to inculcate a spirit of caution in publishers of potentially actionable statements which we regard as salutary' was the response

---

[58] *Thorpe* v *Waugh* (unreported). See (1979) Court of Appeal Transcript No 282, and Borrie and Lowe's *Law of Contempt*, 2nd edn, Butterworths, 1983, p. 101.

of this committee to a reasonable reform that would bring libel law into line with other civil actions. A reform of this sort might inculcate a salutory spirit of caution in those who threaten their critics with writs over stories with a basis in truth.

The meaning of 'malice'

A number of important defences available to the media in libel cases can be defeated if the plaintiff proves that the publication was actuated by 'malice'. In ordinary language 'malice' means 'spite' or 'ill-will'. But in libel law it generally refers to dishonest writing or reporting – the publication of facts that are known to be false, or opinions that are not genuinely held. These qualities may exist without feelings of spite or revenge, so that legal 'malice' can sometimes have a wider meaning than colloquial usage suggests. On the other hand, the mere existence of personal antagonism between writer and plaintiff will not defeat a legitimate defence if the published criticism, however intemperate, is an honest opinion. For the careful and conscientious journalist or broadcaster, the legal meaning of 'malice' provides vital protection for honest comment, the more so because the burden of proving that malice was the dominant motive rests on the plaintiff. Such proof is necessary before a plaintiff can succeed against unfair and exaggerated criticism (the 'fair comment' defence) or against false statements made on certain public occasions (which are protected by the defence of 'qualified privilege').

The importance of the legal meaning of 'malice' in the defence of free speech is emphasized by the House of Lords' decision in the case of *Horrocks* v *Lowe*:[60]

> Lowe was a Labour councillor who launched an intemperate attack on Horrocks, a Tory councillor whose companies had engaged in land dealings with the Tory-controlled local authority. 'His attitude was either brinkmanship, megalomania or childish petulance . . . he has misled the Committee, the leader of his party, and his political and club colleagues' said Lowe of Horrocks at a council meeting. Speeches on such occasions, and reports of them, are protected by 'qualified privilege' – a defence that will fail only if the plaintiff can show that the defendant was actuated by malice. In the ordinary

---

[59] Committee on Defamation, HMSO, 1975, Cmnd 5909, para 141. Compare American libel law, where both public figure and private plaintiffs bear the burden of proving that allegedly libellous statements are false: *Philadelphia Newspapers* v *Hepps* 475 US 767 (1986). The public figure must further prove express malice, although a private plaintiff may recover against a negligent publisher: *Curtis Publishing Co* v *Butts* 388 US 130 (1967).

[60] [1975] AC 135 at p. 149.

sense of the word Lowe *was* malicious – his political antagonism had, the trial judge found, inflamed his mind into a state of 'gross and unreasoning prejudice'. None the less, he genuinely believed that everything he said was true. On that basis the House of Lords held that he was not 'malicious' in law.

A passage in Lord Diplock's speech is generally regarded as the classic exposition of the meaning of legal malice:

> What is required on the part of the defamer to entitle him to the protection of the privilege is positive belief in the truth of what he published . . . If he publishes untrue defamatory matter recklessly, without considering or caring whether it be true or not, he is in this, as in other branches of the law, treated as if he knew it to be false. But indifference to the truth of what he publishes is not to be equated with carelessness, impulsiveness or irrationality in arriving at a positive belief that it is true. The freedom of speech protected by the law of qualified privilege may be availed of by all sorts and conditions of men. In affording to them immunity from suit if they have acted in good faith in compliance with a legal or moral duty or in protection of a legitimate interest the law must take them as it finds them. In ordinary life it is rare indeed for people to form their beliefs by a process of logical deduction from facts ascertained by a rigorous search for all available evidence and a judicious assessment of its probative value. In greater or less degree according to their temperaments, their training, their intelligence, they are swayed by prejudice, rely on intuition instead of reasoning, leap to conclusions on inadequate evidence and fail to recognize the cogency of material which might cast doubt on the validity of the conclusions they reach. But despite the imperfection of the mental process by which the belief is arrived at it may still be 'honest', that is, a positive belief that the conclusions they have reached are true. The law demands no more.[61]

An honest belief will always defeat an allegation of malice, unless the plaintiff can prove that the honestly mistaken defendant was activated mainly by a desire to injure the plaintiff or to obtain an improper personal advantage. This will rarely be the case with media reporting, although it may sometimes poison the motives of informants. Newspapers will not normally be aware of improper motives lying behind otherwise defensible statements they report:

---

[61] ibid.

in such cases the better view is that they are not 'infected' by the improper motivation of the accusers, unless either they ought to have known of it or the accuser was in their employ.[62]

Recklessness as to the truth or falsity of accusations may amount to malice, but not 'carelessness, impulsiveness or irrationality'. Lack of care for the consequences of exuberant reporting is not malice and nor is mere inaccuracy or a failure to make inquiries or accidental or negligent misquotation.[63] The plaintiff must show that the defendant has turned a blind eye to truth in order to advance an ulterior object. An example is provided by one Parkinson, a Victorian clean-up campaigner, whose moral objection to 'public dancing' led him to allege that a ballet at the Royal Aquarium had involved a Japanese female catching a butterfly 'in the most indecent place you could possibly imagine'. Confronted with evidence that the performer in question was neither Japanese nor female, and in any event was dressed in pantaloons, Parkinson confessed that he had difficulty observing the performance and that his object in making the allegation was to revoke the Aquarium's dancing licence. His pursuit of moral ends did not justify his reckless disregard for truth, and his malice destroyed the privilege to which he would otherwise have been entitled.[64]

It is sometimes argued that criticism of the plaintiff after the writ has been issued, and a failure to apologize prior to trial, is evidence of malice. This approach is wrong in principle. Other critical statements made about a plaintiff are irrelevant unless they shed light on the defendant's state of mind at the time he or she wrote the article that gave rise to the action. It is not a sign of 'malice' to refuse an apology, or to repeat the allegations prior to trial or to persist in them at the trial;[65] this is no more than steadfastness in the cause (although if the allegations turn out to be false, such conduct may increase the damages).

Truth as a Defence

The defence of justification

Truth is a complete defence to any defamatory statement of fact, whatever the motives for its publication and however much its revelation is unjustified or contrary to the public interest. The

---

[62] *Egger* v *Viscount Chelmsford* [1965] 1 QB 248.
[63] *Pinniger* v *John Fairfax* (1979) 53 ALJR 691 per Barwick CJ; *Brooks* v *Muldoon* (1973) NZLR 1.
[64] *Royal Aquarium* v *Parkinson* [1892] 1 QB 431.
[65] See *Broadway Approvals Ltd* v *Odhams Press Ltd* [1965] 2 All ER 523.

legal title of the defence is 'justification', and it operates whenever defendants can show, by admissible evidence, that their allegation is, on balance, substantially correct. The question of 'substance' may be significant – it is not necessary to prove that every single fact stated in a criticism is accurate, so long as its 'sting' (its defamatory impact) is substantially true. Minor errors, such as dates or times or places, will not be held against the journalist if the gist of the allegation is justified. Even mistakes that diminish reputation will not count if they pale into minor significance beside the truth of major charges. Section 5 of the 1952 Defamation Act provides that the defence of justification shall not founder by failure to prove every charge, 'if the words not proved to be true do not materially injure the plaintiff's reputation, having regard to the truth of the remaining charges'. Thus a detailed criticism in the *Observer* of the activities of the Workers' Revolutionary Party was justified, despite proof that some allegations were untrue: the jury found that the inaccuracies could not 'materially injure' plaintiffs who had been depicted in an otherwise truthful light. Even where baseless charges do 'materially injure' a plaintiff's reputation, accurate criticisms in the same article will amount to a 'partial justification', which reduces the damages by reducing the value of the reputation. To say that someone is guilty of terrorism and drunken driving will be justifiable if he or she is a teetotal terrorist. It will, however, be gravely libellous if he or she is a drunken driver but not a terrorist.

There are limits, of course, to the distance that truth will stretch. An accurate news story will not justify a headline that gives a false impression. Nor can generalized criticism be justified if it is based on one isolated incident. A statement that a reporter is a 'libellous journalist' implies some proven propensity to defame: it is not justified by the fact that the journalist was once in his or her career obliged to apologize.[66]

Facts should normally be allowed to speak for themselves: to spell out a conclusion may spell danger. For example, it may be a fact that a writer has used the work of others without their permission. But to describe the writer as a 'deliberate plagiarist' may overlook another, but unknown fact: that he or she was assured at the time of using the material that the originator's consent had been forthcoming. It follows that although the writer is a plagiarist, he or she is not a *deliberate* plagiarist. Where there is smoke, there is usually fire, but occasionally there is only a smoke machine. Libel lawyers are nervous of the word 'lie' because it implies that a person said something that he or she *knew* was untrue. Since this is

---

[66] *Wakeley* v *Cooke* (1849) 4 Exch 511.

usually difficult to prove, they will often suggest changing it to 'misled', 'misrepresented' or some other phrase that does not connote a particular state of mind.

The fact that a defamatory statement has been made or the fact that a defamatory rumour exists is no justification for publishing it. The law requires the 'truth' in such cases to be the truth of the rumour, not the truth of the fact that it is circulating. As Lord Devlin has explained:

> . . . you cannot escape liability for defamation by putting the libel behind a prefix such as 'I have been told that . . .' or 'it is rumoured that . . .', and then asserting that it was true that you had been told or that it was in fact being rumoured . . . For the purpose of the law of libel a hearsay statement is the same as a direct statement, and that is all there is to it.[67]

However, the context of the article may remove or reduce the rumour's impact on the plaintiff's reputation. Much will depend on the reaction of the reasonable reader. In most cases the publication of a false statement will give it currency and credit (e.g., the publication by the *News of the World* of rape allegations against Banbury CID officers). But if the gist of the article is genuinely to demolish the rumour, or to demolish the credibility of its mongers rather than its victim, the article as a whole may not bear a defamatory meaning. In other situations a rumour or suspicion may with great care be reported if its existence (irrespective of its truth) has some significance, if its victim is allowed to reply and renounce the allegation and if the publisher is scrupulous not to indicate expressly or impliedly that the allegation is true. In many spheres of public life justice should be seen to be done as well as be done, and officials should not only be impartial but be seen to be above reproach. So a paper might report that a community believed that police officers had been unnecessarily violent in arresting suspects. The report would need to include any denial by the police, but it might go on to comment that whether the allegations were true or not, their existence undermined the confidence of the community in the officers, and for this reason the officers should be transferred.

There was a week in 1986 when Fleet Street and Westminster were convulsed with a rumour that Home Secretary Leon Brittan had been caught interfering sexually with a small boy; no newspaper dared to print what all 'in the know' were discussing until *Private Eye* published the story with the explanation that it was utterly false and circulated to damage the Home Secretary by an

---

[67] *Lewis* v *Daily Telegraph Ltd*, note 1 above, at p. 283.

anti-Semitic faction in MI5. This form of publication reproduced the rumour in order to kill it, and a relieved Home Secretary announced he would be taking no proceedings against *Private Eye*.

Practical problems

Problems with the defence of justification arise from the law's procedures, not its principles. Although truth is a defence, proving it in court may be impossible. There is the burden of proof – squarely on the defendant. There is the cost of preparing a full-blooded counter-attack. There is the difficulty of calling witnesses who may have died or gone abroad, or who may have been promised confidentiality. And then there is the risk of failure, which inflates the damages on the basis that the defendant is not merely a defamer, but a defamer who has persisted in the injury to the last. There is no doubt that difficulties of this sort mean that many true statements are not published, or else are the subject of apologies rather than defences.

Other problems stem from the ambiguities of language and the complex rules of pleading. The plaintiff will plead the most exaggerated meanings that his or her counsel considers the words will conceivably bear in order to maximize the insult and humiliation (and hence the damages). The defence may well be able to prove the words true in some less defamatory meaning, but will fail unless that is the only meaning that the jury chooses to adopt. There will be legal pressure to settle the case: successful defendants do not recover all of their costs, and the simplest of libel actions is likely to run up at least £25,000 in costs for each party prior to trial. Few contested actions are nowadays decided in favour of media defendants.

On the other hand, the difficulties of proving justification should not be exaggerated. The adage that 'truth will out' is assisted by the law. The defendant may rely on facts that emerge after publication – and in such cases the length of time before trial may be a positive boon. Most importantly, the defence may be helped by court rules relating to 'discovery of documents'. Plaintiffs must make available to the defence all documents in their possession that are relevant to the matters in dispute – and sometimes there will be found, amongst office memoranda and other internal documents, material that goes to justify the original allegation. The order for discovery is often the point of no return for the plaintiff in a libel action: it is the stage at which some prefer to discontinue rather than to open their files. Finally, there is always the prospect of cross-examining the plaintiff. Libel plaintiffs are virtually obliged to go into the witness box: the only plaintiff in living memory who failed to take the stand was David Bookbinder, leader of

Derbyshire Council, who in 1991 sued Norman Tebbitt over the latter's criticisms of his political policies. The tactic proved disastrous: Bookbinder was savagely derided for his cowardice by defence counsel, and the jury found Tebbitt's criticisms to be fair comment. Once in the witness box, plaintiffs may be cross-examined in detail about matters relevant to their reputations. Their answers may support the defence of justification – although rarely as dramatically as football manager Tommy Docherty, a libel plaintiff who collapsed so utterly under cross-examination that he was subsequently prosecuted for perjury. A sympathetic jury acquitted him after his counsel had luridly described the terrors and confusions for plaintiffs of undergoing cross-examination in libel actions.

Reporting old criminal convictions

There are special rules relating to publication of past criminal convictions. A conviction – or, for that matter, an acquittal – by a jury is no more than an expression of opinion by at least ten out of twelve people about the defendant's guilt. One ingenious convict, Alfie Hinds, sued a police officer for stating in the *News of the World* that Hinds had been guilty as charged. Hinds convinced the libel jury that he had been wrongfully convicted, so the newspaper's defence of justification failed.[68] Parliament, recognizing the danger – perhaps more to respect for the law than to press freedom – changed the law, so that now the very fact of a conviction is deemed to be conclusive evidence of its correctness. The prosecution's evidence does not have to be presented to the court all over again.[69]

However, this rule – and indeed the basic rule that truth is a complete defence – is subject to one exception in relation to past convictions. It is socially desirable that offenders should be able to 'live down' a criminal past, and the Rehabilitation of Offenders Act 1974 is designed to assist this process. The Act applies only to convictions that have resulted in a sentence of no more than thirty months' imprisonment, and which have been 'spent' – i.e., a certain period of time has elapsed since the passing of sentence. The length of that period depends on the seriousness of the punishment: where there has been any period of imprisonment between six months and thirty months, the conviction becomes 'spent' after ten years have elapsed. Seven years is the rehabilitation period for prison sentences of six months or under; five years for all other

---

[68] *Hinds* v *Sparks (No 2)* (1964) *The Times*, 20 October; see similarly *Goody* v *Odhams Press Ltd* (1967) *Daily Telegraph*, 22 June.
[69] Civil Evidence Act 1968 s 13(1).

sentences that fall short of imprisonment, save for an absolute discharge, which is 'spent' (not that it should carry a blameworthy connotation in any event) after a bare six months. There are short rehabilitation periods for juvenile offenders and persons subject to court orders or disqualifications.

The provisions of the Act are complex, but they have little effect on media freedom. The press may publish details of 'spent' convictions and, if sued, may successfully plead justification or fair comment, unless the plaintiff can show that the publication of this particular truth has been actuated by malice.[70] Since there can be no dishonesty involved in stating the truth, the difficulties of proof are considerable. An improper and dominant motive would have to be shown for revealing matters that would normally be in the public interest. An overwhelming desire to injure the plaintiff rather than to inform the public would have to be proved. Newspapers have routinely reported the 'spent' convictions of National Front leaders, for example. The IBA, with an overabundance of legal caution, did cut such references from a Labour Party political broadcast, apparently on the ground that the broadcasters might be deemed 'malicious' if their dominant motive was to win votes for themselves rather than to inform the public of the truth about persons standing for public office.

Journalists who may be minded to look at court or police records should bear in mind that an official persuaded to show them a 'spent' conviction is liable to a fine, and if they make their persuasion more persuasive by a bribe or obtain access to the record dishonestly, they themselves are liable to imprisonment for up to six months.[71]

In practice, the Rehabilitation of Offenders Act has caused little difficulty for freedom of expression. It does, however, represent an ethical standard that the press should be reluctant to infringe other than for reasons of genuine public interest. Shortly after the passage of the Act, the *Daily Mail* had no hesitation in plastering over its front page the 'spent' conviction of a left-wing member of Hackney Labour Party active in unseating Reg Prentice MP. Newspapers that patrol the moral perimeters of society regularly divine a public interest in reporting the 'spent' convictions of those in social welfare jobs. The 'public interest' is a value judgement, and the ethical impact of the Act depends not on the law of libel, but on the values of the press.

Ironically, there is no inhibition on digging up an old acquittal. Nor does the fact of an acquittal debar the media from alleging that

---

[70] Rehabilitation of Offenders Act 1974 s 8.
[71] 1974 Act s 9.

the defendant was really guilty after all. The jury's verdict is 'final' only so far as punishment by the criminal court is concerned. Naturally, such allegations will rarely be made, although the defence of 'justification' requires them to be proven only on the balance of probabilities, and not on the higher criminal standard, 'beyond reasonable doubt'. Where there is strong evidence of guilt, defendants given the benefit of the doubt by a jury in a criminal trial will be reluctant to chance their luck a second time by bringing a libel action. Criticism of a verdict that casts aspersions on the integrity of jurors may, of course, attract libel actions on that score.

'Opinion' as a Defence

The defence of 'fair comment' protects the honest expression of opinion, no matter how unfair or exaggerated, on any matter of public interest. The question for the court is whether the views could honestly have been held by a fair-minded person on facts known at the time. Whether the jury agree with it or not is ir-relevant. 'A critic is entitled to dip his pen in gall for the purpose of legitimate criticism: and no one need be mealy-mouthed in denouncing what he regards as twaddle, daub or discord.'[72] The defence is called 'fair comment' – a misnomer, because it in fact defends unfair comment, so long as that comment amounts to an opinion that an honest person might express on a matter of public interest, and that has in fact been expressed by a defendant who was not actuated by malice.

> Every latitude must be given to opinion and to prejudice, and then an ordinary set of men with ordinary judgement must say [not whether they agree with it, but] whether any fair man would have made such a comment . . . Mere exaggeration, or even gross exaggeration, would not make the comment unfair. However wrong the opinion expressed may be in point of truth, or however prejudiced the writer, it may still be within the prescribed limit. The question which the jury must con-sider in this – would any fair man, however prejudiced he may be, however exaggerated or obstinate his views, have said that which this criticism has said?[73]

---

[72] *Gardiner* v *John Fairfax & Sons* (1942) 42 SR (NSW) 171 at p. 174 per Jordan CJ.
[73] *Merivale* v *Carson* (1887) 20 QBD 275 at p. 280 per Lord Esher.

Distinction between fact and opinion

The fair-comment defence relates only to *comment* – to statements of opinion and not to statements of fact. This is the most important, and most difficult, distinction in the entire law of libel. A defamatory statement of fact must be *justified* (i.e., proved true) – which is a much more onerous task than defending a defamatory comment on the basis that it was made honestly. The difficulty arises when facts and opinions are jumbled together in the same article or programme. A form of words may, in one context, be opinion (and therefore defensible as 'fair comment') while in another context appear as a factual statement, consequently requiring proof of correctness. There is no hard and fast rule: once again, the test is that of ordinary readers. Would they, on reading or hearing the words complained of in context, say to themselves 'that is an opinion' or 'so that is the fact of the matter'? Unattributed assertions in news stories and headlines are likely to be received as factual, while criticism expressed in personalized columns is more likely to be regarded as opinion, especially when it appears to be an inference drawn by the columnist from facts to which reference has been made. Writers can help to characterize their criticisms as comment with phrases like 'it seems to me', 'in my judgement', 'in other words', etc., although such devices will not always be conclusive. To say, without any supporting argument, 'In my opinion Smith is a disgrace to human nature' is an assertion of fact. To say 'Smith murdered his father and therefore is a disgrace to human nature' makes the characterization a comment upon a stated fact. Where a defamatory remark is made baldly, without reference to any fact from which the remark could be inferred, it is not likely to be defensible as comment, especially if it imputes dishonesty or dishonourable conduct. In these latter cases it will be difficult to defend as comment unless it clearly appears as a mere expression of opinion that a fair-minded man could honestly infer from the facts upon which the comment is said to be based. In deciding the scope of a fair-comment plea and the degree of interpretative sophistication to bring to bear on the question of whether a passage is 'comment' or 'fact', the court should have regard to the constitutional importance of the fair-comment defence as a protection for freedom of expression.[74]

The cause of freedom of expression was damaged, however, by the House of Lords in 1991 in *Telnikoff* v *Matusevitch*, a decision that ignores the realities of newspaper reading and places a burden

---

[74] See *London Artists Ltd* v *Littler* [1969] 2 QB 375; *Slim* v *The Daily Telegraph* (1968) 2 QB 157; *Silkin* v *Beaverbrook Newspapers Ltd* [1958] 2 All ER 516.

on editors to identify fully the subjects commented upon in their 'letters' page.[75]

> The plaintiff wrote an article for the *Daily Telegraph* attacking the BBC World Service for recruiting mainly members of the USSR's national minorities for its Russia service. The defendant wrote, and the *Telegraph* published, a 'letter to the editor' in response, characterizing the plaintiff's views, as expressed in this article, as racist and anti-Semitic. The plaintiff sued and the outcome hinged on whether the words used in the letter could be construed as *comment* (in which case the defendant succeeded) or *fact* (in which case the defendant lost, because they were untrue). This in turn hinged on whether the jury could construe the letter in isolation (when it was read literally, it appeared to be making statements of fact) or in the wider context of the original article (on which the letter was plainly intended as a comment). The House of Lords, reversing the Court of Appeal, held that the jury should be permitted to look at the letter only as published. It did not occur to their lordships that letters to the editor are generally written – and sensibly read – as comments upon articles and opinions previously expressed in the newspaper.

This decision undermines the protection that the defence of fair comment has given to 'free for alls' in letters' columns of local and national newspapers. Lord Keith blandly states that 'the writer of a letter to a newspaper has a duty to take reasonable care to make clear that he is writing comment . . . there is no difficulty about using suitable words for that purpose.' Of course there is difficulty, one that troubles lawyers and will confound ordinary citizens using their ordinary language. The law should encourage them to exercise free speech by writing letters to newspapers, and encourage editors to publish, in the public interest, as many of these letters as possible. The rule in *Telnikoff* deters them, because it requires editors either to reject or censor a letter if its critical statements cannot be proved in court, or else to republish the criticized article again so that its naïvest readers will realize that the letter is stating its author's *opinion*. As the latter course will normally prove impractical, the *Telnikoff* decision will shrink the area of robust criticism permitted to letters-to-the-editor pages by the fair-comment defence.

The opinion must have some factual basis

The defence of fair comment will not succeed if the comment is made without any factual basis. An opinion cannot be conjured out of thin air – it must be based on *something*. And that something

---

[75] *Telnikoff* v *Matusevitch* [1991] 4 All ER 817.

should either be accurately stated in the article or at least referred to with sufficient clarity to enable the reader to identify it. It is not necessary to set out all the evidence for the writer's opinion: a summary of it or a reference to where it can be found is sufficient. Even a passing reference is sufficient if readers will understand what is meant. The leading case is *Kemsley* v *Foot*.[76]

> Michael Foot once launched an attack in *Tribune* on what he termed 'the foulest piece of journalism perpetrated in this country in many a long year', indicating a particular article in the *Evening Standard*. The editor of that paper and the writer could not sue for this honest, if exaggerated, appraisal of their work. However, Foot's article was titled 'Lower than Kemsley' – a proprietor whose stable of news-papers did not include the *Evening Standard*. Did the headline amount to a statement of fact – i.e., that Lord Kemsley was a byword for publishing dishonest journalism – or an opinion about the quality of journalism in Kemsley newspapers? The House of Lords held that the readers of *Tribune* in the context of the copy would regard the headline as a comment on the quality of the Kemsley press, rather than as a factual statement about the character of the proprietor. There was sufficient reference to the factual basis of the comment – namely the mass-circulation Kemsley newspapers – to enable readers to judge for themselves whether the comment was reasonable.

Given the rule that a fair comment must state or refer to the facts upon which it is based, to what extent might the falsity of those facts destroy the defence? Clearly, the comment that 'Smith is a disgrace to human nature' could not be defended if the stated fact, e.g., that Smith was a patricide, was false. Often comments will be inferences from a number of facts – some true, some partly true, and some not true at all. These difficulties have resolved themselves into the question: is the comment fair in the sense of being one that the commentator could honestly express on the strength of such of his facts as can be proved to be true? Take the case of the prudish Mr Parkinson, who attended the butterfly ballet. His opinion that it was grossly indecent was genuine to the extent that his inclination was to think every form of dance indecent. However, his stated grounds for that opinion were a figment of his imagination: his misdescriptions of the performance were so fundamental as to vitiate any factual basis for his criticism. The defence of honest comment would not have availed him. The defence protects the honest views of the crank and the eccentric, but not when they are based on dishonest statements of fact.

The rule will not apply to defeat comments that are based on

---

[76] *Kemsley* v *Foot* [1952] AC 345 at p. 356, and see *Hunt* v *Star Newspapers* (1908) 2 KB 309.

facts that, although untrue, have been stated on occasions protected by privilege. Trenchant editorials are sometimes written on the strength of statements made in court or Parliament. These will be protected as fair comment, even if the 'facts' subsequently prove unfounded.[77] However, a publisher has this additional latitude only if, at the same time, it carries a fair and accurate report of the court or parliamentary proceedings (or other privileged occasion) on which the comment is based. Thus *Time Out* was not entitled to rely, in factual support of a fair-comment defence of an attack on George Walker, on a statement made by a police officer at his Old Bailey trial in 1956 linking him to membership of a criminal gang. Privilege attached to such a statement only in the context of a fair and accurate report of the case in which the future chairman of Brent Walker was gaoled for two years for stealing women's underwear.[78]

Absence of malice

The fair-comment defence is defeated by proof that the writer or publisher was actuated by malice, in the legal sense of that term. That sense will in most cases resolve itself into the question of whether the comment was honestly made, which is no more than a defining characteristic of fair comment in the first place. Where the malice is alleged to be some improper motivation, the plaintiff will require strong evidence of impropriety in order to destroy the defence. Defendants are entitled to give evidence of their honest state of mind, and to explain why their dominant motive, irrespective of any dislike they may feel for the plaintiff, was to comment on a matter of public interest. The courts have repeatedly insisted that 'irrationality, stupidity or obstinacy do not constitute malice though in an extreme case there may be some evidence of it.'[79] A failure to apologize or to publish a retraction will not normally be evidence of malice, but rather of consistency in holding sincere views. But editors who refuse to retract damaging comments after clear proof that they are wildly exaggerated may lay themselves open to the inference from this conduct that they were similarly reckless at the time of the original publication. An outright refusal to give the victim of a damaging comment a reasonable opportunity to reply – a rejection of a polite letter to the editor, for example – may similarly betray a degree of malice behind the original comment.

---

[77] *Mangena* v *Wright* [1909] 2 KB 958; *Grech* v *Odhams Press Ltd* [1958] 2 QB 276; *London Artists Ltd* v *Littler*, note 74 above.

[78] *Brent Walker Group PLC and George Walker* v *Time Out Ltd* [1991] 2 All ER 753.

[79] *Turner* v *MGM* [1950] 1 All ER 449 per Lord Porter at p. 463.

Hard-hitting criticism and savage satire can generally be successfully defended as honest comment so long as the exaggerations are
not so extreme as to indicate malice. Derek Jameson notably failed
to prove that the writers of the BBC satirical programme *Week
Ending* were dishonest in portraying him as stupid and lubricious:
his record as editor of down-market newspapers allowed them to
describe his editorial policy as being 'all the nudes fit to print and
all the news printed to fit'. It would have been a sad day for British
satire had Jameson won this presumptuous action. Former Royal
Shakespeare Company actress Charlotte Cornwell had more luck
when she was awarded £11,000 to compensate for a vile personal
attack on her in the *News of the World* over her performance in a
new television series. The 'malice', in the sense that the virulent
criticisms were not the honest belief of their writer, lay in the
description of her as 'a middle aged star [who] can't sing, her bum
is too big and she has the sort of stage presence that jams lavatories
. . . [she] looks just as ugly *with* make-up.' The defendants knew
that the actress was aged thirty-four and was of normal weight and
appearance: the article had heaped upon her the kind of reckless
insults that could not have reflected an honest opinion.

It is important to remember that defendants do not bear the
burden of proving that their opinion was honestly held and
expressed. All that the defence need show is that the opinion is
'objectively' fair, in the sense that a hypothetically honest (albeit
prejudiced) person *might* genuinely hold the opinion in question on
the facts known at the time. Once this is established, then the
defence of fair comment will succeed unless the plaintiff can plead
and prove that the defendant was, subjectively, motivated by
malice, so that the opinion that he or she expressed was not his or
her real opinion. Had the letter written by the defendant in
Telnikoff v *Matusevitch*[80] been characterized as comment, then,
although exaggerated and misguided, it would none the less have
expressed opinions that a passionate believer in the evils of anti-
Semitism might honestly hold, and so the defence of fair comment
would have succeeded.

In 1990 the British public was entertained by a libel action brought
by the editor of the *Sunday Times* against the editor of the rival *Sunday
Telegraph* over the latter's moral condemnation of his (and the
Observer editor's) dalliance with a woman of easy virtue. The
comparatively puny damages of £1,000 (the cost of a dozen bottles of
champagne at the expensive nightclub where the affair had begun) and
the public ridicule suffered by all parties may serve to remind editors
of the wisdom of the adage that 'dog does not eat dog in Fleet Street'.

---

[80] [1991] 4 All ER 817, HL; and see [1990] 3 All ER 865, CA.

Public interest

The defence of fair comment may be sustained only if the comment is on a matter of public interest. This is an easy test to satisfy: the only cases where it has failed have been criticisms of the private lives of persons who are not public figures. The courts have held that the public is legitimately interested, not merely in the conduct of public officials and institutions, but of private companies whose activities affect individual members of the public. The conduct of a professional person towards a client or an employer towards a worker are also matters that may attract legitimate public interest. Anyone who throws a hat into a public arena must be prepared to have it mercilessly, though not maliciously, trampled upon.

Whose comment is it?

There is an important question about the application of the fair-comment defence to comment by a third party that is published in a newspaper. The editor may not agree with sentiments in a 'letter to the editor'; if sued for libel, does the editor lose the defence of fair comment because it cannot be said that the opinion is honestly his? It is clear that publishers may rely upon the defence of fair comment to the same extent as the person whose comment it was, so if the author of the letter is also sued, or is prepared to testify, the honesty of his or her views will support the newspaper's defence. If the author does not come forward, however, the expression of opinion may still be defended as fair comment if it can be shown to satisfy the test of whether a hypothetical fair-minded person could honestly express the opinion on the proven facts.[81] This was the second – and more satisfactory – decision of the House of Lords in *Telnikoff* v *Matusevitch*, which rejected the plaintiff's contention that the defendant, to succeed on a fair-comment defence, has to prove that the comment was the honest expression of his views. On the contrary, the burden is on the plaintiff to prove that a comment is objectively unfair in the sense that no man, however prejudiced and obstinate, could have held the views expressed by the defendant.[82]

---

[81] The minority view in the Canadian case of *Cherneskey* v *Armadale Publishers* (1978) 90 DLR (3d) 371 is to be preferred to the majority opinion: see *Telnikoff*, note 80 above, and *Lyon* v *Daily Telegraph* [1943] 2 All ER 316.
[82] See note 80 above.

Absolute Privilege

Accurate reports of certain public occasions are 'privileged' – which is to say that any defamatory statements arising from them cannot be made the subject of a successful libel action. Privilege is either 'absolute' – a complete defence – or 'qualified', i.e., lost only if the speaker or reporter is actuated by malice. Although it is unseemly that the law should protect the publication of malicious falsehoods, absolute privilege is justified on the practical ground that without it, persons with a public duty to speak out might be threatened with vexatious actions for slander and libel. In other words, 'absolute privilege' is a recognition of the law's potential for suppressing truth and silencing justifiable criticism. Protection is given to the malicious and the reckless as the price of protecting from the threat of vexatious litigation all who are under a powerful duty to state facts and opinions frankly.

Thus politicians may say whatever they choose in Parliament or at the proceedings of select committees (see Chapter 9). Judges, lawyers and witnesses may not be held responsible for any statement uttered in court. The Ombudsman's reports are absolutely privileged, as are ministers of the Crown, officers of the armed forces and high-level government officials in their reports and conversations about matters of state. In these cases the absolute privilege attaches only to the maker of the statement: when it is reported or broadcast, the organization that does so is protected by a privilege that is qualified and not absolute.

The one occasion when written and broadcast reports of statements made by persons who possess absolute privilege are themselves absolutely privileged is when they concern proceedings in the courts. This important media privilege is explained at p. 363. Court reports in newspapers and on radio and television are absolutely privileged under s 3 of the Law of Libel Amendment Act 1888 so long as they are fair and accurate, and are published as soon as is reasonably practicable, having regard to the schedules of the newspaper or broadcasting organization.

Qualified Privilege

The law recognizes the importance of encouraging statements made from a social or moral duty. It accords them a privilege from action for defamation, on the condition that they are made honestly. However unfounded the allegations made on a protected occasion may subsequently prove, they are privileged unless made with malice. This branch of the law is strongly impressed with considerations of public interest. The notion that lies behind it is that where there is a moral duty to speak out, speakers should not hold their tongues for fear of writs.

The defence of qualified privilege has been developed in accordance with social needs. The early cases were overly concerned to protect the gentry's right to communicate gossip about disloyal or dishonest servants. The growth of commerce saw protection extended to references given by bankers and employers, and to information shared among traders. Parliament has intervened to give special protection to press reports of statements made on significant public occasions, and there are hints – no more – that in certain cases the courts may be prepared to extend protection of qualified privilege to media investigations of major public scandals.

Communications between people who share a common interest in the subject matter of the communication will attract qualified privilege. The communication may be made out of social or moral duty – references between employers, for example, or allegations about criminal conduct made to the police. A communication is protected if it is made to further a common interest – a circular published to shareholders in a company, or to fellow members of a trade union, or an inter-office memorandum. A communication is protected if it is made to a person who has a duty to receive and act upon it: thus complaints to 'higher authority' are privileged whenever the authority complained to is in a position to investigate or discipline or supervise. Journalists who observe what they regard as improper behaviour by judges or lawyers could provide information to the Lord Chancellor's department without running any risk of a libel action.[83]

A general privilege for investigative journalists?

But to what extent will these common-law principles protect the media when they publish allegations of misconduct to the world? So far, the courts have been reluctant to hold that the press has a 'moral duty' to inform an interested public. It may have a duty to inform the public about the misconduct of a candidate for election, but only in newspapers that circulate in the candidate's constituency.[84] A 'moral duty' may similarly exist in the case of a specialist journal circulating only, say to members of a profession, who would have a shared interest in receiving information about discreditable conduct of a fellow member.[85] It may be that the privilege will be held to exist where the only possible mode of communication is via

[83] *Beach* v *Freeson* [1972] 1 QB 14.
[84] *Duncombe* v *Daniell* (1837) 2 Jur 32. See *Gatley on Libel*, para 541.
[85] *Brown* v *Crome* (1817) 2 Stark 297 at p. 301.

the media, for example if the appropriate authority had arbitrarily refused to consider the information. There are some tantalizing references to a defence of 'fair information on a matter of public interest', notably in the case of *Webb* v *Times Publishing Co*:[86]

> Donald Hume murdered Stanley Setty, cut up his body and threw it out of an aircraft over the Essex marshes. He was tried for murder, and acquitted. Ten years later, he committed another murder in Switzerland. At his Swiss trial he admitted murdering Setty, whom he claimed was the father of his wife's child. *The Times* reported this evidence – which, having been given in a foreign court, was not protected by absolute privilege. Hume's wife sued, claiming that she had never met Setty, let alone had an affair with or a child by him. Mr Justice Pearson held that the report was protected by qualified privilege, as it was fair information on a subject of public interest. Importance was attached to the legitimate interest that the English public would have in information that could throw light on a major 'unsolved' crime.

On the strength of this case Lord Denning has argued, extrajudicially, that 'if newspapers or television receive or obtain information fairly from a reliable and responsible source, which it is in the public interest that the public should know, then there is a qualified privilege to publish it. They should not be liable in the absence of malice'.[87] This is a statement of law as it should be, rather than as it is, but there is nothing to stop the courts developing it in this direction. However, it will only be developed in cases where the public advantage in receiving the information clearly outweighs the private injury that may be suffered.[88] For the present it would be advisable not to report such allegations without giving the person defamed an opportunity to refute them in the same report.

Lord Denning's view of the law of qualified privilege was rejected by the Court of Appeal in *Blackshaw* v *Lord*. It declared that 'No privilege attaches yet to a statement on a matter of public interest believed by the publisher to be true and in relation to which he has exercised reasonable care.' The defence of 'fair information on a matter of public interest' was not enough to attract privilege unless the newspaper had a duty to publish the information to the public at large, whose members had a corresponding interest in receiving it. The *Daily Telegraph* had no 'duty' in this sense to publish mere rumours and suspicions that a public servant had been responsible for losing millions of pounds of public money. However, the court did concede that:

---

[86] [1960] 2 QB 535.
[87] Lord Denning, *What Next in the Law*, Butterworths, 1982, p. 192.
[88] See Cantley J in *London Artists Ltd* v *Littler* [1969] 2 QB 375.

there may be extreme cases where the urgency of communicating a warning is so great, or the source of the information so reliable, that publication of suspicion or speculation is justified; for example, where there is danger to the public from a suspected terrorist or from the distribution of contaminated food or drugs . . .[89]

This leaves the door ever so slightly open for the media to claim a public-interest privilege based on a duty to communicate vital information to the public. The Canadian courts have taken the first step, by accepting that the media have a qualified privilege to publish information (which later turns out to be false) about a possible public health hazard.[90] An Australian judge has held that such a privilege arises in cases where the reasonable public would regard the subject as so important that the desirability of the public being informed outweighed the risk of injury to reputation.[91] It may seem a contradiction in terms to assert a public interest in publishing untruths, but there may come a point at which the reliability of the source and the potential danger to the public cohere to impose a duty on those possessed of the information to alert the public.

The most interesting developments in the law relating to qualified privilege may come as a result of Article 10 of the European Convention on Human Rights (see p. 4). Restrictions on press freedom, such as libel laws, must respond to a 'pressing social need' and must be no wider than is 'necessary in a democratic society'. In 1986 the European Court of Human Rights decided in *Lingens* v *Austria* that the Convention requires such restrictions to be relaxed in relation to criticism of public figures during political controversies:

> Lingens, a seasoned political commentator, published attacks on Bruno Kreisky, the President of the Austrian Socialist Party, accusing him of 'immorality' and 'the basest opportunism' for contemplating a political alliance with ex-Nazis. Lingens was privately prosecuted by Kreisky, and convicted and fined for defamation. The court held that this was a breach of the Convention guarantee of free speech, because it would deter journalists from contributing to public discussions of issues affecting the life of the community:

> The limits of acceptable criticism are wider as regards a politician as such than as regards a private individual . . . the former

---

[89] *Blackshaw* v *Lord* [1983] 2 All ER 311 at p. 327.
[90] *Camporese* v *Parton* (1983) 150 DLR (3d) 208.
[91] *Australian Broadcasting Commission* v *Comalco Ltd* (1986) 68 ALR 259 at pp. 283–9 per Smithers J.

inevitably and knowingly lays himself open to close scrutiny of his every word and deed by both journalists and the public at large, and he must consequently display a greater degree of tolerance.[92]

The decision in *Lingens* edges Europe closer to the American 'public figure' doctrine, in which journalists are free to publish what they honestly believe about important persons. However, the European Court carefully distinguished between the publication of value judgements about such persons rather than factual allegations, and it is likely that Lingens (who was expressing his genuine opinion of Kreisky) would have had a fair-comment defence in English law. Nevertheless, it could be argued that the common-law doctrine of qualified privilege can be extended, under the public policy spur of the European Convention, to protect assertions about public figures made in good faith as part of public political discussion. In this context there is an important distinction to be drawn between imputations that are derogatory and imputations that are defamatory. Greater latitude can be permitted to disparagement of politicians and self-promoting celebrities: the sting is less likely to pierce when the hide is thick.[93]

Reply to an attack

The 'right of reply' privilege is often overlooked, but its constitutional significance for the protection of freedom of expression deserves to be recognized. It is based on the simple proposition of self-defence: if you are verbally attacked, you are entitled to strike back with some vehemence to defend your reputation. The media that carry your response share your privilege, so long as the publicity given to your condemnation of your attacker is reasonably commensurate with the publicity given to the original attack. The right-of-reply privilege was established by the House of Lords in the case of *Adam* v *Ward*:

> The plaintiff, an officer but not a gentleman, used his position as an MP to make a vindictive attack upon a general in his former regiment. The defendant, Secretary to the Army Council, issued a statement in support of the general, which defamed the MP and was published in newspapers throughout the Empire. The Law Lords held that this publication was protected by qualified privilege: the Council had a

---

[92] *Lingens* v *Austria* (1986) 8 EHRR 425, and see also *Oberschlick* v *Austria*, European Court, 23 May 1991, and *Gorton* v *ABC* (1973) 22 FLR 181.
[93] *Adam* v *Ward* [1917] AC 309, and also see *Laughton* v *Bishop of Sodor and Man* (1872) LR & PC 495; *Loveday* v *Sun Newspapers* (1938) 59 CLR 503.

duty to leap to the general's defence, and the privilege was not lost by the fact of world-wide publication, because 'a man who makes a statement on the floor of the House of Commons makes it to all the world . . . it was only plain justice to the General that the ambit of contradiction should be spread so wide as, if possible, to meet the false accusation wherever it went.'

The rule in *Adam* v *Ward* offers consolation to victims of attacks made under the 'coward's cloak' of parliamentary privilege: they may reply in kind through newspapers, which will be liable for the defamatory content of their reply only if it is irrelevant to the subject-matter of the attack, or if it defames other persons who bear no responsibility for the attack. The right-of-reply privilege does not merely protect responses to criticisms made in Parliament, of course; it is a privilege of general application, arising from the legitimate interest of individuals in protecting their reputations, and it is shared by the media when it facilitates that interest.

The rule that qualified privilege protects bona fide responses to criticism assists newspapers that offer a right of reply. Editors sometimes justify their refusal to publish letters by victims of attacks in their newspapers on the grounds that they contain passages libellous of their journalists. Such refusals are disingenuous. A person whose reputation is criticized in the press is privileged to make honest, if defamatory, replies to those criticisms, and this privilege will shield the newspaper that publishes the defamatory response.

Parliamentary and court reports

At common law, all fair and accurate reports of Parliament and the courts are protected by qualified privilege. This is a safety net for press coverage that falls outside statutory protection – because, for example, it is not published as soon as practicable after the event. The application of qualified privilege is considered in detail in Chapter 7 and Chapter 9.

Other public occasions

Section 7 of the 1952 Defamation Act grants qualified privilege for newspapers in reporting a wide range of public occasions. 'Newspapers', under the 1952 Act, are defined as periodicals 'printed for sale' at intervals not exceeding thirty-six days (thereby including monthly magazines, but excluding free sheets). The privilege is extended to television and radio programmes by s 166(3) of the Broadcasting Act 1990. Video-cassettes are excluded and are protected, if at all, by common law. The writers of books and producers of films for cinema release are also outside the statutory privilege.

Section 7 is in two parts. The first accords qualified privilege unconditionally; the second grants it subject to the condition that a reasonable right of reply must have been afforded to victims of privileged defamations.

Part I privilege extends to fair and accurate reports of:

- Commonwealth parliaments;
- conferences of international organizations of which Britain is a member or is represented;
- proceedings of international courts;
- proceedings of British courts martial held outside Britain, and of any Commonwealth courts;
- public inquiries set up by Commonwealth governments;
- extracts from public registers;
- notices published by judges or court officers.

Part II privilege extends, subject to affording the victim a reasonable right of reply, to fair and accurate reports of:

- findings or decisions (not necessarily the evidence on which they are based) of any association (or committees of associations) formed in the United Kingdom and empowered by its constitution to exercise control over, or adjudicate on, matters relating to:
  (a) art, science, religion or learning;
  (b) any trade, business, industry or profession;
  (c) persons connected with games, sports or pastimes and who are contractually subject to the association;
- proceedings at any lawful public meeting, (whether or not admission is restricted) that is called to discuss any matter of public concern;
- proceedings of any meeting open to the public within the United Kingdom of:
  (a) a local authority or its committees;
  (b) justices of the peace acting in non-judicial capacities;
  (c) committees of inquiry appointed by Act of Parliament or by the Government;
  (d) local authority inquiries;
  (e) bodies constituted under Acts of Parliament;
  (f) general meetings of public companies and associations;
- 'any notices or other matter' issued for the information of the public by or on behalf of any government department, officer of state, local authority or chief constable. This does not include information that has been leaked from such sources, nor does it include unauthorized and off-the-cuff comments made by junior officials. To be protected, the information must be issued or approved by some person in authority. Journalistic

speculation and inference about official statements are not protected.[94]

These Part II privileges are 'subject to explanation and contradiction', which means that they will not apply where an editor or programme controller has refused the plaintiff's request to publish a reasonable statement in reply, or has done so in an inadequate manner. Plaintiffs must supply their own set of words – a bare demand for a retraction is insufficient to defeat the privilege.[95] So long as it is reasonable in 'tone and length', it must be published with a prominence appropriate to the original report.

These privileges attach to reports of public statements and public documents. They do not extend to the contents of documents (such as pleadings or affidavits) that have not been read in open court or to reports of evidence given in closed court, or to confidential reports that are available to councillors but not specifically read in open debate. The privilege would not stretch to reports of fresh statements made by speakers after the protected meeting has been closed, although it has been held that it does extend far enough to allow those who have spoken in the course of the meeting to repeat their privileged statements to reporters afterwards so that the latter may check the accuracy of their notes.[96]

Qualified privilege will be lost if the defamation is contained in a report that is not 'fair and accurate', or if the defamatory matter 'is not of public concern and the publication of [it] is not for the public benefit' (s 7(3) Defamation Act 1952). The whole point of providing qualified privilege for statements made at tribunals or local authority meetings or parliamentary commissions is that they relate to matters of public concern, and the public-benefit issue serves only to confuse the jury. None the less, the Court of Appeal has recently held that this issue, like the issue of fairness and accuracy, is a question of fact that must be left to the jury rather than be decided by a judge, even in cases where there are 'strong grounds' in favour of a factual finding (of fairness or public benefit) that would conclude the issue in the defendant's favour at the outset.[97]

---

[94] *Blackshaw* v *Lord* above note 89.
[95] *Khan* v *Ahmed* [1957] 2 QB 149.
[96] See decision of Mars-Jones J cited by Callender Smith, *Press Law*, Sweet & Maxwell, 1978, p. 44.
[97] *Kingshott* v *Associated Kent Newspapers Ltd* [1991] 2 All ER 99. The Court of Appeal insisted that the question of whether allegations about corruption of local councillors, given by a mayor at a planning inquiry, was a 'matter of public concern' had to be left to the jury: it was not so obvious that it could be decided by a judge!

Other Defences

Consent

People can – and often do for large sums of money – agree to be defamed. Should they then turn around to bite the hand that takes down their volunteered confessions, they will fail. Consent to publication is a complete defence. The consent must, however, relate to the actual libel published, and not merely to the grant of an interview in which the libellous subject was not specifically canvassed. A person who agreed to participate in a discussion programme in order to refute allegations could not complain about their public repetition, unless they included matters that the interviewee had specifically refused to discuss before the programme was recorded.

Apology

In other cases liability for libel may be avoided or reduced by timely apologies and offers of amends. In cases of 'innocent publication', where the defendant has not intended to criticize the plaintiff (either because the defendant did not realize that the words would be understood to refer to the plaintiff or the defendant is unaware of special circumstances that make them defamatory) liability may be avoided by making an 'offer of amends' under s 4 of the 1952 Defamation Act. An 'offer of amends' entails an offer to publish a suitable correction, together with an apology, and to pay any legal costs incurred by the complainant. The procedure is designed to give a right of reply instead of an action for damages in cases where the media have behaved responsibly: the plaintiff cannot succeed if the defendant proves that an offer of amends was made in good time and is still open at the time of the trial. However, in order to maintain this defence, it must be shown that the publisher exercised 'all reasonable care in relation to the publication' – which means that the publisher took steps to avoid obvious confusion, ensured that sources were checked and that familiar reference works were consulted.

> In *Ross* v *Hopkinson*[98] an actress sued the publisher of a novel in which a character bore her stage name. The defence that an offer of amends had been made failed on two counts: it had not been made 'as soon as practicable' (seven weeks had elapsed since publication) and 'reasonable care' had not been exercised, because a check with current stage directories would have revealed that the name chosen for the fictitious actress was the same as that used by a leading West End lady.

---

[98] (1956) *The Times*, 17 October.

The offer of amends would be a valuable protection for the media in cases of unintentional defamation were it not encumbered by what the Faulks Committee described as 'expensive rigmarole' – a procedure that requires the swearing of a detailed affidavit about how the confusion arose, which must be served at the same time as the offer of amends. This is the reason why it is little used and will fail to fulfil its valuable purpose until the reforms recommended by the Committee are implemented.[99]

In 1991 the Supreme Court Procedure Committee chaired by Lord Justice Neill suggested a much more radical reform, namely that in every case where the libel was not published deliberately or recklessly, the defendant should be permitted to make an 'offer of amends' that would bring the plaintiff's action to a halt. Either the offer would be accepted or the damages in the action would immediately be assessed by a judge and not a jury. This is undoubtedly the most sensible libel reform suggestion ever to emerge from an official committee, and it deserves speedy implementation. It would confine spiralling jury damages to cases where libels had been published maliciously, and would encourage speedy and effective settlements in other cases.

A prompt correction and apology for an indefensible defamation serves two purposes besides setting the record straight. In many cases it satisfies the complainants – and, where it is accompanied by payment of costs, it will satisfy their lawyers as well. If the complainant is still determined to become a plaintiff, the fact that a prompt apology has been made can be relied upon by the defendant to lower the amount of damages. It is obviously prudent, however, for the potential media defendant to seek a disclaimer of further legal action as a condition of publishing the apology. Once an apology is given, the defendant will be hard put to contest liability later.

Limitation

Plaintiffs must normally start their action by issuing a writ within three years of the libel's publication. This does not apply to repeated publications (each starts the clock running again), or to children or other people under a legal disability. If a person remains in ignorance of a publication until after the three-year period has expired, he or she can start proceedings within a year of learning of it, but the court's permission is necessary.[100]

---

[99] *Report of the Committee on Defamation*, HMSO, 1975, Cmnd 5909, Ch 9.
[100] Limitation Act 1980, ss 4A, 32A.

Damages

Damages in libel actions are difficult to predict. Personal injury cases are almost always tried by judges alone and receive recompense on a scale that can be predicted with some accuracy by reference to recent cases. Damage to reputation is a concept that has no equivalent in money or money's worth. It is inflated by the feeling that it should be large enough to 'vindicate' plaintiffs by showing the world that their names deserve respect, and perhaps even larger to 'console' them for the insult and injury of having their names taken in vain by circulation-grabbing newspapers. A refusal to correct or apologize for an obvious mistake will enlarge the damages, as will the seriousness of the libel and the degree to which it is repeated. By the same token, the promptness of the apology, the honesty of the mistake, and pre-existing flaws in the plaintiff's reputation are matters that go to reduce the final sum. Where journalists who give evidence in libel cases do not answer questions that identify their source of information, the Court of Appeal has held that they are in peril of suffering much heavier damages if they lose the case.[101]

The extent of circulation and the prominence given to defamatory remarks are factors that will influence the final award: a libel in the national press comes more expensive than the same libel in a small local newspaper. The plaintiff may also recover damages for repetition of the libel in other publications that the defendant might reasonably have foreseen would follow as a natural and probable consequence of his own publication. Thus the BBC might be compelled to compensate a plaintiff defamed in a drama-documentary not merely in relation to the damage done to his or her reputation amongst those viewers who watched the programme, but also in relation to newspaper readers who had read the 'sting' of the defamation in reviews of the programme. If such repetition is unexpected, then the media may escape wider responsibility, but as the Court of Appeal pointed out in 1991, 'defamatory statements are objectionable not least because of their propensity to percolate through underground channels and contaminate hidden springs.'[102]

Damages are awarded to compensate the plaintiff for the injury to his or her reputation and the hurt to his or her feelings. If 'malice' is proved against a sole defendant or against all defendants, it may aggravate the hurt and hence the final award. The plaintiff's feelings may be wounded if he or she is subjected to aggressive cross-examination, especially if it is designed to support what transpires

---

[101]   *Hayward* v *Thompson*, note 24 above.
[102]   *Slipper* v *BBC* [1991] 1 All ER 165 at p. 179 per Bingham LJ.

to be an unsuccessful plea of justification, so this forensic factor may be brought into account. On the other hand, the jury can be asked to take the plaintiff's own conduct into account in reducing damages – if the plaintiff has taken steps to refute the allegations publicly, or has been cleared of them after a publicized inquiry, or has obtained retractions and damages from other publications, his or her wounds may be considered to have partially healed. Similarly, if the plaintiff has used his day in court to make wild or unjustified attacks on the defendant, this conduct may be taken into account in reducing the damages.

Damages in libel cases are intended generally to compensate the plaintiff for loss of face, and specifically for any loss of work or earnings that can be proved to have been suffered as a result of the libel. They are not meant to punish the press, but when a publisher deliberately or recklessly sets out to defame another, with the object of making a profit out of that defamation (i.e., by increasing circulation), the law permits 'punitive' damages to be awarded, as in *Cassell & Co* v *Broome*: [103]

> David Irving wrote a book about the fate of a wartime convoy, blaming it upon the negligence of a particular captain, Broome. Cassell & Co published the book. The jury awarded punitive damages of £40,000 against Irving, and a further £40,000 against Cassell. The House of Lords upheld the award as a punishment to both author and publisher, as there was evidence that both were reckless about the truth of the defamatory statements in the book, and indeed hoped that they would cause a sensation so that the book's sales would increase.

Punitive damages in libel cases are a legal anomaly. They amount to a fine for misbehaviour, but have no upper limit. They are generally awarded by juries, who have neither the power nor the proficiency to impose a sentence in any other area of law. They do not, like other fines, go into the public purse but into the pocket of victims who have already been compensated by the same jury for damage to their reputation. They are, indeed, difficult to distinguish from the 'aggravated damages' to which a plaintiff is entitled by virtue of the suffering caused by the newspaper's high-handed or insulting conduct. They are not awarded in Scotland, and both the Faulks Committee and the Court of Appeal have recommended their abolition. [104]

There is urgent need to reform the law relating to damages in libel actions. In the hands of juries, without meaningful guidance from judges, they have become entirely unpredictable. Most

---

[103] *Cassel & Co* v *Broome* [1972] AC 1027.
[104] See *Riches* v *News Group Newspapers Ltd*, note 26 above.

lawyers expected that the wife of the 'Yorkshire Ripper' would receive no more than £20,000 for a relatively mild libel in *Private Eye*: instead, she was awarded £600,000. The Court of Appeal overturned the award but no clear guidance emerged from its judgment (see p. 44). In 1984 'Union Jack' Hayward received £50,000 to console him for the untrue allegation that he was involved in a murder plot. A few years later that sum was awarded to Robert Maxwell for the false suggestion that he was angling for a peerage, while ten times that amount was lavished on Jeffrey Archer to compensate him for the false suggestion that he had received a sexual favour from a prostitute he had admitted to paying to leave the country. Reform might come from Parliament simply taking the calculation of damages out of the hands of juries, and allowing judges to develop reasonably predictable scales for assessment after the jury has indicated whether damages in the particular case should be substantial, moderate, nominal or contemptuous. In the absence of legislation it may be that the Court of Appeal will prove more willing to strike down unreasonably high awards or, better still, authorize trial judges to suggest appropriate financial parameters in their summings-up. (Following the Courts and Legal Services Act 1990, the Court of Appeal now has greater power to substitute its own award of damages.) Failing such developments, it is possible that the European Court will find the unprincipled and unpredictable system of libel awards to be a breach of Article 10 of the European Convention, under which all restrictions on freedom of expression must be 'prescribed by law'. The prospect of heavy damages has a chilling effect on freedom of speech, and the blank cheque that juries are allowed at present to write does not constitute the sort of precise and predictable rule that the Convention requires.

Trial by jury

Section 69 of the Supreme Court Act 1981 entitles any party to a defamation action to require a trial by jury, 'unless the court is of the opinion that the trial requires any prolonged examination of documents or accounts or any scientific or local investigation which cannot conveniently be made by a jury'. Even in these cases the court has a discretion to order jury trial, although it will apply a presumption in favour of trial by judge alone if satisfied that otherwise the trial would be so complicated, costly and lengthy that the administration of justice would be likely to suffer.[105] The Court of Appeal has in such cases refused a jury even though the

---

[105] *De L'Isle* v *Times Newspapers Ltd* [1988] 1 WLR 49.

allegation accuses the plaintiff of committing criminal offences, although where the trial affects national interests or the honour and integrity of national personalities it may decide otherwise.[106] This was the case in *Lord Rothermere v Bernard Levin & Times Newspapers*, where the defendants had published an attack ('Profit and dishonour in Fleet Street') on Rothermere's integrity in closing down a newspaper. Although the trial would involve a prolonged examination of financial documents, the Court of Appeal was moved by the personal plea of the editor of *The Times* that free speech issues should be decided by a jury.[107] That was in 1973: the escalation of jury awards in more recent libel cases makes it unlikely that such a plea will be repeated by a defending editor.

A move to restrict the use of juries in libel actions was defeated in 1981, largely as a result of public satisfaction at the performance of the jury that sat for six months to hear the claim for libel brought by the head of the 'Moonies' in England against the *Daily Mail*. The jury not only upheld the newspaper's defence of justification, but added a rider suggesting that the 'Moonies' should be stripped of their charitable status. But unless the plaintiff is unpopular or unpleasant, the media will normally be advised to avoid jury trials, because of the danger of heavier damages.[108] For that very reason, of course, the plaintiff will normally insist on a jury.

Criminal Libel

If a libel is extremely serious, to the extent that a court is prepared to hold that it cannot be compensated by money and deserves to be punished as a crime, its publisher may be made the target of a prosecution. Criminal libel is an ancient offence that is now unlikely to be invoked against the media by prosecuting authorities: the Law Commission has recommended its abolition,[109] and one Law Lord has further pointed out that its scope conflicts with the European Convention on Human Rights.[110] However, there have been two modern instances in which it has been invoked by private individuals as part of a vendetta against their journalist-tormentors.

---

[106] *Goldsmith v Pressdram Ltd* [1988] 1 WLR 64; *Beta Construction Ltd v Channel 4* [1990] 1 WLR 1042.

[107] *Rothermere v Bernard Levin & Times Newspapers* [1973] (unreported).

[108] See *Blackshaw v Lord*, above note 89, where members of the Court of Appeal declined to reduce a jury award of £45,000 although they thought it 'far too high'.

[109] The Law Commission, *Working Paper No 84*, HMSO, 1982. The US Supreme Court has declared laws that punish falsehoods unconstitutional, unless they require proof of express malice: *Garrison v Louisiana* 379 US 64 (1964).

[110] *Gleaves v Deakin* [1980] AC 477 at p. 483 per Lord Diplock.

In 1977 Sir James Goldsmith was granted leave to prosecute the editor of *Private Eye*.[111] The following year a London magistrate, struck by the notion that there should not be one law for the rich unavailable to the poor, permitted a man named Gleaves to bring proceedings against the authors and publishers of a book entitled *Johnny Go Home*, based on a Yorkshire television documentary that had exposed his insalubrious hospitality to feckless youths. Neither case was an edifying example of law enforcement. Goldsmith was allowed to withdraw his prosecution after a settlement with *Private Eye*, and an Old Bailey jury took little time to acquit the authors of *Johnny Go Home* after a two-week trial. These precedents do not hold out great hope for private prosecutors determined to teach their critics a lesson in the criminal courts.

The arcane offence of *scandalum magnatum* was created by a statute of 1275 designed to protect 'the great men of the realm' against discomfiture from stories that might arouse the people against them.[112] The purpose of criminal libel was to prevent loss of confidence in government. It was, essentially, a public-order offence, and since true stories were more likely to result in breaches of the peace, it spawned the aphorism 'The greater the truth, the greater the libel.'[113] Overtly political prosecutions were brought in its name, against the likes of John Wilkes, Tom Paine and the Dean of St Asaph. Most of its historical anomalies survive in the present offence. Truth is not a defence, unless the defendant can convince a jury that publication is for the public benefit.[114] The burden of proof lies on the defendant, who may be convicted even though he or she honestly believed, on reasonable grounds, that what was published was true and a matter of public interest. Breach of the peace is no longer an essential element: all that is required is a defamatory statement of some seriousness, and 'seriousness' may be inferred from the public position of the person about whom it is made. The victim, of course, is permitted to seek rehabilitation through damages in a civil action at the same time as the libeller faces retribution in the criminal courts. In certain circumstances the offence extends to defamation of the dead,[115] and may even be brought where the attack has been published about a class of persons rather than an individual.[116]

For all its theoretical scope, there are several safeguards. Leave

---

[111] See Richard Ingrams, *Goldenballs*, Deutsch, 1979.

[112] ibid., p. 10, and see generally J. R. Spencer, 'Criminal Libel – Skeleton in the Cupboard', [1977] Crim LR 383.

[113] *De Libellis Famosis* (1606) 5 Co Rep 125 (*a*) and (*b*).

[114] In *R* v *Perryman* (1892) *The Times*, 19 January–9 February a jury actually found that an editor's allegation that a solicitor was party to a serious corporate fraud was true, but it was not in the public interest that this truth should be published.

must be obtained from a High Court judge before any prosecution can be brought in relation to an article in a newspaper or periodical.[117] The judge must be satisfied that there is an exceptionally strong prima facie case, that the libel is extremely serious and that the public interest requires the institution of criminal proceedings. In deciding whether these tests are satisfied the judge must look not just at the prosecution's case, but must take into account the likelihood of the newspaper successfully raising a defence.[118] In one 1982 case Mr Justice Taylor refused to allow a man who had been described by the *Sunday People* as a violent and drunken bully to bring a prosecution for criminal libel. He heard evidence from the newspaper that undermined the applicant's evidence, and decided that there was not 'a case so clear as to be beyond argument a case to answer'. He further held that in any event the public interest did not require the institution of criminal proceedings.[119] These same tests should be satisfied before a magistrate commits anyone for trial in relation to a libel that has not appeared in a newspaper or periodical. There is no offence of 'criminal slander', with the result that public speakers appear immune, at least in relation to off-the-cuff remarks.[120]

Criminal libel corresponds to no 'pressing social need' of the sort that the European Court insists should justify restraints on free expression, and its continuing existence is difficult to reconcile with the decision in *Lingens* v *Austria* (see p. 89). Very few cases are brought and those that are generally relate to nuisances who can be dealt with in other ways. Defamations that endanger the peace by being couched in threatening, abusive or insulting language may be prosecuted under the Public Order Act, and most poison-pen letters can give rise to charges under the provisions of the Post Office Act 1953 or the Malicious Communication Act 1988.[121] Private squabbles that motivate one party to advertise the defects of an opponent in handbills, hoardings or on subway walls can always be dealt with by bind-over orders, and sometimes by prosecutions for criminal damage or indecent displays.

---

[115] See *Hilliard* v *Penfield Enterprises* [1990] IR 38, where the deceased's wife sought to prosecute the publishers of a magazine for alleging that her husband had been a member of the IRA. Justice Gannon refused leave, on the grounds that criminal defamation of the dead required a malevolent intention to injure surviving members of his family by the vilification of his memory.

[116] See G. Zellick, 'Libelling the Dead' (1969), 119 NLJ 769, and (in relation to class libels) *R* v *Williams* (1822) 5 B and Ald 595.

[117] Law of Libel Amendment Act 1888 s 8.

[118] *Goldsmith* v *Pressdram Ltd* [1976] 3 WLR 191.

[119] *Desmond* v *Thorne* [1982] 3 All ER 268.

[120] Defamation Act 1952 s 17(2) and see *Gatley on Libel*, para 1600. Words broadcast on television or radio, however, are deemed to be published in permanent form: Broadcasting Act 1990 s 166(1).

[121] See Post Office Act 1953 s 11 and British Telecommunications Act 1984 s 43.

The law of criminal libel is an unnecessary relic of the past that is now generally agreed to have no place in modern jurisprudence. There have been suggestions that it should be replaced by a new law of criminal defamation, which would make it an offence deliberately to publish a serious falsehood. The difficulties of definition and of trial procedure, however, make such suggestions impracticable.[122] Moreover, as the Privy Council pointed out in *Hector* v *A-G of Antigua and Barbuda*:

> it would in any view be a grave impediment to the freedom of the press if those who print or distribute matter reflecting critically on the conduct of public authorities could only do so with impunity if they could first verify the accuracy of all statements of fact on which the criticism was based.[123]

The absurdity of taking the law of criminal defamation seriously was well illustrated in 1990, when the British Board of Film Classification sought to ban the Pakistani feature video *International Guerrillas* on the grounds that it amounted to a criminal libel on Mr Salman Rushdie, whom it depicted, in James Bond-style fantasy, as a sadistic terrorist. Mr Rushdie announced that if criminal libel proceedings were brought on his behalf, he would give evidence for the defence. The Video Appeals Committee decided that the prospect of a prosecution, let alone a conviction, was too far-fetched to justify the ban.[124]

Conclusion

A plaintiff once brought a defamation action over the allegation that he was a highwayman. The evidence at the trial proved that he *was* in fact a highwayman. The plaintiff was arrested in the courtroom, committed to prison and then executed. Few defamation actions end so satisfactorily for the defence.

The media constantly complain about defamation law, with some justice. At the same time they have been reluctant to support the extension of legal aid in libel cases, or to put their own house in ethical order (see Chapter 13). The alarming escalation of damages in recent cases is best explained as the response of ordinary people to falling standards in the popular press. No civilized society can permit a privately owned press to run vendettas against individuals powerless to arrest the spread of falsehoods and innuendoes. In the

---

[122] See G. Robertson, 'The Law Commission on Criminal Libel' [1983] Public Law 208.
[123] [1990] 2 All ER 103 at p. 106.
[124] Video Appeals Committee, Appeal No 0007, 3 September 1990.

United States the Supreme Court held in the great case of *The New York Times* v *Sullivan* that no libel action could succeed if the plaintiff was a public figure and the allegation was honestly and diligently made.[125] This ruling has freed the American media to probe Watergate and Irangate in a depth and a detail that could not be attempted in equivalent circumstances in Britain, where the merest hint of impropriety in public life calls forth a libel writ. But the public-figure doctrine denies virtually any protection to persons who are prominent in public affairs, simply because of that fact. True, public figures voluntarily step into a fish-tank that entails close public scrutiny of their every move, and they ordinarily enjoy greater access to channels of communication that provide an opportunity to counter false statements. But that opportunity is circumscribed, none the less, and in a country where Rupert Murdoch, the Maxwell organization and Lord Rothermere, with their powerful and partisan views, control 80 per cent of national newspapers, there is an understandable reluctance to give their newspapers a blank cheque to attack political enemies.

Two essential freedoms – the right to communicate and the right to reputation – must in some way be reconciled by law. British libel law errs by inhibiting free speech and failing to provide a system for correcting factual errors that is speedy and available to all victims of press distortion. American libel law gives no protection at all to the reputation of people in the public eye. Some European countries have opted for a more acceptable solution in the form of right-to-reply legislation, which allows judges or 'ombudsmen' to direct newspapers to publish corrections and counter-statements from those who claim to have been misrepresented. In 1989 a Right of Reply bill made progress in the House of Commons, attracting all-party support. But it proposed no changes in the law of libel, other than to provide redress to victims of untrue statements that were not defamatory. What is required is a speedy and effective legal procedure that secures corrections and counter-statements by way of an alternative procedure to libel litigation.

Media freedom would be enhanced by legislation of the reforms proposed by the Faulks and the Neill Committees, and even the statutory right of reply advocated by many media critics would be liberating if the exercise of that right were made contingent upon abandoning claims for libel damages. When journalists receive libel writs, they will generally be well advised to seek expert assistance, although there are times where a robust extra-legal response will be more effective.

---

[125] *The New York Times Co* v *Sullivan* 401 US 265 (1964).

The much celebrated correspondence in the matter of *Arkell* v *Press-dram* involved only two letters: the first, from the solicitors Goodman Derrick & Co, to the editor of *Private Eye*, ended with the familiar legal demand: 'Mr Arkell's first concern is that there should be a full retraction at the earliest possible date in *Private Eye* and he will also want his costs paid. His attitude to damages will be governed by the nature of your reply.' To this the magazine responded: 'We note that Mr Arkell's attitude to damages will be governed by the nature of our reply and would therefore be grateful if you could inform us what his attitude to damages would be, were he to learn that the nature of our reply is as follows: fuck off.'

Chapter 3

Obscenity, Blasphemy and Race Hatred

Censorship of writing, drama and film on grounds of morality is achieved by laws that apply two sets of standards. One prohibits 'obscene' articles likely to deprave and corrupt readers and viewers, while the other allows authorities to act, in certain circumstances, against 'indecent' material that merely embarrasses the sexual modesty of ordinary people. Obscenity, the more serious crime, is punished by the Obscene Publications Act 1959, either after a trial by judge or jury or by 'forfeiture proceedings' under a law that authorizes local justices to destroy obscene books and films discovered within their jurisidiction. Disseminators of 'indecent' material that lacks the potency to corrupt are generally within the law so long as they do not dispatch it by post, or seek to import it from overseas, or flaunt it openly in public places. Both 'obscenity' and 'indecency' are defined by reference to vague and elastic formulae, permitting forensic debates over morality that fit uneasily into the format of a criminal trial. These periodic moral flashpoints may edify or entertain, but they provide scant control over the booming business of sexual delectation. Occasional forfeiture orders, based upon the same loose definitions, are subject to the inconsistent priorities and prejudices of constabularies in different parts of the country, and offer no effective deterrent.

The deep division in society over the proper limits of sexual permissiveness is mirrored by an inconsistent and ineffective censorship of publications that may offend or entertain, corrupt or enlighten, according to the taste and character of individual readers. The problem of drawing a legal line between moral outrage and individual freedom has become intractable at a time when one person's obscenity is another person's bedtime reading.

Bedtime viewing, however, is subject to more stringent controls. Reliance is placed upon the statutory duty of the Independent Television Commission to ensure that nothing is transmitted on the commercial airwaves that is in bad taste or is likely to prove offensive to public feeling. Although no similar legal duty has been imposed upon the BBC, the Corporation has undertaken to ensure that its broadcasters also bow to the dictates of public decency.

Television was subjected to the Obscene Publications Act in 1990, although it is difficult to imagine how obscene material could slip through these controls, especially since it is additionally subjected to monitoring, adjudication and general nannying in the interests of good taste by Lord Rees-Mogg and his Broadcasting Standards Council (BSC). Films screened in public cinemas are subject to the test of obscenity, although the film industry, in order to obtain additional insurance against prosecution, has voluntarily bound itself to comply with the censorship requirements of the British Board of Film Classification, a private body established and funded by the industry itself. The importance of the BBFC has been enhanced in recent years by local licensing requirements for sex cinemas, which generally require that all films screened shall have been approved by the BBFC in its 'adult' category, and by the rule that cable television companies and video shops shall carry only films that have been granted an appropriate BBFC certificate. Licensed sex shops are also obliged to sell only videos that have been certified by the Board. In this way a form of pre-censorship is imposed on feature films that is not inflicted upon books or magazines or theatre.

The obscenity and indecency laws, and the arrangements for film censorship, are generally directed against sexual explicitness. However, the tests applied are sufficiently broad to catch material that encourages the use of dangerous drugs or that advocates criminal violence. Distributors of horror movies on video cassettes have been convicted on the basis that explicitly violent scenes are likely to corrupt a significant proportion of home viewers. In this chapter the scope and general principles of laws relating to obscenity, indecency, blasphemy, conspiracy and incitement to racial hatred are examined in some detail. In Chapters 14 and 15 the extent to which their principles are applied to the relatively new media of television, film and video will be considered separately along with the statutory duties and voluntary censorship systems that work in these media to regulate the treatment of controversial subjects.

Obscenity

History

The history of obscenity provides a rich and comic tapestry on the futility of legal attempts to control sexual imagination.[1] The

---

[1] See generally Geoffrey Robertson, *Obscenity*, Weidenfeld & Nicolson, 1979.

subject-matter of pornography was settled by 1650; writers in subsequent centuries added new words and novel settings, but discovered no fundamental variation on the finite methods of coupling. The scarlet woman, pornography's picaresque and picturesque prop, gained one dimension with the development of photography and another with the abolition of stage censorship, but the modern exploits of Linda Lovelace were old hat to Fanny Hill. The Society for the Suppression of Vice was born again in the Festival of Light, but its modern victims were to prove as incorrigible as those jailed and vilified by moral guardians of the past. The central irony of the courtroom crusade – what might be termed 'the *Spycatcher* effect' – is always present: seek to suppress a book by legal action because it tends to corrupt, and the publicity attendant upon its trial will spread that assumed corruption far more effectively than its quiet distribution. *Lady Chatterley's Lover* sold 3 million copies in the three months following its prosecution in 1961. The last work of literature to be prosecuted for obscenity in a full-blooded Old Bailey trial was an undistinguished paperback entitled *Inside Linda Lovelace*. It had sold a few thousand copies in the years before the 1976 court case: within three weeks of its acquittal 600,000 copies were purchased by an avid public. That trial seems finally to have convinced the Director of Public Prosecutions (DPP) of the unwisdom of using obscenity laws against books with any claim to literary or sociological merit.[2]

The courts first began to take obscenity seriously as a result of private prosecutions brought in the early nineteenth century by the Society for the Suppression of Vice, dubbed by Sydney Smith 'a society for suppressing the vices of those whose incomes do not exceed £500 per annum'.[3] A law against obscene libel was created by the judges, although Parliament gave some assistance in 1857 with an Obscene Publications Act, which permitted magistrates to destroy immoral books found within their jurisdiction. The Act did not, however, define obscenity. Lord Chief Justice Cockburn, in the 1868 case of *R* v *Hicklin*, obliged with a formula that has influenced the subject ever since:

> I think the test of obscenity is this, whether the tendency of the matter charged as obscenity is to deprave and corrupt those whose minds are open to such immoral influences, and into whose hands a publication of this sort may fall.[4]

---

[2] *Committee on Obscenity and Film Censorship* (The Williams Committee), HMSO, 1979, Cmnd 7772, Ch 4 para 2.
[3] *Edinburgh Review*, XXVI, January 1809.
[4] (1868) LR 3 QB 360 at p. 371.

Armed at last with a definition of obscenity, Victorian prosecutors proceeded to destroy many examples of fine literature and scientific speculation.[5]

Under the law of obscene libel, almost any work dealing with sexual passion could be successfully prosecuted. The *Hicklin* test focused upon the effect of the book on the most vulnerable members of society, whether or not they were likely to read it. One 'purple passage' could consign a novel to condemnation, and there was no defence of literary merit. D. H. Lawrence's *The Rainbow* was destroyed in 1915, and *The Well of Loneliness* suffered the same fate in 1928 at the hands of a magistrate who felt that a passage that implied that two women had been to bed ('And that night they were not divided') would induce 'thoughts of a most impure character' and 'glorify a horrible tendency'.[6] The operation of the obscenity law depended to some extent upon the crusading zeal of current law officers. There was a brief respite in the 1930s, after a banned copy of *Ulysses* was found among the papers of a deceased Lord Chancellor. But in 1953 the authorities solemnly sought to destroy copies of *The Kinsey Report*, and in 1956 a number of respectable publishers – Secker & Warburg, Heinemann, and Hutchinson – were all tried at the Old Bailey for 'horrible tendencies' discovered in their current fiction lists. The Society of Authors set up a powerful lobby, which convinced a Parliamentary Committee that the common law of obscene libel should be replaced by a modern statute that afforded some protection to meritorious literature.[7] The Obscene Publications Act of 1959 was the result. The measure was described in its preamble as 'an Act to amend the law relating to the publication of obscene matter; to provide for the protection of literature; and to strengthen the law concerning pornography'.

The 1959 Obscene Publications Act emerged from a simplistic notion that sexual material could be divided into two classes, 'literature' and 'pornography', and the function of the new statutory definition of obscenity was to enable juries and magistrates to make the distinction between them. The tendency of a work to deprave or corrupt its readers was henceforth to be judged in the light of its total impact, rather than by the arousing potential of 'purple passages'. The readership to be considered was the actual or at least predictable reading public rather than the precocious fourteen-year-old schoolgirl into whose hands it might perchance fall – unless it were in fact aimed at or distributed to fourteen-year-old schoolgirls, by whose

---

[5] See *R* v *Thomson* (1906) 64 J P456: 'In the Middle Ages there were things discussed which if put forward now for the reading of the general public would never be tolerated.'

[6] See Vera Brittain, *Radclyffe Hall – A Case of Obscenity*, Femina, 1968, pp. 91–2.

[7] See Norman St John Stevas, *Obscenity and the Law*, Secker & Warburg, 1956.

vulnerability to corruption it should then be judged. It was recognized that a work of literature might employ, to advance its serious purpose, a style that resembled, or had the same effect as, the pornographer's: here the jury was to be assisted to draw the line by experts who would offer judgements as to the degree of importance the article represented in its particular discipline. Works of art or literature might be obscene (i.e. depraving or corrupting) but their great significance might outweigh the harm they could do, and take them out of the prima facie criminal category established by s 1 of the Act.

In fact, the 1959 Act has worked to secure a very large measure of freedom in Britain for the written word. It took two decades and a number of celebrated trials for the revolutionary implications of the legislation to be fully appreciated and applied. The credit for securing this freedom belongs not so much to the legislators (many of whom now profess themselves appalled at developments) but to a few courageous publishers who risked jail by inviting juries to take a stand against censorship, and to the ineptitude and corruption of police enforcement. The first major test case – over D. H. Lawrence's *Lady Chatterley's Lover* – enabled the full force of the reformed law to be exploited on behalf of recognized literature. The book fell to be judged, not on the strength of its four-letter words or purple passages, but on its overall impact, as described by leading authorities on English literature. In 1968 the appeal proceedings over *Last Exit to Brooklyn* established the right of authors to explore depravity and corruption without encouraging it: writers were entitled to turn their readers' stomachs for the purpose of arousing concern or condemning the corruption explicitly described. The trials of the underground press in the early Seventies discredited obscenity law in the eyes of a new generation of jurors, and acquittals of hard-core pornography soon followed. These came in the wake of apparently scientific evidence that pornography had a therapeutic rather than a harmful effect. Popular permissiveness was reflected in jury verdicts, and the repeal of obscenity laws in several European countries made it impossible for the authorities to police the incoming tide of eroticism. And if pornography did not corrupt its readers, it certainly corrupted many of those charged with enforcing the law against it. Public cynicism about obscenity control was confirmed when twelve members of Scotland Yard's 'dirty squad' were jailed after conviction for involvement in what their judge described as 'an evil conspiracy which turned the Obscene Publications Act into a vast protection racket'.[8] After the acquittal of *Inside Linda Lovelace* in

---

[8] Barry Cox, John Shirley and Martin Short, *The Fall of Scotland Yard*, Penguin, 1977, p. 158.

1976, the authorities largely abandoned the attempt to prosecute books for which any claim of literary merit could be made. The Williams Committee, which reported on the obscenity laws in 1979, recommended that all restraints on the written word should be lifted – a position that they thought had already been achieved *de facto*.[9]

Since the Williams Report, the only books that have been prosecuted have either glorified illegal activities, such as the taking of dangerous drugs, or have been hard-core pornography lacking any literary pretension or sociological interest. In the late 1980s the need for education about the dangers of transmitting the AIDS virus justified a degree of public explicitness that would have been unthinkable in previous decades. However, the boast of British literary artistic freedom cannot be made with confidence, given a vague law and a swinging moral pendulum. The forces of feminism have done more than the cohorts of Mrs Whitehouse to challenge public acceptance of erotica; there can be no guarantee that some future legal onslaught against sexually explicit art and literature would not succeed. In 1988 a complaint from a Hampshire clergyman had the DPP rereading the works of Henry Miller, and seriously contemplating a test-case prosecution. In 1991 the DPP resisted trenchant demands that he should prosecute Century-Hutchinson for re-issuing the works of de Sade, and Picador for publishing *American Psycho*, a novel by Brett Easton Ellis of debatable literary merit, which included highly explicit descriptions of serial killings of women. The latitude he allowed to respectable white publishers did not extend to black 'rap' artists from the American urban ghetto, and the Island Records group Niggaz With Attitude suffered the first obscenity case brought in relation to a compact disc. It was solemnly played to elderly lay justices at Redbridge Magistrates' Court, who found it impossible to conclude that whatever it was that they were hearing could excite sexually.

The test of obscenity

The complete statutory definition of obscenity is contained in s 1 of the Obscene Publications Act:

> For the purposes of this Act an article shall be deemed to be obscene if its effect or (where the article comprises two or more distinct items) the effect of any one of its items is, if taken as a whole, such as to tend to deprave and corrupt persons who are likely, in all the circumstances, to read, see or hear the matter contained or embodied in it.

---

[9]   Williams Committee, *Obscenity and Film Censorship,* note 2 above.

In any trial the prosecution must prove beyond reasonable doubt that the material is obscene. Its task is complicated by the following interpretations of the statutory definition.

The tendency to deprave and corrupt

'Deprave' means 'to make morally bad, to pervert, to debase or corrupt morally' and corrupt means 'to render morally unsound or rotten, or destroy the moral purity or chastity of, to pervert or ruin a good quality, to debase, to defile'.[10] The definition implies that the tendency must go much further than merely shocking or disgusting readers.[11] Thus 'obscene', in law, has a very different, and very much stronger, meaning than it possesses in colloquial usage. The convictions of the editors of *Oz* magazine were quashed because their trial judge had suggested that 'obscene' might include what is 'repulsive, filthy, loathsome, indecent or lewd'. To widen its legal meaning in this way was 'a very substantial and serious misdirection'.[12]

In *Knuller* v *DPP* the Law Lords considered that the word 'corrupt' implied a powerful and corrosive effect, which went further than one suggested definition, 'to lead morally astray'. Lord Simon warned:

> Corrupt is a strong word. The Book of Common Prayer, following the Gospel, has 'where rust and moth doth corrupt'. The words 'corrupt public morals' suggest conduct which a jury might find to be destructive of the very fabric of society.[13]

Lord Reid agreed that:

> corrupt is a strong word and the jury ought to be reminded of that. ... The Obscene Publications Act appears to use the words 'deprave' and 'corrupt' as synonymous, as I think they are. We may regret we live in a permissive society but I doubt whether even the most staunch defender of a better age would maintain that all or even most of those who have at one time or in one way or another been led astray morally have thereby become depraved or corrupt.[14]

---

[10] See C. H. Rolph, *The Trial of Lady Chatterley*, commem. edn, Penguin, 1990, pp. 227–8. The present law is stated in detail in Robertson, note 1 above, Ch 3.
[11] See *R* v *Martin Secker & Warburg Ltd* [1954] 2 All ER 683.
[12] *R* v *Anderson* [1971] 3 All ER 1152.
[13] [1973] AC 435 at p. 491.
[14] ibid. pp. 456–7.

These dicta in *Knuller* emphasize that the effect of publication must go beyond immoral suggestion or persuasion, and constitute a serious menace.

'Obscenity' is a much narrower concept than 'sexual explicitness'. This important distinction was emphasized by the Divisional Court in the 1991 case of *Darbo* v *CPS* when it held that an Obscene Publications Act warrant authorizing police to search for 'material of a sexually explicit nature' was invalid, because material in this category was by no means necessarily 'obscene' in the sense that it might be likely to deprave and corrupt consumers.[15] Indeed, there is much to be said for the view of the Chief Justice of South Australia in respect of most ideologically vapid pornographic publications: 'I do not think that the arousal of erotic feelings in an adult male is itself an offence – there is, to my mind, something ludicrous about the application of such portentous words as "deprave" and "corrupt" to these trivial and insipid productions.'[16]

The aversion defence

One important corollary of the decision that obscene material must have more serious effects than arousing feelings of revulsion is the doctrine that material that in fact shocks and disgusts may *not* be obscene, because its effect is to discourage readers from indulgence in the immorality so unseductively portrayed. Readers whose stomachs are turned will not partake of any food for thought. The argument, however paradoxical it sounds, has frequently found favour as a means of exculpating literature of merit:

> *Last Exit to Brooklyn* presented horrific pictures of homosexuality and drug-taking in New York. Defence counsel contended that its only effect on any but a minute lunatic fringe of readers would be horror, revulsion and pity. It made the readers share in the horror it described and thereby so disgusted, shocked and outraged them that instead of tending to encourage anyone to homosexuality, drug-taking or brutal violence, it would have precisely the reverse effect. The failure of the trial judge to put this defence before the jury in his summing up was the major ground for upsetting the conviction.[17]

The aversion argument was extracted from its literary context and elevated into a full-blown defence of crudity in the *Oz* case:

> One of the arguments was that many of the illustrations in *Oz*

---

[15] *David John Darbo* v *DPP* (1991) *The Times* 11 July, Divisional Court (Mann LJ and Hidden J) 28 June 1991.

[16] *Popow* v *Samuels* [1973] 4 SASR 594 per Bray CJ.

[17] *R* v *Calder & Boyars Ltd* [1969] 1 QB 151.

were so grossly lewd and unpleasant that they would shock in the first instance and then would tend to repel. In other words, it was said that they had an aversive effect and that, far from tempting those who had not experienced the acts to take part in them, they would put off those who might be tempted so to conduct themselves . . .[18]

The most valuable aspect of the aversion defence is its emphasis on the context and purpose of publication. Writing that sets out to seduce, to exhort and pressurize the reader to indulge in immorality, is to be distinguished from that which presents a balanced picture and does not overlook the pains that may attend new pleasures. For over a century prosecutors thought it sufficient to point to explicitness in the treatment of sex, on the assumption that exposure to such material would automatically arouse the libidinous desires associated with a state of depravity. Now they must consider the overall impact and the truthfulness of the total picture. Books that present a fair account of corruption have a defence denied to glossy propaganda. In deciding whether material depraves and corrupts, the jury must lift its eyes from mere details and consider the tone and overall presentation. Does the material glamorize sex or does it 'tell it like it is'?

In 1991 the aversion defence assisted Island Records to argue successfully that a record by rap musicians Niggaz With Attitude was not obscene. Despite the profusion of four-letter words and aggressively unpleasant imagery, it was inconceivable that anyone in their right mind – or even their wrong mind – would be sexually aroused by songs like 'One Less Bitch' or 'To Kill a Hooker'. These songs were said to be 'street journalism', reflecting the degradation and depravity of life among the drug gangs in the ghetto suburbs of Los Angeles. The magistrates agreed that the record was more likely to arouse distaste and fear than lust, and directed that the 30,000 records, cassettes and compact discs seized by Scotland Yard's Obscene Publications Squad should be released.[19]

The target audience
An article is only obscene if it is likely to corrupt 'persons who are likely, having regard to all relevant circumstances, to read, see or hear the matter contained or embodied in it'. Thus the Act adopts a relative definition of obscenity – relative, that is, to the 'likely'

---

[18] *R* v *Anderson* [1971] 3 All ER 1152 at p. 1160.
[19] See 'Niggaz Court Win Marks Changing Attitude', *Guardian*, 8 November 1991; and 'NWA Cleared of Obscenity Charges', *Melody Maker*, 16 November 1991.

rather than the 'conceivably possible' readership. This is further emphasized by s 2(6) of the Act, which provides that in any prosecution for publishing an obscene article 'the question whether an article is obscene shall be determined without regard to any publication by another person, unless it could reasonably have been expected that the publication by the other person would follow from the publication by the person charged.'

These statutory provisions ensure that the publication in question is judged by its impact on its primary audience – those people who, the evidence suggests, would be likely to seek it out and to pay the asking-price to read it. They reject the 'most vulnerable person' standard of *Hicklin*, with its preoccupation with those members of society of the lowest level of intellectual or moral discernment. They also reject another standard employed frequently in the law, that of the 'average' or 'reasonable' man, and focus on 'likely' readers and proven circumstances of publication. A work of literature is to be judged by its effect on serious-minded purchasers, a comic book by its effect on children, a sexually explicit magazine sold in an 'adults only' bookstore by its effect on adult patrons of that particular shop. The House of Lords has confirmed that 'in every case, the magistrates or the jury are called on to ascertain who are the likely readers and then to consider whether the article is likely to deprave and corrupt them'.[20]

> In *R v Clayton & Halsey* the proprietors of a Soho bookshop were charged with selling obscene material to two experienced members of Scotland Yard's Obscene Publications Squad. These officers conceded that pornography had ceased to arouse any feelings in them whatsoever. The prosecution argument that the pictures were 'inherently obscene' and tended of their very nature to corrupt all viewers was rejected.[21]

Although judges sometimes loosely talk of material that is 'inherently obscene' or 'obscene *per se*', it is clear that this concept is irreconcilable with the legislative definition of obscenity.[22] The quality of obscenity inheres whenever the article would tend to corrupt its actual or potential audience; the degree of that corruption becomes relevant when it is necessary to balance it against the public interest, if a public-good defence has been raised under s 4 of the Act.

---

[20] *DPP v Whyte* [1972] 3 All ER 12 at p. 17. The US Supreme Court has ruled that children must be excluded from the relevant 'community' whose standards are at issue, unless there is evidence that they were intended recipients of the material: *Pinkus v US* 434 US 919.

[21] *R v Clayton & Halsey* [1962] 1 QB 163.

[22] *A-G's Reference No 2 of 1975* [1976] 2 All ER 753.

The significant-proportion test

The 1959 Act requires a tendency to deprave and corrupt 'persons' likely in the circumstances to read or hear the offensive material. But how many persons must have their morals affected before the test is made out? The answer was given by the Court of Appeal in the *Last Exit to Brooklyn* case. The jury must be satisfied that a *significant proportion* of the likely readership would be guided along the path of corruption:

> Clearly s 2 cannot mean all persons; nor can it mean any one person, for there are individuals who may be corrupted by almost anything. On the other hand, it is difficult to construe 'persons' as meaning the majority of persons or the average reader. This court is of the opinion that the jury should have been directed to consider whether the effect of the book was to tend to deprave and corrupt a significant proportion of those persons likely to read it. What is a significant proportion is a matter entirely for the jury to decide.[23]

The significant-proportion test has been applied at obscenity trials ever since. It protects the defendant in that it prevents the jury from speculating on the possible effect of adult literature on a young person who may just happen to see it, although it does not put the prosecution to proof that a majority, or even a *substantial* number, of readers would be adversely affected. This was emphasized by the House of Lords in *Whyte*'s case, where local justices had mistakenly interpreted 'significant proportion' to mean 'the great majority'. Lord Cross accepted that the significant-proportion test was the standard that the justices were required to apply, but stressed that 'a significant proportion of a class means a part which is not numerically negligible but which may be much less than half.[24] If the jury feels that a considerable number of children would read or see the article in question, and would be corrupted by the experience, it may decide that this number constitutes a significant proportion of the class that comprises the likely audience.

The dominant-effect principle

In obscenity trials before the 1959 legislation it was unnecessary for juries to consider the overall impact of the subject matter on its likely readers. Prosecuting counsel could secure conviction merely by drawing attention to isolated 'purple passages' taken out of context. The Select Committee on the Obscene Publications Act

---

[23] R v *Calder & Boyars Ltd*, note 17 above.
[24] *DPP* v *Whyte* [1972] 3 All ER 12 at pp. 24, 25.

had stressed the importance of considering the 'dominant effect' of the whole work:

> The contrary view, under which a work could be judged obscene by reference to isolated passages without considering the total effect, would, if taken to its logical conclusion, deprive the reading public of the works of Shakespeare, Chaucer, Fielding and Smollett, except in expurgated editions. We therefore recommend that regard should be paid in any legislation to the effect of a work as a whole.[25]

This recommendation was duly embodied in the 1959 statute, which provided that 'an article shall be deemed to be obscene if its effect or (where the article comprises two or more distinct items) the effect of any one of its items is, if taken as a whole, such as to tend to deprave and corrupt. . .'. In the *Lady Chatterley* case Mr Justice Byrne instructed his jury to consider the total effect of the work after reading it from cover to cover. 'You will read this book just as though you had bought it at a bookstall and you were reading it in the ordinary way as a whole.'[26]

The effect of the dominant-impact test is to enable the courts to take account of the psychological realities of reading and film viewing, in so far as the audience is affected by theme and style and message, so that isolated incidents of an offensive nature are placed in context. The injunction that an article must be 'taken as a whole' will apply to books and plays and films: in the case of magazines, however, which are made up of separate articles, advertisements and photographs, the dominant-effect principle has less force. In such cases the publication is considered on an 'item by item' basis: the prosecution may argue that obscenity attaches only to one article or photograph, and that the other contents are irrelevant.[27]

The publisher's intentions
The Obscene Publications Act is an exception to the general rule that criminal offences require an intention to offend. It does not matter whether the purpose is to educate or edify, to corrupt or simply to make money. The *effect* of the work on a significant proportion of the likely audience is all that matters in deciding whether it is obscene under s 1. However, the publisher's intentions may be very important when a public-good defence is raised under s 4 of the Act, namely that although the work is obscene, its publication is none the less justified in the public interest. In the *Lady Chatterley* case Mr Justice Byrne directed that 'as far as literary merit

---

[25] *Report of the Select Committee on Obscene Publications*, 1958, para 18.
[26] Rolph, *Lady Chatterley*, p. 39.
[27] *R* v *Anderson* [1971] 3 All ER 1152 at p. 1158.

or other matters which can be considered under s 4 are concerned, I think one has to have regard to what the author was trying to do, what his message may have been, and what his general scope was.'[28]

A limited defence is provided by the Obscene Publications Act for those defendants who act merely as innocent disseminators of obscene material. Section 2(5) of the 1959 Act reads:

> A person shall not be convicted of an offence against this section (i.e. the offence of publishing obscene material) if he proves that he had not examined the article in respect of which he is charged and had no reasonable cause to suspect that it was such that his publication of it would make him liable to be convicted of an offence against this section.

The onus of proof is placed on the defendant under this section. The defendant must show, on the balance of probabilities, both that he or she did not examine the article and that he or she entertained no suspicions about the nature of its contents. It is often possible to judge pornographic books by their covers and a bookseller would probably fail if he or she admitted to catching sight of a provocative cover-picture or suggestive title. In *R* v *Love* the Court of Appeal quashed the conviction of a director of a printing company who had been absent at the time a print order for obscene books was accepted, and who had no personal knowledge of the contents of those books.[29] Even though he had accepted general responsibility for his company's operations, and would probably have agreed to print the books had the decision been referred to him, he could not be convicted unless he had been given specific notice of the offensive material. The defendant who had not 'examined', in the sense of personally inspected, the offending items might none the less be given reasonable cause to suspect obscenity by clandestine or unorthodox behaviour on the part of the supplier. Any evidence that, for example, a printer has specially increased his profit margin to cover a risk factor would be fatal to a s 2(5) claim. Conversely, if the accused can show that the material came to him in the normal course of business from a reputable supplier, he may have a defence. Cases on the liability of distributors for libels in newspapers emphasize the importance for this defence of establishing that the business – of printing, distributing or retailing – was carried on carefully and properly. The test is whether the unwitting distributor *ought* to have known that the material would offend.[30]

---

[28] Rolph, *Lady Chatterley*, pp. 121–2.
[29] *R* v *Love* (1955) 39 Cr App 30.
[30] See *Emmens* v *Pottle* (1885) 16 QBD 354; *Sun life Assurance Co of Canada* v *W H Smith Ltd* (1934) 150 L T 211.

The contemporary standards test

Although the Act does not make reference to the current climate of opinion about sexual explicitness, juries in obscenity trials are enjoined to keep in mind the current standards of ordinary decent people. They 'must set the standards of what is acceptable, of what is for the public good in the age in which we live'.[31] The collective experience of twelve arbitrarily chosen people is assumed to provide a degree of familiarity with popular reading trends, with what is deemed acceptable on television and at cinemas, and with the degree of explicitness that can be found in publications on sale at local newsagents. A publisher is not, however, permitted to argue that he should be acquitted because his publication is less obscene than others that are freely circulated.[32]

The 1959 Act does, however, provide for two situations in which comparisons are both permissible and highly relevant. Under s 2(5), it may be that a defendant has 'no reasonable cause to suspect' the obscenity of a book that he has not personally examined because books with similar or identical titles or themes have been acquitted, to his knowledge, in previous proceedings. And under the public-good defence it may be relevant to the jury's task of evaluating the merit of a particular book to compare it with other books of the same kind, and to hear expert evidence about the current climate of permissiveness in relation to this kind of literature. This exception was recognized by Mr Justice Byrne in the *Lady Chatterley* case when he permitted expert witnesses to compare the novel with other works by Lawrence and various twentieth-century writers, and to discuss the standards for describing sexual matters reflected in modern literature. At one point in the trial he agreed that:

> other books may be considered, for two reasons, firstly, upon the question of the literary merit of a book which is the subject-matter of the indictment . . . [where] it is necessary to compare that book with other books upon the question of literary merit. Secondly . . . other books are relevant to the climate of literature.[33]

Where a public-good defence is raised, juries may be asked to make comparisons in order to evaluate the real worth of the publication at stake, and they may be told by experts about the state of informed contemporary opinion on subjects dealt with in those publications.

---

[31] *R* v *Calder & Boyars*, note 17 above, at p. 172 per Salmon LJ.
[32] *R* v *Reiter* [1954] 2 QB 16.
[33] Rolph, *Lady Chatterley*, p. 127.

Prohibited acts

There are two separate charges that may be brought in respect of obscene publications. It is an offence to *publish* an obscene article contrary to the Obscene Publications Act of 1959, and it is an offence to *have an obscene article for publication for gain*, contrary to the Obscene Publications Act of 1964. A charge under the 1959 Act requires some *act* of publication, such as sale to a customer or giving an obscene book to a friend. There must be some evidence connecting the defendant with movement of the article into another's hands.[34] Mere possession of an obscene book will not satisfy the definition of publication in s 1(3)(*b*), which governs both Acts:

> For the purposes of this Act a person publishes an article who (a) distributes, circulates, sells, lets on hire, gives, or lends it, or who offers it for sale or for letting on hire; or (b) in the case of an article containing or embodying matter to be looked at or a record, shows, plays or projects it . . .

When the Act was passed in 1959 television was specifically excluded from its ambit. The medium later became a favourite target of the 'clean up campaigners', who railed against its legally privileged position, and the 1990 Broadcasting Act grants their wish by repealing the exemption for television and sound broadcasting. An article is 'published' when matter recorded on it is included in a television or sound programme, and there is a defence for producers and participants who are unaware that a programme they are involved with might include obscene material, or that their material might be published in a way that would attract liability. Any seizure of recordings by police, or any prosecution, requires the consent of the Director of Public Prosecutions.[35]

Those who participate in or promote obscene publications are entitled to acquittal if they intend their work to be 'published' in a manner that falls outside the Act, e.g. because they genuinely believe that distribution will be confined to a select group immune from corruption or to those countries that do not have laws against obscene publications. A film producer, for example, who makes a 'blue movie' in England and then takes the negative to Denmark for development and ensuing commercial distribution is unlikely to be held to have committed an offence under English law, unless he or she is aware of plans to re-import copies for sale in Britain.

---

[34] *A-G's Reference No 2 of 1975*, note 22 above.
[35] Broadcasting Act 1990, s 162 and Sched 15. Video cassettes are judicially regarded as 'articles' within the scope of the 1959 Act: *A-G's Reference No 5 of 1980* [1980] 3 All ER 816.

Major English studios sometimes make two versions of feature films, a 'hard' edition for continental distribution and a 'soft' version suitable for home consumption. But the prosecution is not put to specific proof that obscene material is intended for publication in a manner that will infringe the Act, if such publication is a commonsense inference from the circumstances of production. In *R v Salter and Barton* two actors were charged with aiding and abetting by performing in an obscene movie, and they denied any knowledge of the producer's purpose or his distribution plans. The Court of Appeal held that ignorance could not avail them, although positive belief in a limited publication would have provided a defence. They could also have avoided liability if, more than two years before the prosecution was brought, they had taken some step to disassociate themselves from the continuing distribution of the film.[36]

The question of whether production or possession of magazines or films that might be considered obscene if published on the home market is in breach of the law if they are destined for export abroad will depend upon their likely effect on readers and viewers in the country of distribution. The courts cannot apply British standards of morality in such cases: they must consider the standards prevailing in the country of export, and the class of persons in that country who are likely to obtain them. The House of Lords has accepted that in some cases of this kind the court will not have sufficient evidence to form an opinion: since the burden of proof rests upon the prosecution, there should be an acquittal. The same result should be achieved if evidence is received that the material is acceptable under the laws of the country for which it is destined.[37]

The public-good defence

Section 4 of the Act provides that the defendant to an obscenity charge 'shall not be convicted' – despite the fact that he or she has been found to have published an obscene article – if 'publication of the article in question is justified as being for the public good . . .'. The ground upon which the defence may be made out is that publication, in the case of books and magazines, is 'in the interests of science, literature, art or learning, or of other objects of general concern'. The ground for exculpating plays and films is somewhat narrower: they must be 'in the interests of drama, opera, ballet or any other art, or of literature or learning'.[38] Section 3(1) of the

---

[36] *R v Salter & Barton* [1976] Crim LR 514.
[37] *Gold Star Publications Ltd* v *DPP* [1981] 2 All ER 257.

Theatres Act 1968, the counterpart of s 4, was drafted in more restricted terms because the inclusion of 'science' and of 'other objects of general concern' was thought irrelevant to the protection of quality theatre: plays that could not be justified by reference to dramatic 'art' or to 'learning' were unlikely to be redeemed by any other feature. Television and radio programmes have the widest possible defences: the Broadcasting Act of 1990 combines the grounds of public good available for both books and films (Sched 15, para 5(2)).

'In the interests of '
The exculpatory grounds set out in s 4(1) might have been expressed in terms of 'merit', but public good is not served by merit alone. An article may be 'in the interests of' literature and learning without being either literary or learned. Section 4(1) looks to the advancement of cultural and intellectual values, and the expert opinion as to the 'merits of an article' must be able to relate to the broader question of 'the interests of' art and science. A publication of obscene primitive art may lack objective merit, but none the less may be defended on the grounds of its contribution to art history. (The DPP once considered a complaint about the ancient drainage ditch at Cerne Abbas, which forms the outline of a giant with a truly giant-size erection. In the interests of history, and the interests of the local tourist trade, he declined the request to allow grass to grow strategically over the offending area.)

The *Oz* editors contended that although their 'Schoolkids Issue' had no particular literary or artistic brilliance, its publication was 'in the interests of' literature and art because it gave creative youngsters the opportunity to display their potential talents in a national magazine. The end product was in the interests of sociology, not because of any profundity in its contents, but because sociologists were interested in the results of the experiment of giving schoolchildren an uncensored forum to air their grievances.

'Science, literature, art or learning'
The jury must decide as an issue of fact whether and to what extent obscene material serves the interests of any of these 'intellectual or aesthetic values'. The Court of Appeal has construed 'learning' to mean 'the product of scholarship . . . something whose inherent excellence is gained by the work of a scholar'.[39] It follows that a publication cannot be defended under s 4 because of its value as a teaching aid, since this would require assessment of its

---

[38] Law Commission, *Report on Conspiracy and Criminal Law Reform, No 76,* HMSO, 1976, Ch 3 paras 69–76.
[39] *A-G's Reference No 3 of 1977* [1978] 1 WLR 1123.

effect upon readers' minds. A sex education booklet is not defensible because it provides good sex education, but if research has gone into its compilation, then no matter how ineffectual or misguided as an instructional aid, it possesses some inherent worth as 'a product of scholarship'. This result is hardly rational, but it represents a logical extension of the quest for intrinsic merit.

'Learning' overlaps with 'science', which is defined in most dictionaries as 'knowledge acquired by study'. A publication may possess scientific interest if it adds to the existing body of knowledge or if it presents known facts in a systematic way. Recent legislation defines 'science' to include the social sciences and medical research, and works with serious psychiatric, psychological or sociological interest would qualify for a public-good defence. Studies of human sexual behaviour might contribute to scientific knowledge, and even pornographic fantasies, if genuine and collected for a serious sociological purpose, could legitimately be defended.

'Literature' is widely defined as 'any printed matter', and the courts have been prepared to give copyright protection to the most pedestrian writing.[40] In the context of s 4, however, experts would be required to find some excellence of style or presentation to redeem the assumed tendency to corrupt. Excellence of prose style is not the only criterion for literary judgments, however, and books may be defended on the strength of wit, suspense, clarity, bombast or research if these qualities distinguish them in a particular genre of literature or in a particular period of literary history. Similarly, 'art' comprehends the application of skill to any aesthetic subject, and is not conventionally confined to the reproduction of beautiful images.[41]

In both the *Oz* and *Nasty Tales* cases underground comics were accepted as 'art' for the purpose of a s 4 defence. One expert, the painter Felix Topolski, reminded the court that 'unexpected elements, when brought together, produce the act of creation . . . I think one should accept that any visual performance if executed in earnest, is a branch of artistic creation.'[42] In 1975 the New Zealand courts held that drawings of toilet fittings were artistic works – a conclusion that the surrealist school would never have doubted.[43]

---

[40] See cases referred to in Ch 5.
[41] *Hensher (George) Ltd* v *Restawile Upholstery (Lancs) Ltd* [1976] AC 64. See generally P. H. Karlen, 'What is Art? A Sketch for a Legal Definition', 94 LQR 383.
[42] Tony Palmer, *The Trials of Oz,* Blond & Briggs, 1971, pp. 170–1.
[43] *P. S. Johnson and Associates Ltd* v *Bucko Enterprises* [1975] 1 NZLR 311.

'Other objects of general concern'
In *DPP* v *Jordan* the House of Lords ruled that the psychiatric health of the community allegedly served by 'therapeutic' pornography was not an 'object of general concern' for the purposes of s 4. Their Lordships declined to elucidate the phrase, beyond affirming that it had a 'mobile' meaning, which changed in content as society changes, and that:

- it referred to objects of general concern similar to those aesthetic and intellectual values specifically enumerated in s 4;
- it could not comprehend any object that was served by direct impact of publication on the mind of likely readers;
- it related to 'inherent personal values of a less transient character assumed, optimistically perhaps, to be of general concern'.[44]

There are many objects that survive these three tests. Among the 'objects of general concern' advanced on behalf of *Lady Chatterley's Lover* were its ethical and Christian merits: 'I suppose the section is sufficiently elastic to say that such evidence is admissible' remarked the judge, as he permitted the Bishop of Woolwich to testify to the book's contribution to human relations and to Christian judgements and values.[45] Other witnesses testified to its educational and sociological merits, and the editor of *Harper's Bazaar* was called as an expert on 'popular literature'. In the *Last Exit to Brooklyn* case the Court of Appeal conceded that 'sociological or ethical merit' might be canvassed.[46] Other objects of general concern that have been relied upon at obscenity trials include journalism, humour, politics, philosophy, history, education and entertainment.

Expert evidence

Where an s 4 defence is available, experts can be called to give evidence, and indeed it is difficult to imagine the defence carrying any credibility without them. Strictly speaking, the Act requires the jury to conclude that the article is obscene before they consider the public-good evidence, although in reality the impression made by the experts is likely to influence the decision on the obscenity issue. Expert opinion on the *effect* of the article is strictly inadmissible, but the Jesuitical distinction drawn by the courts between the 'effect' of literature (which must not be canvassed) and its merits is wholly artificial. Literature and art have merit precisely

---

[44] *DPP* v *Jordan* [1977] AC 699 at p. 719 per Lord Wilberforce.
[45] Rolph, *Lady Chatterley*, p. 73.
[46] *R* v *Calder & Boyars*, note 17 above, at p. 171.

because of their impact on the mind and their capacity to arouse emotions. Experts called under s 4 will inevitably give evidence about the theme and moral purpose of the work, and this evidence will be relevant, as a matter of common sense if not of law, to the question of whether it depraves or corrupts.

In certain cases the courts have permitted experts to be called by the prosecution and the defence to assist the jury in relation to the obscenity question if the subject matter of the work or its impact upon a restricted class of consumer is not likely to be within the experience of the ordinary person. When a book about the pleasures of cocaine was prosecuted for obscenity, scientific evidence was called to acquaint the jury with the property of the drug and its likely effects, so that they could decide (it being assumed they would not themselves have experienced cocaine) whether, if the book did encourage experimentation, the behaviour of the experimenters could be characterized as depraved and corrupted.[47] Similarly, when a company that had manufactured chewing-gum cards for distribution to very young children was alleged to have depraved their minds with scenes of violence, child psychiatrists were called to give expert opinion as to the likely impact of the cards on the mind and behaviour of children in that age-group.[48]

These precedents were taken further in the Niggaz With Attitude case. Dr Guy Culmberbatch, the Home Office expert on the effects of pornography, had been commissioned by Island Records to carry out field research on the effects of listening to NWA albums, which he did, with the cooperation of large numbers of disc jockeys, school and university students and members of rap clubs. His study was helpful in identifying the age and social profile of likely listeners and in establishing that they understand the lyrics in the context of American black experience, and not as any encouragement to antisocial behaviour. There is no reason in principle why this sort of evidence by social scientists should not be called by parties who are 'showing cause' under section 3 as to why an article should not be destroyed, and are consequently not bound by the rules of evidence in criminal cases. In any event, evidence of this sort is necessary to acquaint courts with what the case is all about: the Redbridge magistrates in the NWA case asked questions such as 'Is rap a cult?' and 'What do people do at rap concerts?' The rules are likely to be more strict at criminal trials for obscenity, where judges are notoriously reluctant to allow defence experts of any sort to 'sway' juries on the central issue of whether material tends to deprave and corrupt.

---

[47] *R v Skirving* [1985] 2 All ER 705.
[48] *DPP v A & BC Chewing Gum Ltd* [1968] 1 QB 159.

Prosecution practice

The enforcement of the obscenity laws is now directed largely at 'hard core pornography'. This has no legal definition, although juries are often told that 'pornography is like an elephant. You cannot define it, but you know it when you see it.'

Despite the uncertainty of the law, there is some consistency in prosecution targets.[49] Descriptions of sexual deviations are much more likely to be attacked than accounts of 'normal' heterosexual behaviour. In practice, prosecution authorities ignore the message of an article and concern themselves instead with the physical incidents photographed or described. Stories may degrade women by depicting them as objects to be manipulated for fun and profit, without attracting a prosecution. DPP officials have their lines to draw, and they draw them fairly consistently at the male groin: nudity is now acceptable and even artistic, but to erect a penis is to provoke a prosecution.

Accounts of straightforward copulation may attract prosecution if they are detailed and explicit and without literary or artistic merit. The House of Lords has held that the arousing of libidinous thoughts fell squarely with the mischief aimed at by the Act.[50] But pictures of orthodox sexual activity short of erection, penetration and ejaculation are usually made the subject of forfeiture proceedings in which no conviction is recorded and no punishment (other than the destruction of the goods) can be imposed.[51] These 's 3' proceedings (so called because the forfeiture code is contained in s 3 of the Obscene Publications Act 1959) serve little purpose other than to waste the time of the police and the local magistrates' courts. An order for forfeiture made by justices in one district is of no use as a precedent in others. The publishers of 'soft porn' magazines cheerfully accept occasional stock losses, usually without even bothering to intervene (which s 3 entitles them to do) to argue that their goods should not be destroyed. If meaningful action is to be taken against sexually explicit magazines on open sale, it should be taken nationally by test-case prosecutions of their publishers, and not by having local justices engage in periodic burnings of magazines they do not like.

The essential quality of pornography is its breach of social taboos. It works – for good or ill – by liberating its readers from social conventions, and enabling them to apprehend a pleasure in sex that some are incapable of realizing in normal surroundings. This is the psychological function of frequent references to

---

[49] See Robertson, *Obscenity*, Ch 10.
[50] *DPP* v *Whyte* [1972] 3 All ER 12.
[51] See Robertson, *Obscenity*, Ch 4.

behaviour that most readers would never wish to emulate in real life – incest, bestiality, necrophilia, coprophilia and so on.[52] The real obscenity of bestiality pictures lies not in their effects on readers' minds, but in the circumstances surrounding their production. Procuring women for intercourse with animals would seem to be an indefensible case of human exploitation, which could be prosecuted and punished under the Sexual Offences Act. The Cinematograph Films (Animals) Act of 1937 may also be relevant: it prohibits the exhibition of films the making of which involves cruelty to animals. This obscure piece of legislation is faithfully applied by the BBFC, which has ordered cuts in a number of Walt Disney films and videos with scenes that may have involved infliction of cruelty on animals. It should not, however, hinder films that are commentaries on cruelty towards animals.

Bizarre strains of pictorial pornography depicting extreme sexual violence, simulated necrophilia and human excretory functions do exist in Scandinavia and are sometimes imported into Britain, where distributors are almost invariably convicted. Juries, which are sometimes inclined to support freedom for voyeurs, are less keen to promote freedom for ghouls.

Drugs

There is no indication in the debates that surrounded the Obscene Publications Act that 'obscenity' pertained to anything but matters of sex. United States legislation and practice is so confined, but in Britain the courts have interpreted the statutory definition of 'obscene' to encompass encouragements to take dangerous drugs and to engage in violence.

The first case to push the notion of 'obscenity' beyond the bounds of sex arouse from forfeiture proceedings in 1965 against *Cain's Book*, a novel by Alex Trocchi that dealt with the life of a New York heroin addict. In the ensuing Divisional Court case, it was held to be

> perfectly plain that depravity, and, indeed, obscenity (because obscenity is treated as a tendency to deprave) is quite apt to cover what was suggested by the prosecution in this case. This book – the less said about it the better – concerned the life, or imaginary life, of a junkie in New York, and the suggestion of the prosecution was that the book highlighted, as it were, the favourable effects of drug-taking, and, so far from condemning it, advocated it, and that there was a real danger that those

---

[52] See Goldstein and Kant, *Pornography and Sexual Deviance*, University of California Press, 1973.

into whose hands the book came might be tempted at any rate to experiment with drugs and get the favourable sensations highlighted by the book.[53]

Cain's Book contained seductive descriptions of heroin consumption; for the courts to go further and to classify cannabis smoking as a 'depraved and corrupt' activity would hardly be compatible with the 1969 Report of the Government Advisory Committee on cannabis, which concluded after a thorough review of the evidence that 'the long term consumption of cannabis in moderate doses has no harmful effect.'[54] None the less in 1983 prosecutions were brought against the publishers of books that gave detailed instructions on how to grow cannabis plants and how to obtain the most favourable sensations from marijuana and cocaine.

> The publishers of some twenty books about prohibited drugs – *Cooking with Cannabis*, *The Pleasures of Cocaine*, *How to Grow Marijuana Indoors under Lights* and the like – were acquitted after a four-week trial at the Old Bailey. The prosecution failed to convince the jury that taking or cultivating cannabis was necessarily a depraved activity, given the widespread use of the drug, or that books that provided factual information about both the pains and the pleasures of harder drugs would be likely to encourage readers to experiment. Subsequently, however, the publishers of a pamphlet entitled *Attention Coke Lovers* were convicted. This unattractive work contained no warnings about the effects of the drug, but gave detailed instructions and recipes as to how to make use of cocaine so as to obtain maximum effects. It exuded enthusiasm for 'freebasing' – a highly dangerous method of inhaling a chemically-enhanced concentration. The Court of Appeal, in *R* v *Skirving*, upheld the trial judge's decision to permit scientific experts to be called to explain the effects of cocaine in general and free-basing in particular. Such matters could not be within the experience of the ordinary person, and the expert testimony was necessary to enable the jury to come to a proper conclusion as to the effect of the drug.[55]

The distinction between, on the one hand, providing factual information about drugs and, on the other, encouraging their use can be difficult to draw. Any publication that deals with drug-taking would be well advised to emphasize repeatedly both the physical dangers and the criminal penalties that attach to drug usage. The rule against 'highlighting favourable sensations' has never been applied to novelists: the favourable descriptions of

---

[53] *Calder* v *Powell* [1965] 1 QB 509 at p. 515.
[54] *Report of the Advisory Committee on Drug Dependence*, 'Cannabis' (Wootton Report), HMSO, 1969.
[55] *R* v *Skirving* [1985] QB 819.

opium-taking in the *Count of Monte Cristo* and the apparently productive use of cocaine by Sherlock Holmes have not led to obscenity prosecutions.

Violence

Any material that combines violence with sexual explicitness is a candidate for prosecution. Yet there are many gradations between a friendly slap and a stake through the heart, and most 'spanking' books and articles escape indictment. 'Video-nasties', however, that combine pornography with powerful scenes of rape and terror have been successfully prosecuted. More difficulty is experienced with the depiction of violence in non-sexual contexts. The Divisional Court in one case approved the prosecution of a manufacturer of childrens' swap cards depicting scenes of battle, on the theory that they were capable of depraving young minds by provoking emulation of the violence portrayed.[56] In the *Last Exit* case the Court of Appeal confirmed that the test of obscenity could encompass written advocacy of brutal violence.[57] The difficulty with these decisions is that they permit the conviction of publications that are not normally regarded as 'obscene', and that require expert evidence to establish the existence of their corrupting potential. The prevalence of violence in the mass media must raise serious doubts as to whether any one publication should be singled out for prosecution under an Act designed to suppress pornography.

None the less, in a climate in which saturation press coverage has been given to the psychological dangers of young children watching violence on video-cassettes designed for home viewing, distributors of video-nasties were at considerable risk of conviction for obscenity in the years before the Video Recordings Act (see p. 575) came into force:

> *Nightmares in a Damaged Brain* was an American cult horror movie, professionally made by a director with some talent. It was shown uneventfully to adults in cinemas in an X-certificate version, but when marketed on video-cassette some scenes of explicit violence that had been cut by the BBFC were reinstated. Much of the violence involved axe-murders, and there were soft-porn scenes with overtones of sexual violence. Although it had some light merits as a film, its distributors were convicted in 1984 after the prosecution had invited the jury to find that children would form a significant proportion of its likely viewers when it was made available for home viewing.

---

[56] *DPP* v *A & BC Chewing Gum Ltd* [1968] 1 QB 159.
[57] *R* v *Calder & Boyars Ltd*, note 17 above.

Horror publications

In one respect the obscenity formula has been specifically adapted to outlaw depictions of non-sexual violence that might prove harmful to children. In 1955 Parliament sought to prohibit the importation and sale of American 'horror comics', which had been blamed by psychiatrists for causing an upsurge in juvenile delinquency. The Children and Young Persons (Harmful Publications) Act 1955 was designed, in the words of the Solicitor-General, to prevent 'the state of mind that might be induced in certain types of children by provoking a kind of morbid brooding or ghoulishness or mental ill-health'.[58] It prohibits the printing, publication or sale of:

> any book, magazine or other like work which is of a kind likely to fall into the hands of children or young persons and consists wholly or mainly of stories told in pictures (with or without the addition of written matter), being stories portraying
>
> (a) the commission of crimes; or
> (b) acts of violence or cruelty; or
> (c) incidents of a repulsive or horrible nature;
>
> in such a way that the work as a whole would tend to corrupt a child or young person into whose hands it might fall.

Although the measure was perceived as urgent and important at the time it was passed, there have been as yet no prosecutions. Criminal proceedings require the consent of the Attorney-General, although this safeguard does not apply to imported comics, which may be seized and forfeited at the instance of customs officials. In 1976 customs officers prevailed upon Southampton magistrates to destroy the illustrated tales of Edgar Allan Poe, although the same bench ordered the release of *The Adventures of Conan the Barbarian* after evidence from a child psychiatrist that the Conan legend would be perceived as moral and even romantic by children inured to the adventures of Starsky and Hutch.

Child involvement

Undoubtedly the greatest concern over sexually explicit publications is manifested at the prospect of the involvement of young people, either as consumers or as models. This concern is reflected in the 1959 Act by its reference to the circumstances of the publication and the likely readership. The test of obscenity varies with the

---

[58] Hansard, HC Debs [1955] vol 539 col 6063. And see Martin Barker, *A Haunt of Fears: The History of the British Horror Comics Campaign*, Pluto, 1984.

class of persons likely to read or see the publication. Instead of imposing censorship at the point of distribution, by making the actual sale of erotic material to children a crime, it must be established that the material on trial is *aimed* at impressionable young people. The case of the chewing-gum cards illustrates how material that could be considered harmless if sold to adults by inclusion in cigarette cartons may be made the subject of obscenity proceedings if it is marketed in children's chewing-gum packets.

No mercy can be expected in the courts for those who involve young persons, even with their consent, in modelling sessions for sexually explicit photographs. Section 1(1) of the Indecency with Children Act 1960 provides that:

> any person who commits an act of gross indecency with or towards a child under the age of fourteen, or who incites a child under that age to commit such an act with him or another, shall be liable on conviction on indictment to imprisonment . . .

This provision would cover most cases in which children were encouraged to pose for erotic pictures, although the requirement of some indecent action 'with or towards' the child may arguably exclude photographic sessions in which an individual child poses provocatively without any physical contact with, or direction from, the photographer or procurer.[59]

The gap in statutory protection for children of fourteen and fifteen[60] was closed in 1978 by the Protection of Children Act. Section 1 of the Act makes it an offence:

(*a*) to take, or permit to be taken, any indecent photograph of a child (meaning in this Act under the age of 16); or

(*b*) to distribute or show such indecent photographs; or

(*c*) to have in his possession such indecent photographs, with a view to their being distributed or shown by himself or others; or

(*d*) to publish or cause to be published any advertisement likely to be understood as conveying that the advertiser distributes or shows such indecent photographs, or intends to do so.

A defendant 'distributes' photographs within the meaning of this section if he merely shows them to another, without any desire for gain. 'Indecent photographs' include films, film negatives and any form of video recording. There is no defence to s 1(*a*) other than

---

[59] *R v Sutton* [1977] 1 WLR 1086, at p. 1089.
[60] See Law Commission, *Report No 76*. Ch 3 para 117.

that the photographs are not indecent; or, if indecent, do not depict persons under sixteen; or that the accused in any event played no part in their production. Section 1(*d*) does not even require the photographs on offer to be themselves indecent – an advertiser is guilty if his wording is 'likely to be understood as conveying' a willingness to sell or show nude pictures of children within the prohibited age group. If the charge is laid under s 1(*b*) or (*c*), however, the distributor or exhibitor is entitled to an acquittal if he can establish on the balance of probabilities:

- that he had a legitimate reason for distributing or showing the photographs or (as the case may be) having them in his possession; or
- that he had not himself seen the photographs and did not know nor had any cause to suspect them to be indecent.

The courts have been unable to provide a meaningful definition of 'indecent', short of 'offending against recognized standards of propriety' or 'shocking, disgusting and revolting ordinary people'. The leading authority in cases concerning photographs of children involved the decision that *Boys are Boys Again*, a book comprising 122 photographs of naked boys, was an indecent import. Mr Justice Bridge accepted that the publication was not obscene, and would not infringe the standards of decency current in 1973 if it depicted naked children without sexual overtones. But he held that this publication, although borderline, lacked innocence:

> . . . the conclusion that I reach is that if the book is looked at as a whole . . . the very essence of the publication, the reason for publishing it, is to focus attention on the male genital organs. It is a series of photographs in the great majority of which the male genitals, sometimes in close-up, are the focal point of the picture . . . they aim to be interesting pictures of boys' penises . . .[61]

In deciding whether the photograph is indecent the jury is not permitted to hear evidence about the defendant's motive for taking it. The only intention that is relevant is the deliberate intention to take a photograph: whether it is indecent depends solely upon whether the jury is satisfied that the resultant picture is a breach of recognized standards of propriety.[62] That decision, however, must at least be informed by the jury's knowledge of the age of the child: it is accepted that this may play a part in the question of whether

---

[61] *Commissioners of Customs and Excise* v *Sun & Health Ltd* (unreported) 29 March 1973, Royal Courts of Justice, transcript pp. 5–6.
[62] *R* v *Graham-Kerr* (1989) 88 Cr App R 302.

the picture is a breach of recognized standards of propriety. Thus a photograph of a topless female model in a provocative pose that may not be accounted indecent if the model is above the age of consent may be held to infringe the Act once the jury realizes that the model is fourteen – much younger than she looks.[63] It is doubtful whether expert evidence would be admitted as to the artistic merit of the photograph, unless this were advanced as a 'legitimate reason' for showing or distributing it. There could be no objection in principle to such a defence being raised to justify an exhibition of photographs of historical interest, or pictures included in a documentary about the evils of child pornography. Photographic evidence of the torture or maltreatment of children may be highly indecent, but should not be the subject matter of a prosecution under this section where the purpose of the exhibition is legitimately to arouse anger or compassion. The legitimate-reason defence is new to the criminal law, but it has a potentially wide application. It would protect investigative journalists who acquire indecent photographs of children in order to expose a corruption racket, so long as they do not pay money to procure the taking of photographs that would not otherwise have come into existence.

There is no logic at all in allowing a legitimate-reason defence to a distributor or exhibitor, but not to a taker, of photographs that are found to be indecent. The decision in *Graham-Kerr* that the circumstances of the photography and the motivation of the photographer are irrelevant means that a paediatrician who photographs children's genitalia for legitimate medical purposes had no defence to a prosecution. The 'safeguard' is that prosecution can be brought only by the DPP, but a bad law is never justified by the hope that it will be sensibly enforced. Doctors will not be prosecuted, but 'artists' who pose children provocatively always will, whether they are C. S. Lewis or Robert Mapplethorpe. Photographers have no defence if the jury finds their pictures indecent, unless they can establish that they took the picture by accident or that the child just happened to run in front of the camera.

Section 7(2) of the Act defines 'indecent photograph' to include 'an indecent photograph comprised in a film', while s 7(3) provides:

> Photographs (including those comprised in a film) shall, if they show children and are indecent, be treated for all purposes of this Act as indecent photographs of children.

This section has complicated the task of the British Board of Film Classification when faced with feature films that include child

---

[63] *R* v *Owen* (1988) 86 Cr App 291.

actors in immodest or disgusting scenes. Such scenes are deemed, by s 7(3), to constitute 'indecent photographs of a child' even if the child is not participating in, or even aware of, the indecency. A plot that calls for a child to discover parents making love may be difficult to film or to distribute without contravention of the Act, and the artistic merit or overall purpose will not redeem an offending scene. One orgy scene from the film *Caligula* was cut by the BBFC because among the onlookers were women suckling babies. The new-born infants were sleeping in blissful ignorance of the catamite revels, but technically the scene contravened the Act, because it was indecent and it depicted persons under sixteen. The Hollywood vogue for casting child actors and actresses in major 'adult' movies means such films may require cuts before distribution in the United Kingdom.

Section 1(*d*) affects film and magazine titles, and requires careful vetting of advertising copy. Even if the product itself does not infringe the Act, 'any advertisement likely to be understood as conveying that the advertiser distributes or shows such indecent photographs' may be prosecuted, without the benefit of a 'legitimate reason' defence. Films with titles that include 'Schoolgirl', 'Lolita', 'Baby' or other words that evoke the thought of under-age sex will be difficult to publicize. In the week that the Act came into force one West End cinema pointedly changed the name of its current offering from *Schoolgirls* to *18-Year-Old-Schoolgirls*.

In 1988 Parliament created a new summary offence of *possessing* an indecent picture of a child (Criminal Justice Act 1988 s 160). This is the first example of the law relating to obscenity extending to material confined to the privacy of the home, without publication or possession for gain. As such, it may amount to a breach of the European Convention guarantee of personal privacy. Another unattractive feature of the offence is that it is not triable by jury – local justices generally apply a more censorious notion of what offends against recognized standards of propriety. The defendant at least is permitted to raise the legitimate-reason defence or to maintain that although the photograph was in his possession he had not viewed it and had no reason to suspect its indecency. He is also entitled to an acquittal if he can prove that the photograph was sent to him unsolicited 'and that he did not keep it for an unreasonable time'. This places a duty upon unwary recipients of child pornography in the post either to destroy it or to hand it in to their local police station.

Procedures and penalties

The offence of obscenity, on conviction by a jury, carries a maximum term of three years' imprisonment and an unlimited fine. Defendants may elect to be tried in magistrates' courts, where the penalty is reduced to a maximum of six months and/or a fine of £2,000. Such an election is rarely made, because magistrates are prone to convict for this offence with little hesitation or regard for legal niceties. Juries, on the other hand, can be reluctant to convict in cases that do not involve children, violence or hard-core pornography. Prosecuting authorities, mindful of the difficulties of jury trial, prefer to use the forfeiture procedure laid down by s 3 of the Act, which entitles them to seize under warrant a stock of obscene material and have it destroyed at the nearest magistrates' court. Any person claiming an interest in the material may contest its forfeiture, but the predisposition of most JPs is to make the order. The procedure has little deterrent effect: the case is brought against the material, rather than its publishers, and has no criminal consequence whatsoever. Section 3 seizures occupy a great deal of court and police time, but judgments in these cases do not serve as precedents and the only object of the exercise is to diminish the profits of soft-core pornographers by destroying some part of their stock. Section 3 is often used by police and prosecuting authorities as a device for avoiding jury trial. If a publisher wished to contest an s 3 seizure before a jury (at the risk of a gaol sentence if convicted) he can invoke a parliamentary assurance that this wish will be granted.[64]

It is open to question whether s 3 forfeiture orders conform with the European Convention on Human Rights. Although states are entitled to use obscenity laws to protect the morals of their citizens, their penalties must be proportionate to the aim of restricting freedom of expression only to the extent that is strictly necessary in a democratic society. In *Handyside* v *UK* the European Court of Human Rights declined to find that s 3 was a breach of the Convention when it was used (with Handyside's consent) to test the lawfulness of circulating *The Little Red Schoolbook*, which gave controversial advice to schoolchildren about sex and drugs.[65] The decision might be otherwise if the forfeiture procedures were used to destroy original artwork. In 1988 the European Court upheld a Swiss decision that had ordered that paintings held to be obscene when publicly exhibited should be deposited in a National Museum for safekeeping and limited viewing: the artist had been entitled to apply for their return, which he successfully did some years later. However, the court recognized a 'special problem' in the confiscation of original artworks, and the implication from its decision is

---

[64] Given by Sir Peter Rawlinson, the Solicitor-General, on 7 July 1964. See Hansard, col 302, and Robertson, *Obscenity*, p. 106.
[65] *Handyside* v *UK* [1976] EHRR 737.

that a forfeiture order under s 3 requiring the destruction of such items would be an infringement of Article 10.[66]

The only two significant countries that still routinely gaol first offenders for obscenity offences are Great Britain and the People's Republic of China. The Court of Appeal bound itself to send all pornographers to prison, irrespective of their circumstances, with a good deal of huffing, puffing and bluffing in 1982. ('When news of this judgment reaches Soho, we think it is likely that there will be a considerable amount of stocktaking within the next seventy-two hours, because if there is not, there is likely to be a depletion of the population of that area in the next few months.')[67]

Deterrent sentencers have a touching faith that their words strike immediate terror into criminal breasts throughout the world, but real life does not work in the way they imagine. Pornographers may take more care about being caught or pay more protection money, or move their stock to licensed sex shops. The gaoling of persons connected with pornography has had no deterrent effect and has served only to waste taxpayers' money on keeping in prison persons who are no danger to the public. Severe fines and suspended sentences would be a more sensible and more civilized alternative.

The cinema and film censorship

Film censorship today operates on three different levels. The distributors of feature films may be prosecuted under the Obscene Publications Act if the Director of Public Prosecutions deems that audiences are likely to be 'depraved and corrupted' by their offerings. Irrespective of the DPP's decision, district councils may refuse to license particular films for screening within their jurisdiction. Most councils rely upon the advice of the BBFC, which may insist upon cuts before certifying the films' fitness for the public screen or for certain age-groups, or may refuse to issue any certificate at all. Councils may also limit the number of sex cinemas in their locality, or prohibit such cinemas altogether. Finally, customs authorities are empowered to refuse entry to any foreign film they choose to classify as 'obscene'. Neither theatre producers nor book publishers suffer institutional restrictions laid down by trade

---

[66] *Mueller* v *Switzerland* (24 May 1988 Series A, No 33).
[67] *Holloway* (1982) 4 Cr App R (S) 128; and see *Nooy & Schyff* (1982) 4 Cr App R (S) 308: 'The word should go round the continent of Europe and the Americas that importing on a commercial basis indecent and obscene matter into the United Kingdom is nearly as hazardous an operation as importing dangerous drugs.' A slightly more humane approach is evident from *Knight* (1991) 12 Cr App R (S) 319, and *Lloyd* v *Ristic*, Court of Appeal, 3 February 1992.

censors or local councillors, and the standards of acceptability imposed by these bodies are such that cinema censorship is more pervasive and more arbitrary than the limitations imposed upon many other forms of artistic expression. These standards are examined in Chapter 14. The present discussion is concerned only with the application of the obscenity law to films and video-cassettes, which is of recent date. It was not until 1977, after ingenious private prosecutors had belaboured film distributors with the old common-law offence of holding indecent exhibitions, that the Obscene Publications Act was extended to cover the public screening of feature movies.[68] In 1979 the Court of Appeal extended the Act to video-cassettes by interpreting its wide language to include a form of entertainment that had not been foreseen when the Act was passed.[69]

Feature films that dilate upon violence and torture fall squarely within the law, although the 'aversion' theory would apply to works that depict scenes of cruelty in order to condemn them, within an overall moral or political framework. The BBFC certified an edited version of Pasolini's *Salo* on the grounds that:

> the sexual and other horrors are presented either in long shot or offscreen, and there is no exploitative sensationalizing. We are meant to hate everything we see, and there is no overt gloating over the spectacle. This is a turn-off film and not a turn-on, and in that sense it is unlikely that it would be found obscene by British law, since the film is intended to cause aversion or revulsion rather than a tendency to imitate . . .[70]

By shifting the emphasis from public outrage to the danger of moral corruption, the Act permits limited screening of artistic films that use explicit sex or violence to make a moral statement while deterring the public distribution of amoral works that glamorize vice and crime.

Limitations on prosecution
The Criminal Law Act 1977 abolishes the common-law offences, including the conspiracies to corrupt public morals and to outrage public decency, in relation to cinemas.[71] The consent of the DPP is required for any prosecution of a feature film, defined as 'a moving picture film of a width of not less than sixteen millimetres', and no order may be made to forfeit such a film unless it was seized pursuant to a warrant applied for by the DPP.[72] The Law

---

[68] Criminal Law Act 1977 s 53.
[69] *A-G's Reference No 5 of 1980*, note 35 above.
[70] British Board of Film Censors, Monthly Report for February 1976, p. 18.
[71] See Criminal Law Act 1977 s 53(3).

Commission recommended these restrictions on proceedings to ensure that uniform standards applied throughout the country, and to discourage vexatious or frivolous prosecutions.[73] These provisions protect the 1,300 licensed cinemas, and those film clubs and societies that show feature films, from arbitrary police harassment of the sort visited upon booksellers and newsagents.

However, once the DPP has approved, the police enjoy the full powers of search and seizure contained in the Obscene Publications Act.

Public-good defence

The public-good defence provided for films by s 53(6) of the Criminal Law Act is narrower than that which applies to books and magazines, omitting the grounds of 'science' and 'other objects of general concern' in favour of those objects enumerated in the Theatres Act, namely the interests of 'drama, opera, ballet or any other art, or of literature or learning'. The Law Commission noted that 'films have themselves an archival and historical value as social records, as well as being used for industrial, educational, scientific and anthropological purposes', and assumed that these merits would be canvassed under the head of 'learning'.[74] Cameramen who film contemporary horrors are providing evidence that will be 'in the interests of' present and future scholarship. Expert evidence is admissible, and if a certified film were prosecuted, representatives of the BBFC could expatiate on the merits of the work. Such testimony might, in any event, be acceptable as evidence of fact: the BBFC certificate, screened at the commencement, would comprise part of the 'article' on trial, and the jury would be entitled to an explanation of what it meant. In cases brought against horror movies, film critics have been permitted to testify to the merits of the film as cinematic art, its technical qualities, its dramatic effects, its message or moral, and its value as popular entertainment.

Television and radio

The 1990 Broadcasting Act applies the Obscene Publications Act to television and radio in much the same way as it has been applied to feature films. The s 4 defence is available (in a wider formulation than that which applies to plays and films) and no prosecution may be brought or forfeiture ordered except by or with the consent of

---

[72] ibid., 53(2) and (5). The DPP's consent should be obtained before application for a summons: See *R* v *Angel* (1968) 52 Cr App Rep 280; *Price* v *Humphries* [1958] 2 All ER 725.
[73] Law Commission, *Report No 76*, part III para 78.
[74] ibid., paras 69–76.

the DPP. The censorship constraints on broadcasting are dealt with in detail in Chapter 15.

Theatre Censorship

In 1737 Sir Robert Walpole, goaded beyond endurance by caricatures of himself in plays of Henry Fielding, introduced legislation empowering the Lord Chamberlain to close down theatres and imprison actors as 'rogues or vagabonds' for uttering any unlicensed speech or gesture. Thereafter political satire was banned or heavily censored for 'immorality', and as late as 1965 the Lord Chamberlain would not allow a stage version of Fielding's *Tom Jones* to be performed with bedroom scenes.[75] In 1843 a new Theatres Act was passed to consolidate the Lord Chamberlain's power to prohibit the performance of any stage play 'whenever he shall be of opinion that it is fitting for the preservation of good manners, decorum or the public peace so to do'.

The Lord Chamberlain's office remained eager to impose political, as well as moral, censorship, up to the time of its abolition in 1968. Commercial managements accepted political discipline without demur but state-subsidized companies had no profits at stake, and the RSC launched an all-out attack after the Lord Chamberlain objected to one of its plays on the grounds that it was 'beastly, anti-American, and left-wing'. In 1966 the Joint Committee on Theatre Censorship commenced its deliberations. Dramatists, state theatre companies and drama critics overwhelmingly demanded the abolition of the Lord Chamberlain's powers, and convinced the Joint Committee that pre-censorship provided a service neither to playgoers nor to dramatic art.[76] Its recommendations were embodied in the 1968 Theatres Act. The 1843 Act was repealed and the test of obscenity installed as the sole basis for theatre censorship:

> a performance of a play shall be deemed to be obscene if, taken as a whole, its effect was such as to tend to deprave and corrupt persons who are likely, having regard to all relevant circumstances, to attend it.

Decisions on the interpretation of s 1 of the Obscene Publications Act now apply with equal force to stage plays, with the exception of the 'item by item' test: all performances, even of revues compris-

---

[75] Richard Findlater, *Banned! – A Review of Theatrical Censorship in Britain*, MacGibbon & Kee, 1967, p. 175.
[76] *Report of the Joint Committee on Censorship of the Theatre*, HMSO, 1967, HC 255; HC 503.

ing separate sketches, will not infringe the law by reason only of one salacious scene, unless it is sufficiently dominant or memorable to colour the entire presentation. Obscenity is defined by reference to the circumstances of the staging and to its impact upon an audience more readily ascertainable than readership for books on general sale. A more stringent test would apply to West End theatres, trading from tourists and coach parties, than to 'fringe' theatres or clubs with self-selecting patronage.

Plays defined

The Theatres Act applies to 'plays', defined as:

> (*a*) any dramatic piece, whether involving improvisation or not, which is given wholly or in part by one or more persons actually present and performing and in which the whole or a major proportion of what is done by the person or persons performing, whether by way of speech, singing or acting, involves the playing of a role; and
>
> (*b*) any ballet given wholly or in part by one or more persons actually present or performing, whether or not it falls within paragraph (*a*) of this definition.

Reference to 'improvisation' includes ad-libbing and extempore performances, although the requirement of role-play excludes the stand-up comedian, unless the routine consists of playing different characters in a series of sketches. It would exclude some variety performances, although music-hall numbers usually require melodramatic characterizations that, arguably, involve the 'playing of a role'. 'Ballet' is broadly defined in the *Oxford English Dictionary* as the 'combined performance of professional dancers on the stage' and subsection (*b*) expressly excludes the requirement of role-play. It may therefore be more embracing than the 1843 Act, which applied only to dancing that was set within some dramatic framework.

In *Wigan* v *Strange*, a case under the 1843 Act, the High Court held that whether a 'ballet divertissement constituted an entertainment of the stage' was a finely balanced question of fact:

> A great number of females, it seems, dressed in theatrical costume, descend upon a stage and perform a sort of warlike dance: then comes a *danseuse* of a superior order, who performs a *pas seul*. If this had been all nobody would have called the performance a stage play. But the magistrate adds that the entrance of the *première danseuse* was preceded by something approaching to pantomimic action. The thing so described

certainly approaches very nearly to a dramatic performance: and it is extremely difficult to tell where the line is to be drawn.[77]

The Law Commission has doubted whether displays of tribal dancing could be classed as 'ballet', and ballroom or discotheque performances, even by professional troupes of dancers, would fall outside the definition.[78]

The Act applies to every 'public performance', defined to include any performance 'which the public or any section thereof are permitted to attend, whether for payment or otherwise', and any performance held in a 'public place' within the meaning of the Public Order Act 1936, namely:

> any highway, public park or garden, any sea beach, and any public bridge, road, lane, footway, square, court, alley or passage, whether a thoroughfare or not; and includes any open space to which, for the time being, the public are permitted to have access, whether on payment or otherwise.[79]

This would cover street theatre, open-air drama and 'end of the pier' shows. It would also include performances in restaurants,[80] public houses,[81] buses and railway carriages,[82] and possibly boats on public hire.[83] But the Act does not apply to any performance 'given on a domestic occasion in a private dwelling' or to a performance 'given solely or primarily' for the purposes of rehearsal, or for the making of a cinema or television film or a radio broadcast.[84] Whether the occasion was 'domestic' or whether the performance was 'primarily' for rehearsal or recording purposes are questions of fact for the jury. Public 'previews' of a play prior to its opening night would not be characterized as exempted rehearsals if tickets were issued to the general public, albeit at a reduced rate. Similarly, out of town 'try-outs' could not be classed as 'rehearsals', although they are designed to test audience reaction and frequently occasion script changes prior to the West End run. A performance staged primarily for the purposes of recording or filming or broadcasting

---

[77] *Wigan* v *Strange* (1865) LR 1 CP 175, per Erle CJ.

[78] Law Commission, *Report No 76*, part III, para 93.

[79] Theatres Act 1968 s 18 and Public Order Act 1936 s 9.

[80] *R* v *Hochhauser* (1964) 47 WWR 350; *R* v *Benson* (1928) 3 WWR 605.

[81] *R* v *Mayling* [1963] 1 All ER 687.

[82] *R* v *Holmes* (1853) Dears CC 207 at p. 209. *Langrish* v *Archer* (1882) 10 QBD 44.

[83] See generally M. Supperstone, *Brownlie's Law of Public Order and National Security*, 2nd edn, Butterworths, 1981, pp. 33–42. *DPP* v *Verrier* [1991] 4 All ER 18 sets out the test to be applied to determine whether an area is a public place.

[84] Theatres Act 1968 s 7.

is exempt from the operation of the Act, even where a large audience is invited to supply appropriate applause. Outrages to public decency that take place at rehearsals and filmed performances could still be prosecuted at common law.[85]

Local councils retain control over front-of-house displays, which they require to remain within the realms of public decency, and they are entitled to withhold licences from theatres that do not comply with fire regulations or other health and safety requirements. They are not, however, permitted to impose any licence conditions relating to the content of plays performed in the theatre. In 1987 Westminster Council contemplated action against the Institute of Contemporary Arts for staging a theatrical performance that featured a 'female Lenny Bruce', but had to accept that it could not use its licensing powers as a back-door method of censorship.

Public-good defence

The Joint Committee recommended that 'every effort should be made to see that the trial takes place in circumstances that are likely to secure a proper evaluation of all the issues at stake including the artistic and literary questions involved'.[86] A public-good defence contained in s 3 admits expert evidence to justify stage performances that are 'in the interests of drama, opera, ballet or any other art, or of literature or learning'. The 'merit' to which experts must testify is not of the play itself, but of 'the giving of the performance in question', so that pedestrian writing may be redeemed by the excellence of acting, direction or choreography. Experts who have not witnessed the performance may none the less testify to its dramatic, literary or educative value by reference to the script, which under s 9 'shall be admissible as evidence of what was performed and of the manner in which the performance . . . was given'.

Limits on police powers

Police have no power to close down the performance, or to seize programmes, scripts or items of stage property unless they feature writing or representations that contravene the Obscene Publications Act. Their power is limited solely to attendance, and is enforceable by warrant issued under s 15 by a justice who is given reasonable grounds to expect that the performance will infringe the Act.

---

[85] Section 7(2), which exempts rehearsals, etc., from the provision of the Theatres Act, also removes from these occasions the protection of s 2(4), namely the restriction on proceedings at common law.
[86] *Report on Censorship*, para 50.

Liability for prosecution

The Theatres Act applies to any person who, whether for gain or
not, 'presented or directed' an obscene performance. In *R* v
Brownson, the defendants 'presented' and 'directed' by their actions in commissioning the script, engaging the cast, directing
rehearsals, organizing the performances, managing the premises
and promoting the production.[87] Although rehearsals themselves
fall outside the scope of the Act, a director will be liable for scenes
prepared under his instruction after opening night, even though
his association with the production may have ended. Section 18(2)
provides that a person shall be taken to have directed a performance
of a play given under his direction notwithstanding that he was not
present during the performance. A director is not responsible,
however, for obscenity introduced after his departure: the Act
applies to 'an obscene performance', and imposes liability only on
those who have presented or directed *that* performance. Promoters,
on the other hand, may be vicariously liable for obscenity inserted
without their knowledge if the play is presented under their
auspices. The wording of s 2(2) suggests strict liability, and in
Grade v *DPP*, a case under the 1843 Act, it was held that a
promoter 'presented' a play with unlicensed dialogue, although the
offending words had been inserted without his knowledge and
without any negligence on his part.[88] Producers who act in a
personal capacity are more vulnerable than those who operate
through a corporate structure, in which case s 16 imposes liability
only on those who act knowingly or negligently.

Actors will not be liable for any offence arising from participation
in an obscene performance unless the obscenity arises from their
own deviation from the script, whereupon they become the 'director' of their own unrehearsed obscenity. Section 18(2) provides:

> (*a*) a person shall not be treated as presenting a performance
> of a play by reason only of his taking part therein as a
> performer
>
> (*b*) a person taking part as a performer in a performance of a
> play directed by another person shall be treated as a person
> who directed the performance if without reasonable excuse
> he performs otherwise than in accordance with that
> person's direction . . .

What constitutes 'reasonable excuse' is a question of fact, and
actors unable to control themselves in shows requiring simulated
sex acts might perhaps plead automatism or provocation. The

---

[87] *R* v *Brownson* [1971] Crim LR, 551.
[88] *Grade* v *Director of Public Prosecutions* [1942] 2 All ER 118.

actors' union, Equity, now insists that theatre managements give written notice of any scenes of nudity or sexual simulation prior to the contract of engagement.[89]

The Theatres Act makes no reference to the liability of dramatists. The Solicitor-General advised the Joint Committee that an obscene playscript would constitute an 'article' within the meaning of s 1(2) of the Obscene Publications Act.[90] A dramatist 'publishes' a playscript by giving it to a producer, but it does not become an 'obscene article' unless it is likely to deprave the people who read it – i.e., members of the theatre company, and not the theatre audience, which does not see 'the article' (i.e., the script itself) but the play, which is not an 'article' and is not 'published' to them by the dramatist. Prosecution under the Obscene Publications Act would therefore be unlikely to succeed, and an author cannot normally be said to 'present or direct' a performance that is contrary to the Theatres Act. It follows that dramatists are liable only if their script calls for blatant obscenity or if they assist in some other way to mount a performance that is likely to deprave and corrupt.

Evidence

Section 10 empowers senior police officers to order the presenter or director of a play to produce a copy of the script on which the performance is based. 'Script' is defined in s 9(2) as the text of any play, together with stage directions for its performance. This script becomes admissible as evidence both of what was performed and of the manner in which the performance was given, thereby ensuring that courts are not obliged to rely upon police recollections of dialogue and action. Neither the effect nor the merit of drama can be fully appreciated from textural study, but there is an evidential obstacle to restaging the performance for court proceedings. In *R v Quinn and Bloom* the Court of Appeal rejected the film of a strip-tease performance taken three months after the date of the offence, because there was no guarantee that the reconstruction exactly mirrored the performance on the date charged in the indictment.[91] *Quinn*'s case was a disorderly house charge, which carried no public-good defence, and it may be that the rule would be relaxed in a Theatres Act prosecution if the defence of dramatic merit were invoked. Comparative evidence has been admitted under s 4 of the Obscene Publications Act,[92] and reconstructions of accidents for

---

[89]   See Leslie E. Cotterell, *Performance*, London, 1977, p. 28.
[90]   *Report on Censorship*, p. 54.
[91]   *R v Quinn & Bloom* [1962] 2 QB 245.
[92]   *R v Penguin Books* [1961] Crim LR 176; see Rolph, *Lady Chatterley*, p. 127.

the benefit of the court are common in civil cases.[93] A restaged performance might be inadmissible on the question of obscenity on the occasion charged, but it would be highly relevant to a jury's assessment of theatrical merit. A better solution would be for the management to video the play, both at a preview performance and early in its run. If the evidence showed that the play was performed in the same way each night, the jury should have the benefit of the video rather than be required to rely on the script.

The Romans in Britain prosecution

In 1981 a private prosecution was brought against Michael Bogdanov, a National Theatre director, charging that he had procured an act of gross indecency between two actors on the stage of the Olivier Theatre as part of a scene in the play *The Romans in Britain*, contrary to s 13 of the Sexual Offences Act 1956. This was a bold attempt to sidestep provisions of the Theatres Act that require the Attorney-General's consent to any prosecution of a stage play, and to avoid the defences that would otherwise be available under that legislation, notably the strict test of obscenity and the public-good defence. The prosecution, in the event, collapsed in mid-trial for technical reasons (a not uncommon risk in private prosecutions) and reportedly left the prosecutrix with a large bill in legal costs. It did, however, occasion some concern in theatrical circles. The Theatres Act does not protect persons connected with a play from prosecution for actual criminal offences simply because they happen to be committed on stage. What it was intended to protect them against, with the possible and very narrow exception relating to s 13 of the Sexual Offences Act, is subjection to any form of legal censorship other than that provided for by the Theatres Act itself.

The *Report of the Joint Committee on Censorship of the Theatre* specifically recommended 'that no criminal prosecution (whether under statute or common law) arising out of the performance of a play should take place without the order of the Attorney-General having been first obtained'.[94] This was to secure 'the prevention of frivolous prosecutions' and to ensure the 'most important' principle that 'there should be an absolutely uniform application of the law throughout the country'. When the bill received its second reading in the House of Commons, its proposer assured the House that 'No prosecution may take place without the consent of the Attorney-General. We considered this necessary to prevent vexa-

---

[93] See *Gould* v *Evans & Co* [1951] 2 TLR 1189 and *Buckingham* v *Daily News* [1956] 2 QB 534.
[94] HC 255, HC 503, para 48.

tious or frivolous prosecutions by outraged individuals or societies and to ensure uniformity of enforcement.'[95] In the course of the debate this passage was approved and adopted by the Government spokesman (the Secretary of State for Home Affairs), who noted that 'It would be particularly oppressive if a prosecution were otherwise launched ... Those concerned with the presentation of plays are entitled to the protection which the Attorney-General's consent gives.'[96] This position was maintained during the bill's passage in the Lords, where the Government spokesman noted that the Attorney was obliged to read a play of which complaint had been made and to ask himself the question 'Is it in the public interest that there should be a prosecution here?'[97] Section 8 of the Theatres Act duly provides that proceedings shall not be instituted 'except by or with the consent of the Attorney-General'.

When *The Romans in Britain* was first performed at the National Theatre there was considerable critical comment about a scene that called for a simulated homosexual rape, perpetrated by three Roman soldiers upon a young Druid priest. Mrs Mary Whitehouse, the 'clean up' campaigner, asked the Attorney-General to prosecute under the Theatres Act: the DPP investigated, and reported that no prosecution would be likely to succeed. The Attorney refused his consent to allow a private prosecution to go forward, whereupon Mrs Whitehouse sent her solicitor to view the play, and he convinced a magistrate to issue a summons against Bogdanov under s 13 of the Sexual Offences Act. This section is directed at male persons who masturbate themselves or others in public toilets and parks. It punishes men who procure the commission of acts of gross indecency in public. The allegation against Michael Bogdanov was that he, being a male, 'procured' a male actor playing the part of a Roman soldier to commit an act of gross indecency with another male, namely the actor playing the young Druid. The artificiality of the proceedings is demonstrated by the fact that had any of the participants been female, s 13 could not have been applicable.

The prosecutrix had discovered a loophole in the law, applicable in a very limited way to plays directed by males that contain scenes calling for simulation of homosexual activity that a jury might find to be 'grossly indecent'. Although the intention of Parliament was to abolish all residual offences in relation to the staging of plays, the section of the Theatres Act designed to achieve this was not comprehensively drafted. It abolished common-law conspiracy offences, obscene and blasphemous libel and the like, but it

---

[95] Mr C. R. Strauss, 23 February 1968, Hansard vol 759 col 830.
[96] ibid., col 866.
[97] Lord Stow Hill, House of Lords, 20 June 1968, Hansard col 964.

overlooked the existence of s 13.[98] It could be argued that the prosecution was so obviously artificial that it would be oppressive to allow it to proceed, or that the Theatres Act by implication excluded a prosecution under s 13 where the purpose of the proceedings was to effect an act of censorship of drama.[99] These issues have yet to be resolved, and the collapse of *The Romans in Britain* prosecution makes that case an unsatisfactory precedent. The judge held that the prosecution had presented prima facie evidence of an s 13 offence. Had the case continued, the defence would have argued that even if s 13 were applicable, no offence had been committed by staging the play, because:

- There was no act of 'procuration' by the director. The acts and dialogue that form the basis of the charge took place by agreement between the author, the director, the actors and others. A person who does something from his or her own free will 'and without any fraud or persuasion on the part of any other person cannot be said to have been procured . . .'[100] At the committal proceedings Sir Peter Hall described how the scene was the result of a consensus between the parties involved and refuted the suggestion that the director had exerted any pressure or persuasion upon the actors.

- The bona fides of the performance precluded a finding that the scene was 'grossly indecent'. The prosecution admitted that the scene was serious, and performed without any hint of eroticism or titillation. As Sir Peter Hall explained:

I think it was done with extreme integrity and extreme care. Certainly the actors, the dramatist and the director knew what they were doing and endorsed it. One of the questions that was asked of me by the director was whether his view that the act, the scene, should be presented downstage in fairly full lighting – very clearly – was right. I advised him that I thought it was absolutely right because the scene is meant to horrify in what is a highly moral play; had it been done in half light behind a convenient tree, it would in my view have titillated.[101]

---

[98] See Theatres Act 1968 s 2(4).
[99] It is apparent from a review of the Joint Report and the debates that Parliament intended the Theatres Act to 'cover the field' of possible criminal offences committed in respect of the performance of plays. Neither the Law Officers (at p. 54 of the Joint Report) nor the Home Office (p. 106) suggested that s 13 of the Sexual Offences Act could be an appropriate charge.
[100] *R* v *Christian* (1913) 78 JP 112.
[101] Evidence in committal proceedings, *R* v *Bogdanov*, Horseferry Road Magistrates' Court.

Section 13 offences are committed for purposes of sexual gratification in circumstances that admit of no argument or ambiguity. The sex scene in *The Romans in Britain* was simulated in circumstances, and with a purpose, that negated the allegation of indecency.[102]

The prosecution evidence was that the act of gross indecency consisted in one male actor holding his penis in an erect position, advancing across the stage and placing the tip of the organ against the buttocks of the other actor. This was the testimony of Mrs Whitehouse's solicitor, who had been seated, appropriately enough, in the gods – some seventy yards from the stage. He admitted, under cross-examination, that he may have mistaken the tip of the penis for the actor's thumb adroitly rising from a fist clenched over his organ. Shortly afterwards the prosecution collapsed, relieving the jury from further consideration of a 'thumbs up' defence, which might have provided a complete answer to the charge.

Indecency Laws

The obscenity laws are designed to ban material that is likely to cause social harm. Indecency, on the other hand, is not concerned with 'harm' in any demonstrable sense, but rather with the outrage to public susceptibilities occasioned by unlooked-for confrontations with unseemly displays.

Obscenity is punished because it promotes corruption, 'indecency' because it is a public nuisance, an unnecessary affront to people's sense of propriety. For the most part, the indecency laws will not affect freedom of expression or art. They are generally confined to maintaining decorum in public places. However, the prohibitions on sending indecent material through the post may affect the distribution of books and magazines, and the ban on importation of indecent articles was continually used to stop controversial feature films from entering the country until the European Court intervened in 1986 (see p. 153). The most important aspect of 'indecency' as a test for censorship does not derive from the criminal law at all, but from the statutory duty imposed on broadcasting bodies to ensure that anything offensive to decency is not broadcast on commercial radio or television. The legal definition can become relevant for the purpose of contesting their rulings.

---

[102] Even if the motive of sexual gratification is proven, the assault must be 'accompanied with circumstances of indecency on the part of the defendant'. *Beal* v *Kelley* [1951] 2 All ER 763. No act can be divorced from the circumstances in which it takes place. See *R* v *George* [1956] Crim LR 52; *Wiggins* v *Field* [1968] Crim LR 503; 112 SJ 656; *Abrahams* v *Cavey* [1968] 1 QB 479, and *R* v *Armstrong* (1885) 49 JP 745.

The test of indecency

'Indecency' has been defined by the courts as 'something that offends the ordinary modesty of the average man ... offending against recognized standards of propriety at the lower end of the scale.'[103] In *Knuller* v *DPP*, Lord Reid added: 'Indecency is not confined to sexual indecency; indeed it is difficult to find any limit short of saying that it includes anything which an ordinary decent man or woman would find to be shocking, disgusting or revolting.'[104] However, the courts recognize that minimum standards of decency change over time, and that 'public decency must be viewed as a whole'; and the jury should be 'invited, where appropriate, to remember that they live in a plural society, with a tradition of tolerance towards minorities'.[105] This consideration assumes importance in those cases where the allegedly offensive article is destined for a restricted group whose right to receive material of minority interest may overcome the adverse reaction of jurors who do not share the same proclivities.

'Indecency' is not an objective quality, discoverable by examination as if it were a metal or a drug. In some cases courts have been prepared to accept that the context of publication may blunt the offensiveness of particular words or phrases:

> *Wiggins* v *Field* arose from a public reading of Allen Ginsberg's poem 'America', which included the line 'Go fuck yourself with your atom bomb'. The reader was charged with using 'indecent language' in contravention of a local by-law, but the Divisional Court said that the case ought never to have been brought. 'Whether a word or phrase was capable of being treated as indecent language depended on all the circumstances of the case, the occasion, when, how and in the course of what it was spoken and perhaps to a certain extent what the intention was.' It decided that in the work of a recognized poet, read without any intention of causing offence, the word 'fuck' could not be characterized as 'indecent'.[106]

That this question may assume crucial importance is illustrated by *Attorney-General ex rel McWhirter* v *IBA*. The Independent Broadcasting Authority, required by statute to ensure so far as possible that television programmes do not include anything that 'offends against good taste or decency', defended its decision to screen tasteless scenes in a programme about avant-garde film-

---

[103] *R* v *Stanley* [1965] 1 All ER 1035 at p. 1038.
[104] *Knuller* v *DPP* [1973] AC 435 at p. 458.
[105] ibid., p. 495, per Lord Simon of Glaisdale.
[106] *Wiggins* v *Field* (1968) 112 SJ 656; [1968] Crim LR 503. For a similar approach in relation to pictures displayed in an avant-garde gallery, see *In the Appeal of Marsh* (1973) 3 DCR (NSW) 115.

maker Andy Warhol on the ground that the dominant effect of the film was not offensive. The Court of Appeal agreed that the film 'taken as a whole' was not offensive, although about 10 per cent of it depicted 'indecent incidents'. Lord Justice Lawton suggested that context was a relevant factor:

> A possible appreciation of the programme could be that it was an attempt to give the television viewing public an opportunity of seeing something of, and understanding what, in modern idiom, has come to be called a 'sick society'. If this was the intention the distasteful and indecent incidents become relevant. It would be no answer to a charge of disregarding the Act for the authority to say that their motives in broadcasting indecent matter were worthy; but whether an incident is indecent must depend upon all the circumstances, including the context in which the alleged indecent matter occurs.[107]

The question is whether 'ordinary decent people' would be horrified, not at the publication itself, but by all the circumstances of its exposure.[108] This approach is consonant with the purpose of indecency offences: 'the mischief resides not so much in the book or picture *per se* as in the use to which it is put . . . what is in a real case a local public nuisance'.[109]

There is no measure of agreement about the extent to which the notion of indecency in law pertains to matters other than sex. It is usually used to denote sexual immodesty, which would exclude some publications that fall within the narrower statutory definition of 'obscene'. On the other hand, descriptions of drug-taking or brutal violence might be perceived as breaches of recognized standards of propriety, along with the expression of extreme social, political or religious viewpoints. Violence coupled with eroticism, such as sado-masochism and flagellation, is clearly within the definition, and full blooded accounts of torture and massacre would probably be held to be within the definition as well. In 1992 Customs and Excise obtained a jury conviction in relation to importation of a video film of pit bull terriers fighting brutally to the death. The indecency, and indeed obscenity, of the film was doubtless found in its tendency to encourage the keeping and organization of fights involving these dogs, which had been made illegal in the UK after recent tragic incidents.

The indecent article must infringe current community standards. A 'community standard' is something that emerges from the consensus reached in a jury deliberation: it is neither a fact capable

---

[107] [1973] QB 629, esp p. 659.
[108] *Crowe* v *Graham* (1968) 41 ALJR 402 per Windeyer J.
[109] *Galletly* v *Laird* (1953) SC (J) 16 per Cooper LJ at p. 26.

of proof nor an idea that can be canvassed by experts. Where the question of indecency turns on the circumstances or meaning of a publication, however, some assistance may be provided. In some cases expert opinion has been introduced as testimony of fact, to explain the reputation of authors and artists and to provide general information about the work at issue. In 1977 customs officers seized a number of books about classic art edited by international experts, despite the fact that many of the original pictures had been displayed at public galleries in England. Art critics testified to the standing of the editors and the artists, and gave details of a recent exhibition of some of the offending works at the Victoria and Albert Museum. In the same year a professor of English literature traced for a court the etymology of the allegedly indecent word 'bollocks', from the literal meaning of 'testicles', which appeared in early editions of the Bible (the King James edition replaced it by 'stones'), to its modern colloquial meaning of 'rubbish' or 'nonsense'. The promoters of the record album *Never Mind the Bollocks, Here's the Sex Pistols* were cleared of displaying an indecent advertisement, thereby relieving them from changing the title to *Never Mind the Stones, Here's the Sex Pistols*.

Indecency offences

It is an offence to deal with indecent articles in the following circumstances.

Using the post
Section 11 of the Post Office Act 1953 prohibits the enclosure in a postal packet of 'any indecent or obscene print, painting, photograph, lithograph, engraving, cinematograph film, book, and written communication, or any indecent or obscene article whether similar to the above or not'. The penalty is a fine of up to £2,000 in the magistrates' court, or up to twelve months' imprisonment as well as a fine if prosecuted at a Crown Court. The prohibition applies whether or not the posting is solicited, and there is no public-good defence available. In practice, prosecutions are generally confined to cases where complaints are made about unsolicited mailings, or where packages containing erotic magazines have broken open in the course of mailing. The possibility of prosecution is an irritant to publishers with mail order business: some, to be on the safe side, deliver their goods by British Rail, which has no equivalent prohibition, although a much higher theft rate.

Section 4 of the 1971 Unsolicited Goods and Services Act provides:

> A person shall be guilty of an offence if he sends or causes to be sent to another person any book, magazine or leaflet (or

advertising material for any such publication) which he knows or ought reasonably to know is unsolicited and which describes or illustrates human sexual techniques.

There is some ambiguity in the meaning of 'human sexual techniques'. The clause originally proscribed 'sexual techniques', the word 'human' being added at the insistence of the Ministry of Agriculture to protect its flow of breeding information to farmers. There was another ambiguity – was it essential for the 'book magazine or leaflet' *itself* to describe human sexual techniques, or did the words in parenthesis make it an offence for a leaflet merely to advertise a book about such techniques? The Divisional Court opted for the latter interpretation in a case where the unsolicited letter announced the firm's catalogue of books dealing with human sexuality without actually describing or illustrating either the catalogue or the books listed in it. The court ruled:

> It is clearly within the mischief of this legislation that there should be a prohibition of advertising material of that kind, even though the advertising material does not of itself contain illustrations or descriptions of human sexual techniques.[110]

Public display

The Indecent Displays (Control) Act of 1981 makes it an offence to display indecent matter in, or so as to be visible from, any public place. A place is 'public', for the purposes of the Act, if members of the public have access to it, although it loses this quality if persons under eighteen are refused admission. It also loses its character as a public place if access is by payment in order to see the indecent display, or the place is a shop with a prominent exterior display of a notice in the following terms:

> WARNING. Persons passing beyond this notice will find material on display which they may consider indecent. No admittance to persons under eighteen years of age.

The prohibition on the public display of indecency contained in this legislation does not apply to:

- television or to licensed cable services;
- exhibitions inside art galleries and museums;
- exhibitions arranged by, or in premises occupied by, the Crown or local authorities;
- performances of a play;
- films screened in licensed cinemas.

---

[110] *DPP* v *Beate Uhse (UK) Ltd* [1974] 2 WLR 50 at p. 52.

The Act provides severe penalties for infringement, but its provisions have been much less dramatic in controlling indecent displays than the licensing powers given to local councils in the Local Government (Miscellaneous Provisions) Act 1982. These powers enable local councils to prescribe conditions to regulate displays and advertising of licensed sex shops and sex cinemas, and to withdraw licences if the conditions (which invariably prohibit public display of indecent matter) are breached. The prospect that the shop will be closed down is a more effective deterrent than the possibility of prosecution.

There are some surviving local by-laws and nineteenth-century police 'town clauses' acts that entitle magistrates to fine persons involved with indecent acts and articles in public places. They are usually invoked by vice squad officers who frequent public lavatories in the hope of catching masturbators, but may have a wider application. The courts have recently been inclined to interpret these offences narrowly, confining them to situations where the public at large is caused genuine offence, as distinct from prying and provocative policemen.[111]

Telephone messages

Section 43 of the Telecommunications Act 1984 makes it an offence to 'send any message by telephone which is grossly offensive or of an indecent obscene or menacing character'. This offence appeared in the earlier Post Office Acts, doubtless to deter unpleasant and unsolicited calls. (Although whether it is apt to catch one breed of telephone nuisance, the 'heavy breather', depends upon whether exhalation of breath amounts to a 'message'.) This section acquired a new importance when the privatization of British Telecom led to the introduction of telephone services that provided allegedly erotic recorded messages at an expensive dialling rate. The exploitation of a former state monopoly to provide crude entertainment was condemned in the press and in Parliament, although providers of this service, carefully supervised by British Telecom, were in fact offering messages so anodyne that to advertise them as 'erotic' was probably a breach of the Trade Descriptions Act. None the less they attracted considerable custom, and became a lucrative service for which telephone subscribers were charged at the same rate as a dialled call to the Republic of Ireland. In 1986, in response to public criticism, British Telecom required its 'telephone information and entertainment providers' to abide by a special Code of Practice, monitored by an independent committee (ICSTIS) empowered to receive complaints and to discontinue any service

---

[111] See, for example, *Cheeseman v DPP* [1991] 3 All ER 54.

that breaches the Code (see chapter 13). Section 43 applies only to telephone messages originating in the United Kingdom, so there is nothing to stop those who wish to experience international dirty-talk from dialling verbally explicit services in the United States or Europe, which are available to credit-card holders.

Customs offences

Section 42 of the 1876 Customs Consolidation Act prohibits the importation into the United Kingdom of 'indecent or obscene prints, paintings, photographs, books, cards, lithographic or other engravings, or any other indecent or obscene articles'.

The test of 'indecency' imposed a different standard for imported books and magazines to that which governs home-produced literature, and the result, if not the intention, was for many years to protect the British indecent publications industry from overseas competition. Imported publications that did not tend to deprave or corrupt and could not therefore be suppressed by internal controls, were destroyed at ports of entry if they shocked or disgusted customs officials – people who have more experience in financial than in moral evaluation. The prohibition was even applied to film transparencies and negatives, inoffensive enough on casual inspection until processing and projection made their indecency apparent.[112] The phrase 'any other indecent ... article' was not interpreted *ejusdem generis* with the preceding references to printed matter: it covered sex toys, statues, chessmen, dildos, inflatable rubber women, penis-shaped plastic mouth-organs and any other objects that the wit or perversity of the human imagination can make for indecent use.

It was a life-size rubber German sex-doll that finally broke the customs barrier and secured the right to import from the EEC films and books that were 'indecent' but not obscene. It became the unlikely subject matter of the important decision of the Court of Justice of the European Communities in *Conegate Ltd* v *Customs and Excise Commissioners* in 1986:[113]

> A sex-shop chain was ordered to forfeit a consignment of rubber dolls imported from Germany that British courts regarded as 'inde-cent' within the 1876 prohibition. On reference to the European court, it was held that the prohibitions on 'indecent' imports breached Article 30 of the Treaty of Rome, which prevents restric-tions on trade between member states. The restriction could not be justified on public-morality grounds under Article 36, because the British government had not legislated to prevent the manufacture or

---

[112] *Derrick* v *Commissioners of Customs and Excise* [1972] 1 All ER 993.
[113] [1987] QB] 254 [1986] 2 All ER 688.

the marketing other than by post or public display of indecent material within Britain. Since the item could be lawfully made and sold in Britain, because it was not obscene, Britain could not discriminate against Common Market suppliers by applying import restrictions.

The consequence of the decision in *Conegate* has, for practical purposes, been to amend the 1876 law by removing the prohibition on indecent articles. Although in strict law this applies only to importations from Common Market countries, the Commissioners of Customs and Excise have accepted that it is impossible in practice to make distinctions between the same goods on the basis of the country of origin of their shipment. As a result, it abandoned the prosecution of Gay's the Word, a bookshop catering to homosexuals, which had imported a wide range of 'indecent' literature from the United States. (The customs' evaluation of 'indecency' may be gathered from the fact that the books included works by Oscar Wilde, Jean Genet, Gore Vidal and Christopher Isherwood.) It follows that prosecutions of literature under customs regulations will henceforth be confined to consignments of hardcore pornography, a ban on which the Court of Justice of the European Communities has held to be justifiable under Article 36 on public morality grounds.[114] There may also be forfeiture proceedings brought in relation to 'borderline' books, in respect of which the decision will hinge on whether the court regards them as likely to be the subject of conviction if prosecuted in Britain under s 1 of the Obscene Publications Act. The Court of Appeal has held that in considering a customs forfeiture claim the court need decide only whether the books 'tend to deprave and corrupt' likely readers so as to fall foul of the obscenity definition in s 1 of the 1959 Act: if so, it may order forfeiture without considering whether they might be exculpated by an s 4 'public good' defence.[115] This decision is difficult to reconcile with the reasoning in *Conegate*: if an obscene book may be manufactured and marketed within Britain because of its literary merit, there can be no logical reason for preventing its importation from other countries on moral grounds.

Customs officers who intercept articles considered obscene may proceed either by seeking forfeiture without criminal consequence to the importer, or by charging the importer with one of a variety of 'smuggling' offences in the 1952 Customs and Excise Act. A criminal charge will be preferred only where there is evidence of a positive and dishonest intention to evade the prohibition, so that cases other than commercial importation of hard-core pornography

---

[114] *R v Henn & Darby* [1980] AC 850.
[115] *R v Bow Street Magistrates ex parte Noncyp Ltd* [1990] 1 QB 123, CA.

will normally proceed to a civil forfeiture hearing, either before local justices or before a High Court judge, sitting with or without a jury.[116] Whenever goods are seized, the importer must be notified and has one month to apprise the Commissioners of his intention to dispute their claim for forfeiture, otherwise the goods will be destroyed. In disputed cases the Commissioners must institute proceedings, unless they decide on reflection that the seizure was overzealous, in which case they are empowered to release the goods subject to 'such conditions, if any, as they think proper'.[117] Conditions can be imposed only if the article has been seized at point of entry: an importer whose goods have cleared customs and who has paid the appropriate duty cannot, in the absence of dishonesty, be subject to any restriction if customs officers think with hindsight that it was an obscene import.

The Common Law

Corrupting public morals

There are several arcane common-law offences that can be revived 'to guard the moral welfare of the State against attacks which may be more insidious because they are novel and unprepared for'.[118] The charge of 'conspiracy to corrupt public morals', for example, could be used against any writing or broadcasting (unlike the Obscene Publications Act, it can apply to television) that a jury might hold to be destructive of the moral fabric of society. In practice it is now confined to publications that carry advertisements seeking to procure deviant sexual liaisons. It was employed in 1981 against organizers of the Paedophile Information Exchange (whose publications had carried advertisements from members that the defendants knew would facilitate the distribution of child pornography) and again in 1986 against the publishers of a 'contact' magazine.

The crime has had a colourful history. Its roots lie in the power exercised by Star Chamber judges to punish offences against conventional manners and morals. It was revived in 1961 to prosecute the publisher of *The Ladies Directory*, a 'who's who' of London prostitutes.[119] Its scope was reduced by the House of Lords in 1971:

> *IT* (*International Times*) was convicted for publishing a 'Gentlemen's Directory' among its classified advertisements. The prosecution evi-

---

[116] Customs and Excise Act 1952 ss 44(*b*) and 275, and Sched 7.
[117] ibid., s 288(*a*) and (*b*).
[118] *Shaw* v *DPP* [1962] AC 220 at p. 268.
[119] ibid.

dence established that these advertisements were answered by homosexuals through a box number service provided by the magazine. The advertisements were worded in a way that could, and apparently did, attract schoolchildren. The House of Lords affirmed the newspaper's conviction, on the ground that these box-numbered advertisements set up an 'apparatus of liaison' that would facilitate homosexual contact with under-age youths.[120]

The Law Lords restricted the future ambit of the offence in the following ways:

- The defendant must *intend* to corrupt public morals in the manner alleged in the indictment. The prosecution had to prove that the editors of *IT* inserted the advertisements with shared intention to debauch and corrupt the morals of their readers by encouraging them to indulge in homosexual conduct.[121] In this respect, at least, the conspiracy charge is more onerous for the prosecution than an obscenity offence, in which the defendant's intention is irrelevant.[122]

- The jury must be told that 'corrupt' is a strong word. It implies a much more potent influence than merely 'leading astray morally'. The jury must keep current standards in mind,[123] and not be given 'too gentle a paraphrase or explanation of the formula'.[124] 'The words "corrupt public morals" suggest conduct which a jury might find to be destructive of the very fabric of society.'[125]

- The essence of the offence was not the publication of a magazine, but the use of that publication to procure the advancement of conduct that the jury considered corrupt. The corruption in the *IT* case did not arise from obscenity, but from 'the whole apparatus of liaison organized by the appellants'.[126] The jury may have decided that the only objectionable advertisements were those that might attract under-age youths, as distinct from practising adult homosexuals, when published in a magazine bought by thousands of young persons.

- The charge does not invite 'a general tangling with codes of morality'.[127] The courts possess no residual power to create

---

[120] *Knuller*, note 104 above.
[121] ibid., p. 460.
[122] See *Shaw* v *DPP* [1962] AC 220 at p. 228, CA.
[123] *Knuller*, note 104 above, p. 457, per Lord Reid.
[124] ibid., p. 460, per Lord Morris.
[125] ibid., p. 491 per Lord Simon.
[126] ibid., p. 446 (*arguendo*), p. 497, per Lord Kilbrandon.
[127] ibid., p. 490 per Lord Simon.

new offences. The conspiracy charge should be applied only to 'reasonably analogous' new circumstances.[128]

- Homosexual contact advertising, or any other sort of encouragement to homosexuality, does not necessarily amount to a corruption of public morality. In every case it is for the jury to decide, on current moral standards, whether the conduct alleged amounts to public corruption.[129] To demonstrate that the advertisers want to stay within the law, it is common for magazines to require 'contact' advertisements for gay men to specify that respondents should be over twenty-one.

- Prosecutions for conspiracy should not be brought against publishers who would, if charged under the Obscene Publications Act, be entitled to raise a public-good defence. An undertaking to this effect was given to Parliament by the Law Officers in 1964, and it should be honoured by the legal profession.[130]

Outraging public decency

A similarly restrictive approach was placed on the allied offence of conspiracy to outrage public decency in the *IT* case. That applied only to circumstances in which an exhibition would outrage those who were invited to see it, and the court stressed that prosecution would be subject to the Law Officers' undertaking that conspiracy would not be charged in any way that might circumvent the public-good defence in the Obscene Publications Act.[131] But the common-law offence of outraging public decency was revived in 1989 to punish an artist and the proprietor of an art gallery who exhibited a surrealist work featuring earrings that had been fashioned from human foetuses. This prosecution, *R* v *Gibson*, was a breach at least of the spirit of the Law Officers' undertaking, since there were a number of distinguished artists and critics prepared to testify that the work had artistic merit but this evidence was inadmissable on the common-law charge, which has no public-good or artistic-merit defence.

> The defendants were charged with creating a public nuisance and outraging public decency by exhibiting the foetal earrings as part of a sculpture displayed within an art gallery open to the public. As the

---

[128] ibid., p. 455 per Lord Reid.
[129] ibid., p. 490 per Lord Simon.
[130] 3 June 1964, Hansard, vol 695, col 1212. See *Knuller*, note 104 above, p. 459 per Lord Reid, p. 466 per Lord Morris, p. 480 per Lord Diplock, p. 494 per Lord Simon.
[131] *Knuller*, above, p. 468 per Lord Morris and p. 494 per Lord Simon.

work of alleged art was not plainly visible from the public footpath outside the gallery, the public-nuisance charge was dismissed. The Court of Appeal upheld the public indecency conviction, because the requirement of 'publicity' for that offence had been satisfied by the general invitation to the public to enter the gallery and view the exhibits. The Crown did not have to prove that the gallery proprietor drew particular attention to the offensive exhibit, or that the artist and proprietor had intended to outrage decency (or were at least prepared to run an apparent risk of outraging the public). This latter ruling leads to the anomaly that although the prosecution must prove intention when it charges common-law conspiracies, this fundamental requirement of criminal law can be avoided simply by charging the substantive offence.[132]

Although the facts of this case were highly exceptional, it showed how the protections for art and literature solemnly enacted by Parliament in 1959 could be circumvented by the device of charging an offence at common law. The test of 'outrage' is vague and subjective, calling for a value judgment verdict, which will depend not on any provable public standard or any deliberate intention to outrage, but on the 'gut reactions' of the jurors who happen to be empanelled to try the case. The majority-verdict procedure, which allows a conviction despite two dissenters, further undermines the protection for minority tastes and views – it is not surprising that in the 'foetal earrings' case, the *Oz* trial and the *Gay News* blasphemy prosecution, conviction was by 10–2 majority. The dissenters represented a substantial minority of citizens who wished either to have access to the material or not to interfere with the rights of those who did.

Exposure to the common law

The drafters of the 1959 Obscene Publications Act made an appalling mess of embodying in legislation the parliamentary intention to protect all art and literature against the philistine presumptions of the common law. They sought to exclude the operation of common law by providing, in s 2(4), that 'a person publishing an article shall not be proceeded against for an offence at common law consisting of the publication of any matter contained or embodied in the article *where it is of the essence of the offence that the matter is obscene*' [our italics].

Prosecutors who wish to circumvent the protection of the 1959 Act need simply claim that the essence of the offence committed by the publication of the book or artwork is indecency (i.e., the arousing of feelings of disgust and revulsion) rather than obscenity (i.e.,

---

[132]   *R* v *Gibson* [1991] 1 All ER 439.

the corruption of the mind). The parliamentary undertaking referred to above may offer some comfort, as may the view of the Court of Appeal in *Gibson* that 'it is unlikely that a defence of public good could possibly arise' in relation to cases properly prosecuted at common law.[133] It would be attractive to believe that the court had in mind the notion that meritorious art and literature could not, by definition, be shocking and revolting, but it is more likely that they were finding it difficult to credit that art that is shocking and revolting could ever be for the public good. The problem of excluding the infinitely elastic common law is not suffered by producers of feature films or television and radio programmes. By 1977 the inadequacy of s 2(4) had been recognized, and the law was amended by adding a new subsection, 4(*a*), which excluded, in relation to films, any prosecutions at common law where the essence of the offence was indecency or conspiracy or offensiveness or disgust or injury to morality. The same blanket formula was used in paragraph 6 of Schedule 15 to the 1990 Broadcasting Act to remove the threat of common-law prosecution from the electronic media. It is regrettable that on neither occasion in amending the 1959 Act did Parliament plug the obvious gap in s 2(4), which permits common-law crimes of elastic definition and strict liability to survive in relation to art and literature, and which are bereft of any public-good defence.

Living theatre, happenings, performance art, strip-tease, discotheque programmes, variety shows and the like may fall outside the definition of a 'play' for the purpose of the Theatres Act, but organizers and managers of premises where the performance takes place may be prosecuted for the common-law offence of 'keeping a disorderly house'. This offence, created by eighteenth-century judges to curb cock-fighting and bear-baiting, is now primarily used against over-excitable hen parties and stag nights. A disorderly house is simply a place of common resort that features performances that are obscene, grossly indecent or 'calculated to injure the public interest so as to call for condemnation and punishment'.[134] The programme should be considered as a whole and not condemned because of an isolated incident of indecency, and the jury should bear in mind the place and circumstances of the performance, and the nature of the audience, in deciding whether there has been an outrage to public decency. ('A film shown in one place – for example a church fête – might outrage public decency, whereas shown in another place it might not.')[135] The

---

[133] ibid., at p. 444.
[134] *R* v *Quinn & Bloom* [1962] 2 QB 245.
[135] *R* v *Cinecentre Ltd* (Bush J) Birmingham Crown Court, 15 March 1976. See generally Robertson, *Obscenity*, pp. 223–9.

prosecution has to prove that the premises were 'habitually' used for indecent performances, which probably means, in practice, more than twice. In 1991 the landlord of the Wagon and Horses in Rochdale had his conviction quashed because the 'exotic dancers' who had excited beyond endurance a party of seventy women had done so only on one isolated occasion.[136]

Blasphemy

Indecent descriptions applied to sacred subjects may amount to the crime of blasphemy. The offence relates to outrageous comments about God, holy personages, or articles of the Anglican faith, and is constituted by vilification, ridicule or indecency. The intention of the publisher is irrelevant and the words must speak for themselves. Once publication has been proved, the only question remaining for the jury is 'whether the dividing line ... between moderate and reasoned criticism on the one hand and immoderate or offensive treatment of Christianity or sacred subjects on the other, has been crossed'.[137]

There has only been one prosecution for blasphemy since 1922, the controversial case of *Whitehouse* v *Lemon*:[138]

> *Gay News* published a poem about a homosexual's conversion to Christianity, which metaphorically attributed homosexual acts to Jesus Christ. Professor James Kirkup intended to celebrate the universality of God's love; in so doing he referred explicitly to acts of sodomy and fellatio. Leave was obtained for a private prosecution against both editor and publishing company for the offence of blasphemous libel, in that they 'unlawfully and wickedly published or caused to be published a blasphemous libel concerning the Christian religion, namely an obscene poem and illustration vilifying Christ in his life and in his crucifixion'. The jury convicted, by 10 votes to 2, and the House of Lords confirmed by 3–2 the trial judge's ruling that the publisher's intentions were irrelevant, and that there was no need for the prosecution to prove any risk of a breach of the peace.

This decision confirms that blasphemy is no longer a crime of disbelief or irreverence. Attacks upon Christianity, no matter how devastating, will not be blasphemous unless they are expressed in an outrageously indecent or scurrilous manner. Although no evidence may be called about literary merit, the jury may be invited to consider the dominant effect of the work. Moreover, evidence of

---

[136] *Moores* v *DPP* [1991] 4 All ER 521.
[137] *R* v *Lemon and Gay News Ltd* (1978) 67 Cr App 70 at p. 82.
[138] *Whitehouse* v *Lemon* (1978) 68 Cr App R 381.

the place and circumstance of publication would be relevant to the likelihood of public outrage,[139] and evidence as to the character of the readership would be admissible on the issue of whether resentment was likely to be aroused.[140]

The prosecution must lead prima facie evidence that the accused was responsible for the blasphemous publication. The defendants may exculpate themselves by proving that the decision to publish was made without their knowledge and without negligence. This defence is provided by s 7 of the Libel Act 1843, which places the onus on the defendant 'to prove that such publication was made without his authority, consent or knowledge, and that the said publication did not arise from want of due care or caution on his part'. Section 7 will normally protect newspaper proprietors who entrust questions of taste to editorial discretion, although it would also avail an editor who was absent at the time of publication or had delegated responsibility for content to the editors of particular sections or pages.[141]

Newspaper prosecutions must be commenced by leave of a High Court judge under s 8 of the Law of Libel Amendment Act 1888 (see p. 101). A 'newspaper' is defined by the Newspaper Libel and Registration Act 1881 as any paper 'containing public news, intelligence, or occurrences, or any remarks or observations therein', published periodically at intervals not exceeding twenty-six days. For leave to be given:

● there must be a prima facie case so clear as to be 'beyond argument';
● the libel must be very serious. A relevant, but not exclusive, factor in assessing its gravity would be that a breach of the peace might be occasioned by further publication;
● the public interest must require the institution of criminal proceedings.[142]

These principles, enunciated in a case concerning criminal libel, are applicable to proceedings for blasphemous libel under the 1888 Act. In a report on the law of blasphemy in 1986 the Law Commission recognized three fundamental defects:[143]

● Its ambit is so wide that it is impossible to predict in advance whether a particular publication would constitute an offence.

---

[139] *R* v *Boulter* (1908) 72 JP 188.
[140] Transcript of summing up in *R* v *Lemon*, Central Criminal Court 11 July 1977, p. 15.
[141] *R* v *Holbrook (No 1)* (1877) 3 QBD 60; *R* v *Holbrook (No 2)* (1878) 4 QBD 42.
[142] *Goldsmith* v *Pressdram Ltd* [1976] 3 WLR 191.
[143] Law Commission, *Working Paper No 79: Offences Against Religion and Public Worship*, 1981.

- The sincerity of the publisher is irrelevant.
- Blasphemy protects only Anglican beliefs,[144] and the criminal law is not an appropriate vehicle for upholding sectional religious tenets.

Although some have suggested that the law should be extended to protect all religions, the Law Commission despaired of any definition that could draw workable distinctions between Baptists, scientologists, Rastafarians, Anglicans and Moonies.[145] The majority of the Commission concluded that a reformed law of blasphemy would serve no purpose necessary to modern society. The claims of public order, morality and the rights of individuals provide insufficient justification. Its conclusion is reinforced by the absence of prosecutions for blasphemy in England between 1922 and 1977; the withering away of the crime in Scotland (there are no recorded cases since the 1840s, and it is doubtful whether the offence any longer exists); and the demise of prosecutions in Northern Ireland, despite the sectarianism of that most tragic 'plural society'. Apparently, the scope of the offence in Wales is uncertain, as a consequence of the disestablishment of the Welsh Church in 1920.[146]

It is unlikely that the DPP would take action against publications with any literary or artistic value. *Whitehouse* v *Lemon* was a private prosecution brought without official support: its wisdom was much doubted by many Anglicans. No action was taken against the feature film *Monty Python's Life of Brian*, which held sacred subjects up to considerable, if clever, ridicule. However, the very existence of a blasphemy law is calculated to encourage some Christians to believe they can enforce a conventional presentation of sacred themes in the arts. Martin Scorsese's film *The Last Temptation of Christ* led to demands (most notably from the retired *Gay News* trial judge) that its distributors should be prosecuted. While its presentation of Christ's humanity was challenging and unorthodox, the film lacked any element of vilification or scurrility, and on this basis the BBFC classified it as appropriate for screening to adults and the DPP declined to prosecute. None the less, religious activists prevailed on some local councils to use their powers to prevent it from being screened in some parts of the country, and the distributors had no protection against private prosecutions that could have been brought. If they had been, the

---

[144] The difficulties in defining 'religion' are exemplified in the Australian High Court decision that scientology qualifies: *Church of the New Faith* v *Commissioner for Pay-Roll Tax* (1983) 57 ALJR 785.
[145] ibid.
[146] Law Commission, *Working Paper* No 79, p. 32.

defence could not have called evidence as to the film's seriousness of purpose or cinematic merit (there being no 'public good' defence to blasphemy), and the punishment in the event of a conviction could have been an unlimited fine or sentence of imprisonment. The episode reinforces the view that a criminal law that holds a publisher strictly liable for an artistic work liable to shock the Christian on the Clapham omnibus is inappropriate to an age in which the creeds of passengers to Clapham, if they have any, are many and various.

The unfairness of a law that protects only Christian sensibilities was highlighted in 1989 by the outrage felt amongst the Muslim community by the publication of Salman Rushdie's celebrated novel *The Satanic Verses*. This grievance was legitimate only to the extent that Muslims could correctly claim that the blasphemy law in Britain discriminated against their religion. But had it been extended to cover all faiths, Rushdie could have been prosecuted without the right to a literary-merit defence, and without even being given an opportunity to argue that he had no intention to blaspheme. He would have been at risk of conviction merely by proof that the book was likely to outrage and insult believers – which it most certainly did, although much of the 'outrage' seems to have been orchestrated by Muslim activists rather than to have arisen as a spontaneous reaction to reading the work. To punish Rushdie in these circumstances would have been offensive to justice, but no more so than the punishment of the editor of *Gay News*. The Secretary of State for the Home Department responded to Muslim demands for the extension of the blasphemy laws in a considered statement of the Government's position. He stressed 'how inappropriate our legal mechanisms are for dealing with matters of faith and individual belief', remarked that a prosecution of *The Satanic Verses* would be 'damaging and divisive', and noted that 'the Christian faith no longer relies on the law of blasphemy, preferring to recognize that the strength of their own belief is the best armour against mockers and blasphemers'. Although the Government showed no desire to follow through the logic of this position by abolishing the blasphemy law, it is difficult to imagine, in the light of this statement, that it would sanction a public prosecution for blasphemy in the foreseeable future.

The Rushdie affair demonstrated the absurdity of blasphemy law, either as a protection for Christianity or (in an extended and reformed version) as a protection for all religious sensibilities. In 1990 the Archbishop of Canterbury declared in favour of abolishing the law altogether, and the Divisional Court seemed of much the same view after examining it for five days at the behest of Muslims who sought to commit Rushdie and his publishers for trial at the Old Bailey.

The Bow Street magistrate had refused to issue a summons in respect of *The Satanic Verses* on the grounds that the offence of blasphemy protected only the Christian religion. The High Court held that this decision was correct: the early precedents established that the crime was confined to attacks upon the Established Church, so that it appears that other Christian denominations are protected only insofar as their fundamental tenets coincide with those of the Church of England. The court accepted that this was a 'gross anomaly', but the anomaly arose from the 'chains of history', which could be unlocked only by Parliament. Even if the court had power to extend the law to other religions, however, it would refrain from doing so because of the 'insuperable' problems in defining religion, in expecting juries to understand obscure theologies, and because of the danger of divisive and obscurantist prosecutions. The court accepted that 'the existence of an extended law of blasphemy would encourage intolerance, divisiveness and unreasonable interference with freedom of expression', and 'would be likely to do more harm than good'.[147]

The Divisional Court in the *Salman Rushdie* case rejected an argument based on the European Convention, pointing out that to extend the blasphemy law to encompass the author of *The Satanic Verses* would offend against Article 7's prohibition on retrospective criminal offences. The Article 9 guarantee of freedom to manifest religious beliefs did not protect believers against having their beliefs criticized or even ridiculed, and a blasphemy law extended to all religions might well contravene the Article 10 guarantee of freedom of expression. The Divisional Court was a good deal more robust on this point than the European Commission, when it pretended that no issue under the Convention was raised by the blasphemy conviction of *Gay News*.[148] The Commission accepted that this interference with freedom of expression could not be justified by the public interest in preventing disorder or protecting morals, but quite erroneously claimed that it was justified by the public interest in protecting Mrs Whitehouse's right not to have her religious feelings offended by publications. The Commission did not explain this supposed 'right' (which, if it really existed, would be capable of exertion by Muslims offended by *The Satanic Verses*). A much more satisfactory approach is that of the United States Supreme Court in holding unconstitutional the conviction of a Jehovah's Witness for vilifying mainstream Christian religions:

> In the realm of religious faith, and in that of political belief, sharp differences arise. In both fields the tenets of one man may seem the rankest error to his neighbor. To persuade others

---

[147]   *R v Bow Street Magistrates' Court ex parte Choudhury* [1991] 1 All ER 306.
[148]   *Gay News Ltd and Lemon v United Kingdom* [1983] 5 EHRR 123.

to his own point of view, the pleader, as we know, at times resorts to exaggeration, to vilification of men who have been, or are, prominent in church or state, and even to false statement. But the people of this nation have ordained in the light of history, that, in spite of the probability of excesses and abuses, these liberties are, in the long view, essential to enlightened opinion and right conduct on the part of the citizens of a democracy. The essential characteristic of these liberties is, that under their shield many types of life, character, opinion and belief can develop unmolested and unobstructed. Nowhere is this shield more necessary than in our own country for a people composed of many races and of many creeds.[149]

Reform of Obscenity and Indecency Laws

The Williams Committee on Obscenity recommended that all existing obscenity and indecency laws should be swept away, to be replaced by the following system:[150]

- No legal restraint at all should be imposed upon literature or any form of explicit writing. Books and magazines comprising only the written word, or the written word accompanied by inoffensive illustrations, should be available over any public counter and could be freely imported or sent through the post.
- Two narrowly defined strains of pictorial pornography, viz., photographs of indecent activity involving persons under sixteen and photographs in which actual physical harm appears to have been inflicted upon participants in a sexual context, should remain subject to specific prohibition. Trade in and importation although not mere possession of such pictures would carry penalties of up to three years' imprisonment.
- The sale of other pictorial pornography should be restricted to persons over eighteen, either by way of solicited mail order or through shops that do not permit entry to persons under eighteen. These sex shops must not display pornographic wares in a way that makes them visible from public streets, and must exhibit an outside warning to the public of the nature of material sold within and the age restriction on entrance.
- The above restriction would apply to any printed material containing pictures or illustrations 'whose unrestricted availability is offensive to reasonable people by reason of the manner in which it portrays, deals with or relates to violence,

---

[149] *Cantwell* v *Connecticut* 310 US 296 (1940).
[150] *Committee on Obscenity and Film Censorship*, HMSO, 1979 Cmnd 7772.

cruelty or horror, or sexual, faecal or urinary functions or genital organs'.

- It should be an offence, triable only by magistrates and punishable by fines of up to £1,000 and imprisonment for up to six months, to display or to sell 'restricted' material by unsolicited mailings, or to persons under eighteen, or in a shop that fails to observe the rules relating to entrance, window display and advertising.

The Williams Report was not favourably received by the Government on its initial publication, but some of its objectives were achieved by the Indecent Displays (Control) Act, 1981 and by sections of the Local Government (Miscellaneous Provisions) Act of 1982. Section 2 of the latter legislation gives local authorities power to insist that sex shops and cinemas within their jurisdiction be licensed. Although the grant of a licence does not confer an immunity from prosecution for obscenity in relation to material stocked in the shop, it has meant in practice that authorities proceed more cautiously by way of inspection, rather than by seizure. The new licensing system has reduced the outlets for sex magazines and videos, as local councils may decide how many (if any) licences to grant on the basis of the needs and character of the locality in question. A shop will require a licence if it occupies premises

> used for a business which consists to a significant degree of selling, hiring, exchanging, lending, displaying or demonstrating:
> (*a*)   sex articles; or
> (*b*)   other things intended for use in connection with, or for the purpose of stimulating or encouraging –
> (i)   sexual activity; or
> (ii)   acts of force or restraint which are associated with sexual activity.

This section applies only to sex shops: it does not cover the premises used by publishers to prepare and edit magazines or videos that deal with sexual activity. Nor would it cover general newsagencies or bookshops that stock small amounts of 'adult' material – although the concept of 'sex articles' is widely defined to encompass books, magazines, videos, records and films dealing with sexual subjects. The Divisional Court has ruled that the 'significant degree of business' test exempts ordinary newsagents and corner stores whose sales of such items form a part of their turnover.[151] There is no requirement that these items should be

---

[151]   *Lambeth Borough Council* v *Grewal* (1985) *The Times*, 26 November.

'indecent': if they deal with sexual behaviour and their sale is a significant part of the business of the establishment, the shopkeeper will require a local authority licence. It is an offence to operate a sex shop without a licence or to breach a licence condition.[152]

The effects of the legislation have varied from council to council: some have decided not to exercise the powers at all, others have used them to ban sex shops altogether, while most have taken the opportunity to exact large licensing fees, limit the number of shops, and lay down rules that exclude them from residential areas or proximity to schools and churches. Sex-shop operators have suffered, but not all that much: licensing has reduced competition rather than demand, and led to some ingenious avoidance devices, such as selling sex articles through 'Tupperware parties' in private homes and reopening sex shops as 'birth-control centres' which solemnly promote 'items which are manufactured as masturbatory aids as an alternative method of birth control'. The legislation has spawned a great deal of planning litigation and judicial reviews of council decisions, but does not seem to have reduced the national turnover in sexual impedimenta (one million vibrators were reportedly sold each year by one sex-shop chain in the early 1980s). It is interesting that a law that was designed to enable local councils to drive sex shops out of town seems to be working to give them some measure of respectability, as local councillors and council officials up and down the country warm to the task of deciding precisely at what distance from a church one may be permitted to purchase an inflatable rubber doll.

Race Hatred

Freedom of expression entails the right to entertain ideas of any kind, and to express them publicly. The mode or the manner of the expression, however, may properly be regulated in the interests of the freedom of others to go about their business in public without being gratuitously assaulted or defamed, and may properly be curtailed in order to avoid public disorder which may follow provocative dissemination of racist ideas. This was the basis of the first anti-incitement laws, passed in Britain in 1965, after several years of racial violence of the most serious kind, by a Labour Government whose commitment to freedom of speech was weakened after the infamous Smethwick by-election in which a Labour majority evaporated in the face of the slogan, 'If you want a nigger for a neighbour, vote Labour.' This law has been amended

---

[152] The prosecution must first prove the defendant's intention to do so: *Westminster City Council* v *Croyolgrange Ltd* [1986] 2 All ER 353.

on several occasions – the 1986 Public Order Act being the last – in an effort to make convictions easier to obtain. Nevertheless, prosecutions, which can be brought only with the Attorney-General's consent, are comparatively infrequent.

Section 18 of the 1986 Act makes it an offence to use threatening, abusive or insulting words or behaviour with the intent of stirring up racial hatred or in circumstances where racial hatred is likely to be stirred up. Section 19 makes it an offence to publish threatening or abusive or insulting material either with an intention to provoke racial hatred or in circumstances where such hatred is likely to be stirred up by the publication. 'Racial hatred' means hatred against a group defined by colour, race, or national origin, thereby including Jews, Sikhs[153] and Romany gypsies, but excluding Zionists, Muslims and 'gypsies' or travellers in general. The term 'racial group' is not defined by reference to religion, so the Public Order Act offered no assistance to Muslims who claimed that *The Satanic Verses* was designed to stir up hatred against them as a group.

Section 22 of the Public Order Act has been amended by s 164 of the 1990 Broadcasting Act so that the offence of inciting racial hatred may now be committed by the transmission of television or radio programmes. Those vulnerable to prosecution are the television company (including the BBC), the programme producer and the person who is recorded making the incitement. This recent and undesirable change in the law will make it more hazardous to produce programmes about racism, because the offence may be committed irrespective of the producer's intention, if 'having regard to all the circumstances racial hatred is likely to be stirred up'. Current-affairs programme makers must henceforth ensure that racists say nothing that might attract the audience, and are editorially depicted in an unflattering light. The fact that this is generally the case when racists are allowed to speak for themselves may not be sufficient.

The offence can be committed by the public performance of a play (s 20) although a drama's propensity to stir up racial hatred is to be judged with regard to all the circumstances and 'taking the performance as a whole'. Racist abuse heaped on Shylock and Othello by Shakespearian characters is therefore defensible, and there have been no prosecutions of stage plays since the offence first appeared in the Theatres Act of 1968. However, the Royal Court Theatre's cancellation of the play *Perdition* in 1987 after pressure from Jewish interests shows that the question may not be of entirely academic interest in the future.

Further potential for inhibiting free speech is contained in the

---

[153] *Mandla* v *Dowell Lee* [1983] 1 All ER 1062.

offence of possessing racially inflammatory material or recordings with a view to publication in circumstances where racial hatred is likely to be stirred up (s 23). Authors and television researchers who collect such material in order to condemn it will not be at risk, but it might be argued that uncritical displays of Nazi memorabilia or unvarnished publications of 'Hitler diaries' and the like could revive old hatreds. The protection of books of genuine historic interest is provided, not by the words of the Act, but by the need to obtain the Attorney-General's consent to prosecution. It is unfortunate that Parliament did not make s 23 subject to a defence that the play or the publication or collection was in the interests of drama, literature, history or other subjects of general concern.

There are various defences to these charges, generally pivoting upon lack of awareness of the real nature of the speech or writing or lack of any reason to suspect that they would be delivered or disseminated in circumstances where racial hatred would be provoked. If an offence is committed on a television or radio broadcast, the programme contractor and the programme producer and director may be prosecuted as well as the person who has uttered the offensive words. In the case of plays liability is limited to producers and directors, unless an actor commits the offence by an unscheduled departure from the script – in which case he is deemed to be the 'director' of his own impromptu performance. Section 25 of the Public Order Act permits a court to order the forfeiture of any written material or recording that has been used to commit an offence. Section 26 precludes reports of parliamentary proceedings and court reports from becoming the subject matter of a prosecution under the Act.

There is no doubt that the race-hate laws have a potential for punishing the expression of genuine political statements, albeit couched in crude or insulting terminology. This can apply particularly to activists from oppressed minorities, whose rhetoric is designed to jolt what they perceive as white complacency. In Britain the law was used, at least in its first decade of operation, more effectively against Black Power leaders than against white racists. The first person to be gaoled for a race-hatred offence was Michael X, convicted by a white jury in 1967 for some fairly routine black-consciousness rhetoric of the period.[154] Although prosecuting authorities have taken care to avoid creating martyrs, the publicity attendant upon acquittals has been counterproductive. When members of the Racial Preservation Society were acquitted for publishing a newspaper claimed to be 'innocently informative' rather than 'intentionally inflammatory', they derived benefit from

---

[154] *R v Malik* [1968] 1 All ER 582.

the publicity surrounding the trial and reissued the edition, overprinted 'Souvenir Edition – the paper the Government tried to suppress'. There was an increase in this type of quasi-educational racist literature after the acquittal. Similarly, racists were encouraged by the acquittal of a National Front speaker who 'joked' in reference to the murder of an Asian immigrant, 'One down, one million to go'. The danger of such counterproductive consequences has caused the Attorney-General to confine prosecution to the worst cases, and he has in recent years refused to act against racially offensive cartoons published in national newspapers. Vile comic-strips in National Front newspapers, however, have resulted in convictions and prison sentences: the Court of Appeal has encouraged sentences of imprisonment within the statutory maximum of two years, with a period of the sentence suspended in the hope of deterring further offences after release.[155]

The law against inciting racial hatred is, in practice, something of a dead letter. There were only two prosecutions in 1988, one in 1989 and one in 1990, notwithstanding that, in the latter year, the Commission of Racial Equality had referred sixteen cases to the Attorney-General as appropriate for punishment. Most complaints of racial incitement never reach the Attorney-General: they are dismissed by local police or Crown Prosecution Service lawyers. In an effort to make prosecution easier still, the Malicious Communications Act was passed in 1988, making it a summary offence to send letters or other articles containing 'indecent' or 'grossly offensive' messages, or malicious threats, or information known by the sender to be false, for the purpose of causing distress and anxiety to the recipient.

In 1991 two prosecutions were brought: of a Cheltenham Conservative who had described the black candidate foisted on the local constituency party by Central Office as a 'nigger' (the defendant died before his trial) and of the Dowager Lady Birdwood, an elderly and obsessive racist. Birdwood made the mistake of defending herself, and was quickly discredited and convicted by a young-ish Old Bailey jury for distributing anti-Semitic pamphlets. Her judge, Brian Capstick QC, wisely declined to make her a martyr. He granted her a conditional discharge and ordered her to pay the prosecution costs. In these circumstances nobody (except Bernard Levin) bothered to complain about the infringement of her freedom of speech.

The common-law offence of seditious libel can be committed by 'promoting ill-will and hostility between different classes of Her

---

[155] See *R* v *Edwards* (1983) 5 Cr App R; (S) 145; *R* v *Morse & Tyndall* (1986) 8 Cr App R; s 369.

Majesty's subjects'. In *R* v *Caunt* [156] the editor of *The Morecambe and Heysham Visitor* faced this charge for suggesting that violence against British Jews might be the only way of stemming Zionist terrorists' activities against British forces in Palestine. He was acquitted. The statutory offences have effectively superseded this aspect of sedition.

In 1990 the Divisional Court held that an attempt to prosecute the author and publisher of *The Satanic Verses* for sedition was misconceived. The allegation that publication of the book was calculated to create hostility between Muslims and other classes of citizens was, even if true, insufficient to constitute the offence: there had to be proof of incitement to violence against the State.[157]

The court also rejected an attempt to prosecute the publisher, Penguin Books, under s 4 of the Public Order Act, for provoking unlawful violence by distributing the books to shops that later suffered bomb attacks. Even if the book's contents could be described as 'threatening, abusive or insulting' for the purposes of s 4, that section required that the unlawful violence should be the direct and immediate result of the publication of the insulting words. The act of distributing a book to retail outlets cannot sensibly be regarded as the immediate and direct cause of unlawful violence to which the bookseller may later be subjected by terrorists or fanatics.[158]

---

[156] Wade (1948) 64 LQR 203. See also Caunt, *An Editor on Trial*, privately published, 1947.
[157] *R* v *Bow Street Magistrates' Court ex parte Choudhury*, note 147 above.
[158] *R* v *Horseferry Road Justices ex parte Siadatan* [1991] 1 All ER 324.

Chapter 4

Confidence and Privacy

The laws that protect individuals and organizations against unfair exploitation of their original work may seem at first to carry little threat to investigative journalism. The purpose, after all, of in-depth media reporting is not to deny others the commercial benefits of their labours, but to alert the public to developments that are newsworthy and that deserve a wider audience. Publishers are, of course, running a business, and scoops may help to build circulation, but it is doubtful whether the profits that accrue to them from investigative journalism compete in any meaningful sense with the profits of the organizations investigated. None the less, in recent years the courts have permitted forms of action designed primarily to stop unfair competition and commercial piracy to be used at the behest of those concerned to avoid the embarrassment of revelations about their private behaviour or their internal organizational plans. Information has become property, something that can be bought and sold, injuncted and embargoed, almost irrespective of its significance to political debate or current public policy. The laws that permit injunctions and damages for breaches of confidence and copyright are powerful weapons against media use of information supplied by 'moles', 'whistle blowers' and others who leak secrets from within organizations. This chapter will examine the defences that the media can raise, on behalf of its public, to dissemination of information secretly extracted from those who are unwilling to part with it.

The plaintiff in an action to stop a publication on grounds of confidence is claiming a right to protect privacy, or at least private property. The court must be persuaded that the public interest requires the confidence to be preserved. This is not difficult for individuals and private organizations, whose expectation of privacy is itself a public interest prima facie meriting protection. It is not sufficient, though, for the government or public bodies to plead embarrassment: they must positively demonstrate the public harm that would follow disclosure. Whoever the plaintiff, the law recognizes that the claim to confidence cannot be absolute and that there will be cases where it is outweighed by the public interest in disclosure. The courts are fond of reminding media defendants that not everything of interest to the public is in the public interest: there is a distinction between stories that appeal merely to prurient or morbid curiosity and those that contribute new and useful information to public debate.

There is also in this area a greater willingness to grant an interim injunction, suppressing publication until trial. This means that plaintiffs will, wherever possible, choose to rely on these doctrines as a pretext for stopping articles and broadcasts that they fear because of criticism contained in them. It is anomalous that Blackstone's rule against prior restraint, soundly embedded in libel law, should be precarious when the case comes within a different legal category. The courts argue that damages can compensate for an unjustified libel, whereas a secret once published cannot be made confidential again.[1] But the danger of injunctions covering up iniquitous behaviour is demonstrated by the fact that six months before Robert Maxwell's corporate villainy came to light on his death, he was able to obtain injunctions preventing the press from publishing any suggestion that his companies had indulged in 'dubious accounting devices' or had 'sought to mislead . . . as to the value of the assets of the company'. The media were even banned from reporting the fact that this order had been made.

The impact of an 'interim injunction' is in practice 'permanent' rather than 'interim'. It amounts to an order suppressing any publication of the information until trial of the action, which may not take place for a year or so. By that time the information may be stale news or have been overtaken by events. Thus media organizations that lose the argument at the interim stage rarely bother to renew it at a trial – and in such cases 'prior restraint' means permanent restraint.

Breach of confidence is a civil remedy affording protection against the disclosure or use of information that is not publicly known, and that has been entrusted in circumstances imposing an obligation not to disclose that information without the authority of the person who has imparted it. Whenever a journalist acquires information that is 'secret', in the sense that the source from which it is generated has taken steps to restrict its circulation, the first question to be asked is whether an obligation of confidence exists in relation to its use. If it does, the further question arises as to whether, notwithstanding that it is the subject of confidence, it may be published because of its public importance. There will usually be a third question of overriding practical importance: can it be published without the danger of an injunction? These matters will be considered in turn.

'Privacy' is not a right that the law recognizes as such. There are periodic attempts by private members to introduce a statutory

---

[1] See *Lion Laboratories Ltd* v *Evans* [1984] 2 All ER 417, 433.

right to privacy when Fleet Street's excesses plumb new depths. The problem is to find a satisfactory test for distinguishing unwarranted intrusions on private lives while allowing the investigation of stories of real public interest. Despite the absence of this comprehensive right, privacy can sometimes be indirectly protected by actions for trespass, copyright and data protection. But there is growing judicial support for developing the law of breach of confidence to provide a remedy for invasion of privacy by the press. The public hostility to 'chequebook journalism' and 'kiss and tell' stories is reflected in the increasing confidence with which judges slap injunctions on 'exclusives' about celebrities and members of the royal family. Many of the recent cases discussed in this chapter can be explained as decisions in support of the right to be left alone, or at least the right not to be embarrassed by the publication of details about private life sold to the media by disloyal or disenchanted friends or retainers. The Press Council issued 'declarations on privacy', which were honoured more in the breach than the observance, and the privacy protection clauses in the NUJ's code of conduct and the recent Code of Ethics promulgated by national newspaper editors have no effective enforcement machinery. In 1990 a Home Office committee chaired by David Calcutt QC reported that self-regulation in this area had failed abjectly. Legislation to protect privacy is on the cards, if not yet on the statute books, and in the meantime it can be expected that courts will increasingly grant 'interim injunctions' for breach of confidence against anticipated publication of private information. Where such information is of genuine public importance, the media will be well-advised to keep details of publication secret until the very last moment. The device used by *The Sunday Times* to avoid a government injunction on its *Spycatcher* serialization by publishing its first edition as a 'dummy' without any reference to the story may be an expedient that will be deployed again.

The Obligation of Confidence

Information cannot be embargoed simply because it is contained in a document stamped 'confidential', or because its original possessors do not wish it to see the light of day. There must be some existing and enforceable legal relationship that purports to restrict publication. The fact that reprehensible methods have been used to obtain the information does not necessarily mean its subsequent use can be stopped. The courts have held that it is not normally a

---

[2] *Oxford* v *Moss* (1978) 68 Cr App R 183.

criminal offence to steal information,[2] and computer 'hacking' was not a crime until made so in, 1990 by the Computer Misuse Act.[3] The owner of stolen documents will not always be able to prevent the publication of information contained in them. In 1988 a Crown Court recorder was refused an injunction to prevent the *Sun* from publishing letters that had been stolen from his homosexual lover.[4] In *Malone* v *Metropolitan Police Commissioner (No 2)*, Vice-Chancellor Megarry said that information obtained from telephone tapping could not be stopped on grounds of confidence because those using the telephone had to take the risk that their conversations might be overheard.[5] However, he specifically confined his decision to tapping by the Government under a Home Secretary's warrant, a situation that is now governed by the Interception of Communications Act 1985 (see p. 434). Private tapping of telephones is an offence[6] and in *Francome* v *Mirror Group Newspapers Ltd*[7] the Court of Appeal held that there was an arguable case that the telephone user could sue the illegal interceptor either for breach of confidence or for breach of statutory duty:

> The *Daily Mirror* was restrained from publishing details of private telephone taps, made in contravention of the Wireless Telegraphy Act, which allegedly revealed breaches of the rules of racing by a well-known jockey. The Master of the Rolls accepted that the media could defend publications in breach of confidence that revealed illegal or 'anti-social' conduct (including 'activities which are seriously contrary to the public interest'), but described the editor's assertion of a right to decide for himself whether to comply with the law as 'arrogant and wholly unacceptable'. Although the courts would seek to avoid a clash between the law and an editor's 'moral imperative' to publish a public-interest story, such occasions were rare, especially in the case of a newspaper with a commercial interest in exposure, where the editor could safeguard the public interest by handing tapes over to the police or the Jockey Club for further investigation. The *Daily Mirror* could not publish extracts from the illegal recordings, although it was free to make its allegations against Francome in bold terms, and use the telephone taps in its defence if sued for libel.

---

[3] *R* v *Gold and Schifreen* [1988] AC 1063.
[4] The Law Commission concluded in its report *Breach of Confidence*, Report No 110, HMSO 8388, 1981, para 4.9 that publication of stolen information probably could not be prevented in England although there is a comment in the English Court of Appeal (*Lord Ashburton* v *Pape* [1913] 2 Ch 469 at p. 475) and an Australian decision (*Franklin* v *Giddins* [1978] Qd R 72) to the contrary. The House of Lords in *Re Goodwin* had little hesitation in ordering a journalist to disclose the name of a source who was assumed to have provided him with confidential information from a stolen document – see p. 200.
[5] [1979] 2 All ER 620, 646.
[6] Interception of Communications Act 1985 s 1.
[7] [1984] 2 All ER 408, CA.

If a newspaper acquires information by its own covert yet lawful activities, such as snooping or eavesdropping, it breaks no confidential relationship and the person whose privacy it has invaded will not have grounds for stopping publication. *The Sunday Times* Insight investigation into Dr Savundra's fraudulent Fire Auto Marine Insurance Company only succeeded because a journalist copied a crucial list of shareholders on an accountant's desk while the owner was out of the room.[8] In December 1982 the BBC broadcast a film taken secretly in the Savoy Hotel, purporting to show a barman pouring short-measure drinks. The Savoy's application for an injunction was rejected.[9]

The most common forms of relationship that are impressed by a duty of confidence are contractual, domestic, governmental and legal.

Contractual relationships

The first matter to be considered by a media organization when information is offered or obtained from an employee is not the civil law of confidence but the criminal provisions of the Prevention of Corruption Act 1906. It is an offence to offer an incentive or reward to any employee for doing any act in relation to his principal's business. These laws against bribery and corruption may in some circumstances 'catch' (i.e., apply to) payments to informers. The media are protected by the requirement that any payment must be proved to have been made 'corruptly' – a jury would doubtless acquit if the payment was necessary to extract information that revealed a public scandal. Payments to ex-employees are not caught so long as they were not promised prior to resignation, and a genuine consultancy fee would not be legally objectionable.

> In 1987 the *Observer* was prosecuted at the Old Bailey for an offence under the Prevention of Corruption Act. It had paid £10,000 to an employee of the Ministry of Defence for documents and information revealing that millions of pounds of public money had been lost through mismanagement and failure to supervise defence contractors. The employee had been gaoled at an earlier trial for corruptly accepting a bribe from the *Observer*, but the newspaper was acquitted of offering the money corruptly. The newspaper's editor and senior

---

[8] Hobson, Knightley and Russell, *The Pearl of Days: An Intimate Memoir of The Sunday Times 1882–1972*, Hamish Hamilton, 1972, p. 424. The authors claim this investigation was the first of a complicated business matter to have been given mass-reader appeal.

[9] *Savoy Hotel PLC* v *BBC* (1983) 133 NLJ 1100, overturning the decision of Comyn J: (1982) 133 NLJ 105.

journalists explained that they had been led to believe that the employee had resigned his office before they paid him for acting as a consultant. This case demonstrates the importance of bearing the Prevention of Corruption Act in mind before any payment is made to a source.

Employment and consultancy contracts generally have 'secrecy' clauses in which employers and advisers undertake to keep information acquired in the course of the relationship to themselves. Even without a specific clause, the courts will imply an undertaking that information given in confidence to the employee will not be used to the employer's detriment.[10] This does not cover everything that employees learn in the course of their business. 'Trivial tittle-tattle',[11] embarrassing *faux pas* or personal mannerisms of colleagues and superiors[12] are not usually within this duty of confidence.

Where there is a clear contractual promise to keep matters confidential – e.g., not to publish or broadcast anything learnt or witnessed during employment – the courts are prepared to grant injunctions to enforce the promise. Thus when a former royal servant breached the secrecy clause in his employment contract by writing a book, aptly titled *Courting Disaster*, the Court of Appeal issued an injunction to stop him from publishing it anywhere in the world. The clause was not limited in territory or time, and the court saw no reason of a public-policy nature not to force the defendant to honour an agreement he had voluntarily made in return for employment. The court did accept that an unlimited covenant might, in some cases, be attacked for obscurity or illegality or on public policy grounds, such as being in restraint of trade.[13] The author of *Courting Disaster* made no claim that the publication of his book would serve any public interest, either in Britain or abroad. Had there been a significant public interest in the

---

[10] *Faccenda Chicken* v *Fowler* [1987] Ch 117, CA. The need for 'detriment' is controversial. The prevailing view in *A-G* v *Guardian Newspapers Ltd (No 2)* [1988] 3 All ER 545 was that if detriment was needed, there might be sufficient for private litigants in the unwanted disclosure of confidential information; but the Government did have to show some harm to the public interest if disclosure took place.

[11] *Coco* v *AN Clark Engineers Ltd* [1968] FSR 415.

[12] *GD Searle & Co* v *Celltech* [1982] FSR 92, CA.

[13] *A-G* v *Barker* [1990] 3 All ER 257. The United States Supreme Court would not permit an injunction to be granted in such a situation, on prior restraint principles, but it might impose a 'constructive trust' so that royalties from the book went to the employer: *Snepp* v *US* 444 US 507 (1980). If Barker's book had been published in the United States, it would seem (from the European Court decision in *Spycatcher*) that prior restraint on its publication in Britain would be an infringement of Article 10. The publishers could, however, be sued for heavy damages for inducing a breach of contract.

publication of the book, it is submitted that this would serve as a defence to a breach of contract action based on a confidentiality covenant, just as it would if the action had been directly for breach of confidence.

The duty to respect the confidence is impressed as well on a newspaper that knows or must suspect that its source acquired the information in confidence. When Granada Television obtained secret documents from a mole at British Steel, it knew that the papers were not intended to go beyond senior officials of the company. Since the documents were labelled 'confidential' and 'restricted', the position would have been the same if they had been sent anonymously through the post.[14] But there is no magic in a 'confidential' label and if there is some other sign that despite this heading, they had been given wider publicity, a newspaper can make use of them.[15] Conversely, even without such a warning, a paper must take care over documents whose contents are manifestly for a restricted audience.

For the most part, the rush to court for an order to 'deliver up' confidential documents is simply closing the gate after the horse has bolted. The media organization that has obtained the confidential documents will already have published the most interesting aspects of them, and often an approach to the court will do no more than verify their authenticity in the public mind. However, journalists should be aware of the danger that an order for 'delivery up' may pose to their source – if, for example, the documents are a numbered copy, if a name has been underlined in a distribution list, if the source has added handwritten comments or if they are likely to carry the source's fingerprints. Copies produced by a word processor may have deliberate minor differences to identify them. This is, apparently, a favourite technique for keeping track of high-level government documents. The *Guardian* newspaper signally failed to protect its source when it disclosed to the Treasury Solicitor the existence of identifying marks on a secret document prior to the commencement of a court action at a time when it was unlikely to have incurred any legal penalty by simply destroying them. Granada Television, more sensibly, took care to excise tell-tale signs from its copies of British Steel documents before returning them. Protecting sources by destroying or mutilating documents they have provided can make the media organization liable for contempt charges if an order for delivery up of these documents has already been made. This problem should not arise if destruction takes place before a court order, but in such

---

[14] *BSC* v *Granada Television Ltd* [1981] 1 All ER 417.
[15] *Dunsford and Elliott Ltd* v *Johnson & Firth Brown Ltd* [1977] 1 Lloyds Rep 505.

a case a public-interest defence might be harder to prove.[16] Since the only physical damage suffered is the replacement cost of the paper, it will add little to the plaintiff's claim. (See further 'Protection of Sources', pp. 196–209). Journalists should be aware that it is a criminal offence dishonestly to destroy the original of a government document.[17]

Authors and programme makers should be cautious about entering into service contracts with organizations that they may later wish to criticize:

> Television-programme maker David Elstein was hired by Schering Chemicals to tutor its executives in how to cope with media interviews on the subject of Primodos, a pregnancy drug that had turned out to have dangerous side-effects. Elstein was paid £200 a day for conducting the three-day course. It gave him the idea of making a programme about the drug, which he subsequently produced for Thames Television. He took care to avoid using any of the confidential information he had acquired during his consultancy. However, the majority in the Court of Appeal injuncted *The Primodos Affair* on the grounds that Elstein had entered upon a personal confidential obligation to Scherings, which he had betrayed by making the programme. Although he did not use confidential information, he had unfairly exploited his confidential relationship with Scherings by accepting further payment from Thames to make a programme about them.[18]

The decision in *Schering Chemicals* is incompatible with the European Convention, and has been criticized on other grounds by the Law Commission.[19] Thames Television, lamentably, did not appeal it. However, the authority of the case can be narrowed so that it applies only to persons in Elstein's special position of divided loyalty. The court was heavily influenced by what it termed the 'treachery' of a man who had been hired to help foster the company's image and then been paid for producing a programme that was critical of the same company's record. Had he instead passed the idea and information to another producer without taking any payment, the position would have been different.

Domestic relationships

Although there is no substantive law protecting personal privacy in Britain, some veil of secrecy may be drawn over domestic intimacy by the doctrine of breach of confidence, which can stop the betrayal

---

[16] *BSC* v *Granada Television Ltd*, note 14 above, at pp. 439, 442.
[17] Theft Act 1968, s 20.
[18] *Schering Chemicals Ltd* v *Falkman Ltd* [1981] 2 All ER 321.
[19] Law Commission, *Breach of Confidence*, at paras 6.67–9.

by one party of the secrets of a marriage. In 1967 a newspaper was stopped from publishing the Duke of Argyll's account of his stormy marriage with the Duchess.[20] The decision was expressed to cover *communications* between husband and wife pursuant to 'the normal confidence and trust' that is judicially assumed to exist in marriage. The *Argyll* decision has been cited with approval in several subsequent cases. However, the courts would be unlikely to stop an autobiography by one partner published some years after the relationship had ended. (The Duke of Argyll's revelations were touted for publication in the immediate aftermath of a bitter divorce, and the court's decision was influenced by the fact that they contained items of evidence that could not have been reported.) The Prince of Wales obtained an *ex parte* injunction against the publication of purported tape recordings of his conversations with his bride-to-be, Lady Diana. This accords with *Francome*'s case (see p. 175) in which a well-known jockey was able to restrain publication of information obtained from illegal taps on his telephone. The relationship need not be marital or even heterosexual:

> Ms Stephens had a lesbian affair with a woman who was subsequently killed by her husband. She talked about it to Ms Avery, another close friend, who passed on the confidences to the *Mail on Sunday*, which published a story. The newspaper attempted to strike out Ms Stephens' claim for damages for breach of confidence on the grounds that the lesbian relationship was immoral and information relating to it should not be protected. It also argued that since Ms Stephens and Ms Avery were merely friends, there was nothing in their relationship to attract a duty of confidence. The judge did not have to decide which party would finally succeed, but he rejected the newspaper's claim that there was no case to be tried. He accepted the principle that the court would not protect a confidence relating to matters with a grossly immoral tendency, but in the late 1980s there was no consensus over what, if any, kind of consensual sexual conduct between adults was grossly immoral. The courts would enforce confidences even between friends.[21]

In *Spycatcher (No 2)* Lord Keith said 'The right to personal privacy is clearly one which the law should in this field seek to protect.' He gave the example of an anonymous donor of a very large sum to a worthy cause. Such a person ought to be able to restrain a breach of confidence in his identity in connection with the donation.[22]

---

[20] *Argyll* v *Argyll* [1967] Ch 302.
[21] *Stephens* v *Avery* [1988] 2 All ER 477.
[22] *A-G* v *Guardian Newspapers Ltd (No 2)*, note 10 above, at pp. 639–40.

A limitation on *Argyll* was imposed when the late John Lennon was denied an injunction to stop publication of his ex-wife's memoirs about their marriage. Both had already written and talked in public about the relationship, so the singer was unable to show that the information was still confidential.[23]

Government confidences

The Official Secrets Acts place restrictions on civil servants leaking information to the press, although Cabinet Ministers will almost always be able to authorize themselves to discuss matters with the media. However, in 1975 the Attorney-General invoked the civil law of confidence to try to stop publication of Richard Crossman's memoirs. The Lord Chief Justice agreed that public secrets could be restrained but the court had to be satisfied that restriction was in the public interest. Cabinet discussions come within this category and could be protected, but not forever. It is not the case that 'once a confidence, always a confidence'. Stale secrets will not be protected and the Crossman memoirs were not injuncted because they related to confidential meetings that took place at least ten years prior to publication.[24] Outside the context of the Cabinet room, it will be hard for the Government to show the necessary public interest in suppression, unless national security is involved. The Australian High Court has refused to accept that its Foreign Minister could stop the publication of diplomatic cables between the Australian Embassy in Djakarta and Canberra on grounds of breach of confidence when no security secrets were revealed and their potential for embarrassment was insufficient to warrant an injunction:

> It is unacceptable in our democratic society that there should be a restraint on the publication of information relating to government when the only vice of that information is that it enables the public to discuss, review and criticize government action. Accordingly, the court will determine the Government's claim to confidentiality by reference to the public interest. Unless disclosure is likely to injure the public interest, it will not be protected. The court will not prevent the publication of information which merely throws light on the past workings of government, even if it be not public property, so long as it does not prejudice the community in other respects. Then disclosure will itself serve the public interest in keeping

---

[23] *Lennon* v *News Group Newspapers and Twist* [1978] FSR 573.
[24] *A-G* v *Jonathan Cape Ltd* [1976] QB 752. See Hugo Young, *The Crossman Affair*, Hamish Hamilton and Jonathan Cape, 1976.

the community informed and in promoting discussion of public affairs. If, however, it appears that disclosure will be inimical to the public interest because national security, relations with foreign countries or the ordinary business of government will be prejudiced, disclosure will be restrained.[25]

This principle was the key to the media's ultimate success in the English litigation over *Spycatcher*:

> The *Guardian* and *Observer* published the main allegations in Peter Wright's book *Spycatcher* at the time when the book was the subject of confidentiality proceedings in Australia. On the eve of publication of the book in the United States, *The Sunday Times* began to serialize it. All were injuncted in England from publishing any further matter from the book until a trial could take place in this country. This injunction was upheld by the House of Lords (see p. 192). In the meantime the book, having been published in the United States, became an international best-seller. The newspapers continued to defend their right to publish at the trial and in the subsequent appeals. They successfully opposed the grant of a permanent injunction. The House of Lords accepted that Peter Wright, like other members and former members of the security services, was under a life-long duty to keep confidential any information he learnt in the course of his work. However, the Lords endorsed the views of the Australian High Court (which are quoted above). The Government, unlike private individuals and organizations, had to show that the public interest would be harmed by publication. Because of the widespread dissemination of the book's contents, the Attorney-General could not do that and the injunction against all the newspapers came to an end. The *Observer* and *Guardian* articles had contained nothing damaging to the public interest and so they did not have to compensate the Government for the stories they had already published. But *The Sunday Times* had jumped the gun and its instalment had included material from *Spycatcher* that had not been published elsewhere previously. It did not help the paper that publication of the whole book in the United States followed days later: it had deliberately engineered a profitable scoop and had to account to the Government for the profits it made by the increase in its circulation.[26]

In 1991 the European Court of Human Rights unanimously ruled that the injunctions upheld by the English courts *after* *Spycatcher* had been published abroad were an infringement of Article 10. Widespread foreign publication had destroyed all claim to confidentiality, and the Government's case had undergone a

---

[25] *Commonwealth of Australia* v *John Fairfax Ltd* (1981) 32 ALR 485. For similar sentiments of US courts see *New York Times* v *US* 403 US 713 (1971).
[26] *A-G* v *Guardian Newspapers Ltd (No 2)*, see note 10 above.

'curious metamorphosis' as a result, using the same language ('the interests of national security') to disguise its real objective, in the post-publication period, of protecting the security service from embarrassment in Britain and deterring its past and present members who might be minded to follow in Wright's footsteps. This was not sufficient reason to bring into play the national security exception to Article 10's freedom of expression guarantee. The Court narrowly held (by fourteen votes to ten) that the Government had been entitled to seek an injunction on national security grounds prior to publication abroad, because of the risk that the book might contain material damaging to the intelligence services.[27]

Documents subject to discovery

The process of discovery, whereby one party to litigation is obliged to disclose private documents relevant to the case, is protected both by the laws of contempt of court and of breach of confidence. A barrister, solicitor or litigant who discloses such documents to the media may be punished for contempt and the media may be restrained from publishing their contents by an injunction for breach of confidence. *The Sunday Times* obtained some of its information about the process of thalidomide manufacture by purchasing documents disclosed by Distillers to an expert witness. Despite the obvious public interest in the matter, the court granted the injunction on the basis that a greater public interest in the proper administration of justice required it to protect the confidentiality of the process of document-discovery.[28]

Public-interest Defence

The media are justified in publishing information in breach of confidence if the public interest in doing so outweighs the public interest in preserving the confidence. This defence originated from the more narrow rule that the courts would not restrain the disclosure of iniquity:[29]

> John McVicar agreed to write a book with Mr Cork, a former police-man, about corruption in the Metropolitan Police. Cork was to have the right to approve the manuscript before publication. In some of his conversations with McVicar he asked the writer to turn off his tape-recorder so as to speak in confidence. Unknown to Cork,

---

[27] *Observer and Guardian* v *UK*, ECHR Strasbourg, 26 November 1991, paras 61–9.
[28] *Distillers Co (Biochemicals) Ltd* v *Times Newspapers Ltd* [1975] QB 613.
[29] *Gartside* v *Outram* (1856) 26 LJ Ch 113, p. 130.

McVicar had a second machine taped to his leg, which continued to record after the open machine had been switched off. Cork never approved the manuscript, but the *Daily Express* wished to publish his allegations of corruption. The publication was undoubtedly in breach of confidence and in breach of contract, but the judge accepted that the corruption was properly a matter of public interest.[30]

Mr Justice Scott said: 'Newspapers had many functions and practices, some more attractive than others, but one function was to provide a means whereby corruption might be exposed. That could rarely be done without informers and often breaches of confidence.'

In other cases the courts held that the wrongdoing alleged did not have to amount to a crime to justify publication. They began to formulate the defence more widely than 'iniquity' and developed a general principle of balancing the public interest in disclosure against the public interest in preserving confidence.

> The sales manager of a large laundry firm resigned and took some of the firm's documents to a newspaper, which used them to allege that the firm was engaging in monopolistic practices and evading tax. The Court of Appeal held that this was misconduct of a kind that disentitled the firm to injunct the newspaper article. The defence extended beyond proof of crime or fraud to 'any misconduct of such a nature that it ought in the public interest to be disclosed to others'.[31]

> An author of a book about scientology described courses offered by that organization, and certain of its practices, based upon information he had obtained in breach of confidence. The Court of Appeal refused an injunction: 'There is good ground for thinking that these courses contain such dangerous material that it is in the public interest that it should be made known.'[32]

> The public relations officer employed by singer Tom Jones sold his memoirs to a newspaper, which began to publish them under the rubric 'Tom Jones Superstud. More Startling Secrets of the Family'. The court refused an injunction, because the article revealed hypocrisy:

> > If a group of this kind seek publicity which is to their advantage ... they cannot complain if a servant or employee of theirs afterwards discloses the truth about them. If the image which they fostered was not a true image, it is in the public interest that it should be corrected ... it is a question of balancing the public interest in maintaining the confidence

---

[30] *Cork* v *McVicar* (1985) *The Times*, 31 October.
[31] *Initial Services Ltd* v *Putterill* [1968] 1 QB 396.
[32] *Hubbard* v *Vosper* [1972] 1 All ER 1023.

against the public interest in knowing the truth . . . The public should not be misled.[33]

In the important case of *Lion Laboratories* v *Evans and Express Newspapers* the Court of Appeal unequivocally ruled that the public-interest defence to an action for breach of confidence and copyright was not limited to situations where there had been serious wrongdoing by the plaintiff. If the media could produce evidence to show that the public had a serious and legitimate interest in the revelation, then publication was excusable even if the plaintiff's behaviour could not be criticized. Thus the *Daily Express* was permitted to publish internal documents extracted from the manufacturer of the intoximeter that revealed doubts about the efficacy of a machine being used by police to obtain convictions to convict for drink-driving offences. Although no 'iniquity' attached to the plaintiff, the possibility of wrongful convictions raised a matter of vital public interest.[34]

The House of Lords in the second *Spycatcher* appeal has authoritatively confirmed that this is the correct approach.[35] Peter Wright did indeed make allegations of serious wrongdoing by the security services, including an assassination attempt on Colonel Nasser and an MI5 plot to destabilize the Labour Government of Harold Wilson. However, these occupied a relatively small part of the book and if *Spycatcher* had not been published abroad, the media may not have been able to show a public interest sufficiently compelling to justify publication in Britain of Wright's descriptions of his life in MI5 and his suspicions about fellow members of the service.

What the courts have decided in the cases culminating with *Spycatcher* and the *Cavendish Memoirs* in the House of Lords is that in every case where public interest is raised as a defence, the court (both at the 'interim injunction' stage and more fully at the trial) must perform a balancing exercise by deciding whether the beneficial effects of publication outweigh the damage that may be caused both to the plaintiff and to the public. It is public interests rather than private interests that must be considered, although the private interest of the plaintiff is dressed up as a public interest by the judicial assumption that there is a general public interest that confidences should be respected. This formula operates in practice

---

[33] *Woodward* v *Hutchins* [1977] 2 All ER 751.
[34] *Lion Laboratories* v *Evans and Express Newspapers* [1985] QB 526.
[35] [1988] 3 All ER p. 649 (Lord Griffiths), p. 659 (Lord Goff). See also *BSC* v *Granada*, note 14 above, where the point was not argued but Lords Fraser and Salmon (the latter in a dissenting judgment) approved the 'balance of public interests' approach: see pp. 468 and 472.

to allow the court (i.e., the judges) to produce an outcome influenced by subjective appreciation of the evidence. The decision will be based on the value judgement of the judge rather than any precise legal rule. In many cases such value judgements will reflect public attitudes – especially where the media are stopped from publishing details extracted by chequebook journalism about the private lives of popular plaintiffs such as television presenters and members of the royal family. The judge's sense of fair play, however, will protect the privacy of some whom the majority might wish to oppress, such as Myra Hindley (the *Sun* was injuncted from publishing her parole request) and persons suffering from AIDS. The unsatisfactory cases are those where judicial attitudes reflect the conditioning of class or professional life, leading to an appreciation of public interest that cannot be objectively supported. Only a lawyer, for example, could so highly value the process of discovery as to accord its confidentiality a status that outweighed the revelation of reasons for the thalidomide tragedy or the benefits of supplying journalists with documents that have been read in open court.[36] One perennial problem is to convince judges that a corporate plaintiff's right to privacy in respect to documents that reveal secret operations should not prevail over the public benefit of knowing about the questionable activities of powerful corporations. The problem is to find acceptance for the principle that the right to impart and receive important information outweighs any rights of property in that information.

The Court of Appeal in *Lion Laboratories* made other important comments on the public-interest defence. It repeated the distinction between matters that were in the public interest and those that were merely interesting to the public (like many epigrams, its superficial simplicity conceals great difficulties in application). It warned the press of the danger of confusing the public interest with its own interests in increasing sales from sensational exposures. It also indicated that the *degree* of disclosure had to be justified in the public interest. The Court of Appeal made the same point in the *Francome* case. Assuming that the telephone taps did indicate breaches of Jockey Club regulations, this might justify disclosure to the Jockey Club or the police, but not to the world at large. Lord Griffiths in *Spycatcher (No 2)* similarly said that a person who came across confidential information of misdeeds by the security services might be entitled to tell the proper authorities, but not necessarily to publish it to the world.[37] Again, these propositions defy rational explanation. If the *Daily Mirror* was obliged to

---

[36] *Distillers (Biochemicals) Ltd* v *Times Newspapers Ltd* [1975] QB 613 and *Home Office* v *Harman* [1983] AC 280.

[37] [1988] 3 All ER at p. 657.

send the Francome tapes to the police, why not oblige the *Daily Express* to forward its documentary evidence to the Home Office, which was responsible for approving the intoximeter? The court accepted that the *Express* was entitled to take the view that publication would put more pressure on the department than a 'discreet behind-the-doors approach'. A campaign of public pressure on authority was 'an essential function of a free press, and we would all be the worse off if the press was unduly inhibited in this field'.[38] Except, it would seem, if the campaign concerns the security services.

Essentially the balance has to be struck in the light of the circumstances of each individual case. *Spycatcher* was a rare occasion when the press persevered and, having been injuncted before trial, carried on to a full hearing, by which time the balance (tipped by publication abroad) came down in its favour. One case where the balance clearly tipped the other way concerned the revelation of medical records:

> A newspaper paid £100 to employees of a health authority for details of two doctors who had been identified as having AIDS. The paper published one story saying that there were doctors continuing to practise although they had AIDS and that the Department of Health and Social Security wished to conceal the fact. A second article intended to name the doctors. The health authority obtained an interim injunction. At the trial the judge found that the public interest in protecting confidentiality of patients generally and AIDS patients in particular (because they might not otherwise identify themselves) outweighed the public interest in publication. The health authority had done no wrong and the injunction did not stop the debate about AIDS or whether doctors with the disease should continue to practise.[39]

The prevalence of references to public interest may be confusing. The wider and now accepted formulation of the defence is available to the media to justify publication once the plaintiff has made out a case for an injunction. However, in order to make out that case when the plaintiff is the Government or a public body, it has to be shown that an injunction would positively be in the public interest. This preliminary hurdle was too high for the Attorney-General in *Spycatcher* (because the book had been widely published overseas), as it had been for his predecessor in the *Crossman Diaries* case (because the Cabinet 'secrets' were old hat).[40]

---

[38] [1984] 2 All ER 434–5.
[39] *X* v *Y* [1988] 2 All ER 648.
[40] *A-G* v *Jonathan Cape Ltd* [1975] 3 All ER 484; see also *Commonwealth of Australia* v *John Fairfax Ltd*, note 25 above.

Public Domain

Information cannot be protected from disclosure if it can be gleaned from public sources or if its originator has already circulated it to a number of outsiders. These general principles are based upon considerable authority.[41] The majority decision in *Schering Chemicals*,[42] so far as it conflicts with these principles, has been doubted by the Law Commission.[43] The case can in any event be distinguished on the basis that Elstein had the idea for the programme while working for Scherings, and sold that idea, in breach of confidence, to Thames Television.

In the second *Spycatcher* case the House of Lords accepted that the Government could not prevent further publication of the Wright book even though, far from being responsible for its initial dissemination, it had done everything possible to stop it. The reality was that the material was no longer confidential. Lord Keith observed that publication abroad might not always prevent an injunction in Britain. Personal confidences (such as medical conditions) about a British resident might, for instance, cause extra embarrassment if published in Britain despite their prior foreign publication.[44] The majority of the Lords thought that Wright himself would not be free to publish his book despite the fact that anyone else could, because he should not be allowed to profit from his own wrong. Their conclusion was prompted by Wright's betrayal of trust and by resentment at the profits he was making from the book, and it compares unfavourably with the view taken by Lord Goff, who pointed out that neither Wright nor his publishers had been represented on the appeals, and it was difficult to see why they of all the world should be restrained from repeating what had become public knowledge.[45] The majority decision means that profits from sales in Britain cannot enter the calculations of retired spies who publish their reminiscences abroad. Once published, they can be 'pirated' by the British press without any concern about copyright.

Spycatcher showed the importance of a foreign publication. The Government made well-publicized attempts to stop publication in other courts but generally without success. The High Court of

---

[41] *Saltman Engineering Co Ltd* v *Campbell Engineering Ltd* (1948) [1963] 3 All ER 413; *O Mustad and Sons* v *S Allcock Co Ltd* (1928) [1963] 3 All ER 416; *A-G* v *Guardian Newspapers Ltd (No 2)*, note 10 above. See also Andrew Nicol 'Breach of Confidence and the Media' (1981) 12 EIPR 348; the Law Commission, *Breach of Confidence*, paras 4.16–17; and Alan Boyle [1982] Public Law 574.
[42] See note 18 above.
[43] *A-G* v *Guardian Newspapers Ltd (No 2)*, note 10 above, at p. 643.
[44] See note 19 above.
[45] ibid., 6.62–4.

Australia, for instance, refused an injunction, holding that there was no Australian public interest at risk and that the English Attorney-General could not use the Australian courts to enforce British governmental interests.[46] The Attorney-General had no better success in the Irish courts in relation to the book *One Girl's War* by Joan Millar.

> The book concerned the wartime experiences of a woman working for MI5, notably the shock she received on discovering that her boss (who had promised to marry her) was happier in the arms of men. None of the events described was later than 1945, and none was germane to current operations. Somewhat reluctantly the English courts granted an injunction because it was arguably a breach of Ms Millar's lifetime duty of confidence and because the Attorney-General had an arguable case that national security would be harmed by any publication by a member of the security services. It reached this conclusion even though the Irish courts had refused to enjoin the book. The latter had held that no Irish public interest was affected.[47]

The decision to injunct *One Girl's War* has been effectively overruled by a decision of the House of Lords (hearing an appeal from the Scottish courts) in 1989:

> Anthony Cavendish, a former member of MI6, was refused authorization to publish his memoirs, *Inside Intelligence*. He none the less had copies printed and distributed them as 'Christmas cards' in 1987 to 279 friends. The English courts granted an interlocutory injunction to prevent Times Newspapers publishing the Cavendish material. The *Scotsman* refused to undertake not to publish. The House of Lords held that although members of the security service were under a life-long duty of confidence, the Crown would be granted an injunction to prevent publication only if the public interest would be harmed. Here, it was conceded that national security was not threatened. Prior publication was the other most relevant circumstance. An interlocutory injunction was refused. Lord Templeman referred to the standard in Article 10 of the European Convention that restraints on free speech should be imposed only where necessary in a democratic society. He said that the courts should be guided by legislation as to what was necessary and not impose restraints different from or more severe than Parliament had thought appropriate. The Official Secrets Act 1989 had not come into force at the time of this decision, but Lord Templeman was guided by its requirement that publication of matters relating to the security services by an 'outsider' would only be punishable if harm resulted.[48]

---

[46] *A-G for England and Wales* v *Heinemann Publishers Pty Ltd* (1988) 78 ALR 449 HCA.

[47] *A-G* v *Turnaround Distribution Ltd* [1989] FSR 169 QBD; *A-G for England and Wales* v *Brandon Book Publishers Ltd* [1989] FSR 37.

[48] *Lord Advocate* v *Scotsman Publications Ltd* [1989] 2 All ER 852, HL. After this decision, the English court accepted that its injunction should not continue.

Procedure

Who can sue?

Actions for breach of confidence can be brought only by the 'person or organization to whom the confidence is owed'.

> *The Sunday Times* obtained, from a source in the Greek military junta, a report commissioned by that government from a British public relations firm advising how the junta could improve its fascistic image. The public relations consultants were refused an injunction: they were owed no duty of confidence by the Greek government, whence the leak had come, and only that government would have the standing to sue. 'The party complaining must be the person who is entitled to the confidence and to have it respected.'[49]

Interim injunctions

In breach of confidence lawsuits the critical stage is usually the application for an injunction pending the trial. If the publisher beats off that challenge and is able to print or broadcast the story, the action will often evaporate, because it would be either pointless or too embarrassing to continue with a claim merely for financial compensation. If the story is injuncted, the publisher will often lose interest, because by the time the case comes to trial, sometimes years later, it will no longer be topical.

The risk of an injunction depends on the owner knowing that copies have escaped. Normally, the media would wish to contact the owner to confirm the authenticity of the documents prior to publishing them, and to give the owner an opportunity to answer any allegations made on the basis of the documents. Such contact would put the owner on notice, and be sufficient evidence for an application for an injunction. The dilemma is real and at times agonizing. When the *Daily Mail* was supplied with apparently genuine documents implicating executives of British Leyland in an overseas pay-off scandal, it chose to publish without notifying British Leyland. The result was enormous libel damages when the documents were revealed as forgeries – a fact that British Leyland would have been able to establish convincingly had it been asked. Had the documents been genuine, of course, British Leyland might have obtained an injunction against their publication. The case shows how the present law of breach of confidence encourages bad

---

[49] *Fraser* v *Evans* [1969] 1 All ER 8.

press practice: had it been clear law that the public interest in the story would have defeated the confidence claim, the newspaper would have had no hesitation in putting its allegations to British Leyland prior to publication.[50]

Applications for these interim injunctions can be made at very short notice and must be speedily resolved. The evidence is frequently incomplete and almost always given on affidavit rather than orally. The courts are conscious of these problems, and most judges are aware of the presumption against prior restraint.[51] In libel cases the courts are extremely reluctant to injunct a publication that the defendant asserts is the truth or fair comment, and similar criteria are used in application for injunctions on the grounds of injurious falsehood or contempt of court.[52] Lord Denning has expressed the view that in breach of confidence cases the courts should accept the defendant's assertion of public interest in the story as enough to defeat the injunction application.[53] Alternatively, the court might base its decision on a preliminary view of the two sides' arguments.[54]

Lord Denning's view attracted support from other judges only when (as in the *Tom Jones* case) the allegation of breach of confidence was interwoven with an action for libel.[55] Otherwise, the general 'balance of convenience' test for pre-trial injunctions has been applied. This requires the plaintiff to show not that it *will* succeed at trial but that it has an arguable case. The plaintiff must also show that its loss (in the event of publication) could not be adequately compensated in damages. Plaintiffs rarely have difficulty in persuading a court that breach of confidence has no easy money equivalent. It is then for the defendant to show that delay in publication until trial will similarly be difficult to compensate in money terms. This is because a plaintiff, as the price of an interlocutory injunction, will usually have to give an undertaking to pay such compensation if at the trial it cannot make out a case for a permanent injunction. An important exception to this rule is that the Crown, when acting to enforce the law, is not required to give

---

[50] See *The Times*, 20 May 1977, 5 May 1979, 28 March 1980.
[51] William Blackstone, *Commentaries*, (1765) Book IV, pp. 151–2.
[52] *Bonnard* v *Perryman* [1891] 2 Ch 269; *Clement & Johnson* v *Associated Newspapers Ltd* (1924) *The Times*, 30 July; *Trevor & Sons* v *Solomon* (1978) 248 EG 779; *Herbage* v *Times Newspapers Ltd* (1981) *The Times*, 1 May (all libel cases); *Bestobell Paints Ltd* v *Bigg* [1975] FSR 421 (injurious falsehood); *A-G* v *BBC* [1980] 3 All ER 161 at pp. 172, 183 (contempt of court; see also Ch 6).
[53] As in *Fraser* v *Evans*, note 49 above, at p. 12 and *Hubbard* v *Vosper* [1972] 2 QB 84; [1972] 1 All ER 1023.
[54] *Commonwealth of Australia* v *John Fairfax*, note 25 above, at p. 491.
[55] *Woodward* v *Hutchins* [1977] 2 All ER 751, 755 per Lawton LJ.

an undertaking of this type.[56] If either party would suffer uncompensatable loss, the court has to consider the 'balance of convenience' between the two; what lawyers describe as the *American Cyanamid* test, after the case in which it was first applied.[57]

In breach of confidence cases this approach favours suppression, simply because allowing publication of the secret is an irreversible step and preservation of the secret is what such actions are usually all about. The plaintiff is not interested in compensation years later, which will be fairly minimal even if in the event the information is true.

In cases involving the security services the courts have been particularly sympathetic to Government applications for interlocutory injunctions. The BBC was injuncted from broadcasting a rather scholarly series of discussions on the moral dilemmas of security work called *My Country Right or Wrong* because it included interviews with former members of the security services.[58] The injunction was lifted only after the Attorney-General had obtained transcripts on discovery and confirmed that the programmes were harmless (see p. 34). The most notorious example of judicial obeisance to Government claims of national security was *Spycatcher (No 1)*, where by a majority of 3–2 the House of Lords held that the Attorney-General could still maintain an injunction despite the massive publicity that the book had received in the United States and elsewhere.[59]

It is doubtful whether this part of the *Spycatcher* saga will leave a lasting impression. There were vigorous dissents from Lords Bridge and Oliver who predicted the Government's subsequent 'condemnation and humiliation' in the European Court of Human Rights. A permanent injunction was, of course, eventually refused on the very ground that attracted Lords Bridge and Oliver but had failed to persuade the majority on the first occasion. This might be dismissed as a product of the difference between the tentative examination that is made at the interlocutory stage to see if the plaintiff has an arguable case and the closer scrutiny of the position at the trial. However, in the second appeal Lord Goff went out of his way to describe the interlocutory orders as a misuse of the injunctive remedy.[60] The House of Lords decision in the Anthony

---

[56] *F Hoffman La Roche A-G* v *Secretary of State for Trade and Industry* [1975] AC 295. A second exception is that a legally aided plaintiff will not be denied an injunction just because he or she is unable to afford to give such an undertaking: *Allen* v *Jambo Holdings Ltd* [1980] 1 WLR 1252.

[57] *American Cyanamid Co* v *Ethicon Ltd* [1975] AC 396.

[58] *A-G* v *BBC* (1987) *The Times*, 18 December.

[59] *A-G* v *Guardian Newspapers* [1987] 3 All ER 316.

Cavendish case suggests that the lower courts acted too swiftly in restraining *One Girl's War*, but Lord Keith warned that where there is no, or only a minor degree of, prior publication and where the Government did not concede that publication was harmless, interlocutory restraint would normally be appropriate.[61]

In its judgment on the *Spycatcher* saga the European Court of Human Rights declined to require the British Government to abolish the *American Cyanamid* test in cases where the injunction is sought so as to impose prior restraint on the media (see p. 183). *American Cyanamid* is in its terms antipathetic to Article 10 and earlier European case law on it, because it requires a simple balance between free speech and other values, in circumstances where those other values are *defined* as being more convenient, and the balance is a balance of convenience! (The majority's failure to make this obvious deduction is an example of its more recent failures to give full force to the principles of Article 10 where governments claim national security considerations, a development that owes much to the practice of appointing government lawyers, rather than independent jurists, to the Court; see p. 9.) The Court did, however, give some comfort to the media, in cases where they are confronted by a demand for an interim injunction, by recognizing the dangers inherent in prior restraints (see p. 22).

Further support for resisting injunctions demanded on *American Cyanamid* principles comes from Lord Oliver, in his speech in a *Spycatcher*-related contempt case:

> In cases of threatened publication of confidential material . . . the important stage of the proceedings is almost always and inevitably the interlocutory one and it is, I think, important that a vigilant eye should be kept on the possibility that the law of contempt may be invoked in support of claims which are in truth insupportable. The guidelines laid down by this House in *American Cyanamid Co. v Ethicon Ltd* . . . have come to be treated as carved on tablets of stone, so that a plaintiff seeking interlocutory relief has never to do more than show that he has a fairly arguable case. Thus the effect in a contest between a would-be publisher and one seeking to restrain the publication of allegedly confidential information is that the latter, by presenting an arguable case, can effectively through the invocation of the law of contempt, restrain until the trial of the action, which may be two or more years ahead, publication not only by the defendant but by anyone else within the jurisdiction and thus stifle what may, in the end, turn out to be

---

[60] [1988] 3 All ER at p. 666.
[61] *Lord Advocate* v *The Scotsman Publications Ltd*, note 48 above.

perfectly legitimate comment until it no longer has any importance or commands any public interest. In cases where there is
a contest as to whether the information is confidential at all or
whether the public interest in any event requires its publication
despite its confidentiality, this could be very important and
experience shows that orders for speedy trial do not always
achieve the hoped for result. I speak only for myself, but I
cannot help feeling that in cases where it is clearly of importance that publication, if it takes place at all, should take place
expeditiously, it may be necessary for courts to balance the
rights of the parties and to decide the issue, as they sometimes
did before the *Cyanamid* case, at the interlocutory stage on the
prima facie merits and on the evidence then available.[62]

Confidential Ideas

In the cases discussed above, breach of confidence has been
deployed to suppress the revelation of embarrassing information
that may have no commercial value. However, it is also relevant to
the media in terms of its prime purpose, namely in preventing, or
compensating for, the unfair exploitation of programme ideas and
treatments. Normally, this form of piracy is combated by an action
for breach of copyright. However, as we shall see, there can be no
copyright in an idea, or even in an elaborated idea that is not
reduced to material form and substantially copied. The planning
stage for television programmes and plays will frequently involve
luncheons and meetings at which ideas are discussed, and the law
will in some circumstances impose obligations to honour the
confidence of those who impart original ideas that have commercial
value. In order for the plaintiff to succeed:

- the concept must be clearly identifiable, and have some
  significant element of originality not already in the realm of
  public knowledge. The originality may consist in a significant
  'twist' or 'slant' to a well-known story;
- the concept must have been developed to the stage at which it
  has commercial potential and is capable of being realized as an
  actuality. A full synopsis is not necessary in cases in which a
  short statement, or oral elaboration, fulfil these criteria;
- the concept must have been given or expressed to the defendant
  in circumstances in which all parties recognize a moral
  obligation not to make further use of it without the consent of
  the communicator.

---

[62] *A-G v Times Newspapers Ltd* [1991] 2 All ER 398 at p. 422.

These principles were laid down in the case of *Fraser* v *Thames Television*:[63]

> Thames screened a fictional series called *Rock Follies* about the experiences of a three-girl rock group. The idea had originated with the manager of an actual group called Rock Bottom, who proposed to Thames that they should produce a series based on the formation of the group and the subsequent experiences of its members. The concept was discussed at a series of meetings with Thames executives, producer and writer, at a time when the latter were seriously considering production using the Rock Bottom group. This arrangement fell through, but Thames, using the other performers, developed the concept into a successful series. *Rock Follies* was substantially based on the characters and actual experiences of the Rock Bottom girls and their manager, and a number of 'twists' and 'slants' in the final treatment were based on information imparted by them in the course of negotiations in which all parties were jointly concerned commercially in the possible use of the idea. These negotiations would be recognized, in the television profession, as covered by an ethical obligation of confidence. The concept was clearly original: although the mere idea of an all-female rock group may be hackneyed, the 'slant' of focusing on the members as characters and professional actresses in their own right, and using the actual experiences of Rock Bottom, put sufficient flesh on the idea to justify its protection. The very fact that it was eventually turned into a much-acclaimed series was evidence of its commercial attractiveness and its ability to be realized in actuality. The plaintiffs were awarded damages in the order of half a million pounds.

For all the difficulties that confidence and copyright may pose to exposure journalism, there is another side to these laws, which protect the creator of original work from having it copied and exploited without authorization. The wire service, the video copier, the vast array of technology now available for mass reproduction has made creative talent exceptionally vulnerable to piracy, and media interests have had to devote a great deal of their resources to protective measures against copyright theft. At the most serious level, this involves well-organized piracy, which can be combated only by severe application of the criminal law. But as an everyday problem for media organizations, the question of giving credit where credit is due can involve the most complicated and delicate considerations. Plots and themes and ideas can be lost over luncheons, borrowed subconsciously, and pass through the minds of a daisy-chain of progenitors. Unless questions of plagiarism are amicably resolved, they can involve authors and programme-makers in bitter and costly legal disputes. A BBC department was

---

[63] *Fraser* v *Thames Television* [1983] 2 All ER 101.

plunged into an unedifying quarrel over Desmond Wilcox and his book of *The Explorers* series. The rights of journalists became hopelessly entangled in the dispute over 'The Ballsoff Memorandum' – a confidential note, mentioning sources by name, passed between a journalist and the editor of the *Observer*, leaked to and published by *Private Eye*.[64] The plaintiff, supported by the *Observer*'s editor, claimed that the magazine's action was a breach of copyright, which damaged the public interest by revealing journalistic sources; *Private Eye* argued that the public interest was served by revealing these sources and by showing the machinations behind the editorial policies of a major newspaper. The case was eventually decided upon a technicality, but it demonstrated, in the course of a long trial and a complicated judgment, how the 'rights' claimed for journalists can be mutually confusing and contradictory when one part of the press seeks to investigate the confidential arrangements of another.

Protection of Sources

The National Union of Journalists' Code of Conduct says: 'A journalist shall protect confidential sources of information.'

In a grudging and partial way, the law has recognized the importance of allowing the press to preserve the anonymity of its informants, but it has never conceded to journalists the virtually unqualified right that it has given to lawyers to keep quiet about their clients' affairs in the face of judicial interrogation. The right of journalists to protect their sources depends on who is asking the questions and why.

The police and other investigators

If the inquiries are being made by the police (for instance, in connection with leaked information), journalists are in the same position as anyone else: they are under no duty to provide answers. Although this may make the police investigation more difficult, the obdurate interviewee is *not* committing the offence of obstructing the police in the course of their duties.[65]

However, the police have an exceptional power to insist on answers to their questions concerning suspected breaches of s 1 of the Official Secrets Act 1911.[66] The Home Secretary is politically responsible for these powers and must normally give his prior approval. The police cannot use them if they only suspect an offence under the Official Secrets Act 1989: Parliament made clear

---

[64]   *Beloff* v *Pressdram Ltd* [1973] 1 All ER 241.
[65]   Police Act 1964 s 51(3); cf. *Rice* v *Connolly* [1966] 2 QB 414.
[66]   The Official Secrets Act 1920 s 6.

by the Official Secrets Act 1939 that compulsory inquisitions can be used only for detecting grave breaches of national security. The limited duty to tell the police of information relating to terrorist activities is considered in Chapter 10.

There is a growing parliamentary trend to give investigators the power to compel answers from their interviewees. Under the Financial Services Act 1986 the Department of Trade and Industry can appoint inspectors to investigate alleged insider dealing. The inspectors can require *any person* to produce documents and/or attend to answer the inspector's questions on oath.[67] The inspector can refer a failure to comply to the court. If the court finds that the interviewee has no reasonable excuse for refusing to answer, it can punish the refusal as if it were a contempt of court.[68] A specific provision prevents inspectors asking about legal advice or other matters covered by legal privilege.

> As Jeremy Warner of *The Independent* discovered, 'any person' can include journalists. The inspectors who summoned him were investigating suspected leaks of price-sensitive information from the Department of Trade and Monopolies and Mergers Commission. Two stories by Warner indicated that he had a source in these departments. Warner refused to identify him or her. There is no specific defence for journalists in the Financial Services Act, but the House of Lords, ruled that s 10 of the Contempt of Court Act 1981 (see p. 199) should be applied by analogy. In Warner's case they found that the disclosure of his source was necessary for the 'prevention of crime' and he could be required to answer. Warner persisted in his refusal and was fined £20,000.[69]

Similar powers to compel attendance and answers to questions are given to inspectors appointed to look into a company's affairs[70] and to the Director of the Serious Fraud Office.[71]

Plaintiffs in libel actions

There is a well-settled rule of practice that a defendant in a defamation action will not be required to name the writer or informant of

---

[67] Financial Services Act 1986 s 177.
[68] ibid. s 178(1) and (2).
[69] In *Re An Inquiry under the Company Securities (Insider Dealing) Act 1985* [1988] 1 All ER 203, HL and (1988) *the Independent*, 27 January, ChD. NB: The 1985 Act has been repealed and replaced by the Financial Services Act 1986.
[70] Companies Act 1985 ss 434 and 436. This does not expressly give a 'reasonable excuse' defence, but the court's power to punish silence as contempt is discretionary and ought not to be exercised where Contempt of Court Act 1981 s 10 would apply.
[71] Criminal Justice Act 1987 s 2. A magistrates' court can punish noncompliance with a fine on level 5 (currently £2,000) or a sentence of six months' imprisonment, but, as with the Financial Services Act, only if there is no reasonable excuse for failure to answer the Director's questions.

the words complained of *at the pre-trial stage*.[72] This means that a publisher cannot be required to name its source in answer to a request for particulars or by interrogatories or any other pre-trial discovery. Although this protection lasts only until trial, it remains important because so many libel actions are settled before then. At trial publishers now have the protection of s 10 of the Contempt of Court Act 1981 and are unlikely to be ordered to disclose a source unless the identity is essential to enable the court to rule on a defence that has been raised. Even then, the problem can be resolved expensively by withdrawing or modifying the defence. The rule has been applied in contempt proceedings so that the courts will not insist that the editor or publisher disclose the name of its source or writer.[73]

Plaintiffs do not normally have difficulty in identifying someone to sue for an alleged libel in a newspaper. Every newspaper should carry the name and address of its printer (who is currently liable for any libel it contains; see p. 61).[74] If this obligation is broken, the plaintiff cannot compel people who had no connection with the libel to reveal the printer's name simply because they are aware of his identity.[75]

The courts

In what circumstances will a court compel journalists to disclose their sources? Journalists may attend court voluntarily to defend or assert their rights, or to give evidence on behalf of others, or they may be forced by a witness order (in criminal trials) or subpoena (in civil cases) to attend to give evidence.

No witness can be made to answer a question or produce documents unless they are relevant to an issue in dispute between the parties.

> ITN successfully resisted a subpoena from a plaintiff in a civil action to produce *all* its untransmitted film of a rock festival at Windsor which had lasted several days. The Court of Appeal held that this was too wide and oppressive since the court was concerned only with one small incident.[76] A TV company will be ordered to produce its 'off-cuts' only if they are clearly important to help court determine an issue.

The common law did not give journalists an absolute right to

---

[72] *Hennessy* v *Wright* (1888) 21 QBD 509; *BSC* v *Granada Television*, note 14 above.
[73] *Re Bahama Islands Reference* [1893] AC 138.
[74] Newspapers, Printers and Reading Rooms Repeal Act 1869 Sched 2.
[75] *Ricci* v *Chow* [1987] 3 All ER 534, CA.
[76] *Senior* v *Holdsworth ex parte Independent Television News Ltd* [1976] QB 23, CA.

preserve the confidentiality of their sources, but it did recognize that the judge had a discretion as to whether to force journalists to name their sources even where their identity was relevant to an issue in dispute.[77]

> Journalist Jack Lundin succeeded in showing that a trial of a police sergeant for corruptly providing information to a gambling casino about its rival's customers would not be assisted by him disclosing the name of his source for an exposé of the whole affair that he had written for *Private Eye*. The prosecution case was already in a shambles and his evidence could not repair the damage. He was not guilty of contempt in refusing to answer because this was not necessary in the interests of justice.[78]

The common-law position has now been strengthened by s 10 of the Contempt of Court Act 1981:

> No court may require a person to disclose, nor is any person guilty of contempt of court for refusing to disclose, the source of information contained in a publication for which he is responsible unless it is established to the satisfaction of the court that it is necessary in the interests of justice or national security or for the prevention of disorder or crime.

Section 10 establishes a presumption in favour of journalists who wish to protect their sources, but that presumption will be rebutted if the court concludes that revelation is necessary on one or more of the four stated grounds. 'Necessary' is the key word in the section – it is not satisfied by proof that revelation is merely 'convenient' or 'expedient'. The name must be 'really needed' in the following situations.

In the interests of justice

This is the widest and most dangerous of the exceptions to the general principle enshrined in s 10, which protects journalists from court orders to name their sources. Regrettably, the House of Lords has chosen to interpret it in a way that inevitably permits subjective judicial value judgements on a journalist's conduct and the importance of his information, rather than by reference to principle. The question the court must ask in any case when an application is made for an order that a journalist name his source is whether the interests of justice in providing the name to the applicant 'are of such preponderating importance in the individual case that the ban on disclosure imposed by the opening words of

---

[77] *A-G* v *Lundin* (1982) Cr App R 90.
[78] *BSC* v *Granada Television*, note 14 above.

the section really needs to be overridden'.[79]

This means that a journalist's ethical duty to protect his source will be overridden whenever the court, conducting a 'balancing exercise', decides that the public interest in the applicant's right (generally to take legal action against the source to protect property in information) outweighs the journalist's qualified right to maintain the pledge of confidence to his source. Some of the factors to be placed in the balance have been described by Lord Bridge:

> One important factor will be the nature of the information obtained from the source. The greater the legitimate public interest in the information which the source has given to the publisher or intended publisher, the greater will be the importance of protecting the source. But another and perhaps more significant factor which will very much affect the importance of protecting the source will be the manner in which the information was itself obtained by the source. If it appears to the court that the information was obtained legitimately, this will enhance the importance of protecting the source. Conversely, if it appears that the information was obtained illegally, this will diminish the importance of protecting the source unless, of course, this factor is counterbalanced by a clear public interest in publication of the information, as in the classic case where the source has acted for the purpose of exposing iniquity.[80]

This approach emerged from a case in 1990 where a young journalist narrowly escaped prison after defying the courts by refusing to name his source.

> Bill Goodwin, a journalist on *The Engineer* magazine, received information from a source that a leading private company in a much-publicized field was, contrary to its publicity, experiencing financial difficulties and urgently seeking to raise a large loan. When Goodwin telephoned the company to seek information and comment, the company responded by obtaining a breach-of-confidence injunction and by seeking disclosure of the name of his source. It produced evidence that convinced the courts that the information leaked to the journalist must have come from a stolen copy of a confidential corporate plan, and that the source may well have been in contact with the thief. It needed the source's name in order to obtain further injunctions and

---

[79] *X* v *Morgan Grampian Publishers Ltd & Others* [1990] 2 All ER 1, per Lord Oliver at p. 16.
[80] ibid., p. 9. This approach would endorse the decision in *Handmade Films* v *Express Newspapers plc* [1986] FSR 463, where a newspaper was held to be protected by s 10 from disclosing to a film company the source from whom it obtained photographs of pop-star Madonna on a film set: no serious damage was threatening the plaintiff, and its loss could be compensated in monetary terms.

perhaps to trace the thief. The Court of Appeal ordered the journalist to place the name of his source in a sealed envelope and to hand it to the court to abide the outcome of final appeal to the House of Lords. The journalist refused to put his source in peril by this device and was found guilty of contempt. The House of Lords subsequently confirmed that 'the interests of justice' outweighed the prima facie protection of s 10, because the source had been complicit in a grave breach of confidentiality, the information did not reveal 'iniquity' and had no great public-interest value, and the company might suffer severe damage unless it was able to identify the employee or consultant who was prepared to pass its secrets on to the press. The journalist was ultimately fined £5,000 for refusing to obey the court's order.

The case illustrates how the judicial value accorded to property rights will tend to prevail over ethical claims by the journalists in balancing exercises that require a subjective appreciation of competing public interests. The case arose from a routine situation where a journalist received unpaid and unsolicited confidential information of a newsworthy nature, and behaved very properly in checking it with the company prior to publication. The courts were not prepared, however, to recognize any public interest in newsgathering that fell short of revelation of 'iniquity', and were overimpressed by allegations of potential damage made by company officials in affidavits that had not been tested under cross-examination. The company ultimately withdrew its attempt to have the journalist committed to prison, perhaps because it feared its identity would be disclosed under parliamentary privilege by angry MPs and it would suffer damaging publicity both from the consequent revelation of its financial problems and from the stigma that would attach to its efforts to gaol a perfectly honourable young man. Other plaintiffs, with less cause to fear such consequences, may be indisposed to charity. The case of Bill Goodwin demonstrates that s 10 will not afford any real protection to journalists until it is amended to exclude the 'interests of justice' exception. (This phrase, in fact, found no place in Lord Scarman's original draft of the clause during the passage of the 1981 Contempt of Court Act – it was inserted at a late stage by way of a Government amendment.) An alternative reform would be to confine the exception to 'the interests of criminal justice', which would confine disclosure to cases where it was necessary to establish guilt or innocence at a criminal trial.

In the interests of national security

Journalists who withhold disclosure on this ground can expect to go to prison for their contumely. The precedent was created when three were gaoled at the Vassall spy tribunal, and in 1985 the editor of the *Guardian* declined similar martyrdom by handing over the documents from which the identity of his unknown source – Sarah Tisdall – was deduced. Peter Preston was much criticized after Tisdall was gaoled for six months, and it is only fair to point out that he had been wrongly advised as to the protection afforded by s 10 (which was why he kept the document in the first place) and that he was more concerned by the prospect of a heavy and continuing fine on his newspaper than by his personal comfort. Moreover, the *Guardian*'s duty to its source was attenuated by the fact that she was not known by name, and it was by no means certain that the identity could be traced from the document. Journalists who have a direct relationship with their source, to whom they have personally promised confidentiality, may feel they have no alternative but to take punishment, even if the name is demanded on grounds of national security. It was some belated consolation to the *Guardian* that when its appeal reached the House of Lords, the final ruling at least applied a more stringent test to the evidence that the Government must produce to overcome the presumption in favour of protecting sources:

> The *Guardian* published extracts from papers that concerned the deployment of Cruise missiles at Greenham Common and that had been sent to it anonymously. The Secretary of State for Defence demanded their return but the newspaper refused, saying that this might reveal their source. The House of Lords held that the value of the documents was negligible and since the purpose of the exercise was to enable the ministry to deduce the source, the paper could invoke s 10. The section applied even though there was only a reasonable chance (rather than a certainty) that the paper's source would be revealed. The burden of proof lay with the Government to demonstrate that one of the exceptions applied. Although three of the five Law Lords were persuaded that national security required the leaker to be identified, all of them stressed that this conclusion could not be reached merely upon the Government's say-so. There had to be realistic evidence that national security was imperilled.[81]

The prevention of disorder

The higher courts have not as yet been asked to consider the meaning of this exception. It is difficult to see how it could be relevant to evidence given at civil trials, although journalists summonsed to criminal courts as witnesses in cases arising from continuing and violent industrial action might be called upon to answer. This exception is probably unnecessary, since the serious 'disorder'

---

[81] *Secretary of State for Defence* v *Guardian Newspapers Ltd* [1985] AC 339.

required to overcome the presumption would inevitably entail the commission of criminal offences.

The prevention of crime

This is a significant exception for all journalists who publish investigations into crime and corruption. The very impact of their work may result in police inquiries or official investigations, and their sources will be sought after to provide the leads. Jeremy Warner suffered in exactly this way (see p. 197). The House of Lords ruled that the phrase 'prevention of crime' in s 10 does not require the investigator to show that disclosure is necessary to forestall a particular crime: it was sufficient if disclosure would enable prosecution for an offence already committed, or would assist in the prevention of crime in the future. The court will, however, be less inclined to order disclosure under this head at the instance of a private plaintiff or a body that has suffered crime but has no public duty to investigate or prevent it. The Health Authority that successfully suppressed the story about doctors with AIDS failed on this basis to obtain an order for the newspaper to disclose the name of its employee who had corruptly and criminally sold its records: it had no public duty to prosecute crime, and the purpose of its action was predominantly to stop publication rather than to stop crime.[82]

Practical considerations

Even when disclosure would be necessary in the interests of justice or for one of the other purposes set out in s 10, the judge still has a discretion not to press journalists to disclose their source. As Lord Justice Donovan has put it:

> . . . over and above [the requirements that the answer is neces-sary and admissible] there may be other considerations, impos-sible to define in advance, but arising out of the infinite variety of fact and circumstances which a court encounters which may lead a judge to conclude that more harm than good would result from compelling a disclosure or punishing a refusal to answer.[83]

One such consideration is the undesirability of ordering disclosure prior to trial. The purpose of interlocutory orders is to preserve the status quo, and in most cases this can be adequately protected by orders prohibiting or limiting the use of the leaked

---

[82] *X* v *Y* [1988] 2 All ER 648.
[83] *A-G* v *Mulholland* [1963] 1 All ER 767, 773 and see Lord Denning at p. 771. Since the qualifying conditions of the 1981 Act are stringent, it will be rare that this discretion is exercised in favour of the journalist.

material. Ordering the disclosure of a source or the return of documents to the plaintiff at the pre-trial stage does more than this. Once the source's identity is made known, the situation cannot be reversed if at trial it transpires that the plaintiffs are not entitled to the order or documents they seek.[84]

Leaked documents

A media defendant sued for the recovery of leaked documents may be tempted to resist the claim on the principle that it cannot be obliged to provide information that might implicate itself in a crime. This would be an arguable defence if, for instance, the circumstances of its obtaining the document could make it an accessory to theft or the handler of stolen goods. Such a defence was raised by Granada when British Steel sued to discover the identity of the television company's informant, but the courts ruled that the risk of prosecution was remote. The defence is a two-edged sword, because to admit to participating in possible criminal behaviour undermines any public interest claim that might be made in the same proceedings. A further problem is s 72 of the Supreme Court Act 1981, which removes the privilege against self-incrimination in civil proceedings that concern 'commercial information or other intellectual property', although it is doubtful whether Government policy documents, for example, would fall into this category. The privilege against self-incrimination may therefore be of value to journalists who refuse to cooperate with Scotland Yard inquiries into breaches of the Official Secrets Act 1989 after leaks to them of Government documents. Section 72 of the Supreme Court Act, designed to facilitate civil proceedings against video pirates, should not be available as a devious method for probing journalistic sources.

In practice, of course, a newspaper would now be advised to destroy any documents that might incriminate a source as soon as it is aware that the owner is likely to demand their return. If this step is taken before legal proceedings have been formally initiated, it will not amount to contempt of court and the owner would be left with only a civil claim of minimal damages for lost property. Granada Television adopted the expedient of mutilating the British Steel documents to remove all identifying marks before returning them. The *Guardian*, however, made the mistake of both admitting to possession of the document and acknowledging the presence on it of identifying marks in correspondence with Government solicitors before legal action was taken. It preserved the document, in

---

[84] *Francome* v *Mirror Group Newspapers Ltd* [1984] 2 All ER 408, 413, 415, 416; *Handmade Films (Productions) Ltd* v *Express Newspapers plc*, note 80 above.

over-optimistic reliance on s 10 of the Contempt of Court Act. If 'leaked' documents are destroyed before the initiation of legal proceedings for their recovery no offence is committed by the media, unless the document is an '*original* document of or belonging to any Government department' [our italics]. Section 20 of the Theft Act makes it an offence dishonestly to destroy or deface such documents.

Police powers of search and seizure

Prior to 1984 the right of the police to search premises and seize evidence was a confusing jumble of common-law powers and statutes passed to cater for specific situations. The Police and Criminal Evidence Act 1984 both rationalized and broadened these powers. It created a threefold division.

Excluded material
This includes 'journalistic material', defined as 'material acquired or created for the purposes of journalism'. The holder need not be a professional journalist if the material was acquired or created for journalistic purposes. The term would cover an anonymous package of leaked material sent to a journalist since it includes material that is sent to a recipient for the purposes of journalism.[85] Importantly, journalistic material is only 'excluded' if it is held in confidence. This means that most film whether taken by broadcasting crews or still photographers is not 'excluded material'. Generally, the police are not entitled to search for or seize (even under warrant) excluded material. Exceptionally, they may do so if some other statue authorizes the grant of a warrant. They must then obtain an order from a circuit judge.[86] The Official Secrets Acts are examples of statutes that may allow such an order to be made (see p. 430).

Special procedure material
This includes journalistic material that is not 'excluded material'.[87] The police must again apply to a circuit judge, but the conditions on which an order will be made are more relaxed than for excluded material. They must show that there are reasonable grounds for believing that a serious arrestable offence has been committed, that the material is likely to be of substantial value (whether by itself or together with other material) to the investigation, and that the

---

[85] Police and Criminal Evidence Act 1984 s 13. If the material is not in the possession of someone who acquired or created it for journalistic purposes, it loses its status as 'journalistic material'.
[86] ibid., Sched 1, para 3.
[87] ibid., s 14.

material is likely to be relevant evidence. Finally and most importantly, the police must show that the public interest requires an order to be made, taking into account the benefit to the investigation of the material and the circumstances in which the material is held.[88]

Applications are made, after notice to the holder of the material, to a circuit judge. Either in the notice or at the hearing the police must describe in broad terms the offences being investigated.[89] Initially, the application is made to a judge in chambers, but in hearing applications against the press, judges have shown themselves willing to adjourn the case into open court so that the public can attend and the case can be reported (see p. 323).

On at least three occasions the police have used these powers to obtain orders requiring the press to hand over film and photographs of demonstrations. The first concerned disorders in Bristol;[90] the second an investigation by the Police Complaints Authority into complaints about the police violence at a major demonstration at Wapping during the Times Newspapers dispute.[91] In every case the photographers argued that their job would be made more dangerous if the crowds they were photographing knew that their pictures could become prosecution evidence. One press photographer had already been killed in the Brixton disorders after capturing a looter on film. If the danger increased, so too would the likelihood that violent confrontations would not be covered by photographers. In consequence, the public would be less well informed and the police investigators would not even have the benefit of photographs that would otherwise have been taken and published. No court has accepted these arguments. Judges in all three cases paid tribute to the courage of the press but were sceptical as to whether the orders sought would appreciably increase the risk they faced.

Once a person has been served with a notice of application for an order under these provisions, concealment, destruction or alteration of the material can be treated as contempt of court.[92] Nothing limits what can be done with the material before a notice is served. Four freelance photographers who were also at Wapping transferred their negatives to the International Federation of Journalists in Brussels and gave up all further rights to them before

---

[88] Sched 1 para 2.

[89] *R v Crown Court at Manchester ex parte Taylor* [1988] 2 All ER 769.

[90] *Chief Constable of Avon and Somerset v Bristol United Press* (1986) *The Independent*, 4 November, application for leave to apply for judicial review refused: *R v Crown Court at Bristol ex parte Bristol Press Agency Ltd* [1987] Crim LR 329.

[91] *Wyrko v Newspaper Publishing plc* (1988) *The Independent*, 27 May.

[92] Police and Criminal Evidence Act 1984 Sched 1, para 11.

they were served with notices. Mr Justice Alliott subsequently ruled that this was not a contempt of court.

Other material

This may be seized subject only to the normal safeguards for search warrants. These may be granted by a magistrate without any right on the part of the media to object and without the need to apply the public-interest test for 'special procedure' material. Once police are lawfully present on premises (whether under a magistrates' warrant or because of some other power) they are entitled to seize (but not to search for) any material that they have reason to believe has either been obtained in consequence of the commission of an offence or is evidence of an offence, and that it is necessary to seize in order to prevent it being concealed, lost, damaged, altered or destroyed. If the material is held on a computer that can be accessed from the premises, the police can demand a print-out. Under these powers the police cannot demand material that is covered by legal privilege, but they can seize 'special procedure' or 'excluded' material.[93]

The debates over the Police and Criminal Evidence Act raised the issue of principle as to whether journalists should claim special protection from the normal process of the law. Although such protection was initially sought by media organizations, many of their members subsequently changed their minds when it became apparent that the special treatment awarded them in the Act would necessarily involve the courts in defining 'journalism' and in operating a special regime that would accord to practitioners favoured treatment by comparison with ordinary citizens. The special status offered by the Act infringes the principle that journalism is not a profession, but the exercise by occupation of the citizen's right to freedom of expression. In retrospect, the media organizations (such as the Guild of British Newspaper Editors) who supported the Government's offer of 'special protection' for journalists fell into an obvious trap, and damaged their members' interests. Prior to the 1984 statute, police had not been granted access to untransmitted material at common law. But once a statutory route for obtaining that material came into existence, albeit with 'special protections', the police naturally exploited it and courts naturally decided that the protection was not very special after all. Judges generally believe that investigation of crime must have a higher priority than journalistic principles, and the decisions in the Bristol, Wapping and Poll Tax demonstration cases were all decided by this judicial

---

[93] ibid., s 19.

preference. It is now likely that police applications for untransmitted material will become routine after every violent demonstration, and the media objections to production will be routinely dismissed.

Private Photographs

The Copyright Act 1988 took a small step to preserve privacy in domestic photographs. Before the 1988 Act a person who commissioned a photograph was the first owner of copyright in it. That rule has been changed and copyright now first belongs to the photographer. However, if the photograph has been commissioned for private and domestic purposes, the person commissioning it has the right not to have the photograph issued to the public, displayed in public, broadcast or included in a cable programme.[94] The right is not infringed if the photograph is incidentally included in an artistic work, film, broadcast or cable programme.[95] More importantly, the right is not infringed if the commissioner has consented to its use.[96] The consent does not have to be in writing, but it would be prudent to obtain a written consent in order to avoid later argument about whether it was given or not. The practical result of these changes is that, for example, a photograph commissioned by a family of a daughter who is later murdered will not be able to be used without the family's consent. Courts are more than willing to award punitive damages against photographers for the 'flagrancy' of a breach of copyright in circumstances where they supply private photographs of suddenly newsworthy people to the press.[97]

The case of *Sports & General Press Agency* v *Our Dogs Publishing Co.* deserves to be engraved on every press photgrapher's lens: it establishes their right to snap and to publish anyone in a public place or, in the absence of trespass, in a private place without their consent. ('No person possesses a right of preventing another person photographing him any more than he has a right of preventing another person giving a description of him.')[98] To the distress of the Ladies Kennel Club, the magazine to which they had sold 'exclusive rights' to photograph their dog show was unable to stop a rival paper publishing pictures taken by a freelance who had paid for an admission ticket, which had no condition excluding

---

[94] Copyright, Designs and Patents Act 1988 s 85. The right lasts as long as copyright subsists in the photograph; see p. 225.
[95] ibid., s 85(2).
[96] ibid., s 87.
[97] *Williams* v *Settle* (1960) 1 WLR 1072.
[98] [1916] 2 KB 880.

photographs. Where, however, the private pictures have been stolen from the photographer, the latter will be entitled to restrain their publication in the press. Pictures of Princess Margaret dressed as Mae West at a private party were denied to readers of the *Daily Mail* at the suit of the woman who took them, and whose son later stole and sold them to the newspaper without his mother's consent.[99]

Data Protection Obligations

Most journalists who store and sort their data on computer will, since the Data Protection Act 1984, have to register with the Registrar of Data Protection. The restrictions apply only to computer data; manually maintained files are not affected. The restrictions apply only to 'personal data', i.e., data that allows living people to be identified, but it includes expressions of opinion about them.[100] Users must adhere to the following data principles:

- the data must be obtained and processed lawfully and fairly;
- it must be held for only specified and lawful purposes;
- it must not be used or disclosed incompatibly with the purposes;
- it must be adequate, relevant and not excessive in relation to the purpose;
- it must be accurate and, where necessary, kept up to date;
- it must not be kept longer than is necessary for the purpose;
- an individual is entitled to be told at reasonable intervals and without undue delay or expense whether personal data on him is held, to have access to it and where appropriate to have the data corrected or erased if these principles are violated.[101]

The Registrar can issue an enforcement notice if the principles are violated.[102] It is an offence not to comply with the notice, but the user can appeal to the Data Protection Tribunal against the notice.[103] The particulars of users and the purposes for which they hold data are kept by the Registrar in a register to which the public has access.[104]

---

[99] *Lady Anne Tennant* v *Associated Newspapers Group* [1979] FSR 298.
[100] Data Protection Act 1984 s 1.
[101] ibid., Sched 1.
[102] ibid., s 10.
[103] ibid., s 13.
[104] ibid., s 9.

Privacy

English law is far more attuned to property rights than to human rights; privacy is protected, if at all, through a collection of quasi-proprietary actions. Breach-of-confidence remedies have been built on the notion that confidential information is akin to property whose owner ought to be able to control its use.

Similarly, actions for trespass have been brought against intrusive snoopers. Damages were awarded in one case against a defendant who secretly installed a microphone above the plaintiff's bed.[105] But this remedy is of limited use. Apart from the time that it takes to obtain even an *ex parte* injunction, it can only restrain entry on the plaintiff's own land.[106] Where a defendant stands on public ground or in a place where he is permitted to be and spies through binoculars or telephoto lenses, no trespass takes place. In *Bernstein* v *Skyways Ltd*[107] Lord Bernstein failed to obtain an injunction to stop aerial photography of his house and grounds. A flight several hundred feet up from his land did not interfere with his right to enjoy it and there was no general right to stop the taking of photographs. The court warned that it might be different if there was constant surveillance amounting to nuisance.

Of course, there is no trespass in doing what a landowner permits:

> A cinema owner agreed to pay a percentage of each day's takings to the owners of the films that he rented. The film owners employed inspectors to visit cinemas and check attendances. The cinema owner alleged that the inspectors were trespassing, because they came with a secret purpose for which they had no permission. The court held there was no trespass. The inspectors did nothing they were not invited to do and their motives for being present were irrelevant.[108]

The case is important for journalists whose observations and reports are often unwelcome to those they visit. However, its limits are also important. A journalist would not normally exceed his or her licence by observing, remembering and reporting, but the operation of a television camera might well go beyond a general invitation to the public to enter the land. This is why film crews have to submit to the sometimes irksome business of obtaining consent from landowners to film. Unless paid for, licences to come on to land can also be revoked. The landowner must allow a reasonable

---

[105]   *Sheen* v *Clegg* (1967) *Daily Telegraph*, 22 June.
[106]   *Victoria Park Racing Co* v *Taylor* (1937) 58 CLR 479.
[107]   [1977] 3 WLR 136.
[108]   *Byrne* v *Kinematograph Renters Association* (1958) 2 All ER 579, 593.

time for invited journalists to depart, but after this elapses, the former invitees become trespassers.

Even where the behaviour of media employees plainly amounts to a trespass, the courts are most reluctant to deprive the media of the fruits of the civil wrong by granting injunctions against publication of photographs or films obtained in the course of the trespass. The common example is 'footage in the door' television journalism, whereby alleged conpersons, shysters and religious hucksters are confronted at their place of business by victims accompanied by television cameramen and reporters. Although the cameras may continue to roll long after any licence to enter has been withdrawn, the courts will generally take the view that damages will be an adequate remedy and will decline to injunct broadcast of the film.[109]

The case that most profoundly influenced the Calcutt Committee in recommending criminal sanctions against press intrusion was *Gorden Kaye* v *Andrew Robertson & Sport Newspapers:*[110]

> The *Sunday Sport* obtained what its editor described as a 'good old fashioned scoop' when its reporters walked into actor Gorden Kaye's hospital room while he was recovering from brain surgery, photographed him and recorded his ramblings for publication as a 'world exclusive'. Kaye's family was unable to obtain an injunction for libel (as the *Sunday Sport* indicated its intention of defending the claim) or on the basis of trespass (there was no unlawful entry, and no evidence that the photography caused physical distress or damage). All that the court could do was to grant a limited injunction preventing the newspaper from pretending that Gorden Kaye had voluntarily consented to the interview, this being a 'malicious falsehood' in that it represented that he had abandoned a valuable property right (i.e. the right to tell the exclusive story of his accident). All three judges in the Court of Appeal lamented their inability to give a satisfactory remedy for this 'monstrous invasion of privacy'.

Such a remedy is available under American law, where ordinary people have a right to protect themselves against unreasonable intrusion on their physical solitude,[111] and celebrities have an exclusive legal right to control and profit from the commercial use of their names and personalities. (Johnny Carson was able to stop

---

[109] See *Church of Scientology* v *Transmedia Productions Pty Ltd* (1987) Aust Torts Reports 80–101; *Lincoln Hunt (Aust) Pty Ltd* v *Willesee* (1986) 4 NSWLR 457.
[110] [1991] FSR 62 CA.
[111] e.g., *Barber* v *Time Inc* (1942) 159 SW 2nd 291, where a woman with an insatiable appetite won damages against *Time* for publishing a photograph of her taken without her consent in hospital, captioned 'starving glutton'. See also *Cantrell* v *Forest City Publishing* 419 US 245 (1974), where a newspaper was held to have invaded privacy by inventing facts of a personal and sensitive nature about the plaintiff.

the manufacture of the 'Here's Johnny portable toilet'.)[112] The criminal law in England provides some minimal protection against harassment[113] and public provocation,[114] but the vagaries of injunctive remedies convinced Calcutt that specific legislation was required to outlaw media trespass.[115] The report recommended new crimes of uninvited entry on private property to obtain information for publication, using surveillance devices surreptitiously for the same end, and photographing individuals without their consent while they are standing on private land.[116] The criminal offences, although subject to a public interest defence where exposure of 'seriously anti-social conduct' is intended, are misconceived, and would give police unparalleled powers to arrest reporters and television camera crews as they go about ordinary business. Law should not be used actively to suppress publication of the truth. It can, however, usefully work to *deter* publication of unimportant private truths if it provides an effective remedy for victims of invasion of privacy. An effective remedy – the right to bring a civil action, legally aided where appropriate, and to obtain compensation and damages – is precisely what English law does not, at present, offer. In 1992 the Paddy Ashdown 'affair', in which the media handled stolen documents and harassed the woman in question, demonstrated that self-regulation through the Press Complaints Commission is a hollow pretence (see Chapter 13). A private body, funded by the newspaper industry, comprised mainly of editors, which has no power other than to tick off fellow editors when they breach the privacy provisions of a 'code of conduct', is no longer publicly acceptable as a privacy safeguard. If, however, that code were made the basis of a statutory tort, so that any breach of it that could not be justified on public-interest grounds would render the newspaper liable in damages, a significant advantage would be made in the protection of human rights in the United Kingdom.

---

[112] *Carson* v *Here's Johnny Portable Toilets Inc* (1983) 698 F 2d 831. Compare *Byron* v *Johnston* (1816) 2 Mer 29, where Lord Byron stopped a bad poem being falsely attributed to him.
[113] Under s 7 of the Conspiracy and Protection of Property Act 1875.
[114] Section 5 of the Public Order Act 1986.
[115] Trespass on private property is only an offence at present if violence is used to secure entry (see s 6, Criminal Law Act 1977).
[116] *Report of the Committee on Privacy and Related Matters* (Calcutt Report), HMSO, 1990, Cmnd 1102, para 6.33–5.

Chapter 5

Copyright

The sweat of a man's brows, and the exudations of a man's brains, are as much a man's own property as the breeches upon his backside.

Laurence Sterne, *Tristram Shandy*.

The law against breach of copyright protects creative work that has been reduced to material form from being used by others without permission. It is without doubt the most complicated branch of the law dealt with in this book. Its essential purpose, shared with the law against breach of confidence, is to prevent the plagiarism or unfair exploitation of creative work. As such, it affords vital protection to writers, and is the basis of the measures taken by publishing and broadcasting organizations to combat piracy. But as a corollary to this purpose, it may inhibit the media's freedom to report and expose matters of public interest, where such reportage necessarily involves publication of documents written by or belonging to persons or organizations who wish to keep them private.

Most occasions on which the media will wish to use copyright material do not pose problems, either because the originator is only too happy for his or her exudations to be publicized, or because arrangements have been made to pay a suitable royalty or licensing fee. Difficulties are encountered, however, when use of copyright material is made without formal acknowledgement, or in the context of an article or broadcast that makes use of private documents for the purpose of criticizing those to whom copyright belongs. Even with the best will in the world, the egos of artists involved in the different stages of putting together a feature may provoke irreconcilable differences of opinion as to the due credit to be given in the final product. Untangling such disagreements is hard for several reasons. The law of copyright was revised in the Copyright, Designs and Patents Act 1988,[1] but its reforms generally apply only to works created after the statute came into effect. The Copyright Act 1956 (which it replaced) will therefore be important for years to come. In some cases it will be necessary to consult even earlier (and now repealed) legislation. The structure of the new law is still highly complex and a book of this type can be only a guide to its most important aspects for those writing, producing or editing new material. Yet at the same time this mass of rules is often unable to deliver clear answers to common problems. Journalists who consult their lawyer expecting to be led through the labyrinth emerge frustrated when told that the proposed use of a leaked document will infringe copyright if a 'substantial' part is taken but not if its use is 'fair'.

There are five basic questions in copyright law.

- *Does copyright exist in the source material?* The 1988 Act establishes the following categories of copyright:
  - (a) original literary, dramatic or musical works
  - (b) original artistic works
  - (c) sound recordings
  - (d) films
  - (e) broadcasts
  - (f) cable programmes
  - (g) published editions.

The legal meanings of these categories are broader than their everyday use. Moreover, multiple copyrights can exist in a particular work. In the case, for instance, of a television documentary, there will be literary copyright in the script, dramatic copyright in the screenplay and musical copyright in any background music. The totality will be entitled to copyright as a film, and once aired will have a further copyright as a television broadcast.

Copyright begins from the time the work is made. There is no longer any need to register the work, and even the copyright symbol © is not necessary in the United Kingdom, although it is if the work is to be published in a country that is a member of only the Universal Copyright Convention (see p. 225). Until the 1988 Act it was common for this effective monopoly to last a very long time, particularly in the case of unpublished literary, dramatic and musical works, which could, in theory, enjoy perpetual copyright. The scope for rights to be perpetual has been almost completely abolished. A rare exception is *Peter Pan*, for whose exploitation the Great Ormond Street Hospital is still entitled to collect royalties, thanks to the will of J. M. Barrie and a special amendment to the 1988 bill. All other works (such as those that were published under

---

[1] The background to the Act can be traced through the *Report of the Whitford Committee on Copyright and Designs Law 1977*, HMSO, Cmnd 6732; a Green Paper, *Reform of the Law Relating to Copyright, Designs and Performers' Protection*, HMSO, 1981, Cmnd 8302; and a White Paper, *Intellectual Property and Innovation*, HMSO, Cmnd 9712.

the 1956 Act) have finite protection, and once this is over, the work can be reproduced in any fashion. For example, the emergence of the Gilbert and Sullivan operas from the fifty year copyright cocoon ended the D'Oyly Carte monopoly on their staging, and outraged Savoyard purists with *The Rock Mikado*, *The Jazz Mikado* and *The Black Mikado*.

- *Does the proposed use of copyright material infringe the law?* Copyright gives the owner an exclusive right to use the work in specific ways. Infringement is the use of the work in one of these ways without the owner's consent. The possible means of infringement may differ according to the type of work, but each involves some element of copying, reproduction or performance. Ignorance of the owner's rights is no excuse, but it may diminish the amount of compensation that has to be paid. A secondary type of infringement is committed by those in the chain of distribution of infringing copies who know that the merchandise is pirated.

- *Who owns the copyright?* Ownership will decide who has the right to license use of the copyright and who has the power to take legal action against infringement. The Act lays down rules for determining who is the first owner: usually this is the author or maker of the work. It also envisages the transfer of rights to others and specifies certain formalities if these are to be effective. The new 'moral rights' created by the Act cannot be transferred except to the estate of the author or maker on their death. They can, however, be waived.

- *Is there a defence?* There is no infringement if the reproduction was permitted or licensed by the copyright owner. Nor is it an infringement if publication is justified in the public interest. In addition, there is an important statutory defence of 'fair dealing' with the work for the purpose of criticism, review or reporting current events. There are other defences, including court reports, old films and preparation for broadcasting.

- *Will the publication infringe some other right similar to copyright?* Although a publication has successfully steered clear of the shoals of copyright, it may still run into legal difficulties because of other similar rights. Manufacturing quotes may not infringe copyright, but it can lead to a claim to damages for false attribution of authorship. Malicious falsehoods about a rival's goods can be costly. Performers now have rights that are akin to copyright. The 1988 Act also brought English law into line with the Berne Convention on Copyright and introduced the concept of 'moral rights' for authors and directors: (a) to be identified as such and (b) not to have their work subjected to 'derogatory treatment'.

The civil claim of 'passing off' will sometimes provide a remedy for plaintiffs whose name or work or goodwill is misappropriated by others for commercial gain. Thus Dow Jones Inc was able to force Ladbrokes to disband 'The Ladbrokes/Dow Jones Index', a gambling operation related to the rise and fall of the Dow Jones Index, which wrongly implied that Dow Jones had consented to or benefited from the operation. The *Mail on Sunday* was able to obtain an injunction, on grounds of passing-off, to stop an advertiser from arranging with distributors and newsagents to insert printed advertising leaflets in its colour supplement. The newspaper successfully argued that the public would assume that the advertisements had its approval and were under its control, and that the connection might damage its goodwill.[2]

Existence of Copyright

Original literary, dramatic or musical works[3]

This is the first classification of material that is subject to protection. 'Literary' work does not imply any particular quality of language.[4] Even the most turgid prose can be a literary work, as can programme schedules, letters, football fixture lists, opinion polls and even railway timetables if reproduced in detail. However, the work must be 'recorded in writing or otherwise'.[5] There can be no copyright in a literary idea, or suggestion for a story, though it may be imparted in circumstances that would be protected by the law of confidence (see p. 194). Copyright can exist in a literary work only if it is recorded, but it need not be recorded in writing. Memoirs dictated on to a tape are protected even before the tape is transcribed. Similarly, a speaker delivering a lecture from prepared notes will have copyright in the speech. Conversely a spontaneous or extempore speaker will not have copyright, unless, that is, the speech is recorded with or without the permission of the speaker.[6]

---

[2] *Associated Newspapers plc* v *Insert Media Ltd* [1990] 2 All ER 803.
[3] Copyright, Designs and Patents Act 1988 s 3.
[4] *University of London Press Ltd* v *University Tutorial Press Ltd* [1916] 2 Ch 601 at p. 608.
[5] Copyright, Designs and Patents Act 1988 s 3(2). 'Writing' includes 'any form of notation or code. Whether by hand or otherwise and regardless of the method by which or medium in or on which it is recorded': ibid., s 178.
[6] ibid., s 3(3).

The position was doubtful under the 1956 Act[7] but the 1988 Act has made it clear. This will mean that people interviewed by reporters will now have copyright in the words they utter if the journalist has taken an accurate note or recorded them. However, there is a new defence to prevent this extension of literary copyright acting as a new form of censorship (see p. 248).

Copyright apart, journalists must exercise care in attributing quotations or in ghosting articles for others. False attribution of remarks to which exception is taken can lead to a claim for damages.

> Dorothy Squires obtained £100 damages for false attribution of authorship in 1972 from the *News of the World*, whose reporter had inaccurately written up an interview concerning her marriage to Roger Moore. This sum was in addition to libel damages that were awarded in the same case. The paper was not excused because it was following an apparent Fleet Street custom of making up quotes for willing interviewees. The paper was liable if the 'author' disliked 'her' lines.[8]

False attribution can provide a useful remedy for freelance writers whose copy is misused.

> Geoffrey Cannon, a respected authority on nutritional values of different foods, was commissioned to write an article for *Today* newspaper. He did so, but the article was never published. Instead, his name was appended to another article on the same subject, expressing opinions with which he profoundly disagreed. He was awarded substantial damages in 1988 for the false attribution.

The 1988 Act substantially enlarged the scope of false attribution, which it categorizes as a matter of moral rights. It prohibits the false attribution of authorship of a literary, dramatic, musical or artistic work and falsely describing someone as the director of a

---

[7] In the absence of a prepared text the interviewee had to have been so closely involved in writing up the story that they became a joint author (*Donoghue* v *Allied Newspapers Ltd* [1938] Ch 106; *Evans* v *E Hulton and Co Ltd* (1924) *The Times*, 20 March, (1923–8) MCC 51; *Tate* v *Thomas* [1921] 1 Ch 503).

[8] *Moore* v *News of the World* [1972] 1 All ER 915. Cf *Jenkins* v *Socialist Worker* (1977) *The Times* 28 February, where the General Secretary of ASTMS recovered £1,000 for a satirical letter published by the defendants over his facsimile (and unauthorized) signature: Copyright Act 1956 s 43. The work that is falsely attributed to the plaintiff must be a literary, musical, dramatic or artistic one: ibid., s 43(1). Damages were also payable if an altered artistic work is published or sold as the unaltered work of the artist. Similar care must be taken with quotes attributed to the dead. Their estates could and can claim damages for false attributions made up to twenty years after their death: ibid., s 43(5) Copyright, Designs and Patents Act 1988 s 86(2).

film. It prohibits falsely representing a literary, dramatic or musical work as an adaptation of a person's work or a copy of an artistic work as having been copied by the artist. An altered artistic work must not be knowingly passed off as the original. The section now spells out in detail who is to be liable for these wrongs: in some (but not all) cases they are confined to those who knew or had reason to believe that the attribution was false; in certain cases the liability is limited to those who deal with the falsely described article in the course of business.[9]

The term 'originality' is also misleading. The work must require some skill and labour, but it need not also be novel. It is enough if the creator of the work can truthfully say 'this is all my own work'.[10]

An 'original' work for the purposes of the Act has been variously described as a work the creation of which has involved the expenditure of 'skill, labour and judgement'; 'selection, judgement and experience'; or 'labour, skill and capital'. These tests operate to exclude protection only where compilations are basic and commonplace. In consequence, protection has been afforded to mathematical tables that the compiler had worked out for himself, hire-purchase forms, broadcast programme schedules and even street directories. The 1988 Act now unambiguously provides that a computer program can be a literary work with its own copyright protection.[11]

Copyright can also be acquired in compilations, translations, abridgements and anthologies. So, for instance, a list of Stock Exchange prices and a football pools coupon have copyright. The requirement is the same: the author's own contribution must have required a degree of skill and labour that led to the new work having some recognizably different quality to its source or sources. A person who translates a speech into a different language clearly transforms it sufficiently to satisfy this test. Copying the translation would then infringe the rights of both the original author and the translator. A slavish copy, that adds nothing, rearranges nothing or selects nothing would have no claim to be literary work unless, possibly, the text of the original were inaccessible.

The skill and labour expended by a reporter or stenographer in taking down a speech in shorthand may be sufficient to attract copyright protection against other newspapers who 'lift' a substantial part of the report. Thus in *Walter* v *Lane*,[12] a *Times*

---

[9] Copyright, Designs and Patents Act 1988 s 84. The prohibitions apply to *any* part of a protected work, not just substantial parts: see 1988 Act s 89(2).
[10] Whitford Committee, *Copyright Law 1977*, para 33.
[11] Copyright, Designs and Patents Act 1988 s 3(1)(*b*).
[12] [1900] AC 539.

reporter was entitled to damages when his version of a politician's public speech was copied word for word by a rival newspaper. This would not mean, of course, that no other paper could report the speech: another reporter present would have an equal right to file a separate account of it. Though both accounts might be identical, neither would be derived from the other and both would enjoy copyright. As each of these reporters would have copyright, both papers could prevent their less diligent rivals from copying their reports. (The politician in *Walter* v *Lane* would, after the 1988 Act, have copyright in his speech because of the act of the reporter in recording it, but the reporter's defence (see p. 248) would mean that the politician could not prevent its appearance in the paper.)

News stories and programme formats

There is 'no copyright in news itself, although there is copyright in the form in which it is conveyed'.[13] This means merely that a newspaper cannot obtain exclusive rights to cover an event by being first on the scene, or stop rivals from repeating facts of public importance that it is first to report.

The *Daily Express* sued *Today* newspaper for breach of copyright because, in time-honoured press tradition, *Today* had 'copied', in its second edition, an 'exclusive' *Express* story on prostitute-about-town Pamela Bordes. *Today* responded by suing Express Newspapers for breach of copyright when its own exclusive story – from a royal relative it had paid to criticize the royal family – was pirated. The Vice-Chancellor, Sir Nicholas Browne Wilkinson, refused to find that there could be copyright in the substance of a news story, although there would have been a breach if a substantial part of the original reporter's words had been copied verbatim:

> I would hesitate a long time before deciding that there is copyright in a news story which would be infringed by another newspaper picking up that story and reproducing the same story in different words. Such a conclusion would strike at the root of what I think is the practice of the national press, namely to search the columns of other papers to find stories which they have missed and then using the story so found in their own newspaper by rewriting it in their own words. If it were the law that such practice constituted breach of copyright, the consequences, as it seems to me, would be that a paper that obtained a scoop from a confidential source would obtain a monopoly on that piece of news. That would not be in the

---

[13] *Springfield* v *Thame* (1903) 89 LT 242. Note that this case was decided before Parliament gave the press a 'fair dealing' defence for reporting current events.

public interest as it would prevent the wider dissemination of the news to the public at large.[14]

What *is* protected by copyright, under the rubric of 'form' or 'mode of expression', is not merely language and paragraph arrangement, but *original work*, which in the case of a news article would include the skill, labour and judgement that had been expended upon research, 'putting together' and presentation. The principle is that 'the plaintiff has a right to say that no one is to be permitted . . . to take a material and substantial part of his work, his argument, his illustrations, his authorities, for the purpose of making or improving a rival publication.'

Journalists who find their stories 'borrowed' in detail by other publications, without an agency agreement and without an appropriate attribution, may have a good cause of action. If what is pirated is merely the facts, retold in different words, then the courts may well find that this is a custom engaged in by newspapers over a very long time, and impliedly consented to by all who work on them. But where the borrowing is substantial and verbatim, and reproduces quotations from third parties (who have a separate copyright), then the principle in *Walter* v *Steinkopf* is likely to be applied:

> Rudyard Kipling's news dispatches, printed in *The Times*, were regularly and substantially reproduced without that newspaper's consent in the *St James Evening Gazette*. Mr Justice North held that its copyright had been infringed:

In the present case what the defendants have had recourse to is not a mental operation involving thought and labour and producing some original results, but a mechanical operation with scissors and paste, without the slightest pretension to an original result of any kind; it is a mere production of 'copy' without trouble or cost . . . it is not immaterial to look at the number and character of the passages taken, in the whole; and also to bear in mind that it is not a mere casual trespass on the plaintiff's right, occurring now and again at long intervals, and not likely to be repeated; but deliberate, persistent abstraction of matter from the plaintiff's paper, which the defendants justify and insist on their right to continue. For the purposes of their own profit they desire to reap where they have not sown, and to take advantage of the labour and expenditure of the plaintiffs in procuring news for the purpose of saving labour and expense to themselves.

It is said there is no copyright in news. But there is or may

---

[14] *Express Newspapers* v *News (UK) Ltd* [1990] 3 All ER 376.

be copyright in the particular forms of language or modes of expression by which information is conveyed, and not the less so because the information may be with respect to the current events of the day . . .[15]

The problem of deliberate borrowing in journalism will be considered further in relation to the requirement of 'substantiality' and the defence of 'fair dealing'.

Literary copyright will obviously exist in the scripts of television and radio programmes. In some cases they will also have protection as dramatic works. However, the badge or characteristic of other programmes may be less easy to define. Hughie Green discovered how difficult it was to prevent others using the same idea.

> Hughie Green had compered *Opportunity Knocks* in the United Kingdom for many years. He had devised the use of a 'clapometer' to measure the audience's reaction to the different acts that appeared in his talent contest. Certain stock phrases, such as 'For X . . . opportunity knocks', were used in most programmes, but the content of each programme changed each week and Hughie Green's own words were usually ad lib. New Zealand Television took the same idea and used similar techniques in a television programme with the same name. Hughie Green failed to injunct them. The title was too trite to attract copyright. The clapometer and the other features of the programme's format were too nebulous to be described as a 'dramatic work' and too imprecise to be protected as 'literary copyright'.[16]

There is a lively current debate over the fairness of the *Opportunity Knocks* decision, and a lobby (enthusiastically joined by lawyers in the entertainment industry) for its reversal by legislation and for the creation of 'format rights' that would entitle creators of ideas for game shows to stop others from copying these ideas. Our view is that freedom of expression is better advanced by retaining the present copyright rule, which protects the way in which ideas are expressed, but not the ideas themselves.

Published editions[17]

In addition to protecting the content of a literary, musical or dramatic work, the 1988 Act also gives copyright to its typographical arrangement (assuming that it has been published). It is a more restricted right in that it lasts for only twenty-five years from the end of the year of publication (by comparison with fifty years after the death of the author(s) for published literary works), but for

---

[15] *Walter* v *Steinkopf* [1892] 3 Ch 489.
[16] *Green* v *Broadcasting Corporation of New Zealand* (1989) *The Times*, 24 July.
[17] Copyright, Designs and Patents Act 1988 ss 8 and 15.

that period, facsimile copies can be made only with the consent of the owner of this copyright as well as the owner of the literary or other work itself.

Artistic works[18]

Copyright can subsist in the following original artistic works:
>   (a) irrespective of artistic quality: paintings, drawings, diagrams, maps, charts, plans, engravings, etchings, lithographs, woodcuts or similar works (collectively referred to as 'graphic works'), photographs, sculptures or collages;
>   (b) works of architecture, being either buildings or models for buildings;
>   (c) work of artistic craftsmanship not falling within (a) or (b).

The first of these categories is likely to be most important for journalists – in particular, paintings, drawings and photographs. These words are given a wide definition. In one case a picture of a hand holding a pencil that was marking a cross next to the name of a favoured election candidate was said to be a sufficient drawing to have copyright.[19] Cartoon comic strips also have copyright under this head.[20]

'Photograph' means 'a recording of light or other radiation on any medium on which an image is produced or from which an image may by any means be produced and which is not part of a film'.[21] Films are excluded because they are separately protected. This apart, the definition is broad and would include, for instance, holograms and also the photographic 'plates' that are used in photolithographic printing.

As with literary works, artistic works in the first category are protected whatever their aesthetic value. Similarly, all 'artistic works' are only protected if they are 'original', in the sense that some skill and labour must have been involved in producing them. Buckingham Palace is a hackneyed subject for tourists' photographs but each picture enjoys copyright, as in each case the photographer will have chosen the distance and angle from which to take it. Similarly, a photocopy montage of clippings or headlines may have sufficient originality to have photographic copyright, but a photocopy of a page of someone else's work falls on the other side of the line: as an exact copy it lacks originality and no particular skill and labour has been required to produce it.

---

[18] ibid., s 4.
[19] *Kenrick & Co* v *Lawrence & Co* (1890) 25 QBD 99, decided under the Copyright (Works of Art) Act 1862.
[20] *King Features Syndicate Inc* v *O & M Kleeman Ltd* [1941] AC 417, HL.
[21] Copyright, Designs and Patents Act 1988 s 5.

Sound recordings[22]

This expression is widely defined as
- (*a*) a recording of sounds from which any sounds may be reproduced, or
- (*b*) a recording of the whole or any part of a literary, dramatic or musical work from which sounds reproducing the work or any part may be reproduced, regardless of the medium on which the recording is made or the method by which the sounds are reproduced or produced.

Consequently while this type of copyright is commonly used to protect recordings of music, it would include, for example, a tape recording of a conversation. There is no test of originality, but a copy of a previous sound recording does not acquire its own copyright. Under the 1988 Act the sound recording of a film sound track has copyright; under the 1956 Act this was only the case if a record or tape was separately issued.

Films[23]

'Films' are again broadly defined as 'a recording on any medium from which a moving image may by any means be produced'. It is therefore irrelevant whether the film is shot on an ordinary camera or by using a magnetic videotape. The recording of a computer program that produces abstract patterns when fed through a machine would also qualify as a 'film'. Dramatic works or sound recordings that are only embodied in a film can now enjoy a separate copyright (unlike the position before the 1988 Act), but a photograph that is part of a film does not have its own copyright.[24] This limitation is less appropriate to cartoon films. Each drawing made for the animation has a separate artistic copyright. This was clearly the case when animators like Walt Disney commissioned separate paintings for each frame. The huge costs of that method of production can now be cut by using a single drawing and washable inks. The picture can then be re-photographed for the following frame, by altering only the part that needs to 'move'. The picture in each state lasts only a few minutes and this impermanence creates a doubt as to whether each enjoys artistic copyright. Of course, each picture is captured on the film, but a photograph can be an artistic work only if it is *not* part of a film.

No court has yet had to decide on whether a series of still photographs taken by motordrive cameras are protected as artistic

---

[22] ibid., s 4(2).
[23] ibid., s 5.
[24] ibid., s 4(2).

works or as a film. Clearly they are intended to be developed singly, but if (as is sometimes the case) they are 'capable of being shown as a moving picture', then the spool would be protected only as a film.

Broadcasts and cable programmes[25]

'Broadcast' is defined as 'a transmission by wireless telegraphy of visual images, sounds or other information which is capable of being lawfully received by members of the public or is transmitted for presentation to members of the public'. Thus, television and radio have their own copyright in addition to that which pre-recorded programmes enjoy as sound recordings or films. 'Wireless telegraphy' is defined[26] as 'the sending of electromagnetic energy over pathways not provided by a material substance or arranged for that purpose' and therefore excludes cable (which now has its own form of copyright – see below), or the services that rely on telephone lines. It is no longer the BBC and the ITC who exclusively enjoy the broadcasters' copyright: the 1988 Act removed this limitation, no doubt with an eye to future deregulation. Satellite broadcasts are protected if decoding equipment for their encrypted signals has been made available to the public by or with the broadcasters' permission.[27]

Cable programmes in a service 'which consists wholly or mainly in sending visual images, sounds or other information by means of a telecommunications system, otherwise than by wireless telegraphy, for reception (*a*) at two or more places [whether simultaneously or not], or (*b*) for presentation to members of the public'[28] have their own copyright. This wide definition not only catches what would colloquially be called cable programmes, but a variety of other telephonic means of communication. The scope is cut back by some complex exceptions. Broadly, the Act excludes from cable copyright services that are solely for the internal benefit of a business, for a single individual or for use in premises that have a single occupier. The 'catalogue' of interactive services, e.g., home banking or home shopping, is protected by cable copyright (as well as, of course, by any literary copyright that it might also have) but the consumer's response is not.

As with sound recordings and films, there is no requirement that

[25] ibid., ss 6 and 7.
[26] ibid., s 178.
[27] Under s 298 the broadcasters are given remedies against unlicensed producers and sellers of equipment that decodes their signals, whether in the United Kingdom or abroad. See *BBC Enterprises Ltd* v *Hi Tech Xtravision Ltd* [1991] 3 All ER 257.
[28] Copyright, Designs and Patents Act 1988 s 7(1).

a broadcast or a cable programme be original. However, as with sound recordings and films, a simple copy of a previous broadcast or cable programme would not be entitled to a fresh copyright.

Territorial connection

Copyright can be claimed only if there is a connection between the work and either the United Kingdom or a country that is a party to an international copyright convention giving reciprocal rights. In general terms, *unpublished* works are protected if the author or maker was a national of, or resident or domiciled in, Britain or one of the other countries that have subscribed to the Berne Copyright Convention or the Universal Copyright Convention. Where a company may own copyright, it is sufficient if it is incorporated in one of these countries.[29] Most of the developed countries are parties to one or both of these conventions, although some have joined relatively recently. So, for instance, an unpublished Russian manuscript written by an author who died prior to 1973 will not have copyright protection in the United Kingdom.[30] The personal connection between the author and Britain is also sufficient to give copyright in *published* works. Alternatively, they will be protected if the work's first publication took place in Britain or one of the Convention countries.

Television, radio broadcasts and cable programmes are protected if made or sent from a place in the United Kingdom or from a Convention country.

Period of copyright

The 1988 Act has simplified and (generally) shortened the period of copyright that works enjoy. For works created after 1 August 1989 (the commencement date of the 1988 Act) the period of copyright is stated below; in each case 'from the year' means from 31 December of that year.

- literary, dramatic, musical and artistic works, fifty years from 31 December of the year in which the author died except for computer-generated works, where copyright lasts for fifty years from the year in which the work was made;[31]
- sound recordings and films, fifty years from the year of release

---

[29] ibid., ss 1(3) and 153–155.
[30] Copyright (International Conventions) (Amendment No 3) Order 1973 (SI 1973 No 963).
[31] 1988 Act s 12(3).

to the public or fifty years from the year of making if not released within fifty years;[32]

- broadcast and cable, fifty years from the year first broadcast or inclusion in a cable programme;[33]
- published edition, twenty-five years from the year of first publication;[34]
- literary, dramatic, musical and artistic works by unknown authors, fifty years from the year it was made available to the public, (but there is no infringement if it is reasonable to believe that the author had been dead for at least fifty years);[35]
- Crown copyright in literary, dramatic, musical and artistic works, 125 years from the year of making or fifty years from the year of commercial publication (whichever is the shorter);[36] in other works, the normal term;
- parliamentary copyright in literary, dramatic, musical and artistic works, fifty years from the year the work was made;[37] in other works, normal term.

For works that were created before commencement of the 1988 Act, the position is much more difficult.[38] First, it is necessary to decide whether copyright subsisted on the date the 1988 Act came into effect. Second, it is necessary to apply the transitional provisions of the 1988 Act. These are very detailed and the Act should be consulted. The most important provisions are that unpublished works (which under the 1956 Act generally had perpetual copyright) are (in most cases) now protected for only fifty years from the commencement of the 1988 Act and that conversion damages (see p. 257) cannot be obtained even for infringements before 1 August 1989 unless the action was also commenced before that date.

Infringement of Copyright

Copying

Literary, dramatic, musical or artistic works
The most common method of infringing copyright in these types

---

[32] ibid., s 13.
[33] ibid., s 14.
[34] ibid., s 15.
[35] ibid., s 12(2).
[36] ibid., s 163(3).
[37] ibid., s 165(3).
[38] ibid., Sched 1.

of works is by copying them – that is, by reproducing all or a substantial part of them – in any material form.[39] The reproduction need not be exact. Obviously, copyright would be of no value if it could be avoided by a sham alteration of a word or two. It is a more difficult question as to whether drastic alterations of language or form exonerate a story whose substance is taken from an earlier work. The question is particularly important for the media. Can a story from a rival newspaper or broadcaster be reproduced if it is rewritten first? In the United States the answer would clearly be no, as the Hearst newspaper chain discovered. Its war reporters in World War I were not as effective as those of Associated Press. Hearst therefore lifted its war news from AP's East Coast editions and telegraphed them to California in time to compete with AP's West Coast editions. The United States Supreme Court held that this misappropriation of AP's skill and labour was wrongful competition and could be stopped.[40]

Under United Kingdom copyright legislation the question would turn upon whether the borrowing was 'substantial'. This test would be satisfied if a story in newspaper A, based on original research and interviews, was repeated in newspaper B. Thus, each paper in the *Today/Express* litigation (see p. 219) was found to have infringed the other's copyright in the quotations that had appeared in the original articles and that were copied by the rival paper.[41]

Parliament has accepted and catered for the peculiar position of news. It has given the media a limited licence to plagiarize literary, dramatic and musical works for the purpose of reporting current events, if they provide a sufficient acknowledgement of their source (see 'Fair Dealing', p. 236). Consequently, it is only if a newspaper has failed to acknowledge its indebtedness to a rival that it would need to argue that it had not infringed the other's copyright. It is not at all clear that a court would be sympathetic in such a circumstance. A clue to the likely attitude is the response to the *St James Gazette*'s argument that in copying Rudyard Kipling's dispatches in *The Times* the paper was only following a hallowed Fleet Street custom. A highwayman, the judge caustically remarked, might as well plead the frequency of robbery on Hounslow Heath.[42]

In 1980 the High Court of Australia held that journalists who had obtained secret government cables could, without breaking the

---

[39] ibid., ss 16(1) (*a*), (3) and 17(2).

[40] *International News Service* v *Associated Press* 248 US 215 (1918).

[41] *Express Newspapers plc* v *News (UK) Ltd* [1990], note 14 above.

[42] *Walter* v *Steinkopf* [1892] 3 Ch 489, 499. The *Daily Express* tried a similar arrangement in its litigation with *Today* but was precluded from blowing hot and cold: the existence of the action would have fatally undermined its own claim that the copyright in its quotations had been enjoyed.

government's copyright, relay the content and essence of the documents if they chose their own language.[43] They could summarize the effects of the cables and pick out the highlights, but verbatim reproduction would be an infringement. The courts can grant injunctions where the reproduction (although quite different in form) draws on the skill and labour that the plaintiff had invested in making the original:

> The script of an historical event (the Charge of the Light Brigade) had been drawn from facts recounted in a history book without further original research. An injunction was granted even though the language of the book had not been reproduced, the order of events was different and fresh material had been added.[44]

As the court stated in a similar case:

> No man is entitled to avail himself of the previous labours of another for the purpose of conveying to the public the same information, although he may append additional information to that already published.[45]

Substantial part

The test is whether, irrespective of language, a 'substantial part' of the original work has been reproduced. For this reason, the courts would not prevent others from using a commentator's apt epithet or a dramatist's smart pun. One way of deciding whether the part copied is 'substantial' is to consider whether on its own it would attract copyright protection.[46] Most titles – of plays, books, stories and newspapers – are not copyright, because by themselves they do not have sufficient originality. Consequently, it is not a breach of copyright for a competitor to use a title that is very similar. In *Dicks* v *Yates*[47] both plaintiff and defendant had called respective (and different) stories 'Splendid Misery'. Since there was no likelihood of the public being misled, there was no remedy. Inventing a new word as a title or name (e.g. 'Exxon') does not give rise to copyright if it has a meaning only when used with other words.[48]

---

[43] *Commonwealth of Australia* v *John Fairfax and Sons Ltd* (1981) 32 ALR 485. High Court of Aust.

[44] *Harman Pictures NV* v *Osborne* [1967] 1 WLR 723.

[45] *Elanco Products Ltd* v *Mandops (Agrochemicals) Specialists Ltd* [1980] RPC 213 CA. See also *Independent Television Publications Ltd* v *Time Out Ltd* [1984] FSR 64.

[46] But this test must be used with care: *Ladbroke (Football) Ltd* v *William Hill (Football) Ltd* [1964] 1 WLR 273 at 276.

[47] (1881) 18 Ch D 76.

[48] *Exxon Corporation* v *Exxon Insurance Consultants* [1981] 3 All ER 241. Cf. the 'Wombles' case *Wombles Ltd* v *Wombles Skips* [1975] FSR 488 and the 'Kojak' case *Taverner Rutledge* v *Trexapalm Ltd* [1975] FSR 479.

However, if the name is so close that it will create confusion as to whether the new product is the responsibility of, or linked with, the established title, it can be stopped as a wrongful attempt at 'passing off'.[49] On the same principle, while a cartoon can be artistic copyright, the joke behind it cannot: it is too ephemeral. Other cartoonists can raise the same laugh so long as their drawings are different.[50]

The degree of change that a defendant must make may vary according to the degree of skill that has gone into producing the original. Although a picture of a hand holding a pencil and making a cross might be entitled to copyright, the fact that it had taken no great skill to produce is recognized by protecting it only against close imitations: a picture of a hand in a slightly different position was not an infringement.[51] In the same way, copyright in an anthology of quotations is not infringed by a later work that uses some of the same material, but in combination with other sources and in a different arrangement.[52]

The main purpose of copyright is to allow the inventors of original works to exploit them commercially. Where the plaintiff's and the defendant's works do compete and more than minimal effort has gone into producing the original work, it is not easy to persuade a court that the copying is insubstantial. It will not use a crude quantitative criterion, but rather a qualitative one. The most frequently cited judicial test looks to the commercial reality: 'what is worth copying prima facie is worth protecting.'[53]

Copyright is not just a battleground between commercial rivals. Satire and parody may involve the repetition of a large part of the work that is being lampooned. It, too, will be judged by the 'substantial part' test in deciding whether there has been an infringement.[54] However, the satirist and the parodist may have a fair-dealing defence (see pp. 235–9). In any case, the targets of their

---

[49] *University of Oxford* v *Pergamon Press* (1977) *The Times*, 19 October, CA, where Pergamon were injuncted from publishing *The Pergamon Oxford Dictionary of Perfect Spelling*. Contrast *Baylis & Co (The Maidenhead Advertiser)* v *Derlenko* [1974] FSR 284 where the *Maidenhead Advertiser* was unable to stop a free sheet using the name the *New Advertiser*. Despite some inevitable misunderstanding, 'Advertiser' was just descriptive and the word 'New' made the title sufficiently distinctive.
[50] *McCrum* v *Eisner* (1917) 117 LT 536; (1917–23) MCC 14.
[51] *Kenrick* v *Lawrence*, see note 19 above.
[52] *Warwick Film Productions Ltd* v *Eisinger* [1967] 3 All ER 367.
[53] *University of London Press Ltd* v *University Tutorial Press Ltd* [1916] 2 Ch 601, 610. This attitude is strikingly manifest where the compiler of a directory has made use of a rival publication rather than carry out the original research itself. There may be an infringement of copyright in the competing work even if it is only used to compile a mailing list for a questionnaire for the new work; *Waterlows* v *Butterworths* (unreported, but see *The Independent* 5 October 1990).

barbs may risk making greater fools of themselves by taking legal action.

If they should do so, there are two other (vaguer) principles that the courts can invoke either in assessing whether there has been an infringement or in deciding whether to grant a discretionary remedy such as an injunction. The first is a recognition that copyright law must not be used as a means of oppression:

> *Red Star Weekly* used the four lines of a popular song called 'Her Name is Mary' as the opening paragraph of a serial story. The court said this was not a breach of copyright. Care had to be taken not to allow the Copyright Acts to be used as a means of oppression. Here the defendant was using part of the plaintiff's work for a totally different purpose: a purpose that would have no adverse effect on the defendant's sales.[55]

The second principle is that the courts are unlikely to interfere (especially at the interlocutory stage) where the alleged infringer adapts the owner's work to make a political point:

> The Campaign for Nuclear Disarmament printed a pamphlet *30 Questions and Answers about CND*. On its cover the CND symbol was interwoven with a map of Britain. The Coalition for Peace Through Security, a group opposed to CND, produced a counter-publication, *30 Questions and Honest Answers About CND*. The design of the cover was very similar except that the CND symbol had been adapted to resemble a hammer and sickle. CND was refused an interlocutory injunction because it had suffered no financial loss and the judge was reluctant to restrain political controversy.[56]

Programme schedules

One example of how copyright law can operate to prevent one part of the media announcing what another part is doing was for many years provided by the monopoly that the BBC and the ITV companies, respectively, gave to the *Radio Times* and *TV Times* for publishing their weekly programme schedules – an indulgence that made these the largest selling journals in Britain. Although other newspapers and magazines were permitted by the fair-dealing provision of the Act to preview a number of programmes, and the broadcasting authorities allowed their full schedules to be

---

[54] See *Schweppes* v *Wellingtons* [1984] FSR 210, *Williamson Music Ltd* v *The Pearson Partnership* [1987] FSR 97; contrast *Joy Music Ltd* v *Sunday Pictorial Newspapers* [1960] 1 All ER 703.

[55] *Chappell & Co Ltd* v *D. C. Thompson & Co Ltd* (1928–35) MCC 467. See also *British Leyland Motor Corp* v *Armstrong Patents Co Ltd* [1986] AC 577.

[56] *Kennard* v *Lewis* [1983] FSR 346.

published twenty-four hours ahead, there could be no publication in Britain like the American *TV Guide*, which gives all the listings of all channels a week in advance. This was the result of a ruling in 1926:

> A group of radio enthusiasts started a magazine that set out the week's radio programmes, in opposition to *Radio Times*, published by the BBC. The interlopers gave advance notice of the BBC's most popular programmes – with names like *Old Memories* and *Humour and Request* – and announced in advance songs to be broadcast, such as 'When two that love are parted'. The court held that BBC programmes were a valuable compilation involving skill and effort, and so the Corporation owned the copyright, which it had exclusively granted to the *Radio Times*.[57]

The BBC and ITV companies defended their copyright monopoly on the grounds that they ploughed the heavy profits back into broadcasting, and used the magazines to promote programmes that were worthy but otherwise unpublicizable. Their opponents – notably *Time Out*, which unsuccessfully challenged the 1926 decision in the courts[58] – claimed that programme information is public information, because it is provided on public airways by public authorities. Their further claim, that the monopoly is an anti-competitive practice that led to dull and unimaginative magazines, was surely correct.

In 1990 the Government finally legislated to end the broadcasters' copyright monopoly in programme schedules. An early attempt to challenge such monopolies under the European Convention of Human Rights had failed, on the grounds that Article 10 guaranteed freedom to exploit information only to those who produced it.[59] However, subsequently the EC Commission held that the programme monopoly schedule infringed Article 86 of the Treaty of Rome, and directed broadcasters to provide weekly advance listings of their programmes to all who requested them.[60] In order to conform with this ruling, the British Government introduced Section 176 of the Broadcasting Act 1990, which requires the BBC, Channel 4 and all services regulated by the ITC or the Radio Authority to provide a list of a full week's programmes at least fourteen days in advance to those wishing to publish this information. The information may be limited to

---

[57] *BBC* v *Wireless League Gazette Publishing Co* [1926] Ch 433.
[58] *Independent Television Publications Ltd* v *Time Out Ltd* [1984] FSR 64.
[59] *De Geillustreede* v *The Netherlands* [1979] FSR 173.
[60] *Magill TV Guide* v *Independent Television Publications* [1990] FSR 71, EC Comm., and see the judgment of the European Court in Luxembourg (10 July 1991) that approved the Commission's view that the BBC and ITV had used copyright law as 'an instrument of abuse'.

programme titles and must be paid for by those wishing to publish it, at rates that, if they cannot be agreed, should be decided by the Copyright Tribunal in terms of what it considers 'reasonable in the circumstances'.[61] The BBC and independent television companies reacted churlishly to the loss of their monopoly, and demanded an astronomical £8 million per year for allowing national and local newspapers and magazines to publish their programme listings. Two hundred publishers appealed to the Copyright Tribunal, which proceeded to adjudicate on the charges after a five-week public hearing.

Derivation

From the examples given so far it should be apparent that a copy will be an infringement only if it is derived from the plaintiff's work. A picture of a winning goal cannot be lifted from one newspaper by its rivals without committing a breach of copyright, but if two photographers took identical pictures from the same spot, both pictures could be published without impinging on each other's copyright. If a newspaper were to copy a table of fixtures from a football pools coupon, it would breach the pools organizer's copyright, but it could publish an identical table if it obtained the information by its own researches.

This casual connection need not be direct. The owners of the *Popeye* cartoon copyright were able to stop an infringer from producing Popeye dolls. The dolls had been copied, not from the cartoon, but from other dolls that had been produced under the plaintiff's licence.[62] This case, incidentally, also illustrates the possibility of infringing a two-dimensional artistic work by a three-dimensional copy.[63]

A photographer or painter can also indirectly copy an earlier work by recreating the model or scene from which the first artist worked. The copying can then be in the similarity of composition, angle, lighting and general effect,[64] although, as with other examples of infringement, the less skill that was invested in the first work, the closer must be the resemblance to the second before the courts will accept there has been infringement.

Once the link between the original and the copy is proved, it is unnecessary for the copyright owner to show that the defendant intended to plagiarize.[65] Unconscious imitation is still an infringe-

---

[61] Broadcasting Act 1990 Sched 17.
[62] *King Features Syndicate Inc* v *O & M Kleeman Ltd*, note 20 above; see also Copyright, Designs and Patents Act 1988 s 16(3)(*b*).
[63] Copyright, Designs and Patents Act 1988 s 17(3).
[64] *Gross* v *Seligman* (1914) 212f 930 (1911–16) MCC 219; *Turner* v *Robinson* (1860) 10 I Ch R 121, s 10.

ment, though, as will be shown, the defendant's innocence may affect the remedies available to the plaintiff.

Other types of infringement

Copying other works

Copying a published edition means making a facsimile copy of it.[66] Copyright in a film, television broadcast or cable programme can be infringed by taking a photograph of any image forming part of the work.[67]

There can be copying of any type of work even if the copy is transient or incidental to some other use.[68] This can be important for the protection of copyright in computer programs or material stored on computer discs. Calling up a file to be read on a computer would be to make an infringing copy (assuming, of course, it was without the permission of the copyright owner), even if the copy disappears without trace when the machine is switched off. Although incidental copying is prima facie an infringement, there are important defences (see p. 247)

Broadcast and cable

Any type of copyright (apart from a published edition) will be infringed if the work is included in a broadcast or cable programme.[69] Responsibility is shared between the broadcaster who actually transmits the programme (e.g. the BBC, the IBA) and the company contracting to provide the programme (e.g. Granada, TVS, Capital Radio).[70] A similar position has been reached by the courts under the earlier legislation.[71]

Adaptation

Literary, dramatic and musical (but not artistic) works are also protected against adaptations. This includes turning a non-dramatic work into a dramatic one and vice versa; translating the work into a different language, and turning the work into a strip cartoon. An arrangement or transcription of a musical work is an adaptation. A computer program can be 'translated' by converting it into or out of a computer language or code or into another

---

[65] e.g., *Byrne* v *Statist Co* [1914] 1 KB 622.
[66] Copyright, Designs and Patents Act 1988 s 17(5).
[67] ibid., s 17(4).
[68] ibid., s 17(6).
[69] ibid., s 20.
[70] ibid., s 6(3).
[71] *Independent Television Companies Association Ltd* v *Performing Rights Society Ltd* (1982) *The Times*, 23 November.

language or code but this is not an infringement if it is done only incidentally in the course of running the program.[72]

Publication and public performance

Sometimes the owner of the copyright will make or authorize copies to be made, but wish to keep them for his own use. The unauthorized issuing of such copies (as well as infringing copies) to the public is an infringement.[73] Liability is here limited to the person who puts the copies into public circulation (the newspaper publisher, for instance) and, with one exception, does not apply to others in the chain of distribution. Thus, wholesalers or retailers would not be liable for 'issuing to the public'. They will be liable, if at all, for secondary infringement (see below), which depends on knowledge that the merchandise is an infringement. The one exception relates to sound recordings, films or computer programs. So far as these are concerned 'issuing to the public' includes renting copies to the public.

The public performance of a literary, dramatic or musical work is another matter in which the copyright owner is entitled to control. 'Performance' includes lectures, addresses, speeches and (parsons beware!) sermons. It will also include a presentation by means of sound or visual aids. Owners of the copyright in sound recordings, films, broadcasts and cable programmes can similarly restrict the public playing of their works.[74]

Authorizing infringement

In addition to suing the person who actually does these prohibited acts, the copyright owner can also pursue those who 'authorize' them.[75] 'Authorizing' includes sanctioning, approving or countenancing the infringement. So contributors who supply articles or photographs to magazines would be liable for authorizing the infringement if they did not own the copyright. Attempts have been made to hold newspapers liable for 'authorizing' infringement of musical copyright when they have carried advertisements for, or stories about, home-taping. These have generally failed because the plaintiffs were unable to prove that the publication had any influence on the readers' actions.[76] A similar action against the maker of twin-deck tape recorders also failed.[77]

---

[72] Copyright, Designs and Patents Act 1988 s 21.
[73] ibid., s 18.
[74] ibid., s 19.
[75] ibid., s 16(2).
[76] *RCA Corporation* v *John Fairfax & Sons* [1982] RPC 91 Sup Co of NSW; *A & M Records Inc* v *Audio Magnetics Inc (UK)* [1979] FSR 1 (where the advertiser was the defendant).
[77] *CBS Songs Ltd* v *Amstrad Consumer Electronics plc* [1988] 2 All ER 484, HL.

Secondary infringement

All the methods of infringement considered so far in this section and the last are regarded as 'primary infringement' by some form of copying, performing or broadcasting. The Copyright Act goes further and allows the copyright owner to take action against others in the chain of distribution and exploitation of infringing copies. Thus importing, possessing in the course of a business, selling, letting for hire, offering or exposing for sale or hire, exhibiting in public for trade or other purposes, and certain types of distributing in each case of infringing copies makes the person concerned liable to the copyright owner.[78] Secondary liability is also imposed on a range of other people who might be commercially involved in primary infringement by, for instance, dealing in articles specifically designed or adapted for making infringing copies or taking steps to enable an infringing performance to take place.[79]

Whereas primary infringement does not depend on guilty knowledge, these secondary infringements do require knowledge or reason to believe that the copies are illegitimate. For this reason, plaintiffs who assert that their rights have been abused will sometimes write to major wholesalers putting them on notice of their claims. This step should not be taken lightly, for the plaintiffs may be liable in damages for lost sales if their claims are not later substantiated.

However, printers are under no separate duty to inquire into the purpose to which their copies will be used and so will not be liable for general damages in the tort of negligence if they print infringing copies.[80]

Defences

Fair dealing

The use of reasonable extracts from the work of others is not an infringement of copyright if it is for the purpose of:

- research or private study, where a literary, dramatic, musical or artistic work is used, or
- criticism or review, or
- reporting current events.[81]

---

[78] Copyright, Designs and Patents Act 1988 s 23.
[79] ibid., ss 24–6.
[80] *Paterson Zochonis and Co Ltd* v *Merfaken Packaging Ltd* [1986] 3 All ER 522, CA.
[81] Copyright, Designs and Patents Act 1988 ss 29–30.

The fair-dealing defences require that an acknowledgement be given to the originator if the work is used for criticism or review or, in the case of the print media, if it is used for the purpose of reporting current events. News stories on television, radio, film or cable television or in a sound recording are not required to give an acknowledgement. Where an acknowledgement is required, it must identify the work by its title rather than by general description. It must also identify the author unless he or she is anonymous.[82] As long as the source and author are identified as such in the text, neither the word 'acknowledgement' nor expressions of gratitude are required.

The dealing must be fair. A publisher or broadcaster will not need to resort to the defence unless a substantial part of the work has been taken, for only then will there be a prima facie infringement to which a defence is necessary. However, the defence will be lost if the taking is 'unfair' in the sense of being out of all proportion to the permitted purpose. Critics can illustrate their points by quotations, and where the original work is short, it can be reproduced in its entirety, but the quotation must be a basis for criticism or review; if the purpose is only to convey the same information as the original, and so compete with it, the use will be unfair.[83] Fairness depends on individual circumstances. The question of fairness is judged by the amount taken in order to achieve the permitted purpose: the justice or otherwise of the comments upon the extract is irrelevant.

Copyright protects the form of literary, dramatic or musical works, but the criticism need not be limited to the language or means of expression that the author has chosen. It is legitimate to copy substantial parts of the original in order to criticize its substance, content and values.

> *The Mind Benders* was a book written by a former member of the Church of Scientology. It included extracts from manuals by and directives of Ron L. Hubbard, the cult's founder, in order to expose and criticize its practices and beliefs. Although the documents had not previously been published, the court refused an interim injunction. Lord Denning said:

> We never restrain a defendant in a libel action who says he is going to justify. So in a copyright action, we ought not to

---

[82] ibid., s 178.
[83] *Hubbard* v *Vosper* [1972] 1 All ER 1023 at p. 1027, per Lord Denning; *Johnstone* v *Bernard Jones Publications Ltd* [1938] 1 Ch 599; *Associated Newspapers Group* v *News Group Newspapers* [1986] RPC 515.

restrain a defendant who has a reasonable defence of fair dealing . . . the law will not intervene to suppress freedom of
speech except where it is abused.[84]

In this case, the defendant was commenting on the plaintiff's
own works. This is not essential. Extracts of a reasonable length
can be used as part of a review of some third party's work (for
instance, if used for the purpose of comparison).[85]

The scientology case also shows that, at least in some circumstances, the fair-dealing defence is available in connection with
unpublished works. Some of the extracts were taken from bulletins
and letters that had been sent only to scientology initiates. Lord
Denning said that this was a sufficiently wide circle to make them
subject to public criticism.[86] A company circular sent only to
shareholders or a management study report distributed to top executives and union officials[87] may come within the same category.
Even where the document has been seen by only a very few people,
the fair-dealing defence is not automatically excluded.

> In 1968 a secret report written for the Greek military junta was
> leaked to *The Sunday Times*, which proposed to publish extracts
> from it along with a commentary. The Court of Appeal agreed that
> the newspaper had an arguable defence of fair dealing because it was
> only going to use extracts from the report in the course of a story
> commenting upon it and criticizing it.

> Copyright does not subsist in the information contained in the
> report. It exists only in the literary form in which the informa-
> tion is dressed. If *The Sunday Times* were going to print this
> report in full, thus taking the entire literary form, it might
> well be a case for an injunction.[88]

However, the restricted circulation of the original document and
the absence of consent to publication are certainly factors that the
courts have taken into account in deciding whether a dealing is
fair. The court in *Fraser* v *Evans* may have been influenced by the
fact that the document was a government (albeit foreign government) document and a matter of public concern. In an Australian

---

[84] *Hubbard* v *Vosper*, note 83 above.
[85] Copyright, Designs and Patents Act 1988 s 30(1).
[86] *Hubbard* v *Vosper*, note 83 above, at p. 1028.
[87] *Sun Printers Ltd* v *Westminster Press Ltd* [1982] 1 IRLR 292.
[88] *Fraser* v *Evans* [1969] 1 All ER 8. These cases qualify an earlier decision saying
that an unpublished work could never be reproduced for criticism and review:
British Oxygen Co Ltd v *Liquid Air Ltd* [1925] Ch 383 at p. 393.

case the judge hinted that the fair-dealing defence might be wider for criticism or review of government papers.[89] This indicates how the fair-dealing defence has become blurred with the separate defence of publication in the public interest. The latter would seem more appropriate in the case of leaked documents when the media's real intention is to reveal their contents and the plaintiff's real desire is to frustrate that purpose. In these situations a breach of copyright claim is a disguised action for breach of confidence and it is sensible to apply a common defence of public interest to both.

Fair dealing for the purpose of reporting current events is obviously of importance to the media. Before this statutory defence was introduced, a newsreel film was held to have infringed the musical copyright in *Colonel Bogey*. The film had included a twenty-second shot of a high-school band playing that tune as the Prince of Wales opened a new hospital.[90] Today such a newsreel would be protected as a report of a current event and, since it was part of a film, no acknowledgement would be necessary.

The meaning of *current* event has yet to be fully explored. The court thought it at least arguable in 1974 that the details of the effect of thalidomide were not then 'current' because the drug had been withdrawn twelve years previously.[91] This is a doubtful interpretation, given that the consequences of thalidomide last a lifetime. In any event, had the case gone further, *The Sunday Times* (which wanted to publish substantial extracts from Distillers' private documents) could well have argued that there was a contemporary debate over the morality of Distillers' delay in reaching a settlement, and that its proposed story was highly relevant to this 'current event'. However the *Sun* was unable to argue that it was reporting a current event when it copied letters from the Duke and Duchess of Windsor to which the *Daily Mail* had obtained exclusive rights for a limited period.[92]

The 1988 Act significantly broadened the fair-dealing defence. Thus, under the earlier law, none of the aspects of fair dealing applied to the use of film, sound recording, broadcast or cable copyright. This restriction still applies to the research and private study aspect of the defence, but these works can now be used for criticism, review or news reporting. Therefore, there is no longer a copyright obstacle to the BBC presenting a critical and illustrated review of TV programmes on ITV, or vice versa. The ramifica-

---

[89] *Commonwealth of Australia* v *John Fairfax*, note 43 above at p. 495.
[90] *Hawkes and Son (London) Ltd* v *Paramount Film Service Ltd* [1934] Ch 593.
[91] *Distillers Co (Biochemicals) Ltd* v *Times Newspapers Ltd* [1975] QB 613 at p. 626.
[92] *Associated Newspapers Group* v *News Group Newspapers* [1986] RPC 515.

tions of the extended fair-dealing defence were considered by Mr Justice Scott in 1991 in *BBC* v *British Satellite Broadcasting*:[93]

> BSB, shortly before its absorption into Sky, successfully defended as fair dealing its use of short excerpts from BBC live broadcasts of World Cup matches in its sports-news programmes. Mr Justice Scott held that fairness was ultimately a matter of impression, and what impressed him was the fact that the excerpts were short (between 14 and 37 seconds) and were replayed no more than four times in genuinely informational sports-news bulletins. They were also acknowledged as having been shot by the BBC, not a statutory requirement, but an indication of overall fairness. There was no oblique motive rendering the use unfair, and although the BBC complained that the satellite channel was using only the best bits (i.e., the scoring of the goals), it was these clips that had obvious relevance to the news updates. The judge refused to limit the fair-dealing defence to general news programmes, and confirmed that sporting clashes were as much current events as any other newsworthy incidents. The judgment is notable for giving the defence a wide scope, consonant with the Government's intent to end the 'cosy duopoly' and promote competition within the broadcasting industry.

The 1988 Act also allows artistic works to be used for reporting current events. Significantly, this liberalization was not extended to photographs. This means that a newspaper still cannot reproduce a rival's 'scoop' photograph, even with acknowledgement, in order to report a news story. The law of copyrights thus gives special force to the newsroom adage that a picture is worth a thousand words. One rather unsavoury aspect of chequebook journalism involves the purchase by newspapers or news agencies of an exclusive right to exploit family snapshots of notorious criminals. If relatives are paid large sums by a particular news group for the exclusive copyright in a photograph, the law will prevent rival papers from publishing the same picture, however much a matter of public interest it has become. This market in the memorabilia of mass murder and the like would collapse if the law were changed to permit all media to publish such photographs for the purpose of reporting current events. News should not be the subject of copyright, and photographs that are specially newsworthy should not be confined to one newspaper merely because it happened to be the highest bidder.

Public interest

In a number of cases the courts have developed a defence of 'public interest' to claims for copyright infringement. The 1988 Act does

---

[93] [1991] 3 All ER 833.

not spell out this defence, but it does recognize its existence.[94] Thus in *Beloff* v *Pressdram*[95] the court agreed that *Private Eye* would have been entitled to publish a memorandum written by Nora Beloff to the editor of the *Observer* about the future of Reginald Maudling in the Heath Government, if the magazine had been able to show that the memo disclosed an 'iniquity'. It is not now necessary to point to misconduct on the part of the plaintiff for a public-interest defence to succeed. The ruling to this effect in *Lion Laboratories* v *Daily Express* (the intoximeter case) was made in relation to a claim for breach of copyright as well as for breach of confidence. The Court of Appeal indicated that the public-interest defence applied to both civil actions. Documents supplied by 'moles' will generally be subject to copyright: in order to contest the grant of an interim injunction the media must raise a serious public-interest defence that might succeed at the trial.

In the important 1990 case of *Express Newspapers* v *News Ltd* the Vice-Chancellor accepted unhesitatingly that there was a defence to breach of copyright, as to breach of confidence, 'if the information was such that it was in the public interest to know it'. In that case, however, the whining of a minor member of the royal family amounted to 'sensational journalism, not a serious discussion of matters of public interest'.[96]

Most government publications are covered by copyright, which is vested in either the Crown or Parliament. The Government has announced that it will not generally enforce its rights in the following publications, the wide diffusion of which is obviously in the public interest:

- bills and Acts of Parliament, statutory rules and orders, and statutory instruments,
- other parliamentary papers, including reports of select committees laid before Parliament,
- Hansard reports.

The right to enforce copyright in exceptional cases, e.g. where the reproduction would cause a significant loss to public funds, is reserved. The copies must also not purport to be authorized publications. For non-parliamentary publications, permission must be obtained and a fee usually paid, although HMSO can waive or reduce this 'where the need for fuller dissemination of official information is paramount and the commercial and other aspects are relatively unimportant.[97]

---

[94] Copyright, Designs and Patents Act 1988 s 171(3).
[95] [1973] 1 All ER 241.
[96] *Express Newspapers* v *News (UK) Ltd*, note 14 above, at p. 382.

Immorality

Public policy may *restrict* the plaintiff's ability to make out a cause of action. In 1916, one judge held that Elinor Glyn's novel *Three Weeks* was incapable of enjoying copyright protection because of its shocking moral values – it advocated free love and justified adultery.[98] In the early nineteenth century Lord Chancellor Eldon enthusiastically exercised this power and ruled that on grounds of public policy there was no copyright in Southey's subversive poem 'Wat Tyler' nor in Byron's blasphemous poem 'Cain'. Other works were denied copyright protection because they were blasphemous, defamatory or likely to deceive the public.[99] Public policy moves (albeit slowly) with the times. While the courts will still refuse their assistance to material that has a grossly immoral tendency, there is no common view as to what kind of sexual conduct between consenting adults is grossly immoral. The Vice-Chancellor remarked in 1988 that 'works of Elinor Glyn if published today would be widely regarded as, at the very highest, very soft pornography'.[100] In the second *Spycatcher* appeal the House of Lords thought that Peter Wright would be unable to assert copyright in his book because it represented a gross breach of trust.[101]

There can be an element of hypocrisy in raising a 'gross immorality' defence to excuse a publication made in breach of confidence. In the case that prompted the Vice-Chancellor's comment (*Stephen v Avery* – see p. 180) the *Mail on Sunday* had argued that a lesbian affair was so grossly immoral as to produce a tendency in others to immoral conduct. Not, the Vice-Chancellor observed, an easy argument for a paper that had just given nationwide publicity to the material. The consequence of accepting the argument that a work is too outrageous to be protected by copyright is that others may copy it at will and, since no licence fees can be charged, a good deal more cheaply than works that are copyright protected.

There is currently a refreshing unstuffiness about moral issues amongst judges in the Chancery Division of the High Court, which deals with copyright and patents. Their brethren in the criminal courts are likely to find most things indecent, and in this tradition a dour Comptroller General of Patents Designs and Trademarks refused to register a design for a model of a Scotsman doll with 'mimic male genitalia' under his kilt. This design was, in his opinion, 'contrary to law or morality' and hence unsuitable for

[97]   General Notice GEN 75/76.
[98]   *Glyn* v *Weston Feature Film Co* [1916] 1 Ch 261.
[99]   Phillips (1977) 6 Anglo-Am LR 138.
[100] *Stephens* v *Avery* [1988] 2 All ER 477 ChD.
[101] *A-G* v *Guardian Newspapers Ltd (No 2)* [1988] 3 All ER 545, HL.

registration under the Registered Designs Act 1949. The court noted that the design was to commemorate a wedding at which at least one guest had apparently worn nothing beneath his kilt, and that while some would find the doll distasteful, its registration could hardly be injurious to morality. The Registry had been wrong to apply a rigid taboo against the design of the penis, and to imagine that registration would give the design 'an official stamp of approval'.[102]

Licences

Who owns the copyright?

Owners of copyright cannot complain of infringement if they have licensed or granted permission for the use in question. This begs the important question: who is the owner? Analysing this issue is a two-stage process: determining who was the first owner of the work, and then assessing whether ownership has subsequently been transferred.

The first owner of a literary, dramatic, musical or artistic work is the author, i.e. its creator.[103] Under the earlier law copyright in photographs normally belonged first to the owner of the film or other material on which the picture was taken. Now the rule for photographs is the same as for other artistic works. Computer-generated works belong to the person who made the arrangements for their creation.[104] The author of a sound recording or film is similarly defined as the person who makes the arrangements necessary for the recording or filming.[105] This means that normally the producer of a film owns its copyright. The director, though, is given moral rights in the work (see p. 251).

The author of a broadcast is the person who makes it.[106] This will include the owner of the transmitter (e.g. the IBA and BBC), but only if that person has responsibility for the broadcast's content. British Telecom may facilitate direct broadcasting by satellite but has no involvement in its content and therefore does not share in the copyright. The 1988 Act enlarged the first owners in a broadcast to include the persons providing the programmes and who contract for their transmission. In future, therefore, commercial TV and radio stations will share copyright in their broadcasts with the IBA (or its successor, the ITC).

---

[102] In *Re Masterman's Application* (1990) *The Times*, 19 December.
[103] Copyright, Designs and Patents Act 1988 s 9(1).
[104] ibid., s 9(3).
[105] ibid., s 9(2)(*a*).
[106] ibid., ss 9(1)(*b*) and 6(3).

Copyright in a cable programme is first owned by the programme provider, and copyright in a published edition (i.e., typographical arrangement) is first owned by the publisher.[107] A work (such as this book) may have joint authors, in which case they will jointly be the first owners of the copyright. However, if their contributions are distinct (e.g., if the chapters of a book were divided between them), then each would have a separate copyright in his or her own part.[108]

Literary, dramatic, musical or artistic works made by employees in the course of their employment are first owned by their employers.[109] This can provoke difficult and delicate questions as to whether a relationship is one of employment or whether the author is self-employed and acting under a contract of services. Similarly, it may not be easy to determine whether a work was part of the employment or whether it was an independent venture of the employee.

Journalists used to enjoy a favoured position. Even though they were employed and even though their writing was done as part of their job, their employers had copyright only for the purpose of publishing their works in a newspaper, magazine, etc. Other uses (e.g., publishing anthologies of their stories in book form) could be controlled (and sold) by the journalist.[110] The 1988 Act has removed this right, and now the works of journalists are treated in the same way as other copyrights produced by employees.

Another exception removed by the 1988 Act concerns commissioned photographs, portraits, engravings and sound recordings. First copyright used to belong to the commissioner.[111] Now the general rule is reasserted. The impact of the change will be softened because of the new moral right in favour of those who commission photographs or films for private and domestic purposes (see p. 208), which will limit the power of the copyright owner to exploit it.

Employers can agree to allow their employees to have first copyright, [112] but there is no other statutory provision for altering the first allocation of the right. None the less, the courts have shown a willingness to introduce ideas of equity and trusts. In one case an advertising agency that was undoubtedly the first legal owner of the copyright was found to hold the copyright on trust for the commissioner of its drawings.[113] In the *Spycatcher* case the House of Lords suggested that if copyright could subsist in such a

---

[107] ibid., s 9(1)(*c*) and (*d*).
[108] ibid., s 10.
[109] ibid., s 11(2).
[110] Copyright Act 1956 s 4(2).
[111] ibid., ss 4(3) and 12(4).
[112] Copyright, Designs and Patents Act 1988 s 11(2).

scandalous book, it belonged in equity to the Crown.[114]

Once the first owner of the copyright is settled, the possibility of transfer must be considered. Copyright can be assigned, but to be fully effective the transfer needs to be in writing and signed by the assignor.[115] An assignment can be made in advance of the creation of the work, in which case it takes effect as soon as the work is made and the first owner's rights are fleetingly passed on.[116] An oral or unsigned transfer is not wholly ineffective: it allows the transferee to call for a proper assignment and will bind third parties who have notice of it, but it can be disregarded by a bona fide third party who purchases the copyright without notice of the informal assignment.

Implied licences

No special formality is required for a licence to be granted. It need not be express, but can be implied from the circumstances or by custom. A reader who sends a letter to the editor of a newspaper impliedly consents to its publication, and impliedly agrees as well to any editing that is necessary for reasons of space.[117] Submission of a feature article connotes a similar implied licence, albeit subject to payment of an appropriate fee.[118] Press releases clearly carry an implied licence to copy, at least if publication is made after any embargo.

Exclusive licences

Although an informal licence is effective to protect the media, it is less satisfactory if there is a danger that the publication will be pirated by others. A publisher who is merely a licensee can take action only against the pirates indirectly by calling on the owner of the copyright to sue them. This is inconvenient: authors, even if protected by an indemnity against costs, are sometimes shy of litigation. The problem can be avoided if the publisher takes an assignment. If the author is unwilling to part completely with the copyright, an almost identical advantage can be obtained by taking an exclusive licence: again the licence must be in writing and signed by the licensor.[119]

---

[113] *Warner* v *Gestetner* [1988] E IPR D–89 see also *Antocks Lairn* v *Bloohn* [1971] FSR 490.
[114] *A-G* v *Guardian Newspapers Ltd (No 2)* [1988] 3 All ER 545.
[115] Copyright, Designs and Patents Act 1988 s 90(3).
[116] ibid., s 91.
[117] *Springfield* v *Thame* (1903) 89 LT 242; *Roberts* v *Candiware Ltd* [1980] FSR 352.
[118] *Hall-Brown* v *Iliffe and Sons Ltd* (1928–35) MCC 88.
[119] Copyright, Designs and Patents Act 1988 s 92.

Adequate licences

Publishers and broadcasters must take care to obtain a licence from owners of all the copyrights in the item that they wish to use. If a copyright is owned by two or more people, each of them must give consent. Copyright can be infringed by a publisher who acted in good faith, and a number of reported cases concern licences that were inadequate because they were incomplete or obtained from the wrong person.[120] It is also important for the media to obtain a licence adequate for all intended purposes. For example, a broadcaster dealing with a playwright must obtain permission to film (if the play is to be pre-recorded) as well as to broadcast. The broadcaster need not, however, expressly provide for the right immediately to retransmit the material via cable television; a licence to broadcast a work carries with it the right to include it in a cable programme.[121]

Copyright Tribunal

Collective licensing, the Copyright Tribunal and competition

It is obviously impractical for individual copyright owners to police all possible infringements. The music industry first recognized the advantage of collective enforcement of copyrights. Now the Performing Rights Society and Phonographic Performance Ltd respectively control practically all performing and sound recording rights in music in the United Kingdom. Similar societies represent the interests of publishers and authors. Equally, there is the potential for these monopolies to act against the public interest. The 1956 Act established the Performing Rights Tribunal to adjudicate on disputes between rights owners and those who needed licences. The 1988 Act renamed the Tribunal the Copyright Tribunal and extended its jurisdiction.

The Tribunal's principal role is to hear disputes about either licensing schemes (standard terms, conditions and tariffs) or one-off licences in three areas.[122]

- the schemes of societies in relation to literary, dramatic, musical or artistic works or films that cover the work of more than one author;
- schemes or licences (whether by societies or individual owners) in relation to sound recordings (other than the sound tracks of films), broadcasts, cable programmes and published editions;

---

[120] e.g. *Byrne* v *Statist Co*, note 65 above.
[121] Copyright, Designs and Patents Act 1988 s 73.
[122] ibid., ss 116–135.

- schemes or licences (whether by societies or individual owners) in relation to the rental of sound recordings, films or computer programs.

In these areas the Tribunal can determine whether the offered terms are reasonable and whether an excluded category or use under a scheme ought to be licensed. The Tribunal must particularly try to prevent unreasonable discrimination by the copyright owners.[123] 'Discrimination' does not mean just unequal treatment on grounds of race or sex (though that would no doubt be unreasonable) but any discrimination between lincensees or potential licensees. Thus, under the 1956 Act the Tribunal held that it was unreasonable for the PRS to offer a discount to the Cinema Exhibitors Association but not to the smaller Association of Independent Cinemas.

The 1988 Act introduced two new statutory licences.[124] The first concerns rental of sound recordings, films or computer programs. The Secretary of State is empowered to introduce statutory licences for these.[125] The second concerns the Monopolies and Mergers Commission (MMC) and requires some explanation.

Under the Competition Act 1980 anyone can refer to the Office of Fair Trading an 'anti-competitive practice'. A good example was the practice of the BBC and ITV companies refusing to allow anyone other than the *Radio Times* and *TV Times* to print radio and television listings a week in advance. The London magazine *Time Out* referred this practice to the Director-General of Fair Trading. He found that the practice was anti-competitive and referred the matter to the MMC. The Commission was obliged to reconsider the issue of anti-competitiveness and, in this case, upheld the Director-General's view. It then had to consider the critical question of whether the practice worked against the public interest. In *Time Out*'s case the Commission were evenly divided and the challenge failed; it was left to Parliament finally to end the broadcasters' monopoly by s 176 of the 1990 Broadcasting Act shortly before the European Court of Justice ruled that a similar practice in Ireland breached EEC competition principles.[126] However, in a reference concerning the refusal of the Ford Motor Company to authorize the independent manufacture and sale of spare parts, the MMC found that the practice was both anti-competitive and against the public interest.[127] Yet the Commission

---

[123] ibid., s 129.
[124] A third concerns photocopying by educational establishments, ibid., s 141.
[125] ibid., s 66.
[126] *Radio Telefis Eirann* v *Commission of the European Community and Magill TV Guide Ltd*, Luxembourg, 10 July 1991.

was then powerless to order Ford to grant licences to the independents.[128]

The 1988 Act has now allowed the creation of a statutory licence in cases such as Ford where the MMC finds that the refusal to grant a licence is both anti-competitive and against the public interest.[129] For both types of statutory licence the Tribunal can fix terms in the absence of agreement.

The 1956 Act introduced a statutory licence to replay musical works once a record of the work had been issued to the public. The 1988 Act abolished this. The Broadcasting Act 1990 brought back something similar. It allows the broadcasting of sound recordings in the absence of agreement from the copyright owner and in advance of the Copyright Tribunal fixing the terms. There are complex and stringent conditions for the exercise of this new right. In outline, the broadcaster must have been refused a licence by the appropriate licensing body, have given notice of his intention to exercise the new right, be ready to pay the charge agreed or set by the Tribunal, be prepared to include in the broadcast a statement reasonably required by the licensing body and provide reasonably required information about the programmes that incorporate the recording. A similar scheme is established to prevent licensing bodies prescribing maximum 'needletime' – the proportion of any period of broadcasting that can be given over to records.[130]

Other defences

Incidental inclusion
Copyright in any work is not infringed by its incidental inclusion in an artistic work, sound recording, film, broadcast or cable programme.[131] This is a considerable advance on the 1956 Act, which allowed the incidental use only of an artistic work, and then only in a film, broadcast or cable programme. The use of music or lyrics will not be treated as incidental if they are deliberately included.

Reports of judicial and parliamentary proceedings
Reports of judicial or parliamentary proceedings will not be a

---

[127] HMSO 1985 Cmnd 9437.
[128] The House of Lords discovered another way out of the dilemma by ruling that the seller of an article like a car could not withhold the right to make spare parts since this would be a 'derogation from grant' (see *British Leyland Motor Corporation Ltd* v *Armstrong Patents Co Ltd* [1986] AC 577).
[129] Copyright, Designs and Patents Act 1988 s 144.
[130] ibid., ss 135A–G added by the Broadcasting Act 1990 s 175.
[131] Copyright, Designs and Patents Act 1988 s 31.

breach of any copyright as long as the report is first-hand.[132] Plagiarizing the published report of a rival is not protected. Interestingly, the proceedings do not, apparently, have to be in public. Copyright is not therefore among the restrictions that curtail the reporting of private court hearings (see Chapter 7). 'Judicial' is widely interpreted to mean any court, tribunal or person having authority to decide any matter affecting a person's legal rights or liabilities. [133]

Other aspects of public administration
There is no copyright objection to reporting the proceedings of a Royal Commission or statutory inquiry.[134] There is more limited right to copy material from public registers, but this is hedged with restrictions, notably the need to obtain the permission of the keeper of the record.[135] Material in the Public Record Office can be copied.[136] If any other statute specifically authorizes an act, then that act will not involve infringement of copyright.[137]

Contemporaneous notes of a speaker
Since the 1988 Act copyright can be claimed by a speaker in his extempore pronouncements if the words are recorded, whether or not the recording is done for the speaker's benefit. Prima facie it would restrict a journalist who took a note or made a tape-recording in order to report the event. This new development would have been a major handicap for the media were there not also a new defence that limits its extent. This defence applies if the speaker's words have been recorded directly (and not, for instance, copied from someone else's record) and not taken from a broadcast or cable programme. The person in lawful possession of the record must sanction its use. If these conditions are satisfied, the record can be used for reporting a current event or in a broadcast or cable programme without infringing the speaker's copyright.[138]

Public reading
A reasonable extract from a literary or dramatic work can be read

---

[132] ibid., s 45.
[133] ibid., s 178.
[134] ibid., s 46.
[135] ibid., s 47; only plans and drawings marked in a specified manner can be copied without infringing copyright under s 47(2): Copyright (Material Open to Public Inspection) (Marking of Copies) Order 1990 SI 1990 No 1427.
[136] Copyright, Designs and Patents Act 1988 s 49.
[137] ibid., s 50.
[138] ibid., s 58.

or recited in public without infringing copyright. A sound recording, broadcast or cable programme can be made of the reading, but
only if the record or programme consists mainly of material that
does not have to rely on this defence.[139]

Abstracts of scientific or technical articles

Technical articles are often accompanied by an abstract or summary
of their contents. Unless a licensing scheme has been certified by
the government, these abstracts can be copied and issued to the
public without infringing copyright.[140]

Special use of artistic work

Buildings, sculptures, models for buildings and works of artistic
craftsmanship on permanent public display can be photographed,
graphically represented, included in a film, broadcast or included
in a cable programme without infringing copyright.[141]

An artistic work that is put on sale can be included in a catalogue
or otherwise copied for the purpose of advertising the sale.[142]
Although an artist may dispose of copyright in a work, he or she
will not infringe the copyright by copying the work in the course
of making another, provided the main design of the first is not
repeated.[143]

Broadcasts and cable

Radio and television broadcasts and cable programmes can now be
legitimately recorded for private and domestic use, but only for the
purposes of time-shifting.[144] This limitation will be unenforceable.

A photograph of a television screen that is taken for private and
domestic purposes will not infringe copyright in the broadcast or
cable programme.[145] A copyright owner who has licensed its use in
a broadcast or cable programme gives an implied right to make
ephemeral recordings and film of it for the purpose of preparing
the broadcast.[146]

The BBC, IBA and Cable Authority can make use of copyright
works for their regulatory functions without being guilty of infringement.[147]

---

[139] ibid., s 50.
[140] ibid., s 60.
[141] ibid., s 62.
[142] ibid., s 63.
[143] ibid., s 64.
[144] ibid., s 70.
[145] ibid., s 71.
[146] ibid., s 68.
[147] ibid., s 69.

Television, radio and cable can be relayed in pubs and other places to which the public are admitted without being charged for admission.[148] There will be no infringement in the broadcast, cable, film or sound recordings, but copyright permission is still needed in relation to any musical, literary, dramatic or artistic works that are included in the broadcast or cable programme. In practice, use of these copyrights is licensed by collectives of copyright owners (see p. 245).

Moral Rights

Four 'moral rights' were created by the 1988 Act:

- the right to be identified as author or director (the right to be identified);
- the right not to have the work subjected to derogatory treatment (the right of integrity);
- the right not to be falsely described as author or director;
- the right to privacy in certain types of photographs.

The latter two are dealt with elsewhere (see p. 217 for false attribution of authorship; p. 208 for privacy in photographs).

These first two rights were introduced to bring English law into line with the Berne Copyright Convention. They depend on there being a copyright work and they last as long as copyright in the work,[149] but the owner of the copyright may be quite different from the owner of these moral rights. Copyright can be assigned and, to assist in its exploitation, it frequently is. Moral rights are intended to protect the integrity of the author or director. They cannot be assigned, except on death, when they pass to the author's or director's estate.[150]

The rights are new to British law. For all the qualifications and conditions with which they are hedged, their meaning and impact will become clearer only with judicial interpretation and application. Their significance will also depend on commercial practice, for while the rights cannot be sold, they can be waived,[151] and the right to be identified as author or director depends on a positive act of assertion. In many European countries the law does not

---

[148] ibid., s 72.
[149] ibid., s 86.
[150] ibid., ss 94 and 95.
[151] To be fully effective a waiver must be in writing, but an oral or informal waiver may estop the author or director from asserting the right against those to whom it was directed, ibid., s 87.

allow waiver of moral rights. But in Britain powerful television and publishing companies set their lawyers in motion immediately the Act came into force to devise standard clauses to waive or exclude moral rights. Lawyers for Granada Television and the BBC came up with one disgraceful clause that requires creative artists to waive 'so-called moral rights'; in 1990 the Writers' Guild of Great Britain condemned film and television companies for the pressure they were exerting on artists and writers to sign such waivers.

It will clearly take some time before the right not to have one's original work distorted is accepted as properly belonging to all creative artists.

Right to be identified as author or director

The right belongs to the author of a literary, dramatic, musical or artistic work or the director of a film.[152] It does not apply to a computer-generated work, a computer programmer, the designer of a typeface, an employee (whose employer is the first owner of the copyright) or a director when someone else has made the arrangements for the film (and so that other person is the first owner of the copyright in it).[153] The right is not infringed if any one of the defences to an infringement action apply (notably if there is a fair dealing with the work of reporting current events on a sound recording, film broadcast or cable).[154] The right does not apply at all to the author or director of a work made for the purpose of reporting current events.[155] Nor does it apply in relation to the publication in a newspaper, magazine or similar periodical (an encylopedia, dictionary, yearbook or other collective work for reference) where the work was made for that purpose or used for it with the author's consent. [156]

The right must be asserted. This is a formal act that must be done in writing: the Act specifies precise forms of assertion for the different types of work.[157]

If all of these conditions have been fulfilled and the right has not been waived or given up by consent, then the author or director must be identified as such in connection with various public promotions of the work or any substantial part of it.[158]

Derogatory treatment

The right not to have a work subjected to derogatory treatment applies also to authors of literary, dramatic, musical or artistic

---

[152] ibid., s 77(1).   [153] ibid., s 79(2) and (3).   [154] ibid., see s 79(4) for details.
[155] ibid., s 79(5).   [156] ibid., s 79(6).   [157] ibid., s 78.
[158] ibid., ss 77 and 89(1).

works and to film directors.[159] As with the right to be identified, it applies to specified public dealings with the altered work.[160] It goes further, though, in applying to the public use of *any* part of the work (whether substantial or not).[161]

The exceptions to this right are a more limited version of those to the 'identity' right.[162] Employees may not have copyright or the right to be identified, but they do (subject to their waiver or consent) have the right not to have their work subjected to derogatory treatment if they are or have been publicly identified in the work.[163] Most of the defences that apply to both infringement of copyright and the right to be identified do not permit derogatory treatment. Fair dealing, which is sufficient to excuse an infringement of copyright, will not necessarily be a defence to this new moral right.[164]

So what is 'derogatory treatment'? The Act answers that treatment is derogatory 'if it amounts to distortion or mutilation of the work or is otherwise prejudicial to the honour or reputation of the author or director'.[165] This gives little guidance except that there must be something objectively prejudicial in the treatment. It will be for the courts to work out a balance between this new right and the right of satirists and cartoonists to lampoon and ridicule.

The first person to assert his new 'integrity right' in British courts was pop singer George Michael, who alleged that five compositions he had originally recorded with Wham had been subject to derogatory treatment by being remixed to alter some of the lyrics and to introduce 'fill-in music' provided by others between his compositions, on an album entitled *Bad Boys Megamix*. The court found that he had established an arguable case of derogatory treatment, and granted an interim injunction until the action could be tried.[166]

Not all derogatory dealings will offend the right of integrity. There must be derogatory 'treatment' and this means that something must be done to alter the work or add to it. The juxtaposition of the work and a context that is objectionable to the author is not a breach: a feminist photographer could not complain under this head if her pictures were displayed amongst an exhibition of pornography.

There is an echo here of the law's reluctance to allow famous (or, indeed, any) people a monopoly over the use of their names and faces. Two of the Beatles were refused an injunction to prevent the

---

[159] ibid., s 80(1).   [160] ibid., s 80.   [161] ibid., s 89(2).   [162] ibid., s 81.
[163] ibid., s 82.   [164] ibid., s 81.   [165] ibid., s 80(2)(*b*).
[166] See Deborah Stone, 'Moral Rights in the Recording Industry', *International Media Law*, September 1991, p. 66.

sale of a record of interviews with them. The LP was called *The Beatles Tapes* and had pictures of the group inside the sleeve. The maker had a licence from the photographer but not from the Beatles. However, the musicians had no copyright to assert, and the LP was not passed off as their work.[167]

The new moral right not to have work derogatorily treated is also infringed by those who deal in articles that infringe it. Like secondary infringement of copyright, however, there is only liability if the dealer knows or has reason to believe that it is an infringing article.[168]

Rights in Performances

'Bootlegging', or the making and selling of illicit recordings of a live performance, has been another unwanted side-effect of the growth in recording technology. It can harm the commercial interests of both the performer and anyone to whom the (lawful) recording rights have been awarded. A related issue is the extent to which the performer (or recording company) ought to be able to control the subsequent use of legitimate recordings. Until the 1980s the legislation was unsatisfactory. It created criminal offences but with such small penalties that they were disregarded with impunity. Civil liability was ill-defined until the courts ruled that recording companies could not take action against bootleggers. [169] Then, in the *Pink Panther* case the Court of Appeal held that the estate of Peter Sellers was entitled to damages (assessed at £1,000,000) for the compilation of 'out-takes' from the earlier *Panther* films into a new film that neither the actor nor his estate had authorized.[170] It should be stressed that the right asserted here was independent of any copyright in the clips. Because this new civil right was not linked to copyright, it was not subject either to the qualifications that were imposed on copyright, e.g., as to duration of the right or the statutory defences that limited actions for infringement.

The 1988 Act has completely revised the law. The rights are still independent of copyright,[171] although the provisions now

---

[167] *Harrison and Starkey* v *Polydor Ltd* [1977] 1 FSR 1. Other celebrities have failed because their names or likenesses were borrowed for use in a quite different area of business (see the Uncle Mac case *McCulloch* v *May* (1947) 65 PRC 58 and the Abba case, *Lyngstad* v *Anabas* [1977] FSR 62. Australian courts have been more sympathetic: *Henderson* v *Radio Corp'n Pty Ltd* [1969] RPC 218.
[168] Copyright, Designs and Patents Act 1988 s 83.
[169] *RCA* v *Pollard* [1983] Ch 135.
[170] *Rickless* v *United Artists Corporation* [1988] QB 40.
[171] Copyright, Designs and Patents Act 1988 s 180(4)(*a*).

frequently run parallel to each other and an infringement of the performance rights will often also involve a breach of copyright. However, because they are independent, the people who enjoy the rights may be different to the persons who hold the copyright.

Rights are given to performers themselves and to those who have exclusive recording rights. All the rights are conditional on there being a 'performance', which can be dramatic, musical, a reading or recitation or a performance of a variety act or similar presentation.[172] As with copyright law, the performer qualifies for protection only if he or she has some connection with the United Kingdom or another country that is party to the relevant international convention[173] or another member of the EEC.[174]

The Act then controls 'recordings' of a performance. This term is not synonymous with 'sound recording' in copyright law. It can mean a film or a sound recording made either directly from the live performance or indirectly from a broadcast, cable programme or another recording.[175]

The performer's rights are infringed by a person who makes a recording (otherwise than for private and domestic use) or broadcasts the performance live or includes it in a cable programme without the performer's consent.[176] This would obviously include the bootlegger. It would also embrace the users of the *Pink Panther* out-takes since their composite film would be an indirect recording of the original Sellers performances. Other infringements of the performers' rights are committed by showing, playing in public, broadcasting or including in a cable programme an unauthorized recording.[177] In all cases the prohibition extends to a substantial part of the performance. As with copyright, there are 'secondary infringements' of commercial dealing with infringing recordings.[178] Like moral rights, the performer's rights cannot be assigned, although they can be transmitted on the performer's death. [179]

Exclusive recording contractors have similar, though slightly narrower, rights to control the use of unauthorized recordings.[180] 'Authorized' here means permitted either by the contractor or the performer.

---

[172] ibid., 180(2).
[173] The 1961 Rome Convention for the Protection of Performers, Producers of Phonograms and Broadcasting Organisations.
[174] Copyright, Designs and Patents Act 1988 s 206.
[175] ibid., s 180(2).
[176] ibid., s 182(1).
[177] ibid., s 183.
[178] ibid., s 184.
[179] ibid., s 192.
[180] ibid., s 185–8.

All the rights in performances now have time limits and exceptions broadly comparable to the duration and defences to copyright actions.[181] The civil and criminal remedies for the infringement of the rights also resemble the copyright remedies.[182] If performers cannot be traced or if they unreasonably refuse their consent, the Copyright Tribunal can give a licence in their place and fix appropriate terms.[183]

Remedies

Injunctions

Injunctions are normally granted if the plaintiff succeeds at the trial of a copyright action, though they have been refused because the infringement was trivial, the chance of repetition was slight or the plaintiff had delayed unreasonably before going to court.[184] In the case of moral rights the court is given a discretion to order that the act be prohibited unless it is accompanied by a sufficient disclaimer dissociating the author or director from the work.[185] More significant for the media is the prospect of a pre-trial or interim injunction against the use of copyright documents in a book or as part of a news story. The principles upon which such 'prior restraint' may be resisted are discussed earlier (see p. 19).

Private search warrants and compulsory disclosure

The growth of video and other copyright piracy has led the courts to grant powerful orders for obtaining and preserving evidence of infringement. If there is strong evidence to show that copyright has been or will be infringed in a way that would cause serious harm to the owner of the copyright, and if the owner can prove that vital evidence might be destroyed as soon as word of the institution of proceedings reaches the suspected pirates, then the court can in effect issue a private search warrant. It is prepared to do so *ex parte* (i.e., in the absence of the proposed defendant), and before notice of the proceedings has been served on the defendant. Applications are usually heard in camera. These orders are known

---

[181] ibid., time limits s 191, exceptions Sched 2.
[182] ibid., ss 194–200 and see below.
[183] ibid., s 190.
[184] Laddie, Vitoria and Prescott *The Modern Law of Copyright*, Butterworths, 1980, paras 12. 17–18.
[185] Copyright, Designs and Patents Act 1988 s 103(2) and see s 178 for the meaning of 'sufficient disclaimer'.

as *Anton Piller* orders[186] after the case that established the court's jurisdiction to make them. They require the defendants to allow the owners to inspect their premises, usually in the company of the owner's solicitor, and to copy or photograph relevant articles and documents or to detain them until the action is heard.

The courts can also order the defendants to disclose on oath information that the plaintiffs need to enforce their rights, such as the names of their suppliers and customers.[187] These *Norwich Pharmacal* orders can also be made to discover the source of leaked confidential information (see p. 199). Some infringements of copyright are criminal offences (see below) but defendants cannot refuse to answer questions on the grounds that the answers may incriminate them: their privilege against self-incrimination has been taken away by statute.[188] Instead, there is a bar on the answers being used in any subsequent prosecution for a related offence.[189]

Defendants can apply to have these orders set aside. They are rarely successful, but if they are, or if the plaintiffs fail in their action at the trial, the defendants would be entitled to compensation.

In 1985, in the first contested case involving an *Anton Piller* order, the High Court awarded £10,000 damages in trespass against a firm of solicitors that had overzealously executed an order that had been obtained upon unsatisfactory evidence. Mr Justice Scott emphasized the need for applicants to produce overwhelming evidence of piracy causing considerable damage, and of the imminence of the danger of destruction of evidence, before *Anton Piller* orders should be made:

> What is to be said of the *Anton Piller* procedure which, on a regular and institutionalized basis, is depriving citizens of their property and closing down their businesses by orders made *ex parte*, on applications of which they know nothing and at which they cannot be heard, by orders which they are bound, on pain of committal, to obey, even if wrongly made? . . . even villains ought not to be deprived of their property by proceedings at which they cannot be heard.[190]

---

[186] *Anton Piller KG* v *Manufacturing Processes* [1976] Ch 55.
[187] *Norwich Pharmacal* v *Commissioners of Customs and Excise* [1974] AC 133.
[188] Supreme Court Act 1981, s 72.
[189] Defined in Supreme Court 1981 Act s 72(6); see *Universal City Studies Inc* v *Hubbard* [1983] 2 All ER 596.
[190] *Columbia Picture Industries* v *Robinson* [1987] Ch 38.

Damages

Successful plaintiffs can claim compensation for damage to the value of their copyright, which will either be the amount of profits lost as a result of the competitor's action or the fee that they could properly have charged the defendant for using their copyright material.[191] Until the 1988 Act a copyright owner had the further right to the value of the infringing article (i.e. damages in conversion).[192] This could far exceed the harm to the copyright and was accurately described as draconian. The present Act has abolished the conversion damages remedy except for actions that had begun when the Act went into effect. The court has also a power to award additional damages where the infringement has been particularly flagrant, or where the defendant's profit was so large that compensatory damages would not be adequate.[193] There must have been some 'scandalous conduct, deceit and such like which includes deliberate and calculated copyright infringement'. In one case a photographer sold to the press a wedding photo of a man who had subsequently been murdered. The photographer had neither the copyright nor permission from the family, and he was made to pay extra damages.[194]

Breach of copyright does not require guilty knowledge. However, if defendants do not know that copyright subsists in work that is infringed, they are excused from paying damages.[195] They may be subjected, though, to other remedies, such as an injunction or an account of any profit that they have made out of the infringement.[196]

Breach of all four moral rights is actionable as breach of a statutory duty.[197] This means that the plaintiff can claim compensation to be put in as good a position as if the wrong had not been committed. In considering remedies for breach of the right to be

---

[191] Copyright, Designs and Patents Act 1988 s 96(2).

[192] Copyright Act 1956 s 18.

[193] Copyright, Designs and Patents Act 1988 s 97(2).

[194] *Williams* v *Settle* [1960] 1 WLR 1072. The court described its award differently, but in a comparable situation today additional damages would be likely.

[195] Copyright, Designs and Patents Act 1988 s 97(1). This is a narrow exception. It does not help those who make a mistake as to who is the copyright owner. Nor can a publisher plead ignorance of the copyright – everyone is presumed to know the law. All reasonable care must have been taken, including any appropriate inquiries. After making these, the defendant must still have no grounds for believing that copyright exists. Because of all these restrictions, the defence is really only of benefit where the copied work is old or originates from a country where it is not reasonably possible to discover whether the necessary conditions for copyright are fulfilled.

[196] ibid., s 97(1).

[197] ibid., s 103(1).

identified the court must specifically take account of any delay in asserting the right.[198]

Account of profits

Damages compensate plaintiffs for what they have lost, but an enterprising defendant may have used the plagiarized work in a way that yielded a profit in excess of what the plaintiff could have obtained for it. The courts can order the defendant to 'account' for this excess profit to the plaintiff.[199]

An account is a discretionary remedy. It will be refused if the breach was trivial or if the plaintiff delayed unreasonably before starting proceedings.

Delivery up of copies

The court can order the defendant to hand over to the plaintiff any infringing copy and articles specifically designed for making copies of a particular copyright that the owner of the article knows or has reason to believe has been or is to be used for making infringing copies.[200] The application must be brought within six years of the infringing article being made.[201] Like an account of profits, delivery up is a discretionary remedy, and the court must consider whether the rights of the owner can be adequately protected in some other way. Anyone with an interest in the article is entitled to make representations as to why delivery up should not be ordered and to appeal against the order.[202]

Criminal offences

The Copyright Act 1956 criminalized certain types of infringement, but the penalties were low and the scope of the offences was haphazard. The criminal sanctions were progressively toughened, particularly in response to the growth of the trade in pirated videos and music cassettes. The 1988 Act continues that trend.[203]

A wide range of offences has now been created for those who are both commercially and knowingly involved in copyright infringe-

---

[198] ibid., s 78(5).
[199] Laddie, et al., *The Modern Law of Copyright*, para 12.28.
[200] Copyright, Designs and Patents Act 1988 s 99.
[201] ibid., s 113: the period is extended if the copyright owner is under a legal disability, e.g., is still a minor, or if the owner was prevented by fraud or concealment from knowing the facts of the case.
[202] ibid., s 144.
[203] ibid., s 107.

ment. On summary conviction magistrates can sentence to prison for six months and fine the statutory maximum (currently £2,000). Conviction on indictment can lead to a fine (for which there is no upper limit) and a two-year prison sentence.[204] The criminal court can make forfeiture orders similar to the civil courts' powers to order delivery up.[205] Magistrates can issue search warrants where there are grounds for believing that an offence of manufacturing, importing or distributing infringing copies is or is about to be committed.[206] This power now relates to infringement of any type of copyright work (no longer just sound recordings or films, as under the previous law). In executing the warrant the police may seize any evidence of dealing in infringing copies, but cannot take items subject to legal privilege, excluded material or special procedure material,[207] (see also p. 205).

An interesting precedent was established in 1991 when a freelance photographer, David Hoffman, brought a private prosecution against a local liberal councillor in Tower Hamlets, who had used one of his photographs in a leaflet attacking the Labour Party. The councillor was convicted of criminal infringement of copyright, fined £200 and ordered to pay the photographer's legal costs. Victims of copyright infringement may find this an extreme remedy, and one that brings them no financial compensation, although it would undoubtedly prove effective against persistent violaters and those who use copyright material for purposes that the copyright holder finds particularly deplorable.

Copyright owners can also enlist the aid of customs officers in their fight against pirated works. The owner of copyright in a published literary, dramatic or musical work can give notice in writing asking that infringing copies of the work be treated as prohibited goods for a period not exceeding five years. Owners of copyright in sound recordings and films can make a similar request if the time and place of the arrival of the expected infringing copies can be specified. Classifying the infringing copies as 'prohibited goods' does not make their importation a criminal offence, but it does mean that they are liable to be seized and forfeited unless the importer has them only for his private and domestic use.[208]

The Bank of England is given a monopoly over all representations of legal tender, and it is a criminal offence against s 18 of the Forgery & Counterfeiting Act 1981 to 'reproduce on any substance whatsoever, and whether or not on the correct scale, any part of a

---

[204] ibid., s 107.
[205] ibid., s 108.
[206] ibid., s 109.
[207] ibid., s 109(2); Police and Criminal Evidence Act s 9(2).
[208] Copyright, Designs and Patents Act 1988 s 111.

British currency note' without the Bank's consent. The Bank's singular lack of any sense of humour (or indeed common sense) led to the Old Bailey prosecution in 1987 of an artist named Boggs over paintings of banknotes, which were worth considerably more than the notes themselves and were much increased in value by the publicity that attended his trial. The paintings had been clumsily seized from an art gallery exhibition, and witnesses from the Bank asserted the astonishing proposition that any artist who wished to depict a banknote in a painting had first to submit a sketch in triplicate for approval. The legal argument turned on the meaning of the word 'reproduction' as applied to art (is the *Mona Lisa* no more than the reproduction of a sixteenth-century Italian woman?) and experts solemnly placed Boggs in the tradition of *trompe-l'oeil* painters. The jury, doubtless surprised to be summonsed to Court No 1 of the Old Bailey to judge an art exhibition, acquitted after a ten-minute retirement.[209]

---

[209] See Lawrence Wechsler, 'Onward and Upward with the Arts – Boggs' (Pt I and II) *New Yorker*, 18, 25, January 1988.

Chapter 6

Contempt of Court

The power to punish for contempt of court is the means by which the legal system protects itself from publications that might unduly influence the result of litigation. The dilemmas caused by conflict between the demands of a fair trial and a free press are real enough. We pin a certain faith on the ability of juries, judges and tribunals to resolve disputes, so we are justified in being concerned about the effect of outside influence on their deliberations, especially the sort of pressure generated by circulation-seeking sensationalism. The smooth working of the legal system is a very important, but not always overriding, consideration in holding the delicate balance of public interest between the rights of suspects and litigants to a fair trial and the need for society to know about the issues involved in their cases and about the effectiveness of the system that resolves those issues. Too many contempt decisions, especially before the 1981 Contempt Act, treated 'the public interest' as synonymous with 'the interests of those involved in the legal process', imposing secrecy and censorship without regard for the countervailing benefits of a free flow of information about what happens in the courts.

The rationale behind the contempt law is an abiding British fear of 'trial by newspaper' of the sort that often disfigures major trials in America, where the First Amendment permits the press to comment directly on matters involved in litigation. The principle is firmly ensconced in the value-system of lawyers and legislators, and the media ignore it at their peril, even in relation to the trial of the most obviously guilty or most unpopular defendants. When the *Daily Mirror* published sensationalized suggestions that a man arrested for one particularly foul murder was not only guilty, but guilty of other murders as well, its editor was gaoled for three months.[1] More recently, the *Sun* was fined £75,000 for publishing

---

There are three principal textbooks on contempt: Arlidge and Eady, *The Law of Contempt*, Sweet & Maxwell, 1982; Miller, *Contempt of Court*, 2nd edn, Clarendon Press, 1989; Borrie and Lowe, *The Law of Contempt of Court*, 2nd edn, Butterworth, 1983. Recommendations for reform following the thalidomide story injunction were made by the Phillimore Committee's *Report on Contempt of Court*, HMSO, 1974, Cmnd 5794. Sir John Fox's book *The History of Contempt of Court* (1927) explains lucidly the history of contempt, with an appropriate sense of the absurd.
[1] *R v Bolam ex parte Haigh* (1949) 93 SJ 220.

prejudicial material about a man whose private prosecution the newspaper had agreed to fund. The penalty for the massively prejudicial publicity surrounding the arrest of 'Yorkshire Ripper' Peter Sutcliffe came in a more permanent form: Parliament refused to amend the Contempt Bill, then under consideration, to make it easier for the press to report newsworthy developments in criminal investigations between the time of arrest and the time of charge.

The power to punish for contempt may be justified by reference to the European Convention on Human Rights: Article 6 provides that:

> In the determination of his civil rights and obligations or of any criminal charge against him, everyone is entitled to a *fair and public hearing* within a reasonable time by an independent and impartial tribunal established by law [*our italics*].

This is one of 'the rights of others' that can justify a restriction on freedom of speech guaranteed by Article 10 if the restriction is 'prescribed by law' and not disproportionate to the aim of securing a fair trial.

The purpose of the law of contempt in relation to the media is to prevent publications that might realistically bias the tribunal or tilt the balance of its procedures unfairly against one side. It is normally a criminal offence, carrying a maximum penalty of two years' imprisonment and an unlimited fine, although the High Court may injunct a potentially contemptuous article or film if action is taken prior to publication. Contempt is the only serious criminal offence that is punishable without trial by jury: cases are decided by High Court judges, who are, inevitably, judges in their own cause in relation to material that reflects adversely upon the administration of justice. The vagueness of the concept, and its intimate relationship with the operation of the legal process, force the media to rely upon professional legal advisers rather more heavily than in other areas of media law. A feature of recent prosecutions against national newspapers has been the appearance in the defence evidence of affidavits by newspaper lawyers setting out the considerations that prompted editors to approve the offending article; reliance on professional advice will not preclude a finding of guilt, but it will always mitigate the penalty and hopefully exclude the possibility of imprisonment.

The law of contempt serves a valuable purpose in so far as its operation is confined to placing a temporary embargo on publication of information that would make a jury more likely to convict a person who is on trial, or shortly to face trial. Without such a law, the legal system would be forced to adopt the expensive, and not entirely successful, expedients used in notorious trials in America, where jurors are quizzed at length as to what they have seen in the press or on TV and are then sequestered under guard in hotels, denied access to family, newspapers and television programmes for the duration of the case. There has, in fact, been only one occasion when English courts have upheld an appeal on the grounds of prejudice caused by media coverage, and in that case the media was in no way at fault. The prejudice was caused by Tom King, Secretary of State for Northern Ireland, who chose to announce abolition of the right to silence on the grounds that it was being exploited by Irish defendants guilty of acts of terrorism, on the day after three Irish defendants had claimed their right to silence on a charge accusing them of plotting to murder the self-same Tom King. The publicity resulting from the Minister's action was devastating to their prospects of acquittal, and the ensuing conviction had to be quashed.[2]

It is easy, however, to exaggerate the dangers of 'trial by media'. Publicity at the point of arrest is generally forgotten by the time the case struggles to trial, through congested court lists, a year or so later. Juries do heed judges' admonitions to decide cases entirely on the evidence. As the Court of Appeal said in *Gee* v *BBC*:

> more importantly an inward-looking atmosphere built up during the trial and the jury and judge tended less and less as the trial proceeded to look outwards and more and more to look inwards at the evidence and arguments being addressed to them.[3]

Juries are remarkably resilient to newspaper comments: Jeremy Thorpe was acquitted after years of media speculation, and defendants in the second trials of the Kray twins and Janie Jones were acquitted in the teeth of enormous publicity given to convictions in their earlier trials. By the time a case comes to trial, initial press comment is the least of a defendant's worries. As Lord Hutchinson QC pointed out during the debates on the Contempt Bill, 'the greatest potential prejudice that he faces is to find a judge, magistrate or lawyer who is incompetent, unfair, simply ignorant or too old'.[4] Exposure of judicial prejudice depends much upon the media – but it is precisely this sort of exposure that the law of contempt sometimes makes difficult.

The fear of 'trial by media' was taken to extremes when British

---

[2] *R* v *Cullen, McCann and Shanahan* (1990) 92 Cr App R 239.
[3] *Gee* v *BBC* (1986) 136 NLJ 515, CA, and see *A-G* v *News Group Newspapers Ltd* [1986] 2 All ER 833, 842, CA.
[4] Hansard HL Debs Vol 415 col 679.

courts stopped publication of editorial criticism by *The Sunday Times* of the moral position of Distillers, the giant corporation that had marketed the deforming drug thalidomide, in relation to its offer of financial settlement to parents of the drug's victims. The newspaper was campaigning to increase that offer, against a background of protracted and complicated High Court litigation, which might never have come to trial. In 1973 the House of Lords held that contempt law prohibited the publication of material that pre-judged the issue of whether Distillers had been negligent in marketing the drug. Two of the judges also said that editorial comment designed to put moral pressure on Distillers to abandon its legal defence and to negotiate a higher settlement was contempt.[5] This decision was widely condemned by Parliament and the press, and an official committee, headed by Lord Justice Phillimore, was established to recommend reforms in the law of contempt.[6] In due course the European Court of Human Rights confirmed that the British contempt law, as declared by the House of Lords in the *Sunday Times* case, was in breach of the convention guarantee of freedom of expression[7] (see p. 6). In order to bring British law into conformity with the European Convention, the Government was obliged to legislate. This was one of the purposes of the Contempt of Court Act 1981, which now governs most (but not all) aspects of what was previously judge-made law.

Types of Contempt

For media purposes, contempt may be divided into five categories.

- *Strict-liability contempt*. So called because it may be committed by journalists and editors without the slightest intention of prejudicing legal proceedings. This class of contempt is perpetrated by publication of material that creates a substantial risk that justice, in relation to a case presently before the courts, will be seriously impeded or prejudiced. It can be committed only when a particular case is 'active'. In a criminal matter this is generally after an individual has been arrested, and in civil litigation this stage is reached after the action has been set down for trial. This form of contempt is often committed accidentally (e.g., when newspapers publish details of an individual's previous convictions without realizing that he or she is facing fresh criminal charges). Its harshness is mitigated

---

[5] *A-G v Times Newspapers Ltd* [1974] AC 273.
[6] Phillimore Committee *Contempt of Court*.
[7] *Sunday Times v United Kingdom* [1979] 2 EHRR 245.

by special defences that apply when the publisher has taken particular care to avoid the danger, or when the prejudicial matter has been published as part of a discussion of matters of public importance. The media is protected from frivolous cases at the hands of disappointed litigants by the rule that any prosecution must be sanctioned by the court or by the Attorney-General.

- *Deliberate contempt*. This occurs on the rare occasions when a publisher deliberately sets out to influence legal proceedings. Greater use has been made of this category of contempt to sidestep the protections for the media in the 1981 Act. Deliberate contempt may also be committed by placing unfair pressure on a witness or a party to proceedings.
- *Scandalous attacks on the judiciary*. This is an anachronistic relic of eighteenth-century struggles between partisan judges and their vitriolic critics. It survives only as a threat to publications that make false and 'scurrilous' attacks on the judiciary. The little recent authority suggests that honest and temperate criticism of the administration of justice can be published without risk of prosecution.
- *Jury deliberations*. The Contempt of Court Act 1981 introduced a new offence of publishing accounts of how jurors reached their verdict.
- *Disobedience to an order of the court*. This has been given a special significance for the media by the sections of the Contempt Act that give courts a limited power to order postponement of reporting and the suppression of evidence. These rules will be considered, together with other specific restrictions on court reporting, in Chapter 7.

Strict-liability Contempt

Contempt is committed if a publication 'creates a substantial risk that the course of justice in particular proceedings will be seriously impeded or prejudiced.'[8] Liability is 'strict' in the sense that the prosecution does not have to prove that the publisher intended to prejudice legal proceedings. However, it still bears the burden of showing, beyond reasonable doubt, that the publication created a substantial risk of serious prejudice. The prejudice need not have materialized but the degree of its risk must be 'substantial', as distinct from merely possible or remote. Thus a BBC programme that was broadcast only in the south-west region was not in

---

[8] Contempt of Court Act 1981 s 2(1).

contempt of a trial that was about to take place in London.[9] Of course, a local story might be picked up by the press agencies or by the national media, but if this endangered the trial, it would be the responsibility of those who had given it the broader coverage. The original broadcaster could be liable only if it had sold the story or otherwise been instrumental in giving it a wider audience.

The impediment or the prejudice risked by the publication must itself be of a serious kind. This means, at least in criminal cases, that it must be of a nature that could tip the final verdict one way or the other.[10] A useful test of whether the prejudice is 'serious' is to consider whether it can readily be cured by the court itself, rather than by a prosecution or an injunction against publication. The simplest device is for the trial judge to ask jurors who may have seen the prejudicial material to stand down from the panel. This was the solution adopted by Mr Justice Cantley at the commencement of the Thorpe trial in relation to two books that set out evidence given months before at the committal proceedings, not all of which would have been admissible at the trial. Prospective jurors were asked to stand down if they had read the book.[11]

A trial involved allegations of corruption against police officers made by a special investigation team known as 'Operation Countryman'. Its opening in London coincided with the opening of a play at the Royal Court about police corruption, which, although not directly concerned with the allegations against the defendants, was avowedly based on material from 'Operation Countryman' and depicted widespread corruption in the Metropolitan police. The defence asked for action to be taken against the play, but the trial judge chose instead to minimize any danger of prejudice by ordering the jurors not to see it.

Another example of a situation where a reasonable alternative course of action was available to reduce the seriousness of apprehended prejudice is the 1991 case of *Re Central Television*:[12]

> A trial judge feared that the jury in a much publicized fraud case might be affected by radio and television reports of the case on the night they were to be sent to a hotel while considering their verdict. He therefore used Contempt Act powers to 'postpone' all radio and television reports about the trial until the verdict had been delivered, and told the jurors that they could relax and watch television without the danger of prejudice. The Court of Appeal criticized the judge's priorities: the public right to have trials reported overrode the com-

---

[9] *Blackburn* v *BBC* (1976) *The Times*, 15 December.
[10] *A-G* v *English* [1982] 2 All ER 903 at p. 919.
[11] David Leigh, *The Frontiers of Secrecy*, Junction Books, 1980, p. 74. Leigh was a co-author of one of the books. To his disappointment, none of the jurors had read it.
[12] *Re Central Television plc* [1991] 1 All ER 347.

fort of jurors. If the judge had any real reason to fear prejudicial media comment, he should simply have directed that the jurors were to have no access to radio and television during their overnight stay at the hotel.

A 1992 case has emphasized that the 'substantial risk' of prejudice must be a *practical* risk, in the sense that it must carry a prospect that the outcome of the trial would be different without the offending publication, or that it would necessitate the discharge of the jury:

> An article in the *Guardian* criticized the over-sensitivity to the press of judges in big fraud trials. It referred to a current Manchester trial where a judge had imposed reporting restrictions for no better reason than that some of the defendants were facing further committal proceedings. The Attorney-General argued that any revelation that a defendant was facing other charges would amount to contempt if it created 'more than a remote risk' of prejudice. The High Court held that this proposition was too wide. For example, revelation of the fact that a defendant was also facing minor charges would not bias a jury against him.[13]

The twin burdens on the prosecution, under the Contempt Act, to prove both '*substantial* risk' and '*serious* prejudice' give considerable latitude to the news media in reporting the background to a sensational case. This was confirmed by an early test of the legislation in respect of national newspaper reporting of the arrest of Michael Fagan, a trespasser who had found his way into the Queen's bedchamber in Buckingham Palace:[14]

> Fagan had been charged with burglary (by stealing part of a bottle of wine he had found in the Palace). He faced other unconnected charges of taking a car without permission and of assaulting his stepson. The *Sun* described Fagan as a 'junkie', a glib liar and a thief of palace cigars. None of these descriptions were held to be likely to cause a substantial risk of prejudice. The *Daily Star* referred to an alleged confession by Fagan to theft of the wine. This went to the heart of the case against him and was found to be contempt. The *Mail on Sunday* alleged that Fagan had had a homosexual affair with Commander Trestrail (the Queen's bodyguard) and called Fagan 'a rootless neurotic with no visible means of support'. This was found to pose a sufficiently serious risk of prejudice to be prima facie contempt, but the paper successfully relied upon the public-interest

---

[13] *AG v Guardian Newspapers Ltd* (1992) *The Times*, 28 February. Another media-friendly application of this principle is found in *Schering Chemicals v Falkman* [1981] 2 All ER 321, where the Court of Appeal thought that no civil judge would be influenced by a TV programme about a case that had to be tried, and the appearance on it of experts who would give evidence was perfectly proper: they could be cross-examined in court.

[14] *A-G v Times Newspapers Ltd* (1983) *The Times*, 12 February.

defence in section 5 (see p. 281) because the story was part of a report on a matter of general public interest, namely the Queen's safety. Finally, *The Sunday Times* was found guilty of contempt because it exaggerated the charge against Fagan in relation to his stepson: the paper implied he was accused of wounding when in fact he was charged with the less serious crime of assault occasioning actual bodily harm.

Which court?

The seriousness of the risk and the degree of the prejudice will hinge in the first place on the nature of the tribunal that is to try the issue that is the subject of media treatment. The first question for a journalist writing about a pending case is, therefore, 'who will judge it?'

Trial by jury
Jurors, drawn at random from the general public, are assumed to be most susceptible to media influence. The publication of prejudicial information about any person awaiting jury trial is consequently dangerous. Jurors are not expected to remember, let alone to believe, everything they happen to read in newspapers. As the judge at the much-publicized Kray trials commented, 'I have enough confidence in my fellow-countrymen to think that they have got newspapers sized up and they are capable in normal circumstances of looking at the matter fairly and without prejudice even though they may have to disregard what they read in a newspaper'.[15] *Gee v BBC* was an example of a civil case to be heard by a jury that the court did not think would be seriously prejudiced by another programme on a similar subject shortly after the case had been set down but months before the likely trial date.[16]

Trial by magistrates
Most criminal cases are tried in magistrates' courts, either by stipendiary magistrates or by a bench of lay justices. The stipendiary is a full-time professional lawyer and unlikely to be influenced by media reports. More care must be taken in cases that are to be decided by lay justices, who have minimal legal training, although their experience as regular members of the tribunal and the guidance they receive from their clerk would make them more difficult to influence than jurors sitting on a case for the first time.

---

[15] (1969) 53 Cr App R 412.
[16] See note 3 above.

Trial by judge

Almost all civil actions (other than libel and claims against the police) are now heard by judges sitting alone. The Court of Appeal in *Schering Chemicals* v *Falkman* found it impossible to say that a documentary programme could affect the views of a High Court judge.[17] Indeed, Lord Salmon has said 'I am and have always been satisfied that no judge would be influenced in his judgment by what may be said by the media. If he were, he would not be fit to be a judge.'[18] Publicity in relation to a case to be heard by a single judge would need to be trenchant and intemperate before contempt proceedings would be likely to succeed. As a former Chief Justice has explained:

> A judge is in a very different position to a juryman. Though in no sense a superhuman, he has by his training no difficulty in putting out of his mind matters which are not evidence in the case. This indeed happens daily to judges on Assize. This is all the more so in the case of a member of the Court of Appeal, who in regard to an appeal against conviction is dealing almost entirely with points of law and who in the case of an appeal against sentence is considering whether or not the sentence is correct in principle.[19]

The courts will be rather more protective of civil cases where a judge sits with non-lawyer assessors, e.g., a Crown Court judge hearing appeals from a magistrates' court, or a County Court judge hearing complaints of sex or race discrimination. But even so, it will be unusual for there to be a real risk of prejudice.[20]

Appeal hearings

No publisher or broadcaster has been punished for contempt of an appeal court in the last fifty years, and there have been only four attempts to do so. This record reflects Lord Reid's comment in the *Sunday Times* case:

> It is scarcely possible to imagine a case when comment could influence judges in the Court of Appeal or noble and learned Lords in this House. And it would be wrong and contrary to existing practice to limit proper criticism of judgments already given but under appeal.[21]

However, the Court of Appeal has been more sensitive where the appeal included the hearing of new evidence from witnesses.

---

[17] See note 13 above and also *Re Lonrho plc and Observer* (1989) *The Independent*, 28 July.
[18] Quoted by Robin Day in his note of dissent to the Phillimore Report para 4.
[19] *R* v *Duffy ex parte Nash* [1960] 2 QB 188 at p. 198.
[20] *R* v *Bulgin ex parte BBC* (1977) *The Times*, 14 July.

Channel 4 was enjoined from broadcasting a dramatic re-enactment of the appeal of the 'Birmingham Six' until after the decision had been given. Although painstaking care had been taken to produce a fair programme, it remained a theatrical performance and could give an impression of the truthfulness of a witness that was different from his or her credibility as assessed by the court.[22]

The worrying aspect of this decision was that it was essentially a public relations management exercise. None of the judges would have been influenced by the programme, 'but it would or might affect the public view of the judgment of the court'. The impression given by this unusual case is that the court was misusing its Contempt Act powers in order to spike the guns of those who might criticize its published decision by reference to what they had seen on the television re-enactment. It was, in effect, a reverse application of the 'pre-judgment test' disapproved of by the European Court in the *Sunday Times* case: the court interfered with freedom of expression by postponing the programme, in order to prevent the public from pre-judging the judges. The ban appears particularly unattractive in hindsight: the Court of Appeal's confident assessment in 1987 that the 'Birmingham Six' were guilty was reversed three years later, when the credibility of police and scientific evidence was finally demolished.

The most recent and authoritative case on contempt of appellate courts is the most permissive so far as media comment is concerned. It arose, in quite extraordinary circumstances, in the course of 'Tiny' Rowland's crusade to damnify the Al Fayed brothers and the government decision that had allowed them to defeat him in the battle to take over the House of Fraser, which owns Harrods:

> Rowland brought legal proceedings against the Secretary of State for Trade and Industry to compel him to disclose an unpublished report of an investigation into the take-over, which was critical of the Al Fayeds and their supporters. Lonhro (Rowland's company) lost the case in the High Court and in the Court of Appeal, but shortly before it was due to be heard in the House of Lords the company was sent, anonymously, a copy of the report. This it managed to publish in a special Thursday edition of the Sunday newspaper the *Observer*, which was also owned by Lonhro. Many copies were distributed before the Government managed to obtain the inevitable injunction, and amongst the list of distinguished personages who

[21] *A-G v Times Newspapers* (above note 14) at p. 301, and see Lord Simon p. 321. The unsuccessful attempts were *R v The People* (1925) *The Times*, 5 April; *R v Davies ex parte Delbert-Evans* [1945] 1 KB 435; *R v Duffy ex parte Nash*, note 19 above; *Re Lonhro*, note 23 below.
[22] *A-G v Channel Four Television Co* (1987) *The Independent*, 3 December; (1987) *The Times*, 18 December, CA.

were sent copies of the newspaper were four of the five Law Lords listed to hear the appeal. The members of this panel were scandalized that Lonhro should apparently have attempted to influence their decision, and ordered that the company (together with the *Observer*) should stand trial before the House of Lords Appellate Committee on charges of contempt. Lonhro succeeded in removing from the Committee those Law Lords who had determined that the prosecution should be brought, on the grounds that they would otherwise be seen as 'judges in their own cause'. The Law Lords who eventually ruled that Lonhro had not been guilty of contempt did so on the basis that:

- the Contempt of Court Act 1981 must be construed so far as possible to conform with Article 10 of the European Convention, with its requirement that legal suppression of information must be justified by a 'pressing social need';
- the possibility that a professional judge would be influenced by anything he might read about a case he has to decide is remote;
- 'it is difficult to visualize circumstances in which any court in the United Kingdom exercising appellate jurisdiction would be in the least likely to be influenced by public discussion of the merits of a decision appealed against or of the parties' conduct in the proceedings';
- Lonhro's action had pre-empted the very remedy it was seeking from the court, namely publication of the report. But it was not a contempt for it to have taken the law into its own hands and to have achieved its purpose extrajudicially, at least in the absence of any injunction against publication having been granted in aid of the party resisting disclosure in the legal proceedings that were pre-empted.[23]

These rulings make it highly unlikely that public discussion of any case that is subject to appeal will be treated as a contempt on the basis that it is likely to prejudice the course of justice in appeal proceedings. If it is couched in foul or scurrilous language, or falsely impugns the integrity of the judge at first instance, it may amount to contempt by 'scandalizing the court', although even then it may not be made the subject of prosecution (see p. 296).

Contempt risks

The risk of contempt may arise in numerous situations, and it is impossible to lay down hard and fast rules. The following areas, however, present clear dangers.

---

[23] *Re Lonhro plc and Observer Ltd* [1989] 2 All ER 1100, HL.

Criticizing the decision to prosecute

The decision to prosecute is not mechanical. It involves the exercise of a discretion and consideration of the public interest, and as such can legitimately be the object of comment and criticism at the time when it is taken; objectors need not wait until the case is over. Consequently, much greater latitude is given to comments hostile to the prosecution than to those critical of the defendant, especially if they deal with issues of principle and do not purport to settle facts in dispute.[24] The use by prosecuting authorities of unusual or discredited laws can always be a subject of debate even at the time of trial. In 1974 the Attorney-General refused to halt a television documentary critical of incitement to disaffection laws at a time when pacifists were standing trial under this legislation, despite a request from the trial judge.

Anti-prosecution commentaries are on much more dangerous ground if they attack prosecution witnesses or are likely to influence their evidence. The Director of Public Prosecution and the police must tolerate a greater degree of criticism, because of their public role.

Anticipating the course of the trial

Predicting the outcome of a trial, or even giving odds on a particular jury verdict, would in most cases amount to contempt. However, considerable freedom is given to the media in publishing informed speculation as to the issues that are likely to be raised, so long as no opinion is expressed as to the way they should be resolved:

> Shortly before the trial of a company fraud, a newspaper published details of the case that would be of interest to investors in the company concerned, and added that 'mourners over the fiasco are likely to hear a little inside history of the business'. The Court of Appeal said that the contempt proceedings should not have been brought, because the speculation would cause no substantial prejudice to parties to the action.[25]

It is commonly – and wrongly – believed that a defendant must stay silent throughout the long period between arrest and trial. In cases where the arrest has been attended with publicity (invariably prejudicial to the defendant) there can be no objection to his repeated public assertion of innocence (which is, after all, echoing the law's most sacred presumption). Nor is it necessarily contempt

---

[24] Old examples of criticism of a prosecution, e.g., *R* v *Mason* (1932) *The Times*, 7 December; *R* v *Nield* (1909) *The Times*, 27 January would now be unlikely to be contempt under the strict-liability rule because the risk of prejudice would not be substantial.

[25] *Hunt* v *Clarke* (1889) 58 LJQB 490.

to publish a book by or about him. John Stonehouse, MP, published an account of his disappearance before his trial on insurance fraud charges, and Ernest Saunders and his son gave an account of his stewardship of Guinness in a book that received considerable publicity a few months before his trial on matters arising from the Guinness take-over of Distillers. Such literary effusions carry the danger for the author that they will be used in evidence against him, but this is not a problem relevant to contempt of court. Where great caution is required is in any references to prosecution witnesses, and any comment on specific charges or issues that the jury will have to decide. Mere repetition of matters already published should not be a problem, but overt attempts to elicit sympathy and support for a defendant must be avoided (the title of Saunders' book was changed, on legal advice, from *Scapegoat* to *Nightmare*).

Contempt creates a difficult problem for individuals who are not witnesses, but who receive adverse publicity as a result of references to them at the trial or in pre-trial proceedings. Can they rebut false allegations while the trial is in motion? Not, it seems, when the result would be to suggest that a party to it is a liar. When a man on trial at the Old Bailey for serious offences made the fantastic claim that Edward Heath (in company with an Inspector of Police) had raped his wife, Heath instructed counsel to attend the court to put his denial on public record. This was not permitted until after the verdict. When Greville Janner MP was falsely and irrelevantly accused of buggery by a witness at the trial of Frank Beck in 1991, he maintained a stoic silence 'on legal advice' until the jury convicted, and then launched a parliamentary campaign to remove the absolute privilege attached to press reports of court proceedings where allegations are made against third parties. (Janner and his supporters showed no enthusiasm for removing the absolute privilege attaching to reports of MPs' speeches in Parliament, a source of much greater unfairness to third parties.) When a victim of outrageous allegations, made under privilege in court in which he is neither a party nor a witness, puts on public record immediately a short and emphatic denial, he does not in our view commit contempt of court. When Lord Goodman was mentioned in an unattractive light by a witness in the Thorpe committal hearings, it is said that he went to the Attorney-General to demand redress, only to be advised that the best thing he could do was to stand on a soapbox in Trafalgar Square and proclaim his innocence.

Defendants' convictions and life-style

Publishing derogatory information about a defendant's life-style or previous convictions before the verdict is almost invariably contempt. These are deliberately kept from the jury so that they will not judge the defendant on his bad character rather than on evidence of his involvement in the offence with which he is charged. Publishing the information frustrates that purpose. For these reasons 'backgrounders' must generally wait until after the verdict.

> In 1968 the Black Power leader Malcolm X was awaiting trial for incitement to racial hatred. *The Times* published his photograph and referred to a previous conviction for brothel-keeping. The paper had a system for checking copy, but the story had slipped through. It was fined £5,000.[26]

However, as the Fagan case demonstrated, not every adverse comment or description of a defendant will be contempt. It must be one that would be substantially likely to affect seriously the outcome of the case.

A similar type of contempt is exaggerating the charge against the defendant. *The Sunday Times* did this in its Fagan story. A newsreel film company was likewise fined in 1936 when it featured the case of a man charged with unlawful possession of a firearm at a royal parade. The piece was entitled 'Attempt on the King's life' and wrongly suggested a much more serious crime than was actually alleged.[27]

Particular care must be taken by the press when it publishes articles about criminal trials before they have concluded. These may unintentionally refer to matters that the jury is not permitted to hear in evidence. The *Guardian* was heavily fined in 1985 for making a passing reference to the fact that a defendant had escaped from police custody, thereby causing his trial (which had been going on for several months) to be aborted, at enormous public expense. The Lord Chief Justice was critical of the *Guardian*'s lawyer (an expert in libel who did not practise criminal law) for failure to inquire from the prosecution whether evidence of the escape had been introduced at the trial before approving the article.

In 1990 the Court of Appeal held that *Private Eye* had created a serious risk of prejudice to Sonia Sutcliffe's libel action against it by blackguarding her character only three months before the trial.[28] This result was reached by reference to the gravity of the allegations falsely made against her (that she had provided her husband with false alibis to murder and was defrauding the DHSS), the proximity of the jury trial at the time they were published, and the likelihood that one juror at least would read and recall them, in view of *Private Eye*'s large circulation in the London area, where

---

[26] *R v Thomson Newspapers Ltd ex parte A-G* [1968] 1 All ER 268.
[27] *R v Hutchison ex parte McMahon* [1936] 2 All ER 1514.
[28] *A-G v Hislop* [1991] 1 All ER 911.

the trial was to be held. Although a newspaper that defends a libel action on grounds that its initial allegations were justified is entitled to repeat them prior to trial (at the risk of aggravated and even exemplary damages) the new *Private Eye* defamations were irrelevant to the issue in the libel action (which related only to whether Sutcliffe had accepted payments from newspapers) and were intended to put pressure on her to withdraw. The publication was therefore a contempt under the strict-liability rule, and also an 'intentional contempt' at common law (see p. 286).

Defendants' photographs

Publishing defendants' photographs can be contempt in criminal cases where the correctness of identification is in issue. The danger is that eyewitnesses for the prosecution may then describe the person in the newspaper's picture, rather than the person they saw at the scene of the crime. The *Evening Standard* was fined £1,000 for printing Peter Hain's photograph on the very day he was to attend an identification parade in relation to a bank robbery. It did not matter that its caption was 'Hain, He's No Bank Robber'. The picture created a serious risk of prejudicing his trial by making it more likely that he would be picked out at the identity parade.[29] It may be difficult to know whether identification will be in issue. Defendants must tell the prosecution of an alibi defence within two weeks of their committal for trial, but the media are likely to want to use their pictures long before this deadline. Defence solicitors may be prepared to say whether mistaken identity will be alleged, but they are under no duty to do so and may well prefer not to reveal their client's case prematurely.

The problem becomes acute when an arrest warrant has been issued for a suspect who is still at large. For example, photographs of Neville Heath, wanted for a sex murder in 1946, were not published after his first victim was discovered, for fear of contempt. If the press had published the photographs, he might have been arrested before he struck a second time.[30] In recognition of this problem, the Attorney-General has now said that pictures of wanted persons issued by the police can be published by the media without risk of contempt.[31] Since he has a monopoly on this type of prosecution for contempt, his assurance gives the media a practical immunity.

---

[29] *R* v *Evening Standard ex parte A-G* (1976) *The Times*, 3 November. See also Peter Hain, *Mistaken Identity*, Quartet, 1976, pp. 39, 42, 85; cf. *R* v *Daily Mirror ex parte Smith* [1927] 1 KB 845.
[30] Steve Chibnall, *Law and Order News*, Tavistock, 1977, p. 53.
[31] Hansard HC Debs [1981] vol 1000 col 34.

Witnesses

Many eyewitness accounts of crimes appear in the press without attracting contempt charges. It will be relatively rare for this to cause a 'substantial risk of serious prejudice' and so satisfy the strict-liability test. Since strict-liability contempt can be committed only once a prosecution is under way, there is not even this risk if a suspect has not been arrested, charged or been made the subject of a warrant. However, any publication that seeks to deter or intimidate prospective witnesses will certainly be vulnerable to contempt proceedings. When a trade union journal severely criticized anyone who might give evidence against the union in a forthcoming case, this was held to be an illegal attempt at intimidation.[32] It will not be contempt, however, to publish an advertisement for witnesses to come forward to assist a particular party, so long as the advertisement is worded neutrally and any reward is not extravagant.[33] It is also an offence under the Theft Act 1968 s 23 to advertise for the return of stolen goods and promise to ask no questions. Advertiser and publisher can be fined.

Payment to witnesses for their stories before they give evidence is usually undesirable and will attract judicial criticism, although no contempt case has yet been brought to deter the practice. There is an obvious danger that bought witnesses will become sold on their stories. They are tempted to exaggerate evidence in order to increase its saleability, and they may become commited to inaccurate stories ghosted by reporters, and have a financial inducement to stick to them in the witness box. The worst example was the *Sunday Telegraph* arrangement to pay Peter Bessell an additional fee of £25,000 if his evidence secured the conviction of Jeremy Thorpe. This deal wholly discredited Bessell's evidence in the eyes of the jury.[34] The paper claimed that Bessell had already been committed to his story when he signed the contract, but there is no doubt that the 'escalation clause' in the contract substantially prejudiced the prosecution case. The newspaper was fortunate not to be prosecuted for contempt: it would probably have been held strictly liable for causing a substantial risk of serious prejudice to the trial. At present, payments to witnesses are contrary to the Press Council's declaration on 'chequebook journalism' (see p. 536), although the widespread disregard for that declaration may cause the Attorney-General to take action for contempt in an appropriate case.

Not all payments to witnesses are objectionable. Experts who are

---

[32] *Hutchinson* v *AEU* (1932) *The Times*, 25 August.
[33] *Plating Co* v *Farquharson* (1881) 17 Ch D49 at p. 55; cf. 'Payment to Witnesses and Contempt of Court' [1975] Crim LR 144.
[34] See *New Statesman* 27 July 1979.

due to give evidence, for instance, might be paid for summarizing their conclusions on television. In the *Schering Chemicals* case the Court of Appeal said it was unlikely that their evidence would thereby be affected.[35]

The press has on many occasions aided the administration of justice by finding important witnesses. For instance *The Sunday Times* in 1976 discovered and interviewed a crucial witness who had set up drug deals on behalf of the police. The newspaper supplied a transcript of his evidence to the prosecution and defence: his allegations of police misconduct caused charges against thirty-one defendants arrested by the police team to be dropped.[36]

Sometimes witnesses have been jealously hidden from journalistic rivals. Again, this is not in itself contempt, though it may sow suspicion that the witness's evidence has been affected. The line is crossed if the witness's evidence is tampered with or the witness is concealed from the police or prosecuting authorities. In 1924 the *Evening Standard* was fined £1,000 for contempt when, amongst other things, it hid a key murder witness with the wife of a sub-editor.[37]

Revealing a 'payment into court'

'Payment into court' is a common tactical ploy by defendants in civil litigation. It is a formal offer to settle for the paid-in sum. If the offer is refused and less than that sum is eventually awarded, the plaintiffs cannot recover their legal costs after the date of the payment in. Rules of court require such a payment to be kept secret, even from the judge. A newspaper that disclosed the fact would run a serious risk of contempt.[38]

Television coverage of criminal trials

It is common for television to set up outside courts to cover the entries and exits of participants in notable trials. So long as there is no element of harassment, there can be no question of contempt (see p. 359) unless members of the jury are pictured or otherwise identified. The court's traditional concern to protect jurors from any kind of embarrassment or reprisal would incline them to rule that such media conduct would pose a serious threat to the administration of justice. This result would certainly be reached where the identified juror is sitting in a court where special security arrangements preclude a view of the jury box from the public gallery.

---

[35] *Schering Chemicals Ltd* v *Falkman Ltd*, note 13 above.
[36] *R* v *Ameer and Lucas* [1977] Crim LR 104.
[37] *R* v *Evening Standard ex parte DPP* (1924) 40 TLR 833.
[38] *R* v *Wealdstone and Harrow News; Harley* v *Sholl* [1925] WN 153.

One difficulty that British justice has yet to confront stems from mass-media coverage of security arrangements, especially at trials of alleged IRA terrorists. Television news eagerly shows the sharpshooters on the court roof, the police helicopters overhead and the sniffer dogs in the courtyard. There is no doubt that such reports conduce to an atmosphere in which the defendant's guilt as a terrorist comes to be generally assumed, and this factor may have played a part in the wrongful convictions of Irish defendants for the Guildford and Birmingham pub bombings. The position is that highly prejudicial press and television reports of security arrangements have not in the past been prosecuted as amounting to a contempt, and are unlikely to be prosecuted in the future without legislative amendment. But where it is possible to withhold details of security arrangements from jurors, to avoid prejudice to the defendants, it will be difficult to resist rulings prohibiting the media from informing them of these arrangements, at least until the trial is over.

The *sub judice* period

The restrictions imposed by strict-liability contempt do not apply from the moment that a crime is committed or a civil dispute flares up: legal proceedings must have been started and reached a particular stage at the time the story reaches the public. This section will examine these points at which a case becomes *sub judice* or, in the terminology of the 1981 Act, 'active'.[39] Unless a case is 'active', there is no risk of committing strict-liability contempt, but it is important to remember that 'activity' is a necessary and not a sufficient condition. Stories can be written, even about active cases, as long as they do not then pose a substantial risk of serious prejudice.

Commencement of strict-liability periods

Criminal proceedings become active as soon as the first formal step in launching a prosecution is taken. This may be an arrest by a police officer, or the charging of a person who has gone voluntarily to a police station or to court. The first step may alternatively be the issue of a warrant by a magistrate for a suspect's arrest or the issue of a summons ordering a person to appear at court on a specified day.[40] If one case involves several of these steps, it becomes active on the first.

Although these tests are more precise than the previous common

---

[39] Contempt of Court Act 1981 s 2(3).
[40] ibid., Sched 1, para 4.

law (by which the media could commit contempt if proceedings were 'imminent'), they are still ambiguous. A man 'helping the police with their inquiries' may or may not be arrested. An arrest warrant may or may not have been issued for a suspect. The media have no right to be told, although they have a defence (see p. 283) if, after taking all reasonable care, they have no reason to suspect that one of the critical steps has been taken. If they know enough to realize that one of the steps might have been taken and they guess wrongly, they may be in contempt.

Press reporting is not frozen indefinitely if a suspect for whom an arrest warrant has been issued is not caught: twelve months after its issue the proceedings cease to be active and the media are then free to comment until the actual arrest.[41] Until Lord Lucan is caught, therefore, it would not be contempt to describe him as a murderer (although it would be libellous to do so if he turns out to be innocent).

Civil proceedings become active when a trial date is fixed or when the case is 'set down for trial'.[42] This is a stage in a High Court lawsuit after the pleadings (the formal statements of each party's case) have been exchanged and the plaintiff has given notice to the court that the case is then ready to be tried. Even so, the trial will not commence immediately. The case will be put in the appropriate queue or 'list' and it may be as long as two years before there is a judge available to hear it.

A party to civil proceedings may seek an order of the court on a procedural or interim matter before trial. These interlocutory applications are also shielded by contempt, although because the application will be heard by a legally qualified master or registrar the chance of it being prejudiced by press comment will in most cases be too remote. These applications are regarded as 'active' from the time a date is fixed for the hearing until the hearing is completed.[43] When several applications are made, the case will resemble a restless poltergeist, passing through periods of activity and repose.

County court cases are not set down for trial in the same way. Trials are usually preceded by a 'pre-trial review' at which procedural directions are given by the registrar. The pre-trial review is active from the time its date is set until it is concluded. Similarly, the trial is active from the time the date for it is set until it is concluded.

Journalists ought to be able to find out if a case has been set

---

[41] ibid., Sched 1, para 11.
[42] ibid., paras 12 and 13.
[43] ibid.

down for trial or if a date has been fixed for a hearing by inquiring at the court where the case will be heard. The Attorney-General has instructed court officials to assist journalists.[44] However, when one writer undertook the task, she found that unless the exact names of the case and the relevant court were known, the information could be discovered only by a long and tedious search.[45]

Termination of strict-liability periods

Criminal proceedings are over if the jury returns a 'not guilty' verdict, or if the prosecution drops the charges.[46] A guilty verdict is more complex. The proceedings continue to be active until the offender is sentenced. The courts have expressly disapproved of a premature press clamour that might give the appearance of affecting the sentence, although it is unlikely that contempt proceedings would be brought unless the publication amounts to a deliberate attempt to put pressure on a judge to hand down a particular sentence.

The period of activity can continue, at least in theory, for some time after a conviction if the court remands the defendant for a social inquiry report or if the case has been tried by magistrates who think their powers of sentence are insufficient and they decide to commit the defendant to the Crown Court for punishment. The case ceases to be active if sentence is formally deferred for a fixed period to allow the defendant a chance to show that he or she can make good.[47] If the jury disagrees, the proceedings remain active unless the prosecution indicates that it will not seek a new trial.[48]

Civil proceedings end when they are disposed of, discontinued or withdrawn.[49]

Appeals

Appeal proceedings are active from the time when they are launched by the lodging of a formal notice of appeal or application for leave.[50] The losing party's declaration of intent to appeal is not enough. There will often be a period, perhaps quite short, between the end of active trial proceedings and the commencement of active appeal proceedings during which the strict-liability rule does not apply at all and comment is quite free. Even if appeal proceedings

---

[44] During the Committee stage of the Contempt of Court Bill: Standing Committee 'A' 12 May 1981 col 141.

[45] Frances Gibb, 'Riddle of When Comment Must Stop' (1981) *The Times*, 19 May.

[46] Contempt of Court Act 1981 Sched 1 para 5.   [47] ibid., para 6.

[48] *A-G* v *News Group Newspapers* (1982) 4 Cr App R (S) 182.

[49] Contempt of Court Act 1981, Sched 1, para 12.   [50] ibid., para 15.

have become active, it is most unlikely that appellate judges will be influenced by what appears in the media. When an appeal is disposed of, abandoned, discontinued or withdrawn, even this restraint is removed unless the case is remitted to the trial court or unless a new trial is ordered, in which case the strict-liability rule applies until these proceedings are over.[51]

Defences

Public-interest defence

An important new defence is provided for the media by s 5 of the Contempt of Court Act. This is intended to ensure that public debate and criticism on matters of importance can continue, although a side-effect of expounding the main theme is that ongoing proceedings might be prejudiced. The section reads:

> A publication made as or as part of a discussion in good faith of public affairs or other matters of general public interest is not to be treated as contempt of court under the strict-liability rule if the risk of impediment or prejudice is merely incidental to the discussion.

Section 5 was given a liberal interpretation by the House of Lords in the first test-case:

> The Attorney-General accused the *Daily Mail* of prejudicing the trial of a doctor who was charged with allowing a Down's syndrome baby to die. The *Daily Mail* had published an article by Malcolm Muggeridge in support of a 'Pro-Life' candidate in a contemporaneous by-election. He spoke disparagingly of what he described as the common practice of doctors deliberately failing to keep deformed children alive. The House of Lords said the defence was applicable. Even if the public understood the article as a reference to the trial, it was not contempt. Academicians might enjoy abstract discussions, but the press was entitled to make great issues come alive by reference to concrete examples. 'Gagging of bona fide discussion of controversial matters of general public interest merely because there are in existence contemporaneous legal proceedings in which some particular instance of those controversial matters may be in issue is what section 5 . . . was intended to prevent.'[52]

Sir John Junor was fined £1,000 and the *Sunday Express* £10,000

---

[51] ibid., para 16.
[52] *A-G* v *English* note 10 above. See also the recommendation of the Phillimore Committee, para 142, on which the section was based, and the Australian decisions that spell out a similar defence: *Re 'Truth & Sportsmen' ex parte Bread Manufactures* (1937) 37 SRNSW 249; *Brych* v *The Herald and Weekly Times* [1978] VR 727.

for a comment that prejudiced the same trial.[53] This piece directly criticized the doctor, on the basis of facts reported in the prosecution case that were subsequently proved incorrect. Section 5 was not applicable, because there was no discussion of wider issues. Neither writer nor newspaper tried to defend this blatant contempt, committed in mid-trial.

In 1989 the Divisional Court said that in deciding whether the risk of prejudice was incidental, it was necessary to look at the subject-matter of the discussion and see how closely it related to the particular legal proceedings.

> In the middle of a trial of a Reading landlord charged with conspiring to defraud the Department of Health and Social Security, TVS broadcast a programme called *The New Rachmans* about sham bed-and-breakfast accommodation in Reading. The court accepted that the programme attempted to analyse the cause of the new wave of Rachmanism in the South of England, but it focused on a small number of landlords in Reading. The programme included still photographs of two of the defendants, who were recognizable although their faces had been blacked out. The trial of the defendants was aborted at a cost of £215,000. The broadcaster and a newspaper that had previewed the programme under the headline 'Reading's new wave of harassment . . . TV focus on bedsit barons' were found guilty of contempt.[54]

The defence is dependent on good faith. 'Bad faith' means more than unreasonable or wrongheaded opinions. There must be an element of improper motive, such as a deliberate attempt to prejudice proceedings under cover of a public discussion. The burden of proving 'bad faith', or of negating the defence generally, rests on the prosecution throughout[55] – another factor that makes the new 'public discussion' defence a broad shield for investigative reporting.

Section 5 does not afford protection only where the subject of general interest has already been under discussion before the proceedings commenced. It would apply in situations where the public interest has been generated by the proceedings themselves. Had the Muggeridge article not been tied to the platform of a by-election candidate, but had rather taken the form of a general discussion of the morality of euthanasia in relation to deformed babies, a topic given prominence by the trial, it should still have been protected by s 5.

---

[53] (1981) *The Times*, 19 December.
[54] *A-G* v *TVS Television*; *A-G* v *HW Southey & Sons Ltd* (1989) *The Independent*, 7 July.
[55] *A-G* v *English*, note 10 above.

Innocent distributors

Strict-liability contempt is committed only by publishing an infringing story, but the definition of 'publishing' is a wide one.[56] It applies to anyone in the chain of distribution from printer or importer to newsvendor. However, distributors can usually rely on the defence that they did not know (having taken all reasonable care) that their wares contained a contempt and they had no reason to suspect that they were likely to do so.[57] To demonstrate this, distributors sometimes insist that magazines provide them with a lawyer's opinion that the publication is free of contempt. Even if the lawyer is wrong, the distributor will then have taken all reasonable care and can rely on the defence.

Innocent publishers

This defence is open to publishers and broadcasters, but it is much narrower. It helps only those who did not know and had no reason to suspect that the proceedings in question were active. Again all reasonable care must have been taken.[58] The burden lies on both distributor and publisher to show that the defence is established, although that burden may be satisfied on the balance of probabilities.[59] It is very important, therefore, that journalists should make contemporaneous notes of all their inquiries (e.g., to police or lawyers acting for the parties or at the court). These notes should be kept as evidence that the appropriate inquiries were made, and that nothing was said to alert the reporter to the fact that the case was 'active'.

This defence does not help a paper that knew that the proceedings were active, but (like *The Sunday Times* at the time of Michael X's trial) published by mistake a reference to the defendant's murky past.[60] Even if the paper takes ordinary precautions to eliminate prejudicial material, it is guilty of contempt. The requirement that the publisher had 'no reason to suspect' that the proceedings were active narrows the defence still further. A journalist who knew that a man was helping the police with their inquiries would probably have reason to suspect that the man might be arrested before the paper was published, unless the police had said something to suggest otherwise.

If care has been taken to establish a sound vetting procedure, there is no realistic danger of a prison sentence. When mistakes occur, as they inevitably do, even in well regulated and 'night-

---

[56] Contempt of Court Act 1981 s 2(1).
[57] ibid., s 3(2).
[58] ibid., s 3(1).
[59] ibid., s 3(3); *R v Carr-Briant* [1943] KB 607.
[60] *R v Thomson Newspapers Ltd ex parte A-G*, note 26 above.

lawyered' newspaper offices, an apology to the court will normally mean a fine, and this will be visited upon the newspaper rather than the editor personally. But this is still unnecessarily restrictive. It would be fairer and pose no threat to the administration of justice to allow publishers a simple and complete defence that the contempt was published despite all reasonable care.

Fair and accurate reports
No contempt is committed by contemporaneous publishing in good faith of a fair and accurate report of court proceedings, however prejudicial that report may be to a party involved in the case. The requirements of this defence are considered further at p. 341.

Gagging writs

A 'gagging writ' is the device of attempting to suppress media criticism by issuing a writ for libel against one critic, and threatening contempt proceedings if the criticism, now the subject of litigation, is repeated. The courts have declined to allow their contempt jurisdiction to be exploited in this fashion by the likes of fascist leader Oswald Mosley and company fraudsman Dr Wallersteiner.[61] The interests of the administration of justice will prevail over freedom of speech only if the proposed publication would constitute 'strict liability' contempt. That means, in turn, that the defence of public interest is not applicable and the publication would be likely to cause a substantial risk of serious prejudice.

> When the *News of the World* wanted to write about Ian Botham's alleged involvement with drugs, the cricketer's libel action against the *Mail on Sunday* for similar stories had been set down for trial. However, the trial would still not take place for at least ten months. The Court of Appeal decided that there was not a substantial risk of serious prejudice and lifted an injunction that the Attorney-General had obtained.[62]

This case marks an important judicial recognition of the psychological phenomenon that involvement in the immediate drama of a trial will help to eradicate dim memories of media content. As Lord Donaldson put it:

> This trial will not take place for at least ten months, by which time many wickets will have fallen, not to mention much water having flowed under many bridges, all of which would blunt

---

[61] *R* v *Fox ex parte Mosley* (1966) *Guardian*, 17 February; *Wallersteiner* v *Moir* [1974] 3 All ER 217.
[62] *A-G* v *News Group Newspapers Ltd* [1986] 2 All ER 833, CA.

any impact of the publication . . . the fact is that for one reason or another a trial, by its very nature, seems to cause all concerned to become progressively more inward-looking, studying the evidence given and submissions made to the exclusion of other sources of enlightenment.[63]

The significance of the gagging writ is now much reduced by the rule that strict liability for contempt does not begin with the issue of a writ, but is only activated after the case has been set down for trial. None the less, the pertinent words of Lord Salmon may still need to be quoted to solicitors who try to bluff the media out of publishing criticisms of their clients with threats that the matter is '*sub judice*':

It is a widely held fallacy that the issue of a writ automatically stifles further comment. There is no authority that I know of to support the view that further comment would amount to contempt of court. Once a newspaper has justified, and there is some prima facie support for this justification, the plaintiff cannot obtain an interlocutory injunction to restrain the defendants from repeating the matters complained of. In these circumstances it is obviously wrong to suppose that they could be committing a contempt by doing so. It seems to me equally obvious that no other newspaper that repeats the same sort of criticism is committing a contempt of court. They may be publishing a libel, and if they do so, and they have no defence to it, they will have to pay whatever may be the appropriate damages; but the writ does not, in my view, preclude the publication of any further criticism; it merely puts the person who makes the further criticism at risk of being sued for libel.[64]

Deliberate Contempt

The 1981 Act is not an exhaustive treatment of the law of contempt. It deals principally with strict-liability contempt, which is committed irrespective of the publisher's intentions, and it expressly preserves other forms of contempt developed by the courts through their powers at common law. The 1981 reforms have worked to restrict the ambit of strict-liability contempt, and in consequence the forces antagonistic to media freedom (notably the British

---

[63] ibid.
[64] *Thomson* v *Times Newspapers Ltd* [1969] 3 All ER 648 at p. 651.

Government) have sought to exploit the residual powers of the court to punish for 'intentional' or 'deliberate' contempt at common law.[65] They were notably and regrettably successful during the *Spycatcher* saga, when the courts strove mightily to staunch what judges perceived to be treasonable leaks from the security services by holding newspapers in contempt for breaching the spirit of interim injunctions. The two other important areas of deliberate contempt relate to the creation of prejudice against a defendant before proceedings are 'active', and the arcane crime of 'scandalizing the courts'. Deliberate contempt does not attract the public-interest defence in s 5 of the Act, although the requirement that the prosecution must prove a specific intention to prejudice the administration of justice offers some comfort to media defendants.[66] Most regrettably, the offence carries no right to trial by jury – a factor that undoubtedly secured convictions for the Government against newspapers that published Wright's memoirs, which it might not have obtained from a 'gang of twelve'.

Intentionally prejudicing potential criminal proceedings and civil jury trials

It is an offence at common law to publish material that is designed to prejudice criminal proceedings that are 'imminent' although not yet under way. There is an important distinction between agitating for a prosecution to be brought against a particular individual, which is permissible, and deliberately poisoning the public perception of an individual whom you know is about to be prosecuted. This distinction was crucial to finding the *Sun* guilty of deliberate contempt in 1988 for viciously whipping up hostility to a doctor against whom it had already decided to bring a private prosecution:

> The editor of the *Sun* heard that the DPP had declined to prosecute a distinguished doctor over an allegation that he had raped a young child. He decided that the newspaper would pay for a private prosecution, to be brought by the child's mother, on the secret condition that the mother would provide interviews and pictures exclusively to the

---

[65] Contempt of Court Act 1981 s 6(*c*).

[66] It may be that a form of public-interest defence exists at common law, in so far as the court may find that the public interest in freedom of expression outweighs, in the instant case, the public interest in the administration of justice. This 'balancing act' has been adopted by the High Court of Australia: see *Hinch* v *Attorney-General (Vic)* (1987) 74 ALR 353, and Sally Walker, *The Law of Journalism in Australia*, Law Book Co., 1989, pp. 70–5. It will be rare for a deliberate attempt to prejudice a trial to escape a contempt finding on this test – although one example might be the right of a defendant publicly to proclaim his innocence prior to his appearance in court.

Sun and would not talk to any other media. The day after this deal was signed, the *Sun* published a vitriolic front-page character assassination of the doctor ('a beast and a swine'), declared him guilty of rape, and boasted that it was going to fund his prosecution. The next day, after the 'dial-a-quote' MP Geoffrey Dickens had helpfully named the doctor under parliamentary privilege, the *Sun* continued its character-assassination, accusing the doctor of other sexual crimes and of permanently injuring his victim. Despite such blatant attempts to destroy the doctor's right to a fair trial, he was subsequently acquitted, unlike the *Sun*, which was convicted of criminal contempt and fined £75,000. The verdict itself cannot be questioned – the *Sun*'s conduct would be regarded as wrong in any country that seriously endorses the principle that a defendant is entitled to a fair trial. The decision may be interpreted as turning upon the fact that the newspaper negotiated its agreement with the mother *before* it embarked upon the campaign to discredit the person whose prosecution it had undertaken to support. Had this course not been contemplated, and had the articles been designed instead to criticize the DPP (or even to put pressure on him to change his mind), this should not have been regarded as contemptuous.[67]

Thus, the *Sun* case does not prevent publishers or broadcasters trying to sting the authorities into bringing proceedings. Encouraging the initiation of a prosecution is not by itself prejudicial to the administration of justice. What made the *Sun* articles prejudicial was the newspaper's intention to finance a private prosecution coupled with the article's assumption of guilt, the inflammatory language and the reference to allegations of similar but unrelated offences, which would (even if true) have been kept from a jury. Equally, it is not intentional contempt for defence campaigns to urge the police or the Attorney-General to abandon a prosecution. The decision to prosecute involves a consideration of the public interest, and defence committees are entitled to urge their view of what this entails. The same is true when the prosecution is brought by a private individual. The Attorney-General can always take over and stop a private prosecution, and a campaign pamphlet calling on him to do this would not be contempt. Any attempt to go further and to threaten prosecution witnesses with ostracism or calumny is much more dangerous (as was shown on p. 276) and might well constitute contempt.

Although the House of Lords declined to hear an appeal by the *Sun* some doubt about the correctness of the Divisional Court's decision that contempt could be committed by publications prior to arrest arises from the subsequent case of *Attorney-General* v *Sport Newspapers*:

---

[67] *A-G* v *News Group Newspapers* [1988] 2 All ER 906.

A man with previous convictions for rape went 'on the run' after a fifteen-year-old schoolgirl disappeared from her home. Police treated him as a suspect and notified all newspapers (through the Press Association) about his previous convictions, with a warning that nothing should be published about them lest this jeopardize his possible trial. It is no business of the police to tell newspapers what they may or may not print; it is their business to obtain arrest warrants for suspects, which in this case they failed to do until ten days had elapsed and the *Sunday Sport* had treated its readers to a lurid account of the man's 'sex monster' past, thanks no doubt to the police tip-off. The man was later caught and convicted of murder. The *Sport* could not be prosecuted for strict-liability contempt, as the proceedings were not active at the time it published. The Divisional Court held that its editor had not been proved to have the necessary specific intention to prejudice a trial for the purposes of common law contempt, but the two judges were divided on the legal question of whether it was possible, at common law, to commit contempt in relation to proceedings that had not yet begun. Lord Justice Bingham, with some reluctance, held that the *Sun* case should be treated as correctly decided; Mr Justice Hodgson said that it was plainly wrong.

In the *Sport* case[68] Mr Justice Hodgson relied on previous authorities, both in Britain and Australia, to show that contempt could not be committed at common law in relation to proceedings that were not yet in existence, even if they were 'imminent'.[69] He justified this position with a number of powerful policy arguments anchored on the right of journalists to freedom of expression and the right of all individuals to fair trial when alleged to have committed a crime. It was an everyday occurrence, and entirely in the public interest, that the media should be free to expose wrongdoers and demand that they should face trial. To render them liable for contempt at this stage would deter them from providing a useful public service. Moreover, it would extend a criminal offence for which defendants were deprived of their right to jury trial, a position that could be justified only by the need to give parties to active proceedings a swift and effective protection by High Court judges. Moreover, there was no safeguard against a private prosecution for intentional contempt brought by rich and powerful wrongdoers 'exposed' in order to jolt the authorities into action: section 7 of the Contempt Act, which required the Attorney-General's consent to contempt proceedings, is limited to contempt under the strict-liability rule. Despite the unprepossessing newspaper whose opportunistic conduct was the springboard for the

---

[68] [1992] 1 All ER 503.
[69] See *In re Crown Bank, In re O'Mally* (1890) 44 Ch D 649; *Stirling* v *Associated Newspapers Ltd* (1960) SLT 5; *James* v *Robinson* (1963) 109 CLR 593.

judgment, and the obnoxious behaviour of the *Sun* in the case that preceded it, Mr Justice Hodgson's reasoning, both as to law and as to public policy, is to be preferred. It is unlikely, however, that it *will* be preferred when the issue finally falls for decision by the House of Lords.

A further difference between strict-liability contempt and the intentional variety is that distributors and importers are more vulnerable because they cannot in the latter case rely on the defence of innocent distribution (see p. 283). Moreover, the *Sun* case indicates that the prosecution must prove only a real risk of prejudice and need not satisfy the more exacting standard of showing that the article created a substantial risk of serious prejudice.

On the other hand, if the risk of prejudice is remote, there will be no contempt. Sir James Goldsmith failed in his contempt case against *Private Eye* for articles it published while his libel action was pending against the magazine. The articles were intended to persuade Goldsmith to drop his case and suggested he might have 'nobbled' witnesses, but all this was unlikely to have any effect on the libel action's outcome.[70]

The court took more seriously a trade union paper's castigation of a member for taking his grievance to law, and its hint of the retribution he might face from his comrades.[71] Menacing a litigant with spiritual excommunication can also be contempt.[72] It is irrelevant that the black sheep would be expelled with full procedural regularity; the courts will punish threats, even threats of lawful acts, if they are intended as a deterrent, and have a real chance of success.[73]

A more difficult question is whether a modern day thalidomide-style campaign would constitute contempt. The majority of the House of Lords found *The Sunday Times* guilty because the paper had prejudged the litigation between Distillers and the children. This constituted contempt irrespective of the paper's intention. That part of the decision was overturned by the 1981 Act. Two Law Lords, however, thought that, in addition, the newspaper was guilty of deliberate contempt because it was intentionally trying to pressurize Distillers into paying compensation. Theirs was a minority view. Lord Cross expressed a more liberal opinion:

> To seek to dissuade a litigant from prosecuting or defending proceedings by threats of unlawful action, by abuse or by

---

[70] *R v Ingrams ex parte Goldsmith* [1977] Crim LR 240; see also *R v Duffy ex parte Nash* [1960] 2 QB 188, 200.
[71] *Hutchinson v AEU* (1932) *The Times*, 25 August.
[72] *Hillfinch Properties Ltd v Newark Investment Ltd* (1981) *The Times*, 1 July.
[73] ibid.

misrepresentation of the nature of the proceedings or the circumstances out of which they arose and such like is no doubt a
contempt of court, but if the writer states the facts fairly and
accurately and expresses his view in temperate language the
fact that publication may bring pressure – possibly great pressure – to bear on the litigant should not make it a contempt of
court.[74]

A majority of the judges would have allowed a *Venetian Times* to
make a fair and temperate appeal to Shylock to abandon his legal
right to a pound of Antonio's flesh, but they would doubtless have
drawn the line at vituperative Jew-baiting from a *Rialto Gutter
Press*. Of course, the wilder the language, the less likely it is to
have any real impact, and for that reason even an intemperate
appeal might not be guilty of contempt. Publishers may also take
some comfort in the infrequency with which private litigants go
the expense of initiating contempt proceedings of this kind. In the
course of the lengthy litigation over the alleged side-effects of the
drug Opren the judge sounded a contempt warning over media
campaigns to persuade the manufacturers, Eli Lilley, to pay generous compensation, but the issue was never tested by actual
contempt proceedings.[75]

The intemperate nature of a *Private Eye* attack on Sonia Sutcliffe
very nearly earned its editor, Ian Hislop, a prison sentence for
intentional contempt in 1990:

> Three months before Sutcliffe's action against *Private Eye* (for alleg-
> ing she had accepted money from a newspaper for telling of her
> marriage to the 'Yorkshire Ripper') was fixed to be tried by a jury,
> Hislop threatened in print that if the action went ahead, she would
> be cross-examined about defrauding the DHSS and providing her
> husband with alibis for his murders which she knew to be false.
> Although Hislop believed these allegations at the time he published
> them, his intention in so doing was to deter her from proceeding with
> her case. His impropriety turned on the fact that the articles went far
> beyond 'fair and temperate criticism', and amounted to 'plain abuse',
> over matters that had nothing to do with the issues in the libel action.
> The purpose of the articles was to place improper pressure on Sutcliffe
> to abandon her right as a litigant, and hence amounted to an interfer-
> ence with the administration of justice and an intentional contempt at

---

[74] *A-G* v *Times Newspapers Ltd* [1974] AC 273 at p. 326 per Lord Cross. Lords
Reid and Morris appear to agree, contrary to the less liberal view of Lords Diplock
and Simon. In Australia this authority has been used to exculpate public statements
calculated to bring pressure on a party to litigation, unless the expression is intemperate or full of factual errors. See *Commercial Bank of Australia* v *Preston* [1981] 2
NSWLR 554, per Hunt J.
[75] *Davies* v *Eli Lilley and Co* (1987) *The Independent*, 23 July.

common law. The court accepted that Hislop had no intention to prejudice the jury, so he was not guilty of common law contempt on this score, although the fact that the publication had objectively created a serious risk of prejudicing them meant that it was additionally a contempt under the strict-liability rule. Hislop and his journal were fined £10,000 each.[76]

Of course, an essential ingredient of this type of contempt is 'intent' to prejudice the proceedings. This is a difficult and confusing legal concept. It is not enough that the publisher simply intends to publish the newspaper or magazine. The law is concerned with the effect the contents are intended to have. 'Intent' is not the same as 'desire' or 'motive'. Nor, in this context, is it to be equated with recklessness.[77] But it is enough if the publisher foresees prejudice as a likely consequence and carries on regardless. The court can usually only infer such an intent from all the circumstances since there will rarely be direct evidence of a prejudicial intent.

> After the preliminary issue had been found against them (see p. 293), *The Independent*, *The Sunday Times* and the *London Daily News* were found guilty of intentional contempt by publishing material from Peter Wright that other newspapers had been ordered to keep confidential. The judge rejected the argument that a person who knew of such an injunction and published anyway would necessarily be guilty of intentional contempt. These were matters from which intention could be inferred, but the court had to look at all the circumstances, including what legal advice was given, its basis and how it was understood. The editors did not desire to interfere in the administration of justice, but this did not negate their intent. Each paper was fined £50,000. The individual editors were not imprisoned since it was accepted that they believed on legal advice (albeit erroneously) that they were not committing contempt. The judge saw no point in fining the editors since they all had indemnities from their papers.[78]

The fullest discussion of the 'intention' that has to be proved against a newspaper in order to obtain a conviction for deliberate contempt is found in the verdict against the *Sun* for prejudicing a prosecution that it had decided to fund. The court held that it was

---

[76] *A-G* v *Hislop* [1991] 1 All ER 911.

[77] *A-G* v *Newspaper Publishing plc* [1987] 3 All ER 276, 304, 309, 313, CA; *A-G* v *News Group Newspapers Ltd* [1988] 2 All ER 906.

[78] *A-G* v *Newspaper Publishing plc* (1989) *The Independent*, 9 May. The fines were quashed on appeal, on the grounds that it would be wrong to punish editors in circumstances where the law was unsettled and their erroneous legal advice had coincided with the view taken by the judge who had decided a preliminary issue in their favour (see *The Independent*, 28 February 1990).

necessary for the Attorney-General to prove a specific intention to prejudice a fair trial; it was insufficient to show that the publication had been reckless or that the newspaper had some generalized intention to interfere with the course of justice. Newspaper editors, of course, will always deny criminal intentions, and the courts will not take them at their word; the issue will be decided by examining what they published and the circumstances surrounding publication, and asking whether they must have foreseen, for all practical purposes, that a real risk to the fairness of a trial would result. The editor of the *Sun* was held to have had the requisite intention, despite his disavowals, as he was plainly campaigning for the doctor's conviction in circumstances where that conviction would have proved financially beneficial to the newspaper: it would not only have recovered its legal costs, but it would have boosted its circulation on the back of the 'world exclusive' for which it had bought up the alleged victim's mother.

Honest mistake is a complete defence to common law contempt. The banking correspondent of the *Daily Telegraph* was writing a story about Homes Assured Corporation PLC, some of whose directors were facing proceedings for disqualification. She visited the registry of the companies court and was told (correctly) that to inspect the file she would have to obtain the leave of the court. She was given the file to take to the registrar. While waiting forty minutes for her appointment, she openly made notes from the report of the official receiver, which was in the court file, and told the registrar she had done so. The registrar telephoned the city editor to complain, but the latter thought the problem was ethical rather than legal, and published two stories based on the report. The Chancery Division dismissed an application by the directors to commit the editor (Max Hastings) and his journalist for contempt. The essential vice of the offence lies in *knowingly* interfering with the administration of justice. The journalist had apparently never before inspected a court document and the court accepted that she did not know she was acting in breach of the rules. There had been no trickery or dishonesty.[79]

Campaigns over criminal proceedings raise different considerations. No decision to prosecute Dr Savundra had been made at the time of David Frost's televised interview in 1967 over his handling of the Fire and Auto Marine Insurance Company. At the time, the programme was criticized because Savundra's arrest was imminent.[80] Now 'imminence' of an arrest is not enough; the proceedings would not be active and so there would be no risk of infringing the strict-liability rule (see p. 278). However, part of the

---

[79] *Dobson* v *Hastings* (1991) *The Independent*, 12 November.

programme's apparent intention (like that of consumer programmes such as *Checkpoint*) was to sting the authorities into action. Even so, this is not intentional contempt, because encouraging the initiation of a prosecution is not prejudicial to the administration of justice.

Frustrating court orders against others

Court orders primarily affect another party to the lawsuit in which they are made. Basic fairness requires that before a person is ordered to do something by a court, he or she should have a chance to argue that the order would be wrong. There are statutory exceptions to this that affect the media. Thus, reporters do not have a legal right to be heard before banning or postponement orders are made under the Contempt of Court Act (they do now have a right to seek an appeal or review of the order – p. 346). In addition, it is contempt for one person to aid or abet another to break a court order. However, in one of the most serious elements of the *Spycatcher* saga the courts created a new inroad on the principle that court orders do not affect third parties:

> The Attorney-General obtained injunctions preventing the *Guardian* and the *Observer* from printing material derived from Peter Wright's memoirs. Subsequently *The Independent*, the *London Daily News*, the *London Evening Standard* and, later, *The Sunday Times* published various parts of Wright's allegations. These three newspapers had not obtained their information from the first two, and they certainly did not publish their stories as their agents. They were not parties to the proceedings in which the injunction was obtained. The House of Lords accepted that the newspapers could not break an injunction that was not addressed to them. However, it held that their publications could amount to deliberate contempt of court. It was contempt to destroy or seriously damage the subject matter of an action if this impeded or prejudiced the administration of justice: the subject matter of the first action was the allegedly confidential nature of the material in *Spycatcher*, which would be destroyed if someone else published it. The consequence of the publication was to nullify the purpose of the trial by placing in the public domain information the Attorney-General contended was confidential and this amounted to interference with the course of justice in the confidentiality action.[81]

When the case was heard in full, the judge decided that the newspapers had been in contempt (see p. 291). It was immaterial

---

[80] *R v Savundranayagan and Walker* [1968] 1 WLR 1761, see Frost's letter in reply to *The Times*, 18 July 1968. The Board of Trade had been investigating the companies but nothing had happened for months and there was no indication that it would.

[81] *A-G v Times Newspapers* [1991] 2 All ER 398, HL, and see CA.

that the Attorney-General's action had not in fact been prejudiced. It did not matter that the House of Lords subsequently found that the injunction was unjustified following the widespread circulation of the Wright material. In the contempt proceedings some of the newspapers argued that there could be no contempt because by the time they published, the American edition of *Spycatcher* had appeared and other papers had printed extracts. However, the judge said that each publication played its part in destroying the confidentiality; each newspaper committed contempt; and he drew no distinction in the penalties he imposed between the early and the late publishers.

This case shows just how far the law of contempt can be stretched when combined with the supple common-law doctrine of breach of confidence. The subject-matter of the initial confidence action against the *Observer* was a report of Wright's allegations. This subject-matter was likened to an ice-cube: it would 'evaporate' if exposed to the light of day by *The Independent* and *The Sunday Times*. There would be no point in the Attorney-General continuing his action against the *Observer* if Wright's revelations were published elsewhere. Since the contempt jurisdiction is a power deployed by the courts to prevent interference with the due administration of justice, the courts were entitled to punish the editors of *The Independent* and *The Sunday Times* by way of a criminal action for contempt of court on the ground that by publishing Wright's allegations they had destroyed the confidential nature of information that another court had injuncted the *Observer* from publishing pending the trial of the Government's claim to exclusive possession of this information. It was, said Lord Donaldson in the Court of Appeal, as if the Government and the *Observer* had commenced a legal action over the ownership of a racehorse, and the court had ordered the horse to be kept alive until the dispute over its possession could be resolved after a full trial. The editor of *The Independent* had shot the horse prior to that full trial, and thereby rendered the proceedings pointless. The Attorney-General, in his role as guardian of the administration of justice, was entitled to seek to commit *The Independent* editor to prison for intentionally aborting legal proceedings in which, quite coincidentally, the Attorney-General happened to be a party.

There can be no objection to the principle that courts should have power to protect judicial proceedings from third parties who deliberately set out to prejudice or subvert them, and the cases relied on by the House of Lords, which related to third parties who cut down trees or disposed of assets that were the subject of a court order, cannot be faulted. But they concerned property, not information. Where the argument in this case becomes metaphysical is in assimilating Wright's allegations (that MI5 plotted to assassinate Nasser, bug foreign embassies and destabilize the Wilson Government) to items of physical property like ice-cubes and racehorses. Information of this kind is not 'subject-matter' that can be possessed exclusively by a department of state, any more than a conspiracy to murder is the exclusive property of the conspirators. The subject-matter of an action for breach of confidence is not the information itself, but the confidential relationship in the course of which it was acquired. In fact, *The Independent*'s publication did not abort the proceedings in the case against the *Observer*, which continued to trial and appeal, irrespective of the fact that over a million copies of *Spycatcher* had been published throughout the world and many copies had been imported into Britain. The ice-cube had by this stage been transformed into a flood of dirty water, but what was at stake in the litigation was the question of whether the *Observer* had become party to Wright's breach of his duty owed to the Crown by publishing his allegations. *The Independent* did not frustrate the administration of justice in that case by further publishing Wright's allegations, although by so doing it may well have become a party to his breach of confidence. *The Independent* should have been sued for breach of confidence, not prosecuted for the crime of contempt.

None the less, the case stands for the proposition that it can be a crime for one newspaper to breach the spirit of an injunction imposed upon another, despite the fact that it has had no opportunity to present a case against the imposition of any restraint. It must go cap in hand to the court and ask for permission to publish. This was the course taken by Derbyshire Country Council to request permission for its local library to stock a copy of *Spycatcher*.[82] Although numerous copies of the book had by this time been imported into the country, and were being sold by enthusiastic entrepreneurs at inflated prices, the High Court held that the book's availability in a public library would 'constitute an interference with the due administration of justice' in the ongoing cases against the *Guardian* and the *Observer*. This decision shows just how far the contempt confidentiality doctrine has moved in the direction of prior restraint: had the council simply ordered a copy of the book pursuant to its duty to provide a comprehensive and efficient library service, it is doubtful whether it would have been charged with intentional contempt. This crime is committed only by those who specifically intend to impede or prejudice the administration of justice, and even recklessness as to whether such prejudice may be caused is insufficient to ground a conviction.

---

[82] *A-G* v *Observer Ltd*; *Re An Application by Derbyshire County Council* [1988] 1 All ER 385. The argument advanced in the text is developed in Geoffrey Robertson, *Freedom, the Individual and the Law*, Penguin, 1989.

Scandalizing the Court

'Scandalizing the court' was a type of contempt invented in the eighteenth century to punish radical critics of the establishment, such as John Wilkes.[83] It has been defined as: 'any act done or writing published calculated to bring a court or judge into contempt or to lower his authority'.[84] Editorial barbs were thus equated with cat calls in court, both being treated as affronts to judicial dignity. In Scotland the crime is called 'murmuring judges'.

Despite its apparent breadth, scandalizing the court should not prevent criticism of the judiciary even when expressed in strong terms. 'Justice is not a cloistered virtue' a senior Law Lord once said,[85] and comment about the legal system in general or the handling of particular cases once they are over sometimes deserves to be trenchant.

The Victorian press was outspoken in its condemnation of the bench. Charles Dickens led a campaign of press criticism against one magistrate ('Mr Fang' in *Oliver Twist*) that resulted in his removal.[86] This was not an isolated example. Press attacks on the judiciary were so frequent that the Lord Chancellor retaliated by refusing to make editors Justices of the Peace.[87] None of these papers was punished for scandalizing the court, and by 1899 the Privy Council considered that the offence was virtually a dead-letter in England.[88] However, it was revived the following year when the *Birmingham Daily Argus* described Mr Justice Darling, accurately enough, as an 'impudent little man in horse-hair' who was 'a microcosm of conceit and empty-headedness'. It was fined

---

[83] *R* v *Almon* (1765) Wilm 243; 97 ER 94. This authority is distinctly shaky. It was an undelivered judgment of Justice Wilmott, published posthumously by his son, and uncritically accepted by Blackstone. It cites no authority for the proposition that judges have power to punish their press critics, and the better view is that it was wrongly decided; see Sir John Fox, *The History of Contempt of Court*, Oxford, 1927; reprinted Professional Books, 1972. In the context of eighteenth-century politics it was an attempt to protect Lord Mansfield from reasoned criticism of his oppressive judicial behaviour towards Wilkes and other critics of the Government; see D. Hay, 'Contempt by Scandalising the Court: A Political History of the First Five Hundred Years' (1987) 25 *Osgoode Hall Law Journal* 431.

[84] *Badry* v *DPP of Mauritius* [1982] 3 All ER 973 at p. 979 quoting *R* v *Gray* [1900] 2 QB 36 at p. 40. The offence does not apply in respect of a defamatory attack on a judge in his personal rather than his official capacity: *In re the Special Reference from the Bahama Islands* [1893] AC 138; *Debi Prasad Sharma* v *Emporer* [1943] AIR 2020.

[85] *Ambard* v *A-G for Trinidad and Tobago* [1936] AC 322 at p. 335 per Lord Atkin.

[86] His real name was Allan Laing. See Marjorie Jones, *Justice and Journalism*, Barry Rose, 1974, p. 27.

[87] (1883) Justice of the Peace 750; cf. Jones, note 86 above, p. 43.

[88] *McLeod* v *St Aubyn* [1899] AC 549.

for contempt. In the late 1920s the *New Statesman* was convicted of scandalizing the court for doubting whether birth control reformer Marie Stopes would receive a fair trial from a Roman Catholic judge, and the *Daily Worker* was fined for labelling a Tory judge 'a bewigged puppet exhibiting a strong class bias'.[89] In retrospect, both comments had an element of truth, and it is inconceivable that similar remarks would be prosecuted today. Judges who have exhibited anti-women attitudes in rape cases have been condemned by the press, while attacks on the judges of the National Industrial Relations Court were made without punishment. The modern attitude is exemplified in this 1968 case:

> Raymond Blackburn, the indomitable pursuer of pornography and gambling, tried to commit Quintin Hogg MP (later Lord Chancellor Hailsham) for contempt after he had written an article in *Punch* that was severely but inaccurately critical of the Court of Appeal. The Court of Appeal itself dismissed the application. Lord Denning said:

> It is the right of every man, in Parliament or out of it, in the Press or over the broadcast, to make fair comment, even outspoken comment on matters of public interest. Those who comment can deal faithfully with all that is done in a Court of Justice. They can say we are mistaken, and our decisions erroneous, whether they are subject to appeal or not.[90]

> Lord Salmon added: 'No criticism of a judgment, however vigorous, can amount to contempt of court if it keeps within the limits of reasonable courtesy and of good faith.'[91]

Scandalizing the court is an anachronistic form of contempt. Lord Diplock has described it as 'virtually obsolescent in the United Kingdom[92] and it has not been used for fifty years.[93] But

---

[89] *R v Gray*, note 84 above; *R v Wilkinson* (1930) *The Times*, 16 July; *R v New Statesman ex parte DPP* (1928) 44 TLR 301.

[90] *R v Metropolitan Police Commissioner ex parte Blackburn (No 2)* [1968] 2 QB 150.

[91] ibid.

[92] *Secretary of State for Defence v Guardian Newspapers Ltd* [1985] AC 339, 347.

[93] It has, though, been dusted down and used in the Commonwealth (see Clive Walker's 'Scandalising the Eighties' [1985] 101 LQR 359. A Canadian provincial minister was fined for describing a judge's verdict as 'insane' and a 'disgrace' (*R v Ouillet* (1977) 36 Crim Reps (Nova Scotia) 296). An Indian state premier was likewise punished for damning the judges as bourgeois and class-biased (*Nambooripad v Mambiar* [1970] All India Reps 1318), and when a Trinidadian paper (*The Bomb*) published a thinly disguised 'fictional' account of dishonesty and drunkenness in the local judiciary, its editor, Paddy Chokolingo, was imprisoned (*Chokolingo v A-G for Trinidad and Tobago* [1981] 1 All ER 244 PC). By contrast, an American judge who fined an attorney for a critical newspaper article was himself impeached and very nearly convicted by the US Senate for encroaching on the writer's constitutional freedom of speech (Sir John Fox, *Contempt of Court*, p. 202 ff).

newspaper lawyers sometimes use its existence as an excuse to advise editors and columnists to temper their criticism of the judiciary. This may be one reason why the British media have failed to make much contribution to improving the standards of justice. It is inconceivable that action could be brought against publications that criticize the courts in moderate language, even if the criticism is misplaced. Lord Hailsham has said 'nothing really encourages courts or Attorneys-General to prosecute this type of contempt in all but the most serious example, or courts to take notice of any but the most intolerable instance.'[94] The Law Commission has proposed that the only circumstances under which scandalizing-the-court charges should be brought are when false allegations of corrupt judicial conduct by judges or magistrates are published when the publisher knows they are false or is reckless as to their truth but intends them to be taken as true.[95]

The bounds of 'reasonable courtesy' may well have been exceeded by the *Daily Mirror* in 1987, when it published upside-down photographs of the Law Lords who had injuncted *Spycatcher* under the banner headline 'YOU FOOLS!' No prosecution was forthcoming. The danger, however, of leaving such a crime on the books is well illustrated by recent contempt prosecutions in other countries that have inherited the common law, where robust condemnation of court decisions (Trinidad), suggestions that a decision was influenced by trade-union demonstrations (Australia) and minor inaccuracies in justifiable criticism of the conduct of proceedings against an opposition MP (Singapore) have all been treated as contempt.

In certain Commonwealth countries there does exist an unhealthy relationship between the judges and the Government that appoints them (or, in the recent example of Malaysia, the Government that unseats upright judges and replaces them with time-servers), and scandalizing the court is a crime that has been invoked as an instrument of oppression, to silence honest criticism of biased judges. In *Badry* v *DPP of Mauritius*[96] the Privy Council urged ex-colonial courts to punish only 'the most intolerable instances' of scandalization, and held that the crime was not committed by asserting that a judge had made false statements and had not taken into account relevant evidence. Regrettably, however, it upheld the conviction of a political leader for a rabble-rousing speech accusing the Supreme Court of bias in favour of wealthy

---

[94] *Badry* v *DPP of Mauritius*, note 84 above.
[95] Law Commission, Report No 96, *Criminal Law: Offences Relating to Interference with the Court of Justice*, (1979), HC 213 para 370. Compare the slightly wider proposal of the Phillimore Committee, paras 162–3.
[96] [1982] 3 All ER 973.

companies, because this was 'clearly meant to shake public confidence in the administration of justice in Mauritius'.

The history of contempt by scandalizing the court, both in Britain and especially in the Commonwealth, argues strongly for its abolition. Its impact might be mitigated if it were held to contain a requirement of *mens rea* – an undecided issue, although the judgment in *Almon* is authority for intention as an ingredient of the offence.[97] The crime has no counterpart in American law, where similar offences have been declared unconstitutional,[98] and it is difficult to reconcile with Article 10 of the European Convention. The fullest forensic analysis of the concept is to be found in the Canadian case of *R* v *Kopyto*: the majority of the court held that the British law of contempt by 'scandalization' was incompatible with the 'freedom of expression' guarantee in the Canadian Charter of Rights and Freedoms.[99]

It may be that the British press has itself to blame for Parliament's refusal to abolish this archaic head of contempt in the United Kingdom. During the 1981 reforms an amendment to this effect was rejected, after Lord Hailsham recalled a recent incident that had arisen after the Court of Appeal denied a divorce to a woman who claimed that her husband was unreasonable in having sex with her once a week. A journalist from the Fleet Street gutter telephoned the wives of the three appellate judges to ask how often a week they regarded as reasonable. The offence of scandalizing the court, said the Lord Chancellor, was still required to deal with such conduct.

Publishing Details of Jury Deliberations

Section 8 of the Contempt of Court Act makes it an offence for a journalist 'to obtain, disclose or solicit any particulars of statements made, opinions expressed, arguments advanced or votes cast by members of a jury in the course of their deliberations in any legal proceedings'. This extension of the law came after the *New Statesman* was acquitted of contempt for publishing an interview with one of the jurors in the Thorpe trial, in which the juror revealed how the jury had reacted to certain witnesses and aspects of the evidence when considering its verdict. The public interest in publishing the interview was considerable: it revealed that the *Sunday Telegraph*'s deal with chief prosecution witness Peter Bessell (whereby he would receive £50,000 for his 'exclusive' story

---

[97] *R* v *Almon*, note 83 above.
[98] *Bridges* v *California* 314 US 252 (1941).
[99] *R* v *Kopy To* (1987) 47 DLR 213.

were Thorpe convicted, but only £25,000 were Thorpe acquitted) had irreparably damaged Bessell's credibility as a witness in the eyes of the jury.

It also suggested that the jury would have convicted the defendants had the DPP charged them with conspiracy to assault (rather than to murder) Norman Scott. The Attorney-General should have brought contempt proceedings against the *Sunday Telegraph* for prejudicing the Thorpe trial; instead, he brought them against the *New Statesman* for producing evidence that the *Sunday Telegraph* deal had prejudiced the case. The Divisional Court dismissed the charges, in a judgment that some lawyers thought might open the door to a new form of chequebook journalism: secrets of the Old Bailey jury rooms in notorious criminal trials.[100]

The Government's Contempt Bill was designed to stop this development, but it applied only to publications that named particular trials or jurors. If the *New Statesman* decision was to be cut back at all, these exceptions were sensible. They would have prevented vendettas by convicted defendants or their families without stifling all discussion of jury deliberations. Jury duty is a rare occasion when ordinary people take an active part in government. In can be a memorable experience. Others can benefit from their stories. In addition, like any aspect of government, it is an eminently appropriate subject for study and research. Regrettably, the clause was amended so as to ban even anonymous accounts of unnamed trials. The change was made at the instigation of peers who feared that the jury system might not survive the full glare of publicity if reporters were permitted to cross-examine jurors about the reasons behind their verdict. Lamentably, Section 8 has worked to preclude any sensible or scientific research into the operation of the jury system: it notably frustrated the work of the Fraud Trials Committee (chaired by Lord Roskill), which could produce no hard evidence on the question of whether complex fraud cases were suitable for jury trial.[101] It also breaches Article 10 of the European Convention by destroying a juror's right to freedom of expression in circumstances that find no justification consonant with Article 10(2). The section is ripe for amendment to permit research and voluntary post-trial disclosure, while specifically prohibiting unsought identification of jurors, and the soliciting or purchasing of their stories.[102]

Section 8 is not intended to hinder the working of the trial itself. The judge can ask the jury its verdict, and the jury can solicit help

---

[100] *A-G v New Statesman and Nation Publishing Co Ltd* [1981] QB 1.
[101] Fraud Trials Committee Report, HMSO, 1986, para 8.10.
[102] See the sensible recommendations of the NSW Law Reform Committee Report No 48, *The Jury in a Criminal Trial*, 1986, Ch 11.

even if this hints at the way its members are thinking. The appearance of justice requires that these communications should be in open court,[103] and so they are freely reportable.

The media should not be frightened of making approaches to jurors for information after a trial is over. Section 8 prohibits the media only from intentionally soliciting information about the jury's *deliberations* in reaching their verdict. As the Attorney-General noted in the debate on the clause, it is not an offence to solicit or publish a juror's view of the desirability of the prosecution, of the quality of the advocates, of the sobriety of the judge or the attentiveness of the court usher.[104] Nor would it be contempt to interview trial jurors about their opinion of the length of the sentence. Shortly after the Act went into effect *The Sunday Times* published a story on the trial of the doctor charged with killing a Down's syndrome baby; the article included the opinion of a juror that the prosecution should never have been brought. The BBC has broadcast interviews with jurors complaining about coroners who tried to dictate their verdicts. In 1980 some of the jurors who had acquitted four anarchists on bomb conspiracy charges wrote to the *Guardian* in response to the trial judge's attack on their good faith. Although this touched on what had taken place in the jury room, the Attorney-General has said that the new offence would not prevent jurors in a comparable situation from publicly responding to judicial rebukes.[105] Section 8 does not apply at all to trials where the jury has been discharged prior to the stage at which it is asked to retire to consider the verdict. It follows that jurors may be interviewed without legal difficulty when cases are dismissed by the judge at 'half-time' because of insufficient prosecution evidence. A prosecution under s 8 can only be brought by the Attorney-General,[106] and it is likely to be confined in practice to cases where journalists pester jurors for the sake of sensationalism. Reporters need not hesitate to interview jurors, but they must remember to avoid any question designed to elicit an answer about what was said or done in the jury room.

Procedure and Punishment

Contempt proceedings can be initiated by the judge or court that is affected. This is now rarely done except where there has been a

---

[103] *R* v *Townsend* [1982] 1 All ER 509 CA; *R* v *Rose* [1982] AC 822.
[104] Hansard HC Debs [1981] Vol 9 col 426.
[105] Hansard HC Debs [1981] Vol 9 col 425.
[106] Contempt of Court Act 1981 s 8(3), though proceedings can be brought on the motion of a court having jurisdiction to deal with it (ibid.).

disturbance in court or where the court's own order has been allegedly disobeyed. The more usual, and the proper, course is for the matter to be referred to the Attorney-General.

If a judge does threaten reporters with immediate committal for contempt, they should respond by asking for an adjournment to obtain legal advice. Freelancers or journalists for newspapers without a lawyer should also ask for emergency legal aid. The Contempt of Court Act gives courts the power to grant this on the spot (subject to the normal means-tested contributions).[107] When the lawyers come back before the judge, they should try to have the matter referred to the Attorney-General: this is now accepted as the proper course, even for alleged misbehaviour by a journalist in the face of the court. Thus when *Observer* journalist Jack Lundin refused under oath to answer questions that would have revealed a source, the trial judge (Mr Justice Webster) agreed to refer the matter to the Attorney-General, so that it could be considered and dealt with in the calmer arena of the Divisional Court.[108] It is invidious for the judge immediately concerned to double up as contempt prosecutor. It is also contrary to the normal principle, enshrined in the European Convention, that a person does not act as a judge in his own cause.[109]

If the affected court accepts these arguments and does not mete out instant punishment of its own, contempt proceedings will be started by an application to the Divisional Court of the Queen's Bench Division of the High Court.[110] This must also be the procedure if a publication is said to be in contempt of magistrates. They can punish only for contempts committed in or near their own courtroom and not those committed by the press or by broadcasters.[111] These have to be referred to the Divisional Court.

The Attorney-General's consent is essential where the contempt was unintentional but was in breach of the strict-liability rule.[112]

---

[107] ibid., s 13.

[108] *A-G v Lundin* (1982) 75 Cr App R 90.

[109] Art 6(1) of the European Convention on Human Rights, which requires that any punishment for a criminal offence be imposed by an impartial tribunal.

[110] The procedure is set out in Rules of Supreme Court Order 52.

[111] Contempt of Court Act 1981 s 12.

[112] ibid., s 7 – unless, contrary to the principles in the text, the court acts on its own motion. In 1991 the House of Lords questioned earlier judicial views (e.g., *Peacock v LWT* (1985) *The Times*, 27 November, CA) that a person who would be affected by a statutory contempt could apply for an injunction without the backing of the Attorney-General. The matter was left unresolved because the applicants in any case failed to make out their case for an injunction (*Pickering v Liverpool Daily Post and Echo Newspapers PLC* [1991] 1 All ER 622, 631–3 and 636, HL). This follows an earlier pronouncement by the High Court that even injunctions to restrain intentional contempts should be narrowly confined. (*Taylor v Topping* (1990) *The Times*, 15 February).

In all cases (even those brought by the Attorney), the court has to give its permission for contempt proceedings to begin.[113] This is considered on an *ex parte* application (i.e., on hearing only the applicant's side). Sometimes the publisher is informed in advance, but this is not obligatory. The proper time for the Attorney-General to make his application is after the conclusion of the jury stage of the proceedings alleged to have been prejudiced. This will obviate any danger that publicity given to the contempt action will repeat the alleged prejudice, and will enable the court to consider, with the benefit of hindsight, whether the risk of prejudice at the time of publication was really real.

Once the Divisional Court has given leave for the case to go ahead, the publisher will be served with a 'notice of motion', accompanied by an affidavit setting out the applicant's case. In Divisional Court proceedings evidence is normally given on affidavit rather than orally, but publishers should scrutinize carefully the draft affidavits that their lawyers prepare because they might be cross-examined on them, and it is perjury to swear a false affidavit. Most contempt trials take the form of polite exchanges, in legal jargon, between counsel and judges; the atmosphere is that of an Oxford common-room rather than an Old Bailey courtroom. Publishers can insist on having their say by giving oral evidence;[114] this gives them a day in court and may have publicity value, but it is unlikely to swing the judges in their favour. Applications to commit for contempt must be heard in open court except in certain cases to do with children (wardship, adoption, guardianship, custody, maintenance, upbringing or access), the mentally ill, secret processes, or where for reasons to do with national security or the administration of justice the court decides to sit in private. Before making a committal order in these cases the court must state in open court the name of the guilty person, in general terms the nature of the contempt, and the period of committal.[115] Contempt is the one serious criminal charge not decided by a jury. Although the Divisional Court is preferable from a publisher's point of view to the court that was allegedly prejudiced, it is still composed of judges who cannot avoid the appearance of partiality as they weigh freedom of speech against the preservation of the administration of justice.

In June 1982 a man was tried at the Old Bailey before a jury for contempt of court by disobedience to a court order. The Court of Appeal disapproved of this procedure, but against the background of a defendant who did not want to be tried by a jury. However,

---

[113] RSC Order 52 rule 2.
[114] ibid., rule 6(4).
[115] Contempt of Court Act 1981 s 7.

there is little likelihood of publishers charged with contempt being able to invoke trial by jury. The experiment has not been repeated, and a passing comment by the House of Lords in *Re Lonrho* firmly discourages such a course.[116]

A publisher found guilty by the court can be fined an unlimited amount. Individuals who are convicted can in addition be sentenced to up to two years' imprisonment.[117] An appeal can be taken directly to the House of Lords, but the permission of either the Divisional Court or of the Lords themselves is necessary.[118] If the application to commit is heard by a single judge, the appeal is made in the first place to the Court of Appeal. If that is unsuccessful, but a certificate is given that the case raises an issue of public importance, and either the Court of Appeal or the Lords consent, a further appeal can be made to the Lords.[119]

---

[116] *Re Lonrho* [1989] 2 All ER 1100 at p. 1106.

[117] Contempt of Court Act 1981 s 14(1). This is also the maximum that a county court can impose: County Courts (Penalties for Contempt) Act 1983. Other inferior courts, e.g., magistrates' courts, can imprison for only one month: Contempt of Court Act 1981 s 14(1). A person committed for contempt can apply at any time to the court for an earlier release (RSC Order 52 r 8(ii)). Thus even dilatory contrition may result in a shorter sentence.

[118] Administration of Justice Act 1960 s 12.

[119] This was the course taken in *Home Office* v *Harman*. It is also the course where the Attorney-General applies for an injunction in advance of publication as in the *Sunday Times* thalidomide story.

Chapter 7

Reporting the Courts

The most fundamental principle of justice is that it must be seen to be done. Lord Halsbury, in the great constitutional case of *Scott* v *Scott*, proclaimed that 'Every court in the land is open to every subject of the King'.[1] The rule became established almost by historical accident from the fact that courts in the Middle Ages were badly conducted public meetings in which neighbours gathered to pass judgment on their district's notorious felons. The Star Chamber followed the practice and heard all its cases in public, in order that its vicious punishments would have a general deterrent effect. In time, jurists like Blackstone and Bentham elevated the practice into a fundamental precondition of justice. They acclaimed it on a number of grounds, principally as a safeguard against judicial error or misbehaviour. In Bentham's words, 'Publicity is the very soul of justice. It is the keenest spur to exertion and the surest of all guards against improbity. It keeps the judge himself, while trying, under trial.' Moreover, publicity deters perjury, in that witnesses are likely to come forward to confound lies when they learn that they are being told. Press reporting of court cases enhances public knowledge and appreciation of the workings of the law, it assists the deterrent function of criminal trials and it permits the revelation of matters of genuine public interest. On the other hand, of course, it can at times be shallow, sensational or just plain incompetent. Courts have some corrective powers and can usually protect parties from any prejudice. A more persuasive reason for restricting the right to report is the desire to protect witnesses against loss of face or loss of job, or even, where police informers are concerned, against possible loss of life. Does it really matter if a few cases go unreported so that prosecution witnesses are relieved from the anxiety of reading their names in newspapers? It does, for the reasons given by Blackstone and Bentham. Trials derive their legitimacy from being conducted in public; the judge presides as a surrogate for the people, who are entitled to see and approve the power exercised on their behalf. Those who assist the prosecution can and should be protected by other means. No matter how fair, justice must still be seen before it can be said to have been done.

---

[1] *Scott* v *Scott* [1913] AC 417. The open-justice principle is reflected in Article 6 of the European Convention and in Article 14(1) of the International Covenant on Civil and Political Rights.

The open-justice principle is now firmly embedded, with the help of Blackstone and Bentham, in the constitutional jurisprudence of the United States and Canada. The Supreme Courts of both countries have endorsed Wigmore's reasoning as to the evidential consequences of the requirement for hearings in public:

> Its operation in tending to *improve the quality of testimony* [*our italics*] is two-fold. Subjectively, it produces in the witness's mind a disinclination to falsify; first, by stimulating the instinctive responsibility to public opinion, symbolized in the audience, and ready to scorn a demonstrated liar; and next, by inducing the fear of exposure of subsequent falsities through disclosure by informed persons who may chance to be present or to hear of the testimony from others present. Objectively, it secures the presence of those who by possibility may be able to furnish testimony in chief or to contradict falsifiers and yet may not have been known beforehand to the parties to possess any information.[2]

The United States Supreme Court has gone further, by regarding openness as a defining characteristic of the integrity of a trial process,[3] while the Supreme Court of Canada has struck down legislation preventing the reporting of evidence in divorce cases as contrary to the guarantee of freedom of expression.[4] Justice Bertha Wilson concluded in that case:

> In summary, the public interest in open trials and in the ability of the press to provide complete reports of what takes place in the courtroom is rooted in the need (1) to maintain an effective evidentiary process; (2) to ensure a judiciary and juries that behave fairly and that are sensitive to the values espoused by the society; (3) to promote a shared sense that our courts operate with integrity and dispense justice; and (4) to provide an ongoing opportunity for the community to learn how the justice system operates and how the law being applied daily in the courts affects them.[5]

In the US and Canada the open-justice rule is strictly enforced by reference to a 'freedom of expression' guarantee. In Britain the courts pay lip-service to the rule, but enforce it, as we shall see, haphazardly and at times inconsistently.

For all the opportunities presented by the open-justice principle,

---

2 *Wigmore on Evidence*, para 1834.
3 *Richmond Newspapers* v *Virginia* (1980) 448 US 555.
4 *Edmonton Journal* v *A-G for Alberta* (1989) 64 DLR(4th) 577.
5 ibid.

it must be said that the standard of legal journalism in Britain is not particularly high, certainly when compared to the United States. It may be that reporters, sitting snugly in their privileged 'press bench', have come to regard themselves as part and parcel of the court process, rather than as 'the eyes and ears of the public' (see p. 18). It is often claimed on behalf of the media that it enjoys no special privileges over and above those enjoyed by ordinary citizens. In the case of court reporting, however, this is manifestly untrue. The media do enjoy special rights – to sit in the press bench and to be present on some of the occasions when the general public are excluded – and it is important for journalists to understand the reason why the courts recognize those privileges. In the words of the present Master of the Rolls, Lord Donaldson:

> It is not because of any special wisdom, interest or status enjoyed by proprietors, editors or journalists. It is because the media are the eyes and ears of the general public. They act on behalf of the general public. Their right to know and their right to publish is neither more nor less than that of the general public. Indeed it *is* that of the general public for whom they are trustees.[6]

If British journalists have been reluctant to probe the processes of justice, they are certainly concerned to report sensational stories that emerge in evidence in the course of legal proceedings. It has been thus for centuries; indeed, the first newspapers consisted of nothing but court reports. Daily 'chapbooks' of Old Bailey trials were hawked in the streets of seventeenth-century London at one penny apiece, catering to the curious, the pitying, the righteous and the prurient, who will always be interested in the crimes and punishments of the court calendar.[7] Coverage of the latest excitement in a sensational criminal case will attract circulation, especially if the press report is spiced with some of the colour and drama of the trial. There is another great attraction to the modern newspaper in court reports: they are 'privileged' against actions for libel. The courtroom is one of the few places where an Englishperson can say *'J'accuse'* and have the accusation reported to the country. Dozens of journalists turned up to hear Norman Scott answer a trivial summons with an entirely irrelevant allegation that Jeremy Thorpe had been his lover and would-be murderer; they knew that once the words were out in open court no injunction or libel writ could stop their publication. During the

---

[6] *A-G* v *Guardian Newspapers Ltd (No 2)* [1988] 3 All ER 595, 600, applied in *Re M* [1990] 1 All ER 205.
[7] Langbein, 'The Criminal Trial Before Lawyers' (1978) 45 U of Chicago LR 263, 267.

Helen Smith inquest, the nurse's father muttered an accusation that two named persons had killed her. Court reporters, who could not hear what he said from the press gallery, worked out his words from a specially amplified tape of the proceedings. Ron Smith's accusation was headlined in all the papers the following day, where-upon the coroner fined him for an 'outburst' in court that he (the coroner) had not noticed at the time it was made.[8] The fact that the newspapers were reporting a statement, albeit made *sotto voce*, in open court, protected them from libel action. There may be doubts about the wisdom of a rule that gives parties to court proceedings the privilege of exploiting them to make defamatory statements that cannot be proved. None the less, the probability that the privilege will be abused on occasions is the price that must be paid for allegiance to the open-court principle.

There are always those who are willing to find the price of this principle too high. The case of *Home Office* v *Harman*, in which solicitor Harriet Harman was held in contempt for showing docu-ments to a journalist after they had been read in open court, is one example (see p. 356). That decision has been reversed by a change to the Rules of Court following a decision in her favour by the European Commission on Human Rights. The media must be prepared to fight all attacks on the open-justice principle, wherever they occur. In 1982 lay justices in Surrey were prevailed upon to sentence a 'supergrass' in secret: the local newspaper protested, and the behaviour of the justices was condemned by the Divisional Court.[9] That judgment had the result, of course, of publicizing the very facts that the justices had sought to keep secret. The media have, in their ability to publicize, the best antidote against attempts to close the courtroom doors. Whenever there is secrecy, there must inevitably be some suspicion of impropriety. Those who seek to defy the open-justice principle often find that machina-tions to this end prove counterproductive.

The open-justice principle is based, however, on public-interest considerations. It must give way when the public interest dictates a degree of privacy. The names of rape and blackmail victims, for example, are suppressed in the interests of mitigating their pain and encouraging other victims to come forward. Family disputes are heard in private when details might damage the children of a disrupted marriage. Postponement of publication of certain evidence in criminal trials is justified on occasions when it might cause irredeemable prejudice to other trials. These exceptions are reasonable, but the media must be on constant guard against allow-

---

[8] Paul Foot, *The Helen Smith Story*, Fontana, 1983, pp. 334–8.
[9] *R* v *Reigate Justices ex parte Argus Newspapers Ltd* (1983) 5 Cr App R CS 101, CA.

ing them to be extended or exploited to prevent genuine public-interest revelations.

There are four categories of exception to the open-justice principle:

- The most serious inroad is where journalists are neither admitted to the court nor able to report what happened. This will be the case where the court sits in camera. Literally this means 'in a room', but its technical meaning is 'in private'. Despite the secrecy, the hearing is still conducted with the ordinary formality of wigs and robes.
- There are occasions when press and public are banished, but an account gleaned from the participants *can* be published. An example of this is a hearing for an injunction before a judge 'in chambers'. It will be in private (and, unlike an in-camera hearing, free of the paraphernalia of legal garb), but it is not generally contempt to report what took place.
- The press may be allowed access to the court, but be restricted in what it can report; e.g., when the press can attend and report the proceedings but without identifying rape victims or juveniles involved.
- The press may be allowed to be present subject to a temporary ban on publication. Most committal proceedings (the preliminary inquiry by magistrates into whether there is enough evidence to justify a jury trial) are of this type. The 1981 Contempt of Court Act has also given courts a power to make an order postponing publication where this is necessary in the interest of justice.

These exceptions need to be considered in detail, but the space devoted to them is not indicative of their relative importance. They are all still regarded as departures from the general norm of openness. In the great majority of court cases the press are free to attend and report everything said in the course of the legal proceedings. The following sections of this chapter deal with cases in the first category, enumerate the rules that restrict reporting in the other categories, look at the means that the press can use to gather and record information about legal proceedings, and examine in more detail the defences of absolute and qualified privilege against claims for libel and slander that court reports enjoy.

Public Access to the Courts

The general principle is that every court is open for citizens to see justice being done. Reporters are generally present exercising their right as citizens rather than any special privilege of the press (though there are circumstances when the press *does* have a privileged access (see p. 17)). A court is not 'open' if the judge takes deliberate steps to keep the press at bay:

> A Government minister wanted to avoid the publicity of a divorce trial, so the judge obligingly agreed to hold the hearing in his library. The only access was through a door marked 'private'. This was left ajar and the judge announced to the parties and their representatives before he started that the court was open. On appeal, the Privy Council said this was a sham and in reality the hearing had been in private. Because there was no jurisdiction at the time to hear such cases in secret, the proceedings were a nullity.[10]

English magistrates have not been averse to similar expedients, and there are instances where they have heard cases earlier than normal or at some unannounced venue.[11] When they are trying a prosecution, they must now sit in open court and they must use their ordinary courthouse or a formally designated substitute.[12]

Whenever a magistrates' court deviates from the open-justice principle it is subject to correction by the High Court, which has recognized that journalists and newspapers have a right to enforce the principle in the public interest. This right was most firmly established in a case brought by investigative reporter David Leigh:

> The magistrates of Felixstowe adopted a policy, which was on the increase in magistrates' courts, of refusing to allow the press and interested members of the public to know the names of individual JPs who tried particular cases. They feared that JPs would be exposed to nuisance calls and reprisals over unpopular decisions. David Leigh and his newspaper, the *Observer*, took an opportunity to challenge this policy, and the Divisional Court declared it unlawful and unconstitutional. It was an unwarranted obstruction of the fundamental right to know the identity of persons who sit in judgment ('There is no such person known to the law as the anonymous JP'). The court traced the history of reporting in magistrates' courts, and described the court reporter as 'the watchdog of justice', who plays an essential role in the administration of the law by noting any possible unfairness or impropriety on the part of the bench. The magistrate 'will be more

---

[10] *McPherson* v *McPherson* [1936] AC 177.
[11] Marjorie Jones, *Justice and Journalism*, Barry Rose, 1974, pp. 28, 88–91.
[12] Magistrates' Courts Act 1980 ss 121(3), (4), 147. Magistrates must also by statute sit in public when considering an application to deport a person to the Republic of Ireland to face criminal charges – see Backing of Warrants (Republic of Ireland) Act 1965 Sched 2 para 2.

anxious to give a correct decision if he knows that his reasons must justify themselves at the bar of public opinion'.[13]

A 1989 Home Office circular recommends that the media should have copies of the court lists on the day of the hearings and, as a minimum, these should contain the defendant's name, address, age, profession (where known) and the alleged offence. Where provisional lists are prepared in advance, copies of these should be available to the media on request. Courts are, however, also strongly recommended to charge the full economic cost of this service.[14]

Usually a bench or table is set aside for the press close to the witness box and to counsel. Reporters may be exercising a public right, but they do so from a privileged position. Any attempt to commandeer the press bench, or to relegate reporters to barely audible positions at the back of the court, should be challenged. (see p. 18).

Exclusion in the public interest

What exceptional circumstances permit a court to sit in secret without rendering its proceedings a nullity? Firstly, those circumstances in which Parliament, by express statutory enactment, has given permission to expel the public. The statutes containing such express powers are summarized below. Secondly, where for convenience of handling interlocutory applications the case is heard by judges sitting in a private room, the public is effectively barred, although generally there is nothing to stop the press from publishing accounts of what went on in chambers, if details can be discovered and the publication will not prejudice a future trial. But is there an inherent power in the court to exclude both press and public in the interests of justice?

---

[13] *R* v *Felixstowe JJs ex parte Leigh* [1987] 1 All ER 551, DC.
[14] Home Office Circulars 80/1989. Following computerization, some court clerks are worried that disclosing the list to the press will infringe the Data Protection Act 1984. There is a principle that personal data should not be disclosed other than to those specified by the user on registration. A simple solution is, therefore, for the court to include the press in its registered particulars. In any case, these worries are probably groundless. Section 34(1) of the 1984 Act exempts from the principle of non-disclosure data that the holder is required by any enactment to make available to the public. The name and charge will always be given in court and the Divisional Court has said that it is a well-established practice that, save for a justifiable reason, the defendant's address will also be publicly mentioned (*R* v *Evesham Justices ex parte McDonagh* [1988] 1 All ER 371, 384 QBD). Since the court must, by statute, (see note 12 above), sit in public, there is an indirect obligation to disclose these particulars: an obligation that is statutory.

In *Scott* v *Scott*[15] the Law Lords were divided on the subject. Several said that a court had no power other than that given by statute. One thought that the public were only to be excluded if 'administration of justice would be rendered impracticable by their presence'. Viscount Haldane put the test thus: 'To justify an order for a hearing in camera it must be shown that the paramount object of securing that justice is done would really be rendered doubtful of attainment if the order were not made.'[16]

This rightly stresses the rigorousness of the test. Convenience is not enough: 'It must be necessary to avoid the subordination of the ends of justice to the means.'[17] There must also be material (though not necessarily formal evidence) on which the court can reasonably reach its conclusion.[18] This can be tendered or submitted in writing or agreed in private,[19] but the decision whether the case should proceed in camera must normally be publicly announced.[20]

> An extreme example in 1983 concerned the New Cross Building Society's challenge to the legality of government directions that it should cease taking money from the public. The Society claimed that the directions were invalid. It successfully persuaded the High Court that its reputation would be irreparably harmed if it had to contest the directions (which had not been announced) in public proceedings. There would be a run on its deposits if the public appreciated that there was even a chance that the directions might have to be implemented. An appeal to the Court of Appeal was also heard in camera. The secrecy of the court proceedings was lifted only when the Court of Appeal dismissed the Society's claim and upheld the validity of the directions.[21]

This approach was repeated in 1991 when the Court of Appeal agreed to hear some applications in respect of the Polly Peck collapse in private.[22] Lord Donaldson justified the secrecy on the grounds that banks, building societies and other financial institutions that depend on investor confidence might be irreparably damaged if the allegations against them in civil proceedings were made public at an early stage, and later proved false. This prospect is

---

[15] [1913] AC 417.

[16] ibid., at p. 439, and see pp. 442, 446 and 448.

[17] Lord Devlin in *Re K* [1965] AC 201, 239 and see Lord Haldane in *Scott*, note 1 above, at p. 438, Viscount Reading CJ in *R* v *Lewes Prison (Governor) ex parte Doyle* [1917] 2 KB 254, 271 and *A-G* v *Leveller Magazine Ltd* [1978] 3 All ER 731 at pp. 750, 761 per Lords Diplock and Edmund-Davies.

[18] *A-G* v *Leveller Magazine Ltd*, note 17 above, at p. 766 per Lord Scarman.

[19] *R* v *Tower Bridge Magistrates' Court ex parte Osborne* (1989) 88 Cr App R 28, QBD.

[20] *R* v *Ealing Justices ex parte Weaver* (1982) 74 Cr App R 204.

[21] *R* v *Chief Registrar of Building Societies ex parte New Cross Building Society* (1984) *The Times*, 14 January.

somewhat fanciful and, in any event, overlooks the interests of customers and investors who continue dealing with the bank in ignorance of allegations that are subsequently found to be true. There is no real distinction between private hearings for civil claims against banks and building societies, and private hearings for a restaurateur accused of violating health standards to avoid adverse publicity that will reduce custom (which the Divisional Court will not permit).[23]

The Haldane exception has much less force since the 1981 Contempt of Court Act introduced postponement orders. The court ought now to consider whether justice might not be sufficiently served by making a more limited order permitting the press to remain but postponing reporting until such time as it will do no harm to the interests of justice.[24]

In 1982 the Divisional Court issued a clear warning to magistrates and their clerks against excluding the press:

> A 'supergrass' appeared before the Reigate justices on charges of burglary and theft. These offences had been committed after he had received a lenient sentence for informing, and after police had given him a new identity. The defence asked the justices to hear his mitigation in secret, and the bench succumbed when the prosecution supported the application. The defendant was given an inexplicably light sentence. There was a press outcry, and several newspapers ensured that the secrecy was counterproductive by identifying the defendant and giving details of his unrepentant criminal career. The Divisional Court, on an application by the *Surrey Mirror*, held that the justices had been wrongly advised: they were entitled to go in camera only if proceedings in open court would 'frustrate the process of justice'. The question was whether secrecy was *strictly necessary*, rather than merely convenient or expedient.[25]

The warning was reiterated in 1988:

> A woman motorist who had pleaded guilty to a charge of driving with excess alcohol persuaded a magistrates' court to hear her arguments in mitigation in camera. She was divorcing her husband. This had caused emotional problems and suicidal tendencies. She would not be capable of giving evidence of these matters unless the court sat in private. The prosecution did not oppose the application, which was allowed by the bench. Having heard the evidence in private, the court disqualified the defendant for only three (as opposed to the usual twelve) months. A local journalist and his publishers applied

---

[22] *Polly Peck International Plc* v *Nadir* (1991) *The Times*, 11 November, CA.
[23] *R* v *Dover Justices, ex parte Dover District Council* (1991) *The Times*, 21 October, DC.
[24] *Argus Newspapers* note 9 above.
[25] ibid. The background to this case is discussed by Ole Hansen in 'Secret Justice: Questions Remain' [1983] LAG Bull, June p. 6.

for judicial review of the decision to sit in camera. The Divisional Court said that while magistrates did have jurisdiction to sit in camera, they should do so only if there were compelling reasons, the existence of which were likely to be rare. The order in the present case appeared wholly unsustainable and out of accord with principle. It was not surprising that in this case justice had neither been seen nor done. The court also held that the magistrates acted unlawfully in failing to apply the full disqualification period.[26]

Regrettably, the court in the *Malvern Justices* case rejected a submission that magistrates, as creatures of statute, cannot sit in secret since they have no statutory power so to do. Such a ruling would have finally put an end to temptations dangled by skilled advocates before lay justices to protect their clients from the punishment of publicity, which is usually more severe than any financial penalty the court can impose. The worst recent development for the open-justice principle is that advocates are now permitted to make secrecy applications in secret, where they may advance reasons that would not stand up to public scrutiny.

This ruling, which has done more in practice to encourage breaches of the open-justice principle than any other decision, comes as a result of an entirely exceptional case in 1987, when a defendant's counsel found that he could not explain at committal proceedings why his client wanted her address kept from her husband (who was also charged) without revealing in open court sensitive matters relating to the evidence that would be called on her behalf at a subsequent trial.[27] This is a special situation, which may justify an in-camera hearing to avoid prejudice to a trial; what it did not justify was the Divisional Court's decision that magistrates should always sit in secret to hear applications that they should sit in secret or impose a reporting restriction. The consequence has been an increase in secret courts, as magistrates hear the applications behind closed doors and then, if the application is granted, keep the doors closed while they consider the merits of the case. The court reporters do not, at either stage, know what is going on. Lawyers, who will do everything ethically possible for their clients, have no hesitation in asking (in secret) for courts to cover-up their clients' distress and humiliation by sitting in secret. In one case, counsel appearing for a reporter on *The Independent* asked that charges against her (of possessing a small amount of cocaine) should be heard in secret because of the 'undue

---

[26] *R* v *Malvern Justices ex parte Evans* [1988] 1 All ER 371 QBD. See also *R* v *Epping and Ongar Justices ex parte Breach* [1986] Crim LR 810.

[27] This appears, from the judgment, to have been the nature of the information in question: *R* v *Tower Bridge Magistrates' Court ex parte Osborne* (1989) 88 Cr App R 28.

hardship' that publicity would bring. The magistrates rightly refused the application, perhaps having been influenced by the campaign against 'secret courts' being run by *The Independent* at the time.

Committal proceedings

A criminal charge is either tried by magistrates or by a judge and jury at a Crown Court. The latter is known as trial on indictment, the indictment being the formal accusation of the offence. Most indictments are preceded by committal proceedings. These are conducted by magistrates, who, when acting in this capacity, are called examining justices. Their job is to examine the evidence presented to see if there is a case to answer. They must sit in open court except where a statute provides to the contrary or where it 'appears to them as respects the whole or any part of the committal proceedings that the ends of justice would not be served by their sitting in open court'.[28] This will rarely, if ever, be the case, because if the normal reporting restrictions are not lifted, reports of the proceedings must be postponed until after the full trial; and if reporting restrictions are lifted, the magistrates now have power to postpone reports of any evidence that may cause serious prejudice to the trial (see p. 341). In consequence, committal proceedings are hardly ever reported other than in the barest of details.

Most committals are purely formal. Prior to 1967 all prosecution witnesses had to be taken orally through their evidence, which was then transcribed into a written statement called a deposition. The Criminal Justice Act 1967[29] provided a short cut and now, if the defence consents, statements may be submitted to the court in written form. The defendant can argue that these do not contain sufficient evidence to justify a trial, but if it is accepted that there is a case to answer, the magistrates need not consider or even read the statements.[30] Consequently, the press in court will not know their contents, except for the name and address of the maker, which must be read out.[31]

Voluntary bills of indictment

Instead of asking magistrates to commit a defendant for trial, a prosecutor can apply to a High Court judge for a voluntary bill of

---

[28] Magistrates' Courts Act 1980 s 4(2).
[29] ibid. s 6(2).
[30] ibid.
[31] This is obligatory unless the court otherwise directs. Magistrates' Courts Rules 1981 (SI 1981 No 552) r 70(6).

indictment.[32] This is considered by the judge in private and neither the prosecution nor the defendant, let alone the press, has the right to be present.[33] It is an exceptional step, which may be justified where a magistrate has unreasonably refused to commit the defendant or where a suspect is caught shortly before any co-accused have been committed to stand trial.[34] However, there is evidence that it is used increasingly as a way of avoiding protracted or heated committal hearings. The voluntary-bill procedure circumvents the rights of defendants as well as of the media; it can cause serious injustice, and the DPP should be asked to justify its exercise in every case.

Official secrets

There is a presumption that prosecutions for breaches of the Official Secrets Acts are to be treated in the same way as any other prosecution and must be held in public. However, the Crown can apply for all or part of the public to be excluded during all or part of the evidence.[35] It must persuade the court that publication of the evidence would be prejudicial to national safety. It will be a rare judge who will deny the prosecution application, though secret hearings ought to be confined to the minimum necessary. The restrictions can be applied to committal hearings, trial and appeal, but the sentence must be passed in public.[36] If the Crown (or defendant) in a criminal trial intends to ask the court to sit in camera for reasons of national security, it must now give seven days' advance warning to the court, which must then prominently display a notice in the court stating that the application is to be made. The application must be made after the defendant has pleaded to the charge but before the jury is empanelled. If the court decides that it will sit in camera, it must adjourn for twenty-four hours to allow an appeal against this decision to be made to the Court of Appeal.[37] In civil cases the court can hear technical information about defence contracts in camera if this is necessary

---

[32] Administration of Justice (Miscellaneous Provisions) Act 1933 s 2(2).
[33] Indictments (Procedure) Rules 1971 (SI 1971 No 2084) r 10.
[34] *R* v *Raymond* [1981] QB 910, CA.
[35] Official Secrets Act 1920 s 8(4), now extended to offences under the Official Secrets Act 1989 (except in relation to careless loss of documents, 1989 Act s 11(4)). Sir Compton Mackenzie was tried in camera in 1932 for alleged disclosures in his book *Gallipoli Memoirs*. So, too, was a postman for giving away information that led to a mail robbery – see written evidence of NCCL to the Franks Committee, vol II p. 297. More recently, almost the whole trial of Michael Bettaney took place in camera.
[36] Official Secrets Act 1920 s 8(4).
[37] Crown Court Rules 1982, r 24A added by SI 1989 No 1103.

or expedient in the public interest or in the interest of the parties to the proceedings.[38]

Private secrets

Some actions are brought to restrain the defendant from publishing or using information that the plaintiff alleges was acquired in confidence or over which the plaintiff has monopoly control. If these actions and those concerning secret inventions had to be held in public, their whole purpose would be frustrated. However, the court should agree to sit in camera only so far as is necessary and any part of the evidence that would not give away the secret should be heard in public in the normal way. In *Lion Laboratories* v *Evans*[39] (the intoximeter case) the Court of Appeal declined to direct or request the press not to publish the confidential material set out in its judgment: appreciation of this material was necessary to enable the public to understand its decision.

In commercial cases applications are sometimes made for the court to sit in camera to prevent the disclosure of price-sensitive information. Even these should be considered critically and the courts should be wary of displacing the normal principle of open justice.

> When a company stopped paying its lawyers so that its application for the removal of a provisional liquidator had to be abandoned, the Vice-Chancellor dismissed the application in open court, even though all the argument had taken place in camera. He said that hearings in closed court 'were contrary to the public interest and should only take place if it was clear that there was a contrary public interest which overrode the need for public justice'. Once the application had been abandoned 'the general public should be aware of what has been happening'.[40]

Family cases

A court hearing wardship proceedings is acting in a quasi-parental role. Full publicity is not appropriate and consequently these cases are usually (though not invariably) heard in private.[41] The judgment, however, will usually be given in public, with the deletion of material that would identify the child. Guardianship matters may,

---

[38] Defence Contracts Act 1958 s 4(3).
[39] *Lion Laboratories* v *Evans* [1985] QB 526.
[40] *Re London and Norwich Investment Services Ltd* (1987) 16 December, Ch D. See also *British and Commonwealth Holdings plc* v *Quadrex Holdings Inc* (1988) *The Independent*, 13 December.
[41] *Re F (a minor: Publication of Information)* [1977] 1 All ER 114.

and adoption applications must, be heard in the absence of press and public.[42]

Parliament has given the courts power to sit in camera when hearing petitions for a declaration of marital status, the effectiveness of an overseas adoption, and legitimacy (though since the Family Law Reform Act 1987 was brought into effect, this may also be a declaration as to parentage).[43] The hearing will not automatically be in private. The courts must take into account the effect of publicity on the petitioner, including his or her health and occupation, and on third parties who might be affected by the revelation of family secrets. It must then weigh this against the traditional rule of public policy that justice should be administered openly.[44] The section confers the power to sit in camera only in connection with proceedings for a declaration of parentage. If questions as to parentage are raised in other proceedings, they must be publicly resolved unless there is some other power to consider them in secret.[45]

Court rules now provide that evidence in divorce and nullity proceedings should normally be given in open court,[46] though in the common case where the divorce is undefended and the spouses have lived apart, the evidence will be heard in private and only the decision announced in open court.[47] Ancillary proceedings concerning such matters as maintenance and custody of children are normally heard in chambers.[48] Applications for injunctions (e.g., to oust one party from the shared home) are also normally made in chambers.[49] Further, where it is alleged that a marriage is a nullity because one spouse was unable to consummate it, evidence on the question of sexual capacity should be heard in camera unless the judge is persuaded that in the interests of justice it should be heard in open court.[50] As with Official Secrets, the press and the public should be excluded only while the sensitive evidence is being given.

---

[42] Rules of Supreme Court Order 90 r 7. Magistrates' Courts Act 1980 s 69(4); Children Act 1975 s 21.

[43] Domestic and Appellate Proceedings (Restrictions of Publicity) Act 1968 s 2; which reversed the decision of *B (P)* v *A-G* [1965] 3 All ER 253, and see Family Law Reform Act 1986 ss 55–60 and Family Law Reform Act 1987, s 22.

[44] *Barritt* v *A-G* [1971] 3 All ER 1183 Wrangham J.

[45] *Prior* v *Prior* (1970) 114 SJ 72 PDA Div Latey J.

[46] Matrimonial Causes Rules 1977 (SI 1977 No 344) r 37.

[47] ibid., r 48.

[48] For claims by a wife for maintenance or by either spouse for financial relief see Domestic and Appellate Proceedings Act 1968, s 2(1)(*b*) and (*c*).

[49] *Practice Direction* [1974] 2 All ER 1119. Senior Registrar, Family Division.

[50] Matrimonial Causes Act 1973 s 48(2).

Magistrates must sit in private when sitting as a youth court, although the press is entitled to be present.[51] This duty overrides the provision in the Backing of Warrants (Republic of Ireland) Act 1965 Sched 2 para 2 that applications for deportation to the Republic to face criminal charges must be heard in open court.[52] The public, but not the press, can be kept out of an adult court while a child or young person gives evidence in relation of a sex offence.[53]

Although *Scott* v *Scott* said that the indecency of evidence was no ground for closing the court at common law, magistrates have by statute the power to sit in private for this reason when hearing domestic proceedings.[54]

Outside these areas and wardship proceedings (see p. 332) the general principle of open justice applies even in cases involving children. In October 1988 Mr Justice Boreham agreed to hear in chambers the settlement details of a medical negligence claim brought on behalf of a young child because the agreed damages were for a very large sum and the plaintiff's mother feared receipt of begging letters. The media protested. The judge recanted and apologized for exceeding his power.[55]

Possession actions

Landowners who wish to evict squatters or other trespassers can choose to bring their application in the Queen's Bench Division of the High Court.[56] The case will be heard before a judge in chambers. The public and the press are not admitted. A different procedure has to be followed against tenants or licensees. Most residential lettings will be within the jurisdiction of the county court and eviction proceedings will normally be heard there in public. Even so, where the landlord claims that the court has no discretion and must make a possession order, the case may be heard in private if the judge or county court registrar thinks this desirable.[57]

There are no sufficient reasons to justify this derogation from the open-justice principle. The actions of landlords and property

---

[51] Children and Young Persons Act 1933 s 47.
[52] *In Re L* (1990) *Guardian*, 5 December.
[53] Children and Young Persons Act 1933 s 37(1).
[54] Magistrates' Courts Act 1980 s 69(4).
[55] (1988) *Guardian*, 10 October.
[56] Rules of Supreme Court Order 113.
[57] The Rent Act (County Court Proceedings for Possession) Rules 1981 (SI 1981 No 139) r6(2). The cases where the court *must* order possession are set out in Part II of sched 15 of Rent Act 1977.

owners are matters of public interest, and it is quite wrong that legal action to enforce their private rights should be taken in secrecy. This was brought home in 1983 when a controversial order was given at the request of Newbury Council by a High Court judge to remove women anti-cruise-missile protesters from parts of Greenham Common. The judge declined to sit or to deliver judgment in public, apparently fearing disorder from protesters in the courtroom.

Appeals

An appeal court has a statutory power to sit in camera, if the trial court could do so. An application to adopt this procedure can itself be heard in the absence of the public. The decision on the merits of the appeal must be given in open court unless there are good and sufficient reasons for doing so privately.[58]

Although the Court of Appeal cannot sit in chambers,[59] it has the same common-law power as other courts to exclude the public and proceed in camera. It is reluctant to do so. A rare example is when it is hearing an appeal concerning a private search warrant to detect pirated or bootlegged copies of tapes or films and a public hearing would give the defendant a chance to hide his stock.[60] Even here, it is questionable whether some lesser restriction might not sometimes be adequate. For instance, the Court of Appeal could follow Lord Justice Lawton's suggestions in *R* v *Waterfield* (see p. 17) and allow the press to remain to see the kind of evidence on which the court is prepared to make these awesome orders. An order postponing publication would prevent the defendant being given advance notice.[61] Nor will the court generally conceal the name of a party to an appeal. It refused the cloak of anonymity to a building society that was fighting a government ban on the taking of further deposits. Where a party to the appeal is under a disability – e.g. by being a mental patient – an order granting anonymity will often be made.[62]

'In chambers' hearings

Registrars in the county court and Masters in the Queen's Bench

---

[58] Domestic and Appellate Proceedings (Restrictions of Publicity) Act 1968 s 1, based on a Report of the Law Commission Cmnd 3149 (1966).

[59] *Re Agricultural Industries* [1952] 1 All ER 1188 CA.

[60] *Practice Note (Anton Piller Orders: Appeals)* [1982] 3 All ER 924.

[61] A similar procedure was adopted in *EMI Records Ltd* v *Kudhail* (1983) *The Times*, 28 June, where argument was heard in camera but judgment was given in open court subject to a ten-day postponement order. But see *Re Crook*, p. 349.

[62] *R* v *Registrar of Building Societies ex parte A Building Society* [1960] 1 WLR 669.

Division of the High Court hear pre-trial applications in chambers. In the Queen's Bench the more important applications (particularly injunctions) can be heard only by a judge, but each day a judge-in-chambers sits to consider these. The judge in chambers will also hear appeals from Masters. Despite its Dickensian image, the Chancery Division is more open. Pre-trial applications there are heard in open court. Many cases can be brought in either division and a desire for pre-trial privacy is often a motive for choosing the Queen's Bench. Appeals to the Crown Court against the refusal of magistrates to grant bail are also heard in chambers. So, too, are small claims arbitrations in the county court. This will be of greater significance if the proposals of the Civil Justice Review Committee are adopted and the financial limit on this jurisdiction (now generally £500) is substantially increased (though the Review Body also canvassed the possibility that case papers ought to be publicly available for a limited period after the hearing).

It is a common but erroneous belief that the privacy of a chambers hearing means that it must also be kept secret. This is not necessarily so. The Administration of Justice Act 1960 s 12(1) says: 'The publication of any information before the court sitting in private shall not of itself be contempt of court.' In general, if reporters can persuade either of the parties to divulge details of the hearings in chambers, they can publish what they have been told without being in contempt. This is important, particularly in connection with pre-trial injunctions. Where, for instance, the plaintiff claims that the defendant intends to publish a libel, break a confidence or call a strike, the hearing of an application for a pre-trial injunction may be more important than the ultimate trial of the action. There are rich pickings to be had in the Bear Garden (the ante-room to the judges' chambers in the High Court). The main handicap is that since the proceedings have not taken place in open court, the media cannot take shelter behind privilege if sued for defamation arising from a report of what happened in chambers. Similarly, if the press learns of details of a bail appeal, it must be careful about contempt: if the proceedings were not in open court, the press will not have the protection of s 4(1) of the Contempt Act (see p. 341).

The exceptions to the general rule, where publication of chambers hearings can constitute contempt, are reports of proceedings concerning:[63]

- wardship, adoption, guardianship, maintenance or upbringing of children or rights of access;
- Mental Health Act applications;
- national security;

---

[63] Administration of Justice Act 1960 s 12(2).

- secret processes and inventions;
- 'where the court (having the power to do so) expressly prohibits the publication of all information relating to the proceedings or of information of the description which is published'.

Even in these cases it is not contempt:

- to publish the text or summary of any order made by the court (unless it expressly prohibits this);[64]
- to publish material that came from one of these types of private proceedings if the publisher was ignorant of this fact;[65]
- if the publication is made a sufficiently long time after the proceedings were held that the justification for privacy has passed;[66]
- if the court gives permission for publication.[67]

It is not a defence for the publishers to say that they did not intend to commit contempt, nor can they obtain an acquittal by pleading that in the case of proceedings, such as wardship, that are regularly held in private they did not know that the public had been excluded.[68]

At some of the larger criminal courts it is common to hold a 'pre-trial review' in chambers. It will be contempt to publish a report of the arguments on such occasions only if publication would create a serious risk of substantial prejudice to the forthcoming trial. Details of jury-vetting orders given at several pre-trial reviews have been discovered and published by the media, without action. On one such occasion a trial judge had justified vetting in order to discover whether any jurors had been drawn from Kilburn, 'where there is a high content of Irish people and most of them go round to pubs collecting money for the IRA'.[69] It may be embarrassing for such judicial prejudice to see the light of day, but publication would not amount to contempt.

The High Court always has power to adjourn a chambers hearing into open court, in which case the press, like the rest of the public, has a right to be present.[70] This is sometimes done to allow the

---

[64] ibid.
[65] *Re F* (above note 41). This case concerned reports to the court by the Official Solicitor and a social worker. These should carry a warning that they must be kept confidential on penalty of proceedings for contempt. *Practice Direction (Divorce: Children: Welfare Officer's Report)* [1982] 1 All ER 512.
[66] *Re F* note 41 above.
[67] *Re R (MJ) (Publication of Transcripts)* [1975] 2 All ER 749.
[68] *Re F* note 41 above.
[69] Proceedings of the anarchist trial in 1979 quoted in David Leigh, *Frontiers of Secrecy*, p. 70.
[70] Rules of Supreme Court Order 32, rule 13; *Hardie and Lane Ltd* v *Chiltern* (1927) 43 T LR 477.

public to hear the argument, although more commonly it is limited to delivery of the judgment. The Court of Appeal in 1988 adjourned an application into open court to prevent a false market in a company's securities.[71] There has been a welcome willingness in the Crown Court to adjourn applications by the police for special procedure material (see p. 206) into open court.[72] Both the Court of Appeal and the Divisional Court have said that a decision to take this course is a discretionary one and cannot generally be quashed on judicial review or varied on appeal.[73]

Disorder in court

Courts have an inherent power to control their own proceedings. This includes the power to limit numbers in the courtroom and to clear the public entirely if disorder is threatened or actually occurs. However, as with the other qualifications to the open-justice principle, the court should depart from it no more than necessary, and it would be quite wrong to exclude journalists who are not joining in the disorder.

> Members of the Welsh Language Society appealed against their conviction for refusing to pay television licence fees, on the grounds that the court trying them had improperly excluded members of the public. These members of the public were, in fact, supporters of the defendants, who had begun to create a disturbance. The Divisional Court, rejecting the appeal, noted that a journalist from a local paper had been allowed to remain. The Lord Chief Justice said: 'I find it difficult to imagine a case which can be said to be held publicly if the press have been actively excluded.'[74]

Reporting Restrictions

Attending court is merely the means to the end of publication. What takes place in open court 'is necessarily and legitimately made public and being public property may be republished'.[75]

---

[71] *British and Commonwealth Holdings plc* v *Quadrex Holdings Inc* (1988) *The Independent*, 13 December.

[72] *Chief Constable of Avon and Somerset* v *Bristol United Press (unreported)* Bristol Crown Court, Stuart-Smith J., 23 October 1986; *Re An Application under s 9 of Police and Criminal Evidence Act 1984* Central Criminal Court, Alliott J. (1988) *The Independent*, 27 May.

[73] *R* v *Central Criminal Court ex parte DPP* (1988) *The Independent*, 31 March, *British and Commonwealth Holdings*, note 71 above.

[74] *R* v *Denbigh Justices ex parte Williams and Evans* [1974] 2 All ER 1052. See also an *ex cathedra* speech by the Lord Chancellor to Nottingham justices reported in the *Magistrate*, June 1983, p. 90.

[75] *Richardson* v *Wilson* (1879) 7 R 237.

This section considers the exceptions to that general principle. Where reporters are admitted to court, when are they limited or prohibited from publishing what they hear? Where reporters are not allowed into court, when *can* they publish information from other sources?

Remands and committal hearings

Restrictions

Prior to 1967 committal hearings could be reported in full. Since it was common for the defence to reserve its case until the trial, there were many complaints that the public and potential jurors received a distorted impression of the strength of the prosecution's case. A departmental committee was set up in 1957 after lurid reports of the committal of Dr Bodkin Adams on a murder charge seemed prejudicial because much of the published committal evidence was not repeated at the trial. The press strongly opposed the committee's proposals[76] for a ban on reporting of committal proceedings, and no action was taken for nine years. It was the Moors Murder case that finally prompted the government to act, and then more to spare the public a double dose of grisly details than to avoid prejudice to defendants.[77]

The Criminal Justice Act 1967 introduced reporting restrictions on committals.[78] Unless the restrictions are lifted a written report, broadcast or cable programme about committal proceedings in Great Britain can refer only to:

● the names of the examining justices and their court;
● the names and addresses and occupations of parties and witnesses, and the ages of the defendant and witnesses;
● the charge;
● the names of counsel and solicitors;
● the decision to commit or how the case was otherwise disposed of;
● the charges on which each defendant was committed;
● the date and place to which the hearing was adjourned;
● arrangements for bail;
● whether legal aid was granted or refused.

Consequently, the reasons given by the police for opposing bail or the magistrates' grounds for refusing it cannot be published.

These restrictions apply only temporarily. Full details of the committal can be reported after the trial.[79] But by then these are

---

[76] Tucker Report Cmnd 479 (1958).
[77] Jones, *Justice and Journalism*, pp. 109–15.
[78] These are now contained in s 8 of the Magistrates' Courts Act 1980.
[79] ibid., s 8(3).

usually stale news and many editors consider it uneconomic to have a reporter in a court whose proceedings cannot be promptly reported.[80]

All the details can be reported if the magistrates decide not to commit or if they exercise their right (with the defendant's consent) to change their role part way through the examination and try the case themselves. Where there are several defendants of whom some are committed for trial and some are dealt with by the magistrates, a reporter must take care to observe the restrictions in connection with those who are sent for trial.

Breach of these restrictions can lead to a maximum fine of £2,000 on the editor, publisher or proprietor of the paper. Other publishers are also liable and so are broadcasters: the BBC was the first to be prosecuted under the Act.[81] The Attorney-General must approve a prosecution, a safeguard intended to prevent proceedings for harmless or trivial breaches.[82] It did not stop prosecution of the *Eastbourne Herald*, which was fined £200 in 1973 for referring to the defendant as a 'New Year's Day Bridegroom . . . bespectacled and dark-suited' and for describing the charges he faced as 'serious'.[83] This decision is mistaken, and the newspaper could have succeeded on an appeal by arguing that these matters were not 'part of the proceedings'. Certainly the purpose behind the restrictions was not to silence such descriptions. The case was an aberration: minor violations that do not pose a risk of prejudice will not be prosecuted.

Lifting the restrictions
A defendant has a right to have the restrictions lifted[84] and must be told of this at every hearing.[85] The right can be exercised at a first appearance, though no evidence is then called.[86] If the restrictions have been lifted at an earlier date, the clerk must announce this when the hearing is resumed.[87]

Until 1981, where there were a number of defendants, any one of them could apply for restrictions to be lifted. All the defendants had to accept publicity, even though they may have been added to the proceedings only after the restrictions had been lifted.[88] There

---

[80] 'Criminal Proceedings in English Magistrates' Courts and the Local Press' Stephen White (1977) *Justice of the Peace* 457 and 472.
[81] Jones, *Justice and Journalism*, p. 120.
[82] Magistrates' Courts Act 1980 s 8(6).
[83] (1973) *The Times*, 12 June.
[84] Magistrates' Courts Act 1980 s 8(2).
[85] Magistrates' Courts Rules 1981 (SI 1981 No 552) r 5(1).
[86] *R v Bow St Magistrate ex parte Kray (Reginald)* [1969] 1 QB 473.
[87] Magistrates' Courts Rules 1981 r 5(3).
[88] *R v Russell ex parte Beaverbrook Newspapers Ltd* [1969] 1 QB 342; *R v Blackpool Justices ex parte Beaverbrook Newspapers Ltd* [1972] 1 WLR 95.

was massive publicity after George Deakin, alone of the defendants, applied for restrictions to be lifted at the Minehead committal hearings relating to himself, Jeremy Thorpe and two others on charges of conspiracy to murder. The result was the Criminal Justice (Amendment) Act 1981. Now if any defendant objects to the application to lift reporting restrictions, the magistrates must refuse it if persuaded that retaining the restrictions is in the interests of justice.[89] The presumption is in favour of delayed reporting, and the High Court has said that only 'powerful' arguments in favour of publicity will prevail. In a 1982 case a defendant's wish to publicize his allegations that police had reneged on a promise to drop charges against him was held not to be sufficient to override a co-defendant's objection to publicity.[90]

Magistrates who wrongly refuse an application to lift restrictions are acting beyond their powers. Newspapers, broadcasters, individual reporters and probably the NUJ can challenge such a refusal by applying to the Queen's Bench Division of the High Court for an order of mandamus to compel the magistrates to follow the law.[91] The court can act quickly. In one case the application was heard on one day's notice. The procedure is not an appeal. It must be shown that the justices were wrong in law: either by refusing to lift restrictions when the Act required them to do so or by exercising their discretion in an unreasonable way. In some cases, particularly for broadcasters, even this procedure may take too long. If they are sure that the restrictions ought to have been lifted (e.g., because a lone defendant asked for them to be) and they broadcast a full account, they are most unlikely to be prosecuted for breach of a restriction order that was invalidly made or retained.

Serious fraud

The length and complexity of some fraud trials has worried governments for many years. In 1986 the Roskill Committee recommended wide-ranging changes,[92] and the Criminal Justice Act 1987 made substantial procedural alterations in the way that major fraud prosecutions are conducted.

From the media's point of view the most important concern is the 'preparatory hearing'. In serious fraud cases the prosecution can now dispense with committal hearings by making a transfer order to an appropriate Crown Court. The Crown Court, in turn,

---

[89] Criminal Justice (Amendment) Act 1981 s 1.
[90] *R v Leeds Justices ex parte Sykes* [1983] 1 All ER 460.
[91] *R v Horsham Justices ex parte Farquharson and Another* [1982] 2 All ER 269.
[92] *Fraud Trials Committee Report*, HMSO, 1986.

can order a preparatory hearing. This can be used by the defence to argue that there is no case to answer. It can also be used by the judge as a pre-trial review. Uniquely, the judge can compel both prosecution *and defence* to set out their respective cases in considerable detail.

The preparatory hearing is treated as part of the trial[93] and the press and public have their common-law right to attend, but reporting restrictions apply in the same way as to committal hearings.[94] They also apply to applications by the defence for the charges to be dismissed for failing to disclose a sufficient case. As with committal proceedings, a single defendant has the right to have these reporting restrictions lifted; where multiple defendants disagree, the court has a discretion to act in the interests of justice.[95] There is no discretion to lift the restriction partially.

If the restrictions are not lifted, the permitted details are virtually the same as those of a committal hearing. The principal difference is that 'relevant business information' may also be published. This means, in brief, the name and address of any business that the accused was carrying on on his own account or in which he was a partner or of which he was a director.[96] The addresses can be those at the time of the events giving rise to the charges and those at the time of publication. These restrictions apply until either the charges are dismissed against all the defendants who make pre-trial applications or until the trial of the last of the defendants is concluded.[97]

Breach of the restrictions is an offence for which the editor, proprietor and publisher (or their equivalents in the case of a broadcast or cable programme) can be fined by a magistrates' court up to level 5, currently £2,000.[98] The Attorney-General's consent is needed for a prosecution.[99]

Juveniles

Reporters permitted to attend youth courts can report the proceedings, but they must not reveal the name, address, school or any particulars that would lead to the identification of any person under eighteen as a witness or as the person who was the object of the proceedings.[100] Photographs of juveniles involved in any way in the

---

[93] Criminal Justice Act 1987, s 8.
[94] ibid., s 11.
[95] ibid., s 11(2)–(4) and see Henry J's ruling in *R* v *Saunders* [1990] Crim LR 597.
[96] 1987 Act, s 11(4).
[97] ibid., s 11(5)–(7).
[98] ibid., s 11(12).
[99] ibid., s 11(13).
[100] Eighteen was substituted for seventeen by the Criminal Justice Act 1991 s 68.

proceedings are also prohibited.[101] It is the link between the proceedings and the young person to which the law objects. Consequently, background stories or interviews that do identify the person can be published if all mention of the court case is scrupulously avoided. Conversely, feature articles can be written about the juvenile court backed by anonymous examples. The trivial nature of some charges that are brought and the wholly inappropriate style of cross-examination that is sometimes used in these courts deserve wider publicity.

The court or the Home Secretary can give permission for a juvenile to be identified. This ought not to be done as a form of punishment, but only when necessary to avoid injustice to the child or young person.[102] An example would be to scotch local rumours that a child was attending court as a defendant when in reality he was a witness. In practice the power to allow identification is rarely used.[103]

Anonymity is required as a matter of course only in youth court proceedings and in appeals from these to the Crown Court or High Court.[104] There are many other cases that can involve young persons in appearances before adult magistrates' courts, Crown Courts or in civil proceedings. In none of these cases is there an *automatic* ban on identification. Children who kill are often the subject of wide press coverage. However, any court can choose to impose restrictions of the same kind as a youth court.[105] The power to restrict reports of proceedings in adult courts in which a child or young person appears should be exercised only where there are reasons to do so that outweigh the public's legitimate interest in receiving fair and accurate reports of the proceedings, including knowing the identity of those in the community who have been guilty of criminal conduct. However, the fact that the defendant is a child will normally be a good reason for applying the restriction and only in exceptional cases should no direction to suppress the child's identity be given.[106]

Courts have sometimes tried to prohibit the identification of a young murder victim, but they have no power to do so since a corpse is neither a party nor a witness. Similarly, the courts cannot

---

[101] Children and Young Persons Act 1933 s 49(1), based on Departmental Committee's Report on the Treatment of Young Offenders, HMSO, 1927, Cmnd 2831.
[102] Children and Young Persons Act 1969 s 10.
[103] John Watson, *Juvenile Courts*, p. 126.
[104] Children and Young Persons Act 1963 s 57, based on the Ingleby Committee on Children and Young Persons, HMSO, 1960, Cmnd 1191.
[105] Children and Young Persons Act 1933 s 39 as amended by Children and Young Persons Act 1963 s 57.
[106] *R v Leicester Crown Court ex parte S* (1990) *The Independent*, 12 December, QBD.

prevent the press naming adults involved (unless indirectly they disclose the child's identity). An order in an adult court can prohibit publication of any information calculated to lead to the identification of a child, but it cannot go further and give the media directions as to what material it can or cannot publish to give effect to this order. This was established in the 1991 case of *R v Crown Court ex parte Godwin*:[107]

> A trial involved serious allegations of child molestation against two members of a close and very orthodox Jewish community living in Stamford Hill. The children were also from that community, and the trial judge was prevailed upon by defence counsel to make an s 39 order prohibiting publication of the names and addresses of the defendants, on the grounds that such publication might lead to the identification of their alleged child victims. The Divisional Court held that s 39 gives no power to direct how the order not to identify children shall be implemented: this is up to the media. If their judgement is wrong, they can be proceeded against subsequently, but they must not be subjected to 'prior restraint' by a judge giving directions as to what information would produce an identification. A judge was perfectly entitled to give 'advice' to the journalists in court as to what might or might not breach the order, but such advice was not legally binding or part of the order itself. (This case was also notable for the fact that a court reporter, Caroline Godwin, was permitted to address argument to the trial judge, a feature of the case that was not criticized by the Court of Appeal, before whom she also appeared in person.)

Of course, even in those cases where there is no legal restriction on identifying a young person, there may be an ethical question as to whether identification and the trauma that it can cause is really necessary to any story about the case.

All these restrictions apply to television, cable and radio coverage of juvenile cases as well as to the press.[108] In each case the maximum fine is £2,000.[109]

Family cases

At one time the popular press thrived on divorce-court scandals, and every salacious detail would be reported. One 1886 case involving a duke and a general was reported over sixty-two columns of the *Daily Telegraph*.[110] This practice has declined dramatically, in part because of the restrictions on access to certain evidence (especially in undefended divorces) and in part because it is no longer

---

[107] *R v Crown Court ex parte Godwin* [1991] 3 All ER 818.
[108] Children and Young Persons Act 1963 s 57(4).
[109] Children and Young Persons Act 1933 ss 39(2), 49(2).
[110] Jeremy Tunstall, *Journalists at Work*, Constable, 1971, p. 91.

necessary to establish cruelty or adultery in order to obtain a divorce. Irretrievable breakdown is the sole ground, and this can be demonstrated merely by a period of separation. However, even where evidence of sensational adultery is given and discovered by journalists, they must be circumspect in their reports. Reports of proceedings for divorce, nullity, separation, financial provisions for a spouse or declarations of marital status, overseas adoption, legitimacy or parentage must be limited to the following:[111]

- names, addresses and occupations of parties and witnesses;
- a concise statement of the charges, defence and counter-charges in support of which evidence is given or (in the case of a declaration as to status), the declaration sought;
- submissions on points of law and rulings of the court;
- the judgment of the court and observations by the judge.

The charges and counter-charges may be the most interesting to a journalist, but they can be reported only if evidence is given in support of them. If the allegations are withdrawn, publication is prohibited.

In practice, the judgment of the court is usually very full and will review all evidence. Judicial comment of the sort: 'the wife (of a merchant banker) was well-dressed, well-preserved, stupid in many ways but not uncultured' and the co-respondent (a window cleaner) was a 'good physical specimen'[112] can be acidic and grossly unfair. Publication of such comments can be justified in the public interest on the grounds that they say more about the judges than about the subjects of their comments. One High Court judge retired after a storm of protest over comments he made about the morality of Chelsea dustmen.

As with juvenile cases, the editor, proprietor and publisher are at risk rather than the journalist. The maximum penalty is a fine at level 5, currently £2,000, and four months in prison. The Attorney-General's consent is necessary for any prosecution.[113]

This last safeguard is imperfect. While the persons affected by the report may not prosecute, they may apply for a civil injunction to restrain its publication. Normally, the courts will not enjoin in advance the commission of a criminal offence.[114] They say that the proper course is to bring a prosecution after the event. However,

---

[111] Judicial Proceedings (Regulation of Reports) Act 1926 s 1(1)(*b*); Domestic and Appellate Proceedings (Restrictions of Publicity) Act 1968 s 2(3); Matrimonial Causes Act 1973 s 45; Family Law Reform Acts 1986 and 1987.
[112] *Daily Express* (1969) 25 January quoted in Cretney, *Principles of Family Law*, 3rd edn, Sweet & Maxwell, 1979, p. 158.
[113] Judicial Proceedings (Regulation of Reports) Act 1926 s 1(3).
[114] *Gouriet* v *Union of Post Office Workers* [1978] AC 435.

where a person stands to suffer particular hardship, the position is different and in *Argyll* v *Argyll* the court granted the Duchess an injunction to prevent the Duke reporting details of charges in their divorce proceedings that had not been backed by evidence.[115] The case is important because its rationale is capable of being applied to most, if not all, the restrictions on reporting examined in this section. An injunction should be refused if the threatened breach was trivial, but the publisher would be put to time and expense in opposing the action. This was the very vice against which the Attorney-General's veto was intended to guard, and the time and cost of High Court proceedings are much more serious than the cost of defending a prosecution in the magistrates' courts. But when this argument was put to Mr Justice Ungoed-Thomas in *Argyll* v *Argyll*, he disregarded it. However, the difficulty of learning what a paper intends to publish in advance and the cost of obtaining an injunction have meant that there are few cases in this context where the *Argyll* precedent has been followed.

The Children Act 1989, which came into force in October 1991, gave magistrates greater responsibilities in care proceedings. These 'family proceedings' are subject to similar restrictions as apply in divorce cases.[116] In addition, when the Act is fully in force magistrates will have a clear statutory discretion to exclude the public in any family proceedings.[117] Media reports of any proceedings under the Act must not include material that is intended or likely to identify the child (i.e., a person under eighteen) as being involved in the proceedings or an address or school of such a child. It is a defence to show that the publisher was unaware, and had no reason to suspect, that the material was likely to identify the child. The maximum penalty is a fine on level 4 (currently £1,000). Either the Secretary of State or the court can dispense with anonymity in whole or to some limited extent.[118]

In adoption proceedings the restrictions go further: the parties must be anonymous, the charges cannot be summarized and nothing must be published that would identify the child; nor can the child's photograph be printed.[119] The maximum penalty is a fine at level 4, currently £1,000, on the editor, proprietor or publisher of a newspaper or periodical. Again the Attorney-General must consent to a prosecution. These restrictions now apply to the electronic as well as the print media.[120]

---

[115] [1967] Ch 302.
[116] Magistrates' Courts Act 1980 s 71; Children Act 1989 s 97(8).
[117] Children Act 1989 s 97(1).
[118] ibid., s 97(2)–(8).
[119] Magistrates' Courts Act 1980 s 71(2).
[120] ibid., s 71 as amended by Broadcasting Act 1990 Sched 20 para29.

The new power of magistrates hearing cases under the Children Act 1989 to exclude the public will also be used to exclude the press. One unsatisfactory feature of the Act is that it gives no guidance as to when magistrates should use their discretion to sit in secret, and, since they will usually prefer to do so, it will mean that press coverage of juvenile justice will shrink alarmingly. Whatever Dickensian tendencies these new courts develop in dealing with children, there will be no latter-day Dickens to inform the public about them. Even when the reporters are permitted to remain, their reports will be limited to bare details and to the court's 'observations' in giving its decision.[121] They may, if present, at least point out to the court, should the occasion arise, that it has power, under s 97(4) of the Act, to lift the ban on identification 'if satisfied that the welfare of the child demands it'.

Ex parte applications for injunctions to oust one party from the family home are usually heard in chambers. However, when a power of arrest is attached to the injunction, this should be announced when the judge next sits in open court. A person who is arrested under this power has to be brought before a judge within twenty-four hours (excluding only Sundays, Good Friday and Christmas Day). If a regular court will not sit within that time, the arrested person can be taken before a judge elsewhere. In theory this will be a hearing in open court and there is a Practice Direction that no impediment should be put in the way of the press or any other member of the public who wishes to attend. In practice, of course, it will be rare for the press to learn that such a hearing is due to take place. If the person arrested is committed for contempt, there must be an announcement at the next regular sitting of the court. The name of the person committed, the period of the committal and the general nature of contempt should be given.[122]

Wards of court

Neither press nor public has access to wardship hearings and it is contempt of court to publish any information relating to the proceedings. This was the position at common law[123] and it has been preserved by statute.[124] The Court of Appeal has said that 'proceedings' include such matters as statements of evidence, reports, accounts of interviews and such like that are prepared for use in court once the wardship proceedings have been instituted.[125]

---

[121] Magistrates' Courts Act 1980 Sched 11.
[122] *Practice Direction* [1991] 2 All ER 9.
[123] *Re F (a minor)* note 41 above.
[124] Administration of Justice Act 1960 s 12(1).
[125] Geoffrey Lane LJ in *Re F*, note 41 above, at p. 135.

This reporting restriction is paralleled by the imposition of a high degree of confidentiality on reports made by relatives, social workers and professionals that find their way into the court files. The confidentiality is given in order to encourage candour, and the reports will be protected from newspaper lawyers who seek to inspect them in order to defend libel actions.[126]

The ban does not mean that nothing can be published about a ward. The usual position is that it is not contempt to name the child, to identify him or her as a ward of court or to write about some event in which he or she was involved outside the wardship proceedings. Thus the *Daily Mail* was not in contempt for describing the funeral of a couple who had been killed in the Zeebrugge disaster in 1987 and referring to the reactions of their child, who had been made a ward of court.[127]

The legitimacy of media interest in wards of court has been accepted since the press helped to expose the 'Cleveland crisis', where local JPs had separated numerous children from their parents on insuffcient evidence of sexual abuse. For the media to investigate possible abuses of power by social workers and other state agents charged with protecting children, they must have some latitude to publish – a latitude that local councils will generally oppose in the interests of the welfare of the child, not to mention their own interests in avoiding public criticism. There have been many recent conflicts that the courts have resolved by seeking compromises between the right to impart information and the traditional concern for the welfare of the child.

Where the information does not relate to court proceedings, there is a presumption in favour of publication. The key case is *Re X* (see p. 25), where the Court of Appeal made some ringing declarations in favour of freedom to publish, even though the publication (a book that made references to the sexual behaviour of the deceased father of a ward of court) would psychologically damage the ward were she to read it. The case still stands for the proposition that the courts will not normally protect a child from publicity unconnected with court proceedings relating to it.

There are, as always in this area, highly exceptional cases:

> The child killer Mary Bell was released on licence. She had a child, who was made a ward of court. The judge refused a request for an order prohibiting publication of the fact of the birth, because the possible harm to the child did not justify such a wide order, but he did later make an order prohibiting publication of the new name of Mary Bell, or the child as her child, or the name of the father. He

---

[126] *In Re X, Y and Z (minors)* (1991) *The Times*, 20 March, Waite J.
[127] *Re L (a minor) (Wardship: Freedom of Publication)* [1988] 1 All ER 418, Booth J; see also *Re F*, note 41 above.

was satisfied that the potential harm to the child if this order was not made justified the interference with the freedom to publish which it entailed.[128]

In the Mary Bell case the child might have been directly affected by publicity. That was not the case with 'Baby C', who had been born with severe brain damage and who the court in wardship proceedings had ruled should be allowed to die. Baby C would always remain ignorant of anything written or spoken about her. None the less, the Court of Appeal imposed injunctions that not only preserved the child's anonymity, but also restrained disclosure of the hospital where the ward had been treated or the identity of any of the individuals who had cared for the ward. It further prohibited the solicitation of information relating to the ward (other than information already in the public domain) from the ward's parents or staff at any hospital where she had been treated.[129]

The courts should hesitate long and hard before making an order interfering with the right of free publication.[130] The courts, after the Cleveland affair, have been more ready to accept the legitimacy of press investigations of the way local authorities exercise their draconian powers to remove children from parents and foster-parents, for reasons that may be unsubstantiated (as with some sexual abuse allegations) or based on what are perceived to be 'political' rather than humane reasons. At the same time, the courts have become more worldly wise to the entrapment techniques used by some newspapers to elicit information from school-children and unwary relatives and teachers. The result now is often a limited restriction on publication, which permits investigation and criticism of local authority actions, but without reference to details that might identify the children and with a specific ban on 'soliciting information' from children, parents or foster-parents, relatives and teachers. The leading authority is the decision of Lord Justice Butler-Sloss (who chaired the Cleveland Inquiry) in the 1989 case of *Re M*:

> Two children were removed from the care of foster-parents without notice to them. The foster-parents were told by a later letter some of the reasons for removal, but not of the fact that one child had alleged sexual interference by one foster-parent. The local newspaper proposed to publish the story to spotlight a possible abuse of the local authority's powers. The Court of Appeal recognized that there was a genuine public interest in the story. It stressed that injunctions against publicity in relation to wards should never be of a common

---

[128] *X County Council* v *A* [1985] 1 All ER 53, Balcombe J.
[129] *Re C (a minor) (Wardship: Medical Treatment) No 2* [1989] 2 All ER 791, CA.
[130] *X (a minor) (Wardship: Restriction on Publicity)* [1975] 1 All ER 697, 706, CA.

form or nature and that they should be no wider than necessary to protect the interests of the child. However, an injunction against identifying the children, their parents, foster-parents, schools and any relevant addresses was upheld. It also gave some protection against intrusive interviewing by the media of the foster-parents, although not of employees of the local authority.[131]

In the Zeebrugge case the registrar did not specifically order that the ward remain anonymous; he only expressed a hope that this would happen. This is not uncommon, and the press often acquiesces in such requests. However, contempt proceedings can be brought only if the judge has gone further and made an order (having weighed the balance between the interests of the ward and the freedom of the press). The court in that case said that any order should be clear and precise and the people against whom it was intended to be effective must be identified.[132]

In *Re W*[133] the local authority placed a fifteen-year-old boy, who in the past had been homosexually abused, for fostering with two men who had a long-standing homosexual relationship. Although the boy was a ward of court, the court was not informed of the arrangement. The council obtained an *ex parte* injunction restraining publication of a newspaper article about the affair. It argued that even if names and addresses were withheld, there was serious risk that the boy would be identified, and that he would suffer psychological damage as a result. The Court of Appeal distilled from the past cases the following guidelines:

- The court attached great importance to safeguarding freedom of the press and to Article 10 of the European Convention.
- These freedoms were subject to exceptions, including restrictions imposed for the protection of children.
- In the balancing exercise, the welfare of the ward is *not* the paramount consideration.
- An important factor is the nature and extent of the public interest in the matter which it was sought to publish.
- In almost every case the public interest in favour of publication would be satisfied without any identification of the ward to persons other than those who already knew the facts. However, the risk of some wider identification might have to be accepted on occasions if the story was to be told in a manner that would engage the interest of the general public.
- Any restraint was for the protection of the ward and those who cared for the ward. The restraint must therefore be in

---

[131] *Re M (a minor)*; *Re N (a minor)* [1989] 3 WLR 1136, CA.
[132] *Re L*, note 127 above, 418, 423.
[133] *Guardian*, 7 August 1991; (1991) NLJ 1263.

clear terms and no wider than was necessary for that purpose. Save in exceptional circumstances, the ward could not be protected from any distress that might be caused by reading the publication himself.

The court held that it would be wrong to prohibit the naming of the local authority. Although this might increase the risk of the ward's identification, it was the action of that particular council that gave rise to the matter of public interest on which the newspapers wished to comment.

Although the order can be directed to the world at large and although it does not have to be personally served, the newspaper or broadcaster must know of the order and its terms before a publication in breach of it can be a contempt.[134] Wilful blindness, however, is unlikely to be accounted a good defence.

Rape

In 1975 the Heilbron Report[135] recommended that rape complainants should be promised anonymity in an effort to improve the rate of reporting to the police. A study in the same year had shown that in about half the press reports of rape prosecutions the victim was named and in about a third her address was given as well.[136]

The recommendation was adopted by the Sexual Offences (Amendment) Act 1976 and it is now an offence to identify a woman as the complainant in a rape case.[137] Since the Criminal Justice Act 1988 there is no restriction on identifying the defendant in a rape case (unless this indirectly reveals the identity of the victim). The restriction applies only to 'rape offences', and while this includes attempt, conspiracy and incitement to rape, and burglary with intent to rape, it does not extend to forms of sexual assault other than penile penetration of the vagina.[138]

Once a woman has alleged that she has been the victim of a rape offence, neither her name nor address nor a still or moving picture may be published, broadcast or included in any other programme service.[139]

---

[134] *Cleveland County Council* v *W* (1988) *The Independent*, 29 April, 4 May; and *Re L* note 127 above.

[135] Advisory Group on the Law of Rape Cmnd 6352, (1975).

[136] Keith Soothill and Anthea Jack, 'How Rape is Reported', *New Society*, 19 June 1975.

[137] Sexual Offences (Amendment) Act 1976 s 4. The ban applies also to radio, television and cable operators. For the latter, see Cable and Broadcasting Act Sched 3 para 31.

[138] Sexual Offences (Amendment) Act 1976 ss 1, 7.

[139] ibid., s 4(1)(*a*); 'picture' is not confined to photographs but includes a likeness however produced, s 4(1A).

This restriction lasts for her lifetime. It would therefore apply if, for instance, the man was not prosecuted but was sued by the woman for damages for assault. After a person has been accused of a rape offence, the restrictions are more stringent: thereafter no matter likely to lead members of the public to identify a woman as the complainant may be published, broadcast or included in any other programme service.[140]

There are three important exceptions to the anonymity rule. First, the woman may consent to being identified. Her agreement must be given in writing and it must not have been obtained as a result of unreasonable interference with her peace or comfort.[141] Secondly, the media are free to identify a woman as a rape complainant as part of a report of criminal proceedings other than the trial or appeal of the person allegedly responsible. This was apparently intended to cater for those (rare) cases where a complainant is herself later charged with perjury.

The court can itself allow a woman to be named. It may do so if this is necessary to persuade witnesses to come forward, if anonymity would otherwise prejudice the defence[142] or if it would 'impose a substantial and unreasonable restriction on the reporting of proceedings at the trial' and identification would serve the public interest. By itself, the defendant's acquittal is not sufficient reason.[143]

> In a trial of a man for rape and murder a newspaper applied for an order allowing identification. The Crown, defence and the victim's mother (in an affidavit) consented. The murder could not be practicably reported without identifying the victim. The order was granted.[144]

The press has no formal standing to apply to the trial judge for a lifting order, but a discreet note to the court clerk or one of the lawyers in the case may prompt the judge into considering whether one should be made. The maximum penalty for infringing these restrictions is a fine on level 5 (£2,000).

---

[140] ibid., s 4 (1)(*b*) as amended by the Broadcasting Act 1990 Sched 20 para 26. For an interesting study of how these reporting restrictions are applied by the media, and how the anonymity of victims is often ignored in law reports, see Stephen White, 'Rape Reports and Law Reports' (1991) 12 *Jo. of Int. Media Law and Practice* 2.

[141] ibid., s 4(5A) and (5B): the burden is on the media to show written consent and on the prosecution to show that it was obtained improperly.

[142] ibid., s 4(2).

[143] ibid., s 4(3)

[144] *R* v *Gilligan* [1987] Crim LR 501.

Attorney-General's reference to the Court of Appeal

A jury's verdict is final. However damning the evidence, a jury has an unreviewable power to return a verdict of not guilty. Since 1972, however, a legal ruling of the trial judge made before the acquittal can be referred by the Attorney-General to the Court of Appeal.[145] The court may decide the point of law in the Attorney-General's favour, but still cannot reverse the acquittal. To protect defendants, court rules require their identity to be kept secret unless they consent to be named.[146] It is different where the Attorney-General refers to the Court of Appeal a sentence that he considers unduly lenient.[147] Here the court is not just concerned with the abstract question of whether the sentence was wrong in principle, but can increase or alter the sentence actually imposed. Consequently, there is no need for any special protection for the defendant and these references can be reported in the usual way.

Indecent evidence

An Act of 1926 prohibits publication in relation to any judicial proceedings of 'any indecent matter or indecent medical, surgical or physiological details being matter or details the publication of which would be calculated to injure public morals'.[148] The vulnerability of public morals must be judged by current standards,[149] and the complete absence of recent prosecutions indicates that this section is now in practice a dead letter. The proceedings in both the *Lady Chatterley's Lover* and *Oz* magazine trials were published in book form and in television re-enactments without objection.

Secrecy Orders

Section 11 orders

In certain circumstances the courts may invoke an inherent power to order that the names of witnesses should not be published. Blackmail cases have provided one example.[150] The policy, as with rape cases, is to encourage victims to come forward to testify against

---

[145] Criminal Justice Act 1972 s 36.
[146] Criminal Appeal (Reference of Points of Law) Rules 1973 (SI 1973 No 1114) r6.
[147] Criminal Justice Act 1988 ss 35 and 36.
[148] Judicial Proceedings (Regulation of Reports) Act 1926 s 1(1)(*a*).
[149] *Knuller* v *DPP* [1973] AC 435.
[150] *R* v *Socialist Worker Printers & Publishers Ltd ex parte A–G* [1975] QB 637.

their tormentors. Blackmail victims are rarely likely to testify unless assured that their guilty secrets will not leak out. The power is now formalized by s 11 of the Contempt Act, which provides:

> In any case where a court (having power to do so) allows a name or other matter to be withheld from the public in proceedings before the court, the court may give such directions prohibiting the publication of that name or matter in connection with the proceedings as appear to the court to be necessary for the purpose for which it was so withheld.

Section 11 does not give courts a new power to take evidence in secret where one did not previously exist, but, where this is appropriate, it provides the means for punishing disclosure. In the absence of a statutory power this means that there must be some overwhelming reason in the interests of the administration of justice why the normal principle of open justice should be abrogated.

> The defendant to a minor road-traffic offence was a former MP. His home address was not given orally to the court because, he said, he feared further harassment from his ex-wife. The magistrates agreed and made an order under s 11 forbidding its publication. The Divisional Court held that while evidence could be communicated to the court in writing if the proper administration of justice demanded it, there were no good reasons in the present case. Many defendants would prefer that their identity was not revealed, 'but s 11 was not enacted for the comfort and feelings of defendants'. The order was quashed.[151]

> At a kidnapping trial an Old Bailey judge ordered that the identity of the main prosecution witness (the alleged victim) should not be publicized. She was a member of a wealthy and famous family. She was also undergoing treatment for heroin addiction and it was said

---

[151] *R v Evesham Justices ex parte McDonagh* [1988] 1 All ER 371, 384 QBD. It is a common failing of common-law judges to supress names for reasons that appear reasonable, but that have nothing to do with the strict needs of the administration of justice. Powerful appellate rebukes of this behaviour are to be found in the Australian cases of *Raybos Australia Pty Ltd v Jones* (1985) 2 NSWLR 47 (reversing a suppression order on the name of a leading solicitor accused of conspiracy in a civil action, made because of damage to his professional reputation from possibly unfounded accusation) and *John Fairfax & Sons v Police Tribunal of NSW* (1986) 5 NSWLR 465 (reversing a suppression order on the name of a police informant, because it had already been mentioned in public and so the order could not have been necessary to secure justice in the particular proceedings). See also *R v Dover Justices ex parte Dover District Council* ((1991) Divisional Court, 14 October), where 'exceptional circumstances' justifying restrictions on publicity did not include the fact that it might have dire economic consequences leading to the closure of the defendant's business. (The defendant was a restaurateur who failed to win approval for a ban on the reporting of proceedings brought against him by a council health department.)

that publicity would damage her recovery. The judge's s 11 order
was challenged in the Divisional Court, which indicated that it would
have quashed the order if it had jurisdiction to do so. There was a
danger that the witness had been accorded special treatment because
of her family connections. It was common for witnesses to be faced
with embarrassment as a result of facts that were elicited in the
course of proceedings or of allegations made without real substance.
However, it was an essential part of British justice that cases should
be tried in public and this consideration had to outweigh the individual interests of particular persons.[152]

A further reason for criticizing the order of the judge in the
last case was that the witness's name had been openly used in
court. In a subsequent case in 1985 the Divisional Court
confirmed that an order under s 11 cannot be made to prevent
publication of a name (or other evidence) once it has already been
spoken in open court.[153] If the prosecution or defence apply to a
Crown Court for an order that all or part of a trial should be
held in camera in order to protect the identity of a witness or
any other person, advance notice must be given to allow an
appeal against these restrictions on open justice to be taken to
the Court of Appeal. The requirements are the same as where a
court is invited to sit in camera for national security reasons (see
p. 316).

Before an editor or reporter can be held in contempt for disobedience of a partial secrecy order, there must be a clear ruling
expressed as a formal order. So much is clear from *Attorney-
General* v *Leveller Magazine Ltd.*[154]

> During committal proceedings in the 'ABC' Official Secrets case
> (see p. 417) the prosecution called an expert witness. The magistrates
> allowed his real name to be written down and shown to the parties,
> but said that he was to be referred to publicly as Colonel B, since the
> prosecution claimed that revelation of his true identity would preju-
> dice national security. In the course of giving evidence, the Colonel
> provided information from which reporters in court, by subsequently
> consulting army publications, deduced his name and position. The
> *Leveller* and other magazines gleefully published this discovery, and
> were prosecuted for contempt on the basis that they had flouted a
> court order. The House of Lords held that the press action was not
> contempt, for a number of reasons:

---

[152] *R* v *Central Criminal Court ex parte Crook* (1984) *The Times*, 8 November;
(1985) LS Gaz 1408 QBD.
[153] *R* v *Arundel Justices ex parte Westminster Press Ltd* [1985] 2 All ER 390, QBD.
[154] *A-G* v *Leveller Magazine Ltd* [1979] AC 440, and see the principles applied in
relation to orders restricting publicity about wards of court (p. 332).

- It had not been shown to interfere with the administration of justice.
- The magistrates' action may well have amounted to an implied request that the press should not publish the name, but before contempt could be proved there had to be disobedience to a clear order by the court.
- The Colonel had effectively 'blown his own cover' by his answers to questions in open court.

As a result of s 11, any partial secrecy order should be in writing, state its precise scope, the time it should cease to have effect (if appropriate) and the specific purpose of making the order. Courts must normally give notice to the press that an order has been made and court staff should be prepared to answer specific inquiries about orders.[155]

Postponement orders

Reports of evidence in a trial will not generally pose any risk at all since they convey to the public at large only what has been presented in open court. Consequently, they cannot be contempt of court.[156] Section 4 of the Contempt of Court Act 1981 formalizes this position. It gives an express right to publish in good faith a fair, accurate and contemporaneous report of public legal proceedings. A report is 'accurate' if its gist is correct even if not word perfect. Reports are contemporaneous if they are published as soon as practicable after a temporary legal restriction on reporting ends.

Section 4(2) of the Act gives the court a power to make an order postponing the publication of certain matters heard in open court:

> In any such proceedings the court may where it appears to be necessary for avoiding a substantial risk of prejudice to the administration of justice in those proceedings, or in any proceedings pending or imminent, order that the publication of any report of the proceedings, or any part of the proceedings, be postponed for such period as the court thinks necessary for that purpose.

Before the 1981 Act the judges identified two situations where a contemporaneous report of public proceedings might be prejudicial. The first was where part of the proceedings were conducted in the absence of the jury; for instance, a person facing several charges might plead guilty to some of them before a jury

---

[155] *Practice Direction: (Contempt of Court Act: Reports of Proceedings: Postponement Orders)* [1983] 1 All ER 64 and see note 167 below.
[156] *Buenos Aires Gas Co Ltd* v *Wilde* (1880) 42 LT 657.

was sworn to try the others; or the defence might contest the admissibility of certain evidence, in which case the jury would retire while the matter was argued before the judge in a 'trial within a trial'. These matters were heard in public, but it would probably be prejudicial to the defendant if the jury were able to read in the press about his or her other crimes or of evidence that the judge ruled inadmissible. It was therefore contempt to publish a contemporaneous account of them.[157] The second situation was where one trial was part of a series, and a premature publication of the evidence common to them all might jeopardize the later proceedings. From time to time the courts have ordered the press to desist from publication until the last of the series is heard. This was first done by Chief Justice Abbott in connection with the Cato Street Conspiracy trials in 1821. The *Observer* printed a 'fair true and impartial' account of one of them but was nevertheless fined the (for those days) staggering sum of £500.[158] Mr Justice Waller similarly warned the press not to disclose certain evidence in the first of the Poulson local government corruption trials, lest it prejudice the trials that were to follow.[159] A more respectful attitude to jurors was shown by Mr Justice Lawton, who did not think the jury trying a second murder charge against the Kray twins would be prejudiced by the publicity a few weeks earlier surrounding their first murder trial. This confidence was well placed. The Krays were acquitted in the second trial.[160]

Section 4(2) of the Contempt Act confirms the court's power to order the postponement of particular reports for such period as is necessary to avoid a substantial risk of prejudice to the proceedings it is hearing, or to others that are pending or imminent.

Orders are common to prevent the premature disclosure of trials within trials and guilty pleas. To this extent they are unexceptionable. The difficulty is that judges may gag the press when the danger to the administration of justice is more speculative, and may make gag orders that are unnecessarily wide. Both tendencies were disapproved of by the Court of Appeal:

> The Horsham justices were hearing an 'old-style' committal in a case involving allegations of gunrunning. A part of the prosecution evidence suggested that the conspiracy might be linked with recent political assassinations in London. Reporting restrictions had been lifted, but the defence was anxious to prevent publicity being given to evidence that was sensational, but of very little relevance to the

[157] *R* v *Newcastle upon Tyne Justices ex parte Vickers* (1981) *The Times*, 18 April.
[158] *R* v *Clement* (1821) 4 B & Ald 218; 106 ER 918.
[159] See Phillimore Committee Report on *Contempt of Court*, HMSO, 1974, Cmnd 5794, paras 134–40. The common-law basis for such orders is by no means clear.
[160] *R* v *Kray* (1969) 53 C App R 412.

actual charges. The Horsham justices made an order postponing publication of the entire proceedings. The Court of Appeal held that this 'blanket ban' was far too wide: the magistrates should have waited until the evidence was led, and postponed only the reporting of any part that it was necessary, in the interests of justice, to suppress for the time being. The court permitted the NUJ as well as the local newspaper and its reporter, to challenge the order.[161]

Since the *Horsham Justices* case, postponement orders have been used more sparingly. The court must not reach for its powers to suppress or postpone reporting unless it plainly appears:

● that the reporting in question would carry a substantial risk of serious prejudice (i.e., not a small risk, or a risk of mild prejudice); and

● that an unacceptable level of risk cannot be reduced by some reasonably available alternative action.

This approach was confirmed in 1990 by the Court of Appeal in *Re Central Television* PLC, condemning a trial judge's order postponing television and radio reports of the case while the jury was deliberating on its verdict, having been taken to a hotel overnight. The order fell at both hurdles, since there was no reason to suppose that press reporting would be prejudicial, and if there had been, the judge could have avoided the risk (or reduced it to an acceptable level) by directing that the jurors should not have access to television and radio while at their hotel. He had failed to take proper account of the importance of the open-justice principle and of the public interest in freedom of expression.[162]

This approach should normally prevent the success of applications to postpone reporting of trials that are part of a series of prosecutions. Thus Mr Justice Hodgson refused on public-interest grounds to postpone the trial of Winston Silcott for the murder of PC Blakelock during the Tottenham riots, although the trial of other persons allegedly involved in that murder were shortly to follow. The position has also been considered in relation to the special problems of a series of fraud trials. At the first *Guinness* trial Mr Justice Henry refused an application to postpone reporting made on behalf of the defendant Ernest Saunders, who was also to be a defendant in a subsequent trial. His decision turned on the presumption that media coverage of the first trial would be fair and accurate, as the law of contempt requires.[163] The Court of Appeal found no flaw in this presumption, and it was applied by Mr Justice MacKinnon in 1991 in rejecting an application to postpone

---

[161] *R v Horsham Justices ex parte Farquharson and Another* [1982] 2 All ER 269.
[162] *Re Central Television plc* [1991] 1 All ER 347.
[163] *R v Saunders* (1990) *The Independent*, 8 February; [1990] Crim LR 597.

reporting of the first Nat West/Blue Arrow trial until the conclusion of the second. Although the charges in the two trials were closely connected (and the prosecution had supported a partial ban) the judge applied the presumption that reporting of the first trial would be fair and accurate. The jury at the second trial was bound to know that the first had taken place, and informed reporting was better than inaccurate speculation. Any prejudice would be minimized by directing members of the jury to concentrate on the evidence presented to them, and to put out of their minds whatever memories they might have of press reports of the first case.[164]

It should go without saying that s 4(2) applies only to reports of 'proceedings', and does not empower a court to postpone the reporting of matters connected with the case but which form no part of the record of events that take place in court. In 1986 magistrates attempted to use s 4(2) to prohibit the broadcasting of a film of an arrest. The Divisional Court quashed the order because the arrest was not part of the court proceedings. It warned that the broadcast might constitute strict-liability contempt, but the remedy was for the defendant (or anyone else directly affected) to apply to the High Court for an injunction.[165] There was particular criticism of blanket bans on reporting a series of trials of Rampton Hospital nurses at Nottingham Crown Court. When nurses took industrial action in protest against the charges, the press found it could not fully cover the reasons for the dispute. The *Observer* and one of its journalists, David Leigh, courageously broke the order, and the Court of Appeal refused to injunct future breaches on the ground that the order was too wide. The *Observer* and the NUJ then sent counsel to Nottingham to challenge the judge who had made the orders: he backed down and rescinded them.[166] Partly as a result of this case, the Court of Appeal in December 1982 issued an important Practice Direction, which stressed the limits on future postponement orders:

> It is necessary to keep a permanent record of such orders for later reference. For this purpose all orders made under s 4(2) must be formulated in precise terms having regard to the decision of *R* v *Horsham Justices ex parte Farquharson* [1982] 2 All ER 269; [1982] QB 762, and orders under both sections must be committed to writing either by the judge personally or by the clerk of the court under the judge's directions. An order must state (a) its precise scope, (b) the time at which it

---

[164] *R* v *Nat West Investment Bank Ltd* (unreported) 11 January 1991 (Central Criminal Court, MacKinnon J.).

[165] *R* v *Rhuddlan JJs ex parte HTV Ltd* [1986] Crim LR 329.

[166] *Observer*, 11 July 1982.

shall cease to have effect, if appropriate, and (c) the specific purpose of making the order.

Courts will normally give notice to the press in some form that an order has been made under either section of the 1981 Act and the court staff should be prepared to answer any enquiry about a specific case, but it is, and will remain, the responsibility of those reporting cases, and their editors, to ensure that no breach of any order occurs and the onus rests with them to make enquiry in any case of doubt.[167]

It is not sufficient, as used to be the practice at the Old Bailey until 1991, to rely on the shorthand writer's note of the order; the order itself must actually be put into writing.[168]

The rule, derived from the decision in the *Leveller* case, that the press can be guilty of contempt only if it publishes in defiance of a specific order applies to postponement orders as well as suppression orders. That this fact is occasionally overlooked by trial judges, as well as by journalists and newspaper lawyers, is demonstrated by an illuminating feature of the reporting of Clive Ponting's trial for breach of the Official Secrets Act. The jury was excluded from court during legal submissions as to whether Ponting had any defence in law to the charges brought against him. The trial judge indicated his view that there was no defence, and that he was minded to direct the jury to convict. He was prevailed upon by the prosecution, after a hurried conference with the DPP in person, to leave the case for the jury to decide. The judge forgot to make a postponement order, and David Leigh, alone of all the reporters in court, published these exchanges in the *Observer*, thereby revealing the judge's real attitude to the defence. The episode is an interesting example of how our 'public watchdogs' are reluctant to slip their leash, even on those rare occasions when it is left unfastened.

Challenging postponement and partial secrecy orders

Judges and magistrates have been tempted into making wide and unnecessary orders because frequently none of the parties before the court opposes them. It is usually defendants who make the application. The prosecution generally either supports it or stands aloof and indifferent. The media interests who are affected and

---

[167] *Practice Direction: (Contempt of Court Act: Reports of Proceedings: Postponement Orders)* [1983] 1 All ER 64. A journalist who inquired about a verdict of a court clerk and who was not told of an order postponing its publication was found not guilty of contempt by Judge David Roberts at Wolverhampton Crown Court: *Guardian*, 25 January 1984.

[168] *R v Nat West Investment Bank*, note 164 above.

who do oppose them are not heard. As the Rampton cases showed, the media themselves must sometimes take action to protect the public right to know.

How can such orders be challenged? There are four ways.

Application for revocation of order
The first is for the media representatives to ask the judge to revoke his or her order. It is unusual for outsiders like journalists to make applications to the trial court, and the Divisional Court has disapproved of the procedure. None the less, practice varies. In the *Rampton* case, in the Guinness trials, in the Nat West/Blue Arrow trials and in an analogous application under the rape restriction provisions[169] counsel were heard on behalf of media interests. The judge almost certainly has a discretion under his inherent jurisdiction to hear the representatives, and it is a sensible and pragmatic solution.

In a case heard by the Divisional Court in 1992 Mr Justice Brooke warned trial judges to show diligence in accommodating the legitimate interests of the media, and to think long and hard before banning contemporaneous reporting of important trials under Section 4(2). The need for any reporting restrictions could be discussed at a preliminary hearing, which should be adjourned if necessary to enable the press to be represented. When the media did not instruct counsel, judges should be prepared to appoint counsel to act as *amicus curiae*.[170]

Publish and be damned
The second (and by far the most risky of the four) is to publish the report in defiance of the order. If the order is made without jurisdiction, it is most unlikely that contempt proceedings would be brought or, if they were, that they would result in any penalty. The risk is in gauging whether a court would subsequently agree that the order was not merely unwise but so badly wrong as to have been made without jurisdiction. This route remains a last option if the circumstances preclude any of the other methods of challenge and the order is blatantly erroneous.

Judicial review
The third way is for the journalist or the publisher to apply to the High Court for judicial review to quash the order. The procedure is the same as described for challenging the continuation of committal reporting restrictions (see p. 325). Again, the court will not come to its own view as to whether the order was right or wrong,

---

[169] *R v Gilligan*, note 144 above.
[170] *A-G v Guardian Newspapers Ltd* (1992) *The Times* 28 February.

but only whether it was lawfully made. This will include judging whether it was an order that any reasonable tribunal could have made. This route is available if the order has been made by a magistrates' court or by the Crown Court when it is hearing an appeal, a committal for sentence or a civil matter. However, nothing relating to a trial on indictment can be judicially reviewed.[171] In *Crook* (see p. 339) the Divisional Court found that because of this the media were barred from using judicial review to challenge secrecy orders erroneously made in the course of a Crown Court trial. This unhappy position led Tim Crook to complain to the European Court of Human Rights at Strasbourg, which, in turn, obliged the Government to provide a statutory right to appeal (see below) but only to the Court of Appeal and not further to the House of Lords. There is some prospect that the Divisional Court will take a more expansive attitude to its jurisdiction than it did in *Crook*, and thereby provide an appellate route to the House of Lords (which lies directly from Divisional Court decisions in criminal matters, and indirectly – via the Court of Appeal – in civil cases). Thus in 1990 it agreed to accept jurisdiction to review a decision to restrict reporting of the identity of a child (a power given by s 39 of the Children and Young Persons Act 1933) on the basis that the decision was not 'relating to a trial on indictment'.[172] The position is, at time of writing, somewhat confused, and may well be resolved by requiring all challenges to decisions to impose or not to impose gag orders to be made under the statutory procedure laid down by s 159 of the Criminal Justice Act 1988.

Appeal
The changes that the Government made to the law as a result of Tim Crook's complaint to Strasbourg were incorporated in s 159 of the Criminal Justice Act 1988. It allows an aggrieved person to appeal against any of the following:

● partial secrecy (s 11) and postponement orders (s 4(2)) made in relation to a trial on indictment (i.e., to a criminal trial at a Crown Court);
● any order restricting the access of the public to the whole or any part of a trial on indictment or any ancillary proceedings;
● any order restricting the publication of any report of the whole or any part of a trial on indictment or ancillary proceedings.

This new avenue of appeal extends beyond Contempt Act orders.

---

[171] Supreme Court Act 1981 s 29(3).
[172] *R* v *Leicester Crown Court ex parte S* (1990) *The Independent*, 12 December, following *R* v *Central Criminal Court ex parte Randle and Pottle* (1990) 92 Cr App R 323.

It would include, for instance, orders restricting the publication of the identity of young witnesses or parties; orders under the Official Secrets Act requiring part of the trial to be in camera; and orders under the common-law power to conduct part of the trial in the absence of the public where the administration of justice is said to demand it. Arguably, the public's access to part of the trial is also restricted if the court accepts evidence (e.g., a name or an address) in writing that is not read aloud.

There are, however, important limitations on this new route. It is not a *right* of appeal. Leave must first be obtained from the Court of Appeal. Because it applies only to criminal cases tried by juries, it is powerless to correct the decisions of magistrates or civil courts that, though wrong, are not so wrong as to be unreasonable or otherwise amenable to judicial review. It is also unusual in that the Court of Appeal has the last word. There is no further appeal to the House of Lords. Despite these qualifications, it is an important reform, which provides a long-needed avenue for curbing the proliferation of exclusion, secrecy and postponement orders.

Where the Crown Court has made an order restricting reporting, the application for leave to appeal must be made within fourteen days (although there is power to extend this). The application will need to set out the case fully because it can be determined without a hearing. If leave is granted the Court of Appeal can take evidence, but this will normally be in writing.[173] The court will not hesitate to quash an order even though its force has long since been spent. In *Re Central Television plc* the order banning television and radio reports had applied for only one night, while the jury was at a hotel. Six months later, when the appeal was heard by the Court of Appeal, it ruled that s 159 could not provide an effective remedy unless it could be used to reverse spent orders, which might otherwise appear to have been made properly.

Appeals against an in-camera hearing on national security grounds or for the protection of a witness's identity are highly unsatisfactory. The rules allow only twenty-four hours for an application for leave to appeal (although a precautionary notice can be set down in advance). In these cases both the leave application and the appeal itself are determined without a hearing.[174] It is inconceivable that Parliament intended the new right of appeal to be so restricted.

There are many situations where public access is restricted to a trial or its ancilliary proceedings that are not covered by these regulations. There is, therefore, no prescribed time for appealing

---

[173] Criminal Appeal Rules 16A added by Criminal Appeal Amendment Rules 1989 (S I 1989 No 1102).

against such orders (although a long delay would make the Court of Appeal unwilling to allow the appeal). The press would have the usual right of an appellant to argue orally as to why leave should be granted and why the appeal itself should be allowed.

The first case to be brought by the media under its new right to challenge Crown Court secrecy was an application by, appropriately enough, Tim Crook, the Old Bailey newshound whose persistence in taking his case to Strasbourg had forced the government to concede a right of appeal.

> Two Old Bailey judges had decided to exclude the public and the press while they considered matters relating to juries. One was a prosecution application that the jury should be seated so that its members could not be seen from the public gallery, presumably because it was feared that relatives or friends of the particular defendants would make attempts to 'nobble' jurors whom they could identify. In the second case, the judge decided to sit in chambers to consider the fitness of a particular juror to continue with jury service. Obviously, the first matter was sensitive, and an s 4(2) order would have been required to postpone reporting of allegations prejudicial to the defendants, although the second case related to the general administration of justice and could quite unobjectionably have been conducted in open court. The Court of Appeal declined to fault either judge, and approved the procedure (which is inimical to the open-justice principle) whereby secrecy applications are themselves made in secret, with no right of subsequent media access to the transcript. It rejected an argument that the judge should have considered allowing the press to remain in court subject to an s 4(2) postponement order.

However, the court did formulate two important principles:

- A judge should adjourn into chambers only where he has a positive reason for believing that this is an appropriate course, and

---

[174] ibid., r16B. A prosecutor or defendant who intends to apply for an in-camera order on grounds of national security or for the protection of a witness must give seven days' notice to the Crown Court before the start of the trial, and a copy of the notice should be displayed forthwith by court officials in a prominent place within the precincts of the court. This will give the press some advance notice that an application is to be made and an opportunity to prepare for any necessary appeal. The application will normally be considered after the defendant has made his plea but before the jury is sworn. If the application is successful, the trial must be adjourned for a minimum of twenty-four hours to allow for an appeal against the decision. The adjournment will continue until any appeal is disposed of (Crown Court Rules 1982 r 24A as added by SI 1989 No 1103). A trial judge should not use the inherent power of the court to sit in camera to circumvent a failure to comply with these provisions (*R v Middlesex Crown Court ex parte Godwin* (1990) *The Independent*, 15 October).

- once in chambers he must resume sitting in open court 'as soon as it emerges that the need to exclude the public is not plainly necessary.'[175]

These rules do not go far enough to protect the open-justice principle. The only exception allowed by *Scott* v *Scott* – the rare occasion where justice cannot be done at all if it is done in public – needs further entrenchment, perhaps by a rule permitting the press to have access to the transcript of a chambers hearing at a future date to be determined by the judge. In one much-publicized case shortly before the media right to appeal came into effect, a notorious criminal named Garner persuaded a judge to hear evidence from his defence witness – the controversial Scotland Yard detective Inspector Lundy – in chambers. It was said to relate to criminals upon whom Garner had informed, and from whom (once this information was made public) he feared reprisals. The detective's evidence was heard in closed court and not subsequently released to the press. David Leigh, however, obtained a transcript, from which it appeared that no criminal had, in fact, been identified, but that matters of considerable public interest relating to the conduct of the detective had been exposed. The *Observer* took the risk of publishing the evidence on the basis that, if it were subsequently prosecuted for contempt, it could show that the decision to go into closed court had been made under a misapprehension. The Attorney-General declined to prosecute. This example shows the importance of establishing a procedure whereby an appeal court can scrutinize the transcript of what has gone on behind closed doors, and determine whether it should be released to the press.

Gathering Information

There is more to a trial than meets the eye or catches the ear. What is said in open court is only the tip of an iceberg of investigation, documentation and analysis that goes into the preparation of a case for trial. If the accused pleads guilty, the prosecution counsel will provide a brief outline of the facts to help the judge decide on the appropriate sentence. In murder cases the judge has no discretion and must impose a life sentence, but the Lord Chief Justice has directed that a similar summary should nevertheless be given so that the public can know at least the outline of the offence.[176] This brief outline may give no more than a smattering of the hundreds

---

[175] *Re Crook's Appeal* [1991] 93 Cr App R 17 CA.
[176] *Practice Direction* [1968] 2 All ER 144.

of pages of witness statements and documentary exhibits. Even in a lengthy and contested trial there will be interesting material not put in evidence – because it is tangential to the charges or legally inadmissible. In civil cases judges may prefer to read important documents in their spare time rather than to have them tediously read out, word for word. Journalists and authors covering a particular trial will naturally wish to have access to this class of material. In British law very little of it can be obtained by right, although when in a civil trial witness statements have been exchanged in advance, they come into the public domain when they stand at trial as the witness's evidence in chief. Accordingly, the solicitor to the party calling the witness should make available copies of the statement for the press and public.[177]

These limited rights stand in contrast to the position in the United States, where the media have the right to inspect the 'court record', which includes all matters produced in evidence, and under the Freedom of Information Act all prosecution documents, even in spying cases, must eventually be disclosed.[178] In a 1981 anti-corruption operation (known as Abscam) the FBI filmed leading politicians accepting bribes. The videotapes were the backbone of several prosecutions and the federal courts acknowledged that television stations had a right to transmit copies of the film.[179] The Supreme Court would similarly have allowed the Nixon tape recordings to be broadcast, but for a special statute dealing with presidential materials.[180] Although the American press has a privileged constitutional status, these cases did not depend on it. The courts looked back to the common-law principle of open justice and saw the copying and supplying of all prosecution evidence to the media for publication as a natural and logical corollary.

Tape-recording

The right to attend court includes the right to take notes of what is said there. This applies to the public as well as to the press, although court officials will sometimes (wrongfully) try to stop those in the public gallery from putting pen to paper.

It is only recently that the law has grudgingly recognized the invention of the tape recorder. The Contempt of Court Act 1981 bans the use of tape recorders unless the leave of the court has been obtained.[181] The judge has a discretion to give or withhold

---

[177] *Practice Statements: Witness Statements* (1989) *The Independent*, 28 August.
[178] James Michael, *The Politics of Secrecy*, Penguin, 1982.
[179] *National Broadcasting Company Inc* v *Meyers* 635 F2d 945 (1980).
[180] *US* v *Mitchell, Appeal of Warner Communications* 551 F2d 1252 (1976).
[181] 1981 Act s 9.

leave, but in the House of Lords debates the Lord Chancellor envisaged that it would normally be given and that regular court reporters would be given indefinite, if revocable, permission.[182] A Practice Direction for the High Court and Court of Appeal, and a Home Office circular for magistrates have given guidance on when permission should be granted.[183] Each lays down that there is no objection in principle to the use of tape recorders, and applications from the press and broadcasting institutions should be given sympathetic consideration.[184] The court must, however, take into account disturbance from noisy machines, and may attach conditions to its permission. The House of Lords in its judicial capacity has not issued any equivalent guidelines and the first application there (by Christopher Price at the hearing of the GLC cheap-fares appeal) was turned down. Permission for the media to tape-record an inquest was given by coroner Philip Gill at the Helen Smith inquest in December 1982.[185] In addition to the ordinary penalties for contempt a journalist or any other person who uses or intends to use a tape recorder that he or she has brought into court stands to forfeit the machine and any used tapes.[186]

Even where leave is granted, the tape cannot be broadcast. It is contempt of court subsequently to play the recording in the hearing of the public or a section of the public.[187] The Practice Direction recommends that a court giving permission should remind the user of this.

Transcripts and skeleton arguments

Whenever the High Court or Court of Appeal is sitting, official shorthand writers will take a note of the proceedings. They have a statutory right to use tape recorders, although the tapes are transcribed only on request.[188] The rules allow (but do not require) the sale of transcripts to people, like journalists, who are not parties to the action.[189] When shorthand writers have refused to provide

---

[182] Hansard HL Vol 416 col 383.
[183] [1981] 3 All ER 848. The Lord Chancellor has extended it to county courts – (1981) *The Times*, 9 December. See *Justice of the Peace*, 12 September 1981, p. 553.
[184] The circulars, but not the Practice Direction, speak of 'accredited' representatives.
[185] Elaine Potter, 'Going on Trial Off the Record', *The Sunday Times*, 5 December 1982.
[186] Contempt of Court Act 1981 s 9(3). This happened at Horseferry Road Magistrates' Court when a member of the public was spotted recording his wife's committal proceedings: (1981) *The Times*, 4 December.
[187] ibid., s 9(1)(*b*). It would also be wrong to use the tape to coach waiting witnesses in what to say in order to be consistent.
[188] Contempt of Court Act 1981 s 9(4).

transcripts, applications have been made to the Lord Chief Justice. Rupert Furneaux was allowed to have a transcript of the trial of Gunther Podola, but Ludovic Kennedy was wrongfully refused one for his book on Dr Stephen Ward.[190] Even when offered for sale, transcripts are expensive items – up to £400 for a day's proceedings. No official shorthand note is kept of other courts, such as magistrates' or county courts. Disputes as to what was said are often insoluble because of the inadequacy of the note taken by the court clerk or judge. It is these difficulties that increase the demand for tape recordings not only by journalists but by the parties themselves.[191]

The Court of Appeal asks barristers to produce in advance outlines or 'skeletons' of their arguments and legal submissions. It has asked counsel to produce an extra copy for the press (except when reporting is restricted).[192]

Court records

The public has access to High Court writs, but not to other pleadings or affidavits filed in court (see p. 354). Judgments and orders made by the High Court and Court of Appeal are also a matter of public record if they are given in open court.[193] There is a record of steps taken and orders made in bankruptcy and winding-up proceedings, which is open to public inspection,[194] although the registrar of the Companies Court may refuse access if he 'is not satisfied as to the propriety of the purpose for which inspection is required'. In this case the inquirer has the right to appeal against the ban forthwith and *ex parte* to a judge.[195] There is no American-style right to inspect the High Court file, and journalists who wish to inspect expert reports often ordered by the court must make an application to the court. Obtaining access to court files by deceit or trickery is a punishable contempt.[196]

When High Court judges give reasons for their decisions orally, the text is embargoed until the judge has finished speaking. The BBC was reproved in 1983 for quoting the advance text on its new

[189] Rules of Supreme Court Order 68 r 1(2). Except in divorce and nullity cases, where leave of the court is needed: Matrimonial Causes Rules 1977 r 53(7).
[190] Ludovic Kennedy, *The Trial of Stephen Ward*, Gollancz, 1964, Preface; Rupert Furneaux, *Gunther Podola: A Crime Documentary*, Stevens, 1960, Acknowledgements.
[191] Potter, 'Going on Trial Off the Record', note 185 above.
[192] *Lombard North Central plc* v *Pratt* (1989) 139 NLJ 1709, CA.
[193] Rules of the Supreme Court Order 63 r 4.
[194] Insolvency Rules 1986, (SI 1986 No 1925) r 7.27, 7.28.
[195] ibid., r 7.28(2).
[196] *Dobson* v *Hastings* (1991) *The Independent*, 12 November (the Vice-Chancellor).

bulletin before the judge had finished speaking.[197] House of Lords judges, in theory, give 'speeches' rather than 'judgments', but Parliament's time is too precious for these to be actually delivered. Printed copies are delivered to the parties and sold to the press as their lordships go through the motions of adopting the majority views. Practice in the Court of Appeal varies, though there is some trend towards adopting the Lords' procedure.[198] Transcripts of all Court of Appeal decisions are kept in the Supreme Court Library. In 1985 *The Sunday Times* retained a barrister to analyse them in order to pinpoint those circuit judges with the worst record when their decisions went to appeal. When the authorities discovered the purpose of his research, they refused him further access to the records. This attitude, by the Lord Chancellor's department, can be described only as churlish and contrary to the public interest.

There is a privatized central register of county court judgments involving sums in excess of £10 that are outstanding more than one month. This can be inspected by the public [199] or a search can be commissioned. Magistrates are more secretive. The registers on which their clerks record the courts' decisions are not public documents, and only the justices themselves or their nominees have a right of access to them.[200] This secrecy is indefensible. When a proposal was made to open the register to inspection, the only argument against it was advanced by the *Magistrate*, on the grounds that 'it would allow neighbours to pry on each other and unearth old convictions as well as causing much extra work for court staff'.[201] A Home Office circular now recommends that magistrates' courts arrange to provide a copy of the court register to the local news media, albeit charging the economic cost of doing so.[202]

Writs, pleadings and affidavits

Pleadings are the documents that are exchanged by parties to civil proceedings. They set out formally their respective contentions. They are allegations only and do not include supporting evidence. This is normally given orally at the trial, but in some proceedings,

---

[197] *A-G* v *Able* [1984] 1 All ER 277.
[198] *Practice Note (Court of Appeal: New Procedure)* [1982] 3 All ER 376, 378.
[199] Register of County Court Judgment Regulations 1985 (SI 1985 No 1807). The Register is kept by Registry Trust Ltd at 173/5 Cleveland Street, London W1P 5PE (telephone 071 380 0133). Admiralty and equity judgments and administration orders are no longer registered, although pre-1985 ones are preserved. 'Judgment' does not include a *Tomlin* order staying the proceedings on agreed terms.
[200] Magistrates' Court Rules 1981 r 66(12).
[201] *Magistrate*, October 1969, p. 144.
[202] Home Office Circular 80/1989.

particularly pre-trial applications, evidence is received in written form as an affidavit on oath or as a solemn affirmation. Unlike testimony in court, an affidavit or affirmation can include information that the maker has learnt from others. It is usually accepted without cross-examination.

Pre-trail publication of pleadings and affidavits is not by itself contempt.[203] Since almost all civil cases are tried by a judge alone, it is extremely unlikely that he would be affected by publication of documents that he will anyway have to read at the trial.[204]

In extreme cases the High Court can exercise its inherent power to restrict publicity or use of affidavits outside the litigation. However, there is a heavy onus on the party seeking the restriction to show that without it the documents would be improperly used.[205] Libel is a greater hazard. No privilege will attach to documents that have not been read in open court, and a publisher must consider carefully whether they are defamatory and, if so, whether there is a defence to an action for libel.

Although pleadings and affidavits are filed in court, the parties alone are entitled to see them.[206] The public and the press have a right to see only the writ or other document that started the litigation.[207] Often these have just an uninformative statement of the order that the plaintiff wants the court to make. Sometimes the writ will include a more detailed statement of the plaintiff's claim, which journalists then also have a right to inspect. Should the court office refuse to allow access, the right can be enforced by an application to the High Court for judicial review.[208]

Discovered documents

Before trial
In the course of most civil litigation the parties must disclose to each other all the documents in their possession that are relevant to the case. The obligation is a broad one, and a document must be listed and produced however damning it is to the case of the party disclosing it. In a very limited category of cases a party can plead privilege from discovery. It is not necessary, for instance, for parties

---

[203] *Re F (a minor: Publication of Information)* [1977] 1 All ER 114.
[204] *Gaskell and Chambers* v *Hudson and Dodsworth and Co* [1936] 2 KB 595.
[205] *Esterhuysen* v *Lonrho plc* (1989) *The Times*, 29 May, CA.
[206] The court can grant leave to inspect any other document on its file (Rules of the Supreme Court Order 63 r 4(1)(c)), although it is likely to require particularly compelling reasons to persuade it to do so (Supreme Court Practice 1991 para 63/4/1).
[207] Rules of the Supreme Court Order 63 r 4.
[208] *Ex parte Associated Newspapers* [1959] 3 All ER 878.

to show to the other side correspondence with their lawyers. Public-interest immunity can be claimed for government documents that are particularly sensitive. The fact that a document is confidential is not enough for it to be privileged, and some litigants settle their cases rather than show their most private papers to their opponents or have them read aloud in a public court.

Although this potential for publicity is inherent in discovery, the law will normally protect the confidentiality of the documents unless and until they are used in court. The recipient of the documents impliedly undertakes to the court not to use them for any purpose other than one related to the litigation in question. But, as with other confidential documents there may be an important reason for publicizing their contents that outbalances the normal duty. In the course of the thalidomide litigation *The Sunday Times* bought some of the documents produced by Distillers on discovery, which had also been given to a research chemist who had been retained as an expert witness for the injured children. The court enjoined the paper from making any further use of the documents. The paper's argument that the story was important was accepted, but the court did not agree that the public interest in publication was so great that the ordinary confidence could be broken.[209] *The Sunday Times* could be restrained only because it *knew* that the documents had been produced on discovery. If the paper had received them anonymously with no suggestion of their origin, its chance of defeating the injunction would have been much greater.

Again, English concepts of free expression lag behind those in the United States, where discovered documents are considered part of the public record and are in the public domain from the time that they are produced. The courts can make 'protective orders' restricting the use of documents, but this is recognized as an exceptional interference with the free speech of lawyer and litigant, and requires substantial justification.[210]

After trial
The extent to which discovered documents may be shown to the media by an opposing party was the subject of a controversial decision in the case of *Home Office v Harman*.[211]

> Harriet Harman, solicitor for the National Council for Civil Liberties, conducted an action on behalf of a prisoner who alleged that his confinement in a 'control unit' was illegal. The Home Office was forced to disclose embarrassing internal memoranda about the setting

---

[209] *Distillers Co (Biochemicals) Ltd* v *Times Newspapers Ltd* [1975] 1 All ER 41.
[210] *In Re Halkin* 598 F2d 176 (DC CA 1979).
[211] [1982] 1 All ER 532, HL.

up of such units. These were read out in open court during the four-week trial. Journalist David Leigh approached her at the end of the trial and was shown copies of the discovered documents, which he quoted in an article attacking the Home Office prison policy. The House of Lords narrowly decided, by 3–2, that Ms Harman's action was a contempt in that she, as a solicitor, was bound by the obligation to use discovered documents only for the purposes of the litigation. Leigh could have sat through the trial and taken notes or purchased an expensive transcript, but he could not be assisted by direct access to the documents themselves. The impracticabilities of these alternatives for the working journalist were recognized in the minority opinion, which regarded the ruling as a breach of the freedom of communication guaranteed by the European Convention.

The European Commission on Human Rights found this a prima facie breach of Article 10 (freedom of expression). Had the government chosen to take the case to the European Court, the response would have been similar to that in the *Weber* judgment in 1990. A campaigning environmentalist had been punished by the Swiss courts for disclosing details of judicial proceedings held in private, and the court found this to be a violation of Article 10 – in part because the material was already public knowledge.[212] A friendly settlement of the *Harman* case was reached with the Government and Rules of Court now provide:

> Any undertaking whether express or implied, not to use a document for any purposes other than those of the proceedings in which it is disclosed shall cease to apply to such a document after it has been read to or by the court, or referred to, in open court, unless the court for special reasons has otherwise ordered on the application of a party or of the person to whom the document belongs.[213]

The undertaking ceases even if the document is not actually read aloud in court as long as it has been 'read by the court, or referred to, in open court'.[214] The new rule came into effect on 1 October 1987 and does not apply to documents used in court before that date.[215]

Some affidavits are covered by the *Harman* rule because they are

---

[212] *Weber* case (10/1989/170/226) European Court of Human Rights 22 May 1990, Series A No. 177.
[213] Rules of Supreme Court Order 24, rule 14A.
[214] *Derby and Co Ltd* v *Weldon* (1988) *The Independent*, 20 October ChD; some discovered documents that were included in affidavits were in turn, included in a bundle of documents for the Court of Appeal. They were 'referred to in open court'.
[215] *Bibby Bulk Carriers Ltd* v *Cansulex Ltd* [1988] 2 All ER 532.

the method by which a litigant is required to make discovery (discovery of assets or income is often ordered by affidavit). However, other affidavits are not restricted and journalists should beware of unwarranted attempts to rely on *Harman* as an excuse for not allowing access to them. The filing of certain affidavits may be necessary for litigants to continue their fight, but *this* type of compulsion does not attract the *Harman* protection.[216] Similarly, the reports of potential expert witnesses that litigants exchange are *not* subject to the implied obligation since it is ultimately for the parties to decide whether or not to call experts. On the other hand, when the court orders a pre-trial exchange of other witness statements, the *Harman* rule *does* apply. This is because rules of court specifically restrict the use to which these documents can be put.[217]

Documents in criminal proceedings

The principal documents involved in criminal proceedings will be the statements or depositions of prosecution witnesses that are used at the committal hearings. They cannot be published as part of a report of the committal unless reporting restrictions have been lifted (see p. 325). If, after a committal at which restrictions were lifted, the prosecution gives notice of additional evidence, this can be publicized. However, because the evidence was not given in open court, no privilege will attach to it and a newspaper must consider another possible defence if it is defamatory.

The decision to publish other, leaked documents, may involve a nice balancing of political consequences. For example, on the morning before the trial of four anarchists opened in 1979, the *Guardian* published a confidential prosecution memorandum about potential jurors – a document prepared from police files for the purpose of 'vetting' the jury. It contained the gossip now routinely recorded on police files about citizens whose relations had been in trouble, who lived in squats and who had made complaints against the police. The trial judge angrily discharged the jury and urged the Attorney-General to prosecute the newspaper for contempt – presumably because its revelation that police had invaded their privacy might bias jurors against the prosecution. No action was taken, the Attorney perhaps concluding that the police action had been rather more upsetting than the newspaper's revelation of it.[218] Nor was action taken against London Weekend Television when one of its programmes revealed that the foreman of a 'vetted' jury in the 'ABC' Official Secrets case was an ex-member of the SAS

---

[216] *Derby and Co Ltd* v *Weldon (No 2)* (1988) *The Independent* November.
[217] *Prudential Assurance Co Ltd* v *Fountain Page Ltd* [1991] 3 All ER 878.
[218] David Leigh, *The Frontiers of Secrecy*, Junction Books, 1980, p. 171.

(see p. 417), an outfit that the defendant journalists had regularly criticized. The trial was stopped as a result of this disclosure, but contempt proceedings, which might well have succeeded, would have been highly embarrassing to an Attorney-General already under attack for approving jury-vetting. These cases illustrate the extra-legal considerations that give the media a tenuous freedom to publish more than the strict letter of the law would allow.

Photographs and sketches

Other forms of recording apart from note taking and tape-recording are prohibited by s 41 of the Criminal Justice Act 1925. It is an offence to take any photograph or to make with a view to publication a sketch of any juror, witness, party or judge in the courtroom, the court building or its precincts. The offence can be committed even though the photographer or artist is standing outside and well clear of the court if the subject of the snap or sketch is entering or leaving the court. It is also an offence to publish such a photograph or sketch. The ban applies to civil and criminal proceedings.

The extent of this embargo has never been authoritatively decided. Parties and witnesses have always been photographed in significant cases as they enter or leave the court building, and no exception has been taken to this practice until 1989, when the Recorder of London directed that photographers, should not lay in wait in Old Bailey, the street that runs alongside the Central Criminal Court. This ruling was not tested, (the Recorder retired, and the photographers returned) and is too wide: 'precinct' strictly means the space enclosed by the walls or outer boundary of a court building (i.e. the court yard) rather than public streets or highways surrounding court. No exception has ever been taken to television and stills photographers standing on the public footpath outside the High Court, although it is understandable that judges should be concerned about media circuses at the gates of criminal courts, which witnesses and jurors may find intimidating. The open-justice principle would seem to imply the media's right to photograph defendants and witnesses as they turn up for a public trial, although any attempts to photograph jurors would probably lead to a prosecution.

The above approach is supported by the Court of Appeal decision in *R* v *Runting*:[219]

> Runting was a photographer for the *Sun* newspaper. He was charged with contempt of court for his efforts to snap a camera-shy defendant, commencing as he emerged from court and continuing for some

---

[219] *R* v *Runting* [1989] Crim LR 282.

minutes as he made a dash for the nearest tube station, colliding with a lamppost in his flight. The Court of Appeal quashed Runting's conviction: although his behaviour caused inconveniences, it did not amount to 'molestation' sufficient to form the basis of a contempt charge. The court warned photographers against hindering, jostling, 'threatening with persistent following' and assaulting defendants and witnesses as they go to or from court. Significantly, however, it made no reference to s 41, and appeared to accept that photographing defendants as they emerged from court would be lawful in the absence of intimidating conduct.

If the sketch is a doodle made by someone in court but *not* with a view to publication, then a newspaper that obtains and publishes it would not commit the statutory offence. Commissioned sketches of courtroom incidents often appear in the press and on television. Those that are drawn from memory are unobjectionable. The Press Council has recognized a long-standing tradition of such sketches being published.[220] Even drawings deliberately made in court for publication rarely attract a prosecution – perhaps because the sketches are flattering, perhaps because the maximum fine is only £400. In 1986 a solicitor's wife was fined £100 for photographing a judge in court.[221] Photography that disturbs the court's proceedings (e.g. by use of flash) might also be contempt of court, for which heavier penalties can be imposed.

Television and the courts

Section 41 has also effectively precluded televising the courts. In 1977 the BBC wished to include footage of a consistory court (see p. 373) sitting in a village church as part of a documentary on rural life. The parties approved, as publicity of Church court proceedings had in the past brought in sorely needed cash, but the judge ruled that s 41 prevented filming of the actual proceedings.[222] He referred to the 'necessary privacy' of judicial proceedings, but this was at odds with the principle of open justice, and the 'pressures, embarrassment and discomfiture' that he wished to spare the participants are, in any event, experienced by a witness awaiting cross-examination.

These traditional arguments against televising the courts were

---

[220] Adjudication on complaints against *The Sunday Times* over publication of a sketch of the jury in the Thornton Heath murder case (1982) *The Times*, 13 December.

[221] (1980) *The Times*, 15 July cited by Miller, *Contempt of Court*, 2nd edn, Oxford University Press, 1989, p. 131.

[222] *Re St Andrews* [1977] 3 WLR 286 Salisbury Consistory Court, Judge Ellison Chancellor.

convincingly refuted by the Report of the Royal Commission into arms shipments to Colombian drug cartels.[223] This Commission was televised throughout its sittings in Antigua, and extracts were screened in the United Kingdom. The Royal Commissioner concluded that the public and professional benefits of media coverage were 'incalculable': it discouraged time-wasting and irrelevance and enabled the public to make up its own mind about the testimony. The proceedings were in no way disrupted by a single, discreetly placed television camera, and the witnesses were in no way disquietened. The report accepted that electronic media coverage of criminal trials 'requires careful and gradual introduction', but hoped that it would become routine for public inquiries (which are beyond the scope of s 41 – see p. 381).

Dramatic reconstructions of courtroom dramas are unaffected by s 41. *The Trials of Oz* were relived in the West End by the Royal Shakespeare Company after the verdict but before the appeal and the BBC made a dramatized documentary of the *Gay News* trial, mainly from court transcripts. When the director of *The Romans in Britain* was charged with procuring an act of indecency (see p. 144), public readings were given each evening of that day's proceedings at the Oxford Playhouse. This neither offended s 41 nor (in the absence of prejudicial comment) could it constitute contempt.

Channel 4 has taken the lead in exploring the possibilities of contemporaneous television coverage of major trials. There are no difficulties in transmitting a 'dramatic reconstruction' once the proceedings have concluded, and it is difficult to comprehend how jurors would be prejudiced by hearing evidence spoken by actors on television when they have already heard it delivered by witnesses in the courtroom, and can read it in summary form in the morning newspapers. None the less, Channel 4 was not allowed by the Ponting trial judge to employ actors for their nightly *Court Report* of the trial – they had to be replaced by a panel of news-readers, whose presentation of the evidence the judge found unexceptional. Ironically, the very experienced producer of the programme had chosen to use actors precisely because they could be directed to avoid imparting emotion or conceivably prejudicial mannerisms to the script; news-readers were more liable to impart drama to the 'parts' they were playing.

It is difficult to defend Britain's absolute prohibition on the broadcasting of legal proceedings. Many states in America permit both radio and television coverage of the courtroom. After initial doubts, there is now an acceptance that the result has been to make

---

[223] The report of the Royal Commissioner, Louis Blom-Cooper QC, is published by Duckworth on behalf of the Government of Antigua and Barbuda, as *Guns for Antigua*, 1990; see pp. 44–6.

the judiciary better behaved, the advocates better prepared and the public better informed. The danger of distracting witnesses has not materialized. Even if it may be thought unseemly to broadcast the highlights of notorious criminal trials, this objection does not apply to appeal hearings. Until cameras are allowed in the courtroom, the media will have to make do with 'dramatic reconstructions' of trials after they have taken place.

In principle, if every court in the land is open to every subject of the King, does it not logically follow that subjects should be entitled, quite literally, to see justice done through the medium of television? The communications revolution can bring benefits to justice, and we are beginning to accept the advantages of videotaped testimony of child witnesses and the possibility of cross-examining overseas witnesses via satellite link-up. Appeal courts would be better able to evaluate the testimony of trial witnesses if they could see and hear it being delivered, and most barristers have had occasion to regret that they could not include in grounds of appeal against judges' summings-up some reference to prejudical tones of voice or body language, which are not apparent from a typed transcript.

The danger of course, is that witnesses may prove camera-shy and that television's coverage of the day's play in a sensational Old Bailey trial will feature heavily edited 'highlights' chosen for entertainment value rather than as fair and accurate reporting. None the less, the public is genuinely interested in significant court cases, and the arguments in favour of open justice apply with even greater force to aural or visual coverage. Present television news reporting, in sixty-second 'slots' with breathless presenters pictured outside court quoting snatches of evidence, sometimes over inaccurate 'artists' impressions' of the courtroom, is of minimal value. When Channel 4 launched its *Court Report* programme, on which news-readers read large slabs of the day's transcript in the Ponting trial for half an hour on every evening of the three-week trial, over 500,000 viewers watched every edition. There would seem to be little objection to radio coverage of important appellate proceedings, but the BBC has been refused permission to go even this far.

Protection from Libel

One great attraction of court reporting is that it is virtually immune from actions for libel, whatever the gravity of the allegations bandied about in the courtroom and republished in the media. They do not have to be defended on grounds of justification or fair comment: they are privileged so long as the report is reasonably fair and accurate.

Absolute privilege

The privilege defence is discussed in Chapter 2. Absolute privilege is a complete defence, irrespective of the malice of the newspaper in publishing the account. It is granted by s 3 of the Law of Libel Amendment Act 1888,[224] which provides that 'a fair and accurate report in any newspaper of proceedings publicly heard before any court exercising judicial authority shall if published contemporaneously with such proceedings be privileged.'

Although Parliament in 1888 believed it was granting only qualified privilege (i.e. a privilege lost if the publication is malicious) to court reporting, the section has been consistently interpreted as conferring a privilege that is absolute.[225] In 1952 it was extended to radio and television[226] and in 1984 to cable programmes. In 1990 the Broadcasting Act extended the privilege further to any programme service.

To attract absolute or even qualified privilege, the report must be 'fair and accurate'. The privilege is not lost if the inaccuracy is minor – 'trifling slips' are to be expected.[227] But major errors – such as reporting a contentious piece of evidence from a particular witness as though it were a proven fact, or recounting an incorrect charge or the wrong verdict – will lose the protection. Erroneous headlines composed by sub-editors who were not in court and have not understood the copy are a familiar danger. The proceedings must have been held in public, but the privilege applies whether or not both parties are present or whether an application (such as for a warrant or a summons) is made by one in the absence of the other.[228] Only words spoken in open court are covered by the privilege. Reporters taking their notes from a charge sheet, court list or other documents are at risk if magistrates deviate from the text.[229] It is partly to give the media the full protection of this privilege that the Home Office has told justices to be sure to identify defendants by reading aloud their names and addresses.[230]

The question of 'fairness' is more difficult. The guiding principle

---

[224] This was sponsored by Sir Algernon Borthwick MP who, as editor of the *Morning Post*, had been successfully sued for a libellous court report: Marjorie Jones, 'The Relationship Between the Criminal Courts and the Mass Media' in Colin Sumner (ed.), *Crime & Justice*, Cropwood Conference Series, 1982, p. 88.

[225] *Farmer* v *Hyde* [1937] 1 KB 728 at pp. 740, 744; see *Gatley on Libel and Slander*, 8th edn, Sweet & Maxwell, 1981, para 631.

[226] Defamation Act 1952 s 9(2).

[227] *Kimber* v *Press Association* [1893] 1 QB 65.

[228] ibid.

[229] *Furniss* v *Cambridge Daily News Ltd* (1907) 23 TLR 705, CA; *Harper* v *Provincial Newspapers Ltd* (1937) SLT 462.

[230] Home Office circulars 78/1967: 50/1969, approved in *R* v *Evesham Justices ex parte McDonagh*, note 151 above.

is that reports should be impartial, carrying some account of both sides of the case. The exigencies of both the courts and newspapers make this a counsel of perfection. Trials can last for weeks or months, and often all the evidence given on a particular day will be in support of one side only. Additionally, the space available for court reports is limited. The most workable test is whether the report, as published, gives a reasonable impression of the proceedings thus far. Concentration on one sensational aspect of a witness's evidence in chief, without reference to a significant retraction made under cross-examination, could amount to a serious misrepresentation of the proceedings. Reporters are present with their privileges in the courtroom as representatives of the public; if, by calculated selection or omission they give an impression of the proceedings that no fair-minded member of the public could have formed in their place, the report will lose both absolute and qualified privilege under the statute, and the qualified privilege that remains at common law will be open to challenge for malice.

The likelihood, of course, is that it will not be challenged; defendants cannot obtain legal aid for libel and will, in any event, be reluctant to revive matters that had led them into the dock in the first place. The best solution when court reporters err is for the lawyers involved in the case to mention the mistake in open court the following day. If there is no dispute about the error, the newspaper should be prepared effectively to correct it by reporting the fact that it was drawn to the court's attention. It should not be necessary to use the law of libel to obtain a correction of a matter of public record.

The most unfair aspect of contemporary court reporting is the tendency of reporters to attend the beginning of a trial in order to publish the prosecutor's opening statement, which puts the allegations at their most sensational. The reporters then disappear for several weeks while the allegations are painstakingly questioned and undermined. But the press returns, vulture-like, for the verdict. If there is an acquittal, a newspaper will sometimes not even bother to report it, or will mention the matter without giving it anything like the prominence accorded to the discredited opening statement. This is *not* fair reporting: the original report, at the time it was published, was fair and accurate, but failure to follow it up with a report of the acquittal could retrospectively entail loss of the privilege.[231]

An interesting question is raised by the not uncommon occurrence of 'outbursts' in court – from the public gallery or from the defendant in the dock. Does a report of defamatory statements made by persons with no right to speak attract absolute privilege?

[231] *Wright* v *Outram* (1890) 17 R 596 and *Turner* v *Sullivan* (1862) 6 LT 130.

Old cases suggested that they did not, but a more liberal view was taken in *Hope* v *Leng Ltd*, when absolute privilege was accorded to the report of a shout of 'It's all a pack of lies' from the well of the court during the plaintiff's evidence.[232] The decision could be artificially distinguished on the ground that the disruptor was a witness who had already given evidence and was then still technically under oath, but the court indicated its approval for a wider and more sensible view for the protection of court reporters. Outbursts in court are generally followed by admonitions from the judge; as a matter of common sense, they are part of the 'proceedings' publicly heard before the court, and should therefore attract privilege.

The report must be published 'contemporaneouly'. This does not mean 'immediately', but as soon as reasonably practicable, having regard to the schedules of the newspaper or the broadcasting organization. A daily newspaper would be expected to carry the report on the following day; a fortnightly magazine would not lose the privilege if it published at the next reasonable opportunity, even though it was reporting matters said in court up to two weeks before. Summaries in Sunday newspapers of the events of the week in a long trial would be protected. Oddly, the definition of 'newspaper' includes 'any paper containing public news or occurrences . . . printed for sale . . . at intervals not exceeding 26 days', so absolute privilege cannot be claimed by monthly magazines or by free sheets that are not 'printed for sale.' At the end of a big trial, feature articles and programmes sometimes appear recapitulating parts of the evidence and, in the case of television, even re-enacting aspects of the trial. The protection is not limited to 'day-by-day' proceedings and there seems no reason why it should not extend to cover such accounts of an entire trial, if they are reasonably fair and published as soon as practicable after the verdict. The protection of absolute privilege extends to reports published within reasonable time of the lifting of a postponement order made under the Contempt of Court Act 1981 or of restrictions on reporting committal proceedings.[233]

Qualified privilege

At common law all fair and accurate court reports are protected by qualified privilege. This remains a safety net for coverage that falls

---

[232] (1907) 23 TLR 243; *Farmer* v *Hyde* [1937] 1 KB 728 concerned a heckler's interruption, but, fortunately for the paper, he began 'May I make an application'. He could not, but he was therefore treated as a party. Compare 'Nothing short of perjury' shouted from the gallery and held not privileged: *Lynam* v *Gowring* (1880) 6 LR Ir 259.
[233] 1981 Act s 4. Magistrates' Courts Act 1980, s 8(9). Curiously, there is no comparable provision for postponed reports of preparatory hearings in serious fraud cases.

outside the statutory protection of s 3, because, for example, it is not 'contemporaneous'. The privilege is 'qualified' in the sense that it is lost if the court report is published 'maliciously', i.e. for an improper motive such as to frighten off potential witnesses. Media court reports are unlikely to be deemed malicious, so the protection is for practical purposes as effective as absolute privilege. To enjoy the common-law privilege, the report must still be fair and accurate, and the words must have been spoken in a public court. The criteria for fairness and accuracy are the same as with absolute privilege. The principle is that a reporter is 'entitled to report on the proceedings or that part of it which he selects in a manner which fairly and faithfully gives an impression of the events reported and will convey to the reader what he himself would have appreciated had he been present during the proceedings'.[234]

To attract qualified privilege a report need not be contemporaneous, and it is not limited to newspapers or broadcasting. It is therefore of great significance for authors whose books about famous trials come out months or years after the case is over. It would also protect accounts on Prestel.

---

[234] *Cook* v *Alexander* [1974] 1 QB 279 at p 290 per Buckley LJ.

Chapter 8

Reporting Lesser Courts and Tribunals

There are about five hundred separate types of tribunal that have some of the features of a court, and that make decisions with some legal force and often considerable public interest. A few, such as courts martial and consistory (Church) courts, have powers to punish, and procedures similar to criminal trials. Professional disciplinary bodies cannot jail ethical transgressors, but may fine them or suspend them from practice. Immigration adjudicators affect the fate of families, industrial tribunals decide the rights and wrongs of behaviour in the workplace and deal with allegations of racial and sexual discrimination, while a myriad of assessment bodies decide the level of rates and rents and pensions, and settle disputes over such disparate matters as mines and quarries, performing rights, plant varieties and seeds and VAT. Public inquiries may fix the responsibility for a riot or the site of a new airport, while inquests at coroners' courts sometimes attract as much press attention as a sensational murder trial. The multiplicity of these potentially newsworthy tribunals, and the present uncertainty as to which of them are protected by the laws of contempt, justifies a treatment separate from that accorded to civil and criminal courts.

The bewildering array of tribunals has no simple explanation. In some cases, tradition has prevailed over consistency and even fairness; military courts, for example, have a criminal jurisdiction that inflicts upon members of the armed services an officer-class justice that may be very different from that received by civilians from a jury of their peers. Other tribunals have been established to facilitate the Welfare State, to provide a basis for decision-taking that is fair (in that it allows public arguments from both sides), yet more informal and expeditious than that available from the regular courts. Some tribunals, such as accident inquiries, adopt an inquisitorial model, in the sense that tribunal members themselves call witnesses, interrogate them, expound and test conflicting hypotheses, and then prepare a report examining the different causal theories and making recommendations to avoid similar accidents in the future. Other tribunals exist to make administrative decisions – whether a licence should be renewed, whether an income-tax assessment should be paid and so on. In many other countries the decisions made by British tribunals would be taken, without argument, by state administrators. The 'tribunal', with its quasi-legal procedures, its opportunities for both sides to state a case and to ask questions, is some concession to the concept of natural justice in public administration. Openness is a characteristic of natural justice, and in the absence of a Freedom of Information Act, tribunals and inquiries sometimes do provide important opportunities to scrutinize and oversee the activities of public servants.

'When is a court not a court?' may sound an absurd question, but upon the answer hinge consequences of great importance to the media. For example, magistrates normally sit as a court of law, protected against prior media coverage that might seriously prejudice their deliberations. But when they sit to decide whether to grant liquor licences or whether to withdraw gaming licences, they are in law meeting as administrators, and the law of contempt does not apply. The question of the application of contempt to various tribunals is important and difficult; it will be considered in this chapter after an outline of the characteristics of those lesser courts and tribunals that are most frequently in the news.

Inquests

Inquests can be particularly newsworthy events, as the cases of Helen Smith, Blair Peach, Roberto Calvi, Jimmy Kelly, Liddle Towers, the Deptford fire victims, the SAS killings in Gibraltar, the King's Cross fire disaster and the Lockerbie crash demonstrate. It is easy to liken the attraction of reporters to inquests to the interest of the vulture in the dead body, but the public interest in picking at the circumstances in which a life has been lost is not unworthy or unimportant. Any society that values life must look closely at death. And when death comes unnaturally and unexpectedly – behind the closed doors of police cells or prisons, or in a foreign country, or through the oversight of employers or doctors or public officials – it deserves to be looked at very closely indeed. Some agency is needed that is sufficiently independent and impartial to satisfy the public conscience. Frequently, the only agency in England and Wales that attempts to fill this need is the coroner, and sometimes the coroner's jury, deliberating in a special procedure called an inquest.

In the Middle Ages the office of coroner was created because the king wanted a local official to keep a watchful eye on corrupt sheriffs. The coroner was given the task of inspecting dead bodies to discover the cause of their death – a matter of great financial interest to the king, who would benefit from the estates of the slain. To assist him, in an age long before police forces and medical science, the coroner summoned a jury from the neighbourhood areas. The medieval coroner and his jury would squat around the body – often by a roadside or in a ditch – and look for tell-tale signs of disease or violence or suicide. Pooling their local knowledge, they would often come up with the name of a likely suspect, whom they would present for trial. Although these important functions were taken over by professionals – policemen and doctors and lawyers – the coroner survived, as a public official appointed by local councils to investigate unnatural deaths, receiving a fee for each body inspected. Unlike other local public officials, the coroner, owing to his origin as the king's man, could not effectively be disciplined or removed. In this century the coroners lost most of their powers of criminal inquiry; in cases of suspicious deaths they, in effect, unveil to the public the evidence upon which the police have failed to reach any conclusion.

There are about 25,000 'unnatural' deaths each year, handled by some 200 coroners in different parts of the country. Their task is to determine exactly how the deceased met with death. When this does not become apparent from initial inquiries, they must hold an inquest: a formal investigation, clad in the trappings of a court, to which witnesses may be summoned and examined, ending with a 'verdict', which is officially recorded. In certain limited cases the coroner is obliged to summon a jury: these are cases of deaths in prison, death by poison, or deaths in circumstances 'the continuance or possible recurrence of which is prejudicial to the health or safety of the public or any section of the public'.[1] In 1980 the Court of Appeal compelled the Hammersmith coroner to sit with a jury for the inquest of Blair Peach, a New Zealand teacher who had been killed in the Southall disturbances. The family claimed he had died from a blow inflicted by an instrument wielded by an unidentifiable policeman from the Special Patrol Group. The court agreed that it would be prejudicial to public safety if the police were issued with dangerous weapons, or if senior officers turned a blind eye to their use.[2] Since 1983 any death resulting from injury caused by a police officer must be investigated by a jury.[3]

Inquests are unlike any other judicial proceedings. Coroners need not be lawyers; they may be doctors of at least five years' standing. Unlike lay justices, they do not have the assistance of a

---

[1] Coroners Act 1988 s 8(3)(*d*).
[2] *R v Hammersmith Coroner ex parte Peach* [1980] All ER 7 CA. After protracted proceedings, the police made a payment of £75,000 (without admitting liability) to the family of Blair Peach.
[3] Administration of Justice Act 1982 s 62.

legally trained clerk. The closest equivalent at an inquest is a policeman, who acts as the 'coroner's officer'. This does not help to create an appearance of impartiality where the death is alleged to have been caused by the police. In addition, an inquest does not follow the usual adversarial pattern of most legal proceedings, where the truth is expected to emerge from the clash of opposing evidence and submissions. Instead, the coroner takes the initiative and leads the investigation. An inquest takes place after police investigations, which have been made available to the coroner. But the coroner is not obliged to show material collected by the police to representatives of the interested parties, and many coroners now habitually refuse to give lawyers a sight of the evidence available to them.[4] This means that lawyers are sometimes unprepared for the evidence that the coroner decides to call. It means, too, that at inquests where police misconduct is alleged, the police lawyers will have exclusive access to statements taken by police officers, and so have an unfair advantage.

Coroners cannot behave like impartial judges. They receive and study the police evidence beforehand, usually discuss it privately with the police, and will in most cases have formed a view before the inquest opens. There are coroners who behave like conjurors, putting witnesses into the witness box to make statements that the parties have been given no opportunity to check with other witnesses, or to rebut. The parties and their lawyers are present, as one judge put it, merely as 'guests of the court'.[5]

At inquests, no advocate may address the coroner or the jury on the facts. There are no final speeches. So the jury never hears the contentions of the parties about the cause of death put in a coherent form. This prevents a comprehensive account, a logical theory of the cause of death, from being presented by anyone other than the coroner. Where the evidence is complicated and confusing, the only coherent account that is ever given to the public is provided by the coroner in the summing up. This may be an unsatisfactory account. It may even be, as in the Helen Smith case, a preposterous account.[6] But there can be no alternative.

In cases where coroners sit with juries public esteem for the jury system in criminal courts invests the 'verdict' with a degree of acceptability. But the most recent official inquiry into the coroners'

---

[4] *Ex parte Peach*, note 2 above, and see *The Death of Blair Peach: A Supplementary Report of the Unofficial Inquiry Chaired by Professor Michael Dummett*, NCCL, 1980; and Paul Foot (with Ron Smith), *The Helen Smith Story*, Fontana, 1983, p. 296.

[5] The 'interested parties' who can be represented are now listed in the Coroners' Rules 1984 (SI 1984 No 552).

[6] See *The Helen Smith Story*, pp. 389–96.

system, the Broderick Report, concluded that the role of the coroner's jury today is no more than symbolic.[7] It conceded that the final verdict is usually dictated by the coroner. All the coroner's jury can do is to announce one simple fact: how the deceased met with death. The law requires a narrow answer to a narrow question, but in some cases the public rightly expects much fuller answers to a whole range of questions. Coroners' juries cannot provide these answers – they are not even allowed by law to attempt them. Coroners immediately stop any questions about public-interest issues not specifically relevant to the actual cause of death. Until 1980 a coroner's jury could add a rider to its verdict making recommendations to prevent the recurrence of similar deaths. The Blair Peach jury used this power to make several critical comments about the Special Patrol Group.[8] An amendment to the rules has now taken away this right.[9]

The inquest must be held in open court unless the coroner thinks that it is in the interest of national security to exclude the public.[10] In December 1983 the *Observer* successfully obtained an interim injunction to prevent a coroner holding in camera the inquest on a British businessman who had died in Moscow after expressing fears that his life might be threatened. The Government had denied that the man was a spy and the judge accepted that prima facie there was no reason why the death should not be publicly investigated.

The right for reporters to be present was not won without a struggle. Until 1951 coroners had an almost unfettered discretion to exclude the public and were often particularly tender to the relatives of suicides. Bertha Hall's death in 1887 was a not untypical suicide following an unwanted pregnancy. Atypically, the *East Anglian Daily Times* fought the coroner's ruling to sit in camera. After being physically ejected, its reporter persuaded the jury to go on strike and for ten days they refused to sit without the press. During the First World War the Ministry of Munitions was eager that deaths of poison-gas workers should not be reported in such a way 'as to affect the supply of labour to these processes',[11] and in

---

[7] HMSO, 1971 Cmnd 481.

[8] It recommended that the SPG should be better controlled by its officers, that its relations with local forces should be improved, that no unauthorized weapons should be available at police stations and that regular inspections should be carried out. It also suggested that the police should be provided with maps of the area of a planned demonstration. *The Death of Blair Peach*, p. 47.

[9] Coroners' Rules 1984 (SI 1984 No 552) r 36(2).

[10] ibid., r 17.

[11] Rule 17 of the 1984 Rules overturns the discretion given by the common law in *Garnett* v *Ferrand* (1827) 6 B & C 611. The examples in the text are taken from Public Record Office file HO 45/23968.

the 1930s coroners were ready to investigate railway and aircraft tragedies in private inquests and any coroner today who sought to close the doors of the court would be ordered to re-open them by the High Court.

Documentary evidence will normally be read aloud and an interested party can usually insist that it is, although the coroner does have a discretion to direct that it should be tendered in writing.[12]

The law of contempt has been applied, without any sensible thought, to coroners' courts: their inquisitorial procedures do not, as a matter of principle, require or deserve the suppression of media comment. On the contrary, since the fundamental object of the inquiry is to establish the cause of death, any light that can be shed on this from any source, including the media, should be welcome. This principle was accepted at the Helen Smith inquest: a Thames Television *This Week* documentary, which was transmitted the week before the inquest opened, was re-screened for the benefit of the jury, because it featured interviews with vital witnesses who refused to come to Britain for the coroner's proceedings. The point that inquests are inquisitorial rather than adversarial was overlooked by the Court of Appeal in its haste to ban an LWT documentary about the death in police custody of a black 'Hell's Angel': it used as its pretext the concern that the coroner's jury might be prejudiced, although no jury had been sworn and the inquest stood adjourned indefinitely while police 'investigations' proceeded.[13]

Courts Martial

Courts martial try offences against military, naval or air force law. Some of these correspond to civilian crimes, but others are of more questionable validity. The notoriously vague offence of 'conduct prejudicial to good order and discipline' appears in all three codes, and can be used to punish behaviour that would be unexceptional from civilians. Insufficient press scrutiny is given to whether punishments are always justified by the exigencies of service life. For example, should male homosexuality in the forces continue to be punished (as it is at present, and with considerable severity), given that it was decriminalized for civilians in 1967? Is lesbianism, which has never been an offence outside the services, rightly regarded as prejudicial to good order and discipline?

---

[12] Coroners' Rules 1984 r 37.
[13] *Peacock* v *London Weekend Television* (1985) 150 JP 71.

Courts martial are composed of officers with no particular legal training. They are advised by an official misleadingly called a 'judge advocate'. He is neither a judge nor an advocate, but acts like a clerk to a magistrates' court and advises the courts martial on points of law. However, courts martial have far greater powers of punishment than magistrates, and the 'justice' they dispense in the absence of jury trial deserves greater attention from the press.

The press, like the public, have a right of access. A court martial can sit in camera in the same circumstances as a civilian court (see p. 311) and, in addition, the public can be excluded if it appears that there might otherwise be a disclosure of information useful to an enemy.[14] At the end of the trial the court will be cleared while the officer-judges deliberate. They give their finding in public and then retire to consider the sentence. This is imposed in public, but does not come into effect until it is confirmed by the defendant's commanding officer.

Church Courts

Ecclesiastical courts have had a colourful history. Once, they dispensed soft justice to all who could claim 'benefit of clergy', and so escape death sentences from the courts of the king. They decided questions of heresy, divorce, wills and defamation. Now they are limited to deciding disputes about Church property, and hearing charges of misconduct levelled against clergymen in their capacity as such.

Each diocese has a consistory court, and the Bishop's Chancellor – a senior lawyer – usually sits as judge. Clerical intermeddling is discouraged: when Bishop Mervyn Stockwood tried to adjudicate a dispute personally, he was roundly rebuked by his Chancellor, who suggested that the bill for unravelling the ensuing mess might be sent to His Grace.[15] The Chancellor sitting alone hears disputes about Church property, but in cases of clerical misconduct sits with a 'jury' of four assessors. An appeal can be taken to the appropriate archbishop's court (the Arches Court of Canterbury and the Chancery Court of York) and then, ultimately, to the Privy Council, which advises the Queen, as the formal head of the Anglican Church, on whether the appeal should be allowed. The general principle of openness applies to these courts. The High Court is reluctant to overturn an order to exclude the press and public if this was made 'reasonably' to serve the ends of justice –

[14] Naval Discipline Act 1957 s 61(2); Army Act 1955 s 94(2); Air Force Act 1955 s 94(2).
[15] *Re St Mary's, Barnes* [1982] All ER 456.

e.g., to obtain evidence that would not be given at all if it had to be given in public. But there is no power to exclude because of the intimate or embarrassing nature of the evidence, or merely to deprive the gutter press of the opportunity to pander to the prurience of its readers.[16]

Industrial Tribunals

Industrial tribunals consider a wide range of employment disputes. Claims of unfair dismissal, disputes over redundancy payments, and allegations of sex and race discrimination by employers are the most familiar issues, but industrial tribunals can also decide whether an organization is an independent trade union for collective bargaining, whether an employer has allowed adequate time off for trade union or public duties, and appeals against health and safety improvement orders.

Each tribunal comprises a legally trained chairperson, a trade union representative and an employer's nominee. This mix is not intended to ensure that each side can depend on one vote, but rather to give the appearance of a balanced tribunal. Their affiliations are not publicly announced and it can sometimes be difficult to tell them apart. An appeal can be taken on a point of law to the Employment Appeal Tribunal, which is chaired by a High Court judge flanked again by two lay people.

Industrial tribunals must sit in public unless, in the opinion of the tribunal, a private hearing is appropriate for the purpose of hearing evidence that relates to national security matters, where disclosure would break a confidence, or where a witness would be seriously prejudiced (other than in negotiations with employees).[17] In practice, tribunals sit almost always in public.

Immigration Appeals

Immigration adjudicators hear appeals against the Government's refusal to allow immigrants or visitors to enter or to stay in the country, and against deportation decisions. An Immigration Appeals Tribunal decides appeals on points of law. Although most

---

[16] *R* v *Chancellor of the Chichester Consistory Court ex parte News Group Newspapers* (1991) *The Times* 15 July.

[17] Industrial Tribunal (Rules of Procedure) Regulations 1985 (SI 1985 No 16) r 17. Similar provisions apply to the Employment Appeal Tribunal. There is a register of Industrial Tribunal decisions (with their reasons), which the public can inspect, ibid., r 9(8).

appellants are black, it is rare for adjudicators or tribunal members to be other than white. Appellants have an opportunity to present their case, but they cannot test the assertions of the Home Office by cross-examination. The Home Office's case is contained in an 'explanatory statement'. This is often contentious, but its maker is rarely compelled to attend the hearing for cross-examination.

Adjudicators and the Appeals Tribunal sit in public, although they do have power to exclude any or all observers at the request of a party, or if the evidence of a third party should be given in private (and neither of the parties objects) or if a person is causing a disturbance.[18] Oddly, the appellant does not always have the right to be present. Where he or she is alleged to have forged a document and disclosure of the method of detection would be contrary to the public interest, the adjudicator must exclude both the public and the appellant while considering the allegation.[19]

Mental Health Review Tribunals

A matter of perennial interest to certain sections of the press is the danger to the public supposedly created by the release of once-manic murderers. In law they are technically manslaughterers who have pleaded guilty on grounds of diminished responsibility and have been consigned to one of the four top-security mental hospitals. In many cases their mental illness will, in time, be cured or brought under control so that in fact their release will pose no danger to the public. But the horrendous nature of the original killing (the 'index offence') is such that release is politically unpalatable to the Home Secretary and sensibly requires extreme caution. That decision is entrusted to a Mental Health Review Tribunal, a panel usually chaired by a circuit judge and comprising a consultant psychiatrist and a layperson. 'Release' comes in stages – to a less secure mental hospital, and then, under restricted conditions, into the community. This last stage is not reached until after many years of psychiatric evaluation and screening, with every opportunity given to the Home Office to oppose it where any risk to the public is apprehended. There are rare cases of reoffending, attended with massive publicity that tends to obscure the overwhelming majority of releases that cause no problems. However, since reassertion of the original mental illness will pose a danger to life, there is a legitimate public interest in press coverage of Mental Health Review Tribunal decisions.

---

[18] Immigration Appeals (Procedure) Rules 1984 (SI 1984 No 2041) r 32(3).
[19] Immigration Act 1971 s 22(4) and 1984 Rules r 32(2).

In the interests of the patient, however, very little coverage is permitted by law. The tribunal is a 'court' for the purposes of the law of contempt, so that any story about an imminent hearing that puts pressure on the tribunal members or upon expert witnesses may give rise to a prosecution.[20] The Mental Health Tribunal rules require that the tribunal shall sit in private, other than in the rare cases when the patient asks for a hearing in public and the tribunal is satisfied that this would not be contrary to the patient's best interests. The rules additionally ban publication of information about tribunal proceedings, including the names of individuals who have been involved in them.[21]

In the important 1991 case of *Pickering* v *Liverpool Daily Post and Echo Newspapers plc* the House of Lords interpreted narrowly the ban on publication of tribunal 'proceedings' so as to permit the press to publish the fact that a particular patient had made an application for discharge, details of the date, time and place of the tribunal hearing, and the result. The ban was limited to reporting 'the substance of the matters which the court has closed its doors to consider', such as evidence and expert reports, or the reasons for the decision and any condition imposed on the patient's release. Alongside this bare information, however, editors are free to republish lurid details of the applicant's original offences. The Law Lords, while conceding the great public concern about release of persons detained for horrifying acts of violence, warned editors against using this freedom as part of a 'media campaign' against the discharge of an offender whose case is about to be considered by a tribunal. Inflammatory articles, especially if repeated in connection with a published hearing date, will readily be judged to create a 'substantial risk of serious prejudice' to the tribunal proceedings and amount to a contempt of court.[22]

This is one of the few areas where some restriction on publicity is justified, in the interests both of the privacy of the patient and of protecting the tribunal system from a particularly obnoxious form of pressure. The decision in *Pickering* that a tribunal was a 'court' for the purposes of contempt overruled a previous High Court decision to the contrary, which had permitted hysterical press campaigns of vilification against certain patients and those psychiatrists who supported their release. The present restrictions seem to strike a reasonable balance: they do not preclude the press from describing an applicant's previous history or fears that may

---

[20] *Pickering* v *Liverpool Daily Post and Echo Newspapers plc* [1990] 1 All ER 335, CA overruling *A-G* v *Associated Newspapers plc* [1989] 1 All ER 604.
[21] Mental Health Review Tribunal Rules (SI 1983 No 942) r 21.
[22] *Pickering* v *Liverpool Daily Post and Echo Newspapers plc* [1991] 1 All ER 622, HL; see also note 20 above.

still be entertained about his or her stability, but require such stories to be moderate in tone and balanced in factual presentation. It will amount to a breach of confidence for the media to publish details of private psychiatric reports prepared for the purposes of a tribunal hearing; the High Court has held that the public interest defence will in such cases be of no avail. However dangerous the patient may be depicted in the report, the public interest is satisfied if it is transmitted to the authorities, but not to the public at large.[23]

Licensing

Some licences (e.g. for sex shops, dancing, cinemas and taxis) are granted by local authorities, but others (e.g. pubs, hotels, off-licences, betting shops) are considered by magistrates. JPs have this job because before the establishment of a unified system of local councils, local administration was in their hands. The licensee must be a 'fit and proper person', and the police or others can object and draw attention to the applicant's unsavoury past. The premises must also be suitable. Fire prevention and environmental officers are the most common objectors on this score, but local residents also have an opportunity to protest at the effect that the use would have on their neighbourhood. When exercising a licensing power, the justices are still acting in this administrative capacity – and here press reports are not constrained by contempt. The justices must hear the applications, and any objectors to them, in public.[24]

Planning Inquiries

Local authorities have a variety of powers to control development and land use in their areas. They can, for instance, refuse planning permission, make orders (enforcement notices) to stop or reverse unpermitted development, and compulsorily purchase land. They must also draw up long-term strategic plans for the development of their area. Objections to these actions are determined by the Secretary of State for the Environment, but in most cases an inspector will be appointed to hear both sides. In general, the inspector takes evidence and hears argument in public, and documentary evidence is open to inspection, although it can be kept private if it relates to

---

[23] Scott J in *W* v *Egdell* [1989] 1 All ER 1089.
[24] *R* v *Redditch Justices* (1885) 2 TLR 193 DC; *Boulter* v *Kent Justices* [1897] AC 556; Betting, Gaming and Lotteries Act 1963 s 1 and Gaming Act 1968 s 2.

national security or if disclosure would jeopardize the security of any premises in a way that would be contrary to the national interest.[25]

For major planning inquiries a Department of Environment Code recommends that a register of participants be prepared, divided into those playing a major part in the proceedings, those wishing to give oral evidence but not otherwise play a major part in the proceedings, and those submitting written representations. The register should be publicly available. The Code also provides that outline statements and certain written submissions will be available to members of the public, who ought also to be able to attend pre-inquiry meetings and programme meetings.

Disciplinary Hearings

Disciplinary complaints against doctors are first considered in private by the Preliminary Proceedings Committee of the General Medical Council. If it finds a case to answer, the issue is tried by the Professional Conduct Committee. This committee sits in public, although it can exclude observers if it considers such an action is in the interests of justice, or desirable in regard to the nature of the case or the evidence. But while the committee has these powers to deliberate in private, it must give its decision in public.[26] Similar procedures apply to veterinary surgeons, opticians, nurses and pharmacists. [27]

By comparison, lawyers, who proclaim professionally the virtues of open justice, are somewhat coy when it comes to the misdemeanours of their own colleagues. Allegations of professional misconduct against a solicitor or a barrister are heard in private unless the defendant requests a public trial – an option that few find palatable.[28] The decision must be publicly announced, an obligation that the Law Society discharges by giving minimal information, and that the Bar Council fulfils by placing a notice on a board in the relevant Inn of Court.

---

[25] Planning Inquiries (Attendance of Public) Act 1982 s 1.

[26] General Medical Council Preliminary Proceedings Committee and Professional Conduct Committee (Procedure) Rules 1988 (SI 1988 No 2255).

[27] Veterinary Surgeons and Veterinary Practitioners (Disciplinary Committee) (Procedure and Evidence) Rules 1967 (SI 1967 No 659) r 15(1). General Optical Council (Disciplinary Committee) (Procedure) Rules, Order of Council 1985 (SI 1985 No 1580) r 11; Nurses, Midwives and Health Visitors (Professional Conduct) Rules 1983 (SI 1983 No 887) r 16. Pharmaceutical Society (Statutory Committee) Order of Council 1978 (SI 1978 No 20) reg 16.

Public Inquiries

A familiar Government response to a crisis is to appoint a committee or announce an inquiry. The openness of the inquiry will depend upon the particular power that is used to set it up. Royal Commissions and departmental or interdepartmental inquiries can be instructed to sit in public or in private; usually, they are allowed to exercise their discretion. When formal gathering of evidence is necessary, a tribunal of inquiry may be appointed. Such a tribunal was set up after the Aberfan coal-tip disaster in 1966. Lord Radcliffe investigated the national security implications of the Vassall affair sitting as a tribunal of inquiry, and the same mechanism was used to investigate leaks of the Budget in 1936 and the Bank Rate change in 1957. In 1981 the scandal surrounding the Crown Agents was investigated by a Tribunal of Inquiry. Tribunals of Inquiry will take all their evidence in public, unless in the tribunal's opinion privacy is expedient for reasons connected with the subject-matter of the inquiry or the nature of evidence.[29]

Inquiries into police-related matters, such as the Scarman investigations of the Brixton riots in 1981 and the death of Kevin Gately in the Red Lion Square demonstration in 1974 are usually held in public, but this is at the discretion of the Home Secretary, who sets up the inquiry.[30] Disciplinary proceedings against individual police officers are taken in private.[31]

Internal inquiries into transport accidents are usually private affairs, but greater publicity is given to an investigation by an outside appointee. A Department of Trade inspector considering the cause of a rail accident must sit in open court;[32] inquiries into sea deaths or casualties must generally be in public,[33] and a court inquiry into an air disaster sits publicly unless the interests of justice or the public interest require all or part of it to be held in private.[34]

---

[28] Solicitors (Disciplinary Proceedings) Rules 1985 (SI 1985 No 226) r 24. Bar Disciplinary Tribunal Regulations reg.12: The Tribunal can be held in public against the wishes of the barrister if the judge holding a preliminary hearing so directs; reg. 9(3)(*a*). Appeals to the judges as the Visitors of the Inns of Court are heard in private unless the barrister elects a public hearing and there is no public-interest reason why this should not be allowed: Hearings before the Visitors Rule r 10(4).

[29] Tribunals of Inquiry (Evidence) Act 1921 s 2.

[30] Police Act 1964 s 32(2).

[31] The Police (Discipline) Regulations 1985 (SI 1985 No 518) r18(2) and the Police (Discipline) (Senior Officers) Regulations 1985 (S1 1985 No 519), r 13(1).

[32] Regulation of Railways Act 1871 s 7.

[33] Shipping Casualties and Appeals and Rehearing Rules 1923 (SR & O 1923 No 752) r 11.

[34] Civil Aviation (Investigation of Accidents) Regulations 1969 (SI 1969) No 752.

Other Inquiries

The pattern that we have observed – namely a presumption of publicity coupled with a discretion to sit in private – is common to most other tribunals. The extent of the discretion varies widely. It may be dependent on proof of 'special circumstance'[35] or 'exceptional reasons'[36] or where one party would be prejudiced by publicity,[37] or be limited to cases where disclosure would be 'contrary to the public interest'.[38] This means that mere bureaucratic embarrassment should not be enough to put the hearing into closed session. At the opposite end of the spectrum are those inquiries that must be held in private if one party requests it,[39] or where the presumption is in favour of a private hearing unless the applicant requests publicity.[40]

But Rent Assessment Committee hearings are open to the public.[41] Oral hearings by Social Security Adjudication Officers and Appeal Tribunals are conducted in public unless the claimant requests a private hearing or the chairman believes that intimate, personal or financial circumstances may have to be disclosed or considerations of public security are involved, when the hearing must be in private.[42]

---

[35] e.g. Rent Assessment Committes, which consider 'fair rents' for private rented accommodation, Rent Assessment Committees (England and Wales) Regulations 1971 (SI 1971 No 1065) reg 3.

[36] e.g. Independent Schools Tribunals, which judge complaints by the Government against such schools, Independent Schools Tribunal Rules 1958 (SI 1958 No 519) r8; Agricultural Land Tribunals, which decide whether a farmer has acted fairly in evicting tenants from a tied house, Agricultural Lands Tribunal (Rules) Order 1978 (SI 1978 No 259) r24.

[37] Regulations determine when the Valuation and Community Charge Tribunals must sit in public (Local Government Finance Act 1988, Sched 11, para 8(3)(*a*) and Valuation and Community Charge Tribunals Regulations 1989 (SI 1989 No 439).

[38] e.g., the Gas (Underground Storage) (Inquiries Procedure) Rules 1966 (SI 1966 No 1375) r 8(4).

[39] e.g., the Lands Tribunal, which, for instance, assesses a reasonable price for the sale of a freehold to long leaseholders. Lands Tribunal (Amendment) Rules 1977 (SI 1977 No 1820) r 33A. As the long leases granted over nineteenth-century housing come close to their end, property companies have begun to buy up freeholds. In areas such as South Wales conflicts over the valuation of freeholds have become acute.

[40] e.g., National Health Service Tribunal, which considers whether GPs should be struck off the NHS approved list, National Health Service (Service Committees and Tribunal) Regs 1974 (SI 1974 No 455) r 38.

[41] Rent Assessment Committees (England and Wales) Regulations 1971 (SI 1971 No 1065) reg 3(1).

[42] Social Security (Adjudication) Regulations 1986 (SI 1986 No 2218) reg 4(4).

Televising Tribunals

Royal Commissions and ordinary tribunals are not 'courts' for the purposes of s 41 of the Criminal Justice Act 1925, which contains the only formal prohibition on televising proceedings (See p. 360). It follows that the tribunal will have a discretion to permit the electronic media to record and broadcast proceedings. Permission to televise has rarely (if ever) been granted, but this is partly due to the fact that media interests hardly (if ever) ask for such permission, with the object of seeking to overturn any refusal by judicial review proceedings. The attitude towards televising courts has undergone a sea change in recent years: the Bar is now in favour, and the electronic media could well begin their incursions by televising some tribunal proceedings.

In the case of Royal Commissions and major public inquiries the argument for the right to broadcast proceedings is overwhelming. The very purpose of establishing a Tribunal of Inquiry is to restore public confidence by establishing the truth about allegations that have caused grave disquiet; and public confidence is best restored after the public have been able to see or hear for themselves the testimony and the procedures.[43] The Australian High Court has pointed out that any restraint on publicity at a Royal Commission:

> seriously undermines the value of the inquiry. It shrouds the proceedings with a cloak of secrecy, denying to them the public character which, to my mind, is an essential element to public acceptance of an inquiry of this kind and of its report. An atmosphere of secrecy readily breeds the suspicion that the inquiry is . . . oppressive.[44]

More positively, the public character of such an inquiry can best come from the broadcasting of its proceedings. This was the conclusion of Louis Blom-Cooper QC, who in 1990 opened to radio and television his Antiguan Royal Commission on the smuggling of arms to the Colombian drug cartels. His report concludes:

> My fears of physical obstruction were entirely misplaced: one single television camera behind Counsel, trained for the most part on the witness, soon went entirely unnoticed. No lights or other studio impedimenta were required. It was observed that some Counsel, who at first disdained microphones, very quickly and effortlessly learned to use them. The witnesses

---

[43] Lord Salmon, *Tribunals of Inquiry*, 1967 Lionel Cohen Memorial Lecture, published by the Hebrew University, Jerusalem.
[44] *Victoria* v *Australian Building Construction Employees and Building Labourers Federation* (1982) 152 CLR 25, at 97 per Mason J.

were in no way flustered or deterred, or for the most part even conscious of the recording. I am confident that they remained blissfully unaware that their evidence was going to be relayed to the populace. If they were aware, they raised no objection and showed no sign of disquiet, let alone dissent. Several senior Counsel indicated to me that they felt an extremely beneficial discipline to ask relevant and comprehensible questions, and not to waste time. I felt, myself, the sense of Jeremy Bentham's argument in favour of open justice, namely, that 'it keeps the judge, while trying, under trial'. That the Commission proceeded as effectively and efficiently as it did, is, in my view, due in some measure to the fact that we could all be heard and seen . . . each evening on radio and television. The benefits of electronic media coverage, in terms of public understanding, were incalculable. It meant that citizens could receive accurate information about a great public scandal, and make up their own minds about the testimony. Although I accept that electronic media coverage of criminal trials requires a very careful and gradual introduction, I hope that it will come to be considered routine for public inquiries.[45]

Contempt[46]

The 1981 Contempt of Court Act imposes strict liability in relation to stories that create a substantial risk of serious prejudice to active 'legal proceedings'. 'Legal proceedings', for the purposes of the Act, are proceedings that take place in a court, defined to include 'any tribunal or body exercising the judicial power of the state'.[47] Most of the lesser courts and tribunals discussed in this chapter have no power to take action of their own volition against the media, but the High Court has an overall supervisory power to punish contempt of 'inferior courts'.[48] The question thus becomes one of deciding whether a particular body is a court, albeit an 'inferior' one. That question, an absolutely crucial one for the media, Parliament infuriatingly failed to answer in the Contempt Act by the simple expedient of listing in a schedule all tribunals protected by the law of contempt. So the answer must be found in general principles, applied on a case by case basis.

---

[45] Louis Blom-Cooper, *Guns for Antigua*, Duckworth, 1990, p. 46.
[46] See further Lowe and Rawlings, 'Tribunals and the Administration of Justice' [1982] Public Law 418.
[47] Contempt of Court Act 1981 s 19.
[48] Rules of Supreme Court Order 52 r1(2)(*a*).

The general rule is that contempt covers all bodies that exercise the judicial power of the state. The only assistance in giving meaning to this phrase is provided by the important 1980 case of *Attorney-General* v *BBC*:[49]

> The BBC had made a programme that was extremely critical of the Exclusive Brethren. One branch of the sect had applied for rate relief to a local valuation court, and the case was to be heard a few days after the BBC proposed to transmit the film. The Attorney-General was granted an injunction to stop it, on the grounds that it would prejudice the Brethren's claim. The House of Lords held that the injunction was wrongly given: a local valuation court did not exercise the judicial power of the state, and hence could not be protected from contempt. The judgments of the Law Lords will be sifted for dicta of help in deciding the issue in relation to other tribunals; their individual approaches to the question were as follows:
>
> Viscount Dilhorne drew a distinction between courts that discharge judicial functions and those that discharge administrative ones, and said that contempt did not apply in relation to the latter. He suggested, albeit in passing and inferentially, that immigration adjudicators, immigration appeal tribunals, the Lands Tribunal, pension appeal tribunals, the Transport Tribunal, the Commons Commissioners and the Performing Rights Tribunal were not to be regarded as courts that would put the media at risk of a contempt action.
>
> Lord Salmon adopted an approach particularly favourable to the media. He said:

Public policy requires that most of the principles relating to contempt of court which have for ages necessarily applied to the long-established inferior courts such as county courts, magistrates' courts, courts martial, coroners' courts and consistory courts shall not apply to valuation courts and the host of other modern tribunals which may be regarded as inferior courts; otherwise the scope of contempt of court would be unnecessarily extended and accordingly freedom of speech and freedom of the press would be unnecessarily contracted.

Lord Scarman accepted that courts martial and Church courts exercised, for historic reasons, the judicial power of the state and were protected in consequence. However, he took the view that legal policy was against protecting administrative courts and tribunals: if Parliament wanted to provide special protection, it must say so in the legislation establishing the body in question:

I would not think it desirable to extend the doctrine (of contempt) which is unknown, and not apparently needed, in most

---

[49] [1980] 3 All ER 161 (HL).

civilized legal systems, beyond its historical scope, namely the proceedings of courts of judicature. If we are to make the extension, we have to ask ourselves, if the United Kingdom is to comply with its international obligations, whether the extension is necessary in our democratic society. Is there a 'pressing social need' for the extension?

> Lord Edmund-Davies and Lord Fraser were more circumspect, although the former echoed Lord Scarman's view that contempt protection to tribunals and other bodies ought to be given specifically by Parliament, and that the courts themselves should not extend contempt proceedings 'unless it is clear beyond doubt that the demands of justice make them essential'.

The upshot of those judicial approaches is that contempt protection will not readily be extended, in the absence of statutory provision, to any 'lesser' court or tribunal. It can be said with confidence that courts martial[50] and Church courts[51] are protected, although since the former are conducted by senior army officers and the latter by a distinguished lawyer, the danger of a media story creating a serious risk of substantial prejudice is relatively small. Lord Salmon, in the passage quoted above, assumed that coroners' courts were protected and the Divisional Court has since confirmed that this is the case.[52] A coroners' court becomes 'active' for the purpose of the strict-liability rule as soon as the inquest is opened (which will usually be shortly after the death) even though the proceedings are then adjourned for a considerable time while the police carry out their investigations.[53]

There is some doubt about the status of industrial tribunals in relation to the contempt laws. Their jurisdiction to award compensation after deciding, often after consideration of complex case-law, the rights and wrongs of a dismissal, is similar in process and effect to decisions made in the ordinary civil courts. Mental Health

---

[50] The *Daily Sketch and Graphic* was fined £500 for contempt because, at the time, the sentence could not be published at all until it was confirmed by the defendant's commanding officer. *R v Gunn ex parte A-G (No 2)* (1953) *The Times*, 14 November; [1954] Crim LR 53. This is no longer the case. Instead the 1981 Act provides that the proceedings are active until confirmation (Sched 1 para 8). This means that reporting and comment are permitted as long as they do not cause substantial risk of serious prejudice.

[51] Ecclesiastical Jurisdiction Measure 1963 s 81(2) expressly gives the High Court power to punish for contempt of Church courts. For a rare example see *R v Daily Herald ex parte Bishop of Norwich* [1932] 2 KB 402.

[52] *R v West Yorkshire Coroner ex parte Smith* [1985] 1 All ER 100.

[53] *Peacock v London Weekend Television*, note 13 above, but see the argument on p. 372 that this case was wrongly decided.

Review Tribunals are 'courts' and therefore are protected by the strict-liability rule (see p. 376).

In all other cases the presumption must be that contempt does not apply. Planning inquiries make administrative rather than judicial decisions. Although professional bodies must act judicially, they do not wield the state's authority. Similarly, arbitrators who are appointed to resolve a contractual dispute derive their authority from the private parties and not from the government. Magistrates, as we have seen, act in an administrative capacity when sitting as licensing justices. A pet-shop owner once protested that his application to local magistrates for a licence was prejudiced by the BBC's *Checkpoint* programme. The Court of Appeal ruled in favour of the BBC: the magistrates were acting administratively and the strict-liability inhibition on comment did not apply.[54] For the same reason the media are free to comment on applications for liquor or gambling licences. On the eve of the sitting that was to decide whether the Playboy Club should retain its gaming licence, the BBC broadcast a documentary alleging that the club had consistently breached the Gaming Act. The programme was devastatingly prejudicial, pre-judging the issues that the magistrates would have to decide in the days that followed. It was not contempt, however, because a licensing body is not a court exercising the judicial power of the state.

Even if the body in question does exercise 'the judicial power of the state', the High Court could penalize a newspaper or broadcaster only if the story satisfied the other requirements of contempt. In brief, the proceedings must have been active (i.e. the publication must have taken place before a hearing date was fixed, and before final disposal). The story must also pose a substantial risk of serious prejudice. None of the tribunals considered here (except on occasions the coroner's court) has a jury. Most are presided over or advised by persons with some legal experience. It will be rare for a story to create the necessary risk of prejudice to amount to contempt. And it must be remembered that even prejudicial material of this kind can be published if it is part of a discussion in good faith of public affairs and the risk of prejudice is only incidental (see further p. 281).

If the body is a 'court', then reports of its proceedings have the same protection from contempt as other fair and accurate reports of legal proceedings. These cannot breach the strict-liability rule unless the tribunal has made a postponement order (see p. 341). Lesser courts probably do not have power to make postponement orders or to ban publication of evidence that was not given publicly

---

[54] *Lewis* v *BBC* [1979] Court of Appeal Transcript 193.

– the matter is undecided, although one appeal judge has said that if they do possess this power, they should hardly ever use it.[55]

The Attorney-General has warned the press to be careful about reports of bodies like licensing justices, which are not exercising the judicial power of the state. He has said that if reports of evidence contain details of discreditable conduct by licence applicants who also happen to be awaiting a criminal trial, this report might amount to a contempt of the criminal court. It is true that the publisher of such a report could not then shelter behind the defence created by the 1981 Act for reports of *legal* proceedings, but if the objections to the licence were matters of public importance, and the report only incidentally prejudiced the forthcoming proceedings, the press would have a 'public interest' defence under s 5 of the Contempt of Court Act.[56]

Tribunals of Inquiry have special statutory powers. They can refer to the High Court any matter that would have been contempt if it had taken place in High Court proceedings.[57] The Vassal Tribunal into the activities of the Russian spy in the British Admiralty was a Tribunal of Inquiry, and it used this power to refer the cases of journalists who refused to reveal their sources. Three were jailed by the High Court for sticking to their professional ethics.[58] Following the flurry of interviews with witnesses to the Aberfan disaster, the Attorney-General warned the press of the danger of contempt, but it is highly unlikely that mere press comment would ever lead to contempt proceedings, especially after Lord Salmon's 1969 report, in which he discouraged the idea that such stories could influence a judge conducting an inquiry. He thought it important to preserve freedom of discussion, even if some witnesses might feel inhibited as a result.[59] There has been no case in which a newspaper has been punished for this type of contempt. The Contempt of Court Act assumes that the strict-liability contempt may apply to Tribunals of Inquiry because it states that the proceedings are active from the time of the Tribunal's appointment[60] until its report is presented to Parliament. Given Lord Salmon's views however, this provision should in practice prove academic.

---

[55] *R* v *Horsham Justices ex parte Farquharson and West Sussex County Times* [1982] 2 All ER 269, 284 per Lord Denning.
[56] It might also be argued that such reports would not have been contempt at common law and so could not be contempt under the 1981 Act (cf s 6(2) of the 1981 Act. *Felkin* v *Herbert* (1861) 30 LJ Ch 798; *R* v *Payne* [1896] 1 QB 577).
[57] Tribunals of Inquiry (Evidence) Act 1921 s 1(2)(*c*).
[58] *A–G* v *Mulholland*; *A–G* v *Foster* [1963] 1 All ER 767 CA, *A–G* v *Clough* [1963] 1 QB 773.
[59] Report of the Interdepartmental Committee on the Law of Contempt in Relation to Tribunals of Inquiry (1969) Cmnd 4078 para 26.

Libel

Media reports of proceedings and decisions of lesser courts and tribunals are protected from libel actions, but with varying degrees of efficacy. Reports about lesser courts that, none the less, exercise the judicial power of the state (i.e. those to which contempt law is applicable) will be fully protected by absolute privilege. Reports of proceedings in most other bodies will be protected by qualified privilege at common law, while in a few cases a special statutory privilege can be claimed only if the newspaper carrying the defamatory report has offered the victim a right of reply.

Absolute privilege

The best defence that a newspaper can have to a defamation action is that the report is absolutely privileged. This means that the person libelled has no claim, even if it can be shown that the paper acted maliciously in publishing its story (see pp. 6, 363). This defence, not surprisingly, is reserved to a narrow class of reports.[61] It applies only to contemporaneous newspaper or broadcast reports of proceedings of courts exercising judicial authority within the United Kingdom, i.e., to courts of law, together with courts martial, Church courts, and, possibly, to industrial tribunals and coroners' courts. This means that in those cases where a newspaper is at risk of committing contempt under the strict-liability rule for prejudicing proceedings, it at least has the benefit of absolute privilege against libel actions for reports of those proceedings.[62]

Qualified privilege

Common law
The second best defence to a libel action is qualified privilege (see p. 365), which is lost only if the publisher is malicious. The defence is not restricted to newspapers or broadcasters, but can be relied upon, for instance, by writers of books and pamphlets. The report need not be contemporaneous. Most importantly, it applies to a wide range of tribunals. It is enough if the body acts like a court, if it sits in public and if its decisions or its proceedings are

---

[60] This would be when both Houses of Parliament have passed the necessary resolution. 'Time' was deliberately chosen over 'date' to allow the media to comment on the morning prior to the establishment of the inquiry: Lord Hailsham on the Contempt of Court Bill, Hansard HL Debs Vol 416, col 390.
[61] Law of Libel Amendment Act 1888 s 3.
[62] For coroners see: *McCarey* v *Associated Newspapers Ltd* [1964] 3 All ER 947.

matters of legitimate public interest. The findings of the General Medical Council on a disciplinary complaint against a doctor satisfied these tests[63] and the Privy Council has ruled that extracts from an official report of an *ad hoc* government commission on bribery were similarly covered.[64] As with the court reports, the story need not record the proceedings verbatim or even in detail: it is enough if they are accurate and fairly selected.

Defamation Act 1952
The preceding two defences are not contingent upon the victim being offered a right of reply. The special statutory defence of qualified privilege, however, applies only if the publisher has been prepared to offer a right of reply. The Defamation Act 1952 allows newspapers,[65] and providers of programme services[66] to report cases where magistrates act administratively (e.g. as licensing justices),[67] the proceedings of any government[68] or local council instituted inquiry,[69] or the proceedings of any other statutory tribunal, board, committee or body. Only reports of proceedings open to the public are protected.[70] The Act also gives qualified privilege to reports of private sports, trade and cultural associations when acting in a 'quasi-judicial' capacity (e.g. disciplining their members) or deciding matters of general concern to the association.[71] None of these reports attracts the defence unless it is fair and accurate,[72] the matter is of public concern and publication is for the public benefit.[73] Since the privilege is qualified, it is lost only if the publisher is malicious, or if the newspaper or broadcasting organization has not been prepared to publish a reasonable

---

[63] *Allbutt* v *General Council of Medical Education and Registration* (1889) 23 QBD 400.
[64] *Perera* v *Peiris* [1949] AC 1.
[65] A newspaper is defined in *this* Act as any paper containing public news or observations thereon or consisting wholly or mainly of advertisements which is printed for sale and published in the United Kingdom either periodically or in parts or numbers or intervals not exceeding thirty-six days, s 7(5). Consequently, monthlies can take advantage of this privilege, though they do not come with the absolute privilege (see above).
[66] Broadcasting Act 1990 s166.
[67] Broadcasting Act 1952 Sched para 10(*b*).
[68] 'Any commission, tribunal, committee or person appointed for the purpose of any inquiry by Act of Parliament, by Her Majesty or by a Minister of the Crown', ibid., Sched para 10(*c*).
[69] 'Any person appointed by a local authority to hold a local inquiry in pursuance of any Act of Parliament', ibid., Sched para 10(*d*).
[70] ibid.
[71] This is a summary of the Defamation Act 1952 Sched para 8. Consult the Act for details.
[72] ibid., Sched paras 8 and 10.
[73] ibid., s 7(3).

reply. The burden is on the victim to propose the wording: a newspaper is not obliged to compose its own correction if it received only a general demand for an apology.[74] A reply can also be rejected as being unreasonable if it is unduly long, if it is immoderate or if it attacks third parties (see p. 93).

[74] *Khan* v *Ahmed* [1957] 2 All ER 385.

Chapter 9

Reporting Parliament and Elections

Reporting Parliament has some parallels with reporting the courts, and, indeed, Parliament's full title is the High Court of Parliament. There are similar defences to defamation actions. Both institutions have a power to punish for contempt if their sense of dignity is offended. Both set aside special facilities for the media: in Westminster there is a press gallery, special writing rooms and even a restaurant for journalists. But while judges welcome journalists only to their public performances, politicians give a select few an audience behind the scenes.

'The lobby' is a group of about a hundred journalists from the daily and Sunday press, the news agencies, BBC and ITN. Weeklies and representatives of foreign media are not admitted. The name derives from their privileged right of access to the Members' Lobby of the House of Commons, a convenient place to meet ministers and other MPs. Twice a day the lobby is given a briefing by the Prime Minister's press staff and, less regularly, it hears from the Leader of the Opposition, the Leader of the House and other ministers. The latter tend to acquire a constellation of journalists to whom they give confidential briefings on the same lines. Lobby correspondents are also fed advance copies of Government publications, which are under embargo until they are formally published.

The lobby has its own rules, the most important of which is that correspondents shall respect the basis on which information is fed them. There are three grades: 'for attribution'; 'for use without attribution'; and background information – 'not for use at all'. The advantage of this system is said to be that ministers can be more frank and open with correspondents whose discretion they can trust. Its disadvantages are its exclusivity, the cosiness that can blunt criticism and its encouragement of anonymous pronouncements that, were it not for the lobby, might still be made on an

---

[1] On the lobby, see Hartley and Griffith, *Government and the Law*, 2nd edn, Weidenfeld & Nicolson, 1981, pp. 266–7; Peter Kellner, 'The Lobby, Official Secrets and Good Government' (1983) 36 Parliamentary Affairs 275.

attributed basis.[1] Particularly when pressed by schedules and budgets, it is also tempting for correspondents to accept and repeat what has come straight from the horse's mouth without scrutinizing the evidence for the judgements they hear. The lobby's rules are not law, but breach can lead to expulsion from the club. Outside the lobby, journalists have few formal rights of access to information, although they can, of course, obtain the flood of papers that are printed by order of the Commons and Lords. Amongst these is a register of MPs' outside interests, which purports to call attention to potential conflicts of interest.

Parliament has a special importance to the media quite apart from its function as a forum for announcement and debate of Government policy. It shares with courts the privilege of being a place where allegations can be made, on any matter at all, and reported without risk. The privilege of free speech is guaranteed to all members of both Houses in the ninth article of the Bill of Rights of 1688, which declares 'That the freedom of speech and debates or proceedings in Parliament ought not to be impeached or questioned in any court or place out of Parliament.'

The language of the Bill of Rights is unambiguous. Ever since the House of Lords reversed the conviction of Sir John Eliot and fellow MPs for seditious speeches made in Parliament,[2] the principle has remained that no MP or peer may be brought before the civil or criminal courts for any utterance in parliamentary proceedings. With limited exceptions of largely theoretical interest, the media is entitled to a similar immunity in publishing these utterances. It follows that matters that cannot be mentioned in the media may, if ventilated in the course of a parliamentary question or debate, become public knowledge. There have been many occasions on which journalists have primed MPs to raise matters that could not otherwise be made public: the truth about Kim Philby, Sir Anthony Blunt and Colonel H. A. Johnstone ('Colonel B') were revealed by this device. Journalists who use an MP to raise a matter that cannot otherwise be put into print will lose exclusivity in the story (in the sense that other media will pick it up), but may be the first with the background detail that can be published in consequence.

The extent to which parliamentary privilege may be used to avoid a court injunction was explored both in the courts and in Parliament when Labour MPs booked a Committee Room in the House of Commons in order to show a private copy of the 'Zircon' film in Duncan Campbell's *Secret Society* series, which was subject to an injunction on the grounds that its television transmission was not in the national interest:

[2] Journal of the House of Lords 1666–75, p. 166.

The Attorney-General asked a High Court judge to prohibit the screening within parliamentary precincts, arguing that this would amount to a contempt of court. Mr Justice Kennedy refused on the grounds that it was for Parliament to regulate its own proceedings. The Speaker of the House of Commons was reluctant to ban the screening; he did so only after being privately briefed by the Attorney-General that the screening would be 'seriously harmful' to national security. The Committee of Privileges concluded that he had acted correctly in exercising his power of control over the Palace of Westminster. He was not interfering with Parliamentary privilege, since an MP's private arrangement to show a film within the precincts of the House was not 'a proceeding in Parliament'. But the Committee reaffirmed the principle that 'there is nothing (other than their own judgement)' to prevent MPs from divulging information that may damage national security in the course of parliamentary debates or committees. The Privileges Committee endorsed, as an absolute rule, the principle that any MP 'must be free to make public, in the course of proceedings in Parliament, information which he believes should be published'.[3]

The Bill of Rights does not protect MPs from the legal consequences of their statements outside the House, and reports of such statements are vulnerable to actions for libel and contempt. (In 1986 Tam Dalyell MP was threatened with an action for contempt by the judge at the Ponting trial, who had read reports of his criticisms of the proceedings made outside Parliament while the proceedings were taking place.) Nor does the Bill of Rights safeguard MPs against discipline imposed by their colleagues for abuses of privilege. On numerous occasions MPs have been censured or admonished for breaches of the rules of the House, which oblige the Speaker to disallow questions and comment on a wide range of issues, including matters in current litigation in the courts. An MP who is determined to ventilate an issue of public importance can often 'slip it past the Speaker' and consequently into print, at some risk of a retrospective reprimand. Questions of breach of parliamentary privilege by MPs or by the press are generally referred to the Privileges Committee, which reports back to the House.

Article 9 of the Bill of Rights has been interpreted in a succession of cases as meaning that proceedings in Parliament cannot be examined in courts of law without the permission of the House itself. Thus the Church of Scientology, attempting to sue an MP for his criticism (made outside the House) of its methods could not rebut his plea of 'fair comment' with evidence of malice relating to

[3] First Report from the Committee of Privileges, 'Speakers order of 22 January 1987 on a matter of national security', HC 365 (1986-7).

what had taken place in Parliament.[4] Equally, an MP suing the *Guardian* over allegations that he had conflicts of interest could not give evidence that the article's publication had caused him to be deselected from a standing committee of the House. Both sides could, however, give evidence about the practice and procedure relating to the Register of Members' Interests, as this was a public document and not part of 'proceedings in Parliament'.[5] Hansard may be quoted in courtrooms in relevant cases without the leave of the House.[6]

The Privileges for Reporting Parliamentary Debates

In the course of his decision in *Attorney-General* v *Times Newspapers*, Lord Denning stated: 'Whatever comments are made in Parliament, they can be repeated in the newspapers without any fear of an action for libel or proceedings for contempt of court.'[7] This is a sound enough summary of the practical position, although it may not strictly accord with the law. In 1813 an MP was convicted of criminal libel contained in a copy of a speech delivered in the House that he afterwards circulated.[8] The authority of the case today is doubtful, although it was relied upon by the Director of Public Prosecutions in rather extraordinary circumstances in 1977:

> The controversial prosecution of journalists Duncan Campbell and Crispin Aubrey under the Official Secrets Act featured an expert witness from the Ministry of Defence, 'Colonel B'. The acronym was alleged by the Crown to be necessary in the interests of national security. The falsity of this claim was exposed by the *Leveller* and *Peace News*, which published the Colonel's true identity, which was discoverable from regimental magazines. The Attorney-General commenced proceedings against the newspapers for contempt of court (see p. 340). Before the case was heard, four sympathetic MPs contrived to mention the Colonel's real name – H. A. Johnstone – in the course of oral questions in the House. The DPP immediately issued a statement to press and broadcasting organizations advising them not to disclose the identity of Colonel B in their reports of the day's proceedings, on the grounds that it might amount to contempt of court. Almost every national newspaper ignored this advice, and radio and television news programmes broadcast the tape of the MPs asking

---

[4] *Church of Scientology of California* v *Johnson-Smith* [1972] 1 All ER 294.
[5] *Rost* v *Edwards* [1990] 2 All ER 641.
[6] Resolution of Houses of Parliament, 31 October 1980.
[7] [1973] 1 All ER 815, 823, reversed on other grounds [1973] 3 All ER 54.
[8] *R* v *Creevey* (1813) 1 M and S 273; 105 ER 102.

their cover-blowing questions. There was an immediate constitutional rumpus, as the media invoked its privilege to publish proceedings in the House and some MPs demanded that the DPP be punished for contempt of Parliament. The Attorney-General, who was compromised in the whole affair, had the behaviour of the four MPs referred to the Committee of Privileges, but declined to test the position by prosecuting any media organization for contempt of court.[9]

The 'Colonel B' affair shed little light on the technical question of whether the media can ever be liable for contempt or any other criminal offence by reporting words uttered, in breach of the rules of the House, by truculent MPs. It did, however, underline the practical impossibility of taking action, given the simultaneous broadcasting of parliamentary sessions. The DPP's advice was wrong in that no contempt could have been committed in any event, either in relation to the Divisional Court hearing or to the magistrates' court, which made the original secrecy arrangement. For all practical purposes the media may rely upon their possession of a privilege to report all proceedings in Parliament without criminal consequences.

Reports of parliamentary proceedings that are fair and accurate and made in good faith enjoy qualified privilege from libel actions. This was established in the famous nineteenth-century case of *Wason* v *Walter*:[10]

> *The Times* had printed extracts from a House of Lords debate, which included unflattering comments about the originator of an allegation that an eminent Law Lord had once lied to Parliament. The paper successfully defended a libel action. The court said that just as the public had an interest in learning about what took place in the courts, so it was entitled to know what was said in Parliament. Only malice or a distorted report would destroy the privilege.

Editorials or other comment based on the report of a parliamentary debate are also protected[11] and so too are 'sketches' written to capture the spirit rather than the detail of a debate. These may be cryptic, amusing and highly selective, but so long as they give a fair and honest representation of what took place as it impressed the journalist, the defence can be invoked.[12] Reports of

---

[9] Second Report of the Committee of Privileges HC 667 (1977–8). Three Australian High Court judges take the view that an accurate report of statements made in Parliament cannot amount to a contempt of court: see Mason C J and Gaudron J, *Hinch* v *Attorney-General (Vic)* (1987) 74 ALR 353 at pp. 361–2 and 405 respectively; McHugh J A in *A-G (NSW)* v *John Fairfax & Sons Ltd* (1986) 6 NSWLR 695 at p. 714.
[10] (1868) LR 4 QB 74.
[11] ibid.
[12] *Cook* v *Alexander* [1974] 1 QB 279.

committee hearings are similarly protected.[13] So, too, is publication or inclusion in a programme service of an extract or summary of a parliamentary report or paper.[14] Of great importance is a newspaper's right to make honest comment on apparently factual statements made in the debate that it has reported, even though these statements are later shown to be untrue.[15]

In 1989 the House of Commons finally, and by a narrow majority (318–264) allowed its proceedings to be televised – after a fashion. The rules devised by the Supervising Committee are calculated to avoid embarrassment when MPs misbehave. Whenever there is disorder, the cameras must switch immediately to the Speaker. No 'reaction shots' or close-ups are allowed, and the public gallery and the press gallery must not be shown. It is difficult to disagree with Bernard Levin that these rules are 'designed to make MPs look better behaved than they actually are' and to cocoon electors from the reality of 'the jeering, the slapping of knees and pointing, the sniggering at an unintended *double entendre*, the late-dining drunks arriving and lurching towards the division lobbies, the barracking, the unwillingness to listen to speakers from the opposite side (or, frequently, from their own)'. The rules were slightly relaxed by the Committee after the first six months of television had produced no obvious danger to the democratic process.

Contempt of Parliament[16]

Each House of Parliament has the power to punish both members and outsiders for contempt. The offence of Contempt of Parliament is defined by Erskine May as 'any act or omission which impedes either House of Parliament in the performance of its functions or impedes any member or officer of such House in the discharge of his duty, or which has a tendency directly or indirectly to produce such a result'. 'Indirect tendencies' can include articles which 'bring the House into odium, contempt or ridicule or lower its authority'.[17] These definitions are vague in the extreme, and it is

---

[13] *Gatley on Libel and Slander*, 8th edn, Sweet & Maxwell, 1981, para 635.

[14] Parliamentary Papers Act 1840 s 3, Defamation Act 1952 s 9(1). Broadcasting Act 1990 Sched 20; see Patricia Leopold, 'The Parliamentary Papers Act 1840 and Its Application Today' [1990] PL 183. This includes not only reports that the House orders to be published, but also any paper that the House orders to lie on the table. *Mangena* v *Wright* [1909] 2 KB 958.

[15] *Grech* v *Odhams Press Ltd* [1958] 2 QB 275.

[16] See generally Sir Thomas Erskine May, *Parliamentary Practice*, 21st edn, Butterworth, 1983, Chs 9 and 10; Hartley and Griffith, *Government and Law*, pp. 243–50.

[17] May, *Parliamentary Practice*, pp. 115, 125.

ironic that an institution whose function is to formulate rules of law with precision has been unable or unwilling to do the same for its own powers and privileges.

In modern practice, the power to punish for contempt may be justified in relation to MPs who take bribes or fail to declare interests, or in respect of outsiders who interrupt debates by throwing refuse from the public gallery. There is no justification for using it against hostile newspapers, and, despite some unedifying decisions in the 1950s, there is little danger that Parliament will run the risk of public obloquy by using it to stifle criticism. Its most relevant use is to reprimand the press for breaking embargoes on the publication of committee reports, or leaking evidence heard in secret. Thus Tam Dalyell MP was reprimanded by the House in 1967 for leaking to the *Observer* secret evidence given by the Porton Down Chemical Warfare Research Laboratory to a Commons Select Committee.[18] The publication of witnesses' submissions must officially await the authorization of the committee.[19] It is also a breach of the rules of the House to disclose or publish a committee's report before it is presented to the full House.[20] For this reason the *Guardian* and the *Daily Mail* were found in contempt for publishing a draft report from the Select Committee on Race Relations.[21] Similar breaches were committed by the *Economist* in 1975 (for publishing a wealth-tax story) and the *Daily Mail* in 1972 (publishing advance details of the Civil List).[22] However, it is now unlikely that newspapers and their reporters will be made to suffer for publishing such leaks. In 1986 Parliament rejected a recommendation from the Committee of Privileges that *The Times* should suffer the loss of a lobby pass and its journalist should be suspended from the lobby for six months for publishing a draft report leaked from the Environment Committee.[23]

Parliament's power to punish disrespectful publications is a parallel to the court's power to punish for scandalizing the judiciary. British judges have deliberately played down this aspect of their power and not exercised it since 1931 (see p. 296), but the House of Commons has not been so self-restrained. At the time of the Suez invasion there was a flurry of allegations of contempt. The

[18] HC 357 (1967–8). An appendix by the Clerk to the House gives further illustrations.
[19] See the House of Commons Resolution of 21 April 1837 and House of Commons Standing Order 85(A); May *Parliamentary Practice*, p. 123.
[20] May, *Parliamentary Practice*.
[21] HC 376 (1977).
[22] *Economist* HC 22 (1975–6); *Daily Mail* HC 180 (1971–2).
[23] HC Debs 1 Vol 98 Col 293 20 May 1986 and see Environment Committee 2nd Special Report HC 211 (1985–6): Committee of Privileges 1st Report HC 376 (1985–6).

Sunday Graphic criticized one MP's attitude to Egypt, and encouraged its readers to make their opinions known to him direct on his home telephone number, published by the newspaper. It was found to be in contempt.[24] Several papers criticized MPs for rationing petrol for others while voting themselves generous allowances, and the *Romford Recorder* and the *Sunday Express* were held in contempt.[25] It is difficult to conceive that action would be taken in relation to similar criticisms today. When, in 1975, the *Liverpool Free Press* was accused of contempt for an article that alleged double standards by an MP, no action was taken. The MP was told to pursue his grievance in the courts.[26] In the current climate of escalated libel awards MPs are only too happy to take this advice and sue for libel, and substantial damages have been won for unjustified allegations of absenteeism and alcoholism.

In 1978 the Commons resolved that its penal power should be used 'sparingly' and

> only when the House is satisfied that to exercise it is essential in order to provide reasonable protection for the House, its members or officers from such improper obstruction or attempt at or threat of obstruction as is causing or is likely to cause substantial interference with the performance of their respective functions.[27]

In future, it would take into account the mode and extent of the publication.[28] Although there is no formal defence of truth or fair comment to a charge of contempt,[29] the Commons again decided to

---

[24] HC 27 (1956–7).

[25] HC 74 (1956–7). The *Recorder* made an unsuccessful appeal to the Press Council, 1957/8, 33–4. See H. Phillip Levy, *The Press Council*, Macmillan, 1967, p. 355; 2nd Report from the Committee of Privileges. HC 38 (1956–7), 563 HC Debs 5th Series, col 403. The *Evening News* was found in contempt for a cartoon on the same theme. HC 39 (1956–7); but Baroness Stocks was acquitted for remarks on *Any Answers*. 4th Report of the Committee of Privileges (1956–7), HC 74.

[26] HC 43 (1975–6). The article is reproduced in Brian Whitaker, *News Ltd*, p. 147. Compare the Committee's condemnation of a passage in *Travel Trade Gazette* accusing Gwyneth Dunwoody of attacking the Association of British Travel Agents for ulterior motives. No action was proposed because the editor apologized. HC 302 (1974–5).

[27] These and the following proposals were first made by the Committee of Privileges in 1967. HC 34 (1967–8). They were brushed off the shelf by a further report in 1977. HC (1976–7). They were adopted by the Commons on 6 February 1978. Hansard, Vol 943, 5th Series, col 1155–1198.

[28] Reports of an improper disclosure are now automatically referred to the Committee of Privileges to assess its significance and to try to discover its source (see Committee of 2nd Report HC 555 (1984–5)).

[29] This may be because the issue has never been squarely raised. Whether truth should be accepted as a defence is, according to the Clerk to the House, an *ad hoc* decision. See HC 302 (1974–5) Annex 1 para 5 quoting HC 34 (1967–8) p. 5.

take into account the truth of, or the publisher's reasonable belief in the truth of, the allegations if all reasonable care had been taken and if the publication was in the public interest and was published in a manner appropriate to the public interest. On the other hand, it rejected a proposal that contempt should be a procedure of last resort to be used only where the Member concerned has no legal remedy. It agreed that, as in the *Liverpool Free Press* case, this was a relevant consideration, but was not willing for it to be an inflexible bar. These changes are an improvement, and the number of complaints referred to the Privileges Committee appears to have fallen sharply. It remains to be seen whether the change is permanent. In 1948 the Committee said that the contempt power should not be administered to discourage free expression of opinion however exaggerated or prejudiced.[30] Eight years later that opinion was ignored or bypassed in the petrol-rationing cases. Old powers, like old habits, die hard and the Commons has a collective phobia of placing binding limits on its contempt power.

Contempt of Parliament has survived as an offence in modern times only because punishments have been mild. Although the House can banish culprits from the Palace of Westminster, and even imprison them, no one has been locked under Big Ben since the atheist MP Charles Bradlaugh in 1880. The Lords, but not the Commons, can impose a fine.[31] In 1975 the Committee of Privileges recommended that the editor and a journalist on *The Economist* be banished from the precincts of the House for six months for publishing a draft report on a proposed wealth-tax, but on a free vote the House decided to take no action.[32] Indeed, few reprimands have been administered since the Second World War.[33] John Junor received one for his attack in the *Sunday Express* on MPs' special petrol allowances during the Suez crisis. His half-hearted apology and failure to check his facts caused the Committee to recommend the reprimand.[34] When Junor returned to the fray in 1983, claiming that MPs who suggested a pay-rise for themselves were hypocrites with 'greedy snouts in the trough', Parliament's response was much more sophisticated than calling him to the Bar of the House for contempt. MPs enthusiastically tabled motions that allowed them to debate Junor's own salary – which they claimed was £100,000 a

---

[30] Investigating a complaint in the *Daily Mail* that Labour MPs were Communist moles. HC 112 (1947–8).
[31] May, *Parliamentary Practice*, p. 110. The 1967 Committee proposed that a power to fine should be revived and when considering *The Economist*'s leak of the wealth-tax report in 1975, made it clear that it thought this an appropriate offence to fine.
[32] HC 22 (1975–6).
[33] Hartley and Griffith, *Government and the Law*, p. 245. 1967 Report, para 18.
[34] HC 74 (1956–7).

year – and to draw attention to the tax perks of egregious Fleet Street editors. The threat of sanctions for contempt need concern only lobby correspondents, who identify closely with the House. Others, at least those who are confident of the public interest in their story, should not be averse to the publicity that a reprimand would bring. However, MPs who are caught leaking can face suspension and, in one post-war case, expulsion.[35]

The objections to the offence of contempt of Parliament go beyond the vagueness of definition and the self-aggrandizement implicit in many of the cases. The procedure for 'trial' breaches every important rule of natural justice, and shames a Commons proud of its historical opposition to the Star Chamber of the Stuart kings. The procedure begins, reasonably enough, with a private complaint by an MP to the Speaker.[36] If the Speaker thinks there is a case to answer, he gives the MP leave to raise it as a matter of procedure over the day's business, and the House may, if impressed with it, pass a motion referring it to the Committee of Privileges, a fifteen-strong body dominated by lawyer MPs with the governing party in a majority.

There are no procedural safeguards. Accused persons may be condemned unheard, or summonsed for cross-examination without legal representation or notice of the charges, and without any right to challenge the evidence given against them or to call witnesses in rebuttal. The Committee sits in secret, and reports in due course to the Commons. The House decides whether and what punishment to inflict, after a further debate in which biased MPs vote entirely as judges in their own cause.

The procedures for dealing with contempt of Parliament are in blatant breach of at least three articles of the European Convention on Human Rights. Article 5 prohibits loss of liberty except by conviction for a clearly defined offence; Article 6 guarantees defendants a fair hearing by an independent and impartial tribunal, and specifically endorses the rights to present a defence, to legal representation, and to call and to cross-examine witnesses; and Article 10 upholds freedom of expression. Fifteen years ago the Committee of Privileges itself recommended some modest procedural reforms, but no action has been taken.[37]

---

[35] Gary Allingham MP, who alleged that MPs traded information for food and drink. The Committee of Privileges was particularly irked by his hypocrisy, since he had done precisely what he accused his colleagues of doing. It recommended a six-month suspension but the House went further and expelled him. HC 138 (1947–8).

[36] In the past a Member had to raise the matter in the Chamber at the earliest opportunity. The publicity this aroused sometimes prompted trivial complaints.

[37] See note 27 above.

At present, the very unfairness of the Committee's procedures can be a boon to those summonsed before it, in the sense that they can make great play of their role as victims. The contraventions of natural justice inherent in the Committee's traditional procedures are indefensible, and any journalist threatened by it should adopt the defiant stance of the 'gang of four' MPs who were summonsed over their naming of 'Colonel B'.

> The gang, led by journalist MP Christopher Price took issue with each and every unfair power that the Committee proposed to use to 'try' them for contempt of Parliament. In a legal memorandum submitted at the outset of their 'trial', they demanded:

1. That we should be accorded the fundamental rights which follow from the application of natural justice:
>   (a) notification of any adverse recommendation the Committee may be minded to make;
>   (b) a summary of any evidence or submission received which reflects on our character or conduct;
>   (c) the rights to appear and explain our conduct at a public hearing;
>   (d) the right of legal representation;
>   (e) a grant of legal aid to cover (d) above;
>   (f) opportunity to call evidence and to cross-examine any hostile witness.
2. That the Committee exclude from membership, at least during its deliberations on our conduct, the Attorney-General (Mr Sam Silkin) who would not appear to be impartial insofar as our conduct, and our submissions in justification of it, may be seen to reflect upon him personally in the conduct of his office.

> The Committee, more used to grovelling apologies than to full-blooded insistence upon legal rights, shrank from confrontation. The Attorney-General played only a very limited part in the proceedings, effectively conceding the demand that justice should be seen to be done, and the Committee issued an anodyne report, which made no recommendations for punishment of the MPs.[38]

These procedural inadequacies are compounded by the extremely limited prospect of obtaining judicial review. The courts may decide whether or not a parliamentary privilege exists, but must not question the practical application of an undoubted privilege in any particular case. The resolution of the House and the Speaker's warrant will be treated as conclusive. The only exception is where

---

[38]   HC 669 (1977–8); HC 222 (1978–9).

the House of Commons exercises its power to imprison for contempt by issuing a warrant that specifies the conduct that is to be punished; in such cases the courts may decide whether the specified conduct is capable of amounting to a contempt – i.e., whether it could have a tendency to impede the performance of parliamentary functions.[39] But Parliament may readily exclude even this limited form of judicial review merely by issuing a general warrant.

MPs' Conflicts of Interest

Following the scandal involving the architect Poulson in 1974 and the growing suspicion that certain MPs had received benefits from him, the House of Commons resolved to take two steps to compel MPs to disclose their private financial interests. In any debates or committee hearings they were to announce any relevant financial interest.[40] This would be recorded in Hansard. The House also set up a register of MPs' interests.[41] Each MP is supposed to report any of the following interests:

- remunerated directorships, employment, offices, trades, professions or vocations;
- the names of clients when the interest referred to includes personal services by the member that arise out of or are related in any manner to his membership of the House;
- financial sponsorship as a parliamentary candidate where this is known to contribute more than one quarter of their election expenses;
- financial sponsorship as an MP, including a statement as to whether the MP is paid or receives any benefit or advantage, direct or indirect;[42]
- overseas visits relating to or arising out of membership of the House where all or part of the cost is not paid by public funds;

---

[39] The most recent authority, which reviews all the eighteenth- and nineteenth-century English cases, is the Australian High Court in *R v Richards ex parte Fitzpatrick and Browne* (1955) 92 CLR 157, upholding the Federal Parliament's foolish decision to imprison two journalists for a defamatory article about an MP.
[40] Hansard 22 May 1974.
[41] On 22 May 1974, the House set up a Select Committee to consider the matter. It reported in December 1974 (HC 102 (1974–5)) and its recommendations were accepted with only a few minor changes on 12 June 1975 (HC Debs (1974–5) vol 893 col 735–803). The requirements for registration are set out in an Appendix to the Committee's Report and in May, *Parliamentary Practice*, pp. 384–90.
[42] Any MP who sponsors a function at Westminster from which he receives a taxable benefit should also declare the source. Report of Select Committee HC 337 (1979–80).

any payment or material benefit or advantage received from or on behalf of foreign governments or organizations;

- land and property of substantial value or from which an income is derived;
- the names of companies or other bodies in which the MP or spouse or infant child has a beneficial interest in shareholdings of at least 1 per cent of its nominal share capital.

The register is published at least once each session as a House of Commons paper.[43] It is also available at the House, where more recent changes can be examined. It is open each day while the House is sitting and once a week during the recess. Appointments must be made by phone and normally confirmed in writing, giving at least forty-eight hours' notice.[44] When the 1990 list was issued, the *Guardian* published it in full. The register is not a 'proceeding in Parliament', and so may become the subject of an action for libel. It may also be introduced as evidence in court actions, without Parliament's consent, where an issue about an MP's conflicts of interest is raised.[45]

Although the registrable interests seem quite comprehensive, the measure is a half-hearted attempt to discover potential conflicts of interest. When the register was first set up, Enoch Powell refused to cooperate, and in the next session four other MPs followed his lead.[46] No action was taken by the House. For three years the Select Committee refused to publish the register until the House attached sanctions to the obligations, but nothing happened and the Committee was forced to climb down.[47] All the information is self-reported, and the paucity of interests registered by some of the wealthier members is difficult to accept as accurate. Failure to register may be a contempt of the House, but no action has been taken against an MP for failure to report a registrable interest. Even where information is reported, it is often vague in the extreme, although in 1990 Winchester MP John Browne was suspended for one month for such a failure. MPs are particularly coy about their landholdings. As for payments, only the source need be registered, not the amount. The register, however, may provide a vital piece to the jigsaw of a puzzling story. As with other disclosure duties, an omission to register may be significant, particularly if the Member has participated in decisions that would affect a personal interest.

---

[43] The latest was published in 1989 HC 115 (1988–9).
[44] See 1974 report (see note 41).
[45] *Rost v Edwards and Others* [1990] 2 All ER 641.
[46] HC 337 (1979–80).
[47] See Introduction to the March 1981 register HC 249 (1980–81).

In addition to the House of Commons register, two trade associations of public relations consultants, the Institute of Public Relations and the Public Relations Consultants Association, maintain a register of MPs and peers who have been employed by their members in an executive or consultative capacity.[48] This has the defects of all voluntary trade association agreements: it is difficult to police and enforce, and it does not apply to non-members. The information that is reported is open to public inspection at the offices of each association.

Election Reporting[49]

Injunctions

Free speech is an essential part of the democratic process, but there must be some safeguard against its deliberate misuse to distort that process at election time. Otherwise, an unscrupulous newspaper editor could influence the result by publishing a story, known to be false, about a party leader or candidate shortly before polling day. Publication could not be restrained by an injunction for libel if the editor stated he was prepared to defend it. A safeguard against such conduct is provided by s 106 of the Representation of the People Act 1983:

> (1) Any person who . . . (a) before or during an election, (b) for the purpose of affecting the return of any candidate at the election, makes or publishes any false statement of fact in relation to the personal conduct or character of the candidate shall be guilty of an illegal practice unless he can show that he has reasonable grounds for believing, and did believe the statement to be true and (2) may be restrained by interim or perpetual injunction by the High Court or the county court . . . from any repetition of that false statement or of a false statement of a similar character in relation to the candidate . . . prima facie proof of the falsity of the statement shall be sufficient . . .

Since there can be no 'candidates' before an election campaign begins, these injunctions can relate to publications only after the

---

[48] Evidence to the 1974 Committee, pp. 75–82.
[49] This section refers to local as well as parliamentary elections. Except where indicated, the same rules also apply to elections to the European Assembly: see European Assembly Elections Act 1978 s 3 and Sched 1 para 2(3), and European Assembly Elections Regulations 1984 (SI 1984 No 137).

writ for the election has been issued or the other formal commencement of the campaign.[50]

This law requires only 'prima facie evidence' of falsehood – an affidavit to that effect by the candidate (who is thereby lain open to a perjury charge if he or she has sworn falsely) might suffice. The false statement need not be defamatory, so long as it is calculated to influence the minds of electors. (It was once held that the false statement that a candidate had shot a fox would be sufficient in a country constituency – the electors presumably being outraged that he had not done the gentlemanly thing and hunted it with dogs.)[51] The false statement must be about 'personal character and conduct', not political performance or allegiance. To say, on the eve of an election, that the leader of the Labour Party is a Communist, would not merit an injunction,[52] to say that he is in the pay of the CIA most certainly would. Finally, the statement must be one of fact rather than opinion. The assertion of CIA paymastery is a statement of fact; the description 'radical traitor' has been held to be a statement of opinion.[53]

The candidate's affidavit of falsehood is not conclusively accepted. No injunction will be granted if the publisher can show reasonable grounds for believing that the story is true.[54]

It is an offence knowingly to publish, in order to promote the election of one candidate, a false statement that a rival candidate has withdrawn.[55]

Advertisements

Newspapers can print election advertisements, but they must take care that these are authorized by the candidate or the election agent. Any other advertisement (by private supporters or well-wishers, for example) for the purpose of procuring a candidate's election is an offence.[56] The advertisement might praise the virtues of the favoured candidate or denounce the failings of the opposition:

---

[50] Parliamentary elections start with the dissolution of Parliament, the announcement by the Government that it intends to dissolve Parliament, or the issuance of a by-election writ. Local government elections run from five weeks before the date fixed for the poll or the publication of notice of the election: 1983 Act s 93(2).

[51] *Borough of Sunderland Case* (1896) 50 M & H at p. 62.

[52] *Burns* v *Associated Newspapers Ltd* (1925) 42 TLR 37.

[53] *Ellis* v *National Union of Conservative and Constitutional Associations, Middleton and Southall* (1900) 44 SJ 750 and see generally *Gatley on Libel and Slander*, 1581 et seq.

[54] *Gatley on Libel and Slander*, paras 1581–2: strictly the burden is on the plaintiff to show the statement is false, but to challenge the plaintiff's affidavit successfully, the defendant must do more than assert that the story is true.

[55] 1983 Act s 106(5).

either way it must be authorized.[57] On the other hand, the press is free to carry advertising concerning general party policies. An advertisement in the 1951 election damned the Labour Government's socialist programme and called for Ministers 'who may be relied upon to encourage business, enterprise and initiative'. This was held to be merely propaganda, which was not related to any particular candidate, and so it was not an advertisement that had to be authorized by a candidate or agent.[58]

In 1984 the Government legislated to restrict trade unions from spending money on political objects unless the expenditure came directly from contributions to a political fund by members who approved of such expenditure. At the 1987 elections NALGO's literature condemning cuts in the Health Service was distributed in marginal constituencies with the object of discomforting Tory candidates: it was held that this action was unlawful because the money for the leaflets did not come from the political fund.[59]

Newspapers and periodicals are free to support or oppose individual candidates in their news and editorial columns. Free publicity of this sort is not included in computing the maximum election expenses that a candidate can incur.[60] But newspapers must still be conscious of defamation in deciding whether to publish election addresses. The Defamation Act 1952 is unequivocal: an election address has no special privilege.[61]

Broadcasting coverage of the campaign

The limitation on advertisements, the absence of privilege for election addresses, the possibility of an injunction for a false statement about a candidate's character, and the penalty for falsely announcing a candidate's withdrawal apply equally to broadcasters. They are also able to transmit statements by or in support of candidates

---

[56] Representation of the People Act 1983 s 75(1) (*b*) and s 75(5). There is an offence only if the paper intends to enhance a candidate's chances. If its motive is *only* to inform the public, it has a good defence: *Grieve* v *Douglas-Home* 1965 SLT 1861. But if one motive is to assist the candidate, then altruistic intentions are irrelevant: *DPP* v *Luft* [1977] AC 962.

[57] *DPP* v *Luft*, note 56 above.

[58] *R* v *Tronoh Mines and The Times Publishing Co Ltd* [1952] 1 All ER 697. In *Meek* v *Lothian Regional Council* (1983) SLT 494 a newssheet put out by the majority party and which explained its rate increases was stopped by the opposition, who persuaded Lord Ross that there was a prima facie case of breach of what is now s 63 of the Representation of the People Act 1983. The judge dismissed *Tronoh Mines* as not applicable to a Scottish regional election, a distinction that is hard to understand.

[59] *Paul* v *NALGO* [1987] IRLR413.

[60] 1983 Act s 75(1)(c)(i).

[61] 1952 Act s 10 reversing *Braddock* v *Bevins* [1948] 1 KB 580.

without committing an election offence.[62] However, there are special controls to make sure that no individual candidate gains an unfair advantage.

Candidate's veto

From the start of an election campaign until the close of the poll, it is unlawful to broadcast a programme that is about the constituency or electoral area and in which a candidate takes part unless the candidate concerned gives his or her consent.[63] The provision allows candidates to approve any editing and to insist on the exclusion of answers in an interview that they later regretted.[64] This control is exercisable only if the candidate has taken an active part in the programme. Candid camera shots of their canvassing would not require consent. They are then the object of the film rather than participants in it.[65]

If the candidate participates and consents, there are further restrictions. The programme cannot be aired until nominations have closed, and even then all the candidates must consent to the programme.[66] Effectively, this means that every candidate for a particular constituency can insist on taking part. It is regrettable that the Act should give one camera-shy candidate the power to block a broadcast with all other candidates in a programme that is fair and balanced. Bernadette McAliskey (Bernadette Devlin) complained that the BBC had divided a candidate's programme into two parts, and she had been placed with 'minor' candidates, who were given less air-time. The judge thought the division was fair but acknowledged that the BBC had to obtain Ms McAliskey's consent or scrap the programme.[67] This 'candidate's veto' means, in practice, that sitting MPs who decide they have nothing to gain by appearing will often refuse to appear or to consent to the programme going ahead without them. It means, in addition, that a single candidate can veto a programme in order to stop the public from hearing the views of a specific opponent (many Labour candidates for this reason veto programmes that would include a candidate from the National Front). These consequences are wholly unacceptable. The voting public in a democracy should be entitled to see the candidates for local and national elections ranged against each other, and local radio and television stations perform a public service by setting up such debates. The law at present permits

---

[62] Representation of the People Act 1983 s 75(1)(c)(ii).
[63] ibid., s 93(1)(a) and s 93(3).
[64] Lord Denning in *Marshall* v *BBC* [1979] 3 All ER 80.
[65] ibid.
[66] 1983 Act s 93(1)(b).
[67] *McAliskey* v *BBC* [1980] NI 44.

individual candidates to ban them, from motives of self-interest or censorship. A provision that was drafted with the reasonable purpose of giving candidates some assurance against unfair editing has, by loose drafting, become a serious infringement of freedom of communication. It should be replaced by a provision entitling election items to be broadcast so long as all candidates are invited and they consent to any editing of their contributions.

Balance

The Independent Television Commission is under a duty to do all it can to ensure that 'due impartiality is preserved on the part of persons providing the service as respects matters of political . . . controversy or relating to current public policy'.[68] By self-denying assurances, the BBC accepts similar standards, although it has no legal or statutory obligation to do so:[69]

> The BBC in Northern Ireland planned to cover the General Election with a series of programmes in which all parties that had polled more than 5 per cent of the vote at a previous election would be allowed to participate. The Workers' Party had not achieved that level of support, so its candidates were excluded. The court held that the BBC was not under any legal duty to act with impartiality in political matters, and that its Royal Charter and Licence did not by implication impose such a duty.[70]

Balance can be achieved through a series of programmes,[71] but at election time broadcasters are super-sensitive to charges of bias. In the run-up to the 1987 elections the BBC turned down a play that depicted Mrs Thatcher behaving heroically and compassionately during the Falklands War. In February 1974 *The Perils of Pendragon*, a comedy programme, was rescheduled because of its unflattering portrayal of a Communist. In 1964 the BBC agreed to move *Steptoe and Son* from peak time on polling day at the request of Harold Wilson, who feared it would keep Labour voters at home. The BBC declined his further suggestion to 'replace it with Greek drama, preferably in the original'.

---

[68] Broadcasting Act 1990 s 6(1).

[69] Letter from Lord Normanbrook, Chairman of the BBC to the Postmaster General in 1964, which is now annexed to the BBC's charter. It is reproduced in Colin Munro, *Television Censorship and the Law*, Saxon House, 1979, p. 10.

[70] *Lynch* v *BBC* [1983] 6 Northern Ireland Judgments Bulletin, Hutton J. The BBC may be the subject of a complaint to the Broadcasting Complaints Commission (see chapter 13), which has statutory powers that could be activated speedily during an election to require the broadcasting of its adjudication that a political party had been unfairly treated.

[71] Broadcasting Act 1990 s 6(2).

Party political broadcasts
A limited number of party political broadcasts are allowed each
year on all channels, determined by the Party Political Broadcast
Committee, comprising representatives from the BBC and ITC
together with the major parties, chaired by the Lord President of
the Council. Air-time is parcelled out according to seats held in
Parliament and performance at recent polls, although no definitive
formula has been adopted. Party propaganda is not welcomed by
viewers other than at election time, and, after thirty years of
complaint, the BBC and ITC have finally abolished the rule that
party broadcasts should be carried simultaneously on all channels.
The SDP/Liberal Alliance felt that it was losing out, not merely in
the number of permitted broadcasts but also in news coverage: an
analysis of major television news programmes in 1984 showed that
70 per cent of political comment reflected Tory views, 25 per cent
Labour and only 5 per cent Alliance. It is natural that Government
policy should obtain substantial coverage, but the Alliance
complained to the Broadcasting Complaints Commission that it
was being denied, as a matter of policy, a coverage in which viewers
might perceive it as an alternative Opposition. The courts upheld
the Commission's refusal to adjudicate the question, on the ground
that it raised issues of policy that were for the broadcasting authorities to determine.[72]

Section 36 of the 1990 Broadcasting Act empowers the Independent Television Commission to require licence-holders to carry party
political broadcasts on Channel 3 (ITV), Channel 4 and the new
Channel 5, and permits the ITC itself to determine which political
parties shall be allowed such broadcasts, how often and for how
long. The Radio Authority is given similar powers. The cosy arrangements between the broadcasters and the major political parties
can come unstuck if their deal contravenes the due-impartiality
requirements of the Broadcasting Act. In 1979 the IBA was
injuncted from showing a set of four party political broadcasts,
agreed with the major parties, three of which favoured a 'yes' vote
for the form of Scottish devolution offered by the referendum.
Three of the four political parties favoured such a vote, but the
court held that the statutory duty on the IBA to maintain a proper
balance required approximately equal time for each case.[73] That
duty has not been imposed on the ITC, but if the situation were to
recur, a similar result might be achieved by reference to the due-
impartiality duty.

---

[72] *R* v *BCC ex parte Owen* [1985] 2 All ER 522, and see *Wilson* v *IBA (No 2)*
(1988) SLT 276.
[73] *Wilson* v *IBA* (1979) SLT 279.

Party political broadcasts during election periods have become an influential part of the democratic process. In 1987 Hugh (*Chariots of Fire*) Hudson produced a remarkable propaganda film that boosted Neil Kinnock's personal rating by 16 per cent overnight, while the Tories counter-attacked with a theme tune specially composed by Andrew (*Evita*) Lloyd-Webber. These broadcasts, too, are allocated by the Party Political Broadcast Committee: by tradition, the Opposition has the penultimate broadcast and the Government has the very last one before the election. These arrangements have worked satisfactorily, although a decision in 1974 to give propaganda time to every party fielding more than fifty candidates led to an inevitably controversial broadcast by the National Front. Much less satisfactory has been the broadcasting authorities' craven acceptance of the right of parties to dictate the choice of spokespeople. Election discussion programmes have become a cosy dialogue between chosen broadcasters and chosen politicians, with none of the fire traditionally associated with the hustings. Questions at carefully arranged press conferences and studio discussions are predictable and deferential – professional broadcasters were put to shame in the 1983 elections, when the only person to subject the Prime Minister to searching questions about the sinking of the *Belgrano*, the Argentinian warship, was a housewife who took part in a phone-in programme. In the 1987 elections the Labour Party was allowed to keep its left-wing candidates well away from the television screen; while much was heard about Ken Livingstone from other parties, he was never permitted to speak for himself to national audiences.

Ministerial broadcasts
The BBC accepts a special duty to permit ministerial broadcasts on matters of national importance, which may range from a declaration of war to emergency arrangements for coping with a drought. So long as there is general consensus on the subject-matter of the broadcast, no right of reply will be given to the Opposition. Where there is, however, an element of partisan controversy in a ministerial broadcast, the Opposition must be given equal time to broadcast a reply.[74] When Mr Tony Benn sought to make a ministerial broadcast in 1975 on the Petroleum and Submarine Protection Act, the BBC detected political controversy in his script and informed him that the Opposition would be entitled to put its

---

[74] See the 'Aide-Memoire' of 3 April 1969, between the BBC and the Conservative and Labour parties.

point of view. He cancelled the broadcast rather than allow his opponents free air-time. Section 10 of the Broadcasting Act places a statutory duty on the ITC to comply with a notice from a minister of the Crown requiring it to direct licence holders to publish an official announcement, 'with or without visual images'. Licence holders will be contractually bound to comply with such a direction, but they may reveal the direction's existence to their viewers.

Foreign radio and television stations must not be exploited by interested parties to influence British elections, but otherwise their programmes can be broadcast by arrangement with the BBC or ITC.[75]

Access to meetings

At election times schools and public meeting rooms have to be made available to candidates so that they can promote their campaigns.[76] Consistent with this objective, a candidate can book one of these venues only for a *public* meeting. A popular or controversial candidate may not be able to accommodate every member of the public who would like to be admitted, but, as in other contexts, it is difficult to see how a meeting could be correctly described as 'public' if the press were actively excluded. Journalists who are ordered to leave election meetings by organizers unhappy with press coverage should insist on their right to remain. If forcibly ejected, they could obtain damages for assault.

Access to register and candidates' returns

The lists of electors are public documents, which the media are free to inspect and copy. Reporters have this access not just at election times but during normal business hours. One copy of the register is kept at the electoral officer's office (normally the town hall) and usually at public libraries as well.[77]

Within thirty-five days of the announcement of the result, the election agents for all the candidates must file a return with the electoral officer detailing the candidates' expenses. The electoral officer has ten further days to advertise in two newspapers that circulate in the constituency giving notice of where and when the returns can be inspected. The returns and accompanying docu-

---

[75] Representation of the People Act s 92.
[76] ibid., s 95 (parliamentary elections) s 96 (local government elections).
[77] Representation of the People Regulations 1983 (SI 1983 No 435) reg 18.

ments can be inspected and copied there (usually at the town hall) by any member of the public for two years after the election.[78] A fee of £1 can be charged for the inspection and a fee of 10p per page for copies.[79]

---

[78] Representation of the People Act 1983 ss 81, 88 and 89. Parish Council returns are kept for only one year: ibid., s 90(1)(*b*) and Sched 4 para 8(1); as are returns of European Assembly elections: European Assembly Election Regulations 1984.
[79] Representation of the People Regulations 1983 reg 70(2), (3).

Chapter 10

Reporting Whitehall

It is an official secret if it is in an official file.

Sir Martin Furnival-Jones, Head of MI5,
evidence to Franks Committee on Official Secrets.[1]

Secrecy, said Richard Crossman, is the British disease. Government administrators catch it from the Official Secrets Act and supporting legislation. It is aggravated by bureaucratic rules and arrangements that conspire to place the United Kingdom toward the bottom in the league table of openness in Western democratic government. Against those who would hide their publicly paid behaviour from the public eye, the professional journalist can have only one response: to press on with investigating and publishing, irrespective of the law. Most of the secrecy rules described in this chapter deserve to be broken, and many are, in fact, broken by the media regularly and without repercussions.

'Whitehall' stands for the executive and military branch of central government. The Palace of Whitehall was the home of the first civil servants, who served the despotic Stuart kings. They now serve a democratic government, and justify the secrecy of their service by reference to an outdated theory that 'ministerial accountability' requires information requested by representatives of the public to be forthcoming only from, or with the approval of, ministers responsible for Whitehall departments. In practice, however, ministerial involvement in departmental decisions occurs only at levels of high policy, and executive errors must be of the magnitude of the failure to foresee the invasion of the Falkland Islands before a minister will resign a portfolio. The truth is that ministers neither control nor are answerable for thousands of decisions made by middle-ranking departmental officers – decisions that may vitally affect individuals and communities. If executive accountability is ever to be made a reality in Britain, the press and the public must be given the power, through a Freedom of Informa-

---

[1] *Report of the Departmental Committee on the Reform of s 2 of the Official Secrets Act 1911*, Cmnd 5104 Vol III p. 249.

tion Act, to inspect the information accumulated and acted upon by administrators. Such legislation is fast becoming a defining characteristic of democratic government in other Western countries, not merely in Europe and the United States, but in Australia, Canada and New Zealand, with their 'Westminster Model' parliaments. The evidence is accumulating that public participation in government leads to better government. As *The Sunday Times* put it in an editorial following the *Crossman Diaries* case:

> Secrecy should be radically re-examined not so that errors can be exposed – although that is important – but because in a system where disclosure is more nearly the norm, errors are less likely to occur . . . Many events of recent history might have turned out not merely different but better if public opinion had been allowed to play upon them.

Freedom of information legislation would challenge the prevailing ethos of bureaucratic secrecy. By establishing a presumption in favour of disclosure, backed by a legal right enforceable in court, it would become a socially subscribed value that civil servants would ignore at their peril.[2]

None of the justifications for our present level of secrecy is convincing. National security might be threatened by the revelation of a limited class of information to foreign powers, but too often this danger is used as a pretext for the Government to withhold embarrassing information from its own citizens. The Government does gather many intimate details about individuals that it ought to keep confidential, but privacy as a rationale for secrecy is less persuasive when it concerns the social impact of corporate policies, and still less when it concerns policy discussions within Government. The argument that civil servants would be less frank if their advice were shortly to be made public is a canard; the evidence from other countries suggests that the advice would be better considered and better expressed. Even if some information is no longer written down and, instead, communicated orally, this cannot be routine in bureaucracies the size of Whitehall. The great attraction for blanket secrecy laws within the civil service seems to be that it fosters a sense of self-importance. Mandarins with a high security clearance have a status derived more from the exclusivity of their access to information than from its intrinsic significance. Even junior civil servants, according to a former head of MI5 who approved the discredited and now abolished 'section 2' of the Official Secrets Act 1911

---

[2] Geoffrey Robertson, 'Law for the Press' in James Curran (ed.), *The British Press: A Manifesto*, Macmillan, 1978, pp. 207–12.

... find a kind of pride in being subjected to the criminal law in this way ... the fact that they ... are picked out as being people who are doing work so dangerous if you like that it brings them within the scope of the criminal law if they talk about it, has a very powerful effect on their minds ... it is not that they are deterred by the fear of prosecution, but in a sense it is a spur to their intent.[3]

A vast quantity of information does, of course, pour out of Whitehall in the form of press releases from the press officers now attached to all departments. Even Army officers are taught how to give interviews, and the media give ample space for these official hand-outs. The difficulty is to extract information that is not 'authorized' or 'vetted'; the civil servant who speaks out of turn in some cases faces the vague threat of prosecution, but more often the immediate danger of disciplinary sanction by way of transfer, demotion or dismissal. British law has no equivalent of the American 'Whistleblowers Act', whereby civil servants are protected from internal disciplinary retaliation if they disclose illegal, incompetent or dangerous activities.[4] However, for all the difficulties posed by secrecy laws and conventions, most journalistic attempts to penetrate it will not be punished. The Official Secrets Acts, for all their formidable appearance, have important gaps. The Government must always assess whether it is willing to court unpopularity by prosecuting journalists over revelations of genuine public interest. This chapter will seek to give the Official Secrets Acts and other secrecy conventions a realistic appraisal. It will explain how valuable source material can be obtained through public records legislation and by invoking policy directives, which can help journalists to negotiate the disclosure of more recent public documents.

The Official Secrets Act

The Official Secrets Act 1911 was rushed on to the statute books at a time of national panic, as German 'gunboat diplomacy' at Agadir coincided with sensationalized newspaper stories about German spies photographing the fortifications at Dover harbour.[5] It completed its entire parliamentary progress in one day, hailed by all parties as an urgently necessary measure to protect the nation's secrets from enemy agents. No MP spoke on s 2 of the Act, which

---

[3] Evidence to the Franks Committee, note 1 above, vol III p. 261.
[4] Civil Service Reform Act 1978.
[5] Franks Report, note 1 above, Vol I App III.

had been carefully drafted within Whitehall some time before with the purpose of stopping leakage of official information to the press.[6] This had grown with a rapidly expanding civil service and the concomitant loss of effective ministerial responsibility. Civil service chiefs had bided their time, and cannily slipped the clause into a measure that ostensibly had nothing to do with journalism. The press was soon to suffer: the very first prosecution brought under the new Act was to punish a war-office clerk for supplying information to the *Military Mail* that cast his superiors in a poor light.[7]

Section 2 managed, by tortuous drafting, to create more than 2,000 different offences in a few statutory paragraphs. These could be roughly divided into two groups: those most likely to be committed by inside sources (i.e. by communicating official information to an unauthorized person) and those that directly affected journalists who received or retained official information without authorization. The more serious s 1, which has a maximum penalty of fourteen years' imprisonment, is aimed at spies and saboteurs, although the Government has once, in the 'ABC' case (see p. 417), tried to extend it to journalists. Finally, the Act gave the police extraordinary powers to arrest, seize documents and to question suspects, including journalists. The 1989 Act, which replaced s 2 with narrower (and hence more formidable) offences, may not often be invoked. More than any other piece of legislation, its use is circumscribed by political considerations.

The Attorney-General in the past had to approve every prosecution under the Act (the exception under the Official Secrets Act 1989 is considered below), and take into account the degree of culpability, the damage to the public interest that resulted from the disclosure, and the effect that a prosecution would have on the public interest.[8] A number of top-level spies have gone unprosecuted since the Second World War because it has been deemed inexpedient to expose to the public (and to Britain's allies) the extent of Soviet penetration even with the restrictions available by in-camera hearings. At the other extreme, Attorneys-General were reluctant to prosecute newspapers for routine breaches of s 2 of the Act; the appearance of secret Whitehall documents in the press is usually followed by a 'leak inquiry', conducted by Scotland Yard, with the object of discovering the civil servant responsible. So long as journalists decline to answer questions or supply leaked

---

[6] K. G. Robertson, *Public Secrets: A Study of the Development of Government Secrecy*, Macmillan, 1982, p. 63.

[7] Franks Report, note 1 above, Vol I App III. See also Jonathan Aitkin, *Officially Secret*, Weidenfeld & Nicolson, 1971.

[8] 1911 Act s 8. The criteria in the text were given by the Attorney-General in evidence to the Franks Committee, note 1 above, Vol II p. 7.

copies of documents that might incriminate their source, these inquiries are usually fruitless.

The Attorney-General, as a party politician, will be disinclined to use oppressive and discredited legislation against the press. However, he may come under heavy pressure from the military and security establishment, unswayed by any concern for civil liberties and perhaps anxious to impress American 'cousins' with their resolve to protect Allied secrets. Insecure Labour law officers, desirous of proving themselves 'responsible' in such matters, twice succumbed to this pressure in recent years. The first occasion, in 1970, had the result of discrediting s 2 of the Act:

> Jonathan Aitken, journalist and parliamentary candidate, came by a secret Army document about the state of the Biafran war that contained information at variance with Prime Ministerial statements to Parliament (such a document would be covered by the 1989 Act because it revealed Army logistics and deployment). He was given it by a general, who had received the report from a colonel attached to the British Embassy in Nigeria. Aitken, to the general's embarrassment, arranged for it to be published in the *Daily Telegraph*. The Attorney-General authorized an s 2 prosecution of the colonel, Aitken, and the editor of the *Daily Telegraph*, with the general cutting a sorry figure as chief prosecution witness. Various technical defences were canvassed, based on the prosecution's difficulty in proving that original disclosure by the colonel to the general, his former commanding officer, was 'unauthorized'. Both journalist and editor additionally claimed that they had a moral duty to make the information public in order to rectify false statements in Parliament. The defence claimed the case was a 'political prosecution', initiated by a petulant Labour Government, and the trial judge in a sympathetic summing-up told the jury that it was high time that s 2 was 'pensioned off'. All defendants were acquitted.[9]

The outcry provoked by the Aitken prosecution led to the establishment of a committee headed by Lord Franks to examine s 2 of the Official Secrets Act. It condemned the width and uncertainty of the section, and urged its replacement by a law narrowly defining the categories of information that deserved protection.[10] The Government, in 1976, accepted that mere receipt of secret information by the press should not amount to an offence.[11] Reform of the Act was put in abeyance, however, by the extraordinary security service vendetta against journalist Duncan Campbell:

> Campbell was a young freelance journalist specializing in defence

---

[9] *R* v *Aitken and Others* and see also Aitken, *Officially Secret.*
[10] Franks Committee Report, note 1 above.
[11] Hansard 22 November 1976 [Hansard] HC Debs Vol 919 col 1878 *et seq.*

and working mainly for small-circulation magazines. In company with Crispin Aubrey, a news reporter from *Time Out*, he interviewed a disaffected ex-soldier, John Berry, who ten years before had worked at a signals intercept base in Cyprus. He had written to the magazine volunteering to reveal security 'scandals', although the information he could give the journalists added little to what Campbell had already collected, from published sources, about British Signals Intelligence operations. The three men were arrested, and Campbell's entire home library was removed in a pantechnicon to Scotland Yard. The 'ABC' case, which then commenced its passage, had side consequences already noted. The prosecution, for the first time, used s 1 charges against journalists.

The result was that Campbell alone was charged, under s 1, with collecting information of use to an enemy relating to a number of defence installations. The count collapsed after two weeks of evidence demonstrating that Campbell's information and photographs had come from published sources – in some cases, Ministry of Defence press hand-outs. The incompetence of the security services, which had instructed the Attorney-General that Campbell's information was top secret, was, in effect, conceded by the Crown prosecutor when withdrawing this ill-conceived charge.

The two journalists were charged under s 1 with obtaining information of use to an enemy (Berry's account of his time in Cyprus) for a purpose prejudicial to the security of the state. The 'purpose prejudicial' was alleged to be their intention to publish it in *Time Out*. These charges were withdrawn at the insistence of the judge, Mr Justice Mars-Jones, who described them as 'oppressive'. Although the wide wording of s 1 of the Act was not necessarily confined to spies and saboteurs, he said that its harsh provisions (including a reversal of the burden of proof and facilitation of guilt by association) made it undesirable for use against persons not alleged to be in league with a foreign power.

Section 2 charges were brought home against each defendant. Berry was found to be in breach of the Act by passing information to the journalists, and they were found guilty of receiving this information. Berry received a six-month suspended sentence; both journalists were given conditional discharges.[12]

The effective collapse of the 'ABC' prosecution may make future Attorneys reluctant to use s 1 against investigative journalism. The Attorney-General of the time, Sam Silkin QC, defended his decision to prosecute on the grounds that he had been misled by the Ministry of Defence and the security service as to the sensitivity of the information in Campbell's possession.[13] Colonel B was less impressive under skilled cross-examination than he had been in the Attorney's chambers. The case had the additional importance of

---

[12] Andrew Nicol, 'Official Secrets and Jury Vetting' [1979] Crim LR 284.
[13] Crispin Aubrey, *Who's Watching You?*, Penguin, 1981.

undermining the seriousness of s 2 by the lightness of the sentences visited upon the journalist offenders. In 1975 the crime correspondent of the *Evening Standard* was acquitted on s 2 charges of receiving information from police contacts. The defence was able to show that receipt of such information was a long tradition in Fleet Street, and was effectively 'authorized' by custom and usage. From a cynical perspective, the media was better off with a discredited 'catch-all' s 2 than with a reformed, precise alternative. The Conservative Government sought to introduce just such an alternative in its ill-fated Official Information Bill of 1979: the initiative foundered when it appeared that the proposed law would have made it an offence for journalists to reveal the traitorous activities of Sir Anthony Blunt.[14] They succeeded ten years later with the Official Secrets Act 1989, which would make such a revelation a criminal offence if it emanated from a former employee of the security service.

The 1989 Act offers the media a Faustian bargain: it lifts the possibility of prosecution for much routine information within Whitehall (revelation of which would never in practice have been prosecuted under the old s 2) while it makes much easier the prosecution of revelations about intelligence work, defence and foreign affairs. In these cases it replaces a blunderbuss with an armalite rifle, designed to hit defendants who repeat the conduct of the likes of Aitken, Campbell and Clive Ponting. The Government firmly resisted a public-interest defence, which might have protected the media and their sources in relation to leaks that demonstrate discreditable conduct within the defence and intelligence establishment.

The 1989 Act offences fall broadly into those that are most likely to be committed by 'insiders' and those designed with 'outsiders', such as the press, in mind. We start with the former because they introduce categories and classifications that span both groups.

Offences by 'insiders'

These are subdivided into four groups.

Security and intelligence

This group is further subdivided into members of the security or intelligence services and those who work closely with them, and other Crown servants or government contractors who learn of information concerning security and intelligence in the course of their work.

---

[14] David Leigh, *The Frontiers of Secrecy*, Junction Books, 1980, p. 262.

Persons who are or have been members of the security and intelligence services commit an offence if they disclose any information, document or other article relating to security or intelligence that they have acquired in the course of their intelligence work.[15] There is no stipulation that the information must be secret, and the courts would probably follow their stance under the old s 2[16] and find the offence was committed even though the information was not secret in any meaningful sense.

Significantly, under this offence the Crown does not have to prove any damage or harm. These severe obligations of secrecy can be extended by written notice to others who, though not actually members of the secret services, work closely with them.[17]

For Crown servants and government contractors who are not members of the secret services and who are not made honorary members by notification there is a narrower offence of making a *damaging* disclosure of information relating to security or intelligence.[18] 'Damage' here means damage to the work of, or any part of, the security and intelligence services.[19] It is not apparently sufficient if work in support of the security services is harmed. Although there may, of course, be a knock-on effect, it is harm to the secret services themselves that must be shown. Here and throughout the Act it is enough if damage would be 'likely to occur' as a result of the disclosure. In the present context alone the definition is wider. The prosecution does not have to prove that the particular information would be likely to cause harm. It may merely show that it is of a class that might have this effect.

'Crown servants' are the principle group of 'insiders'. They include civil servants, the armed forces, and the police (and their civilian assistants).[20] The employees of certain privatized corporations and regulatory bodies have been brought within the definition

---

[15] Official Secrets Act 1989 s 1(1) 'security or intelligence includes work in support of the security services'; s 1(8).

[16] *R v Crisp and Homewood* (1919) 83 JP 121; *R v Galvin* [1987] 2 All ER 851.

[17] Official Secrets Act 1989 s 1(1)(*b*) and s 1(6).

[18] ibid., s 1(3).

[19] ibid., s 1(4)(*a*).

[20] ibid., s 12. Employees of a county council seconded exclusively to police stations were 'in employment under a person who holds office under Her Majesty' for the purposes of the 1911 Act: *Loat v Andrews* [1985] ICR 679 and they would no doubt be 'employed . . . for the purposes of any police force' under the present law. The Government has asserted that the decision of the Home Secretary to issue a written notice would be judicially reviewable: see HC Debs Vol 145 col 148 (26 January 1989). As British judges tend to be overimpressed whenever the Government ministers defend their action with the magic words 'national security', this is unlikely to offer much comfort to individuals deprived of their freedom of expression by receipt of a notice. See *R v Secretary of State for the Home Department ex parte Cheblak* [1991] 2 All ER 319.

of Crown servant by ministerial 'prescription' permitted by the Act – without parliamentary debate or public notice.[21] In 1990 the Government moved by 'prescription' to button the lips of all employees of British Nuclear Fuels and the Atomic Energy Authority, together with all persons employed by the Parliamentary Commission for Administration (the Ombudsman), the Auditor General and the Health Service Commissioner – posts that are ostensibly independent of Government.[22] The failure of the Ombudsman to object to the extension of this draconian Act to his staff is a disturbing reflection on his ability to judge where the public interest lies, namely in permitting the public reasonable scrutiny of bodies supposed to act in their interest. Local government employees are not and never have been Crown servants. The 1911 Act expressly applied to colonial governments; the 1989 Act does not, but the Government can extend its reach to the Channel Islands, the Isle of Man or any colony by statutory instruments.[23] The Act also reserves the power to add other groups to the definition of 'Crown servant' by ministerial order with only the minimal protection that a draft of the order must be approved by each House of Parliament.

The definition disingenuously includes ministers.[24] They are undoubtedly Crown servants, but despite the ministerial 'briefings' that are the bread and butter of political reporting, no minister has ever been prosecuted under the Official Secrets Act. This is excused by the 'fig-leaf' theory that ministers are able to authorize themselves to make disclosures. The naked truth is that prosecutions must be approved by the Attorney-General, who in the recent past has always been a member of the same political party as the blabbermouth minister. Resignation is the most severe penalty that has been imposed on ministers who have been indiscrete. J. H. Thomas was not prosecuted for leaking budget secrets in 1936, as the Attorney-General said he had been drunk at the time.[25] George Lansbury passed a Cabinet paper to his son in 1934; the son was prosecuted, the minister was not. The Attorney-General took civil action (see p. 181) against Richard Crossman's publishers over his Cabinet memoirs but conceded that there was no criminal liability.[26] Leon Brittan was not prosecuted for authorizing the leak of legal advice to the Government over the Westland affair, and

---

[21] ibid., s 12(*f*) and (*g*).
[22] ibid., (Prescription) Order 1990 (SI 1990 No 200).
[23] ibid., s 15(3).
[24] ibid., s 12(1)(*a*).
[25] Hansard 10 June 1936 col 206.
[26] see Hugo Young, *The Crossman Affair*, Hamish Hamilton and Jonathan Cape, 1976, p. 33.

Cecil Parkinson survived allegations that he had whispered Falklands War secrets to his mistress during moments of non-connubial bliss.

'Government contractor' means companies and their employees who provide goods or services for a minister, the civil service, the armed forces or the police force. Additionally, it applies to contractors with governments of other states or international organizations.[27]

Defence[28]

Crown servants and government contractors commit an offence if they disclose information that they have acquired in their jobs and that concerns defence. Damage must be proved by the prosecution. In this context 'damage' means damage to the capability of any part of the armed forces, loss of life or injury to its members or serious damage to its equipment or installations. It can also mean jeopardy to, or serious obstruction of, British interests abroad or danger to the safety of British citizens abroad.

International relations[29]

This, again, is a category that applies to Crown servants and government contractors. It concerns information relating to international relations[30] or confidential information that has been obtained from another state or an international organization. The information of either type must be acquired in the course of the defendant's job.

Damage has to be shown by the prosecution. As with defence matters, this can be jeopardy to, or serious obstruction of, British interests abroad or danger to the safety of British citizens abroad. If the information was derived from another state or an international organization, the prosecution can rely on the fact that it was confidential or on its nature or contents to establish that its disclosure would be likely to cause damage. The jury is none the less entitled to find that no damage would be likely to result from disclosure since the section provides only that these elements *may* be sufficient to establish harm.[31]

---

[27] Official Secrets Act 1989 s 12(2). It also applies to contracts that the Secretary of State certifies are for the purposes of implementing the contracts referred to in the text.
[28] ibid., s 2, defence is comprehensively defined in s 2(4).
[29] ibid., s 3.
[30] 'International relations' means the relations between states and/or with international organizations, ibid., s 3(5).
[31] ibid., s 3(3).

Crime[32]

This category is loosely described as information concerning crime, but it is really far broader. It concerns information the disclosure of which would be likely to result in the commission of an offence, facilitate the escape of a detained person, or impede the prevention or detection of offences or the apprehension or prosecution of suspects. There is no further requirement that the prosecution must show that the information is likely to cause damage. The Government argued that the categories of information are, by definition, likely to cause harm.

This dubious argument does not apply to a subcategory that rides on the back of 'crime'. It is an offence to disclose any information obtained from mail or telephone intercepts under a ministerial warrant or information obtained by the security services under warrant. This prohibition extends to information obtained by reason of the intercept or secret service interference or any document or article used for or obtained by the intercept or interference.[33]

Authority and mistake

None of the insider offences are committed unless the disclosure was unauthorized. For Crown servants and 'honorary' members of the security services that means a disclosure that is not in accordance with their official duty. In Clive Ponting's prosecution the trial judge ruled that it was for the Government of the day to decide what was the duty of civil servants.[34] However, the judge could not direct the jury to convict, and Ponting's acquittal showed that the jury took a more robust view of where his duty lay. 'Authorized' means, in the case of a government contractor, disclosure to a Crown servant or in accordance with a Crown servant's directions.[35]

The prerequisite of authorization provides some prospect of a defence for the media: in the *Aitken* case it was argued that if original disclosure by the ex-colonel was 'authorized', the subsequent chain of disclosure could not be in breach of the Act. The more recent s 2 case of *R* v *Galvin*[36] is also of assistance:

> The Court of Appeal quashed an Official Secrets Act conviction on the ground that the issue of 'authorization' had not been left to the jury. The document concerned was an MoD manual that had been classified as 'restricted' and had been obtained by the defendant by

---

[32] ibid., s 4.
[33] ibid., s 4(3).
[34] *R* v *Ponting* [1985] Crim LR 318, see also Clive Ponting, *The Right to Know*, 1985.
[35] Official Secrets Act 1989 s 7.
[36] [1987] 2 All ER 851

subterfuge. None the less, it emerged at the trial that the manual had, in fact, been circulated to some outside bodies by the MoD, without specific restrictions on its further use. It was open to the jury to find, on this evidence, that the MoD had 'impliedly authorized' circulation of the information, notwithstanding the 'restricted' classification stamp on the copy obtained by the defendant.

None of the offences is committed if the defendant can persuade the jury that he did not know or have reason to believe that the information concerned security, defence, international relations or the categories of crime. In cases where the prosecution must prove damage it is similarly open to the defendant to prove that he did not know or have reason to believe that the disclosure would or might have the damaging effect.[37]

Retention of documents and careless loss

Crown servants and honorary members of the security services who have in their possession documents or articles that it would be an offence for them to disclose commit an offence if they retain the document or article contrary to their official duty. They have a defence if they believed they were acting in accordance with their duty and no reasonable cause to believe otherwise.[38]

Government contractors commit a similar offence if they fail to comply with an official direction for the return or disposal of the document or article.[39]

Both Crown servants and government contractors can be guilty of failing to take reasonable care to prevent the unauthorized disclosure of such documents or articles.[40] A Foreign Office civil servant was fined £300 under the predecessor to this provision for carelessly leaving secret diplomatic cables on a tube train. Extracts from the cables were later published in the London magazine *City Limits*. No action was taken against the magazine.[41]

Offences by 'outsiders'

These are the offences of most direct relevance to the media.

Disclosure of leaked or confidential information[42]

The 1989 Act replaces the notorious s 2 with what will in time become known as s 5, although the latter's notoriety will depend

---

[37] Official Secrets Act 1989 ss 1(5), 2(3), 3(4), 4(4), 4(5).
[38] ibid., s 8(1)(*a*), 8(2).
[39] ibid., s 8(1)(*b*).
[40] ibid., s 8(1).
[41] (1982) *Observer*, 5 December.
[42] Official Secrets Act 1989 s 5.

on a number of unresolved questions of interpretation. Broadly, s 5 makes it a specific offence for journalists and editors to publish information that they know is protected by the Act, although the prosecution must additionally prove that they had reason to believe that the publication would be damaging to the security services or to the interests of the United Kingdom. If charged under s 5, editors can at least testify as to their state of mind in deciding to publish, and will be entitled to an acquittal if the jury accepts that there was no rational basis for thinking that the disclosure would damage British interests.

The new offence is complex. It involves looking at the type of information concerned and the outsider's knowledge that it is of this type (we shall assume that the outsider is a journalist). It turns also on the character of further disclosure that takes place and the journalist's awareness that it has this character. Each ingredient needs more consideration.

Type of information.   The information must be protected against disclosure by an insider, i.e. it must relate to security or intelligence, defence or international relations or to crime.[43] The information must also have originated from a Crown servant or government contractor. It is arguable that in this context an offence is committed by an outsider only if the source is a Crown servant at the time of the leak and that the offence does not extend to disclosures by former servants of the Crown.[44] This confusion over whether s 5 extends to publication of the memoirs of *former* employees was exposed (and confounded) by the decision of the House of Lords in *Lord Advocate* v *Scotsman Publications* (the Cavendish Diaries case):

> The Law Lords lifted a breach of confidence injunction on newspaper publication of Cavendish's memoirs of life in the secret services after the war because no danger to national security could be apprehended by publication. Two judges considered whether the publication would amount to a breach of s 5. Lord Templeman considered that the newspaper would fall within the provisions of the section by publishing, notwithstanding that Cavendish was a former Crown servant and s 5 in terms refers only to revelations by 'Crown servants'. Lord Jauncy, however, stated that this interpretation 'may well be unjustified having regard to the obscurity of the language'. Both Law Lords agreed that a newspaper editor could, in any event, be found guilty only if the disclosure of the information was, in fact, damaging to national security.

On principle, Lord Jauncy's approach is preferable: criminal

---

statutes should be narrowly construed, and Parliament has only itself to blame if the words 'Crown servants' are defined to exclude persons who are not Crown servants by the time the offence was allegedly committed. It must not be assumed, however, that this interpretation will be finally adopted by the courts. Section 5(3) refers to documents 'protected from disclosure by s 1 to 3 above' and these sections protect against disclosures by 'retired Crown servants' – a reference that the courts could seize upon to interpret 'Crown servants' in s 5(1) to include 'former Crown servants'.

In addition, the information must have been disclosed without authority (either to the journalist or to someone else), or entrusted in confidence to the journalist or passed in breach of confidence to the journalist or someone else.[45] If the information was leaked by a government contractor or a confidee of a Crown servant or government contractor, there is a further restriction. That disclosure must have been made by a British citizen or taken place in the United Kingdom, the Channel Islands, the Isle of Man or a colony.[46]

Journalist's knowledge of the type of information.   The prosecution has to prove that the journalist knew or had reasonable cause to believe that the information was protected against disclosure and that it has reached him by one of the routes described above.[47]

Type of further disclosure.   There is an offence only if the further disclosure is without lawful authority (see p. 422). More significantly, if the information relates to security, intelligence, defence or international relations, the prosecutions must show that its further disclosure by the journalist will be damaging. The definitions of damage are the same as those for insider offences.[48] The Government refused to concede a public-interest defence or a defence that the disclosed material had already been published before. This obduracy was unfortunate and unnecessary: juries have been loath to convict when disclosures were made on public-interest grounds (e.g. Clive Ponting and Jonathan Aitken) and the 'damage' requirement is not a perfect substitute for a public-interest defence. Prosecutors will no doubt argue that the statute requires only some harm and, once this is proved, it is not for juries to balance the harm against an alleged benefit from disclosure. In any case, damage does not have to be shown where the information relates to crime. None the less, the fact that the material has been published already or that it is in the public

---

[45] Official Secrets Act 1989 s 5(1)(*a*).
[46] ibid., s 5(4).
[47] ibid., s 5(2).
[48] ibid., s 5(3).

interest that it should be made known would be powerful arguments against there being any harm where damage does have to be
proved.

Journalist's knowledge of character of further disclosure. The
journalist must know or have reasonable cause to believe that his
further disclosure would be damaging.[49] The insider offences
include something similar as a defence but the burden of proof is
then on the Crown servant. Here, knowledge by a media defendant
that the further disclosure would be likely to be damaging must be
proved by the prosecution beyond reasonable doubt.

Media complicity with an 'insiders' offence

There is no doubt that s 5 offers the media a considerable advance
on the abolished s 2: the drafting is clumsy and obscure, and the
questions of 'damage' and knowledge may be developed by way of
defence before the jury. The real danger, largely ignored both by
Parliament and the press in the debates over s 5, is that it will not
be used at all. Instead, the publishers of information from future
Wrights and Massiters will simply be charged with offences of
incitement, conspiracy, or aiding and abetting a breach of the strict
liability s 1 of the 1989 Act. This danger will be particularly present
if payment is made for the information, or if the information is
published by agreement with the errant insider. The confusion
over whether s 5 applies to publication of disclosures by former
Crown servants will be side-stepped by charging the media in such
cases with the crime of complicity in an offence against s 1, which
applies to former Crown servants as well as those presently serving
the state. Such charges would leave the media with no substantial
defence. Of course, whether such draconian action would be taken
will depend, as ever, upon political considerations. In 1990 the
Government admitted to having misled Parliament when denying
allegations by Colin Wallace about disinformation exercises by the
security services in Northern Ireland in the early 1970s. Wallace
was not prosecuted under the 1989 Act.

Disclosure of information from spying

A simple offence is created by the 1989 Act of disclosing without
lawful authority any information, document or article that the
defendant knows or has reasonable cause to believe has come into
his possession as a result of a breach of s 1 of the 1911 Act.[50]
Section 1 principally concerns spying (see p. 428) and it will be

---

[49] ibid., s 5(3)(*b*).
[50] ibid., s 5(6).

rare for journalists to come into the possession of such information.

Information from abroad[51]
A separate offence is created by the 1989 Act for the unauthorized disclosure of information that has come from another state or international organization. This offence also needs to be broken down.

Type of information.   This offence concerns only information relating to security, intelligence, defence or international relations. The information must also have been passed by the United Kingdom in confidence to another state or international organization. It must have come into the journalist's possession without the authority of that state or organization.[52]

Journalist's knowledge.   The journalist must know or have reasonable cause to believe that the information is of the type described above.[53]

Type of disclosure.   There is no offence if the journalist's disclosure is made with lawful authority.[54] It is not a defence, as such, that the material has been previously published abroad unless it was published with the authority of the state or organization concerned.[55] However, the prosecution must show that the publication by the journalist is damaging,[56] and if it has been previously published (even without authority), this will be difficult to do.

Journalist's knowledge of the consequences of further disclosure.   The prosecution must again show that the journalist knew or had reasonable cause to believe that the further disclosure would be damaging.[57]

Retention and careless loss[58]
A person given a document or other article in confidence by a Crown servant or government contractor is guilty of an offence if he or she fails to take reasonable care to prevent its unauthorized disclosure.[59] It is also an offence to fail to comply with an official

---

[51]   ibid., s 6.
[52]   ibid., s 6(1)(*a*).
[53]   ibid., s 6(2).
[54]   ibid., s 6(3).
[55]   ibid.
[56]   ibid., s 6(2), 'damage' has the same meaning as under the insider offences.
[57]   ibid.
[58]   ibid., s 8(4) and (5).
[59]   ibid., s 8(4)(*b*).

direction for the return or disposal of a document or article whose disclosure would be an offence under either ss 5 or 6. There is an offence only if the journalist (or other outsider) is in possession of the document or article at the time its return is demanded. This simply adds to the incentive to dispose of leaked documents before their return is demanded (parting with possession is itself a disclosure (see s 13(1)) and so care would have to be taken in deciding whether disposal would be an offence).

These offences are triable only by magistrates, who can impose a fine on scale 5 (currently £2,000) or sentence to prison for up to three months. The price for being categorized as relatively minor offences is that there is no right to trial by jury. This is worrying since juries in the past have played such an important role in keeping the widely drawn Official Secrets Acts within some reasonable limits.

Access information[60]

This offence concerns information that is or has been in the possession of a Crown servant or government contractor and can be used to obtain access to any information, document or article that is protected against disclosure by the Act and where the circumstances are such that it would be reasonable to expect it to be used for such a purpose without authority. It is an offence for anyone (whether insider or outsider) to disclose this type of information.

1911 Act, section 1: 'penalties for spying'

Headed 'penalties for spying', this section is generally used against enemy agents. It carries a maximum penalty of fourteen years, which has often been invoked for serious espionage: George Blake was sentenced to forty-two years imprisonment for three offences.[61] The section makes it an offence:

> if any person for any purpose prejudicial to the safety or interest of the State –
>
> (*a*) approaches, inspects, passes over or is in the neighbourhood of, or enters any prohibited place within the meaning of this Act; or
>
> (*b*) makes any sketch, plan, model, or note which is calculated to be or might be or is intended to be directly or indirectly useful to an enemy; or
>
> (*c*) obtains, collects, records or publishes, or communicates to any other person any secret official code word, or password

[60] ibid., s 8(6).
[61] *R v Blake* [1961] 3 All ER 125.

or any sketch, plan, model, article or note or other document or information which is calculated to be or might be or is intended to be directly or indirectly useful to the enemy.

The actions by themselves may be quite trivial – approaching a prohibited place, such as a nuclear power station (see below), or sketching a map that could be useful to a potential enemy. War need not have been declared: *potential* enemies are included, although it is agents of enemy governments who are targeted – spies for terrorist groups such as the IRA have not been prosecuted under this section.[62] Where the information concerns prohibited places, it is up to defendants to show that their possession of it is not for a disloyal purpose. In addition, contrary to the normal evidential rule against guilt by association, the prosecution can give evidence of the defendants' characters and associations to show that their purpose was prejudicial.[63]

In 1920 the Attorney-General told the House of Commons that the opening words of the section, 'for any purpose prejudicial to the safety or interests of the state' meant that the section was aimed at spies in the employ of foreign powers.[64] This assurance that s 1 was so limited was repeated by another Attorney-General in 1949. But the House of Lords extended it to 'sabotage' by upholding the conviction of anti-nuclear demonstrators for trying to stage a sit-down demonstration at a V-bomber base. The CND protesters wished to argue that their purpose was to preserve the safety of the state by removing nuclear weaponry, but the courts held that it was for the Government to decide the state's best interests.[65] In 1977 s 1 charges were brought against journalists Duncan Campbell and Crispin Aubrey in the 'ABC' case (see p. 417), but were withdrawn after the judge described them as oppressive.

The media should have nothing to fear from s 1. Their right to report and to comment upon issues of national security may boost the propaganda claims of foreign governments, but it is none the less exercised for a legitimate purpose, and not 'for a purpose prejudicial to the safety and interests of the State'. The security services, however, believe that journalism that exposes their activities amounts to 'espionage by inadvertence',[66] and it was upon this theory that the deportation of the American writer Mark Hosenball was based. Indeed, Hosenball was evicted because he had the

---

[62] *R* v *Parrott* (1913) 8 Cr App Rep 186.
[63] Official Secrets Act 1911 s 1(2).
[64] House of Commons 24 June 1948 col 1711. See B. D. Thompson, 'The Committee of 100 and the Official Secrets Act 1911' [1963] Public Law 201.
[65] *Chandler* v *DPP* [1964] AC 763.
[66] Head of MI5 to Franks Committee, note 1 above, Vol III pp. 243–6.

misfortune to put his name to an article about signals intelligence written largely by Duncan Campbell.[67] Section 1 may be wide enough in its literal language to be applied to the press by a determined Government; whether it will be so applied again will depend on the media's efforts to resist.

Police powers and compulsory questioning

Search and arrest

The Official Secrets Act gives the police special powers to investigate suspected offences. If they can convince a magistrate that they have reasonable grounds for believing that a crime under the Act has been or is about to be committed, they can obtain a warrant to search for and seize potential evidence.[68] Such warrants have been issued on two occasions to search Duncan Campbell's home. On the first occasion, in 1977, the police seized his entire library of files, including press cuttings, telephone directories, personal letters, and a collection of novels.[69] On the second occasion, in 1984, the police haul of suspicious items included his copies of photographs that had been produced by the prosecution for the 'ABC' trial. Following the 1989 Act the warrant cannot authorize seizure of items subject to legal privilege.[70] A magistrate cannot grant a warrant to seize excluded material or special procedure material (see p. 205 for the meanings of these terms). The police can, however, apply to a circuit judge for an order that the possessor of this type of material hand it over to them.[71] Normally, these orders can be made only after the judge has heard both sides, but if the material is subject to a restriction on disclosure, the police can apply secretly and without notice to the possessor.[72] The police relied on these provisions to obtain search warrants for the *New Statesman*'s offices after the magazine had published Duncan Campbell's article on the Zircon spy satellite affair. The police occupied the offices for four days and nights and sifted through an enormous amount of material. No prosecution followed. The Scottish police relied on an Official Secrets Act warrant to seize from the Glasgow offices of BBC Scotland not only the Zircon film that

---

[67] Leigh, *Frontiers of Secrecy*, p. 231. No official explanation was given for Hosenball's deportation other than it was conducive to the public good: see *R v Secretary of State for Home Affairs ex parte Hosenball* [1977] 3 All ER 452.

[68] Official Secrets Act 1911 ss 1(2), 9(1).

[69] Including *For Whom the Bell Tolls*. Aubrey, *Who's Watching You?*, p. 24.

[70] Police and Criminal Evidence Act 1984 s 9(2) and Official Secrets Act 1989 s 11(3).

[71] Police and Criminal Evidence Act 1984 s 9(1) and Sched 1 para 3(*b*).

[72] ibid., Sched 1 paras 12 and 14(*c*)(i) and s 11(2)(*b*).

Campbell had made but also all the other programmes in his *Secret Society* series.[73] In an emergency where the interests of the state seem to the police to require immediate action, a magistrate may be dispensed with, and a police superintendent can sign the warrant.[74] No warrant at all is necessary to arrest a person who is reasonably suspected of having committed (or being about to commit) an offence under the Acts.[75]

Police questioning

Those suspected of s 1 offences can be deprived of their right to stay silent under police questioning. The Home Secretary can order an investigation (in an emergency the chief of police's authorization will suffice) and it is a criminal offence to refuse to answer the inquisitor's questions.[76] Suspects can apparently even be required to give self-incriminating answers, which can be used in evidence against them. The staff of the *Daily Telegraph* were compulsorily questioned in the 1930s after the paper leaked the Government's plans to arrest Mahatma Gandhi, and the interrogation stopped only when the proprietor let it be known that the Home Secretary himself was the correspondent's source.[77] A journalist on the *Daily Despatch* was convicted under this section in 1938 for refusing to name a police source who had given him a police circular about a wanted fraudsman.[78] This use of compulsory questioning to trace the source of embarrassing leaks caused a public outcry and in 1939 Parliament amended the Act so that this power can now be used only where there is a suspected breach of s 1 of the 1911 Act.[79]

Judicial questioning

Journalists may also be questioned in court or before a Tribunal of Inquiry about their sources. The Contempt of Court Act 1981 imposes a limited ban on such questions, but it expressly exempts questions that are necessary in the interests of national security.[80]

---

[73] See Peter Thornton, *The Civil Liberties of the Zircon Affair*, NCCL, 1987. The Police and Criminal Evidence Act 1984, with its restrictions on the seizure of excluded and special procedure material, does not apply in Scotland.
[74] Official Secrets Act 1911 s 9(2).
[75] ibid., s 6. Offences under the 1911, 1920 and 1989 Official Secrets Acts (except for retention or loss of documents) are arrestable offences for the Police and Criminal Evidence Act 1984, see 1984 Act s 24(2)(*b*) and 1989 Act s 11(1).
[76] Official Secrets Act 1920 s 6. But journalists can insist on their reasonable expenses for attending and can refuse to answer questioning from an officer junior to an Inspector.
[77] Aitken, *Officially Secret*, p. 79.
[78] *Lewis* v *Cattle* [1938] 2 All ER 368.
[79] Official Secrets Act 1939.
[80] Contempt of Court Act 1981 s 10.

Three journalists were sent to prison in 1963 for refusing to disclose the source of their published stories about the Admiralty spy Vassall to a Tribunal of Inquiry investigating the security implications of his treachery.[81]

Proceedings
With one exception, any prosecution under the Official Secrets Acts must be approved by the Attorney-General. The exception is where the information relates to crime in which case the approval of the Director of Public Prosecutions is sufficient.[82] At a time when meanings of sections of the 1989 Act are still untested by litigation, journalists who come to be arrested under the Act or become the subject of police suspicions will doubtless wish to dissuade the Attorney-General from approving a test-case prosecution. Their submissions to the law officers may find support in the comforting words of the Government's White Paper *Reform of Section 2 of the Official Secrets Act 1911*, which was issued in 1988. Designed to mollify the media, it is full of promises that 'responsible media reporting would not be affected by the Government's proposals' and that criminal offences would not be committed by making 'disclosures which are not likely to harm the public interest'.[83]

All the offences can be tried by a jury at the defendant's election except charges of retention or careless loss of documents. The maximum penalty for these offences is a fine on scale 5 or three months' imprisonment.

For other offences under the 1989 Act, the maximum penalty is two years' imprisonment;[84] magistrates can impose the statutory maximum fine (now £2,000) and a six-month term of imprisonment.

Specific Secrecy Legislation

Nuclear secrets

Nuclear secrets are protected by an adjunct to the Official Secrets Acts. Although employees of the Atomic Energy Authority are no longer deemed to be Crown servants, the Government has

---

[81] *A-G* v *Mulholland and Foster* [1963] 1 All ER 767; *A-G* v *Clough* [1963] 1 QB 773.
[82] Official Secrets Act 1911 s 3; 1989 Act s 9.
[83] Cm 408 (1988) paras 77 and 78.
[84] Official Secrets Act 1989 s 10(1).

designated nine properties owned by the AEA as 'prohibited places' for the purpose of s 1 of the 1911 Official Secrets Act.[85] Disclosure of information about atomic energy processes or plant can additionally be prosecuted under the Atomic Energy Act 1946. There is no requirement that the information must be secret, but the Secretary of State should not give his consent to a prosecution if the information is not important to defence.[86]

Other statutes

The Atomic Energy Act is but one example of the dozens of statutes that prohibit civil servants from disclosing specific types of information received by the Government. The Franks Committee found sixty-six that had been passed between 1911 and 1971. By 1987 the Home Secretary admitted that the list had grown to 137 statutory provisions.[87] A few, like the Atomic Energy Act or the Army Act 1955, deal with security matters. The Rehabilitation of Offenders Act 1974 is intended to protect personal privacy, and several are concerned with secret trade processes. These are not objectionable. Much more questionable is the political deal that is often struck with a regulated industry: government regulators may compel the provision of information on condition that it must be kept secure by special provisions to punish leaks. The reform of s 2 was incomplete because it did not revise these secrecy clauses at the same time. At present, they operate to prevent the disclosure of information of importance to public health and safety.[88] However, industry cannot stop a government department that wishes to publicize the information. The High Court refused an injunction to a trader with a bad consumer record who had been compelled to give an assurance of improvement to the Director-General of Fair Trading and who wanted to stop the Director-General announcing the assurance in his customary press release. Lord Justice Donaldson said the Director-General was entitled to 'bark as well

---

[85] Atomic Energy Act 1954 s 6(3); Atomic Energy Act 1965 Sched 1 para 3. British Nuclear Fuels' works at Capenhurst, Windscale, and Calder, AEA's premises at Dounreay, Harwell, Risely, Culchett and its London Offices at No 11 Charles II Street, London SW1, and Rex House, 4–12 Lower Regent Street, London SW1. Official Secrets (Prohibited Places Orders 1955 and 1975, SI 1955 No 1497, SI 1975 No 182).
[86] Atomic Energy Act 1946 s 11.
[87] The complete list of the 137 statutory provisions prohibiting disclosure of official information is given in Hansard, Parliamentary Debates, Vol 108, Cols 560–561 (21 January 1987) and reprinted in Patrick Birkenshaw, *Government and Information*, Butterworths, 1990, p. 345.
[88] James Michael, *The Politics of Secrecy*, NCCL, 1979, pp. 10–11.

as bite' and that publicity was one way of seeing that the trader lived up to his promises.[89]

Radio eavesdropping and telephone tapping

Air may be free but ether is not. Unauthorized eavesdropping on radio messages is an offence, and so is disclosure of any information thus acquired.[90] The penalty is a fine of up to £2,000.[91] There is little likelihood of prosecution of journalists, although the risk increases in the case of systematic monitoring of radio traffic or if a journalist incorporates the information into a story that makes clear that it was obtained in a prohibited way.[92] *Sunday Times* reporters discovered a plot against the Seychelles Government with the help of a transmitter bug placed (by others) in a London hotel room. When they voluntarily handed over their material to the police to help them prosecute the conspirators, they were threatened with a prosecution for illegal eavesdropping.[93] It did not, of course, materialize.

Unauthorized interception of the post or a public telecommunications system is also an offence. The penalty can be a fine of the statutory maximum in a magistrates' court (currently £2,000) or an unlimited fine and up to two years' imprisonment in the Crown Court.[94] The DPP must approve any prosecution.

Telephone tapping and mail interceptions are conducted by Telecom and Post Office employees at the request of police and security service officials, who should obtain a warrant from the Home Secretary authorizing the intercept for a particular period of time. Under the 1985 Interception of Communications Act, intercept warrants may be issued in the interests of national security, for the purpose of preventing or detecting serious crime, or for the purpose of safeguarding the economic well-being of the United Kingdom. The Government's objective is to remove these surveillance operations from public view entirely. Under s 9 of the 1985 Act they cannot be questioned in any court proceedings, and under the 1989 Official Secrets Act the leaking or publishing of any details about them is an offence. Those who believe their telephone has been unjustly tapped may complain to a tribunal of

---

[89] *S. H. Taylor and Co* v *Director-General of the Office of Fair Trading* 4 July 1980, unreported, but see (1980) *The Times*, 5 July, and R. G. Lawson, 'Fair Trading Act 1973 – A Review' (1981) NLJ 1179.

[90] Wireless Telegraphy Act 1949 s 5(*b*)(i).

[91] ibid., s 14(1)(*c*).

[92] The purpose of the eavesdropping is immaterial. *Paul* v *Ministry of Posts and Telecommunications* [1973] RTR 245.

[93] *Guardian* 24 November 1982.

[94] Interception of Communications Act 1985 s 1.

five Government-appointed lawyers, who are empowered merely to investigate whether a warrant has been issued by the Home Secretary and if so, whether he acted rationally in issuing it. This tribunal has never found occasion to uphold a complaint. There is a 'judicial monitor', who reports directly to the Prime Minister; his public reports have been bland and uninformative, disclosing on more than rare occasions where clerical errors have led to taps being placed on the wrong phone. These arrangements offer little protection to the public and almost total protection to Government eavesdroppers against media investigation of their work.

D-notices

D-notices are the responsibility of the Defence Press and Broadcasting Committee, which consists of representatives of the armed forces, senior civil servants and various press and broadcasting institutions. The Committee's stated purpose is to advise editors and publishers of categories of information the secrecy of which is alleged to be essential for national security.[95] It was realized shortly after the Official Secrets Act 1911 was passed that the legislation was far too vaguely worded to perform this function. The Committee was established in 1912, shrouded in secrecy: for forty years its existence was not publicly known.[96]

The Committee issues general notices of guidance. In addition, 'Private and Confidential Notices' can be sent giving warning that specific stories would threaten national security.[97] The Secretary of the Committee, who has always been a high-ranking officer from the armed forces, is available for advice and consultation on short notice. No part of this system has any legal force. Stories are regularly printed in breach of the notices without attracting proceedings. In 1967, for example, Chapman Pincher revealed MI5's practice of monitoring all overseas cables. The Wilson Government claimed the story contravened a D-notice, but no action was taken.[98] In 1980 the *New Statesman* published a series of articles by Duncan Campbell about telephone tapping despite a warning from the Committee's secretary that this contravened a D-notice,

[95] House of Commons Defence Committee 3rd Report, 1979–80 'The D-Notice System' HC 773, 640 i-v.
[96] D. G. T. Williams, *Not in the Public Interest*, Hutchinson, 1965, p. 85.
[97] One in 1974 concerned the security procedures on North Sea oil rigs, Leigh, *Frontiers of Secrecy*, p. 67.
[98] See Chapman Pincher, *Inside Story*; Hedley and Aynsley, *The D-Notice Affair*; Lord Radcliffe, E. Shinwell and S. Lloyd 'Report of the Committee of Privy Councillors Appointed to Inquire into "D" Notice Matters' Cmnd 3309 HMSO (1967).

yet no prosecution followed.[99] Conversely, an editor who assidu-
ously follows the Committee's advice is not guaranteed immunity
from prosecution under the Official Secrets Acts. The editor of the
Sunday Telegraph faced charges along with Jonathan Aitken for
receiving the Biafran War report, although the secretary of the D-
notice Committee had told him that its publication would create no
danger to national security.[100]

In 1980 a House of Commons committee reviewed the system
and published a damning indictment. It reported that major
newspapers had stopped consulting its notices; that the foreign and
fringe press had never received them; that the notices were so
vaguely worded as to be meaningless; that the notices had not been
amended in the previous ten years; and that some categories of
sensitive information were not covered by the notices. Its
fundamental criticism was that the whole system was based on the
theory, if not the practice, of covert censorship.[101]

The Conservative majority of the D-notice Committee (which
had finally split on party lines) thought the system could be
reformed. It was supported by both the BBC and the IBA, on the
grounds that they welcomed 'official' advice. Evidence to the
contrary was given by *The Sunday Times*, *World in Action* and the
Press Association, which argued that the freedom of the press is
incompatible with the cosy cooperation that the D-notice system
envisages.

The Government responded to these criticisms with 'observations' to the effect that the D-notice Committee would review its
own system, which it duly did to its own considerable self-satisfac-
tion.[102] The only reform of any note was to lift the 'restricted'
classification on D-notices sent to newspapers, so that editors could
henceforth show them to journalists without any risk of prosecution. The Committee rejected the suggestion that its secretary
should move his offices out of the Ministry of Defence, as this
would separate him from close contact with those whose responsibility it was to maintain secrecy.

The D-notice system can be ignored by newspapers, although
statutory arrangements for broadcasting give it a certain impact. In
1974, for example, the IBA insisted that *World in Action* delete a
reference to the existence of Government Communications
Headquarters (GCHQ) at Cheltenham made on the programme

---

[99] Collected in 'Big Brother is Listening: Phone-tappers and the Security State'
(*New Statesman Report No 2*, 1981).
[100] Aitken, *Officially Secret*.
[101] Defence Committee Report, note 95 above, para 24.
[102] *The D-Notice System: Observations by the Secretary of State for Defence*
(Cmnd 8129, 1981) and *Fourth Report from the Defence Committee 1982–3* (HC 55).

by a former diplomat, despite the fact that his comment was contained in a book that he had recently published. A similar difficulty was encountered by the same programme in 1981 when it combined with the *New Statesman* and the *Daily Mirror* to investigate security leaks at the GCHQ station in Hong Kong. The newspaper and the journal published their stories: the television programme, timed to coincide with these publications, was delayed for a fortnight at the insistence of IBA lawyers concerned about a possible breach of the former s 2 and of a D-notice. The meaning of 'national security' has at times been vastly inflated. In 1956 two Oxford undergraduate journalists were sent to prison for writing about their National Service experiences at a signals-intercept (SIGINT) unit, and until 1977 a D-notice covered the revelation of the very existence of GCHQ and other SIGINT bases. These were secrets to be kept from the British public and not from the Russians, whose spy satellites had long been able to identify any communications intercept aerials.

The D-notice Committee is not to be trusted. In 1985 it asked a publisher for an advance copy of a book by Jock Kane about defective security in signals intelligence. The naïve publisher, thinking that the Committee would offer helpful 'guidance', received instead an expensive injunction, which has meant that the book can never be published. The Committee had sent the advance copy directly to the Treasury Solicitor. In 1988 the Secretary of the Committee tried to put a D-notice on certain names mentioned in books about to be published by David Leigh and Rupert Allison MP. Some were dead, while others had served with Philby, who had blown their cover forty years ago. Both authors insisted that their books be published with the names intact. A few weeks before the 1991 Gulf War commenced, a careless RAF officer had a briefcase with secret documents and a lap-top computer containing details of the deployment of British forces in the Gulf stolen from his car. The Government was forced to admit the theft of the briefcase (which was soon found with contents intact), but issued a D-notice on any mention of the missing computer. All editors of all national newspapers and all broadcasters complied for a week, enabling the minister and Ministry of Defence to issue incorrect statements suggesting that all the 'lost' information had been recovered. The true story was published by an Irish newspaper, but the D-notice was not lifted until the *Sun* (of all newspapers) indicated its intention to publish the truth.[103] It is astonishing that certain editors try to give credence to this discredited Committee by remaining members of it.

---

[103] See James Dalrymple, *The Sunday Times*, 6 January 1991.

Ministerial and Civil Servant Memoirs

Ministers

There is little danger of ministers being prosecuted for breaches of the Official Secrets Act even after they have left office. In 1975 the Attorney-General used the civil law of confidence to try to ban the Crossman diaries (see p. 181). The court found the secrets too old to require suppression, but in principle the court accepted that Cabinet confidences could be protected by injunction if they still affected national security.[104] In Australia a High Court judge refused to injunct as a breach of confidence a book that reprinted diplomatic cables between Canberra and Djakarta, because the Government failed to show that the public interest required restrictions on material that might cause diplomatic embarrassment and political criticism.[105] Democracy entails a measure of acceptance of such consequences as incidents of government.

After the Crossman diaries affair, the Government adopted new guidelines proposed by Lord Radcliffe.[106] The Secretary of the Cabinet continues to act as censor of the first draft, but on national security matters and foreign relations the author can now appeal to the Prime Minister, whose decision is final. Publication in defiance of a rejected appeal could be injuncted on grounds of national security. The embargo on confidential material that does not threaten security is lifted automatically after fifteen years. This is a conventional period, not a legal limitation. A minister can choose to ignore the advice of the Secretary of the Cabinet, and publish at an earlier time.[107] Hugh Jenkins refused to delete from his book *The Culture Gap* references to civil servants who had advised him when he was Arts Minister. The book was published shortly after he left office, when most of the civil servants were still in place.[108] Although the Radcliffe guidelines are worded in legalistic terms, they remain no more than guidelines. If a minister defies them, a prosecution will be successful only if a breach of the Official Secrets Act can be established; and a civil injunction will depend on

---

[104] *A-G v Jonathan Cape Ltd* [1975] 3 All ER 484.
[105] *Commonwealth of Australia v John Fairfax & Sons* (1981) 32 ALR 485.
[106] *Report of Committee of Privy Councillors on Ministerial Memoirs*, Cmnd 6386 (1976).
[107] At least in relation to matters not affecting national security or foreign affairs. The guidelines require notice to be given to the Secretary of the Cabinet. This presumably is so that further pressure can be put on the minister, and so that the Government has the opportunity to seek an injunction.
[108] *Guardian*, 19 September 1978. See Michael Supperstone, *Brownlie's Law Relating to Public Order and National Security*, 2nd edn, Butterworths, 1981, p. 266.

whether the liberal public-interest test of the Crossman diaries case is satisfied.

Civil servants

Civil servants' memoirs have occasionally been targets of the Official Secrets Act. In 1926 the Governor of Pentonville prison was fined for publishing his life story in the *Evening News*,[109] and the biography of Pierrepoint, the public hangman, was held up for many years by threats of an Official Secrets Act prosecution.[110] On taking up their employment, civil servants are required to sign a promise to submit any publications for prior written approval. As the head of the Home Office acknowledged to the Franks Committee, this gives the misleading impression that failure to comply is automatically an offence under the Acts.[111] This overstates the risk of prosecution, since sufficient authorization can be given in other ways under the Acts, although a publisher would have to consider the possibility of an injunction for breach of confidence or for breach of the official's contractual obligation. With the abolition of s 2, prosecution is not a realistic prospect so long as members avoid discussion of defence and intelligence issues.

The rules relating to memoirs have been discredited by the inconsistencies in their application. Memoirs by senior civil servants, which show Whitehall in a favourable light, never encounter difficulty. Both Sir Robert Mark, the former Metropolitan Commissioner of Police, and Sir Norman Skelhorn, the former Director of Public Prosecutions, published memoirs within a few years of leaving office, although a more critical book by Kelleher, a controversial detective-inspector prosecuted unsuccessfully for corruption in Mark's time at the Yard, has never been allowed to see the light of day. The Government's reluctance to use the law means that a determined civil servant has little to fear, and the publishers of Leslie Chapman's *Your Disobedient Servant* went ahead without receiving the retribution that had been threatened for his revelations of waste and inefficiency in Whitehall. There was both public and official displeasure expressed when Ronald Gregory, the Chief Constable responsible for the inept hunt for the 'Yorkshire Ripper', cashed in by selling his story to a newspaper shortly after his retirement. A breach of confidence action might well have succeeded against both policeman and newspaper, but the possibility

---

[109] (1926) *The Times*, 16 December.
[110] Franks Report, note 1 above, Vol I App II p. 116.
[111] Sir Philip Allen in oral evidence to the Franks Committee, note 1 above, Vol III p. 13.

was not mentioned by the Home Secretary when he deplored the incident in Parliament. However, such an action has been brought against a former police officer who used material taken from Myra Hindley's statements to police in his autobiography.

In 1991 the political motive behind Cabinet Office vetting of civil service and ministerial memoirs (and the willingness of their publishers to collaborate) was hilariously exposed through a mistake made by HarperCollins, publishers of *Kill the Messenger*, the 'authorized' autobiography of Thatcher press secretary Bernard Ingham. They sent to *The Sunday Times* (which had bought serialization rights) a copy of the book proofs *before* it had been submitted for Cabinet Office vetting, and a comparison with the final version allowed the newspaper to deduce which passages had been censored. The Cabinet secretary, Sir Robin Butler, had not wielded the blue pencil on the basis of national security or justifiable confidentiality, but only to delete or dilute criticisms of still-serving ministers (particularly Michael Heseltine) that might be politically embarrassing to the Government.

Public Records

Most public records are transferred after thirty years to the Public Record Office at Kew, as a result of the Public Record Acts of 1958 and 1967.[112] Although primarily of interest to historians, some journalists have used this right of access to explore the early careers of today's prominent politicians, as well as reviewing old controversies in the light of newly released material. The Government has the power to 'weed out' and withhold records that it thinks should be kept secret for a longer time. The main categories are:

- distressing or embarrassing personal details about living persons or their immediate descendents;
- information received by the Government in confidence;
- some papers on Ireland; and
- 'certain exceptionally sensitive papers which affect the security of the State'.[113]

---

[112] The 1967 Act reduced the presumptive period from fifty years. Technically, the Acts apply only to England; in practice, the Scottish Office follows the same procedure; Paul Gordon, 'Public Records in Scotland', Journal of the Law Society of Scotland, January 1981.

[113] Lord Gardiner, The Lord Chancellor, Hansard [1967] Vol 282 5th Ser Col 1657–8. Certain Commonwealth documents are also restricted.

The weeders are super-sensitive to national security and until recently extended the embargo on a document if it so much as mentioned MI5 or MI6.[114] The period of 'extended closure' may be fifty years or longer. Records 'relating to the private affairs of the royal family' are routinely closed for 100 years. The 'secret' files at the PRO take up about 4,500 feet of shelf space.

On other occasions the purported zeal for protecting personal privacy can look more like attempts to cover up political embarrassment. In 1977 a police report on 1930s hunger marches was clawed back into the restricted category shortly after its release. The report had made allegations that, seen in retrospect, were both false, and, at the time, highly damaging. The report's release was described as a mistake, on the pretext that one of the marchers named in it had been found to be still alive.[115] The man himself had no objection to the release of the information, which suggests that concern for his privacy was a somewhat hypocritical excuse for an attempt to wipe the egg off the historical face of the Metropolitan Police.

A departmental committee recommended more liberal access. It criticized the practice whereby the Lord Chancellor can order an entire *class* of documents to be kept secret for a century without considering the specific documents that make up that class. It proposed that more files should be released before the thirty-year embargo is up, that 'embarrassment' should no longer be a ground for suppression, that the power to keep files secret forever should be abolished, and that there should be a right to appeal from secrecy orders. The Government rejected the report.[116]

The British obsession for secrecy is well-illustrated by the 300 feet of official volumes stored at Kew that cannot be opened for 50 to 100 years. Amongst the official memoranda listed in January 1989 as being closed for a century are:

- prison reform and lengths of sentences (1910–34);
- forcible feeding in reformatory schools (1910);
- the sterilization of mental defectives (1911–30);
- imprisonment and forcible feeding of suffragettes (1913);
- imprisonment of Emily Pankhurst (1913–17);
- internment of Sinn Fein leaders (1918);
- industrial unrest and strikes (1918);
- experiments on animals with poison gas (1913–18);

---

[114] Michael, *The Politics of Secrecy*, p. 185.
[115] Chris Cook, John Stevenson, 'Historical Hide and Seek', *Guardian*, 25 August 1978, reproduced in May and Rowan (eds.), *Inside Information: British Government and the Media*, Constable, 1982, p. 50–2.
[116] *Modern Public Records*, 1981, Cmnd 8024; White Paper Response (1982) Cmnd 8531; see *State Secrecy and Public Records*, State Research Bulletin, 1982, No 30, p. 128; Chapter by M. Roper in Chapman and Hunt (eds.) *Open Government*, 1987.

- Home Office practice in dealings with criminal lunatics (1913);
- coal-miners' strike (1919);
- flogging of vagrants (1919);
- decisions against prosecuting James Joyce's *Ulysses* (1924);
- Fascist marches (1936);
- police reports on the activities of the National Council for Civil Liberties (1935–41);
- opposition to British interests in Palestine (1938);
- Tibetan relations with China (1938–45);
- dental service for police in wartime (1939);
- war crimes – lists of suspects and reports on atrocities (1941–7);
- interrogations of prisoners of war in London (1942–4);
- British scorched-earth policy in Malaya (1943);
- the relief and repatriation of Allied internees (1946); and
- the Albert Speer file (1946).

These topics need only be listed to demonstrate how the notion of 'embarrassment to descendants' is being manipulated to cover 'embarrassment to the descendants of civil servants'. Closure for a century of files relating to official treatment of suffragettes, prisoners and mental patients prior to the First World War cannot conceivably be justified on privacy grounds. Records of field executions in the First World War were withheld for seventy years, ostensibly to avoid embarrassment to relatives of the long-dead soldiers, but when those documents were finally released, it became clear that the secrecy had been used to avoid exposing the arbitrariness and brutality of justice in the trenches. Quite apart from the absurdity of sealing files about arrangements for police dental treatment during the Second World War, the above examples illustrate how a good deal of information of historical significance in relation to British foreign policy is being suppressed, together with material of contemporary importance about the investigation of war crimes.

European Communities

Eurocrats are not servants of the Crown and, generally, leaks from Brussels are not punishable under the Official Secrets Acts. However, as with British civil servants, their conditions of employment require them to preserve the confidentiality of any document or information 'not already made public'. They must exercise 'the greatest discretion with regard to facts and information coming into their knowledge in the course of or in connection with the performance of (their) duties'. Like servants of the British Government the restrictions continue after they have left their office or job. Staff regulations also prohibit them from 'alone or together with others publishing or causing to be published without the permission of the appointing authorities, any matter dealing with the work of the communities'. However 'permission shall be refused only where the proposed publication is liable to prejudice the interests of the Community'.[117]

Breach of these provisions can lay employees open to disciplinary action, and journalists still need to take care to preserve the anonymity of such sources. Leaking cannot, however, lead to a criminal prosecution of an employee or journalist. The only exception concerns EURATOM (European Atomic Energy Community), one of the two other European 'communities', which has the same members and an almost identical structure as the much more complex European Economic Community. Employees and officials of EURATOM and even those who in their 'dealings in any capacity (official or unofficial) with any EURATOM institution or installation or with any EURATOM joint enterprise' acquire 'classified information' commit an offence if they communicate it to any unauthorized person or make any public disclosure of it.[118]

The European Council of Ministers and the European Commission both sit in private. There is no public right of access to their meetings or to minutes of their deliberations.

Reporting Northern Ireland

Information of use to terrorists

Two parts of the Northern Ireland emergency legislation are of particular potential significance for the press. Section 22 of the Emergency Provisions (Northern Ireland) Act 1978 prohibits collecting, recording, publishing or attempting to elicit any information (including taking photographs) concerning the army, police, judges, court officials or prison officers that is likely to be of use to terrorists. It is also an offence to collect or record any information that is likely to be useful to terrorists in carrying out an act of violence, or to possess any record or document containing any of these types of information. Like the Official Secrets Act, this Act's overt purpose is to punish espionage, although the section is broad enough in its terms to cover normal journalistic activities. The Act does allow a defence of reasonable excuse or lawful authority, although the burden of proof is placed on the defendant. These offences apply only to acts done in Northern Ireland, and the

---

[117] EEC Reg 31 and Euratom Reg 11, both of 18 December 1961.
[118] European Communities Act 1972 s 11(2) 'classified information' is defined in Arts 24–7 of the Euratom Treaty.

consent of the Northern Ireland DPP is necessary for a prosecution. A journalist working on a story about Army behaviour would have 'reasonable excuse' to collect information of the sort described in the Act, unless there was evidence of an ulterior motive to assist terrorist intelligence.

Reporting demonstrations

In Northern Ireland it is an offence knowingly to take part in an unlawful procession.[119] In 1987 the Northern Ireland Court of Appeal held that a reporter who had been simply covering the procession for his newspaper had been properly acquitted of a charge under this provision. It required something more than physical presence, and the reporter did not attend to share in or experience the objectives of the marchers.[120] This decision will be a useful guide to the position on the mainland, where reporters may also wish to report demonstrations that have been prohibited.[121]

Prevention of terrorism

The Prevention of Terrorism (Temporary Provisions) Act 1989 applies throughout the United Kingdom. Section 18 creates a positive duty to tell the police of any information that might be of material assistance in preventing an act of terrorism or in apprehending, prosecuting or convicting someone suspected of terrorism in connection with the affairs of Northern Ireland.[122] Its provisions should be carefully considered by any journalist who plans to interview members of the Provisional IRA or any other proscribed organization or even to have any indirect contact with them. Its potential for use against the media was shown in 1980 when the BBC filmed a Provisional IRA roadblock at Carrickmore. The DPP decided not to prosecute, but the Attorney-General deplored the BBC's action and threatened a tougher line in the future.[123] After the murder of two corporals at a Republican funeral in 1988, media photographers and broadcasters were threatened with

---

[119] Public Order (Northern Ireland) Order 1981 (SI 1981 No 609) Article 3.

[120] *McKeown* v *McDermott* [1987] 7 NIJB 93 CA.

[121] Under Public Order Act 1986 s 13.

[122] Prevention of Terrorism (Temporary Provisions) Act 1989 s 18. Other anti-terrorist measures in this Act are not confined to Northern Ireland's affairs. This one is. The maximum penalty is the statutory maximum fine (currently £2,000) and six months' imprisonment by a magistrates' court; an unlimited fine and five years' imprisonment by a Crown Court. The Attorney-General must approve a prosecution: 1989 Act s 19.

[123] Catherine Scorer and Patricia Hewitt, *The Prevention of Terrorism Act: The Case for Repeal*, NCCL, 1981, p. 62.

prosecution under the PTA if they did not hand over their films. After token resistance, all – including the BBC – complied. The procedure available to the police on the mainland under the Police and Criminal Evidence Act (see p. 205) does not apply in Northern Ireland. So far, though, there has been no actual prosecution of a media representative or organization under this legislation.[124]

The Police and Army in Northern Ireland have a power to question compulsorily any person regarding any recent explosion or other incident endangering life or concerning any person killed or injured in such an incident or explosion. It is an offence to refuse to answer their questions or to fail to do so to the best of one's knowledge and ability.[125]

Broadcasting censorship

Television coverage of the province can be directly censored. But even before the broadcasting bans of 1988, broadcasters were censoring themselves. The IBA banned a number of programmes outright, including a *This Week* report on Amnesty International's findings about ill-treatment of suspects. Sometimes it required cuts in emotive scenes – a hunger striker in an open coffin, or flowers on a terrorist's grave. It postponed other programmes, so that some of their topicality was then lost, or pushed them into late-night slots, although in 1988 it withstood Government pressure and permitted transmission of *Death on the Rock*.[126] The IBA was, and the ITC can be, susceptible to official pressure because of the statutory duty to avoid a programme that 'offends against good taste or decency or is likely to encourage or incite to crime or to lead to disorder or to be offensive to public feeling'.[127] The BBC Board of Governors has voluntarily accepted the same obligations, although its work on Northern Ireland has been marginally more robust.[128] In 1972 it refused to buckle under a Government request to stop *A Question of Ulster*, a live debate chaired by Lord Devlin, but its resolve has been weakened, partly as a result of Government appointments to the Board, and in 1987 the governors banned the

---

[124] Although Bernard Falk was sentenced to four days in prison for contempt of court for refusing to identify a man interviewed on television who claimed to be a member of the IRA (Miller, *Contempt of Court*, 2nd edn, Clarendon Press, 1989 , p. 119).
[125] Emergency Provisions (Northern Ireland) Act 1978 s 18.
[126] 'Banned Censored and Delayed' by Paul Madden in *The British Media and Ireland*, The Campaign for Free Speech in Ireland. Alex Schmid and Jenny de Graff, *Violence as Communication: Insurgent Terrorism and the News Media*, Sage, 1982, pp. 158–62.
[127] Broadcasting Act 1990, s 6(1).
[128] See Philip Schlesinger, *Putting Reality Together*, Constable, 1978, p. 214.

Real Lives programme about two factional leaders in the province.

There are other, non-legal pressures that can be used by officials to influence media reporting of Northern Ireland. These range from 'buttering-up' journalists with generous hospitality at Army units, to freezing out hostile critics from regular briefings.'[129] There have been disturbing examples of 'black propaganda', and Colin Wallace has convincingly confessed to planting false stories in the media (especially through the foreign press) in his role as a Government press officer in Northern Ireland. *The Sunday Times* has claimed that the Army has set off explosions that were then falsely attributed to the IRA.[130]

Other Political Offences

Treason

In the heat of the Falklands circulation campaign the *Sun* accused the *Guardian* and the *Daily Mirror* of treason.[131] The allegation was nonsense. As the Commons Defence Committee said,[132] in a democracy the interests of the Government are not synonymous with the national interest, and differences of view as to the value of a Government aim or the cost of achieving it were quite legitimate. The incident echoed the allegation by Edward Hulton, proprietor of *Picture Post*, that a photograph showing the brutality of South Koreans, which the magazine's editor proposed to publish, would give 'aid and comfort' to the North Korean enemy. The editor refused to withdraw it and was dismissed as a result.[133] Treason can be committed by adhering to the Crown's enemies or by giving them aid or comfort, but the prosecution must show that the defendants intended to aid or comfort an enemy contrary to their duty of loyalty.[134] There has not been a treason trial since 1946, when

---

[129] Steve Chibnall, *Law and Order News*, Tavistock, 1977, pp. 178–82.
[130] 13 March 1977.
[131] 'Dare Call it Treason', 7 May 1982. See Robert Harris, *Gotcha: The Media, the Government and the Falkland Crisis*, Faber, 1983, pp. 38–53. The *Guardian*'s cartoon of a shipwrecked sailor on a raft with the caption 'The price of sovereignty has been increased – official' mirrored the cartoon by Zec that the *Daily Mirror* had published in 1942 over the caption 'The price of petrol has been increased by one penny – official' and which together with the consistent criticisms of the Government by the paper very nearly caused the Government to ban the paper. Neil Stammers, *Civil Liberties in Britain during World War Two*, Croom Helm, 1983, pp. 147–51.
[132] Report of the Defence Committee, *The Handling of the Press and Public Information during the Falklands Conflict*, HC 17 (1982–3), para 35.
[133] Phillip Knightley, *The First Casualty: The War Correspondent as Hero, Propagandist and Myth Maker*, rev. edn, Quartet, 1982, p. 330.
[134] Supperstone, *Brownlie's Law*, pp. 230–4.

William Joyce ('Lord Haw-Haw') was convicted for making Nazi propaganda broadcasts.

Sedition

Seditious libel is defined in the criminal law textbooks as

> writing which directly tends (1) to raise discontent and disaffection among or promote ill-will between the Sovereign's subjects; (2) to incite persons to use or attempt to use unlawful means and in particular physical force in any public matter connected with the State, (3) to bring into hatred or contempt the Sovereign, the Government, the laws or constitution.[135]

This definition is frighteningly broad and the crime has been used in the past to suppress radical political views.[136] Even in this century it was used against an Indian nationalist and against Communist organizers.[137] However, the post-war tendency has been to narrow the offence considerably. Firstly, it has been stressed that political speech, even revolutionary speech, should not be punished as sedition unless it is meant to excite people to 'tumult and disorder'.[138] Incitement to violence alone is insufficient: it must be 'violence or defiance for the purpose of disturbing constitutional authority'.[139] Secondly, on one line of authority, it is not enough that 'tumult and disorder' were likely to follow unless the publisher did actually intend these consequences.[140] There has been no prosecution for sedition since 1947, and the offence now serves no purpose in the criminal law. The deliberate provocation of public violence or disorder is amply covered by offences contained in the 1986 Public Order Act.

In 1990 the Divisional Court decisively rejected an attempt to bring sedition charges against the author and publisher of *The Satanic Verses*. It stressed that the gist of the crime was an attack against the state, and that the prosecution must prove that the

---

[135] Richardson *et al.*, *Archbold Criminal Pleading and Practice*, paras 21–117.
[136] e.g., against John Wilkes for his satires in 1764 in *The North Britain* and Tom Paine for *The Rights of Man*.
[137] *R* v *Aldred* (1909) 22 Cox CC 1; Wal Hannington, *Never on Our Knees*, 1967, pp. 188–93.
[138] *R* v *Caunt* (1948) LQR 203, see also defendant's account, *An Editor on Trial*, privately published, 1947; *Boucher* v *R* [1951] 2 DLR 369.
[139] *Boucher* v *R*, note 138 above, and see *R* v *Burns* (1886) 16 Cox 355.
[140] *R* v *Caunt*, note 138 above. A different view was taken in *R* v *Aldred* (above). In *R* v *Lemon* [1979] AC 617 the House of Lords decided by 3–2 that intention of this kind was not relevant for blasphemous libel, but several of the speeches favour the view that a specific intent is required for the crime of sedition.

speech or writing incites readers to violence against democratic institutions.[141]

Incitement to mutiny and disaffection

The Incitement to Mutiny Act 1797 was passed in a panic after naval mutinies at the Spithead and Nore. It covers:

> any person who shall maliciously and advisedly endeavour to seduce any person or persons serving in HM's forces by sea or land from his or their duty and allegiance to His Majesty or to incite or stir up any person to commit any act of mutiny or make or endeavour to make any mutinous assembly or to commit any traitorous or mutinous practice whatsoever.

A critical word in this definition is the 'and' between duty and allegiance. Tempting soldiers from their *duty* was not an offence if it did not also encourage them to be disloyal. This link was broken in the Incitement to Disaffection Act 1934, which created an offence in almost identical terms except that 'or' was substituted for 'and'.

The 1934 Act also added draconian subsidiary offences. Possession of any document became an offence if its dissemination to the forces would be punishable,[142] and a High Court judge can issue a search warrant to the police to look for material that might infringe the Act.[143] The Incitement Acts were also used against radicals. The editors and printers of *The Syndicalist* were convicted in 1912 for publishing a letter calling on soldiers not to fire on workers. In 1925 twelve Communist leaders were convicted for a similar offence. Five received a year's imprisonment from Mr Justice Rigby Swift; the other seven were offered the chance to go free if they renounced Communism and declared that they would not engage in similar activities again. They refused and were given six months' imprisonment.[144] (It was the same judge whom the *Daily Worker* later described as a 'bewigged class puppet' and whose editor was imprisoned for contempt of court as a result.)

In addition to these statutes, the services' legislation makes it an offence to obstruct or interfere with the forces in the execution of their duty or to procure or persuade a member of the forces to

---

[141] *R* v *Bow Street Magistrates' Court ex parte Choudhury* [1991] 1 All ER 306.

[142] Incitement to Disaffection Act 1934 s 2(1).

[143] ibid., s 2(2).

[144] Tom Young, *Incitement to Disaffection*, Cobden Trust, 1976, pp. 15–18, 45–7. The defendants in the latter case drew attention to the failure to prosecute Edward Carson (by then Lord Reading) and F. E. Smith (by then Viceroy of India) for their speeches in 1911 calling on Ulster Protestants to oppose the Home Rule Bill by force, if necessary.

desert or go absent without leave.[145] A comparable offence of doing any act 'calculated to cause disaffection among members of the police force' or 'doing any act calculated to induce any member of the police force to withhold his services or to commit breaches of discipline' was created after the police strike in 1919.[146]

The Aliens Restriction (Amendment) Act 1919 was passed at the same time to stem what was then perceived as foreign Communist agitation. It is an offence for an alien to attempt or do any act calculated or likely to cause sedition or disaffection amongst forces of the Crown or the Crown's allies or the civilian population. It is also an offence for an alien to promote industrial unrest in any industry in which he has not been bona fide engaged for at least two years immediately preceding in the United Kingdom.[147]

Such blatantly political charges can be brought only at times of tension. They were revived in the mid-1970s against the British Withdrawal from Ireland Campaign. Pat Arrowsmith was convicted under the Incitement to Disaffection Act 1934 for distributing to soldiers a leaflet called *Some Information for Discontented Soldiers*, which called on them to leave the Army rather than serve in Northern Ireland.[148] She failed to persuade the jury that the leaflet was to inform rather than incite. Her sentence of eighteen months' imprisonment was reduced on appeal to nine months. Ms Arrowsmith complained to the European Commission that the conviction violated her right to freedom of thought, conscience and religion under Article 9(1) of the Convention. The Commission accepted that pacifism was a protected 'belief', but held the complaint inadmissible because the distribution of the leaflets was not a means of 'practising' the belief: the leaflet expressed a nationalist rather than pacifist philosophy.[149] The prosecution did not stop distribution of the leaflet and in 1974 a further fourteen were prosecuted under the 1934 Act. On all the contested charges the defendants were acquitted. As a result, pending prosecutions against other distributors of the leaflet were dropped.[150] Incitement to disaffection charges have not been used since the Old Bailey acquittals in 1975, and the then Attorney-General, Sam Silkin, expressed regret that this much-publicized case was ever brought. The most powerful incitement to disaffection was made during the 1987 election campaign by the Prime

---

[145] Army Act 1955 s 193 (obstruction), s 97 (persuading desertion); Air Force Act 1955 s 193; Naval Discipline Act 1957 s 94 is on similar lines.
[146] Police Act 1964 s 53, and see Ministry of Defence Police Act 1987 s 6.
[147] Aliens Restriction (Amendment) Act 1919 s 3.
[148] *R* v *Arrowsmith* [1975] QB 678.
[149] *Arrowsmith* v *United Kingdom* Application 7050/75, 19 Decisions and Reports 5. Her complaint under Art 10 was also dismissed.
[150] Young, *Incitement to Disaffection*, pp. 85–94.

Minister, Mrs Thatcher, who announced that service chiefs should consider resigning in protest if the Labour Party were elected and sought to implement its non-nuclear defence policy. It will henceforth be difficult to convince a jury that pacifists should be punished for urging lesser ranks to consider leaving the services in protest against having to implement Government policies on nuclear defence or Northern Ireland.

Reform

The fourteen acquittals under the Incitement to Disaffection Act increased the demand for the repeal of laws that had been hastily passed, were broad in the extreme and would lie dormant for many years until being revived to deal with a political crisis. The Law Commission has since recommended that treason should be limited in peace-time to attempting to overthrow the Government by armed means, and that sedition should be abolished, as should incitement to mutiny and aliens legislation. It thought that the Incitement to Disaffection Act should be confined to seduction of the forces away from their allegiance as opposed to their duty. The latter was amply protected by the Services Acts, but it expressed no views on whether even this was necessary for national security or public safety.[151]

War Reporting

Protection of war correspondents

Journalists who cover armed conflicts will generally be under the protection of the force to which they are accredited. In the case of British forces, the Ministry of Defence will insist that they sign an accreditation document, which includes undertakings to comply with military censorship and to seek permission before interviewing soldiers and filing a wide range of stories. Correspondents will have no alternative but to sign this document, but it is not legally binding and the only sanction for disobedience to its onerous terms will be loss of accreditation, which will normally mean expulsion from the war zone. The accredited correspondent will be assigned an officer rank, which will give entitlement to drink in the officers' mess and to be given priority in an evacuation of the wounded.

Over and above the dangers of injury and death common to all

---

[151] *Codification of the Criminal Law: Treason, Sedition and Allied Offence*, Working Paper No 72, 1977.

who work in war zones, correspondents are at special risk of being arrested and punished for spying on the forces whose activities they are attempting to report, and of being treated by opposing forces as if they were combatants. The international covenants that seek to regulate governments in their conduct of hostilities have attempted to give journalists some protection against these dangers.

Article 13 of the Hague Convention 1907 provides that war correspondents who follow an army without directly belonging to it should, if they fall into the hands of opposing forces, be treated as prisoners of war and receive minimum standards of humane treatment.[152]

The Geneva Conventions of 1949 make similar but more detailed provision for captured war correspondents. If wounded or sick, they are to have the same rights to humane treatment as wounded or sick prisoners of war, including the right to receive assistance from international relief agencies.[153]

The protection afforded by the Hague and Geneva Conventions is contingent upon captured correspondents possessing authorization from the armed forces they are accompanying, attesting to their status. These conventions do not give any special protection to journalists; they simply accord them (along with other non-combatant camp followers) the same basic right as captured members of armed forces.

The only provision in international law that relates specifically to journalists engaged in dangerous missions in areas of international armed conflict is Article 79 of the first Protocol to the Geneva Conventions 1977.[154] It provides that:

> Journalists engaged in dangerous professional missions in areas of armed conflict shall be considered as civilians ... (and) shall be protected as such under the Conventions and this Protocol, provided they take no action adversely affecting their status as civilians ...

Under Article 79, journalists are entitled to immunity from military discipline and must not be made the specific objects of an

[152] Hague Convention IV Respecting Laws and Customs of War on Land Annexed Regulations 1907, Article 13. For the texts of these and the following conventions see Roberts and Guelff, *Documents on the Laws of War*, Clarendon Press, 1982.

[153] Geneva Convention for the Amelioration of the Wounded and Sick in Armed Forces in the Field 1949, Article 13; Geneva Convention for the Amelioration of the Condition of Wounded, Sick and Shipwrecked Members of Armed Forces at Sea 1949, Article 13; Geneva Convention Relative to the Treatment of Prisoners of War 1949, Article 4A.

[154] Protocol Additional to the Geneva Conventions 1949 and Relating to the Protection of Victims of International Conflicts 1977.

attack or the victims of reprisals by any party to the conflict. They should not be manipulated or exploited by the opposing forces. Their entitlement to civilian status is jeopardized by an 'action adversely affecting' it; carrying a gun or rendering special assistance to the armed forces might deprive them of their protection. The rights guaranteed by Article 79 do not detract from the general entitlement of accredited war correspondents to be treated as prisoners of war if captured by hostile forces. Article 79 also entitles a journalist to obtain an identity card attesting to his status from 'the Government of the State of which the journalist is a national or in whose territory he resides or in which the news medium employing him is located'.

International law has no direct sanction to punish breaches of these rules, other than condemnation at the bar of international public opinion. This can, of itself, be a deterrent to combatants, who are usually mindful of the importance of favourable publicity. The Indonesian government has been continually embarrassed in its endeavours to cover up the murder by its forces of British and Australian newsmen covering the conflict in Timor, although the authorities in El Salvador have shown little concern at army killings of several Western correspondents, and Iran has connived at the capture and incarceration of journalists like John McCarthy. Domestic journalists suffer death or disappearance in some countries with a frequency that is hardly noticed in the West. In 1989 fifty journalists were killed, the majority in Latin America[155] (the distinguished British journalist David Blundy died from a sniper's bullet in El Salvador). The following year *Observer* journalist Farzad Bazoft was executed as a spy in Iraq, after his arrest on a mission to investigate an explosion at a missile base. In 1991 eighty-four were killed, many covering the conflict in Yugoslavia. UNESCO has for some years sought agreement on a convention to give journalists special status and a special system of international protection. However, the notable efforts to this end of Sean McBride have been frustrated by Western suspicion that any 'status' given or withheld by a UN agency might eventually restrict the freedom to report, and by converse suspicions on the part of some Third World countries that special status would be a licence for hostile reporters to distort and sensationalize.

Military censorship

There is ample evidence that 'the first casualty when war comes is truth.'[156] The reason for the phenomenon is sometimes the cynical

---

[155] *Attacks on the Press 1989*, The Committee to Protect Journalists.
[156] Senator Hiram Johnson 1917; see Knightley, *The First Casualty*.

opportunism of journalists confronted with chaos and news blackouts, as definitively portrayed in Evelyn Waugh's novel *Scoop*. Frequently, it stems from the acceptance of propaganda claims by rival forces, or the censorship controls instigated in war zones. More subtle pressures of patriotism are involved in coverage of British forces in action. In British military engagements that fall short of declared war, there will be few specifically legal inhibitions on reporting, but heavy censorship will be applied by the military authorities through the control of access to information and their ability to command avenues of communication.

There is an abiding belief in Allied military circles that America lost the Vietnam War by its failure to control correspondents and television news teams. This article of simplistic faith has bred suspicion and hostility towards the media, evidenced by the treatment of reporters during the Falklands and Grenada invasions. The British Navy originally decided to exclude journalists entirely from the Falklands task force: political pressure produced a limited number of places, but only for 'acceptable' newsmen from British organizations. A two-tier level of censorship was imposed: dispatches were censored at source and were then routed via the Ministry of Defence in London, where they were often further censored or delayed. The movement of journalists on the ground was strictly controlled by military authorities, and each group was allocated a 'minder' – civil servants from the MoD with a concern, which was often greater than that of military commanders, to suppress potentially embarrassing information. The authorities refused to set up facilities for television coverage. Some of the correspondents later admitted to self-censorship of stories that would have depicted British troops in a poor light, and confessed to over-credulous acceptance of official claims. In London information was withheld until it was politically acceptable to release it, and on several occasions the media were encouraged to publish false information in the hope that it would mislead Argentinian monitors. The effects of these measures of news arrangement were not necessarily helpful to the British cause: there was concern that Britain had 'lost the information war' by its censorship, which had the inevitable effect of leaving a gap, that was filled by Argentinian propaganda claims.[157] In the parliamentary post-mortem that followed, military and MoD authorities were prepared to concede that some of the restrictions had been overzealous.[158] None the less, draft regulations for war correspondents issued by the MoD

---

[157] Alan Protheroe, 'Why We Have Lost the Information War', *The Listener*, 3 June 1982.
[158] Defence Committee Report, note 132 above.

in 1983 were found to be restrictive to the point of unwork-ability.[159]

In the Falklands conflict the British media loyally accepted all censorship restrictions and refrained even from telling its pubic when its news reports had been subject to military censorship. *The Sunday Times* suppressed its discovery of an important legal document giving some support to historical Argentinian claims to the islands, and the *Washington Post* correspondents in London accused political journalists of withholding known information about the Cabinet involvement in sinking the *Belgrano* in order to avoid Government embarrassment. Among the most virulent enemies of press freedom in this period was the *Sun* newspaper, which falsely accused others of treason for daring to criticize British policy or to provide a balanced coverage of the conflict. There will always be some reasonable grounds for censorship during hostilities to protect lives and the security of operations, and to withhold news of losses until relatives have been informed. News management is unacceptable when it is used to cover embarrassment or to disseminate disinformation. The vetting of journalists and the exclusion of the foreign press are expedients that should not be resorted to again. The view of some military authorities that reports should be censored and pictures disallowed, because presentation of the true horror of war would sap morale back home, does not provide a proper basis for war censorship.

Following the Falklands conflict, a committee set up by the Ministry of Defence under the chairmanship of General Sir Hugh Beach made recommendations on how censorship in future conflicts should be managed.[160] For major conventional wars, they broadly endorsed the system used in the Second World War of 'voluntary' censorship reinforced by emergency regulations making it an offence to disclose information useful to an enemy and by a government power to suppress publications that systematically fermented opposition to the war. They did propose, however, that once information had been made public overseas, there should be no restriction on its dissemination in the United Kingdom.

The Gulf War presented different problems of news management for the British Government. In conjunction with United States authorities, it hit upon the idea of 'pools' of accredited reporters who would be attached to major force deployments, receiving protection and information in return for submitting every report to

---

[159] 'Defence Ministry Reporting Rules lead to Press Freedom Fears', *Guardian*, 24 October 1983, and 'Letter of Law for War Reporters', *Guardian*, 27 October 1983.
[160] *The Protection of Military Information*, Report of the Study Group on Censorship chaired by General Sir Hugh Beach, HMSO, 1983, Cmnd 9112; for the Government response, see Cmnd 9499.

military censorship. Although in theory a 'pool' means that reports of journalists travelling with military units are available to all media, in practice it came to denote a privileged group who were permitted to witness events at the front and to receive official cooperation in return for submitting to military censorship.[161] The British 'pool' reporters were duly spoon-fed information by military authorities, which they had little alternative but to publish, as MoD rules prevented them from publishing virtually anything else without authorization, as the list of banned subjects released by the MoD just before the war broke out in January 1991 makes plain:

Non-releasable information for Gulf reporters:

1. Number of troops.
2. Number of aircraft.
3. Numbers of other equipment (e.g., artillery, tanks, radar, trucks).
4. Names of military installations/specific geographic locations of military units.
5. Information about future operations.
6. Information about security precautions.
7. Photography showing the level of security at military installations.
8. Photography that would reveal the name or specific location of military forces.
9. Rules-of-engagement details.
10. Information on intelligence collection.
11. Information on 'in-progress' operations.
12. Information on special units, unique operations methodology/tactical.
13. Information identifying postponed operations.
14. In case of operational necessity, additional guidelines may be necessary.

These rules, and the discipline of the 'pool', ensured that news from the Allied side of the conflict was controlled and sanitized. Journalists who refused to accept military supervision were refused access to the front and opportunities to go on special assignments; some had equipment confiscated while others were threatened with deportation from Saudi Arabia. Still photographs were carefully vetted, and the Saudi authorities allowed visas for only three British photographers, from pro-war popular newspapers. The Allied command was anxious to prevent the Western media from showing images of carnage of a sort that affected public morale during the

---

[161] See Robert Fisk, 'Free to Report What we're Told', *The Independent* 6 February 1991; *The Gulf War and Censorship*, Article 19, February 1991.

Vietnam War; it could not, however, prevent Western correspondents from accepting invitations to return to Bagdad, where Iraqi authorities were anxious for them to depict civilian casualties, but without permitting them to report damage to military targets or to civilian morale.

The most absurd casualties of the war were scheduled films and songs and comedies, which were banned from television and radio for the duration of the Gulf conflict. Otherwise sensible media executives determined to help the war effort by removing all jokes about Hitler (*'Allo 'Allo!*), the American military (*M.A.S.H.*) and English soldiers (the BBC solemnly replaced *Carry on up the Khyber*, with *Carry on Cowboy*). Even Channel 4 cancelled a programme that showed American bombing of Vietnam, while the BBC warned its radio stations against playing no less than sixty-seven popular songs, ranging from 'Light my Fire' and 'Killing Me Softly' to 'Everybody Wants to Rule the World'. These ludicrous decisions showed that for broadcasting executives, the first casualty of war is the right of viewers and listeners to be treated as intelligent adults.

Negotiating Civil Service Disclosure

In the absence of a full-scale Freedom of Information Act, British journalists cannot legally compel civil servants to disclose information or documents. Under a rare exception, the Treasury must make available its economic models and forecasts; the public is entitled to use this information, at least, to draw its own conclusions.[162] Whitehall can, of course, choose to release information: the Official Secrets Act does not bar 'authorized' releases. The Public Records Acts also permit the Government to *shorten* as well as lengthen the thirty-year rule for all or selected categories of documents.[163] However, the official position remains that stated in Notes of Guidance issued by Sir Robert Armstrong after the Ponting trial, emphasizing civil servants' absolute duty to the Government of the day, and their duty, until death, to keep confidential any information that comes their way.[164] These guidelines are a fitting memorial to the man who drafted them, whose 'economies with the truth' in the pursuit of *Spycatcher* made him and his country an international laughing stock. In 1987 the Government approved procedures to enable a civil servant to

---

[162] Industry Act 1975 s 27 and Sched 5.
[163] S 5(1) of Public Records Act 1958 as amended by the Public Records Act 1967.
[164] 'The Duties and Responsibilities of Civil Servants in Relation to Ministers' (see written answer, 26 February 1985, 74 HC Debs Col 128).

report improper or illegal directions – so that any such reports could be hushed up within the system. However, now that s 2 of the Official Secrets Act has been restricted mainly to defence and security information, and the public-interest defence to breach of confidence actions has widened, journalists may be able to convince more civil servants to speak out about unethical and incompetent behaviour, secure in the knowledge that they will not fall victim to the criminal or civil law.

The Croham Directive

In their efforts to tease information out of government departments, journalists can invoke a number of Civil Service Directives. In July 1977 Lord Croham, the head of the Home Civil Service, wrote to all departments setting out guidelines for greater openness.[165] Background material was to be separated from policy advice so that the former could be made publicly available. Consideration was to be given to the issuing of bibliographies and digests by each department. The letter made clear that its real purpose was to stave off demands for more changes on the lines of the American or Swedish Freedom of Information Acts. Nevertheless, it was intended to constitute a 'real change in policy'. Its effect has been patchy. The DHSS did publish forty background papers, to its 1978 Supplementary Benefits Review, but a study by *The Times* found little evidence of a shift in practice.[166]

When the Conservatives came to power in 1979, the Prime Minister confirmed that the Croham Directive was still in force, and Paul Channon stated 'it will be the practice of this government to make as much information as possible available including background papers and analytical studies relevant to major policy decisions'.[167] In addition, the Parliamentary Private Secretary to the Prime Minister sent a letter to all Secretaries of State, conveying 'the Prime Minister's wish that Ministers should give close personal attention to and take the initiative in publishing information, especially on matters of Parliamentary interest, to the greatest possible extent'.[168] In practice, though, the Croham Directive has become a dead letter under the Tories.[169]

---

[165] See Leigh, *The Frontiers of Secrecy*, p. 253, and Hansard HC Debs Vol 942 5th Series cols 691–4 (written answer).
[166] *The Times*, 14 November 1979, written up in an expanded version in Colin Bennett and Peter Hennessy, *A Consumer's Guide to Open Government: Techniques for Penetrating Whitehall*, Outer Circle Policy Group.
[167] 23 October 1979 Hansard HC Debs Vol 972 5th Series col 131 (written answer); and HC Debs Vol 968 5th Series Col 1316.
[168] Bennett and Hennessy, *A Consumer's Guide to Open Government*, App: 4.
[169] Patrick Birkenshaw, *Freedom of Information: the Law, the Practice and the Ideal*, Weidenfeld & Nicolson, 1988, pp. 142, 222.

ESTACODE

Criticism of excessive secrecy came from the Fulton Committee, which reported on the Civil Service in 1968.[170] Echoing one of the Committee's recommendations, the manual for senior civil servants (ESTACODE) says:

> The need for greater openness in the work of government is now widely accepted. Openness in this context means two things:
> (a) the fullest possible exposition to Parliament and to the public of the reasons for government policies and decisions when those decisions are formulated and announced;
> (b) creating a better public understanding about the way in which the processes of government work and about factual and technical background to government policies or decisions.[171]

The ESTACODE manual, the Croham Directive and the Channon statement are generalities studded with qualifications. The staff manual, for instance, speaks of disclosing rationalizations for Government decisions that have already been made, rather than releasing data that would allow the public to make a more informed contribution to the formulation of policy. They also share an ignominious history: the Croham letter and ESTACODE were both restricted documents until leaked to the press. For all these deficiencies, these statements of support for openness can be useful to journalists. They will not convince a stubborn bureaucrat to release embarrassing information, but they may ease the decision for a more sympathetic civil servant or at least be a ground for reconsidering an earlier refusal.[172] In addition, the more that civil servants are pressed to disclose information, the less easy it will be for them to assert that open government is merely the preoccupation of a marginal fringe.[173]

---

[170] The Civil Service (1968) Cmnd 3638 para 277–80.
[171] Para 4129. The relevant part is reprinted in full in Bennett and Hennessy, *A Consumer's Guide to Open Government*, and in the Royal Commission's Report *Standards of Conduct in Public Life*, 1976, Cmnd 6524 App II.
[172] Peter Hennessy, 'A Few Simple Techniques for Penetrating Whitehall', July 1980, Journalism Studies Review, p. 11.
[173] Bennett and Hennessy, *A Consumer's Guide to Open Government*, p. 17.

Using the US Freedom of Information Acts[174]

The press in the United States has enviable freedom from the worst restraints of contempt and libel, which would, for instance, have hampered any British equivalent of the Watergate investigation by the *Washington Post*.[175] In addition, it has broad rights of access to government documents, pursuant to Freedom of Information Acts.

The first Act, passed in 1966, established a philosophy of full government agency disclosure except for specified reserved areas.[176] The Act also set up a court procedure for enforcing the new rights. Following Watergate and the subsequent Congressional investigations of the security services, the Act was amended in 1974. The 'national security' exemption had been abused and was significantly narrowed. In particular, courts were directed to consider whether documents had been properly classified and whether a censored version would be safely released. As a result of the Acts, government agencies were compelled to release International Red Cross Reports on prisoners of war in Vietnam, a CIA report on its domestic intelligence activities, and summaries of J. Edgar Hoover's files on his personal enemies.[177]

These Acts, which now have equivalents in Australia and Canada, are more than a model that British law might emulate. They can also be of immediate use to British journalists. *The Sunday Times* was able to obtain a highly critical report on British cruise ships that had been made by an American inspector.[178] Lobbyists against new food additives who were denied test results by the British Ministry of Agriculture were able to inspect them on the files of the US Food and Drug Administration. When two Scottish meat-packing plants were refused an American importer's certificate, British journalists in Washington obtained copies of the inspectors' comments on their appalling standards of hygiene. Questionable payments by British firms were uncovered in the files of the Securities and Exchange Commission (a much tougher American version of the Stock Exchange Council).[179] Journalists

---

[174] Stewart Dresner, *Open Government: Lessons from America*, available from Rowntree Trust, 9 Poland Street, London W1; Supperstone, *Brownlie's Law*, pp. 270–87.
[175] Harold Evans 'The Half Free Press' in *The Freedom of the Press*, Granada Guildhall Lectures 1974.
[176] S 552 of the United States Code, Title 5.
[177] Supperstone, *Brownlie's Law*, p. 284; Michael, *Politics of Secrecy*, pp. 129–38.
[178] James Michael, *Politics of Secrecy*, NCCL, 1979, pp. 10–11.
[179] See 'What the American FoI Act reveals about Britain', Campaign for Freedom of Information, No 22, July 1991.

seeking information to support their defence to a libel action were able to obtain it from Australian authorities, required under that country's Freedom of Information legislation to hand over police and surveillance reports that do not threaten national security and are no longer relevant to current police investigations.

The Thatcher Government adamantly refused to incorporate a 'freedom of information' (FoI) dimension into the 1989 Official Secrets Act. Yet rapid release of official information under such legislation is fast becoming a defining characteristic of accountable democratic government elsewhere in the world. Whitehall's objections on grounds of cost have been greatly exaggerated. Its objection of principle is based on the 'ministerial accountability' theory. But ministerial involvement in departmental decisions occurs only at levels of high policy: ministers neither control nor are in practice answerable for thousands of decisions made by middle-ranking departmental officers, which may vitally affect individuals and communities. It is often claimed that civil servants would be less candid in offering advice and writing reports if they knew their words would be publishable within a year or so rather than after thirty or fifty years' anonymity which the Public Records Act currently provides. This argument does little credit to the civil servants who advance it, and overlooks the fact that statutory privilege from libel action will give no cause for them to fear about frankness.

Overseas experience suggests that the prospect of early public scrutiny does concentrate the mind in helpful ways; judgements are more careful and considered, and advice is not tendered lightly. FoI provides, in fact, an incentive for public servants to perform better, to produce analysis that will withstand contemporary public scrutiny and may often receive accolades a good deal more genuine than the honours routinely handed out in the Queen's Birthday list. There is, of course, a congenital fear of having to defend secrecy decision in the courts, and no amount of logic will convince ministers and mandarins that a High Court judge might be in a better position to determine the public interest than they are. None the less, the skies have not fallen on Westminster-style democracies in Canada and Australia with the advent of FoI; on the contrary, most public servants there have not only come to terms with the legislation, but even come to like it. Tax and social-security forms contain messages about FoI rights, telephone books contain basic instructions on how to make an application, and media campaigns promote awareness of the Act. Not content with merely making memoranda available to the public, in 1978 the United States provided legal protection for civil servants who take the initiative in revealing misconduct. The Civil Service Reform Act of 1978 – known as 'the Whistleblowers Act' – protects civil servants from any form of retaliation, legal action or demotion if they disclose wrongdoing or malpractice.

Chapter 11

Reporting Local Government

Elected Members and officials must deliberately establish and maintain working relationships with those responsible for newspapers, broadcasting and television to seek their help in keeping open the two-way communication between the public and local government.

Royal Commission on Local Government, 1969[1]

Local papers and most local councils have not been slow to respond to this plea from the Royal Commission responsible for the present pattern of local government. Local council reporters have 'established and maintained' a relationship with council contacts who can provide a quick quote to flesh out a dry committee minute or tip the journalist off to agenda items that will spark rhetorical flourishes or have local public interest. Reporting set-piece council debates is safe from a libel action: newspapers can carry, under the shield of qualified privilege, the insults and allegations that rival politicians trade in the public chamber. But these 'working relationships' rarely work to uncover incompetence in local government, let alone the sort of corruption spread by the Poulson gang. This type of investigation ruffles the feathers of regular contacts and jeopardizes reporters' access to information needed for more mundane work.[2] To the shame of the hundreds of reporters covering local government in the North-east, the corruption that riddled that area was discovered and disclosed by lawyers acting for Poulson's creditors. The media saw and heard no evil; certainly they spoke none through the decade in which local authority contracts were awarded by bribery and improper influence.

---

[1] Redcliffe-Maud Report on Local Government Reform Cmnd 4040 (1969) para 319.
[2] See further Dave Murphy, 'The Silent Watchdog: the Press in Local Politics' and 'Control without Censorship' in James Curran (ed.), *The British Press: A Manifesto*, Macmillan, 1978.

The media cannot blame the secrecy laws for their failure; on the contrary, the law provides rights of access to a wide range of council papers. Council electors, including locally based reporters, have rights of inspection that, compared with access to Whitehall, are quite remarkable. This chapter will examine:

- the rights of admission to meetings of councils and other local bodies;
- rights to inspect documents;
- the special rules of libel concerning reports of and by local authorities.

Rights of Admission

Council meetings

Before statute intervened, the courts gave no help to newspapers wishing to report local council meetings. Councillors, like members of a private club, could eject those of whom they disapproved, and a reporter or editor whose stories caused umbrage could be barred from future meetings without legal redress.[3] The courts were out of tune with the times. In 1908 Parliament gave reporters a statutory right to attend council meetings.[4] This was extended in 1960 to the public generally by a statute known after one of its sponsors as the Thatcher Act.[5] Further extensions were made in 1972 and again in 1985.

Consequently, there is no longer a single regime for all public bodies. Journalists will deal most frequently with *principal councils*. These are county, district and London borough councils and also the Common Council of the City of London, a joint authority, a statutory joint committee, a corporate combined police authority, a combined fire authority, and (for most purposes) the Joint Consultative Committees set up for liaison between the National Health Service and local councils and the Community Health Councils (CHCs), which are Health Service user groups.[6] The duties of all

---

[3] *Tenby Corporation* v *Mason* [1908] 2 Ch 457.
[4] Admission of Press to Meetings Act 1908.
[5] Public Bodies (Admission to Meetings) Act 1960. Mrs Thatcher introduced its second reading with her maiden speech. B. E. M. Cotter, 'The Admission of Press and Public to Meetings of Local Authorities' (1974) 138 LGR 174 and 202 has a good description of the Act's legislative history.
[6] Local Government Act 1972 ss 270(1) and 100J as added by the Local Government (Access to Information) Act 1985; Health Service Joint Consultative Committees (Access to Information) Act 1986, Community Health Councils (Access to Information) Act 1988.

these bodies to admit the public and to allow inspection of their documents are set out in the Local Government Act 1972.[7]

The Thatcher Act still determines the obligations of parish and community councils, the Council of the Isles of Scilly, joint boards or committees of any of these authorities or one of these authorities and a principal council, parish meetings of rural parishes, the Land Authority of Wales, Regional and District Health Authorities, and special Health Authorities (if the order setting them up directs so), Family Practitioner Committees as far as their executive functions are concerned, and bodies (other than principal councils) that can set a rate.[8]

Although these lists may seem extensive, there are significant omissions. Decisions regarding the Metropolitan Police are not taken in public: the London police are under the control of the Home Secretary rather than any local authority or joint committee. The Tory government's penchant for protecting private business is reflected in the secrecy with which Urban Development Corporations, Enterprise Zone Authorities and Housing Action Trusts can take their decisions. As a prelude to privatization, water authorities were allowed to meet in private from 1983. The privatized companies are regulated by the National Rivers Authority, but this body can also exclude the public from its meetings.

Committees, subcommittees and caucuses

The Thatcher Act requirements apply only to full meetings of the council or body concerned or committees of the whole organization.[9] Parish and community councils must admit the public to their committee meetings (even if not all councillors are members).[10] The obligations of principal councils to open their doors is much more extensive. Committee and subcommittee meetings must be open to the public except for the limited purposes discussed below.[11] This applies to the committees that a local authority must establish by statute – education, police, local fisheries (where relevant), children, regional planning, social services, superannuation – as well as to committees that an authority sets up voluntarily.[12]

---

[7] For a useful discussion of rights of access to meetings and documents see Tim Harrison, *Access to Information in Local Government*, Sweet & Maxwell, 1988, and Patrick Birkenshaw, *Government and Information*, Butterworths, 1990, Ch 4.
[8] Public Bodies (Admission to Meetings) Act 1960 Sched.
[9] ibid., s 2(1).
[10] Local Government Act 1972 ss 100 and 270(1).
[11] ibid., ss 100A, 100E; Community Health Councils (Access to Information) Act 1988 s 1.
[12] See Local Government Act 1972 ss 101(9) and 102.

However, in many authorities policy is really made at caucus meetings of the majority party, where there is absolutely no right of access. The line is a fine one. There is no automatic legal obstacle to committees composed of just one party, and councils are free to have a 'working party' composed of members of just the ruling party,[13] but if these were to be set up, operate and report back in a way that was indistinguishable from a committee or subcommittee, they could not escape the duty to allow the public to be present.[14]

'Secrecy motions' and other limitations on access

The right of admission is not absolute. The public has to be admitted to committees only 'so far as is practicable',[15] but the courts have insisted that a committee must not deliberately choose to meet in a room that is too small for the expected audience.[16] Although there is power to clear the public gallery to prevent or suppress disorder,[17] the members of the press are unlikely to be part of any disturbance and so they should be allowed to stay when the protesters are swept out. The principle is the same as that which applies to disruptions in court (see p. 323).

Until the Local Government (Access to Information) Act 1985 councils and their committees had a general power under the Thatcher Act to exclude the public when publicity would have been prejudicial to the public interest by reason of the confidential nature of the business to be transacted.[18] This still applies to those bodies governed by the Thatcher Act (see p. 463). But the overfrequent use of this power by the larger councils and the reluctance of the courts to interfere prompted Parliament in the 1985 Act to specify more precisely when the public could be excluded from principal councils, their committees and sub-committees.

The council, committee or subcommittee *must* sit in secret if there would otherwise be disclosed information that it has received

---

[13] *R* v *Eden District Council ex parte Moffat* (1988) *The Independent*, 16 December CA.
[14] See *R* v *Sheffield City Council ex parte Chadwick* (1986) 84 LGR 563, *London Borough of Southwark* v *Peters* (1972) LGR 41.
[15] Local Government Act 1972 s 100(1).
[16] *R* v *Liverpool City Council ex parte Liverpool Taxi Fleet Operators Association* [1975] 1 All ER 379.
[17] Local Government Act 1972 s 100A(8), Public Bodies (Admission to Meetings) Act 1960 s 1(8). See also *R* v *Brent Health Authority ex parte Francis* [1985] 1 All ER 74.
[18] Public Bodies (Admission to Meetings) Act 1960 s 1(2).

from a government department in confidence or information cannot be disclosed because of a statutory duty or court order.[19]

The council or committee *can* choose to debate 'exempt information' in secret session. The price of greater constraint on the ability of local authorities to sit in private session is that this term has a very cumbersome definition. In summary, the categories of exempt information are:[20]

- information relating to council employees, occupants of council accommodation, or recipients of council services or financial assistance; past, present and prospective persons in these categories are included but only if the information relates to an individual of this description in that capacity;
- information relating to adoption, care, fostering or education of any particular child;
- information relating to the financial or business affairs of any particular person (other than the authority), but not if the information has to be registered under the Companies Acts or similar legislation;
- the amount to be spent by the authority under a contract for the acquisition of property or the supply of goods and services, but only if this would give an advantage to a contractor or prospective contractor;
- proposed or actual terms of a contract under negotiation by the authority for acquisition or disposal of property, goods or services if publication of these would prejudice the authority;
- the identity of the authority as a tenderer for a contract for goods or services;
- information relating to consultations or negotiations over a labour relations matter the disclosure of which would prejudice the authority in those or other labour negotiations or consultations;
- instructions to, and advice from, a barrister, and information obtained or action to be taken in connection with legal proceedings or the determination of any matter affecting the authority;
- information showing that the authority intends to give a notice, make an order or issue a direction to a person who might then be given an opportunity to defeat the purpose of the notice, order or direction;
- action in connection with the prevention, investigation or prosecution of crime;

---

[19] Local Government Act 1972 s 100A(2) and (3).
[20] See ibid., Sched 12A.

- the identity of a person giving information about a criminal offence, a breach of statutory duty, a breach of planning control or a nuisance;
- in relation to Joint Consultative Committees and CHCs, information relating to the physical or mental health of any person or information relating to anyone who is, was or has applied to provide services as a doctor, dentist, ophthalmist or pharmacist or their employee.[21]

The Secretary of State for the Environment can add to this list of exempt information.

The authority can exclude the public only if its secrecy resolution states the category of exempt information that will be discussed.[22] Under the Thatcher Act the courts have held that a failure to spell out the reasons for exclusion does not invalidate the resolution.[23] The legislation for principal councils is differently worded,[24] and an authority would probably be acting beyond its powers if it did not conform to these requirements.

> A committee of Liverpool City Council was considering a plan to increase the number of taxi licences. The committee room had fifty-five seats, twenty-two of which were occupied by councillors, and seventeen by officers. The matter had aroused local interest, and many taxi drivers and others wanted to attend and to make representations to the committee. The committee ruled that while the press could stay, the rest of the public should be excluded. The special reasons were, firstly, the lack of space and the impracticability of allowing in only some of the public and, secondly, a preference for hearing representations individually in the absence of other members of the public who generally wished to make submissions. The Divisional Court agreed that these reasons were adequate because the committee had not deliberately chosen a room that was too small, the press had been allowed to stay, and on the special facts of the case it was reasonable to exclude the public who were also potential 'witnesses' before the committee.[25]

The case is important because of the court's emphasis on the presence of the press, and for its indication that deliberate attempts to avoid publicity by a council can be challenged in court on grounds of bad faith.

The secrecy motion is sometimes passed to cover up a council's blunders or to hide an official's embarrassment rather than in the

---

[21] Health Service Joint Consultative Committees (Access to Information) Act 1986 s 2(4); Community Health Councils (Access to Information) Act 1988 s 2(6).
[22] Local Government Act 1972 s 100A(5).
[23] *R v Liverpool City Council*, note 16 above.
[24] See Local Government Act 1972 s 100A(4) and (5).
[25] *R v Liverpool City Council*, note 16 above.

public interest. In one case the public were excluded while the council debated the reasons for the failure of a redevelopment project. Through the gaps in the door frame reporters overheard that the development company had run short of funds and was threatening to abandon the project unless the council increased its subsidies.[26]

If a secrecy motion is proposed, journalists should ask the chair to follow the *Liverpool City Council* case and allow the press to stay. If this request is refused and there is no valid justification for the secrecy motion, the decision could be challenged by applying to the High Court to quash the order and any decision of the meeting taken after discussion behind closed doors. Journalists should in such cases ask the chair either to adjourn consideration of the matter until the challenge is heard by the court or to tape-record the deliberations so that the press can at least hear the tape if the court rules in its favour.

Agendas

Councils and other local government bodies whose meetings are public must give three clear days' notice of all such meetings.[27] Newspapers and news agencies have the right to be sent copies of the agendas and any statements prepared to indicate the nature of the agenda items. They should also be sent copies of any reports for the meeting unless the responsible official believes it is likely to be discussed at a closed session. If the officials think fit, the media should also be sent copies of any other documents supplied to members of the authority in connection with the agenda item. For these services the media can be charged only postage or other necessary costs for transmission.[28] Alternatively, copies of the agenda and reports can be inspected at the authority's offices in the three days before the meeting. The press may still find it worth making an expedition to the authority's offices, because officials of principal councils must now prepare a list of the background papers for each report that is required to be publicly available. Any document that discloses facts or matters on which the report was based

---

[26] Dave Murphy 'The Silent Watchdog', p. 25.
[27] Public Bodies (Admission to Meetings) Act 1960 s 1(4)(*a*). Local Government Act 1972 100A(6)(*a*); unless the meeting is convened on shorter notice, when notice to the public must be given at the same time.
[28] Local Government Act 1972 s 100B(7). A 'newspaper' is defined as including a news agency that systematically carries on the business of selling and supplying reports or information to newspapers, and any organization that is systematically engaged in collecting news for sound or television broadcasts or any other programme service: ibid., s 100K. See also Public Bodies (Admission to Meetings) Act 1960 s 1(4)(*b*) and s 1(7).

and which was relied upon to a material extent in preparing the report must be included on the list. Considerable judgement is left to the officers concerned, but in extreme cases the courts would review the decision. The list and at least one copy of each paper (unless it contains exempt or confidential information) must be open to public inspection, although, unusually, authorities can impose a reasonable charge for this right of inspection.[29] The media might argue that these additional documents should be sent to them with their agendas, but councils, who can charge only postage, might baulk at the cost of copying. Documents inspected at the Town Hall can be copied there, but a charge can be made for this. A reasonable number of agendas and the officers' reports should also be available for the public at the meeting itself.[30] Since the 1985 Act all these provisions apply as well to meetings of committees and subcommittees of principal councils.[31]

Reporting

Accredited representatives of the press at open meetings must be given reasonable facilities for taking notes and for telephoning reports, unless the building in which the meeting is held does not have a telephone or does not belong to the local authority.[32] 'Reasonable facilities' mean chairs and a table conveniently placed to hear and see what is going on.[33] There is no right to take photographs of the meeting, to use any means to enable persons not present to see or hear the proceedings, or to make an oral report of the proceedings as they take place.[34] The authority can thus prohibit tape-recording of the proceedings for the purpose of public broadcasting, but it is doubtful whether it can ban reporters from tape-recording for their own use as an aide-memoire.[35] It is important to note that these restrictions are discretionary; they do not prevent a local council from granting permission to film or record if it wishes. The criminal law does not prohibit this in the way that it prohibits photography in courts. Meetings of local authorities and their committees can be broadcast on radio and television without

---

[29] Local Government Act 1972 ss 100D and 100H.
[30] ibid., s 100B(1)–(6).
[31] ibid., s 100E.
[32] Public Bodies (Admission to Meetings) Act 1960 s 1(4)(*c*), Local Government Act 1972 s 100A(6).
[33] Ministry of Local Government Circular 21/61 Appendix 1 para 8.
[34] Public Bodies (Admission to Meetings) Act 1960 s 1(7) and Local Government Act 1972 s 100A(7).
[35] This interpretation of Public Bodies (Admission to Meetings) Act 1960 s 1(7) and Local Government Act 1972 s 100A(7) would be in line with modern views of tape recorders in courts: see p. 351.

conflicting with any of the statutory duties imposed on political broadcasts.[36]

Inspection of Documents[37]

Accounts and supporting documents

The nearest thing that Britain has to a freedom of information law is buried in an obscure section of the Local Government Finance Act 1982. Section 17 gives to 'any person interested' (including reporters) the right to inspect a local authority's accounts, and 'all books, deeds, contracts, bills, vouchers and receipts related thereto'.[38]

It was by exercising this right that the editor of the *City Enquirer*, a local newspaper, discovered the invoice for two machine pistols purchased by Greater Manchester police. The city's accounts for 1980 also showed a dramatic increase in expenditure on emergency planning for war preparations. These revelations led to inquiries that provoked severe and nationwide criticisms of the chief constable's policies, which he was ordered, in consequence, to reconsider. By exercising the same right, a Nottingham pressure group discovered the hard evidence that they needed to support their claims that local council house sales produced a net financial loss.[39] Details of building contracts can also be demanded under s 17, including the tender price, a copy of the contract itself, the architect's certificates against which payments where made and, if work started before a formal contract was executed, the correspondence which preceded it. It is irrelevant that the contract or, indeed, any of these documents are described as confidential. The duty of disclosure under s 17 overrides such claims.[40] Similarly, a summary

---

[36] This was the position under Broadcasting Act 1981 s 7(*b*) and is unlikely to be different under the ITC's Code.

[37] Harrison, *Access to information in Local Government* App. 2; and Local Government (Inspection of Documents) (Summary of Rights) Order 1986 (SI 1986 No 854).

[38] The right applies as well to accounts and records of committees of local authorities, a port health authority, the Broads Authority a combined police or fire authority, a licensing planning committee, an internal drainage board, a children's regional planning committee and a probation committee (except for Inner London): Local Government Finance Act 1982 s 12(2).

[39] Mike Harris, 'Making Free Use of Section 159', *New Statesman*, 6 November 1981 (s 17 of the 1982 Act replaced s 159 of Local Government Act 1972).

[40] *London Borough of Hillingdon* v *Paullsson* [1977] JPL 518 29 April 1977, Middlesex Crown Court HH Judge McDonnell; and *Oliver* v *Northampton Borough Council* (1986) 151 JP 44. Inspection cannot, however, be demanded of personal information about a member of staff of the authority (Local Government and Housing Act 1989 s 11). Other confidential documents will not come within the terms of s 17. See *R* v *Monmouthshire County Council* (1935) 153 LT 338, which said that applications for student bursaries need not be opened to inspection.

extract of accounts showing only gross payments to employees is not sufficient.[41]

This window on a local authority's affairs is open only for the fifteen full working days prior to the annual audit.[42] An advertisement giving fourteen days' notice of this crucial period must be published in one or more local newspapers.[43] At other times of the year a local elector can demand to see the statement of account,[44] orders for the payment of money by the authority[45] and a breakdown of allowances and expenses paid to councillors.[46] These accounts will not be as detailed as the pre-audit material and a council can fulfil its duty by making a computer printout available.[47] If it chooses to do this, electors will see only the amount of councillors' expenses and not the fuller details on the claim forms themselves.[48]

Journalists who are not trained accountants will find it hard to make sense of the pile of paperwork available under s 17. However, the courts have said that people who are local electors would be entitled to take accountants with them, even though the accountants came from outside the authority's area.[49] It is not necessary to identify the particular document required. It is possible to ask for an entire class of documents, and a request for 'all orders for payment' could be refused only if the class turned out to be unmanageably large.[50] A reporter, like other members of the public, also has a right to make copies of documents.[51] Inspection is free, but copies may be charged for at a reasonable rate. One local authority tried to obstruct inquirers by insisting that they pay for handwritten copies: wisely, it backed down and charged instead for photocopies.[52] It is a criminal offence to refuse a proper demand for a copy or to obstruct a person entitled to inspect one of these documents. The maximum fine is £400,[53] and newspapers could bring private prosecutions against recalcitrant council officials.

---

[41] *Oliver* v *Northampton Borough Council*, note 40 above.
[42] Accounts and Audit Regulations 1983 (SI 1983 No 1761) reg. 9.
[43] ibid., reg. 11
[44] Local Government Finance Act 1982 s 24.
[45] Local Government Act 1972 s 228(2).
[46] Local Government (Allowances) Regulations 1974 (SI 1974 No 447) reg 5.
[47] *Buckingham* v *Shackleton* [1981] 79 LGR 484.
[48] *Brookman* v *Green* [1984] LGR 228.
[49] *R* v *Glamorganshire County Council ex parte Collier* [1936] 2 All ER 168; *R* v *Bedwellty UDC ex parte Price* [1934] 1 KB 333.
[50] *Evans* v *Lloyd* [1962] 1 All ER 239.
[51] Local Government Finance Act 1982 s 17(1); Local Government Act 1972 s 228(2)
[52] Harris, 'Making Free Use of Section 159'.
[53] Local Government Finance Act 1982 s 24(3).

Audit

One purpose of allowing inspection of an authority's books just prior to the audit is to allow local electors to question the auditor about the accounts. Objectors have the right to make oral representations to the auditor.[54] These can be taken in public, but there is a discretion to hear them in private.[55] The Audit Commission's code suggests that the public should be excluded 'if it becomes apparent that injustice may be caused by allegations made without due notice'.[56]

The auditor's report on any objections and on the accounts generally must be sent to newspapers, news agencies, and television and radio stations that receive local authority agendas.[57] Those not on the mailing list will be notified by advertisement in a local paper that the report is available.[58] It can then be inspected as of right by any local elector, who may also purchase copies of all or part of it.[59]

If the auditors come across a matter of particular concern during the course of their investigation, they can make an immediate report, rather than waiting for months until they conclude their final report.[60] From September 1991, these 'immediate reports' must be made publicly available by the council concerned, which must also advertise their existence in the local press. It is a summary offence to obstruct a person trying to exercise his or her rights under the new provision.[61]

Minutes, reports and rating records

For parish and community councils, only the minutes of the authority itself and its committees need to be made public.[62] For principal councils, the obligation extends to any committee and subcommittee minutes. For six years the authority must keep copies of the minutes, the agenda and any report for an item that was considered in public. If the public was actually excluded

---

[54] ibid., s 17(3).
[55] *R* v *Farmer ex parte Hargrave* [1981] 79 LGR 676.
[56] Code of Local Government Audit Practice for England and Wales (Audit Commission 1988) para 22.
[57] Local Government Finance Act 1982 s 18(5).
[58] Accounts and Audit Regulations 1983 (SI 1983 No 1761) reg 11.
[59] Local Government Finance Act 1982 s 24(1)(*a*) and (*b*).
[60] ibid., s 15.
[61] ibid., s 18A as added by the Local Government Finance (Publicity for Auditors' Reports) Act 1991.
[62] Local Government Act 1972 s 228(1).

because exempt information was under discussion, the minutes of that part of the meeting will be sealed. If this means that it is impossible to understand the proceedings, council officials should prepare a summary to give a fair and coherent record without disclosing exempt information.[63] Background papers that are open to public inspection must be kept for four years.[64] During these periods the documents can be inspected. Agendas, minutes and reports can be inspected without charge, but the authority can impose a reasonable fee for inspecting background reports and for copying.[65] Copying can be refused if this would infringe copyright in the document, but not if the only copyright is owned by the authority itself.[66]

Local authorities must maintain registers of councillors showing their membership of committees and subcommittees and a list of officers to whom powers have been delegated.[67] The register and list must be open to public inspection. Councils should also maintain for the public a written summary of rights to attend meetings and inspect documents.[68]

Councillors' conflicts of interest

The minutes should record whether any councillor disclosed a conflict of interest. Councillors with even an indirect pecuniary interest[69] in any matter before the authority must state this fact, take no further part in the debate, and must not vote. If they break these rules, they commit a criminal offence.[70] Instead of declaring an interest orally at the meeting, councillors can give a general notice to the authority.[71] This does not allow them to participate in the debate or to vote, but it does make a public declaration unnecessary, and there will be no explanation in the minutes for their silence. General notices can be examined by other councillors, but

---

[63] ibid., s 100C; three years in the case of CHCs, Community Health Councils (Access to Information) Act 1988 s 1(1)(c).

[64] Local Government Act 1972 s 100D(2); four years in the case of CHCs, Community Health Councils (Access to Information) Act 1988 s 1(1)(c).

[65] Local Government Act 1972 s 100H(1) and (2).

[66] ibid., s 100H(3).

[67] Unless this is for a period less than six months: Local Government Act 1972 s 100G added by the Local Government (Access to Information) Act 1985.

[68] See above and Local Government Inspection of Documents (Summary of Rights) Order (SI 1986 No 854). The register must also list the names and addresses of other members of the committe or subcommittee who are not councillors (Local Government Act 1972 s 100G(17)(b)). Joint Consultative Committees and CHCs must prepare comparable registers and summaries of rights of access: Health Services Joint Consultative Committees (Access to Information) Act 1986 s 3; Community Health Councils (Access to Information) Act 1988 s 2.

there is no right of inspection in England and Wales for the press or the public. Such a right exists in Scotland,[72] and local councils south of the border should be encouraged to allow access to councillors' written declarations of interest.

In the wake of the Poulson affair two committees proposed a statutory public register of councillors' interests similar to that adopted by the House of Commons.[73] Some councils took the initiative and instituted a public register through their own standing orders. The Local Government and Housing Act 1989 belatedly introduced such a statutory register. Only pecuniary interests must be recorded. Councils are prohibited from requiring their members to register other interests (e.g., freemasonry).[74]

Rates and poll tax

Journalists who are also ratepayers have a right to inspect the valuation lists prepared for rating purposes, notices of objection, proposal or notices of appeal in connection with the current list and (if the current one has been in effect for less than ten years) the immediately preceding one, minutes of the proceedings of any local valuation court and minutes of the proceedings of any rating authority for the last ten years.[75]

The transition was first made to the new scheme of local taxation in Scotland, and came into force in England and Wales in 1990. Domestic rates have been replaced and a 'non-domestic' rate (essentially on business premises) is set by central government. Although this is a uniform rate it is applied to updated valuations.

---

[69] A councillor who is a partner, employee or has shares (with a nominal value over £1,000 or 1 per cent of the company's capital) in the proposed contractor is deemed to have a declarable interest: Local Government Act 1972 s 97. Councillors must also declare their spouse's interests (if they know of them, s 95(3)). The statute speaks only of pecuniary interests but the National Code of Local Government Conduct warns councillors to disclose ties of kinship, friendship, membership of organizations or other matters that might give the appearance of a conflict of interests. DOE circular 8/90.

[70] Local Government Act 1972 ss 94, 105. The Secretary of State can give a special dispensation: s 97. A general dispensation has been given for council tenants: DOE circular 105/73.

[71] Local Government Act 1972 s 96.

[72] Local Government (Scotland) Act 1973 s 40.

[73] Committee on Local Government Rules of Conduct (Chairman Lord Redcliffe-Maud) 1974 Cmnd 5636 paras 55–64; Royal Commission on Standards of Conduct in Public Life (Chairman Lord Salmon) 1976 Cmnd 6524 para 179. For the Register of MPs' interests, see p. 401.

[74] Local Government and Housing Act 1989, s 19, reversing *R* v *Newham ex parte Haggerty* (1986) 85 LGR 48.

[75] General Rate Act 1967 s 108 (as amended by Rates Act 1984 Sched 1 para 20.

The valuations generally are still carried out by local authorities and the regime for inspecting the valuation lists, proposals and notices of appeal is essentially the same. Similarly, the minutes of the proceedings of the valuation and community charge tribunals are open for inspection for five years. Copies of all these documents can be taken, or (for a reasonable fee) supplied.[76]

In preparation for the poll tax local authorities (London boroughs and district councils) drew up a community charges register. There is no general public right of inspection of the register. Instead, registration officers are required to prepare an extract of the register for public inspection.[77] The details are left to regulations that provide that the extract must contain just the name and address of each registered person and the addresses of places such as hostels and hotels where a collective community charge is levied. If a person is under threat of violence, the registration officer can omit even these limited particulars from the public register. The regulations forbid registrars supplying copies of the register; unlike the electoral roll, copies of these registers will not, as a matter of Government policy, be put on sale.[78]

Planning

Planning applications are kept on a register that is open to public inspection.[79] If development is carried on without planning permission, the local authority can issue an enforcement notice requiring the owner to restore the land to its previous use or condition, or a breach of condition notice if the terms on which permission was granted have not been followed. The owner can appeal and cannot be compelled to obey the enforcement notice unless the local authority also issues a 'stop notice'. These are not made automatically, because the authority must pay compensation if it loses the appeal. There are public registers of enforcement, breach of condition and stop notices.[80] Applications for certain other kinds of local authority licences (ranging from sex shops to zoos) must also be made available to the public.[81]

---

[76] Local Government Finance Act 1988 Sched 10 para 8.
[77] ibid., Sched 2 para 17.
[78] Community Charges (Administration and Enforcement) Regulations 1989 (SI No 438, reg 11.
[79] Town and Country Planning Act 1990 s 69. It is divided into those that are pending and those that have been finally disposed of. General Development Order 1988 (SI 1988 No. 1813) Art 27. The register should also say what action has been taken on the application.
[80] Town and Country Planning Act 1990 s 188, and General Development Order 1988 Art. 28.

In addition to actions affecting individual properties, local authorities are required to plan strategically. Their plans in draft and as actually adopted, together with supporting documents, must be open to public inspection.[82] Similarly the public are entitled to see the council resolution setting up Housing Improvement Areas and the authority's registers of listed buildings and of tree preservation notices.[83]

Local ombudsmen

Just as a Parliamentary Commissioner for Administration, or ombudsman, has been established to hear complaints of poor administration in central government, so a number of local Commissioners of Administration exist to hear complaints of maladministration against local authorities. The complaint must relate to the procedure of decision-making rather than its merits, and in order to succeed will generally have to reveal bias, neglect, inattention, delay, incompetence, ineptitude, perversity, turpitude or arbitrariness. Complaints are normally made through a local councillor, but unlike the parliamentary ombudsman, the local commissioners can receive complaints directly from the public.[84] The local ombudsman reports back to the authority concerned, which will then normally have to give the public a chance to inspect the report for a three-week period that has been advertised by at least one week's advance notice in the local press. Inspection of the ombudsman's report is free of charge. It can be copied, and it is an offence to obstruct anyone exercising these rights to inspect or copy.[85]

Local parliamentary bills

Certain documents have to be deposited with the local authority under the Standing Orders of each House of Parliament. These are mainly private bills that are sponsored by, or affect, the locality.[86]

---

[81] Sex shops: Local Government (Miscellaneous Provisions) Act 1982 Sched 3, paras (7)–(13); Zoos: Zoo Licensing Act 1981 s 2(3). The Food Safety Act 1990 s 19 allows the government to require a similar system of registering food premises.
[82] Town and Country Planning (Structure and Local Plans) Regulations 1982 (SI 1982 No 555) regs 36–9 (outside London); Town and Country Planning (Local Plans for Greater London) Regulations 1974 (SI 1974 No 1481) regs 25–8.
[83] Inner Urban Areas Act 1978 Sched, para 1(3)(*a*) (housing improvement areas); Town and Country Planning Act 1990 s 214 (tree preservation); Planning (Listed Buildings and Conservation Areas) Act 1990 s 2. (listed buildings).
[84] Local Government Act 1974 ss 23–34; *R* v *Local Commissioner for Administration for the North & East Area of England ex parte Bradford MCC* [1979] 2 WLR 1.
[85] Local Government Act 1974 s 30.
[86] Standing Orders of the House of Commons (Private Business) HC 416 (1980) Orders 27–47.

The detailed plans that must accompany them may be of particular interest in the case of controversial construction projects. These documents are also open to inspection and copying, although the council can charge for viewing them: 10p for the first half hour and 10p per hour thereafter.[87]

Pollution control

Responsibility for controlling pollution rests with local authorities. Traditionally, council officials have preserved the secrecy of the information that they have been given by local industries on the pretext that their cooperation was essential and depended on confidentiality. Environmentalists suspected that the real fears were of greater public pressure for higher standards, and of criticism at the inefficiency of the means of control.[88] Slowly, Parliament has demanded more publicity: waste disposal licences are kept on a public register,[89] information on air pollution that is given under compulsion must also be recorded in a public register;[90] and a local authority that has declared a noise abatement zone has to keep a public record of the noise levels there.[91] In 1974 Parliament decreed that water authorities should keep public registers of discharge consents, analysis of effluent samples and other matters relating to water pollution, but it was only in 1985 that the obligations were brought into effect.[92] Similar rights exist in relation to the discharge of radioactive waste.[93]

Local authorities will have to regulate hazardous substances in their areas and keep public registers of hazardous substances applications, consents, revocations, modifications and direction,[94] but these provisions have still not yet been brought into force.

As a result of the Environment and Safety Information Act 1988, various authorities with responsibility for specific environmental and safety checks must keep public registers of those who have been notified of suspected breaches. Inspection of the

---

[87] Local Government Act 1972 ss 225 and 228(5).
[88] See Maurice Frankel, 'The Environment' in Rosemary Delbridge and Martin Smith (eds), *Consuming Secrets*, National Consumer Council and Burnet Books, 1982, pp. 93–126.
[89] Control of Pollution Act 1974 s 6.
[90] ibid., s 82(3)(*d*); Control of Atmospheric Pollution (Research and Publicity) Regulations 1977 (SI 1977 No 19) reg 6. Polluters are indexed. If they hand over the information voluntarily, they can do so in confidence. Frankel, note 88 above, p. 108.
[91] Control of Pollution Act 1974 s 64.
[92] ibid., ss 41 and 42; Control of Pollution (Registers) Regulations 1985 (SI 1985 No 813).
[93] Control of Pollution (Radioactive Waste) Regulations 1985 (SI 1985 No 708).
[94] Planning (Hazardous Substances) Act 1990 s 28.

register is free, although a reasonable charge can be made for copying. There are important limitations: notices solely for the protection of people at work are excluded; entries on the register are postponed pending an appeal; if the person affected claims that the local authority's proposed entry would disclose a trade secret, only bare details are recorded pending a decision on the claim by the minister; and only notices issued after 1 April 1989 have to be registered.

Further disclosure will be required when the Environmental Protection Act 1990 is fully implemented. To some extent the pressure for greater openness has come from the Council of European Communities, which on 7 June 1990 issued a directive requiring member states to make available to the public information relating to the environment held by public authorities.[95] There are familiar exceptions, however: the information can be withheld if it affects commercial and industrial confidentiality or where the documents or data are 'unfinished' or are internal communications. Where disclosure is required, it must be made within a maximum of two months, and there must be a system of appeal or review so that refusals can be challenged. Member states are obliged to have these systems in place by the end of 1992.

Housing

Public housing authorities must publish details of their arrangements on matters of housing management, policies on allocation of council housing and on transfers. These are open to inspection and copying – the latter for a reasonable fee – although the authority must provide a free copy of a summary of its allocation priorities to anyone who asks for it.[96] If a local authority has established a register of houses in multiple occupation, this must be open to public inspection.[97] Local rent officers must maintain a register of the rents that they have registered in their area for tenants who are 'protected' under the Rent Act 1977.[98] Finally, the authority must make available for inspection its scheme for providing Housing Benefit.[99]

Education and social services

Since 1980, local education authorities (LEAs) must publish their

---

[95] Council Directive 7 June 1990 90/313/EEC OJ No L 158, 23.6.90, p. 59.
[96] Housing Act 1985 s 106.
[97] Housing Act 1961 s 22.
[98] Rent Act 1977 ss 64, 66(1).
[99] Social Security and Housing Benefit Act 1982 s 31(1).

arrangements and policies for admission of pupils to their schools. They must also make known the number of nominations that they have available to make to independent schools and their criterion for filling them. LEAs must also spell out their means for enabling parents to express their preference for schools and the appeals mechanism if the LEA allocates the child to a different school.[100] The authority's policies on school transport, provision of milk and meals and school clothing, and provision for children with special education needs must be published.[101] As the system of local management devolves more power to individual schools, it becomes more important for the public to have a right of access to information about the policies of, and decision-making within, each school. School governors have a discretion to hold their meetings in public, and, in general, the minutes of their meetings must be open to inspection.[102] A school's curriculum policies must likewise be publicly available.[103]

Authorities with social service departments must make known their services for the blind, deaf, handicapped and disabled. They must keep public registers of homes for the old, disabled, drink or drug dependants, or the mentally ill.[104] Local authorities must publish information about the services that they provide for children in need, day-care facilities, and accommodation for children.[105]

Annual reports

The Local Government Planning and Land Act 1980 introduced new mandatory disclosure requirements, which were consistent with the Conservative Government's concern to compare and cut back public spending. Local authorities (including fire authorities and police committees) must produce an annual report that contains the information required by the Environment Minister's Code of Practice.[106] The first code, published in 1981 requires authorities to publish statistics comparing their expenditure for each service with the average for authorities of the same class.[107] Comparisons must be made between projected and actual expenditures, and

---

[100] Education Act 1980 s 8.
[101] Education (School Information) Regulations 1981 (SI 1981 No 630).
[102] Education (School Government) Regulations 1989 (SI 1989 No 1503) regs 21 and 24.
[103] Education (Schools Curriculum and Related Information) Regulations 1989 (SI 1989 No 954).
[104] Chronically Sick and Disabled Persons Act 1970 s 1(2)(*a*); Registered Homes Act 1984 s 7.
[105] Children Act 1989 ss 17, 18, 20 and 24 and Sched 2.
[106] Local Government Planning and Land Act 1980 s 2.

capital expenditure must also be noted. Rate and other income must be given, as well as statistics for major services. The authority's workforce must be tabulated by staff category. The Government has also recommended that local authorities (like companies) should disclose policies for hiring staff who are disabled.[108] The code says that the reports should be made available to the press and to members of the public.[109] More details about the authority's manpower are required by a separate code.[110] The Government has power to compel authorities to comply with these codes by issuing regulations, and has done so in the case of the Manpower Code.[111] The press must be notified of the annual report, and it must be made available at the council's offices and public libraries.[112]

Construction and maintenance work must also be the subject of an annual report by local authorities. (Its content has been determined by Local Government (Direct Labour Organisations) Annual Report Directive 1982, Annex A to circular 6/82.) It is open to inspection and copying by interested parties.[113]

Where authorities continue to use their own workforce for certain tasks,[114] they must make available to the public a statement that compares the in-house bid with any offers to do the same work by private contractors.[115]

Land ownership

Central government requires local authorities to keep a public register of publicly owned land that is unused or under-used.[116] These registers are primarily intended for prospective developers. The duty is based on the fallacious assumption that only publicly owned land is left unproductive. Derelict land is often in private ownership, but there is no power to compile open lists of the speculative holdings of development companies.

---

[107] *Local Authority Annual Reports*, HMSO, 1981; Dept of Environment Circular 3/81.
[108] Clive Walker 'Public Rights to Information in Central and Local Government' (1982) Local Government Review 931, 932.
[109] *Local Authority Annual Reports*, note 107 above, para 1.8.
[110] Publication of Manpower Information (England) Code and DoE Circular 3/83.
[111] Local Government Planning and Land Act 1980 s 3(1); Local Authorities (Publication of Manpower Information) (England) Regulations 1983 (SI 1983 No 8).
[112] *Local Authority Annual Reports*, note 107 above, para 1.8.
[113] Local Government Planning and Land Act 1980 s 18.
[114] Refuse collection, cleaning, catering, maintenance of grounds and vehicles and others specified by the Government: Local Government Act 1988 s 2.
[115] Local Government Act 1988 s 12.
[116] Local Government Planning and Land Act 1980 ss 95–96 and Sched 16.

There is a register of land titles covering most of the country. Legislation has been passed to open this to public inspection, and this law came into force in December 1990.[117] The public can inspect and copy (subject to prescribed charges) entries on the register and documents (other than leases or charges) that are referred to in the register and that are in the registrar's custody. Regulations may prescribe that certain other documents in the registrar's possession may be inspected as of right; any others will be available only at his discretion.

Leaks

Since local authority officials do not hold 'office under the Crown' they are not bound by the Official Secrets Acts and it is not a crime for them or for elected councillors to show secret documents to the press, unless the information has been entrusted in confidence to them by a person who is a Crown servant. However, local government officials show no greater readiness to leak secrets than their Whitehall counterparts. In part this is because officials face dismissal under the National Joint Council's Conditions of Service if they communicate to the public the proceedings of any meeting or the contents of any document relating to the authority, unless required by law or unless they are expressly authorized to do so. There is also considerable social pressure not to undermine colleagues.[118] Councillors caught leaking can be disciplined by their party or struck from circulation lists for sensitive documents.[119] But journalists may at least reassure their sources in local government that they are in no danger of prosecution, unless the information has been supplied as a result of a bribe.

Libel

One of the inducements for the media to cover the formal proceed-

---

[117] Land Registration Act 1988 s 1(1) adding a new s 112 to Land Registration Act 1925 There is a charge of £12 per title to inspect the register. In addition, unless the title number is already known, the inquirer will have to pay to inspect the search index map. This costs £6 if done personally; £12 if the registrar is asked to do it. Further charges are made for copies (Land Registration Fees (No 2) Order 1990 (SI No 2029) and see Land Registration (Open Register) Rules 1990 (SI 1990 No 1362) for the application forms for inspection).

[118] Sisella Bok, 'Whistleblowing and Professional Responsibilities' in Daniel Callahan and Sisella Bok (eds.) *Ethics Teaching in Higher Education* Plenum, New York, 1980.

[119] For a thoughtful analysis of what makes documents politically sensitive see, A. T. J. Maslen, 'Secrecy, Public Information and Local Government' (1979) 5 Local Govt Studies 47.

ings of local authorities is the special protection against libel actions that is given to such reports. The Defamation Act 1952 confers qualified privilege on:

- fair and accurate reports of any open meeting of the local authority (including any of the bodies whose meetings the public can attend) or one of its committees or subcommittees;[120]
- fair and accurate reports of a hearing of objections to the accounts before an auditor or any other person appointed to hold an inquiry;[121]
- a copy or fair and accurate summary of any notice or other matter issued for the information of the public by or on behalf of any local authority.[122] If a meeting is held in private, this provision protects the press if it publishes an official statement about what went on;
- a fair and accurate copy of or extract from any of the registers referred to in this chapter or any other statutory register or any other document which is open to public inspection.[123]

These are defences of qualified privilege.[124] This means that they do not apply if the publisher is malicious (see p. 71). They apply to newspapers and licensed broadcasters. The material covered in the story must also be of public concern and its publication must be for the public benefit.[125] Of the categories listed in the last paragraph, the first three are dependent on the publisher or broadcaster providing a right of reply[126] (see p. 93).

Local coverage of council affairs is relatively anodyne, in part because the privilege does not extend to behind-the-scenes investigations. Stories in greater depth must also contend with the added hazard of a libel writ from the council itself. In 1972 a judge held that Bognor Regis City Council could sue for injury to its 'governing reputation', and awarded £2,000 against the eccentric author of an extravagant handbill.[127] This was followed in 1991 by a further decision holding that the local authority need prove no special or financial loss.[128] This policy is certainly deplorable. Democratic institutions should be sufficiently robust to withstand cranky verbal assaults. Individual councillors who are identifiably

---

[120] Defamation Act 1952 Sched paras 10(*c*) and (*d*).
[121] ibid., paras 10(*c*) and (*d*).
[122] ibid., para 12.
[123] ibid., para 6.
[124] ibid., s 7(1).
[125] ibid., s 7(3).
[126] ibid., s 7 and Sched.
[127] *Bognor Regis UDC* v *Campion* [1972] 2 All ER 61.
[128] *Derbyshire County Council* v *Times Newspapers Ltd* (1991) *The Times*, 8 April.

implicated by the press in wrongdoing should pay their own way to vindicate their reputations; they should not be able to put the council up as the stalking-horse and go to law at the ratepayers' expense.

Local Authority Sponsored Publications

The last decade of Conservative government has been marked by a breakdown of consensus on the role of local authorities. Local council publications and advertisements defending their role and articulating policies that were anathema to Whitehall incurred the Government's wrath. As a result of court action and new legislation authorities are considerably circumscribed in their ability to publish or promote controversial matters.

In 1985 the Greater London Council was enjoined from continuing its anti-abolition advertising campaign because its objective of persuading people to its point of view could not be justified under a statutory power of publishing information on matters related to local government.[129]

An inquiry under David Widdicombe QC recommended further restrictions and these were adopted in two stages in 1986 and 1988.[130] Their net effect is that local authorities are prohibited from publishing, whether directly or through others, material that appears to be designed to affect public support for a political party. The general power that local authorities have of providing information is now restricted to information about services provided by the authority, central government, charities or voluntary organizations or to the functions of the authority. The Government can issue Codes of Guidance on local authorities' publicity, to which they must have regard. By contrast, central government retains a wide discretion over its publicity. As the court said when asked to declare that a 1989 leaflet about the poll tax was unlawful, it will interfere only in the most extreme cases where it could be shown that a government department had misstated the law or if a publication was manifestly inaccurate or misleading.[131]

---

[129] *R* v *GLC ex parte Westminister City Council* (1985) *The Times*, 22 January; see also *R* v *ILEA ex parte Westminister City Council* (1984) *The Times*, 31 December.
[130] Local Government Act 1986 ss 2–6; Local Government Act 1988 s 27.
[131] *R* v *Secretary of State ex parte London Borough of Greenwich* (1989) *The Independent* 17 May.

Clause 28

The 1988 bill also contained the notorious 'clause 28'. This prohibits a local authority from intentionally promoting homosexuality or publishing material with the intention of promoting homosexuality. It is also prohibited from promoting the teaching in any maintained school of the acceptability of homosexuality as a pretended family relationship. None of the prohibitions apply to anything done for the purpose of treating or preventing the spread of disease.[132] The provision aroused anger at the state's censure of a matter that was essentially one for individual choice, and fear that it would lead to an intensification of discrimination against gay men and lesbian women. The Government insisted that this was not its intention and that local authorities would not be debarred from publishing material to do with homosexuality.

It is doubtful whether clause – now section – 28 will have the consequences that its sponsors desired or its opponents fear. It applies only to local authorities, i.e., bodies that have no direct responsibility for, or control over, what is taught in schools. As a result of the 1986 Education Act, the conduct of maintained schools is under the direction of the governing body and it is the ultimate responsibility of the head teacher to determine and organize the secular curriculum within the framework of the national curriculum. Thus section 28 does not permit teachers to be dismissed for discussing homosexuality sensibly and truthfully. Even where local authorities have an advisory role, section 28 must be read subject to the Education Act, whereby the need 'to encourage pupils to have due regard to moral considerations' permits the teaching of tolerance in order to counter pupils' ignorance or hatred of homosexuals.

A local authority does not infringe section 28 unless, at the time it decides to grant funds to a homosexual group, it either desires or is well aware of the fact that its action will 'promote homosexuality', i.e., result in an increase in the number of homosexuals. It follows that there is nothing to stop a local authority from funding gay youth groups or counselling services where the intention is not to 'promote' homosexuality but rather to assist homosexuals to cope with an existing orientation. There is a crucial distinction between promoting homosexuality and promoting tolerance towards homosexuals. None the less, section 28 may have a chilling effect on some local authorities, who will wish to use it as an excuse for withdrawing from homosexuals services similar to those provided

---

[132] Local Government Act 1986 s 2A added by the Local Government Act 1988 s 28.

for other disadvantaged groups. A council that is panicked into misusing section 28 as an excuse for prejudice and discrimination in the provision of services will be open to challenge in the courts. What the advent of clause 28 does show, quite dramatically, is the depth of prejudice that will have to be overcome before discrimination on the grounds of sexual orientation is made unlawful.

Chapter 12

Reporting Business

Investigative business journalism has an honourable history. The term 'muckraker' was first applied by President Theodore Roosevelt to American newspapermen who reported the web of monopolistic practices and price fixing that characterized the heyday of free enterprise. The cabal that operated the meat industry had a particular disregard both for hygiene and for the stomachs of its customers. Upton Sinclair's novel *The Jungle*, set in the meat-packing factories of Chicago, gave a realistic and awesome account. Tinned beef took on a sinister meaning, meat sales dropped by half, and legislation followed as a direct result.[1] Although the United States and Britain now have a wide range of regulatory agencies, they are often stung into effective action only by pressure from the media. Even where no formal action is taken, a press campaign can damage a product's reputation and devastate its sales. Publicity is a potent weapon against businesses that sell to the public, but care must be taken to reserve its use for deserving targets: ruining a business runs the risk of heavier damages than ruining an individual's reputation.

This type of business reporting focuses on production and on dealings with consumers. The financial journalists who write for the business pages will usually be more interested in the efficiency and profitability of companies. Stories of dishonesty and other shady dealings are a speciality of *Private Eye*, whose record for accuracy, in this regard at least, is uncanny. There have been outstanding investigations into the ownership and control of businesses, and the conflict between private advantage and public interest. Charles Raw's analysis of the shaky empire of Slater Walker,[2] Martin Bailey's studies of Rhodesian sanctions busting,[3] and Phillip Knightley's series on the tax avoidance schemes of the Vesteys[4] are notable examples of how this can be achieved despite the laws of

---

[1] Ironically, Sinclair intended his novel as an appeal to socialism. He said ruefully: 'I aimed at the public's heart and by accident hit it in the stomach'. See Robert Downs, *The Jungle*, New American Library, 1960, p. 349.
[2] Charles Raw, *Slater Walker: An Investigation of a Phenomenon*, André Deutsch, 1977.
[3] Martin Bailey, *Oilgate: the Sanctions Scandal*, Coronet, 1979.
[4] Phillip Knightley, *The Vestey Affair*, Macdonald, 1982.

libel and breach of confidence, which are the main legal inhibitions on the business reporter. Investigations of defence contractors and other government suppliers will, of course, have to find their way around the Official Secrets Acts. But the abject failure (with rare exceptions) of British journalism to expose the commercial chicanery of Robert Maxwell until after his death in 1991 – failure both of skill in investigation and in courage in the face of libel actions – serves as a reminder of the blandness and inadequacy of much business coverage.

The non-legal pressures of low budgets, and tedious and often unrewarding research are common to all investigative reporters. Business stories have the added hurdle of incurring advertisers' displeasure. Wales Gas in 1979 withdrew all its advertising from the *North Wales Western News* because of a critical story about its liquid petroleum gas depot in Llandudno.[5] W. D. & H. O. Wills cancelled a £500,000 advertising order with *The Sunday Times* when one of its brands was named as the favourite smoke of a heart transplant patient. In the middle of the article was an advertisement for the same brand. The paper hurriedly prepared a letter to its other tobacco advertisers to assure them that this was not the start of a campaign against them.[6] Pressure of this direct kind is relatively rare, at least in the main news section of national papers.[7]

More importantly, advertisers help set the papers' agenda. Space given to financial news has expanded dramatically since the war, in direct correlation with financial advertising, but the stress on company gossip, Stock Exchange activity and tipster articles reflects the predominance of advertisements for company results, recruitment and unit trusts.[8] This is not a conspiratorial or unyielding influence. Distillers continued its advertisements in *The Sunday Times* while the paper was opposing it editorially over its handling of the thalidomide lawsuits. However, as the *Daily Herald* discovered in the 1950s, advertisers will not support a paper whose values and editorial line appeal to a different market group than the one they wish to reach.[9] From time to time there are calls for

---

[5] *Daily Telegraph*, 19 April 1979. See Hartley & Griffith, *Government and the Law*, 2nd edn, Weidenfeld & Nicolson, 1981, p. 281.
[6] *New Statesman*, 27 February 1981.
[7] James Curran, 'Advertising and the Press' in James Curran (ed.), *The British Press: A Manifesto*, Macmillan, 1978, p. 238. Compare Harold Eley's advice to advertisers in 1932, in *Advertising Media*, Butterworths. The Government used its advertising expenditure to influence papers in the early nineteeth century. *The Times* was particularly vulnerable. (Aspinall, *Politics and the Press 1780–1850*, Ch V). This has gone out of fashion, though Government advertising has always been withheld from the *Morning Star*, except for a brief period in 1970 (O'Higgins, *Censorship in Britain*, p. 107).
[8] Curran, *The British Press*, p. 240.

public libraries not to stock publications in response to their content or the conduct of their publishers. During the Wapping dispute many local authorities banned Murdoch papers from their libraries – the court ruled that this was an abuse of power and quashed the decisions.[10]

This chapter will describe the ways in which the law can help reporters by requiring that certain information is made available to them,[11] and will give a brief outline of the legal structures that a business reporter will have to understand before advantage can be taken of the facilities for corporate investigation.

Companies[12]

A beginner's lexicon

The most important form of commercial organization today is the registered company. It has its own identity, or legal personality, which is distinct from those who contribute its capital or manage its affairs. It can own property, make contracts, and start and defend lawsuits.

Its capital is usually a mixture of long-term loans provided under a formal written agreement called a debenture (by creditors who are thus known as debenture holders) and equity capital. The equity is divided into shares and is held by shareholders, who are also referred to as the members of the company. Loans can be repaid, and commonly bear a fixed rate of interest, although shareholders can be paid a dividend only if the company makes a profit. Preference shares are a hybrid. The holders are members of the company and can take a dividend only if there is a profit. Their payments take priority over those to ordinary shareholders, but their voting rights are usually restricted. The ratio of loan to equity capital is known as the company's gearing and is an important factor in assessing its economic viability.

Most companies are formed by registration with the Companies' Registry, a subdivision of the Department of Trade and Industry

---

[9] ibid., pp. 259–60.

[10] *R v Ealing Borough Council ex parte Times Newspapers Ltd* (1987) 85 LGR 316, QBD.

[11] For imaginative suggestions for lines of inquiry see Charles Medawar, *The Social Audit Consumer Handbook*, Macmillan, 1978, pp. 38–41

[12] Northey and Leigh's *Introduction to Company Law*, Butterworths, 1981, is a good first book; Tom Hadden's *Company Law and Capitalism*, 2nd edn, Weidenfeld & Nicolson, 1977, is more contextual; Gower's *Principles of Modern Company Law* and Supplement 4th edn, Stevens, 1981, is a more detailed textbook.

(DTI), which exercises supervision over companies (see p. 507 for its powers of investigation). Two documents make up the constitution of a company. Its Memorandum of Association specifies its name, initial shareholders, whether its registered office (the company's formal address) is in England and Wales or Scotland, and its objects. The latter are generally drawn so as to give the company the greatest possible latitude and will not pinpoint what the company actually does. The Articles of Association are like the rules of a club, specifying the respective powers of the shareholders, the board of directors and the managing director. They also regulate the summoning and procedure of meetings of the shareholders and the board. If the rights of shareholders are not uniform, the Articles will also prescribe the rights of each class of shares. To restrict ownership of the shares to a select group, the Articles may also prohibit transfer without the board's consent and confer a right of pre-emption, giving the other shareholders a right of first refusal if one of them wishes to sell out.

Companies can be either private or public. The principal requirement for a public company (signified by 'plc' after its name) is that its nominal share capital must be at least £50,000; the main advantage is that it can then raise capital by selling shares to the public at large.[13] Most, but not all, public companies will have a listing or quotation on the Stock Exchange. This makes trading in its shares much easier and consequently increases their value. The Stock Exchange expects a greater degree of frankness from its listed companies, and reporters can gain access to important company documents as a result of its quasi-legal requirements.

When a company wishes to raise equity capital, it announces an issue of new shares. A public company will almost always enlist the services of a merchant bank for this purpose. It must produce a prospectus disclosing information required by law and, in the case of quoted companies, by the Stock Exchange. This can offer a valuable window on the company's past record and dealings.

Some offerings of new shares are limited to existing members (rights issue), and some of these are given free (bonus issue), in which case they simply fragment the existing shares into smaller units. Shares are usually issued as 'fully paid up', which means that once the company has received the initial price, it has no further claim on the shareholders. In those rare cases where shares are not fully paid, the company can make a 'call' for the balance. A nominal value is attached to each share. Shares are issued at par if this is also their actual selling price, or at a premium if they are above par; they cannot be issued at a discount. A company cannot

---

[13] Companies Act 1980 s 4.

generally buy or finance the purchase of its own shares, although this prohibition was relaxed in 1981.

The directors of a company are fiduciaries, which means they owe a duty of trust to the company and must not allow themselves to get in a position where their personal interest conflicts with the company's – or at least not without making full disclosure to the board or its members. Although the most powerful members will have representatives on the board, they cannot ignore the interests of the minority. The court, for instance, prevented Lord and Lady Kagan, the majority shareholders, from compelling Kagan Textiles Ltd to accept the blame for fraudulent trading in indigo dye with which Lord Kagan was also charged. This would have been a fraud on the minority shareholders. Since 1980 directors also have a legal duty to take account of their employees' interests.

The most attractive feature of a company for an investor is the limited liability that it usually enjoys. However small the company – even if it is run by only one person – creditors cannot normally sue the shareholders or the management if the company has insufficient assets to pay its debts. Institutional lenders, like banks and finance houses, that are not satisfied with the creditworthiness of the company will bind the principal shareholders through a guarantee. William Stern, for instance, guaranteed his companies' debts and so became personally liable when they could not pay. He could not pay either, and his bankruptcy was the largest there had then been. Major lenders, in particular those lending long-term capital, will also condition their cooperation on the provision of security. This usually is a mortgage on the business's fixed assets, such as land and machinery, and a floating charge on the circulating assets (those that are bought and sold, accounts receivable, etc.). The lender then has a right to claim this property to satisfy the debt, although other unsecured creditors may be left with only pennies in the pound. Debentures almost invariably include both types of security.

Ownership and control

Registers of share- and debenture-holders
At first blush it seems an easy matter to find out who owns a company. Every member's shareholding is registered and the register is a public document.[14] If the shares are divided into classes, the register will show to which class each shareholder belongs.[15] If a company has issued debentures and maintains a

---

[14] Companies Act 1985 s 356.
[15] ibid., s 352.

register of debenture-holders, this must also be open for public inspection.[16] The shares may be registered in the name of another company. If this is registered in the United Kingdom, the procedure can be repeated. If it is incorporated in other countries with similar disclosure requirements, the chase can be pursued, albeit more expensively. But if it is the creature of tax havens such as the Cayman Islands, the scent will be lost. As well as charging very little tax, these countries allow investors to preserve a veil of secrecy around their holdings by laws that have virtually no disclosure requirements.

Real ownership

Frequently, the registered shareholder is only a nominee for some other person who is really or beneficially entitled to the shares. Many banks have companies holding shares for their clients that include the word 'nominee' in their name. It will then be apparent from the register of such companies that someone else is beneficially entitled to the shares. This will not always be the case with other nominees. A shareholder has generally no obligation to tell the company that it is acting as a nominee.

Automatic registration

Parliament has created exceptions to this principle. Public companies must be notified if anyone has a beneficial interest in a specified percentage (reduced to 3 per cent by the Companies Act 1989)[17] of their shares that carry unrestricted voting rights. This obligation arises when the member knows or learns that the holding has reached the required percentage.[18] It was the failure of a NatWest subsidiary to report that its holding in Blue Arrow had crossed the 5 per cent threshold that led in 1989 to a highly critical report by Department of Trade and Industry inspectors and the resignation of the bank's chairman, Lord Boardman. The requirement does not extend to debentures (which have no voting rights). A person has an interest if the shares are held by his or her family or a company that they control, or if they have an option over them.[19] Agreements amongst shareholders to accumulate a 3-per-cent holding between them must also be notified.[20] This was in

---

[16] ibid., s 190–1.

[17] Companies Act 1989 s 134(2).

[18] Companies Act 1985 ss 198–210. This applies not just to those companies with a Stock Exchange listing. The shareholder's brokers cannot maintain a discreet silence about their clients' acquisitions and dispositions. They are under a duty to inform them of these (s 210).

[19] ibid., s 203 (families); s 208 (options).

[20] ibid., ss 204–5.

response to preparations for the 'dawn raid' on Consolidated Gold Fields, when a group of investors each accumulated just under the declarable percentage of shares before making a sudden bid for control of the company.

When the shareholding reaches the 3-per-cent mark, the company must be told the names in which the shares are registered, the size of the interest and any dealings in the shares.[21] It must maintain a register of the information it receives; this must be indexed and open to public inspection for at least two hours a day. Inspection is free. Copies can be charged for at no more than 10p per 100 words, and must be provided within ten days.[22]

Investigations by the company

The above transactions must be reported automatically to the company. In addition, the company can act on its own initiative to identify its real shareholders and others with interests in the shares.[23] These powers apply to all public companies. The inquiries can relate to shareholders over the previous three years. They can be asked about agreements to buy up shares or to vote in concert. Where shares are held in a United Kingdom company through a United Kingdom nominee holder, the company's right to discover the beneficial owners of its shares under this provision applies even though the beneficiary has no other connection with the United Kingdom.[24] A holder of shares who is obliged to provide this information cannot avoid his duty to answer by undertaking to sell the shares.[25] If the directors are reluctant to delve into these secrets, they can be compelled to do so by the holders of one-tenth of the voting capital.[26] These requests and their answers (so far as they relate to present interests in shares) must be recorded in a separate part of the 3-per-cent register, and must be kept for six years.[27] Some company secretaries have been reluctant to let journalists see this part of the register, but it is clear that the Act requires it to be public and it is clear, too, that this obligation exists whether or not the true owners are shown to have a holding of 3 per cent.

Although the initiative rests with a company to demand disclosure of this kind, the information obtained may have a

---

[21] ibid., s 202. The company must be told within two days: Companies Act 1989. s 134(3).

[22] ibid., s 211 (register), s 219 (inspection). There is an exemption for companies carrying on business, or with subsidiaries, overseas where disclosure would be harmful to business s 211(9).

[23] ibid., s 212.

[24] *Re FH Lloyd Holdings plc* [1985] BCLC 293.

[25] *Re Geers Gross* [1987] 1 WLR 1649.

[26] Companies Act 1985 s 214.

[27] ibid., s 213 (register); s 217 (six years).

spill-over effect. Institutional nominees often use the same account number for all the shares bought by them for a particular client. Sometimes the entry on the register will include this number, and so might appear as 'X Bank Nominees Acc No 12345'. Once one company investigation has identified the owner of an account number, it would not be surprising if the same code in other company registers concealed the same owner. An index of such nominees has been published.[28]

The obligation to require nominees to disclose the names of their clients is principally intended to avoid surprise changes of control. For journalists, however, these registers present a wider opportunity. Owners of shares cannot maintain complete secrecy about their investments, and those who receive a share of the profits from companies that have been the target of widespread public criticism deserve to find some of that criticism turned in their direction.

Major shareholdings by companies

Further clues as to ownership may be traced in company accounts. These must note holdings that amount to one-tenth or more of the voting or total capital in another company.[29] Banking and insurance[30] are excepted, since one defect in these provisions for the investigator is that they apply only to shares held at the end of the accounting company's financial year. If a company wished, it could 'board out' its holdings by lodging them with someone else for the critical few days and lawfully omit any reference to them. A second drawback is that as part of the accounting requirements, the directors can leave out this information if it would be excessive and the ownership of the shares did not materially affect the company's financial position.[31]

Directors' dealings

Shareholdings in their companies

It is accepted that directors will want some stake in the enterprise they manage, but the dangers of this are recognized and their dealings are circumscribed. They cannot, for instance, agree to buy or sell their company's shares for delivery on a future date, and

---

[28] Richard Bellfield and Christopher Hird, *The Index of Nominees and their Beneficial Owners*, 2nd edn, Fulcrum Publishing Ltd, 1988.
[29] Companies Act 1985 Sched 5 paras 7–13.
[30] ibid., s 257; until the Companies Act 1989, the exemption applied to shipping companies as well.
[31] ibid., Sched 5 para 11.

they are restricted in their use of inside information for their own advantage.[32] In addition, directors must make public their holdings in the shares and debentures of the company or its associated companies. They cannot avoid this duty by farming out their shares to spouses or children, because these holdings must also be reported. Nor can they evade the restrictions by taking shares in a parent, subsidiary or sibling company.[33] Any change in their holding must be reported. Most importantly, directors must disclose the price at which their shares or debentures were bought or sold.[34] This registered information must also be indexed and remain open to public inspection.[35]

Contracts of service

Shareholders are also entitled to see copies of a director's contract of service with the company.[36] In the case of companies quoted on the Stock Exchange the public are entitled to see these in two circumstances. The listing agreement, which every quoted company makes with the Stock Exchange, obliges it to make service contracts available 'to any interested person including press representatives' at its registered office, between the date on which the Annual General Meeting is called and the meeting itself – a period of at least twenty-one days.[37] Secondly, when a take-over is imminent, Stock Exchange regulations require the service contracts of the offeree company to be made public.[38] One intention behind these requirements is that those planning a take-over or a coup within the company can assess how much compensation directors will have to be paid for the premature termination of their contracts. However, the contracts can make interesting reading to those sharpening pens rather than long knives. One service contract, for instance, revealed that a director was required to take his wife with him whenever he made an overseas visit. The chairman's earnings must be stated in the annual accounts.[39]

---

[32] ibid., ss 323 and 327.
[33] ibid., s 324 and Sched 13.
[34] ibid., Sched 13 para 17(2).
[35] ibid., s 325 and Sched 13 Part IV. The directors' report will also include details of shareholdings by board members at the year's end, ibid., Sched 7 para 2.
[36] ibid., s 318; unless the contract has less than twelve months to run or the company can terminate the contract within twelve months without paying compensation.
[37] Stock Exchange Admission of Securities to Listing, p. 5.39, s 5, para 43 and see note 43.1 for reference to the press. 1985 Act s 369.
[38] Stock Exchange Admission of Securities to Listing, p. 6.20; s 6, Ch 2, para 6.
[39] Companies Act 1985 Sched 5 para 24(2). The earnings of the highest paid director must also be stated if this was more than the chairman's: para 25(3)–(5). There are exemptions where the board as a whole did not earn more than £60,000 (unless a holding or subsidiary company) or where the chairman/director's job was mainly overseas.

Interests in company contracts

Other contracts or arrangements with the company in which a director has a material interest must be disclosed in the company's annual accounts. In particular, the accounts must disclose any loan, guarantee or credit transaction that a company has made for the benefit of a director or officer.[40] The circumstances in which the company is permitted to enter into these types of transactions are, in any event, narrowly defined[41] They do include the giving of financial assistance to allow a director to buy a house. One company put up about £140,000 for a £200,000 house. No doubt to maximize the tax advantage, director and company owned the house together. The company would enjoy a share of the capital gain in the house and the director was to pay £23 per week for the privilege of living in a mansion. Since directors must disclose their home addresses, an enterprising journalist was able to publish details of the company's generosity alongside a photograph of the residence in question.[42]

Other directorships

The interlocking interests of directors with other companies cannot be so easily traced. However, the company must record present directorships of its board members in the other corporations and any past directorships over the previous five years. The register is also publicly available.[43]

Economic performance

Accounts to be published

Since one of the principal aims of the disclosure requirements is to permit investors and creditors to judge the economic performance of a company, it may not seem surprising that the law lays great emphasis on company accounts, the overriding requirement of which is that they should give a true and fair view of the company's financial state of affairs and profit and loss in the relevant financial year.[44] However, it has been a hard-fought battle; it was only in 1967 that private as well as public companies were required to prepare accounts, and only in 1976 that these had to be made public.[45]

In 1981 there was serious backsliding. 'Small' companies (which

---

[40] ibid., ss 232, 233.
[41] ibid., s 330.
[42] *New Statesman* 24 July 1981.
[43] Companies Act 1985 s 289.
[44] ibid., s 226(2) as amended by the Companies Act 1989 s 4.

must now have at least two of the following: a balance sheet total of less than £975,000; turnover of less than £2 million; fewer than fifty employees) need not prepare a profit-and-loss account and only a perfunctory balance sheet is required. They have no duty to submit a directors' report. 'Medium' size companies (with two of the following: balance sheet total less that £3.9 million; turnover less than £8 million; fewer than 250 employees) have to provide the normal directors' report and balance sheet, but are allowed to submit a modified profit-and-loss account and need not give a breakdown of turnover.[46] 'Small'- and 'medium'-sized groups of companies have similar relief from the duties to provide group accounts.[47] The Companies Act significantly enlarges these definitions. Media interests, lamentably, failed to notice this reverse and the Opposition parties put up few objections, conceding that ordinary disclosure was inappropriate for 'the corner fish-and-chip shop'. The definitions, however, freed much larger enterprises from the need to publicize their accounts. Investors, creditors and journalists will all be the worse off, particularly as information about a private company that is not required to be disclosed by law will generally be protected from disclosure by the courts on grounds of confidence.

Banking and insurance companies are also exempt from particularizing their accounts, but they are subjected to much more rigorous scrutiny by the Department of Trade and Industry.[48]

Auditors
The accounts that a company prepares must be professionally audited. The auditor's report must be sent with the accounts to the

---

[45] Companies Act 1976 s 1. Companies without limited liability could still keep their accounts to themselves, a qualification that spawned new interest in what hitherto had been an historical curiosity. Following the Companies Act 1989 s 7, the conditions on which the exemptions are dependent are more restrictive: see s 254 of Companies Act 1985.

[46] Companies Act 1985 s 247, Sched 8 (duties), s 248 (definitions).

[47] The 1985 Act s 250 treated a group as 'small' or 'medium' if its aggregate characteristics met the tests for individual companies. The Companies Act 1989 s 13 inserts a new s 249 into the 1985 Act and applies the exemption if either the parent company meets the requirements for individual companies or if the group as a whole satisfies two or more of the following conditions (small first, medium in brackets): aggregate turnover: £2 million net or £2.4 million gross (£8 million net or £9.6 million gross); aggregate balance sheet total £1 million net or £1.2 million gross (£3.9 million net or £4.7 million gross); employees 50 (250). A group cannot be exempt if it includes a public company, a company with the power to sell shares to the public, a bank, insurance company or an authorized person under Financial Services Act 1986.

[48] ibid., s 255, 255A and Sched 9 as amended by the Companies Act 1989 s 18.

Companies Registry, where it is open to inspection.[49] Auditors are in a difficult position. They are hired by the directors, but their responsibilities are to the investors, creditors and the public at large. Qualifying the accounts may make the auditors unpopular with the board. Consequently, they can be sacked only by the shareholders and they have a statutory right to put their case to a shareholders' meeting.[50] The auditors are precluded from slipping out quietly to avoid an impending disaster: on resigning they must certify that their departure has nothing to do with the state of the company's affairs, or, alternatively, they must explain in full the circumstances that have impelled them to leave.[51] Some solve the dilemma by adding an inscrutable or unfathomable qualification to the accounts.

Compulsory auditing has certainly improved the standard of accounts. Company accounts contrast markedly with other organizations, such as charities (see p. 511), which can register unaudited accounts.

Even if all auditors were honest and efficient, there are practical limits on the checks that can be run. In a large company the auditors, at best, can run only sample spot checks on stock values and other realities behind the figures presented to them by the company. There have been a number of scandals where grave irregularities have not been spotted by auditors. Ironically, the growing practice among auditors of over-cautiously qualifying the accounts may diminish the impact of any warning they mean to deliver.

Directors' report

Attached to the accounts must also be a report by the directors.[52] This report must give a 'fair review of the business of the company and its subsidiaries during the financial year', particulars of any important events affecting the business during the year and an indication of likely future developments.[53] These obligations tend to produce bland reports. The Stock Exchange regulations require a much more detailed report from quoted companies.[54] This frequently takes the form of a chairperson's statement, which is published in the financial press.

---

[49] ibid., auditor's report: s 235 (as amended by the Companies Act 1989 s 9); duty to send to registrar: ss 239 and 242 (as amended by the Companies Act 1989 s 11); inspection: s 709. For a good account of the auditor's role see Leonard Leigh, *The Control of Commercial Fraud*, Heinemann, 1982, pp. 208–18.
[50] ibid., ss 386 and 387.
[51] ibid., s 390; the resignation statement must be sent to the Registry where it can be inspected, ibid., s 709.
[52] ibid., s 237.
[53] ibid., and Sched 7.

More concretely, the report must note significant changes in the values of the company's fixed assets, record any interests held by directors in the company's shares at the end of the financial year, and report details of any shares in the company that the company itself owns.

Political pressure has achieved an odd assortment of additional disclosure obligations. Perhaps the most interesting is the requirement to disclose details of any donations for political or charitable purposes over £200. Political donations include not only gifts (direct or indirect) to political parties, but also those for purposes that are reasonably likely to affect public support for a political party. Additionally, the directors' report must note any research or development activities, and information specified by regulations concerning health and safety at work. If the company employs over 250 people, the report must give an account of the company's policies for hiring disabled people and for consulting employees.[55]

Public share issue

In addition to these regular reports, a company must expose its financial performance to further scrutiny if it intends to issue shares for public sale. Parallel requirements are imposed by law and by the Stock Exchange.[56] The details are complex but their net effect is that the company must issue a public document setting out in considerable detail its past performance and future expectations.

Penalties for non-compliance

Despite all the legal requirements set out above, a large number of companies do not comply, and there are few prosecutions. However, the courts are habitually lenient where no fraud is proved. Sir Hugh Fraser was fined only £100 in 1976 for describing (without dishonesty) a loan of £4.2 m by the SUITS Investment Trust as 'cash in bank and on hand'. The loan proved irrecoverable.[57] In addition to criminal proceedings, creditors or shareholders can seek a court order requiring the company to make good its default within a specified period, and making it liable to much more substantial penalties for contempt of court if it does not do so.[58] Following the Companies Act 1989, standard civil penalties can be collected by the Registrar for failure to submit accounts on time.[59]

---

[54] Stock Exchange Admission of Securities to Listing, section 5.
[55] Companies Act 1985 Sched 7. There are no regulations yet concerning health and safety at work.
[56] ibid., ss 56–65; Stock Exchange Admission of Securities to Listing s 3.
[57] Leigh, *Commercial Fraud*, p. 128.
[58] Companies Act 1985 s 713.
[59] Companies Act 1989, s 11 inserting a new s 242A into the Companies Act 1985.

A company may fail to comply with its duty because it is inefficient or because it does have something to hide. If reporters ask company secretaries for copies of the documents that should have been filed and they refuse to cooperate, this can safely be mentioned in the story. It will not improve confidence in the company's management.

Inspecting public documents

Not all the public documents and registers can be consulted in the same place. Some are kept at the Companies Registry – known also as Companies House – with branches in London and Cardiff. Some are kept at the particular company's registered office or at a more convenient nominated address.[60] Most of the large public companies nominate a bank to maintain their public documents. This address, or the address of the registered office, will appear in a statement that is lodged with the Registrar prior to the company's formation. The company can change its registered office but must notify the Registrar within fourteen days.[61]

- *At the registered office:* registers of shareholdings;[62] debenture holders;[63] directors' shareholdings;[64] 3-per-cent shareholders;[65] directors' contracts[66] (when available).
- *At Companies House:* annual accounts, reports of auditors and directors,[67] annual return of changes in shareholdings,[68] Memorandum and Articles of Association.[69]
- *At both:* list of directors (including other directorships) and company secretary; register of charges.[70]
- *At the Company's AGM:* any person attending the AGM is entitled to inspect the register of directors' interests.[71]

Companies House keeps records going back five years on microfiche. There are four parts: general (Memorandum and Articles of Association, list of directors and secretary); annual

---

[60] Companies Act 1985 s 353.
[61] ibid., s 287.
[62] ibid., ss 352, 353.
[63] ibid., ss 190, 191.
[64] ibid., Sched 13 para 25.
[65] ibid., s 211(8)
[66] Stock Exchange Admission of Securities to Listing, see notes 37 and 38.
[67] Companies Act 1985 ss 239, 241 (NB changes following Companies Act 1989 (see note 59)).
[68] ibid., s 363.
[69] ibid., ss 10, 18.
[70] ibid., s 288 (directors and company secretary), s 401 (charges).
[71] ibid., Sched 13 para 29.

return (accounts, reports, changes in shareholding); mortgage documents; register of charges. Mortgages are not just of interest to cautious moneylenders. It was by inspecting this section of the fiche for Times Newspapers Ltd that *Sunday Times* journalists discovered in 1982 that Rupert Murdoch had transferred the title of the papers to another of his companies and away from TNL (where it could not have been sold without the approval of a board of directors independent of Murdoch). The ensuing outcry forced Murdoch to transfer the titles back again.[72]

Records over five years old must be consulted at Cardiff. Journalists offered illegible copies have a right to see the originals unless they are over ten years old, in which case the documents will probably have been destroyed.[73]

A journalist, like other members of the public, can be charged a fee for inspecting these documents. The company can charge up to 50p for each register inspected at its office.[74] Companies House levies £3 for each register, account or return examined.[75]

The right to inspect includes, in all cases except directors' contracts, the right to have copies made. A company can charge for this at the rate of 10p per 100 words.[76] The journalist can economize by asking for a copy of only part of a register or document that is needed. It is not clear quite how precise the investigation can be. Journalists may be inclined to avoid the cost of a computer print-out by making their own notes from the register. Can they insist on exercising their right to 'copy' in this way? There is an old Court of Appeal decision holding that the right to have copies made by the company excludes the right to copy in any other way, which might suggest that an antagonistic company official could refuse to allow journalists to make their own notes.[77] This interpretation of the right to copy is unduly narrow. It was not followed when a similar issue arose over the copying of documents produced by a litigant on discovery. Although the Court Rules, like the Companies Acts, prescribed a fee that the discoverer could charge, it was sensibly said that this was intended to set a reasonable limit on the fee and not to preclude the discoveree from making his own copy.[78]

---

[72] *New Statesman*, 18 February 1982.
[73] Companies Act 1985 ss 709, 715.
[74] ibid., s 356 (register of members – 5p); s 191 (register of debentureholders – 5p); Sched 13 para 25 (directors' interests – 5p); s 219 ('3 per cent register' – no charge).
[75] Companies (Fees) Regulations 1991 (SI 1991 No 1206).
[76] Companies Act 1985 ss 356 (register of members); 191 (debenture holders, printed trust deeds are 20p, others 10p per 100 words); Sched 13 para 26 (directors' interests); 219(2) ('3 per cent register').
[77] *In Re Balaghat Gold Mining Co Ltd* [1901] 2 KB 665 CA.
[78] *Ormerod Grierson and Co v St George's Ironworks Ltd* [1905] 1 Ch 505 CA.

Meetings

Most Annual General Meetings of the shareholders of public companies are formal occasions. The institutional investors, who tend to be the predominant shareholders, generally prefer to exercise their influence behind the scenes. In the absence of a crisis, items on the agenda are passed 'on the nod' and the running of the company is left to the directors. Nevertheless, the law gives important residual powers to other shareholders, including a right, which cannot be taken away from them, to dismiss the directors.[79] If the company has been performing poorly or if a take-over is in the air, the shareholders' meetings may be the place for tough questioning. In addition, public-interest groups have sometimes purchased a single share in a company in order to attend a shareholders' meeting and to challenge the board about the social consequences of its policies.

Journalists have no right to attend a general meeting, although they are frequently invited. If the press and public are excluded, reporters may gain admission by buying a share in the company or persuading an existing shareholder to allow them to attend as a proxy.

If there is a crisis and the exchanges become heated, there is more likely to be a newsworthy story. The risk of a writ for defamation is minimal because in the case of the general meeting of a public company the press and broadcast media have a statutory qualified privilege.[80] The privilege is destroyed by malice, or by a refusal of the publisher or broadcaster to print a reasonable letter or statement by way of explanation or contradiction if required by the person defamed (see p. 93).

The privilege does not apply to private companies' meetings, nor to the publications of reports or other documents passing from such companies to their shareholders. The Faulks Committee on Defamation recommended that privilege should apply, but its report has not been implemented.[81]

If for some reason the defence of privilege failed, the publisher or broadcaster can always fall back on the general defences of truth or fair comment. 'Fair comment' can be made only if the matter is of public interest. The affairs of the public company would certainly be of public interest. So, too, would those of a private

---

[79] Companies Act 1985 s 303.
[80] Defamation Act 1952 ss 7, 9 Sched Part II para 11.
[81] (1975) Cmnd 5909 para 339 and App XI part II s 14(*b*).

company if they concerned the reliability of, or deficiencies in, its public documents or the social impact of the company's policies.

Take-overs

Take-over battles present another opportunity for journalists to find out more about the internal workings of quoted companies. A great deal of financial and other information about both predator and prey must be disclosed. It has already been noted that directors' service contracts are publicly available during this period. The rules are primarily intended to ensure that all the participants have common access to certain basic information, and the role of the press in dispersing this information is acknowledged. Thus a company can hold meetings with selected shareholders to explain the terms of an offer only if the press is invited.[82]

These obligations are contained in the Stock Exchange Regulations and the City Code on Take-overs and Mergers. Particularly in the case of the City Code, the sanctions for breach lack sufficient bite to deter some financiers from conducting secretive and shady manoeuvres. The abolition of exchange control has allowed greater access to markets by overseas enterprises, which have even less to fear from the wrath of the City's institutions.[83] Like the Press Complaints Commission, the Stock Exchange and the Take-over Panel lack the power to compel attendance of witnesses, the production of books or the giving of evidence. Their private and confidential investigations of suspected rule violations depend entirely on voluntary cooperation.[84]

The Code discourages participants in a take-over bid from appearing on television programmes. It is feared that the subtleties of the bid will be lost in a simplified discussion. The Code recommends that interviews should be given only if they are recorded and then only on condition that there is no editing and that a transcript is provided before the broadcast. A panel discussion between offeror and offeree or between competing bodies sends shivers down the City Panel's spine and it deprecates anything resembling gladiatorial combat.[85] These views do not reflect any legal requirement, but they may explain why participants in a merger battle are reluctant to put their case to a television test. This attitude is antediluvian and diminishes the legitimate role that the broadcast

---

[82] City Code on Take-Overs and Mergers. The latest edition was published on 25 October 1990 with subsequent amendments.
[83] Leigh, *Commercial Fraud*, p. 192. Even criminal penalties are difficult to apply to foreign companies.
[84] ibid., p. 93.
[85] City Code Rule 19.6.

media should play in exploring the public-interest consequences of take-over. A spate of knocking-copy advertisements in 1985 led the panel to prohibit all advertisements in connection with a take-over offer unless they fell within narrowly drawn exemptions.[86]

Press Monopolies

Over the last thirty years the process of concentration of newspaper ownership in Britain has developed alarmingly. Seventy per cent of all national daily newspapers are now published by four multi-national companies; more than 80 per cent of national Sunday newspapers are published by the same four companies; and in the provinces large numbers of local papers are controlled by four conglomerates: Thomson Regional Newspapers, Associated Newspapers (which also publishes the *Daily Mail*), Westminster Press (linked to the *Financial Times* and *The Economist*) and Reed International. Britain now has one of the most concentrated news-paper ownership arrangements in the Western World. The danger of such monopolistic tendencies was identified by the first Royal Commission on the Press in the following terms:

> The monopolist, by its selection of the news and the manner in which it reports it, and by its commentary on public affairs, is in a position to determine what people shall read about the events and issues of the day, and to exert a strong influence on their opinions. Even if this position is not consciously abused, a paper without competitors may fall below the standards of accuracy and efficiency which competition enforces.[87]

In 1965 the Government gave additional powers to the Board of Trade (subsequently, to the Secretary of State for Trade) to refer proposed newspaper mergers to the Monopolies Commission. The procedure is now set out in ss 57–62 of the Fair Trading Act 1973. The minister is, in certain circumstances, required to refer news-paper sales or mergers to the Monopolies and Mergers Commission. The Commission must report back to the minister within three months on:

> whether the transfer in question may be expected to operate against the public interest, taking into account all matters which appear in the circumstances to be relevant and, in par-ticular, the need for accurate presentation of news and free expression of opinion.[88]

---

[86] City Code Rule 19.4.
[87] Royal Commission on the Press Cmnd 7700 (1949) para 274.

Transfers of newspapers to proprietors whose existing press interests (together with the acquired newspaper) have a circulation in excess of 500,000 copies per day are unlawful without the consent of the Secretary of State, unless the newspaper acquired is 'not economic as a going concern'.

> The Monopolies Commission was involved in an important test case by the 1966 application to sell *The Times* to the Thomson Organisation. In spite of being the owner of two television companies, thirty-three newspapers (including *The Sunday Times*), sixty-two magazines and numerous other interests in publishing, Lord Thomson's purchase of *The Times* from Lord Astor met with the Commission's approval. Dealing with the question of concentration of ownership, the Commission admitted in its report to Parliament that Thomson's take-over of *The Times* would be a continuation of the movement towards concentration in the ownership of the press, which must ultimately tend to stifle the expression of variety of opinion. The report went on, however, to say that the Commission did 'not consider that the proposed transfer would lead to an undue concentration of newspaper power'. It was equally tolerant when laying down the conditions that were to be attached to any transfer of ownership of *The Times*. Although recognizing that a proposal to put four 'national figures' on the main board of Times Newspapers Ltd would be merely 'window dressing' – 'no more than a declaration of good intent by the Thomson Organisation designed to reassure the public' – the Commission agreed to the proposal on the grounds that it could devise nothing better.[89]

In 1981 Times Newspapers was sold to Rupert Murdoch, thereby concentrating a large amount of national newspaper power in one controversial pair of hands. Ownership of the *Sun* and *The Times* gave Murdoch a 30 per cent share of daily newspaper readership, while *The Sunday Times* and the *News of the World* added up to a 36 per cent share of Sunday readership. The ethical record of Murdoch's British papers was questionable, and his reputation in Australia and America for interfering with editorial independence and exploiting his papers for political purposes raised serious doubts about whether the take-over could serve the public interest. All these matters could, and should, have been investigated by the Monopolies and Mergers Commission, on a reference from the Secretary of State for Trade, John Biffen.

The exemption where the minister is satisfied that the newspaper to be purchased is 'not economic as a going concern' may have been an accurate description of *The Times*, but it was not of *The Sunday Times*. The journalists of *The Sunday Times* were advised

---

[88] Fair Trading Act 1973 s 59(3).
[89] The Monopolies Commission: The Times Newspaper and the Sunday Times Newspaper, (1966) House of Commons Paper No 273, esp paras 162–3, 176.

by Queen's Counsel that there was a good case for saying that the minister was obliged to refer the sale to the Commission. Proceedings were started but were dropped two days before the case was due to be heard – largely through concern at the risk of legal costs should it be fought through all appellate stages.[90]

In March 1981, a few weeks after *The Times* take-over, Atlantic Richfield, the American oil company that had owned the *Observer* since 1976, announced that it was selling the paper to Mr 'Tiny' Rowland of Lonrho. Once again, efforts were made by the parties to avoid any detailed examination of the nature of the take-over. Although its tendency to concentrate ownership was much less dramatic than Rupert Murdoch's acquisition of Times Newspapers, Mr Biffen this time agreed to refer the matter to the Monopolies and Mergers Commission. The Commission recommended that the transfer be allowed provided, amongst other things, that 'independent directors' were appointed by Lonrho. It accepted that:

> . . . the proposed transfer involving a major provincial publisher acquiring a national title does represent yet another move in the continuing growth of concentration of ownership of provincial and national newspapers, *which was seriously increased by the recent acquisition of The Times and Sunday Times by companies controlled by Mr Rupert Murdoch.*[91]

The refusal by the Government to refer the take-over of Times Newspapers to the Monopolies and Mergers Commission illustrates the inadequacy of the referral procedure embodied in the Fair Trading Act as a method of scrutinizing concentrations of ownership. Biffen's refusal to refer was plainly unlawful, but when the journalists went to court, there was nobody prepared to ask the courts to enforce the law. The Attorney-General, as guardian of the public interest, refused a request to guard it against dereliction by his fellow minister. If the Commission is to oversee monopolistic tendencies in the press properly, a number of amendments to the Fair Trading Act would be required.

At present the law allows the Secretary of State to give unconditional consent to a transfer without reference to the Monopolies Commission if satisfied that the newspaper to be sold is 'not economic as a going concern'. The very fact that the Government could decide, in 1981, that *The Sunday Times* fell into this category, on the basis of highly questionable projections of future

---

[90] The sorry story is told in some detail by Harold Evans, *Good Times, Bad Times*, Weidenfeld & Nicolson, 1983, Ch 7, 'Biffen's Missing Millions'.
[91] 'The *Observer* and George Outram & Co Ltd', House of Commons Paper No 378, Ch 8 para 33.

income supplied by parties to the sale who were eager to avoid a referral, shows how easily the requirements may be side-stepped. Where the intention is to keep the newspaper alive as a separate publication (a fact that would normally indicate that it was a viable economic proposition), the minister may consent if 'the case is one of urgency'.[92] Again, in the *Sunday Times* case, that urgency was dictated by the timetable devised by the parties to the transaction. In cases where the intention is to close the newspaper, or to absorb it under a rival title, the minister has no alternative but to give unconditional consent to the sale.[93] Such transactions can sometimes be avoided by arrangements that still give the selling proprietor a reasonable recompense.

If the Monopolies and Mergers Commission is to have effective control over concentrations of ownership in the newspaper industry, all such loopholes in the Fair Trading Act will need to be closed. Whether the paper is 'economic as a going concern' would then be one of the factors the Commission could take into account in deciding whether to recommend the transfer, after its own independent assessment of the viability of the newspaper's future and after considering any alternative offers that would preserve publication or avoid further concentration of ownership.

The public-interest test that the Monopolies and Mergers Commission has applied in its nine reports on newspaper transfers since 1965 is also unsatisfactory. Under the Fair Trading Act it is required to report on 'whether the transfer in question may be expected to operate against the public interest'.[94] The burden of proving this speculation falls upon opponents of the transfers. As the third Royal Commission on the Press pointed out: 'In individual cases it is almost impossible to establish this to the Commission's satisfaction and in none of the cases so far referred has it been established.'[95] That Royal Commission recommended that the Monopolies and Mergers Commission should reverse its onus of proof: it should withhold approval unless positively satisfied that the merger would *not* operate against the public interest. This is the test applied in other restrictive-trade practices legislation, and the Royal Commission believed it would 'provide a more satisfactory basis for judgment by the Commission'.

One important aspect in a newspaper transfer is, as all Royal Commissions have recognized, the danger of creating an imbalance in the political affiliations of the press. Newspapers have, as the Press Council has continually held, a right to be politically partisan;

---

[92] Fair Trading Act 1973 s 58(3)(*a*).
[93] ibid., s 58(3)(*b*).
[94] ibid., s 59(3).
[95] Royal Commission on the Press, Cmnd 6810 (1977) Ch 14 para 28.

but it must surely be against the public interest if press outlets in a particular area, or in the nation as a whole, come to favour overwhelmingly one particular side of the political spectrum as a result of monopolistic tendencies. However, when this question was raised by some objectors to the Lonrho take-over of the *Observer* (i.e. the danger that a politically neutral newspaper might, by the decision of its new proprietor, join the ranks of papers supporting the Conservative Party), the Commission declared it inadmissible. 'It would be a serious development of our role for us to take such a point into account' was its reason for refusing to examine the proposed proprietor's political plans for the newspaper.[96] While the Commission's reluctance to examine proprietorial politics is understandable, the Fair Trading Act requires it to take into account 'all matters which appear in the circumstances to be relevant' to the question of whether the transfer would operate against the public interest. This does not call for an evaluation of the merits of political policies, but an assessment of the consequences of the transaction on the availability to the public of a reasonable variety of editorial opinion. It is a serious mistake for the Monopolies and Mergers Commission to interpret the Act so as to disallow consideration of this important dimension.

In cases of newspaper merger referrals the Monopolies and Mergers Commission must report within three months, and must include in that report 'a survey of the general position' with respect to the transfer, 'and of developments which have led to that position'.[97] It may recommend that the Government attach conditions to the transfer that would minimize dangers to the public interest. These statutory duties call for considerable investigation and knowledge of the industry, and up to five additional members may be appointed by the Government to assist the Commission in such referrals.[98] However, this power of *ad hoc* appointment is no substitute for the Commission being placed in a position to judge, from its own monitoring work, what the impact of a particular sale is likely to be. This could be achieved if the Monopolies Commission were given a permanent responsibility to monitor, and from time to time to report publicly on, developments that tend towards greater concentration of press holdings.

Broadcasting and Press Conglomerates

New and complicated restrictions were introduced in the Broadcast-

---

[96] *The* Observer *and George, Outram*, Ch 8 para 28–9.
[97] Fair Trading Act 1973 s 61(1)(*b*).
[98] Fair Trading Act 1973 Sched 3 para 22.

ing Act 1990 to limit the ownership of multiple TV and radio licences and also to restrict the extent to which a person or a company with interests in one medium can branch out into other media.

Broadcasting services are divided into categories. Within each category there is a maximum number of licences that a person (or company) can hold. These maxima are: two regional Channel 3; one national Channel 3; one Channel 5; one national radio; twenty local radio; six restricted radio. The Government can provide similar restrictions for other licensed services, such as satellite TV and radio, and can change the maxima. The Act also establishes a framework for restricting participation by the same person in different categories of service. The details are left to the Secretary of State, but, broadly speaking, a holder of a licence for a national Channel 3 service cannot own more than 20 per cent of a regional Channel 3 or a Channel 5 licensee and vice versa.

Crossover rules prevent newspaper proprietors owning more than 20 per cent of a company with a licence to provide Channel 3, Channel 5 or a national radio service. There is an exception to permit a local newspaper owner having a larger stake in a regional Channel 3 service that covers a different area to his newspaper. A national newspaper owner with a 5 per cent stake in one holder of a Channel 3, Channel 5 or national radio service licence cannot own more than 5 per cent in another similar company. Local newspaper proprietors can own up to 20 per cent of local radio stations in their own area. Matching restrictions apply to broadcasters. Thus, for instance, Channel 3, Channel 5 and national radio licencees cannot own more than 20 per cent of a company that runs a national or local newspaper. The Act has detailed provisions for deciding who controls a company and whose shareholdings are to be compounded in deciding whether the critical thresholds are crossed. The details of all these complex rules can be found in Schedule 2 of the 1990 Act and in the regulations that the Secretary of State makes under it.

DTI Investigations

The Department of Trade and Industry has wide powers to investigate the affairs of a company. It may appoint an inspector to carry out a formal investigation if it believes that the company is untruthful, fraudulent or unfairly prejudicial to part of its members, or if it has failed to disclose information that its members could reasonably expect.[99] Either in conjunction with a formal

---

[99] Companies Act 1985 s 432.

investigation or independently, the Department can call for the production of specified documents.[100] It can also crack the codes of nominees and investigate the true ownership and control of the company.[101] It was an impending investigation of this kind that pushed the shareholders into their dawn raid on Consolidated Gold Fields.

A formal investigation is normally conducted by two specially appointed inspectors, a senior barrister and a chartered accountant. Its proceedings are inquisitorial, although cross-examination is sometimes allowed. They have been held in private since 1932, as the result of an unsatisfactory House of Lords decision.[102] The secrecy of investigations is now additionally buttressed by provisions against revealing documents compulsorily disclosed by the company in response to an order of the DTI, and by a maximum penalty of two years' imprisonment.[103] The offence covers revelations of any oral explanations of the disclosed material but now, apparently, answers given to the inspector's general inquiries on other matters unrelated to the company's documents, nor does the offence cover disclosure of information given by those outside the company.[104]

The inspectors report to the Secretary of State, who may send a copy of the report to the company itself.[105] The minister can also make the report publicly available.[106] This is always done when external inspectors are appointed, although only after any criminal proceedings have finished. Lonrho unsuccessfully challenged the refusal of the DTI in 1989 to publish its report on the take-over of Harrods by the Al Fayed brothers. The minister said that criminal proceedings were still under consideration, and the courts refused to overturn his view that publication might prejudice any future

---

[100] ibid., s 447, as amended by Companies Act 1989 s 63.
[101] Companies Act s 442 and see s 444 (power to obtain information as to those interested in shares) and s 446 (investigation of share dealings).
[102] *Hearts of Oak Assurance Co Ltd* v *A-G* [1932] AC 392. Until this case, investigations were held in public as a matter of course. The Attorney-General's defence of the practice was halfhearted in the House of Lords, but it is still surprising that the Lords left the inspector no discretion to take evidence in public. As a dissenting judge said in the Court of Appeal, the inspector might reasonably believe that witnesses would be less likely to lie in public and that an open airing of the accusations would prevent inflated rumours of more serious wrongdoing. [1931] 2 Ch 370, 396 per Lawrence LJ.
[103] Companies Act 1985 s 449.
[104] ibid., s 447(5)(*a*) unless the outsider was in possession of the compulsorily acquired documents.
[105] ibid., s 437(3)(*a*).
[106] ibid., s 437(3)(*c*), although the Department can appoint inspectors on the basis that their reports will not be published. See Companies Act 1985, s 432(2A) as added by the Companies Act 1989 s 55.

prosecution.[107] Where outside inspectors have not been used, but the Department has called for documents, the results of the investigation are not generally released unless they disclose material of importance that the Department wishes to publicize.[108] The inspectors' reports usually reveal more incompetence than dishonesty, but their reprimands can be severe,[109] and their descriptions (e.g., 'an epidemic loss of money' or 'for this managing director truth was a moving target') acidic.

The DTI can similarly appoint inspectors to investigate suspected insider dealing.[110] It was in the context of such an investigation that the *Independent* journalist, Jeremy Warner refused to disclose his source of information (see p. 197).

Other Businesses

The need to structure a capital base and the attraction of limited liability lead most sizeable businesses to opt for corporate form. This is just as well for reporters, because there is a dearth of disclosure obligations on the principal alternatives: partnership, unincorporated associations (such as clubs) and sole trading. Unless they acquire charitable status or a licence to lend money or one of the other privileges considered below, such businesses have virtually no legal disclosure obligations and the investigator will be dependent on volunteered information or leaks.

Partnerships

Partnerships must reveal the names of their members. This obligation was first imposed in 1916, not to forstall fraudsters but to prevent entrepreneurs of German origin trading under the guise of an Anglicized name. The partnership must keep a list of its partners' names at its principal place of business and allow inspection there.[111]

Co-ops and housing associations

Co-ops and housing associations are normally set up as friendly societies and are registered under the Industrial and Provident

---

[107] *R* v *Secretary of State for Trade and Industry ex parte Lonhro plc* [1989] 1 WLR 525 HL.
[108] Leigh, *Commercial Fraud*, pp. 168, 176.
[109] ibid., pp. 172–4.
[110] Financial Services Act 1986 s 177.
[111] Business Names Act 1985 s 4.

Societies Act 1965. Like companies, they must make an annual return, which must include accounts and an auditor's report.[112] The balance sheet and auditor's report have to be displayed in a conspicuous place at the registered office.[113] The Housing Corporation maintains a public list of registered housing associations.[114]

Building societies

Building societies come under the jurisdiction of the Building Societies Commission. They, too, must submit accounts, though in much more detail.[115] Since 1986 these have been similar to the requirements for companies and banks. As with companies, the purpose of disclosure is principally to reassure creditors and depositors. This overlooks the social role of building societies as the main supplier of loans for private homes. If a society refuses to lend in a particular area ('red-lining'), it can have a devastating effect on property values. The societies may fear that the neighbourhood is in decline and a risky place to invest but, if the area is starved of home loans, this becomes a self-fulfilling prophecy. It is impossible to tell from an annual report whether a society is red-lining, since it is not obliged to say anything about the location of properties on which loans have been made. Building societies, like companies, must disclose any loan made to directors, managers, etc. Only members and depositors are entitled to a copy of the report, but since a journalist could easily open an account, it is normally given out on request without this formality.[116] Building societies must belong to an ombudsman scheme for dealing with complaints. The body administering the scheme must be permitted to publish the whole or any part of an ombudsman's determination.[117]

Nationalized industries

Public sector industries are also remarkably free of disclosure requirements. Some take the form of ordinary companies and are then under the normal obligations. Others are set up by statute, in which case they are usually required to make an annual report to

---

[112] Industrial and Provident Societies Act 1965 s 39.
[113] ibid., s 40.
[114] Housing Associations Act 1985 s 3: the register is open to inspection. Registered housing associations are subject to additional accounting duties: ibid., s 24. The Housing Corporation itself must prepare an annual report (which includes its accounts). The report is laid before Parliament: ibid., s 78.
[115] See Building Societies Act 1986 s 73 and the regulations made under it.
[116] ibid., s 81.
[117] ibid., Sched 12 para 9.

Parliament. In *BSC* v *Granada* Lord Wilberforce thought that this was sufficient to satisfy the public's legitimate interest in the corporation, although investigative journalists would disagree.[118] Information may be given voluntarily or teased out of the relevant ministers at various opportunities given in Parliament to debate the nationalized industries. There is also a Commons Select Committee for Nationalized Industries. In view of the public interest and public money involved in undertakings like British Coal, and the social implications of their employment policies, the level of mandatory disclosure is extremely poor. The Conservative Government has, of course, zealously privatized many former nationalized industries. Where the new commercial corporation or entities are subject to a regulatory agency, it is usual for the agency to keep a register of various formal steps, such as notifications, approvals, and orders, and for this register to be public.[119]

Special Privileges

Charities[120]

Charities do not pay income tax, capital gains or capital transfer tax (unless they engage in trade). They pay no more than half the rates of a comparable occupier and they are entitled to miscellaneous reliefs from VAT, Stamp Duty and National Insurance. It is also easier for them to raise money because they may recover from the Inland Revenue the income tax paid by the donor on a covenanted gift. Donations to charities are free of capital transfer tax and capital gains tax. These are significant state subsidies estimated to be worth over £300 million each year, but there is a paucity of public information about the objects of such largesse.

To secure these advantages, it is in practice necessary for a charity to register with the Charity Commissioners. They will scrutinize its purposes to see if they conform to the legal definition of a charity. This has been developed by the courts by reference to

---

[118] [1981] All ER 417 HL.
[119] e.g., Gas Act 1986 s 36; Telecommunications Act 1984 s 19; Water Act 1989, ss 31 and 117.
[120] The most detailed textbook on the subject is *The Law of Charities* by Hubert Picarda, Butterworths, 1977; *Charities, Trusts and Social Welfare* by Michael Chesterman, Weidenfeld & Nicholson, 1979, examines the development and philosophy of charity law; *The Foundations: an Anatomy of Philanthropy and Society* by Ben Whitaker, 2nd edn, Penguin, 1979 discusses their social and economic significance. See also D. G. Cracknall, *Law Relating to Charities*, Oyez Longman, 1983.

an ancient statute of 1601. Broadly, there are four categories: religious, educational, those for the relief of poverty and those for other purposes beneficial to the community. An organization may run a business and still be a charity if its ultimate object comes within one of these categories.

Some charities will be companies and must therefore comply with the ordinary disclosure requirements, but a reporter investigating those that are unincorporated can look only to the Charities Act 1960. The charity must lodge its trust deed or the instrument specifying its objects for public inspection.[121] This will be drafted more precisely than the objects clause of an ordinary company's Memorandum of Association because the Charity Commissioners will withhold their blessing unless every purpose comes within the charitable definition. Nevertheless, within these limits it will still be drawn so as to give the organization the maximum latitude and may therefore be a poor guide as to what the charity actually does.

The only other documents that the public has a right to see are the accounts of the charity. These must be submitted annually if there is a permanent endowment.[122] The Commissioners have a reserve power to demand to see almost any charity's accounts. Unlike company accounts, they need not be audited. The Charity Commissioners are in a poor position to conduct their own analysis since they have no qualified auditors or accountants on their staff.[123] In any case, there is a high level of default in submitting accounts: 40 per cent of those required to file accounts do not do so.[124] A reporter will therefore have to depend on volunteered sources of information to a much greater extent than with companies. Commissioners have on occasion been spurred to exercise their powers to appoint inspectors, call in documents or conduct a special audit as a result of press stories;[125] but without the basic information that an investigator can gain from mandatory disclosure much more is left to chance and other people's cooperation.

The media have, with a few exceptions, signally failed to alert the public to scandals in charity administration that stem from outdated legal definitions and absence of expert public oversight. There are 140,000 registered charities, with assets of about £5 billion accumulated with the help of tax privileges. Many 'charities'

---

[121] Charities Act 1960, s 4(7).

[122] ibid., s (4)(4)(*c*). Consequently, 'collecting charities' that do not have investment income need not submit annual accounts automatically.

[123] Chesterman, *Charities, Trusts and Social Welfare*, p. 292. In November 1983 the Commission confirmed that this was still the case.

[124] Charities Aid Foundation, *Report on Foundation Activity*, 1976, pp. 6, 21. Austen and Posnett, *Charitable Activity in England and Wales*, 1978.

[125] Charities Act 1960 ss 6, 7, 8(3).

have nothing to do with the relief of poverty or oppression. Some of the wealthiest – private schools and private medical funds, for example – cater only to the wealthy. There is even one charitable organization that specializes in providing well-behaved servants to gentlefolk. Thanks to the idiosyncrasies of interpretation of the 1601 statute embodying the social values of the Elizabethan age, some charities-in-law are positively uncharitable. The *Daily Mail* exposed how the 'Moonies' spent tax subsidies on brainwashing converts and breaking up families. Others are simply eccentric: the Relaxation League, the Fun Palace Trust, the Goat Protection League, the Fund for Polishing Regimental Silver, the Friends of Locomotives of the Great Western Railway.[126] On the other hand, any organization that seeks to change the law – even in order to relieve poverty and oppression – is debarred from registration as a charity. As recently as 1981 it was decided in the High Court that Amnesty International could not obtain tax privileges as a charity because it sought actively to change the laws of fascist and Communist countries.[127] The anomalies stemming from the legal definition of charity are endless: anti-social or downright silly organizations are allowed tax advantages denied to important and humane causes. There have been proposals to rationalize the law, but to no avail. The importance of the Charities Commissioners, and the lack of power to scrutinize the activities of those businesses that batten on to compassionate instincts by raising money for charities that see very little of it at the end of the day, make the entire field a fertile one for exposure journalism. In late 1991 the Government announced its intention to tighten the regulation of charities and require disclosure, but did not propose to alter the test of what constitutes 'charity'.

Investment business

The Financial Services Act 1986 revamped the legislative scheme of investor protection. Anyone engaged in investment business must be authorized by the Securities and Investment Board directly, by a self-regulating organization that has been recognized by the SIB, or by a recognized professional body. The SIB keeps a register of authorized persons, self-regulating organizations and recognized professional bodies.[128] This is open to public inspection without charge.[129] There is a further part of the register that contains details of people whom the SIB has decided are not fit

---

[126] *The Sunday Times*, 17 July 1983.
[127] *McGovern* v *A-G* [1981] 3 All ER 493.
[128] Financial Services Act 1986 s 102.
[129] ibid., s 103.

and proper persons to be employed in connection with investment business.[130] The public does have a right to ascertain whether a named individual is included in this part of the register and, if so, to inspect his or her entry. A more general search of this part can be conducted only if there is good reason for seeking the information. The SIB can also restrict its subsequent use.[131] It was suggested during the bill's parliamentary passage that a bona fide investigative journalist would have a good reason to inspect.[132]

The definition of 'investment business' includes giving investment advice[133] and could therefore have embraced much financial journalism. However, the Act exempts advice given in a newspaper, journal, magazine or other periodical publication if the principal purpose of the publication taken as a whole and including any advertisements contained in it is not to lead people to put money into any particular investment.[134] The mainstream press therefore will not need authorization. If a journal is concerned as to whether it comes within the exemption, it can apply for a certificate from the SIB.[135] A similar exemption has been added for broadcast or cable programmes and teletext transmission.[136]

Financial journalists who predict the stock market performance of particular companies have a serious conflict of interest if they or persons close to them stand to gain by the market reaction to their story. Some newspapers for this reason debar financial journalists from having their own portfolio, while the Press Council has issued some nebulous rules that do not really come to grips with the ethical problems (see p. 542). The temptation to profit personally from foreknowledge of press stories was highlighted by the prosecution in New York of Foster Winans, a journalist who arranged for others to trade in shares about to be 'tipped' by his influential column in the *Wall Street Journal*. In Britain a journalist who entered into similar arrangements could be prosecuted under the Theft Act for dishonestly obtaining a pecuniary advantage for him- or herself or another. A dishonest arrangement with company 'insiders' to affect share prices through the leakage and publication of price-sensitive information would amount to a conspiracy to contravene the Financial Services Act 1986.

---

[130] ibid., s 59.
[131] ibid., s 103(2)–(4).
[132] House of Commons Standing Committee E col 484.
[133] Financial Services Act 1986 Sched 1 para 15.
[134] ibid., para 25(1).
[135] ibid., para 25(2).
[136] ibid., para 25A added by Financial Services Act 1986 (Restriction of Scope) Order 1988 (SI 1988 No 318).

Consumer credit

Almost all business dealings with consumers involving credit must now be licensed.[137] About 100,000 licences are involved.[138] Initially, these are issued almost automatically by the Office of Fair Trading. The register of licences is open for public inspection and includes particulars of applications and licences, and notes whether a licence has ever been suspended or refused.[139] Rogue motor dealers constitute the largest group to have licences refused or revoked, and not merely for mishandling the credit side of their business. Alteration of odometers (mileage recorders) or consistently selling unroadworthy vehicles will justify barring a dealer from further credit transactions. The register is also one of the few public documents that must disclose the officers of *unincorporated* associations. The system has been in operation since 1976 and will be a useful source as time passes and memories of crooked consumer scandals begin to fade.

Restrictive practices

British anti-monopoly law is weak. One of its few requirements is that restrictive-practice agreements relating to goods and certain designated services must be registered.[140] The register is a public document and agreements can be inspected.[141] If inspection would be contrary to the public interest or may substantially damage legitimate business interests, the agreement can be placed on a secret part of the register.[142]

---

[137] Consumer Credit Act 1974 Part III.
[138] 107,000 applications have been received since 1976, Annual Report of the Director-General of Fair Trading HC 354 (1980–81) p. 26.
[139] OFT-Consumer Credit General Notice No 5, 16 January 1976. It is open between 10 am and 4 pm at Government Buildings, Bromyard Avenue, Acton, West London (General Notice No 23, 16 April 1980).
[140] Restrictive Trade Practices Act 1976, ss 6–14 and Restrictive Trade Practices Court Act 1977.
[141] Restrictive Trade Practices Act 1976 s 23. It can be inspected between 10 am and 4.30 pm at the Office of Fair Trading. The Registration of Restrictive Trading Agreements Regulations 1976 (SI 1976 No 183) reg 10. The inspection fee is £1 for any number of agreements or 20p per agreement if less than five are inspected. Registered Restrictive Trading Agreements (Inspection and Copy) (Fees) Regulations 1977 (SI 1977 No 612).
[142] Restrictive Trade Practices Act 1976 23(3) and the Registration of Restrictive Trading Agreements Regulations (SI 1976 No 183) reg 9. Information can be kept secret if in the Secretary of State's opinion it would be contrary to the public interest to disclose it (s 23(3)(*a*)) or if it relates to secret processes, the location of mineral or other deposits, being information which in the Secretary of State's opinion would cause substantial damage to the legitimate business of any person if it were disclosed (s 23(3)(*b*)).

Agreements that are contrary to the public interest are void. The Director-General of Fair Trading can withhold registration and refer a dubious agreement to the Restrictive Practices Court. Thus in 1979 the court ruled that an agreement between London Weekend Television and the Football League for exclusive coverage of *Match of the Day* was void as contrary to the public interest. Referrals are rare, and disclosure through registration remains the only effective deterrent. Failure to register makes the agreement void, but secrecy and oligopoly have a natural affinity, and many price fixers prefer this risk to publicity.[143] Non-registrations may be a significant clue in an investigation, as it was in the 1977 media exposés of local price-fixing rings in the ready-mixed concrete market.

Other registers

There are numerous other public registers. By law the General Medical Council must publish an annual list of doctors.[144] The clerk to most magistrates' courts will also be the clerk to the licensing justices and will keep a register of everyone entitled to sell alcoholic drinks. This will also show the owner of the premises and any conviction of the licensee in his trade or for bribery or treating at an election.[145] The performance of television and radio companies can be measured against their ambitions by inspecting (and copying) the company's contract with the ITC, and that part of its application that sets out its programming policy.[146]

Insolvency

The insolvency procedures (winding-up for companies, bankruptcy for individuals, receivership where the debts are backed by security) are intended to gather in what assets can be traced and to distribute them to the creditors according to set rules of priority.

The whole of insolvency law was reformed in the 1980s. One aim was to harmonize the codes of procedure for individuals and companies. This has largely been achieved but the two regimes continue their separate existence.

A company in financial difficulties has a wide range of options. Normally, the first step is for the major creditors to appoint a receiver, who, at least temporarily, will take over the running of the

---

[143] Restrictive Trade Practices Act 1976 s 35.
[144] Medical Act 1983 s 54 and for dentists see Dentists Act 1984 s 22.
[145] Licensing Act 1964 ss 30–4; Representation of the People Act 1983 s 168(7).
[146] Broadcasting Act 1990.

business. The outgoing directors or others responsible for the company must prepare a statement of its affairs.[147] A copy is filed with the court. The court file is not a public document. It can be consulted as of right only by those immediately connected with the insolvency proceedings. There is a discretionary power to allow any person to inspect the file; conversely, the court can prohibit inspection.[148] The receiver will prepare a report on the company's predicament, which he must make available to all the creditors.[149] He also has to send a copy of the report to the Registrar of Companies, where it can be inspected.[150]

If the company's disease is terminal, it is wound up, or 'liquidated'. This may be done with the company's acquiescence (a 'voluntary winding-up' may be convenient as part of a corporate restructuring for a company that is healthy and solvent). Alternatively, a company may be wound up on its creditors' insistence. The process begins with the presentation of a petition to the court. The petition must then be advertised in the *London Gazette*. The court can exempt a petitioner from this requirement and will ban the advertising of a petition if it is considered an abuse of process.[151] The petition is heard in open court.[152] Following a winding-up order, a statement of affairs by the directors must be produced to the Official Receiver.[153] This will be filed in court and (except in voluntary liquidations) is open to inspection by those immediately concerned in the winding-up, although the court does have power to restrict access to all or part of the statement.[154]

The Official Receiver can apply to the court for the public examination of any officer of the company.[155] This power was widened following the strong recommendation of the Cork Committee, whose proposals led to the transformation of insolvency law.[156] Public examination is no longer dependent on a prior report by the Official Receiver suggesting fraud.

Directors who are found in the course of winding-up to have been involved in fraudulent trading may be disqualified from being a director or promoting, forming or managing a company for a

---

[147] Insolvency Act 1986 s 47.
[148] Insolvency Rules rr 3.5, 7.31.
[149] ibid., s 48.
[150] Companies Act 1985 s 709.
[151] Insolvency Rules 1986 r 4.11.
[152] *Practice Direction (No 3 of 1986)* [1987] 1 WLR 53.
[153] Insolvency Act 1986 s 131.
[154] Insolvency Rules 1986 r 4.35.
[155] Insolvency Act 1986 s 133. There is an alternative power to summon under s 236. This examination is not expressly required to be in public and therefore a registrar must, and a judge can, conduct it in chambers, Insolvency Rules r 7.6.
[156] Review Committee on Insolvency Law and Practice (Cmnd 8558), Ch 12.

specified period.[157] Similar orders can be made against a director who commits a number of Company Act offences, including persistent default in sending accounts, returns or reports to the Registry.[158] This was intended to reduce the shamefully high incidence of noncompliance with these obligations. Even in the absence of a specific offence, a disqualification order can be made if the company is insolvent and the director is considered to be unfit to manage a company.[159] The director must be given an opportunity to be heard at a public hearing before the court.[160] There is a register of disqualification orders, which is kept by the DTI and is open to public inspection.[161]

Bankruptcy proceedings now follow a similar pattern to winding-up. They also begin with a petition to the court, which, again, may be made by either the debtor or one of the creditors. Prior to the 1986 Act it was the norm for bankruptcies to be examined in public. Now the position is the same as for companies: a public examination will take place only if the Official Receiver applies to the court for one.[162]

If the debtor is adjudged bankrupt, he or she will be disqualified from acting as a director,[163] unable to obtain most credit and barred from holding certain public offices. Bankruptcy decisions are advertised in the *London Gazette* and in local papers.[164] The bankruptcy now comes to an end automatically after three years (two if the speedier 'summary administration' method is used) for first-time bankrupts. Others still have to apply to the court to be discharged.

---

[157] Company Directors Disqualification Act 1986 ss 1 and 4.

[158] ibid., ss 2, 3 and 5.

[159] ibid., s 6.

[160] Insolvent Companies (Disqualification of Unfit Directors) Proceedings Rules 1987 (SI 1987 No 2023) r 7(2).

[161] Company Directors Disqualification Act 1986 s 18.

[162] Insolvency Act 1986 s 290; again, there is an alternative power to examine the debtor in private, s 366.

[163] Company Directors Disqualification Act 1986 s 11.

[164] Insolvency Rules 1986 (SI No 1925) r 6.34(2). The court has the power to suspend this obligation, r 6.34(3).

Chapter 13

Public Complaints

The power of the media to damage reputations, invade privacy and conduct partisan campaigns is to a considerable extent unaffected by legal restrictions. Libel is the most obvious constraint, but skilful editing can permit damage to be done at minimal risk to the publisher, and the unavailability of legal aid effectively deters all but the intrepid or wealthy from taking action. There is no direct protection for privacy in British law, and no requirement that inaccuracies that are not defamatory should be corrected. Many European countries oblige the media to publish counter-statements by persons who have been attacked, but in Britain there is no such remedy for the victims of one-sided prejudice. The comparative freedom enjoyed by the media to behave unfairly towards individuals and organizations has led to the establishment of tribunals that aim to regulate media ethics through adjudicating complaints by members of the public who claim to have been unfairly treated by journalists and editors. Complaints about newspapers and journals may be made to the Press Complaints Commission (PCC), a private body funded by newspaper proprietors. It has no legal powers, but its adjudications will usually be published by the paper complained against, and often by rival papers. Allegations of unfair treatment and invasion of privacy by radio and television programmes may be made to the Broadcasting Complaints Commission (BCC) a statutory body set up by Parliament in 1981. The BCC has legal powers to demand transcripts and explanations from broadcasters, and to order its verdicts to be published by the offending station in a manner appropriate to rectify the unfairness. The Advertising Standards Authority is the body that will hear complaints that advertisements in any media are not 'legal, decent, honest and truthful'. Although a private company funded by the advertising industry, it derives a powerful sanction from the preparedness of newspapers and journals to withhold space for advertisements that are in breach of its code.

Journalists should recognize that the political purpose of these organizations – certainly of the Press Complaints Commission, which in 1991 replaced the discredited Press Council – is to protect them from the advent of laws that could restrict their freedom to investigate.[1] They function as a device for condemning journalistic

---

[1] See G. Robertson, *People Against the Press*, Quartet Books, 1983.

behaviour of a kind that, if it were not deterred, would almost certainly be curbed by Parliament. Press proprietors are prepared to invest about £1 million per year in the PCC because its existence offers a form of insurance against new laws to safeguard personal privacy, prohibit chequebook journalism and to guarantee a right of reply. The BCC was established on the recommendation of the Annan Committee to provide an outlet for public complaints against broadcast programmes. These institutions could serve the interests of the media if they were able to demonstrate that a system of self-regulation or, in the case of the BCC, a system of retrospective statutory overview, is better than recourse to criminal law or to pre-censorship. However, neither institution has yet worked to establish satisfactory ethical guidelines for the media, and both are accorded a degree of cynicism, bordering occasionally on contempt, by practitioners of broadcasting and print journalism. In the past editors were disinclined to support Press Council guidelines on chequebook journalism, privacy and race reporting. They generally published its adjudications in respect of complaints against their papers, although often without prominence and sometimes accompanied by editorial statements of defiance. For example, when the editor of the *Sunday Express*, Sir John Junor, was admonished for publishing a racial slur in his own column, he repeated the offensive comment in the next edition, with a side-swipe at the 'po-faced, pompous, pin-striped humourless twits who sit on the Press Council'.[2] It remains to be seen whether Junor and his ilk are any more respectful towards the PCC. The BCC was established in 1981. Its work to date has been of little moment, either in giving guidance to programme-makers or in convincing the public that it is a satisfactory conduit for justified complaints.

None the less, the PCC and the BCC are significant organizations, with a potential for good and a capacity to inhibit investigative reporting. In their adjudications of public complaints, they may pass critical judgement on the ethical standards of individual editors, directors, journalists and researchers. These criticisms will not be enforced by any legal sanction, but the publicity given to them may damage an individual's career. It follows that journalists and broadcasters should be alive to their rights in relation to complaints made against them, and should ensure that the full facts and all extenuating circumstances are presented before any adjudication. A code of practice promulgated by an authorative organization can be of great assistance to journalists in resisting editorial pressures to behave unethically in the quest for

---

[2] John Junor, 'Current Events', *Sunday Express*, 3 September 1978.

circulation-building stories of prurient, rather than public, interest. Some of the journalists who were held to have 'ferociously and callously harassed' relatives of a 'Yorkshire Ripper' victim evinced a sense of shame, but excused themselves on the ground that they were only obeying editorial instructions.[3] A code of conduct may assist journalists to develop the moral muscle to resist unethical orders to invade privacy and sensationalize private grief. It is note-worthy that spokespersons from all sides of the political spectrum have from time to time called for a disciplinary organization with powers to fine, suspend and ultimately expel journalists from the practice of their craft. Unless the PCC and the BCC prove themselves worthy of respect, and achieve a measure of acceptance for their ethical rulings, the arguments for a 'licensed' profession will be more difficult to resist.

The Press Complaints Commission

History of the Press Council

The idea that disputes over the content of newspapers might be resolved by some independent but non-legal body developed first in Sweden, where publishers and journalists established a Press Fair Practices Board in 1916. In due course, all major Swedish newspapers bound themselves by contract to accept the rulings of a press ombudsman – a judge who rules on complaints from the public, orders newspapers to print retractions of false statements, and fines them for proven deviations from a code of conduct drawn up by the country's Press Council.[4] In Britain the idea of a Press Council was first mooted by the NUJ after the lifting of wartime censorship in 1945. The union was alarmed at the decline in the number of national newspapers, the concentration of ownership in the provincial press, the suppression or distortion of news for politically partisan or commercial reasons, and the proprietorial pressures imposed upon editors and journalists. There were debates in Parliament, and journalist-MPs like Michael Foot claimed that some editors were merely 'stooges, cyphers and sycophants'. As a result, a Royal Commission on the Press was established, with the

---

[3] Press Council, *Press Conduct in the Sutcliffe Case*, 1983, Ch 18.
[4] Lennart Groll, *Freedom and Self-Discipline of the Swedish Press*, Swedish Institute, 1980; Lennart Groll and Geoffrey Robertson, 'Legal Constraints on the Press: Swedish and British Viewpoints' in *Freedom and the Press*, Department of Visual Communication, Goldsmith's College, 1979.

object of 'furthering the free expression of opinion through the press and the greatest practicable accuracy in the presentation of news'.[5] It reported in 1949, and suggested that the industry should establish 'a General Council of the Press', which, 'by censuring undesirable types of journalistic conduct and by all other possible means, should build up a code of conduct in accordance with the highest professional standards'.[6] The next four years were spent in desultory and unenthusiastic discussions amongst proprietors, until a private member's bill was introduced in Parliament to set up a statutory council. This prospect brought a speedy end to discussions, and a General Council of the Press commenced operations in 1953.[7] It had no lay membership, and its first chairman was the then proprietor of *The Times*.

The first decade of the Council's operations was unimpressive. Many of its rulings appear today to be oversensitive to Government and the aristocracy, otherwise contrary to the public interest, or faintly ridiculous. Its first declaration was that a *Daily Mirror* readership poll on the question of whether Princess Margaret should be allowed to marry Group Captain Townsend was 'contrary to the best traditions of British journalism'.[8] Its occasional discoveries of press inaccuracy and misrepresentation were greeted by the offending newspapers with no more than polite expressions of regret. Its poor performance was subjected to scathing criticism by the second Royal Commission on the Press, reporting in 1962, which urged the Government to set up a proper disciplinary body with statutory powers if the Council failed to reform itself immediately.[9] The renewed threat of legislation made newspaper proprietors jump to attention: they supplied the Council with increased finance, appointed a retired Law Lord, Lord Devlin, as chairperson, and changed the constitution so that 20 per cent of members were drawn from outside the media. Under Devlin's leadership, the Council began to display a more impressive tone and authority. It began to reprimand press misconduct in positive terms, and evinced a powerful concern for press freedoms, evidenced in its booklets on contempt of court (1967), privacy (1971) and defamation (1973). However, its higher profile on press

---

[5] Royal Commission on the Press, Cmnd 7700 (1949).
[6] ibid., para 650.
[7] The Press Council Bill had its second reading in November 1952. It was moved by C. J. Simmons MP, who reminded the House that 'nearly three and a half years after [the Royal Commission Report] we are still awaiting its formation by the Press of their own volition'. See generally H. Phillip Levy, *The Press Council*, Macmillan, 1967, Chs 1 and 2.
[8] 'A Royal Romance: Princess Margaret and Group Captain Townsend', *Daily Mirror* 21 February 1954 (Press Council).
[9] Royal Commission on the Press, Cmnd 1811 (1962), para 325.

freedom issues caused it to be perceived publicly as a champion of the press rather than a watchdog for the public. The Younger Committee on Privacy, reporting in 1973, urged it to increase its lay membership and to ensure that its adjudications were published with a prominence equal to that given to the offending article.[10]

The first detailed study of the Press Council's work was conducted by the third Royal Commission of the Press, chaired by Lord MacGregor. It reported, in 1977, that 'it is unhappily certain that the Council has so far failed to persuade the knowledgeable public that it deals satisfactorily with complaints against newspapers'.[11] It criticized the Council for displaying too much partisanship towards the press and for failing to draw up codes of conduct to enable the public to judge the press by clear ethical values. It found evidence of 'flagrant breaches of acceptable standards' and 'inexcusable intrusions into privacy'. 'We feel strongly', it stated, 'that the Press Council should have more power over the press . . . There is a pressing call to enhance the standing of the Press Council in the eyes of the public and potential complainants.'[12] It called upon the newspaper proprietors who fund and effectively control the Council to ensure that it had sufficient funds to advertise its services and to monitor press performance. Complaints upheld by the Council should be published on the front page of the offending newspaper, and a written code of conduct for journalists should be produced. The Council should give more support to an effective right to reply, condemn journalistic misbehaviour in a more forthright way and take a stronger line on inaccuracy and bias.

The Council responded to these criticisms by increasing its lay membership to half and by speaking out rather more emphatically against examples of chequebook journalism and invasion of privacy that were the subject of public complaints. In other respects it failed to improve its image. A study of its work published in 1983 revealed that even successful complainants were overwhelmingly critical of the services it offered.[13] Its adjudication procedures were obstacle courses and its delays in judgment ensured that any redress it provided was usually ineffectual. Its principles were confused and inconsistent, rulings were not respected and it did not work to improve the ethical standards of the British press.

In 1984 Sir Zelman Cowen was appointed chairperson. He instituted a number of internal reforms and his adjudications were marked by a greater attention to principle. His period will also be

---

[10] Report of the Committee on Privacy, Cmnd 5012 (1972), para 189.
[11] Royal Commission on the Press, Cmnd 6810 (1977), Ch 20 para 15.
[12] ibid., para 48.
[13] Robertson, *People Against the Press*, Ch 3.

remembered for a number of conflicts with Murdoch-owned newspapers. After he issued a statement calling for Mr Murdoch's take-over of *Today* to be referred to the Monopolies and Mergers Commission, the editor announced that this newspaper would henceforth carry no Press Council adjudications. This dispute was settled by Murdoch himself, who reversed the editor's decision after a meeting with Sir Zelman, who doubtless pointed out prophetically that once the Press Council was seen to be as ineffective as it really was, the demand for legislation to curb invasion of privacy and other excesses particularly associated with the Murdoch press would become politically irresistible.

In 1989 a new chairperson, Louis Blom-Cooper QC, took office and instituted a thorough-going review of the Council's role and function. But despite the new Blom-Cooper broom, the Council's basic problem remained, namely its failure to make its Declarations of Principle stick in the absence of any effective sanction. One persistent problem was the refusal of newspapers to publish adjudications with any prominence (in one month in 1985 the *Daily Express* carried its adverse adjudication in five column inches on page 30; the *Star* tucked away its three upheld complaints on pages 22, 24 and 25; the *Sun* buried two criticisms of its conduct on pages 23 and 24; while the *News of the World* hid its censure in small print on page 36, intermingled with advertisements for G-strings and 'sexsational glamourware'). The Broadcasting Complaints Commission has statutory power to direct the prominence of the publication of its adjudications; if the Press Council had been accorded similar rights by way of contract with newspaper proprietors, it might have survived.

The Calcutt Report

By 1989 the Press Council was a confidence trick that had ceased to inspire confidence. Two Royal Commissions and an independent inquiry had ridiculed its portentous claim to supervise journalistic ethics: it had become an elephantine body, with eighteen nondescript lay members and eighteen press members of no particular distinction in their craft, and its declarations of principle were routinely ignored. Editors at every level defied and derided it: the *Daily Telegraph* publicly refused to abide by its ethical convention on race reporting while the *Sun* took a malicious delight in vilifying individuals who 'successfully' complained about it to the Council. It was no longer serving as an insurance policy against new press laws, and in 1989 support from MPs from all parties threatened to advance the passage of a private member's bill to establish a statutory body to enforce a right of reply. The progress of this bill was halted only when the Government promised to establish a committee to investigate press intrusions into privacy. This committee, chaired by David Calcutt QC, reported in June 1990.[14]

The Calcutt Report was sceptical as to whether the Blom-Cooper reforms, even if implemented, could turn the Press Council into a body with the necessary qualities of authority, independence and impartiality. Calcutt correctly identified its central problem in terms of its contradictory claims both to safeguard press freedom and to condemn press malpractice. It was this latter function that should be performed by a Press Complaints Commission, an expert body with sufficient funding to adjudicate speedily and effectively complaints by members of the public about breaches of an expanded code of practice. The Calcutt Committee was profoundly unimpressed by the cynical attitudes displayed towards the Council in the past by editors and proprietors, and it evinced no great confidence that its proposed Press Complaints Commission would be allowed to work effectively if it remained a voluntary body. So it drew up plans for a statutory complaints tribunal, along the lines of the BCC, which should be legislated into existence if the industry failed to set up and support the new Complaints Commission by June 1991. Failure to act would be 'a clear sign that self-regulation cannot work effectively'. The statutory tribunal would wait notionally in the wings, to be wheeled out if there was a 'less than overwhelming rate of compliance' with the new Commission's adjudications, or else a 'large-scale and deliberate flouting of the code of practice'. As a statutory body, the tribunal would be publicly funded and have the power to take evidence on oath, to order prominent publication of corrections and apologies, and to award compensation to victims of press abuse or abuses. It would also be entitled to injunct publication of any material obtained by, or constituting, a breach of the code of practice. It would be chaired by a judicial figure appointed by the Lord Chancellor, sitting with two assessors drawn from a panel of experts.

The Calcutt 'fallback' recommendation for a statutory tribunal served to concentrate the minds of newspaper proprietors. Hilaire Belloc's advice, to 'always keep a hold on nurse/for fear of finding something worse' was often quoted in newspaper offices in the days following the report's publication as an argument in favour of making a more effective stab at voluntary self-regulation. The power to injunct the press that would be vouchsafed to the statutory tribunal is particularly worrying: newspapers could be stopped a few hours before distribution, while magazines like *Private Eye*

---

[14] *Report of the Committee on Privacy and Related Matters*, HMSO, 1990, Cmnd 1102.

would be regularly withdrawn from sale. The danger lies in giving such draconian powers to infringe press freedom to a body that will be operating a vague and generalized code of practice, deciding each case by reference to ethical considerations rather than clear-cut legal rules. The tribunal might be acceptable if it were to become a fully fledged press court, deciding libel actions as well as passing comment on ethical lapses. As envisioned by Calcutt, however, it would become yet another method for limiting freedom of expression, without the minimal safeguards provided by existing law. The Calcutt Committee was not persuaded to recommend a legal right to privacy, although there is much to be said for the view that such a right, enforceable (and resistable) in the courts would be more satisfactory than back-door demands for injunctions from a statutory tribunal.

The newspaper industry, through the Newspaper Publishers' Association (representing the owners of national newspapers) and the Newspaper Society (representing owners of provincial newspapers), acted speedily to implement the thrust of the Calcutt recommendations for establishing a Press Complaints Commission. It withdrew funding from the Press Council, which wound itself up with a certain amount of ill grace, and hired Lord MacGregor (who had chaired the third Royal Commission on the Press and had presided with considerable success over the Advertising Standards Authority) to chair the new Complaints Commission. It promulgated a code of practice (modelled on a draft prepared by the Calcutt Committee), which the PCC was charged to enforce as from January 1991. The new body would, in practice, abandon the Press Council's more contentious efforts to defend press freedom and combat media monopolies; it would exist solely to adjudicate complaints that editors of newspapers had infringed the published code of conduct.

Although the PCC has, like the Press Council, no power to publicize or enforce its judgments, its supporters hope that the clarity of the code and the distinction of its members will give its adjudications much greater impact and respect throughout the print media than had been accorded to Press Council rulings. The Council had perceived itself as a jury, passing verdicts on behalf of the general public according to notions of decency and fair play; the PCC functions as a judge, deciding only the narrow issue of whether a set of written rules has been contravened. The Calcutt Report suggested that the PCC be given two years to prove that self-regulation can work as a satisfactory alternative to a BCC-style statutory tribunal; many newspapers have additionally appointed 'ombudsmen' or 'readers representatives' to deal with complaints directly.

Structure of the Commission

The PCC operates from a small building at 1 Salisbury Square, just off Fleet Street, which was formerly occupied by the Press Council. Its director (Kenneth Morgan) and his eleven staff have been directly inherited from the Council, unwisely in view of the Calcutt recommendation that there should be a clean break with the past. The Commission comprises a chairperson (Lord MacGregor), paid approximately £40,000 per annum for part-time services, six lay members (paid £7,000 pa for attending monthly meetings) and nine press members. There is no pretence of independent appointment: the industry (in consultation with the chairperson) selects those who are deemed likely to impress politicians and editors. The first lay members are of considerable distinction, and include a former cabinet minister, two ASA councillors, Lady Donaldson (who chairs a voluntary body that effectively oversees the ethics of in-vitro fertilization) and Richard Francis (who drew up the BBC's guidelines for news and current affairs). The nine press members include two distinguished ex-editors (David Chipp and Edward Pickering) and seven active editors, two from the tabloid press, one from a 'quality' daily, and the rest from magazines and provincial newspapers. The editor-members do not sit when complaints against their newspaper are being considered. Nor do they resign when found guilty by the PCC of unethical behaviour. In 1991, the first year of operation, both of the PCC's tabloid editors were responsible for serious breaches of the Code of Conduct.

The Commission is 'charged to enforce' a sixteen-clause Code of Practice. It meets for half a day each month to consider rulings drawn up by the chairperson and the staff, which are subsequently issued in the form of a quarterly bulletin. It has abandoned the 'oral hearings' offered by the Press Council to complainants and editors, and decides each case upon written submissions. Its adjudications will be sent, as a matter of courtesy, to parties a few days before publication of its quarterly bulletin, although it will not entertain any protest prior to publication. It will not consider any complaint about press conduct falling outside its written code, and is not, at this juncture, prepared to undertake the function of monitoring compliance with the Code – a firm recommendation made by the Calcutt Report.

A particular problem is encountered in relation to complaints from individuals who might also have a legal remedy against the newspaper by suing for libel. The Press Council practice – severely criticized by Calcutt – was to extract a 'legal waiver' from such individuals as a quid pro quo for the newspaper's agreement to cooperate with the Council and to publish its adjudication. This waiver was effective to bar any subsequent libel action, but only if it was expressly made and signed – a complaint to the Council did not of itself operate as an implied waiver.[15] As Calcutt pointed out, it is plainly wrong in principle that a complainant should be obliged to surrender a legal right to damages before obtaining an adjudication as to whether an ethical standard has been breached. The PCC has in practice abandoned the waiver, although it exercises a discretion to postpone any adjudication if it relates to a matter that is or may be the subject of litigation.

The complaints procedure

Any member of the public, or any organization, may complain to the Commission about a breach of the Code of Practice by an editor of a newspaper or magazine. The complaint will be accepted against an editor, even if it relates to conduct by a journalist or a freelance. The preamble to the Code provides that 'editors are responsible for the actions of journalists employed by their publications. They should also satisfy themselves as far as possible that material accepted from non-staff members was obtained in accordance with this Code.'

Complaints that appear unrelated to any Code provision are not adjudicated, but are none the less forwarded to the editor concerned.

The PCC exercises a discretion to reject frivolous complaints. It does not insist that complainants be personally aggrieved by the newspaper's conduct, but may reject complaints from sources it perceives as vexatious.

Complaints that are accepted are forwarded to the editor of the publication in question, with an invitation to contact the complainant direct and reach an amicable settlement. In appropriate cases this may be achieved by the newspaper's own ombudsman.

If amicable resolution is not achieved within a short time-frame, the Commission commences its 'investigation'. The editor will be required to provide a written response, which will be sent to the complainant with an invitation to comment. This process will continue until the issues are clear and each party has had an opportunity to deal with the other's contentions.

Where the complaint involves disputed issues of fact, the Commission staff may be required to interview the parties or their witnesses. There will, however, be no contested hearing and no opportunity for parties to cross-examine or even to discover what the other side may be saying in the course of the 'investigation'.

---

[15] *Franks* v *Westminster Press Ltd* (1990) *The Times*, 4 April.

The PCC staff, in consultation with the chairperson, produce a draft adjudication, which is dispatched to Council members, who will communicate their agreement. Draft adjudications that evoke disagreement are debated at the monthly Commission meeting, where they are finalized – if necessary, by a majority vote.

The Commission's adjudications are published in a bulletin issued every three months. There is no obligation on an editor who is held to have breached the Code to publish the adverse ruling, let alone to publish it with any prominence. The PCC has so far shown little concern about the lack of prominence given to most of its rulings.

The Code of Practice

The Code enforced by the PCC has emerged from a number of sources. Much of the language is adapted from the Calcutt Committee's draft, and its report is therefore a primary source for interpretation. This draft was in turn influenced by a series of Press Council 'Declarations of Principle' issued over the thirty-six years of its operation, developed and refined at times by major adjudications or reports. The PCC, in its rulings, will pay some attention to these precedents, which will remain useful for editors and complainants in formulating their written submissions. Editors are warned in the preamble that 'the Code applies in the spirit as well as in the letter', and the PCC will be well advised to avoid over-legalistic interpretations of clauses that, in any event, are drawn in very general terms. The PCC makes great play of the fact that it enforces a code that it did not draft. It is not clear why it imagines this to be a good thing; the Code deliberately obscures several important Calcutt provisions and, in any event, was drafted by a committee chaired by the editor of *News of the World*, who is also a member of the PCC. The Code deals with six subjects: accuracy and fairness, privacy, chequebook journalism, race reporting, financial journalism, and disclosure of sources.

Accuracy and fairness
The first three clauses of the Code provide as follows:

1 *Accuracy*
   (i) Newspapers and periodicals should take care not to publish inaccurate, misleading or distorted material.
   (ii) Whenever it is recognized that a significant inaccuracy, misleading statement or distorted report has been published, it should be corrected promptly and with due prominence.
   (iii) An apology should be published whenever appropriate.
   (iv) A newspaper or periodical should always report fairly

and accurately the outcome of an action for defamation to which it has been a party.

2   *Opportunity to reply*
A fair opportunity for reply to inaccuracies should be given to individuals or organizations when reasonably called for.

3   *Comment, conjecture and fact*
Newspapers, while free to be partisan, should distinguish clearly between comment, conjecture and fact.

Clauses 1 and 3 are 'motherhood' provisions, which need no elucidation. The 'right to reply' duty, however, is couched in vague and question-begging language and is unacceptably limited to replies to factual inaccuracies. It is astonishing that the newspaper industry should so deliberately fudge a principle of basic fairness, noncompliance with which has been a major issue of public dissatisfaction with the British press.

The limitation in Clause 2 marks a retreat from the Press Council's principle that a right of reasonable reply should be provided to any 'attack' on an individual or organization, and from the draft Calcutt code, which called for 'a proportional and reasonable right to reply to *criticisms or alleged inaccuracies*' [our italics]. Clause 2 permits the editor to be the judge of what amounts to an 'inaccuracy', and implies that it may be reasonable to refuse an opportunity to put right a published misstatement of fact. The PCC will earn little public support if it declines to require editors to publish letters from complainants who have been severely criticized by way of comment or conjecture, or by factual statements that cannot be verified but that the complainant alleges to be untrue. That said, there are genuine difficulties in deciding whether a published reply is 'reasonably called for'. Press Council precedents have held that no right of reply arises where the attack is contained in a news report of a speech by a third party, or where the person seeking to reply has threatened or commenced a libel action against the newspaper, or where the reply submitted is overlong or contains defamatory attacks on the newspaper's employees, or where an opportunity to reply has already been afforded in the original story.[16]

The PCC has, in its first year, criticized a number of newspapers for inaccuracy. In rather more cases it has simply declined to resolve basic factual disputes, because it has no investigative powers or resources. It has shown a sensible propensity, in familiar cases where quotations are denied, to find against journalists who have

---

[16] See Robertson, *People Against the Press*, pp. 79–88.

'lost' their notebooks. It needs to go further, and subject journalists' notebooks to ESDA tests, before the public will believe that journalists on some papers have not invented the quotes that the complainant denies. The PCC has not accepted as an excuse for failing to check the accuracy of a story in *The Times* the editor's pathetic defence that a message was left on the victim's answering machine inviting him to call the newspaper.[17]

Privacy
Clauses 4, 6 and 7 of the Code set out the general rules against press incursion into personal privacy unless there is a legitimate public interest in the story:

4   Privacy
Intrusions and enquiries into an individual's private life without his or her consent are not generally acceptable and publication can only be justified when in the public interest. This would include:
(i) Detecting or exposing crime or serious misdemeanour.
(ii) Detecting or exposing seriously anti-social conduct.
(iii) Protecting public health and safety.
(iv) Preventing the public from being misled by some statement or action of that individual.

6   Misrepresentation
(i) Journalists should not generally obtain or seek to obtain information or pictures through misrepresentation or subterfuge.
(ii) Unless in the public interest, documents or photographs should be removed only with the express consent of the owner.
(iii) Subterfuge can be justified only in the public interest and only when material cannot be obtained by any other means.
In all these clauses the public interest includes:

- Detecting or exposing crime or serious misdemeanour.
- Detecting or exposing anti-social conduct.
- Protecting public health or safety.
- Preventing the public being misled by some statement or action of an individual or organization.

7   Harassment
1 Journalists should neither obtain information nor pictures through intimidation or harassment.

---

[17] *PCC Report No 2* (July–September 1991), p. 24 (*Bernie Grant MP* v *The Times*).

2 Unless their enquiries are in the public interest, journalists should not photograph individuals on private property without their consent; should not persist in telephoning or questioning individuals after having been asked to desist; should not remain on their property after having been asked to leave and should not follow them.

The public interest would include: (i) detecting or exposing crime or serious misdemeanour; (ii) detecting or exposing anti-social conduct; (iii) protecting public health and safety; (iv) preventing the public from being misled by some statement or action of that individual or organization.

These rules are largely as drafted by Calcutt. They reflect generally accepted values, which newspapers will continue to flout at the peril of statutory regulation. It is noteworthy that the concept of privacy is confined to an individual's private life and offers no protection to individuals in their business capacity or to any public or private company, unless they are subject to unjustifiable subterfuge or harassment. The justification for invasion of privacy must be based on more specific grounds than 'the public interest': it cannot be contended that press revelation of adultery or homosexuality or run-of-the-mill heterosexual behaviour amounts to the exposure of 'seriously anti-social conduct', unless attended by circumstances of gross hypocrisy. There is an unsatisfactory lack of clarity in the phrase 'serious misdemeanour', an oxymoron that did not appear in the Calcutt draft, but was inserted by newspaper interests as something that might, in addition to 'crime' and 'seriously anti-social conduct', be properly exposed by invasion of privacy. The excuse of 'preventing the public from being misled by some statement or action of that individual' permits the press to invade the privacy of public figures who may in the past have acted contrary to their professed beliefs, so stories about adulterous vicars and the like will doubtless be justified under this exception. The Calcutt draft has been cunningly revised by press interests so that a breach of Clause 4 is constituted by *publication* of the story obtained by invasion of privacy, rather than the intrusion itself. It is difficult to understand why editors who approve unjustifiable invasions of privacy should escape censure merely because this misbehaviour fails to produce a publishable story, unless there was a clear public interest in researching the story to see whether it was publishable. The intrusion may, of itself, be censured if it amounts to subterfuge or harassment, or if it constitutes the particularly obnoxious forms of privacy invasion condemned by Clauses 5 and 9 of the Code:

5 Hospitals

(i) Journalists or photographers making enquiries at hospitals or similar institutions should identify themselves to a responsible official and obtain permission before entering non-public areas.

(ii) The restrictions on intruding into privacy are particularly relevant to enquiries about individuals in hospital or similar institutions.

9 Intrusions into grief or shock

In cases involving personal grief or shock, enquiries should be carried out and approaches made with sympathy and discretion.

Clause 5 was adopted following the outrageous behaviour of a *Sunday Sport* journalist and photographer who sneaked into the hospital room of Gorden Kaye to 'interview' the actor as he was coming round from brain surgery (see p. 211). Clause 9 amounts to a rejection of a key clause in the Calcutt draft, which expressed the view that the press should not intrude unsolicited into personal grief or shock, especially after accidents and tragedies, unless justified by exposure of crime or anti-social behaviour or to protect public health and safety. Quite plainly, the press is not, as an industry, prepared to hold its hand on these occasions, save to offer 'sympathy and discretion' to the newly bereaved it will continue to besiege in efforts to obtain tear-jerking 'human interest' stories. This is an area where the Press Council was notably ineffective in curbing media misbehaviour. Professor Harry Bedson's suicide was partly attributed by the Coroner to press harassment after an outbreak of smallpox in his Birmingham University Department. The Council declared that people under stress as a result of bereavement or involvement in a public crisis should not be put under pressure by the press.[18] In 1981 it upheld a complaint that a newspaper harassed the family of a child heart-transplant donor, and directed newspapers to cooperate in arrangements to relieve the effect of cumulative inquiries on people suffering severe personal grief. In 1983 it was driven to conclude that both Peter Sutcliffe's wife and the relatives of his victims were harassed by the media 'ferociously and callously'.[19] Yet in 1989 it had once again to condemn many newspapers for callous and intrusive behaviour in reporting the Hillsborough tragedy. It is unlikely that the PCC, 'enforcing' the weasel words of Clause 9, will have any more success in mitigating the distress press inquiries cause after

---

[18] Press Council, *People Under Pressure*, 1980.
[19] Press Council, *Press Conduct in the Sutcliffe Case*, Ch 18, para 22.

major tragedies. Calcutt's recommendation was that editors should be held responsible for unjustifiable decisions to dispatch reporters in the first place; Clause 9 is drafted in a way that assumes they will dispatch reporters, and will attract only mild and vicarious criticism if the reporters they dispatch act insensitively.

Four sections of the Code deal with particular privacy problems posed by interviewing children and by identifying persons caught up in criminal offences. They provide:

10 Innocent relatives and friends
The Press should generally avoid identifying relatives or friends of persons convicted or accused of crime unless the reference to them is necessary for the full, fair and accurate reporting of the crime or legal proceedings.

11 Interviewing or photographing children
(i) Journalists should not normally interview or photograph children under the age of 16 on subjects involving the personal welfare of the child, in the absence of or without the consent of a parent or other adult who is responsible for the children.

(ii) Children should not be approached or photographed while at school without the permission of the school authorities.

12 Children in sex cases
The Press should not, even where the law does not prohibit it, identify children under the age of 16 who are involved in cases concerning sexual offences, whether as victims, or as witnesses or defendants.

13 Victims of crime
The Press should not identify victims of sexual assault or publish material likely to contribute to such identification unless, by law, they are free to do so.

Clauses 10 and 11 are unexceptional, and follow Calcutt's recommendation. Clause 12 is more difficult, as it requires newspapers to show more restraint in reporting crime than is required by an exceedingly complex and comprehensive law (see p. 323). While the sentiment is admirable, the effect may be to protect, quite undeservedly, adult offenders who are related to the child, and whose names might have to be suppressed in order to avoid the child's identification.

Clause 13 is otiose (the press should obey the law) and amounts to a justifiable rejection of Calcutt's demand that the press should, even when permitted by law, refuse to identify victims of any crime where to do so would be likely to put their health at risk.

The law relating to court reporting is elaborate and under constant review by Parliament: editors should not be liable to ethical censure for publishing what the law allows, unless the circumstances otherwise amount to a breach of the Code's provisions on privacy or harassment. This was certainly the case when in 1986 the *Sun* published, over three full columns on its front page, a picture of the victim of a rape at an Ealing vicarage, taken as she was leaving her church the following Sunday. The victim's family told the Press Council that the thin black line masking her eyes still left no doubt of her identity and the *Sun*'s coverage had been deeply distressing. A year later the Council condemned the newspaper for taking and publishing the photograph: 'Both were insensitive and wholly unwarranted intrusions into privacy at a time of deep distress for the subject and neither served any public interest.' The *Sun* of course, showed no remorse. Its managing editor had told the Council, with more than the usual display of humbug, that the newspaper had a duty to present rape as sordid crime and the picture was published to highlight the victim's 'ordinary, girl-next-door qualities'.[20] Public outrage at the newspaper's conduct produced a law that now prohibits the media from publishing any picture of an alleged rape victim from the moment a complaint has been made, and this prohibition lasts for her lifetime – even if the complaint is not pursued or the man complained against is acquitted.[21]

The PCC has paid particular attention to privacy complaints, doubtless out of deference to Calcutt, and has upheld some that would have been dismissed by the Press Council. One of its first adjudications, designed especially to impress Members of Parliament, was to condemn Patsy Chapman (one of its own members, and chairman of the committee that drafted the code of conduct) for a *News of the World* vendetta against Clare Short MP. The newspaper had decided to punish the MP for attacking its 'page 3' sexism by trying to dig for dirt on her private life, and found a suitable bedfellow in the police from the crooked West Midlands serious crimes squad (also attacked by Short, for fitting-up suspects), who supplied details of a man with whom the MP had a close friendship twenty years before. The newspaper also offered money to Ms Short's ex-husband (who had been in and out of psychiatric institutions since their marriage break-up twelve years previously) for any revealing pictures of the MP. Neither the newspaper nor its editor bothered to apologize after the adjudication, publishing it in small print on page 8 ('despite it being the longest we've ever seen') alongside the original headline

---

[20] Press Council, *The Press and the People*, 1987, p. 241. This particular managing editor, Mr Keith Donlon, became the *Sun*'s ombudsman.
[21] Criminal Justice Act 1988, s 158.

that committed the code infringement ('Flashback: The *News of the World* story which led to the right to privacy case').[22]

The condemnation of *News of the World* over its vilification of Clare Short was a long and reasoned decision, which attracted national attention. The PCC's other adjudications upholding privacy complaints have received little or no interest from the press. It condemned Raymond's Press Agency for 'picture snatching' by paying £2 to an eleven-year-old boy to obtain a photograph of his mother, but it had no way of obliging the agency to publicize its sleazy conduct.[23] It found the *Sun* guilty of 'inexcusable violation of privacy' by publishing a man's claim that the headmaster's daughter was one of three women at a private school to have sex with him, but could extract no promise from the *Sun* that it would not breach Clause 4 again.[24] It condemned the *People* for publishing a secretly taken picture of the Duke of York's baby daughter frolicking naked in the garden, whereupon the newspaper republished the picture together with a picture of the naked Duke of York, and invited their readers to participate in a telephone poll over whether the pictures were offensive.[25]

So far as section 6 of the Code is concerned, it is already plain that the PCC simply will not enforce it to protect unpopular people from the prying popular press. When one of the over-zealous Cleveland social workers set up in practice to counsel adults who had been victims of sex abuse as children, a *Mail on Sunday* reporter misrepresented herself as a client in order to obtain information about her methods. This subterfuge the PCC found fully justified in the interests of 'protecting public health', although the newspaper had uncovered no evidence that any adult was endangered by the former social worker's activity.[26] Editors can be confident that the PCC will approve of subterfuge whenever used against persons of shaky reputation.

Chequebook journalism

Press payments to criminals, their associates and their relatives have long been a feature of the coverage of sensational trials. In the days before legal aid was routinely granted to defendants charged with murder, newspapers hired fashionable QCs to defend accused persons facing the death sentence, in return for 'exclusives' from them or their about-to-be-bereaved families. The practice of paying 'blood money' in any form for such stories was widely condemned

---

[22] 'MP Clare Short and *News of the World*', *News of the World* 2 June 1991, p. 8.
[23] *PCC Report No 1* (April–June 1991), p. 15.
[24] ibid.
[25] ibid., p. 16.
[26] *PCC Report No 2*, note 17 above, p. 15 (*Sue Richardson* v *Mail on Sunday*).

in the aftermath of the 'Yorkshire Ripper' prosecution, and the Press Council condemned the practice in a detailed declaration after its inquiries revealed a host of unedifying offers of money by editors of national newspapers to friends and relatives of Peter Sutcliffe. Clause 8 of the Code of Practice repeats the rule:

8   Payment for articles

1   Payment or offers of payment for stories, pictures or information should not be made to witnesses or potential witnesses in current criminal proceedings or to people engaged in crime or to their associates except where the material concerned ought to be published in the public interest and the payment is necessary for this to be done.

The public interest will include: (i) detecting or exposing crime or serious misdemeanour; (ii) detecting or exposing anti-social conduct; (iii) protecting public health and safety; (iv) preventing the public from being misled by some statement or action of that individual or organization.

2   'Associates' includes family, friends, neighbours and colleagues.

3   Payments should not be made either directly or indirectly through agents.

The Code does not dissuade newspapers from making arrangements to interview witnesses after the conclusion of the trial, so long as payment is discussed at that later stage. The reference to 'witnesses or potential witnesses' causes practical difficulties, because it is impossible to foretell, in the days after arrest, how the prosecution and defence cases are likely to develop. In the Sutcliffe case the Press Council rejected the excuse that police had informed editors that Sutcliffe had confessed and that there was unlikely to be a contested trial: it pointed out that experienced editors should be aware that defendants frequently repudiate confessions made in police custody. Clause 8 does not make what should in practice be a crucial distinction between a witness to disputed facts (whose testimony must be kept free from any influence) and a witness to matters of formal record or to character. The interests of justice that are served by a rule against paying witnesses do not apply with very great force to witnesses of the latter kind.

The Code does not apply to witnesses who are on the run, or whom journalists discover themselves. One of the most notable pieces of recent investigative journalism was the tracing and interviewing of a potential witness in a drugs trial by David May of *The Sunday Times*, which led to the exposure of police corruption and the abandonment of the prosecution.[27] The newspaper did not,

---

[27]   See *R* v *Ameer and Lucas* [1977] Crim LR 104.

in fact, pay for this interview, although had its informant insisted upon money and protection from police reprisals, the public interest would clearly have justified some measure of accommodation so long as it was not substantial enough to discredit the story.

The Press Council in its Sutcliffe report sought to outlaw payments to criminals:

> While the Council recognizes that conceivably, in an exceptional case, publication of stories or pictures from associates could be justified by some overriding consideration of public interest, and an editor might be able to demonstrate that the disclosure would have been impossible without the payment, generally there is no such justification . . . Associates include family, friends, neighbours and colleagues. Newspapers should not pay them, either directly or indirectly through agents, for such material and should not be party to publishing it if there is reason to believe payment has been made for it. The practice is particularly abhorrent where the crime is one of violence and payment involves callous disregard for the feelings of victims and their families.[28]

This declaration was issued in the context of public outrage over the behaviour of the press in offering enormous sums of money to Mrs Sonia Sutcliffe (who refused them) for no reason other than that she was the wife of a notorious mass-murderer. The 'blood money' amounted variously to £80,000 (*Daily Express*); £100,000 (*Observer*); and £110,000 (*News of the World*). The *Daily Mail* spoke of six-figure sums, the *Daily Mirror* promised to exceed any rival offer, and the *Yorkshire Post* hazarded £1 million as the amount it could obtain for her by syndicating an exclusive story on the day her husband's trial ended.

Those newspapers that reacted editorially to the Press Council strictures pointed out that its ethical rules simply would not work in the harsh realities of the market-place. Some newspapers were gently critical, others openly defiant. The sensible consensus of Fleet Street was best summed up by Michael Leapman in the *Daily Express*:

> The Press certainly will not – and should not – let itself be deflected from its function of telling people as much as they can about issues that interest them, however distasteful. Sometimes such information will have to be bought from people that editors, in a perfect world, would prefer not to do business

---

[28] Press Council, *Press Conduct in the Sutcliffe Case*, Ch 15, paras 5–10.
[29] 'When the Public's Interest Outweighs the Public Interest', *Daily Express*, 4 February 1983.

with. A newspaper's principal obligation is to give its readers the fullest possible story.[29]

In such cases it will be open to editors to argue that the public interest is exceptional. The Council's previous rulings on blood-money payments have been inconsistent. The press was censured for publishing articles by the wife of train robber Charles Wilson, although at different times articles by the wives of two other train robbers were held to be justifiable. The Press Council took the highly unusual course of initiating its own complaint in order to censure the publication of Christine Keeler's memoirs, although it took no action some years later in respect of the more lurid recollections of Mandy Rice-Davies. In 1967 the *Sun* was strongly censured for paying to publish the memoirs of Ronald Biggs; in 1981 it was censured for 'inexcusably repeating' that very offence in a 'flagrant violation' of the Declaration of Principle. This is perhaps an example of consistency at the expense of common sense: Biggs had not been 'engaged in crime' for many years, and his account of an attempt to kidnap and to extradite him was not without some public interest.

> In 1987 the *News of the World* was censured for three blood-money payments to girlfriends of major criminals. The newspaper accepted that it had made payments (although it refused to say how much it had paid) to the girlfriends of a mass murderer (Jeremy Bamford) and a man who had been convicted of both rape and murder, in return for the right to publish prurient 'world exclusives' about their sex lives. Although the girlfriends had been innocent of complicity in the offences (Bamford's had informed on him and given evidence against him), the stories were none the less 'sold on the back of crime' and had no public-interest justification. The third payment, to an Irish barmaid who had been innocently duped by terrorist Nizar Hindawi into carrying a bomb on board an Israeli airliner, elicited a story that was plainly of public interest, but the Council none the less held that this was insufficiently 'overriding' to justify the payment. It is difficult to see how this woman (who had testified against Hindawi) could meaningfully be regarded as his 'associate' – she was intended to be amongst his many victims when the jumbo jet exploded over London. Her story was of enormous public interest, and had been sold to newspapers in many other countries: a strict compliance with the Council's declaration would have denied the British public an insight into a dastardly crime that would have caused many British casualties.[30]

The end result of an absolute rule against press payments to criminals and their associates would be to deter criminals from revealing their associations with powerful people. In such cases

---

[30] Press Council, *The Press and the People*, p. 210.

shady characters with a public-interest story to tell are often in genuine need of some remuneration for telling it. If they are prepared to go public with revelations about policemen or employers or persons in authority, they need financial protection against reprisals. The real question is whether the importance of the story and the exigencies of its author justify the size of the payment, rather than whether payment should be made at all. So long as newspapers continue to refuse to divulge the size of their payments to informants, the Council will be unable to decide this question. It should be noted that criminals who are paid money in return for recounting details of an offence for which they have yet to be convicted may have the payment seized, on the theory that it is part of the profit they have made from the offence. Section 71 of the Criminal Justice Act 1988 gives the sentencing court wide powers to confiscate property obtained 'in connection with' an offence, and the High Court may make charging orders to secure the position until the verdict. These powers were used against Michael Randle and Pat Pottle, authors of *The Blake Escape: How We Freed George Blake and Why*, when a High Court judge directed that their homes be charged to the Crown for an amount equivalent to the royalties they had earned on their book. They argued that the royalties had been earned by recounting an experience rather than in connection with a crime committed twenty-five years before, but the order was allowed to stand until it was discharged on their acquittal.[31]

The PCC has no provision in its Code relating to payments to non-criminal informants, jilted lovers and other familiar sources of kiss-and-tell stories. There is often no public-interest justification for such tales, and on occasion the tabloid press has paid large sums of money to drug addicts and prostitutes in order to tell them. It is ironic that the people who would be prosecuted for the serious crime of blackmail if they threatened their victim with public exposure unless they were paid a sum of money can now obtain that sum quite legally by taking their story direct to a newspaper. It has been suggested that newspapers that purchase sensational stories of this sort should be required to disclose the amount of the payment on publication: this would serve to alert their readers to the possibility that the sensation in the story may be related to the sensation of receiving a large amount of money for telling it.

Discrimination and race reporting
Clause 14 of the Code provides:

> 14   *Discrimination*
>   (i) The Press should avoid prejudicial or pejorative reference

---

[31] *Re Randle and Pottle* (1991) *The Independent*, 26 March, Webster J.

to a person's race, colour, religion, sex or sexual orientation or to any physical or mental illness or handicap.

(ii) It should avoid publishing details of a person's race, colour, religion, sex or sexual orientation unless these are directly relevant to the story.

These simple provisions are the most difficult to apply in practice, and Press Council adjudications on the subject were more than usually conflicting and controversial. In 1987 the editor of the *Daily Telegraph*, Max Hastings, announced his newspaper's intention to defy Press Council censure for describing convicted criminals as 'black', however irrelevant this was to their offence, on the grounds that he could communicate the same information by publishing their photograph.[32] He is now a member of the PCC, and it remains to be seen whether he will join in censuring himself or will convince his colleagues that race is always relevant in stories about serious crime.

The rule that the press should avoid pejorative or prejudicial language in relation to classes of citizens who often suffer from discrimination is welcome, at least when applied to news, features and editorials. The inclusion of 'sexual orientation' affords some protection to sexual minorities, and Clause 14 will doubtless be ignored by some newspapers for this reason. In 1990 the Press Council took the *Sun* to task for using the word 'poofter' to describe homosexuals. It was criticized – and not only by the *Sun* – for its presumption. Yet this adjudication was a good example of the socially valuable role a voluntary standards body can play, discouraging the use of 'socially unacceptable language' that denigrates groups on the basis of race or gender or sexual preference. The Council's critics overlooked the fact that it has no censorship powers and was doing no more than marking the increasing public distaste for newspapers that routinely and gratuitously use language that stigmatizes whole classes of citizens.

The following year the PCC censured the *Daily Star* for encouraging the persecution of homosexuals by a front-page story about the army under the heading 'Poofters on Parade', attacking gay rights groups as 'strident mincing preachers of filth'.[33] The editor of the *Star*, a homophobe named Hitchen, continued the vilification (which was based on falsely stated facts) in his own column. He was the second editor-member of the PCC to be criticized for unethical conduct, a condemnation that, in the interests of his newspaper's circulation, he doubtless bore with fortitude.

---

[32] Press Council, *The Press and the People*, p. 146.
[33] *PCC Report No 2*, note 17 above, p. 9.

Financial journalism

The Press Council, in an effort to ward off requirements for financial journalists to register as 'professional advisers' like other share tipsters, produced a code on this subject, beginning with the platitude 'They should not do a deal of which they would be ashamed if their readers knew.' Clause 15 of the Code of Practice spells out three basic rules:

> 15   *Financial journalism*
>
>   (i) Even where the law does not prohibit it, journalists should not use for their own profit financial information they receive in advance of its general publication, nor should they pass such information to others.
>
>   (ii) They should not write about shares or securities in whose performance they know that they or their close families have a significant financial interest, without disclosing the interest to the editor or financial editor.
>
>   (iii) They should not buy or sell, either directly or through nominees or agents, shares or securities about which they have written recently or about which they intend to write in the near future.

These rules, in fact, reflect the law relating to 'insider dealings', which financial journalists should always bear in mind (see p. 514). Some newspapers insist on a much more rigid code, which requires that their financial journalists should not own shares or securities at all.

Confidential sources

The final clause of the Code of Practice reads simply: 'Journalists have a moral obligation to protect confidential sources of information.' Journalists do not, however, have any legal obligation to protect their sources: on the contrary, they will sometimes have a legal obligation to betray their source (see p. 196). Although the Code is binding only on editors, this provision may be useful to journalists who seek editorial support to defy court orders requiring disclosure. An editor who disciplined or dismissed a journalist for refusing to disclose a source, even in disobedience to a court order, would thus be deserving of PCC censure.

Will the PCC work?

The PCC is a public-relations exercise. It has been established by newspaper interests as a means of convincing politicians and opinion formers that self-regulation can guarantee privacy and rights of reply better than statutory provisions. The Press Council, established to serve the same purpose, was abandoned as soon as its bluff was called by the Calcutt Committee. If the PCC fails, Calcutt's tribunal waits in the Westminster wings, as does a more satisfactory reform, namely a tort (i.e., civil action) of invasion of privacy. The PCC began in 1991 with a media that was anxious to cooperate (at least for a probationary period) and with the advantage of an initial composition of influential press members and distinguished lay persons. It was, moreover, modelled on the Advertising Standards Authority, which has achieved considerable success in making its rulings stick. In the long term, however, it may be doubted whether the PCC will succeed where the Press Council failed. The grounds for this pessimistic prognostication include:

- The ASA works because its rulings are backed by a devastating sanction (advertisements in breach of the code are not published at all). The PCC has no sanction and does not even have the power to require a censured editor to publish its censure, let alone to publish it with any degree of prominence.
- Proprietors and editors are even now unprepared to concede that they have a duty to afford a satisfactory right of reply or to avoid intrusions into grief and shock or to avoid conduct (short of publication) that unjustifiably invades personal privacy. The somewhat devious way in which the newspaper industry has emasculated the Calcutt draft code in these respects is evidence of a reluctance to accept the minimum standards that Calcutt found to be necessary to avoid eventual statutory regulation.
- The PCC has not solved the intractable problem created by maverick newspapers, like the *Sunday Sport*, which will continue to publish circulation-boosting stories irrespective of adverse adjudications, and will welcome the consequent valuable publicity. Calcutt recognized that the improbability of all sections of the print media following PCC adjudications was the factor that would be most likely to fuel demands for statutory regulation.
- The PCC's refusal to monitor compliance with its code or even responses to its own adjudications is a fatal mistake. The ASA is respected precisely because it engages in monitoring and may act against breaches without the need to await a complaint from a member of the public. As Calcutt recognized, a monitoring exercise is essential to any code that purports to regulate intrusions into privacy, as victims (other than of notorious infringements) will usually be reluctant to give the matter further publicity.
- The PCC faces a number of problems over its procedures. Its evident desire to exclude lawyers and to operate informally, with nudges and winks transmitted along a network of editors, is not calculated to satisfy complainants or (inevitably) their

legal advisers. Unsuccessful complainants will feel that they have not been given a fair hearing when they are given no hearing at all, especially when disputed issues of fact are decided against them on the strength of written communications with newspaper representatives. (Although the question has not been tested, the better view is that the PCC is judicially reviewable, and it may be that the courts will in due course correct any procedural unfairness.) A more formidable problem will occur if there are important differences on privacy rulings between the media majority and the lay minority: once the PCC is publicly perceived to be stacked in favour of the press, it will cease to provide the public relations services that its sponsors desire.

At the end of its first year it was clear that the PCC had solved some of the problems of the Press Council by replacing them with others. It was a much more efficient and less portentious body, which raised no expectations that it could not fulfil. On the other hand, its profile was so low that its 'adjudications' were lacking in force: it was difficult for members of the public to perceive how, if at all, they would work to deter breaches of the Code of Practice in future. The PCC was not concerned to publicize its adjudications, or to ensure that they were published with prominence – the only power that could ensure they have any deterrent effect. In 1991 the press was on its best behaviour for many years, with Calcutt's sword of Damocles over it, but the reports of PCC press submissions still provide examples of editorial humbug advanced by way of excuse for distortion and invention.[34] Nor had it solved the problem of the occasional recalcitrant editor who will make circulation capital out of rejecting its judgments. Students of the Press Council (which always kow-towed to royalty and rushed to uphold Buckingham Palace complaints, thereby giving more publicity mileage to the popular press) must have been struck by a sense of *déjà vu* when the PCC produced its fastest ever adjudication condemning the *People* for publishing the photograph of a naked royal baby, thereby providing the newspaper with an opportunity to republish the photo (as the *Sun* banner headline would say in such cases, 'THIS IS WHAT THE ROW'S ALL ABOUT, FOLKS'). The British press and the PCC clearly deserve each other.

---

[34] e.g. *PCC Report No 2*, note 17 above, p. 22 (*Saffron* v *The Sun & Today*). The night editor of *Today* defended a story that had been seriously and deliberately distorted by omitting any mention of the fact that the complainant was a lesbian, on the grounds that 'as a middle market tabloid newspaper, we have to be much more careful of the sensibilities of our readers'. The managing editor of the *Sun* admitted his newspaper had lied by pretending to have interviewed the complainant, but justified its behaviour on the grounds that it was 'common practice' to invent interviews using unchecked quotes from other newspapers.

The PCC has so far failed to raise the tone or the profile of debate over media ethics, although it has encouraged the development of procedures within newspaper offices (including the appointment of ombudsmen and 'readers representatives') that enable complaints to be answered quickly. Its adjudications are short and usually over-simple, reflecting on editors who do not appear discomforted by its statements that they have breached a code of practice. Perhaps its most fateful decision in its first year was to take the *Sunday Sport* seriously and to treat it as a newspaper. When a representative of a regional retail newsagents association complained that his members were 'sickened and appalled' at being 'required to sell to the public' an edition of the *Sport*, the PCC should have told them they were at perfect liberty not to sell it. Instead, the distinguished members of the PCC embarked upon a solemn investigation into a front-page story entitled 'THIS NUN IS ABOUT TO BE EATEN. She's soaked in sauce, barbecued then carved up like a chicken . . . turn to pages 15, 16 and 17 if you dare.' The editor of the *Sport* entered into the PCC's game with relish, describing his article as 'pioneering investigative journalism at its best', which he was proud to have published, and dared the PCC to condemn him for exposing necrophilia in a Buddhist monastery in Thailand, 'a country regularly visited by British tourists'. The PCC rose to the bait, describing the story as 'an extreme breach of the spirit of the Code of Practice and the standards which the newspaper industry sets itself.'[35] In fact, the story was not a breach of the Code of Practice at all, whatever its 'spirit' may be, and if the PCC regards a pornographic paper as part of the newspaper industry that it affects to regulate, then its doom may already be sealed.

The Broadcasting Complaints Commission

The BBC and the IBA have operated a close control over the ethics of the programme makers under their supervision, and serious demands for the equivalent of a Press Council for broadcasters did not come until 1971, when the Labour Party took offence at unfair treatment of its leaders in a programme entitled *Yesterday's Men*. The BBC responded by setting up its own tribunal and the IBA followed suit. These expedients were obviously unsatisfactory: they were not truly independent and their existence was not widely publicized. The Annan Committee on the Future of Broadcasting,

---

[35] ibid., p. 23. The adverse adjudication was not, of course, published by the *Sunday Sport*.

which reported in 1977, recommended their replacement by a single statutory body. Annan conceived the BBC as part and parcel of its proposals for public accountability: it wanted an Inquiry Board to conduct public hearings that would gauge popular dissatisfaction, and an opportunity for individuals to complain about misrepresentation to a tribunal of persons 'skilled in the assessment of evidence and knowledgeable about broadcasting.[36] Successive Governments baulked at the proposal for public hearings, but the generalized recommendation for a complaints commission was finally embodied in the Broadcasting Act of 1981. The BCC began operation in June of that year. The terms of its mandate were vigorously opposed by programme makers and enthusiastically championed by media critics; it has so far done little either to fulfil the fears or to justify the hopes that were expressed at its inception. Towards the end of its first decade, however, its potential threat to freedom of expression was becoming much more noticeable: it was attacking good rather than bad programmes, often at the request of conmen and propagandists, and finding footling faults, which it insisted upon featuring in broadcast adjudications. As a statutory body, it is subject to correction in the courts, but it is also invested with certain legal powers pursuant to which it can oblige television and radio stations to comply with its dictates.

The BCC has operated in a low-key fashion since 1981, unlike the more egregious and controversial Broadcasting Standards Council headed by Lord Rees-Mogg, which sets censorship standards for taste and decency. The 1981 provisions establishing the BCC were re-enacted in the 1990 Broadcasting Act with few modifications other than to extend its remit to programmes screened on Channel 5. The Government, in its White Paper on television, planned to amalgamate the functions of the BCC and the BSC, and it certainly would have made sense (and economy) to have only one complaints body rather than two separate institutions and acronyms to confuse the viewers. However, both bodies lobbied successfully for separate treatment. The 1990 Act places a duty upon broadcasters to advertise the existence of the BCC and BSC, and to spell out the difference between them.[37]

Structure

The BCC comprises at least three (currently, five) paid but part-time members, appointed by the Home Secretary. No member is allowed to have any current interest in broadcasting, although the

---

[36] *Report of the Committee on the Future of Broadcasting*, 1977, Cmnd 6753, Ch 6 para 11.
[37] Broadcasting Act 1990 s 147(2).

Government has undertaken to appoint 'one or more persons . . . with substantial experience in broadcasting'.[38] It is now chaired by Canon Peter Pilkington. The average age of its members is sixty-five: they comprise a retired diplomat, a retired white-collar trade unionist, a retired headmistress and a retired secretary of the BBC. They are part-time and have no judicial or legal experience. The BCC's bill comes to about £350,000 per year and is footed indirectly through contributions from the BBC, ITC and Welsh Authority.

It will be noticed that a fundamental difference between the PCC and the BCC is that the former is largely composed of experienced current practitioners in major aspects of editorial and journalistic endeavour, in the hope that their ethical rulings should impress the industry. The BCC is designed to provide a panel of adjudicators without broadcasting connections (the one exception is generally an ex-newscaster), apparently to impress the public with their objectivity. This may be satisfactory where BCC adjudications relate simply to settling issues of fact, but it has meant that some adjudications appear out of touch with the realities of broadcasting and may explain why the tribunal, in its ten years of operation, has made such an insignificant contribution to developing ethical guidelines for broadcasters.

Jurisdiction

The function of the Commission, defined by the statute, is to consider and adjudicate upon complaints of unjust or unfair treatment in broadcast programmes and unwarranted infringement of privacy in, or in connection with the obtaining of material included in, broadcast programmes.[39] The BCC has no jurisdiction to entertain complaints about bad taste, indecency or offensiveness. This task is undertaken by the Broadcasting Standards Council (see p. 606).

The treatment that is 'unfair' must be 'in programmes to which this part [of the Act] applies' and it applies only to television or sound programmes that are actually broadcast. It follows that the BCC has no jurisdiction to entertain complaints about injustice to persons who are not featured on the final broadcast programme. Complaints of infringement of privacy may be 'in connection with the obtaining of material included in' broadcast programmes, and a nice question arises as to whether the BCC has jurisdiction to deal with a complaint that privacy has been invaded in the obtaining of

---

[38] See G. Robertson, 'The Broadcasting Complaints Commission', *Listener*, 13 November 1980.
[39] Broadcasting Act 1990 s 143(1)

footage that was subsequently dropped from, or edited out of, the programme when it was ultimately broadcast. The better view is that jurisdiction is limited to adjudicating upon behaviour that is connected with obtaining at least some footage that is actually broadcast: if the TV company recognizes the error of its ways, it can cut the footage obtained as a result of the privacy invasion prior to transmission and so avoid an adverse adjudication.

There will sometimes be an overlap between the ITC's duty to ensure due impartiality in coverage of political subjects and the BCC's duty to ensure fair treatment. The two organizations clashed in 1991 over a programme that the ITC found impartial but the BCC found unfair. It featured and contrasted the Labour and Conservative candidates for a particular constituency: there was no reference to the SLP candidate, for the simple reason that no one had at that stage been selected.[40] The ITC pointed out, when the BCC upheld the complaint, that as the programme was broadcast many months before the election, there was no real prospect that the viewers would remember it when they came to vote.

Unjust or unfair treatment

This is defined to include 'treatment which is unjust or unfair because of the way in which material in the programme has been selected or arranged'.[41] There is a sense in which the broadcast medium must be 'unfair' to those it interviews – in fading light, in harsh studio light and with the inevitable pressure of editing for a short sharp slot. In its first decision the BCC accepted that 'fairness' had to be considered in relation to the entire programme rather than its individual elements, and that a short programme could do no more than to highlight a few major issues surrounding a complicated controversy.[42] This is a helpful ruling for programme makers constrained to edit for brevity. In another decision the BCC has accepted the need for current-affairs programmes to be hard-hitting, and for interviewers to play 'devil's advocate' when cross-examining representatives of controversial organizations.[43] In several early adjudications it applied what lawyers would term the *de minimis* rule: that is, while regretting occasional lapses in objectivity and lack of care in editing, it has rejected the complaint because the programme as a whole did not amount to unjust or unfair

---

[40] 'Complaint from Falmouth and Cambourne SLP', *Report of the BCC 1991*, HMSO, pp. 81–4.

[41] Broadcasting Act 1990, s 150

[42] *National Anti-Fluoridation Campaign* v *Medical Express*, *Report of the BCC, 1981–2*, HMSO, 1982, p. 7.

[43] *Life* v '*Nationwide*', Adjudication 25 August 1982.

treatment.[44] By the end of its first decade of operation, however, it had resiled from this sensible approach. Its 1991 Report is full of adjudications that have upbraided, for the most trifling errors, programmes that have been substantially correct and over-whelmingly in the public interest. The 200-word 'broadcast summary' it prepares of its adjudications invariably mentions the most minor errors, and often gives a false impression that the programme has been found 'unfair' when its basic attack on the complainant has been justified.[45]

One early decision is important for radio and television drama, in that it rejects a common complaint about devices that assist verisimilitude:

> *The Brack Report*, a fictionalized drama series focusing on the nuclear debate, depicted the effects of a severe earthquake on a Central Electricity Generating Board (CEGB) reactor in the North of England. The CEGB complained that the realism of the sets and the use of its name and job titles could lead viewers to infer that it had cooperated with the programme, and to conclude that its officials did indeed behave in the cavalier, secretive and dishonest ways depicted in the drama. The BCC decided that viewers should be assumed sufficiently astute to know the difference between fact and fiction: as the CEGB had a monopoly of power stations in England a pseudonym would have been absurd, and the production was entitled to employ a degree of authenticity in its scripts and settings to give the drama an impact. The complaint was rejected.[46]

Not all the BCC rulings have been as sensible as this. In 1990, for example, it solemnly criticized the BBC soap *Eastenders* for unfairness to Brownies over remarks about underage drinking and shoplifting by a few cubs in an imaginary park.[47] The Commission conceded that it would not normally consider complaints about fictionalized story-lines, but on this occasion it considered that the programme had damaged the image of a named organization. Particular difficulties have been caused by a decision that seems to insist that outsiders who supply material for a programme should have some say in its development:

---

[44] ibid., see also *Goldstrom* v *'Reporting London'*, 13 October 1982.
[45] *Report of the BCC 1991*, note 40 above. See, for example, the complaints of Coleman (p. 10), Barker (p. 13), NIPSA (p. 23), Nutrasweet (p. 26), Sultan (p. 30), Brunel University (p. 47), Directors of Polytechnics (p. 51), BNFC (p. 58), BETA (p. 101). This is a constant and justified complaint by broadcasters: Lady Anglesey, former BCC chair, accepts that in 200 words 'it is often impossible to preserve the nuances of the Commission's findings' (*Guardian*, 4 November 1991, p. 29).
[46] Adjudication 5 January 1983. The same approach was adopted in *BECC* v *BBC*, *Report of the BCC 1991*, note 40 above, p. 131.
[47] 'Complaint from Girl Guides Association', *Report of the BCC 1990*, HMSO, p. 93.

Southern Television made a documentary, entitled *All Passion Spent*, that dealt with the unconventional marriage of Harold Nicolson and Vita Sackville-West. Their son Nigel Nicolson agreed to be interviewed and to supply material; he claimed that he understood the programme was to focus upon their writings, careers and characters in the tranquil period of their life spent at Sissinghurst. The programme evolved in production after the interview with Nigel Nicolson was recorded, and without reference to him. When transmitted, it included a dramatized portrayal of sexual incidents in his parents' lives before they settled in Sissinghurst. Although this aspect of the programme had not been discussed with him, the subject had been treated in much more intimate detail in his own book about his parents. The BCC held that Nigel Nicolson had been treated unfairly in that the television company had failed to keep him informed of changes in the programme as it evolved in production.[48]

This adjudication is regrettable. The complainant had not conceived the programme, nor was he engaged to play any part in its creative development. He had presumably been paid for his contribution and had not been averse to the idea of *All Passion Spent*, which gave publicity to his own book of the same name. The Commission did not find that the programme makers had lied to him about the nature of the programme at the time his contribution was solicited, nor that the transmitted programme was unfair to the facts of his parents' lives, which he himself had extensively publicized. It is difficult to see how he could have asserted a right to interfere with the creative development of the programme. The ruling would appear to open the door for contributors to television programmes to insist upon being consulted in the way the programme is shaped and edited.

The BCC has retreated from the logic of the *All Passion Spent* adjudication in some subsequent decisions about the treatment of participants in current-affairs programmes. It has held that persons interviewed on *Checkpoint* and *Nationwide* cannot complain if their statements are put in perspective by other material that broadens the scope of the programme.[49] A person who agrees to be interviewed about a controversial subject on an investigative programme cannot complain if investigations subsequent to the interview turn up material that controverts recorded statements. Thus, having recorded an interview, a public figure cannot dictate that it should be broadcast, or lay down conditions about other participants in the

---

[48] *Report of the BCC 1981–2*, p. 16.
[49] See *Smith* v *'Nationwide'*, 24 November 1982, and *Harley Private Health Care Clinic* v *'Checkpoint'*, 10 November 1982.
[50] *Arthur Lewis MP* v *'Nationwide'*, 1 June 1983. This complaint was upheld on the ground that the BBC producer had given Lewis a firm 'assurance' about the content of the programme.

programme.[50] However, the BCC still upholds complaints where 'the nature of the programme changed' between the time of the initial approach and recording, and the final transmitted version.[51]

The most unsatisfactory aspect of its precedents for current-affairs journalism has been a series of rulings that require 'advance notice' to be given to interviewees of the general areas of exploration. It may on occasion be 'unfair' to confront representatives of an organization with a case occurring years before and with which they cannot reasonably be expected to be familiar, and to film their puzzled or tentative responses. But it is wrong to expect *Checkpoint* journalists and the like to obey Queensberry Rules when exposing fraudsters and charlatans. In 1985 the BCC ruled that people against whom such allegations might be made should be given *written details* of the allegations well before the interview[52] – a ridiculous ruling, as it would simply mean that fraudsters would decline to be interviewed or could take refuge behind their lawyers. There is, inevitably, a 'catch as catch can' quality about investigative journalism of this sort, which would be hopelessly inhibited if this rule were to be strictly applied. (Not even the most dedicated libertarians have suggested that police always give written details of questions they wish to put to suspects.) None the less, in 1989 the BCC was still insisting on the principle that advance warning should be given. In one particularly regrettable adjudication it criticized *World in Action* for failing to make clear to the Economic League – an organization notorious for supplying 'blacklists' of left-wingers to employers – the extent to which the League's activities would be criticized in the programme.[53]

It is naïve to expect that broadcasters will obtain any form of cooperation from such organizations if they make clear at the outset that their scrutiny may be hostile – in practice, the response will either be an absolute refusal to cooperate, or legal action seeking an injunction. The 'advance notice' rule is the most damaging principle for investigative journalism that the BCC has adopted. Allied to it is the rule that 'people who are the subject of serious criticism in a programme should normally be given advance warning of all allegations against them, and be given the opportunity to answer these allegations'.[54] This is hardly practical where the answer would take the form of an application for an injunction, or where the programme makers are certain of their facts and any 'answer' would be tendentious or dishonest.

---

[51] See, e.g. complaint from Mr D. Spooner, *Report of the BCC, 1989*, HMSO, p. 29.
[52] *Report of the BCC 1985*, HMSO, para 2.
[53] *Report of the BCC 1989*, note 51 above , p. 34.
[54] ibid., p. 118.

The 'unfair treatment' test has allowed the BCC to offer a 'right of reply' when programmes put out statements that are erroneous or one-sidedly criticize individuals and organizations. (Where factual errors are publicly and promptly acknowledged, the complaint will be dismissed.) In 1989 the Council of Europe approved a European Convention on Transfrontier Television, Article 8 of which provides:

> every natural or legal person, regardless of nationality or place of residence, shall have the opportunity to exercise a right of reply or to seek other comparable legal or administrative remedies relating to programmes transmitted or retransmitted . . . within its jurisdiction. . . . In particular it shall ensure that timing and other arrangements for the exercise of the right of reply are such that this right can be effectively exercised.[55]

The prospect of complaining to the BCC would seem to satisfy this Convention, given that the remedy can take the form of ordering the adjudiction to be published in magazines widely read by viewers, together with the broadcasting of a summary of the decision at a time when viewers of the original programme would be most likely to watch. The effectiveness of the remedy is somewhat undermined by the long delays that have attended most BCC investigations. In 1990–91 the average time between complaint and decision was five to seven months.

The other adjudications that have upheld complaints of 'unfair treatment' have mostly related to demonstrable errors of fact and involve no question of principle other than a television company's duty to correct misstatements.[56] Where the factual errors have been publicly and promptly acknowledged, the complaint has been dismissed.[57] Regrettably the BCC in recent decisions has been finding programmes 'unfair' because of inconsequential errors. There is no television current-affairs programme that is 100 per cent factual and fair, so wealthy individuals and corporations can now write to the BCC confident that their complaint will probably be upheld 'in part'. Lately, the BCC has been losing sight of the fundamental public interest in freedom of expression. In 1991 a consumer programme that valuably exposed the low meat content of commercially made pasties found itself censured, not for any factual error, but because it had only named one of the corporate culprits.[58] It is, one supposes, 'unfair' to a criminal if he is the only

---

[55] See also Article 23 of the EEC directive on Broadcasting, adopted 3 October 1989.
[56] *Megafoam Ltd* v *'News at Ten'*, 15 June 1983.
[57] *National Front* v *LBC*, 1983 Report, p. 10.
[58] See *Report of the BCC 1991*, note 40 above, p. 84.

member of the gang that is captured, but it is certainly not unjust on any rational principle.

Unwarranted invasion of privacy

The Younger Committee warned that the definition of what constitutes an invasion of privacy was so subjective and uncertain that a set of strict rules and precedents 'might lead to serious inhibitions on freedom of communication.'[59] The intervention of broadcasting lobbies at a late stage in the passage of the legislation led to the insertion of the qualifying adjective 'unwarranted', which should allow the BCC to draw public interest distinctions between mere voyeurism and candid camerawork that illuminates social behaviour. When a motorist, whose vehement kerbside argument with a policeman over a parking ticket had been captured on film by a roving camera crew, complained about the subsequent transmission, she was given short shrift. The BCC ruled that 'in the circumstances we do not consider the filming without her consent amounted to unjust or unfair treatment'.

The BCC's decisions about surreptitious surveillance have depended upon the public interest in the story under investigation:

> *News at Ten* broadcast an item about connections between the National Front and right-wing Italian terrorists. An Italian living in Britain, whom the Italian government had sought to extradite to face terrorist charges, was secretly filmed by concealed cameras entering and leaving his home. The BCC ruled that this amounted to an invasion of his privacy, but it was 'warranted' by the importance of the public interest in the subject and the necessity to use secret surveillance to establish the allegations made in the programme.[60]

In other cases the BCC has regarded the public interest as insufficient to 'warrant' the breach of privacy that surreptitous surveillance represents. Each case will turn on its own facts and involve a judgement on the importance, not only of the allegation made in the programme, but of whether the invasion of privacy has been really necessary to provide evidence to support that allegation. Programme makers who invade privacy must be able to convince the tribunal both that the subject-matter of the programme is a matter of public interest and that evidence could not be obtained without resort to subterfuge or secret surveillance.[61] In its 1990 Report the BCC extended the meaning of 'unwarranted infringement of privacy' in order to criticize a television company for failing to forewarn the parents of a man convicted of manslaughter

---

[59] See Report of the Committee on Privacy.
[60] *Report of the BCC 1988*, p. 33.
[61] ibid., p. 6

that a reconstruction of his crime, inevitably distressing to them, would feature in a forthcoming programme.[62] This may be a reasonable duty to place on broadcasters, but it clearly falls outside the BCC's jurisdiction, which relates only to infringements 'in, or in connection with, the obtaining of material included in, such programmes'.

The BCC has given no general guidance (unlike the Press Council and the PCC) on how broadcasters should behave in situations where privacy deserves respect. Two cases in its 1991 Report deserve comparative study. In one, Thames' *This Week* programme was condemned because its cameraman walked through an unlocked farm gate and openly filmed some of Sainsbury's pigs rolling in their own excrement while caged in metal crates. The point of the story was to show the secrecy surrounding the production of food, and Sainsbury's had refused to cooperate unless Thames promised that it would not be mentioned on the programme. In these circumstances the BCC's decision that the minor infringement of the privacy of Sainsbury's pigs was 'unwarranted' was manifestly wrong. Its adjudication was ordered to be broadcast at 8.00 pm on a week night, and to be published in full in the *TV Times*. The BCC took no action at all, however, over one of Channel 4's most disgraceful excursions into tabloid television, which falsely associated a provincial tour operator and his family with child prostitution.[63] The man's business closed, his child was beaten up at school and he suffered a serious mental illness as a result of both invasions of his privacy (the IBA improperly gave permission to record him secretly, and the camera crew 'door-stepped' him, photographing his wife and child in the background) and unfair treatment (he escorted tours to Thailand, but had never procured women – let alone children – for his tourists). This was a case where a serious subject had been treated by television in a trite and hysterical way, and it deserved the severest condemnation. Instead, the BCC said nothing, and did nothing to undo the damage that this programme had done to the human rights of the victim and his family. On these rare occasions when the BCC should provide condemnation and reddress, its failure is abject.

Who may complain?

Complaints must be made to the BCC in writing, and should be entertained only if lodged by or on behalf of a 'person affected' by

[62] *Parents of Stephen Midlane* v *LWT*, *Report of the BCC 1990*, note 47 above, pp. 1, 122.
[63] See *Report of the BCC 1991*, note 40 above, pp. 36–43.

the allegedly unfair programme within a 'reasonable time' from the date of its transmission.[64] Members of the public who are offended by a programme but who have no connection with it or personal involvement in its subject cannot initiate a complaint. The scheme of the Act is plainly to give remedies to individuals and bodies (including companies) who are personally affected by the offending programme, either because they are themselves shown on it or have had their privacy invaded while it was made. The BCC has chosen, to its own cost as well as that of programme makers, to entertain complaints about matters of fact rather than the treatment of persons. Thus when Jonathon Porritt said that aerosols 'can't be re-used or re-cycled', the BCC upheld a complaint from the British Aerosol Manufacturers Association because a small fraction of aerosols (5 per cent) are in fact re-cycled.[65] Porritt may have been slightly mistaken in his facts, but he had not treated unfairly any 'individual or body of persons'. This is just one of many cases where the BCC would appear to have exceeded its jurisdiction, either by taking up, at the behest of trade groups, arguments made in general terms, or by permitting lobbying groups that are not directly or personally affected to complain.

There is a special provision that permits relatives or others closely connected with a victim of unfairness or intrusion to maintain a complaint if the victim is unable to do so in person, e.g. if he or she is a child or has died less than five years before the programme's transmission. Although the dead are unable to sue for libel, slurs on their recent memory may be redressed in respect of broadcast defamations. The BCC has on one occasion errone-ously extended its jurisdiction by ruling that a false statement about a pop star's death twenty years before was 'unfair' to his daughter because it caused her distress.[66] The BCC is entitled to reject complaints that it considers to be frivolous or otherwise inappropriate for adjudication.[67]

The BCC must not adjudicate if the subject of the complaint has become an issue in legal proceedings:

> A Czech emigré organization complained that it had been treated unfairly in a *TV Eye* programme. After the complaint had been lodged and accepted *The Sunday Times* published an account of the dispute that was severely critical of the conduct of the programme and its reporters. They sued the newspaper for libel, and sought to stop the BCC from proceeding further with its consideration of the complaint. The court held that although the complainant was not a

---

[64] Broadcasting Act (1990) s 144(5).
[65] See *Report of the BCC 1991*, note 40 above, p. 110.
[66] *Valentine* v *Channel 4, Report of the BCC 1990*, note 47 above, p. 33–4.
[67] Broadcasting Act 1990 144(4)(*d*) and s 144(5).

party to the litigation, the fact that the court case called for determination of the same issues as those involved in adjudicating the complaint meant that the BCC was debarred from giving it further consideration until legal proceedings had been concluded.[68]

However, where legal proceedings are open to a complainant but have not yet begun, the BCC has a discretion to continue with its investigations:

> The BBC failed to convince the Court of Appeal that the BCC should be injuncted from proceeding to hear a complaint against *Checkpoint*. The complainant had at first threatened to sue the BBC, and demanded that it supply him with a transcript of the programme. When the BBC declined, he complained to the BCC instead of issuing a writ. The BCC, under its statutory powers, obtained a copy of the transcript, which it supplied to the complainant, who indicated that he would not be commencing a libel action 'at the moment'. The BBC argued that the BCC was allowing itself to be exploited by a potential litigant: if it upheld his complaint, the BBC would be forced to publish its finding, which might be wholly inconsistent with the defence it would raise if libel proceedings were then brought against it. The Court of Appeal held that the BCC had a duty to hear complaints unless it decided that this was 'not appropriate' in the particular circumstances, and the BBC had failed to discharge the heavy burden of showing that the BCC had acted unreasonably in continuing the hearing.[69]

This case illustrates the difficulties that can arise as a result of the BCC's policy of not requiring a 'legal waiver' from complainants who have an alternative remedy in libel. Broadcasters may be placed in 'double jeopardy' when complainants postpone their libel remedy (which they may do for up to three years after the broadcast) in order to extract evidence and a finding in their favour from the BCC. Although the BCC's adjudication would be likely to be ruled inadmissible at a subsequent defamation trial, the advantage of having a 'dry run' is inestimable.

Procedure

Once a complaint is accepted, the BCC has legal powers to view the programme and to call for a copy of the transcript together with relevant correspondence between the complainant and the television company.[70] It will demand from the broadcasting body that has transmitted the programme a written statement in answer

---

[68] *R v Broadcasting Complaints Commission ex parte Thames Television* (1982) *The Times*, 8 October per Stephen Brown J. See also Broadcasting Act 1990 s 144(4)(*d*).
[69] *R v Broadcasting Complaints Commission ex parte BBC* 128 SJ 384; (1989) *The Times*, 17 May. See also Broadcasting Act 1990 s 144(4)(*c*).

to the complaint. None the less, the BCC's procedure can be remarkably unfair to programme makers and to participants whose actions have given rise to a complaint. If the case is considered without a hearing, they have no right to make submissions or even to be told of the complaint. In practice, of course, they will probably be consulted, but there have been occasions where this has been over-looked: LWT was once condemned unheard after its programme had been lukewarmly defended by the IBA.[71] Independent programme makers or participants who fear they are being 'frozen out' of the preparation of an answer to a complaint should approach the BCC direct and insist on receiving copies of all correspondence relating to the complaint and on being given an opportunity to make submissions in response. If the complaint calls their conduct into question and the BCC refuses to hear them, its decision could be challenged successfully in the High Court.

The BCC may deal with the complaint on the basis of written submissions, or may decide to summon the parties to a hearing. Where the complainant is accorded a hearing, the same right must be extended to 'any person . . . who appears to the Commission to have been responsible for the making or provision' of the programme in question or any other person who might be able to assist at the hearing.[72] This may give programme makers an opportunity for a personal explanation if the BCC complies with its statutory duty to invite them. Under its present procedures, the duty is quite improperly delegated to the broadcasting authorities or licensees.[73]

BCC hearings are of two kinds. Either all parties will be summoned to attend on the same occasion, or they will be heard separately. In both cases the hearings are in private and the proceedings are regarded as confidential. This is unsatisfactory and contrary to the Annan Report recommendations, as the BCC is a quasi-judicial tribunal and it should comply with the open-justice principle except in cases where 'invasion of privacy' complaints may be more appropriately heard in secret. Public hearings would allow others to judge the evidence, which can be gleaned only from short summaries comprised in BCC adjudications. There have been occasions when both sides have been represented by QCs.[74]

---

[70] Broadcasting Act 1990 s 145. Broadcasters must retain recordings of all programmes for ninety days in the case of television, and for forty-two days in the case of radio.

[71] *Roehampton Church School* v *LWT*, 1982 Report p. 9.

[72] Broadcasting Act 1990 s 145(2).

[73] See Rule 31, 'Procedural Arrangements' *Report of the BCC 1991*, note 40 above, p. 177.

At a contested hearing the procedure is for the complainant to summarize his case, followed by answers from the BBC or ITC and then statements from the television contractor, programme maker and any other person entitled to be heard. After the complainant's reply, the tribunal may question any of the parties. Although parties may be represented by lawyers, cross-examination is not permitted. The best that broadcasters can do is to request the chairperson to put particular questions – whether the request is granted or not is a matter for the BCC's discretion. There is no appeal from BCC adjudications, although as a statutory body it is amenable to judicial review in the High Court if its procedures breach the basic rules of fairness or if its decisions are unreasonable. It is unlikely that a court would upset a BCC adjudication on the merits, unless it could be shown to have disregarded obviously important evidence or to have taken irrelevant matters into account.

The BCC may pay travelling and subsistence allowances to any person who attends a hearing – on the broadcasters' side as well as the complainants'. It cannot award costs or compensation.

Publication of adjudications

The Commission has power to direct the BBC or the ITC to publish its findings in any specified manner, and at any specified time.[75] The adjudication is issued as a press release, and sometimes features as a news item in newspapers and trade journals. The BCC can order a summary of the complaint, and its findings thereon, to be broadcast 'in any manner specified'. This could include, as one Government minister pointed out in the course of the debate over the legislation, a direction specifying that the findings should be made the first item on the evening television news. This draconian expedient has not yet been used, although the BCC normally directs that a 200-word summary of its findings should be broadcast during a later edition of the programme complained against or at a comparable time. One curious feature of the BCC's mode of operating is that it normally directs a summary of its adjudication to be broadcast irrespective of whether it has upheld the complaint. The use of its statutory powers to oblige broadcasters who have not offended to transmit material of no particular news value is egregious and unnecessary. Equally objectionable is the BCC's nit-picking habit of finding minor faults with outstanding public-interest programmes, and issuing conse-

---

[74] See for example, *Church of Scientology* v *BBC Report of the BCC, 1990*, note 47 above, p. 99.
[75] Broadcasting Act 1990 s 146.

quent adjudications that give the impression to the public that the complaint has been substantially upheld. By its own unsatisfactory practices, the BCC serves to protect some unsavoury people without making any discernible contribution to broadcasters' ethics.

The Advertising Standards Authority

This is a private body set up and founded by the advertising industry to monitor a code of practice designed to ensure that media advertisements are 'legal, decent, honest and truthful'. It derives its powers from the refusal of newspapers and journals to carry advertisements deemed to be in breach of the code, and from the willingness of the ITC to adopt its principles in applying its own statutory powers in relation to advertising. Its chairperson is Timothy Raison (a former Conservative minister), and a majority of its nine members are chosen from outside the advertising industry. Editors and journalists need not wait for it to adjudicate public complaints about advertisements carried in their papers: they can consult the ASA before agreeing to run them if there is any doubt about the claims made in the copy.

The ASA Code on Decency requires that 'no advertisement shall contain any matter that is likely to cause grave or widespread offence', judged in terms of the advertisement's probable effect, taken as a whole, on its likely audience.[76] It follows that a more stringent test is applied to advertisements placed on public billboards than in specialist magazines. 'Grave or widespread offence' is usually predictable, and national peculiarities rule out some advertising – especially featuring naked children – that is acceptable on the Continent. In 1991 an insensitive Italian clothing chain, Benetton, caused grave and widespread offence by plastering a colour picture of a new-born baby on British billboards: offence was caused not because the picture was indecent, but because it was exploitative. The public is quick to protest when bad taste is put to commercial use: 2,000 complaints were received about a billboard advertisement for *Today* newspaper that showed Mrs Thatcher, Mr Kinnock and Mr Owen each hanging from a noose, above the caption: 'Would Britain be better off with a hung Parliament?' More latitude is given to charities, although some are only too willing to manipulate emotions; there was general relief when the ASA banned the RSPCA ad showing a pile of dead dogs. The advertisement was neither decent, nor, as it turned out, entirely truthful. Television advertising is regulated by the ITC,

---

[76] *The British Code of Advertising Practice*, 8th edn, 1988, Rule B 3.1 and A 3.2.

rather more strictly as a result of European initiatives (see p. 641).

In 1988 the Director-General of Fair Trading was given statutory powers to deal with false advertisements, as a result of implementation of the European Community's Directive on Misleading Advertising. These powers will be used only as a last resort, if the ASA's voluntary self-regulation system fails, as it did with the advent of the *Sunday Sport*:

> The ASA upheld complaints against advertisements for a new slimming aid, but the distributors continued to run advertisements in the *Sunday Sport*. The ASA, powerless to prohibit their continuing publication, referred the matter to the Director-General, who was granted an injunction against the distributors preventing them from publishing the same or any similar advertisement.[77]

These proceedings are brought against manufacturers and distributors, rather than newspapers. However, editors should be aware of the potential criminal liability they may incur under the Trade Descriptions Act if they falsely market their own publications:

> *Woman* magazine appeared with a cover announcement 'Exclusive! At last, the real Anne Diamond'. Instead of an interview with the popular television presenter however, the feature to which the cover referred comprised headless pictures of eight women (one of whom was Ms Diamond) together with a 'character analysis' of their clothing. The publishers, IPC Magazines, were fined £600 with £400 costs for applying a false and misleading trade description to the contents of their product.

The crime of applying a false description to a book or magazine is, under the Trade Descriptions Act, a strict-liability offence and committed if a cover is in fact misleading, even if the publisher had no intention to trick potential readers. In 1991 HarperCollins suffered embarrassment and a fine of £6,250 (and an order to pay £4,150 prosecution costs) for some sharp practice exposed at Stratford-upon-Avon by local trading standards officers:

> Alastair Maclean was a popular and prolific author, who bequeathed his publishers a number of 'outlines' for future stories. HarperCollins hired an unknown, never-before-published author, who just happened to be named Alastair MacNeill, to write books based on these story-lines after Maclean's death. The first, *Nightwatch*, was published with a cover description: ALASTAIR MACLEAN'S *Nightwatch* and the name Alastair MacNeill in small print at the bottom. The court had no hesitation in finding that the use of the apostrophe could mislead customers into thinking that the book had been written by the famous novelist, a misrepresentation compounded by the similarity of his name with that of the real author.

---

[77] *Director-General of Fair Trading* v *Tobyward* [1989] 1 All ER 266.

The ASA, although a voluntary body, was in 1989 held to be amenable to judicial review.[78] The Divisional Court in consequence quashed a ruling that had been made on the basis of inadequate information. This decision raises the prospect that the Press Complaints Commission, too, will be held to be subject to the supervisory jurisdiction of the High Court. Although its adjudications do not have the impact of ASA decisions, it none the less claims to exercise a public law function as an alternative to libel proceedings and in lieu of legislative action to protect privacy. Its objective of influencing the ethics of the media through a code of practice and a body of case rulings is similar to the objective in relation to the City of the Panel on Take-Overs and Mergers, which has also been held amenable to judicial review.[79]

Newspapers from time to time suffer reprisals from advertisers as a result of editorials or investigative journalism that is critical of the advertiser's product or personnel. The reprisal usually takes the form of withdrawal of future advertising. The ASA will be of no assistance in cases where the petulant advertiser is a private organization, but the case of *R* v *Derbyshire County Council ex parte Times Supplements Ltd* demonstrates how judicial review may be used to provide redress against local authorities (or government departments) that cancel advertisements for political reasons:

> Derbyshire County Council regularly advertised teaching positions in the *Times Education Supplement*, which is owned by Rupert Murdoch. Another Murdoch paper, *The Sunday Times*, published a series of attacks on the Labour-controlled council and its leader, David Bookbinder. The Labour group on the council vindictively decided to end all advertising in Murdoch publications, and used its majority on the council's education committee to switch the advertising of teaching posts (worth some £60,000 per year) from the *TES* to the *Guardian*. The Divisional Court quashed this decision as a result of evidence that demonstrated that it had been made solely because of the Labour group's vendetta against the Murdoch press, and not for any bona fide reason related to education or to the council's operations; 'It was thus an abuse of power contrary to the public good.'[80]

ICSTIS

The privatizing of British Telecom has led to a mushrooming of 'live conversation' and 'adult entertainment' services available to telephone inquirers at a premium rate (i.e. charged at the rate for

---

[78] *R* v *ASA ex parte the Insurance Service* (1989) *The Times*, 14 July.
[79] *R* v *Panel on Take-Overs and Mergers ex parte Datafin* [1987] QB 815 CA.
[80] (1991) 3 Admin L Rep 241.

dialling the Irish Republic). These services are now subject to codes of practice drawn up and monitored by the Independent Committee for the Supervision of Standards of Telephone Information Services (ICSTIS), a regulatory body comprising ten members appointed by British Telecom and chaired by Louis Blom-Cooper QC. ICSTIS derives its power from clauses in the contracts between service providers and Telecom, which entitles the latter to act on an ICSTIS recommendation to close any service that is found to have breached the relevant code. Complaints may be made, sensibly enough, by telephone, by calling freephone 0800 500212.

The code for live telephone services is considerably more detailed than that for recorded messages, and is regularly monitored. It requires service providers themselves to monitor their services continually, to record all conversations and to retain the recordings for a six-month period in the event that these are required by ICSTIS. They are under a duty to use 'all reasonable endeavours' not to allow talk that might encourage criminal offences, drug-taking or racial disharmony, or that might cause grave offence by reference to sex or violence by use of foul language. They must operate procedures to ensure that persons under eighteen do not use the service, and to warn callers both of the charges they are running up and of the fact that their conversations are being recorded. Under British Telecom, telephone talk is neither cheap nor free, although it has established a compensation fund to help pay the telephone bills of subscribers whose children or guests have incurred heavy premium rate charges without authorization.

These ICSTIS rules have deterred the most explicit 'live sex lines' that flourish in America. British 'adult entertainment services' offer anodyne recorded messages, which must comply with a separate code with strict provisions against indecent speech (see p. 152). Again, service providers are bound by the terms of their contracts with the network operators to abide by the ICSTIS code, on pain of having the service removed from the network following an ICSTIS recommendation. In 1991 ICSTIS promulgated new rules purporting to restrict the manner in which these services are advertised, banning such advertisements entirely from free or unsolicited publications and requiring that all that appear in publications not normally carried on the 'top shelf' of newsagents 'must not contain pictures or words of a sexually suggestive nature which are unacceptably offensive'.

The new rules are an unreasonable restraint on trade, since it must be for newspapers and free sheets to decide for themselves whether to carry lawful advertisements. The providers of adult entertainment services, supported by those newspapers that carry their advertisements (the *Sport*, *Mirror* and *Star*), challenged the new rules on the basis that what is 'unacceptably offensive' is unacceptably subjective and unpredictable. A confused majority judgment finally admitted: 'There is a subjective element to our approach and we regard it as unavoidable.' ICSTIS then moved on to rule that an ad for 'Unzip my suspenders' was not acceptable, but 'Dial-a-Bonk' was. A dissenting opinion by the chairman found this 'an untenable approach for a body such as ICSTIS which operates in an area of public administration'.[81]

NUJ Code of Conduct

The National Union of Journalists has a code with which all members are expected to comply. The code itself is impressive, although attempts to enforce it have been less so. Members occasionally complain about the conduct of colleagues, and the ultimate sanction of expulsion from the union is severe if the offending journalist is employed on a newspaper that accepts an NUJ 'closed shop'. No journalist has been expelled for breach of the code, and disciplinary hearings tend to be unsatisfactory for all concerned. The union has partly opened its disciplinary procedures to the public, in that victims of unethical behaviour can complain to the NUJ branch of which the offending journalist is a member. If any branch member is impressed by the complaint, he or she could formally begin disciplinary proceedings on behalf of the victim. This procedure is not satisfactory: it relies upon journalists to take up cudgels against their colleagues, and provides no assurance that the complaint will be dealt with either independently or impartially.

---

[81] ICSTIS adjudication in respect of advertisements in the *Mirror*, *Star* and *Sport*, 28 August 1991.

Chapter 14

Censorship of Films and Video

The most obvious shift in the British approach to censorship of the visual media has been away from the courts and towards quasi-statutory regulation. The jury – the traditional body for deciding issues of freedom of expression – is no longer trusted to make the detailed judgements required before films and videos are regarded as fit for public exhibition and sale. In practice (although not in theory – films and videos may still be prosecuted for obscenity) the jury's function has been taken over by an institution of state-approved censors, which calls itself the British Board of Film Classification. The term 'classification' is a euphemism – although much of the Board's task involves classification of films as suitable for particular age-groups, the 'cuts' it requires for this certification are in practice censorship directives. In some cases it refuses certification altogether for adult viewing; such a refusal will amount to a legal ban (in the case of a video) or a powerful extra-legal deterrent (in the case of a feature film for cinema release). This distinction arises from the Board's history as a private body set up by the film industry; it retains this advisory capacity in relation to the cinema, but has recently been given statutory powers by Parliament to decide whether video-cassettes are 'suitable for viewing in the home'. Its operations additionally have a determinative influence on the feature films that are shown on television: the licensing bodies for that medium generally insist that films possess a BBFC certificate before they can be screened.

Film censorship is the most complicated and controversial area of legal and extra-legal regulation. Movies that are exhibited in cinemas or viewed in the home on video-cassettes are subject to the Obscene Publications Act, and may be prosecuted on the grounds that they would tend to deprave and corrupt a significant proportion of likely viewers. Additionally, they may be prosecuted at common law for blasphemy or sedition. Cinema films, however, are subject to special pre-censorship arrangements: a classification system operated by the BBFC that is in theory voluntary but, in practice, a requirement insisted upon by local councils, which license cinemas. These councils may themselves prohibit films that have BBFC approval or, indeed, permit the screening of films that have been refused certification. In the case of video-cassettes BBFC certification is required by law before they can be sold to particular age-groups, and must be withheld from movies that are deemed 'unsuitable for viewing in the home', however unexceptionable they may be for screening to adults in licensed cinemas. Neither theatre promoters nor book publishers suffer institutional censorship imposed by bureaucracies or local councillors, and the standards of acceptability endorsed by these bodies are such that cinema censorship is more pervasive, and more arbitrary, than the limitations imposed on other forms of artistic expression.

The reasons for additional layers of censorship in relation to films are partly historic (insofar as cinemas required local authority licences for reasons of health and safety), partly practical (distributors and exhibitors of film have preferred the security of BBFC censorship to protect their profits and their persons from the vagaries of obscenity prosecutions) and partly philosophical. As the Williams Committee put the latter argument, film is a 'uniquely powerful medium . . . the close-up, fast cutting, the sophistication of modern make-up and special effects techniques, the heightening effect of sound effects and music, all combine on the large screen to produce an impact which no other medium can create'.[1] What is left of the insubstantial pageant once the credits have faded and the bus ride home has been taken is a matter of inconclusive evidence, but 'it seems entirely sensible to be cautious'.[2]

In the case of home video, caution is regarded as even more sensible in light of the ability of viewers – especially youngsters – to use the technology to dilate repeatedly upon particular scenes. The BBFC explains that it is much stricter with scenes depicting sexual violence on video than on film, 'since the fact that a scene might be searched out and repeated endlessly out-of-context in the privacy of one's home could condition some viewers to find the behaviour sexually exciting, not just on film, but in real life'.[3] In 1984 this concern led Parliament, after a frenetic campaign about the dangers of 'video-nasties', to designate the BBFC as the body empowered to decide which films were appropriate for home viewing on video-cassette. As a result, this small private body, established and funded by the film industry, has become a bureaucratic apparatus recognized by law and exercising a determinative control over the contents of publicly available films and videos. Its certificate, while not a guarantee of immunity from

---

[1] *Obscenity and Film Censorship: Committee Report* (the Williams Committee), HMSO, 1979, Cmnd 7772.
[2] ibid.
[3] BBFC Annual Report (1986).

prosecution under the Obscene Publications Act, has in practice become just that, and the prospect of proceedings against those who purvey films and cassettes protected by its classification must be regarded as remote. In 1985 the Government undertook that in order to avoid 'local variations in prosecution policy' and to ensure that 'any prosecution should be undertaken only after the most careful consideration of the case', the police would seek the advice of the DPP before prosecuting for obscenity in relation to any work certified by the BBFC.[4]

Film Censorship

History

The BBFC was a voluntary body, established by the film industry in 1912 in an effort to provide some uniform guidance to local authorities empowered to license premises for the screening of particular films. The 1909 Cinematograph Act gave local authorities power to impose conditions on film exhibitions in order to protect the public against fire hazards, but they soon began to use them to quench the flames of celluloid passion. The first banned film – a newsreel of an American prize fight – earned a disapproval 'not unconnected with the fact that it showed a negro defeating a white man'.[5] The film industry took fright at the prospect that distribution might be subjected to the whims of different local councils, and a consensus emerged that 'it would be far better for the trade to censor its own productions than to see all films at the mercy of an arbitrary authority'.[6]

In 1912 the Cinematographic Exhibitors' Association announced the formation of the British Board of Film Censors, whose duty 'would be to induce confidence in the minds of the licensing authorities, and of those who have in their charge the moral welfare of the

---

[4] ibid.
[5] See Neville March Hunnings, *Film Censors and the Law*, Allen & Unwin 1967, p. 50. Until 1932 the annual reports of the BBFC listed the reasons for which cuts had been requested or films refused a certificate. They included 'abdominal contortions in dancing' (1925), 'Bolshevik propaganda' (ibid.), 'complacent acquiescence of husband in adultery of his wife; (ibid.), 'equivocal situation between white girls and men of other races' (1926), 'officers in British regiments in a disgraceful light, (ibid.), 'British possessions represented as lawless sinks of iniquity' (1928), 'police firing on defenceless populace' (ibid.), 'themes likely to wound the just sensibilities of friendly nations' (ibid.), 'unrelieved sordid themes' (1930). The practice was ended because 'for some unaccountable reason critics have seized upon isolated sentences and by taking them out of context have placed mischievous constructions upon them' (1932). The Reports are gathered in PRO file H045/24024.
[6] ibid., p. 51

community generally.[7] In 1924 the BBFC received its judicial imprimatur in the case of *Mills* v *London County Council* when the Divisional Court upheld the validity of a condition that 'no cinematograph film . . . which has not been passed for . . . exhibition by the BBFC shall be exhibited without the express consent of the council'. So long as a council reserved the right to review BBFC decisions, it was entitled to make the grant of a cinema licence contingent upon the screening of certified films.[8] The position was approved by the Court of Appeal in 1976. Lord Denning said:

> I do not think the county councils can delegate the whole of their responsibilities to the board, but they can treat the board as an advisory body whose views they can accept or reject; provided that the final decision – aye or nay – rests with the county council.[9]

The cutting-room counsels of the BBFC avowedly err on the side of caution, in an effort to protect the established film industry from criticism as well as from prosecution. Although the BBFC is (save for its role in approving video-cassettes) an unofficial body, unrecognized by statute and financed through fees imposed upon every film submitted for censorship, it exercises a persuasive and in most cases determinative influence over the grant of local authority licences. 'I freely admit that this is a curious arrangement' conceded the Home Secretary, Mr Herbert Morrison, in 1942, 'but the British have a very great habit of making curious arrangements work very well, and this works. Frankly, I do not wish to be the Minister who has to answer questions in the House as to whether particular films should or should not be censored.'[10]

Section 3 of the 1952 Cinematograph Act (now s 1(3) of the 1985 Cinemas Act) imposed a duty on licensing authorities to place restrictions on the admission of children to cinemas that show works 'designated, by the licensing authority or such other body as may be specified in the licence, as works unsuitable for children'. The reference to 'such other body' was the first parliamentary acknowledgement of the BBFC, and the 1952 Act established its position, if not as a censorship body, at least as an authorized classification tribunal for films unsuitable for young people, and its classification decisions have for this purpose won considerable approval. The present classification, endorsed by all local councils and by the Home Office, is:

---

[7] ibid. p. 54.
[8] *Mills* v *London County Council* [1925] 1 KB 213.
[9] *R* v *GLC ex parte Blackburn* [1976] 1 WLR 550, per Lord Denning, at pp. 554–5.
[10] (1942) 385 HC Debs 504.

U   Universal: suitable for all.
UC   Universal: particularly suitable for children.
PG   Parental guidance: some scenes may be unsuitable for young children.
12   Suitable for persons of twelve years and over.
15   Suitable only for persons of fifteen years and over.
18   Suitable only for persons of eighteen years and over.
18R   Suitable only for restricted distribution through segregated premises to which no one under 18 is admitted.

The 12 category was adopted in 1989, so that the Board could stop children under twelve from seeing films such as *Batman*, *Crocodile Dundee* and *Gremlins*, which it was reluctant to confine to the 15 category, but believed would be damaging to pre-teenagers. (Anomalously, the 12 category does not apply to video.) The Board has become quite obsessive about its arbitrary age-limits (it insisted on twenty-five cuts to *Indiana Jones and the Temple of Doom* before it agreed to a PG certificate) and film exhibitors invariably buckle under its ruling in order to obtain the extra profits that derive from teenage admission fees. They will happily cut scenes from major motion pictures in order to achieve a 15 rating, and will in many cases agree to cut further scenes in order to obtain a 12 rating. The result is that adults in Britain are obliged to see cut versions of major films that are screened unexpurgated in America and in other countries in Europe. The film industry has traditionally preferred the pursuit of profit to the principle of artistic freedom, and rarely appeals against the Board's decisions. Film makers may now, however, be able to assert their new 'moral right' under the Copyright Act against exhibitors who agree to multilate their work (see p. 251).

The BBFC has effectively become the authorized censor for feature films in cinemas and on television, and for those marketed on video-cassettes. Its position derives, not from the law, but from an understanding it has reached with prosecuting authorities, local councils and the Home Office. The basis for the understanding was frankly expressed by the DPP to the Select Committee on obscenity in 1957:

> If I wished to prosecute a film – and it has been suggested on two occasions to me that certain films that had passed the British Board of Film Censors were obscene – my answer would be, as it was in those two cases, I shall have to put the British Board of Film Censors in the dock because they have aided and abetted the commission of that particular offence. So it inhibits me to that extent. As long as I rely on the judgement of the British Board of Film Censors as to the

suitability, under the various categories, of films for public showing, which I do, I do not prosecute.[11]

On this basis the DPP has not prosecuted certified films in connection with cinema screenings, and the only two private prosecutions have both come to grief. A case against *Last Tango in Paris* under the Obscene Publications Act 1959 failed on technical grounds,[12] and a prosecution of the exhibitors of *The Language of Love* for the common-law offence of gross indecency (now abolished in relation to the cinema) was rejected by an Old Bailey jury. Feature films which are certified in the 18 and 18R categories do not receive the same practical immunity from the obscenity law when marketed on video-cassettes, because there is no control over the age of the audience that may view them in the home. For this reason the DPP has authorized prosecutions against distributors of video-cassettes of *The Evil Dead* and *The Burning*, certified films that played without objection to over-eighteen audiences in cinemas.

The DPP now has a monopoly over obscenity prosecutions of feature films, and it is virtually inconceivable that he would prosecute in respect of the exhibition of a film certified by a body like the BBFC, which has parliamentary approval (at least, for the video aspect of its work). If he did, of course, the question would be whether a particular exhibition of the film would be likely to deprave and corrupt its actual or potential audience. It is highly questionable whether the BBFC could properly be charged with 'aiding and abetting' by the grant of its certificate. So far as films are concerned, the certificate is no more than an expression of opinion – it is the local council that is responsible in law for licensing the exhibition.

Local council licensing

The Cinemas Act 1985 consolidates all the previous provisions, dating from 1909, relating to the licensing of cinemas. Subject to certain exemptions for casual or non-profit-making enterprises, it is an offence, punishable by the somewhat extravagant maximum fine of £20,000, to use unlicensed premises for film exhibitions. Local councils may attach conditions to licences, and these normally require that all films shown carry a BBFC classification certificate and that admission be refused to persons outside the certified class. Failure to comply with such conditions is also an offence. On the basis of *Mills* v *London County Council* (see p. 567)

---

[11] See John Trevelyan, *What the Censor Saw*, Michael Joseph, 1973, p. 141.
[12] *A-G's Reference (No 2 of 1975)* [1976] 2 All ER 753.

local authorities must retain a supervisory function over and above the BBFC, and some exercise this power to prohibit particular films that have been granted certification. Thus, controversial releases may be banned in some districts and licensed in others, sometimes only a short bus ride away. (*The Life of Brian* was banned entirely in many jurisdictions, and given a more restricted classification in others.)

Local film censorship is usually delegated to magistrates or entrusted to standing committees: some councils rely upon their Fire Brigade Committees to extinguish any flames of passion that may have escaped the BBFC hose, while one Cornish borough solemnly bans films despite the fact that there are no cinemas within its jurisdiction. This kind of censorship, duplicating the BBFC and the obscenity law, was regarded by the Williams Committee as a waste of public time and money, but the licensing provisions were re-enacted in 1982 and consolidated in the Cinemas Act of 1985. In addition, local councils have powers over 'sex cinemas', provided, as a backstop, by the Local Government (Miscellaneous Provisions) Act of 1982.

Most local authorities adopt the 'model licensing conditions' drafted by the Home Office, which read:

(*a*) No film, other than a current newsreel, shall be exhibited unless it has received a certificate of the British Board of Film Classification or is the subject of the licensing authority's permission;

(*b*) no young people shall be admitted to any exhibition of a film classified by the Board as unsuitable for them, unless with the local authority's permission;

(*c*) no film shall be exhibited if the licensing authority gives notice in writing prohibiting its exhibition on the ground that it 'would offend against good taste or decency or would be likely to encourage or incite to crime or to lead to disorder or to be offensive to public feeling';

(*d*) the nature of the certificate given to any film shall be indicated in any advertising for the film, at the cinema entrance (together with an explanation of its effect), and on the screen immediately before the film is shown;

(*e*) displays outside the cinema shall not depict any scene or incident not in the film as approved.

These conditions import the legal requirements that the local authority should retain the ultimate discretion rather than delegate it entirely to the BBFC. Condition (*a*) allows a liberal authority to permit screening of a film that the BBFC has refused to certify, and condition (*c*) enables a repressive authority to refuse permission to the exhibition of a certified film. The grounds are precisely those on which the television regulators are enjoined to stop television broadcasts. The existence of ground (*c*) does not mean that the BBFC must itself apply these television acceptability tests to what is fit to be viewed in a cinema by paying adults, although the BBFC wrongfully claims that it '*must* observe these tests before granting the certificate without which the film may not be exhibited to the public'. The BBFC is under a duty to apply only the criminal-law test of obscenity; it chooses to adopt the broader Home Office test because that involves more censorship of a sort the BBFC is happy to engage in.

Certain classes of film exhibition are exempted from licensing requirements by ss 5–7 of the 1985 Act. These include occasional exhibitions, children's film clubs, screenings by educational and religious institutions and organizations certified as non-profit-making. The sections are carefully drafted to prevent profit-making cinema clubs from obtaining an exempt status, as many did through a loophole in the 1952 Act. This loophole had fostered the device of the 'sex cinema club' as a means of escaping local authority licensing requirements. Now, any screening that is 'promoted for private gain' is likely to be caught. Those that are not, but that none the less feature sexually explicit films (e.g., demonstration of films that are for sale in sex shops) will probably be caught by the provisions of the 1982 Local Government (Miscellaneous Provisions) Act, which applies to 'sex cinemas' that do not require licences under the 1985 Cinemas Act. Section 3(1) of Schedule 3 to the Local Government Act permits local authority control of any premises used to exhibit films 'relating to sexual activity or acts of force or restraint which are associated with sexual activity or . . . genital organs or urinary or excretory functions'.

The effect of these recent amendments is to bring almost every commercial film exhibition within the local authority licensing powers, with the concomitant requirement for BBFC classifications. This requirement is spelled out by s 1(3) of the 1985 legislation, which imposes a duty on licensing authorities to 'impose conditions or restrictions prohibiting the admission of children to film exhibitions involving the showing of works designated, by the authority or by *such other body* [our italics] as may be specified in the licence, as works unsuitable for children'. 'Such other body' is a reference to the BBFC, and although local councils sometimes disagree with its decisions to grant or withhold certification for adult viewing, its age-group classification decisions are rarely interfered with.

In 1988 the House of Lords decided that video games were not 'an exhibition of moving pictures' for the purposes of the Cinematograph Act 1909 and, consequently, that premises used as an amusement arcade featuring such games did not require to be licensed. It follows that the screening of indecent video games does not fall within the censorship powers of local councils, although the manufacturers and distributors of discs emitting obscene electronic impulses might be dealt with under the Video Recordings Act.[13]

The Advent of Video

The home video market in Britain has been a remarkable success: by 1986 there were over 30,000 outlets selling or renting almost 10,000 separate video titles for home viewing. The earliest scare came when the first court to confront this new technology decided that video-cassettes fell outside the Obscene Publications Act – they had not, after all, been envisaged when that legislation was formulated in 1959. Before pornographers had much time to dance in the streets, the Court of Appeal was urgently reconvened in the middle of a summer vacation to rule, on an Attorney-General's reference, that video-cassettes did comprise 'matter to be looked at' within the scope of the 1959 act.[14] In subsequent prosecutions video-cassettes were treated like books: the question was whether their contents, taken as a whole, would tend to corrupt those likely to see them. In determining their potential audience, the jury could consider the fact that they were for screening in the home, and decide whether children were likely to obtain access to them as a result. Pornographic videos presented no additional problems to those posed at trials of sexually explicit books, magazines or 8mm films. But fears of this novel technology – its fascination for children, its ability to freeze-frame and to replay favourite episodes, its mushroom growth – were soon exploited in a manic press campaign against 'video-nasties'.

Only 10 per cent of the feature films available in 1983 on video-cassette had been certified by the BBFC as suitable for universal viewing. Many had been granted an X certificate for cinema screening, and many more had never been certified at all. Amongst these were many run-of-the-mill horror movies, for which there was an early video vogue; to capitalize on it, distributors promoted films that explicitly depicted violence and brutality. The label 'video-nasty' was used indiscriminately, but it reflected the prevailing fear that meretricious movies that dwelt on rape and mayhem would affect the minds of young children permitted to watch them by negligent parents. The Obscene Publications Act was a suitable

---

[13] *BACTA* v *Westminster City Council* [1988] 1 All ER 740.
[14] *A-G's Reference (No 5 of 1980)* [1980] 3 All ER 816.

tool for prosecution of such films where there was any prospect that a significant number of children might view them, and in 1983 a jury convicted the distributors of *Nightmares in a Damaged Brain* on account of its detailed depictions of sex and violence. But the campaigners – led by the Festival of Light and the *Daily Mail* – saw the opportunity to erect a new censorship apparatus that went far beyond the scope of the Obscene Publications Act. With a remarkable talent for passing off propaganda as scientifically valid research, they convinced politicians and newspapers of the accuracy of such claims as '37 per cent of children under 7 have seen a "video-nasty"' and that 'the nasty video has replaced the conjurer at children's birthday parties'.[15] 'Scientific' research purported to show that very young children in working-class homes up and down the country were watching sadistic sex while their parents were away from home. Sensationalized research claims, timed to coincide with important stages of the Video Recordings Bill, created a mild form of hysteria among politicians of all parties and the bill was rushed through with only two Tory MPs and one Labour peer dissenting. Subsequently, the much-publicized 'research' was largely discredited, but it had served the purpose for which it was apparently designed.

Meanwhile, the climate engendered by the campaign against video-nasties affected police forces throughout the country, who were raiding video shops and prosecuting owners for X-certified horror movies perceived as 'nasties'. There was a two-year period of utter confusion, as some juries acquitted and others convicted the same film, and a few video traders went to prison for stocking films that had been seen by thousands when on previous cinema release. Acquittals were of little use as precedents, because it was usually unclear whether the jury had brought back the verdict because the film was not obscene or because the defendant had successfully made out the special defence under s 2(4) of the 1959 Act, in that he had not examined the film and had no reason to suspect that it was in fact obscene. Under heavy pressure from organizations representing the retail trade, the Attorney-General finally issued a 'list' of some sixty film titles that the DPP regarded as obscene because of depictions of violence. Retailers who wished to avoid police seizures could collect a copy of the list from their local police station and remove any offending titles. The 'DPP's list' was the first modern example of an 'Index' in Britain; video traders greeted it with relief, although many of the films on the list had been acquitted by juries while others, such as *The Evil Dead*

---

[15] See the chapters by Graham Murdoch and Brian Brown in Martin Baker (ed.), *The Video Nasties*, Pluto Press, 1984, and Michael Tracey, 'Casting Cold Water on the Ketchup', *The Times*, 25 February 1984.

and *Andy Warhol's Frankenstein*, had received critical acclaim. Some of the 'nastiest' films have been intelligently defended as containing a moral message or as depicting brutalities such as rape in order to condemn them and their perpetrators. Even *I Spit on Your Grave*, the most frequently condemned film of this genre, has been defended as doing more good than harm by impressing upon viewers an awareness of how traumatic rape is for the victim.[16] The list became something of an embarrassment as titles on it were acquitted by juries, and some distribution companies considered suing the authorities for defaming them by placing their works on the list.

The confusion among police and retailers in 1984 produced not only the DPP's list, but the tabling in the House of Commons by the Attorney-General of the DPP's guidelines for deciding whether a particular video film is obscene:

> The basic factor is the tendency to deprave and corrupt those who are, having regard to all the circumstances, likely to see it. The DPP therefore has to consider who is likely to view videos taken into the home. While this is ultimately for the court to decide in each particular case, the DPP considers that, in many cases, a significant number of the viewers will be children or young people.

In applying this basic factor, the film is considered as a whole. But each episode has to be examined on its own before being considered as part of the film as a whole. The following questions may be relevant:

- Who is the perpetrator of the violence, and what is his/her reaction to it?
- Who is the victim, and what is his/her reaction?
- How is the violence inflicted, and in what circumstances?
- How explicit is the description of the wounds, mutilation or death? How prolonged? How realistic?
- Is the violence justifiable in narrative terms?

A work is likely to be regarded as obscene if it portrays violence to such a degree and so explicitly that its appeal can only be to those who are disposed to derive positive enjoyment from seeing such violence. Other factors may include:

- violence perpetrated by children;
- self-mutilation;
- violent abuse of women and children;

---

[16] Baker, *Video Nasties*, Ch 3 and 7. See also David Edgar, 'Presumption of Innocence', *New Statesman*, 5 October 1984.

- cannibalism;
- use of vicious weapons (e.g., broken bottle);
- use of everyday implements (e.g., screwdriver, shears, electric drill);
- violence in sexual context.

These factors are not exhaustive. Style can also be important: 'The more convincing the depictions of violence, the more harmful it is likely to be.'[17]

These factors, the Attorney concedes, are not conclusive, and, indeed, for the most part these 'guidelines' are unhelpful generalities. How does the DPP divine whether 'a significant number of the viewers will be children'? If it be true that 'the more convincing the depictions of violence, the more harmful it is likely to be', then television news programmes are likely to be most harmful of all. Is the DPP talking about 'harm' as being constituted merely by fear or shock or horror? The 'following questions' simply beg more questions, and the 'other factors' section lists a handful of subjects that could never be taboo in themselves. The most workable test to emerge from these guidelines is to ask whether a work portrays violence in such a way that its only appeal is to those who derive 'positive enjoyment' from seeing violence. On this basis the DPP should not prosecute in relation to a video that appeals to other tastes or that has a modicum of real merit – even if some members of its likely audience will be attracted only to enjoy the violent scenes.

The Video Recordings Act 1984

The scheme of this Act is to require all video-cassettes destined for public availability and dealing in any respect with sex or violence to be submitted to a designated authority (at present and for the foreseeable future, the BBFC) for classification generally as suitable for circulation and particularly as suitable for various age-groups. The only categories of videogram (including both cassettes and discs) that are exempt from the need to be classified are those that, 'taken as a whole' are:

(a) designed to inform, educate or instruct;
(b) concerned with sport, religion or music; or
(c) video games.[18]

However, a video work in the above categories loses its prima facie exemption if 'to any significant extent' it depicts:

---

[17] Statement by the Attorney General, House of Commons, 23 June 1984.
[18] Video Recordings Act 1984 s 2(11).

(*a*) human sexual activity or acts of force or restraint associated
   with such activity;
(*b*) mutilation or torture of, or other acts of gross violence towards,
   humans or animals;
(*c*) human genital organs or human urinary or excretory functions,
   or is designed to any significant extent to stimulate or encourage
   anything falling within paragraph (*a*); or in the case of anything
   falling within paragraph (*b*), is designed to any extent to do
   so.[19]

The maximum fine for offering to supply a non-exempt video-
cassette without a classification certificate is an extravagant
£20,000; the cost of an application to the BBFC for a certificate is
about £500, depending on the length of the video (the BBFC
charges £5.00 a minute). It follows that most distributors will
prefer to err on the safe side and submit videos for classification if
there is any legal doubt about whether they are exempt. It is,
however, a defence to the criminal charges of supply and possession
for supply of non-exempt and non-classified videos created by ss 9
and 10 of the Act to prove that the accused reasonably believed he
was dealing with an exempted work even if he was not. It would be
'reasonable' for a distributor to act on a legal opinion that a work
was exempt, even if a court subsequently construing s 2 of the Act
were to hold that the opinion was mistaken.

The Video Recordings Act does not affect merely the handful of
films that could be deemed video-nasties: it is a measure ultimately
imposing liability to censorship and classification on the vast majority of cinematic works transferred to video-cassette or disc, which
were required to be submitted to the BBFC in stages between
1985 and 1988.[20] The fact that the work has been made by, or
shown on, television is irrelevant: the Minister of State for Home
Affairs took pleasure in announcing that BBC programmes like
The History Man, *Tinker, Tailor, Soldier, Spy* and *The Borgias*
would require classification before they could be sold to the public
on video-cassettes.[21]

There is no requirement that films that contain scenes of torture,
mutilation or other acts of gross violence need to do so in any
sexual context, and it was clearly envisaged by the Act's sponsors
that videos of current-affairs programmes showing the Falklands

---

[19] ibid., s 2(2).
[20] The Act was phased in over three years, each phase relating to the period during
which film titles were registered for theatrical distribution. See British Videogram
Association, *A Trade Guide to the Video Recordings Act*, 1985.
[21] Mr David Mellor, 14 December 1983, Standing Committee on Video Recordings
Bill (fourth sitting).

War, for example, or scenes of football hooliganism or a nuclear holocaust or acts of terrorism would require certification. So, too, do sex-education videos or any video made by a counselling group about 'human sexual activity', unless it were for the purpose of medical training or not distributed as part of a business.

Section 2 of the Act bristles with problems of interpretation. To claim an exempt status for a video work it is necessary to establish first that 'taken as a whole' it is designed to inform or is concerned with sport, religion, music, etc. (Is *Amadeus* concerned with music, or *The Devils* with religion? A narrow interpretation will probably prevail, excluding feature films from these prima facie exempt categories.) If this question is resolved in favour of exemption, that status is none the less lost if human sexual activity, etc., is depicted 'to any significant extent'. It is not clear whether 'significance' is judged in terms of time taken in the film, or importance to plot, or relates to the extent of the depictions. Must, for example, videos of performances of *Il Trovatore* or *Don Carlos* at Covent Garden be submitted for classification? They show acts of gross violence, which are of great significance to the opera, but which are not 'significant' in length nor shown in 'significant detail'. 'Human sexual activity' presumably excludes nudity, but might (or might not) include simulated orgy scenes in the brothels of *The Rake's Progress* or the gondolas of *The Tales of Hoffman*. Nor is it clear whether the 'acts of force or restraint' have to be associated with sexual activity in the film in question or merely in general estimation. 'Acts of gross violence towards humans and animals' would seem to catch news films of bombings and battles and bullfights. How a court will decide whether films designed to inform about the dangers of sexually transmitted diseases depict human sexual activity to any significant extent, or (if they do not) none the less stimulate or encourage it to any significant extent by promoting the use of prophylactics, remains to be seen. The section is so badly drafted that courts should give defendants who can bring their work within s 2(1) the benefit of any doubt as to whether s 2(2) in fact operates to remove the exemption.

If the videogram is not exempted from classification requirements, the offences of supplying, offering to supply and possessing for the purpose of supply will not be committed where the supply concerned is exempt, or the supplier reasonably believes it to be exempt. The main situations in which non-exempt videos may be supplied without classification certificates are:

- where the video is given away free, and without a business purpose (s 3(2));
- where the video is supplied to people within the industry, (s 3(4)) or for television use (s 3(8)) or to the BBFC (s 3(9));

- where the video is made at some special occasion (e.g., a celebration or a conference) and is provided to those who took part in it or to their friends and associates, so long as it does not 'to any significant extent' depict or simulate 'human sexual activity' or the other matters set out in paragraph 2(2) (s 3(5));
- where the video is dispatched for export to a country outside the United Kingdom (s 3(4)(iii)).

Section 4 of the Act contains its main censorship implication: the Secretary of State is to designate an authority to determine whether works are suitable for classification 'having special regard to the likelihood of (certified) video works being viewed in the home'. This test applies to every video submitted for classification, even those that are to be restricted for sale only in licensed sex shops. In one sense it serves to emphasize the 'target audience' test in the Obscene Publications Act, whereby the court must consider the effect of the work on the potential audience, including persons who would view it in the home. Section 4 requires 'special regard' to be accorded to this fact, and was designed to underline the greater potential for harm by the technological capacity to freeze-frame and replay scenes of sex or violence. The Act does not, as some mistakenly assume, lay down that videos must be 'suitable for viewing in the home' in the sense of being appropriate for family viewing: that would be to negate the whole system of age-classification and point-of-sale restriction. The video must be 'suitable for classification' in a particular category, having special regard to the impact it will have upon persons in that age-group and below through the devices available for home viewing.

Thus, a video work that is suitable for the classification 18 or 18R, given that it will be viewed by adults at home, cannot be refused classification because of the danger that children may obtain access to it when it is left in the home by careless parents. It is quite possible, of course, that the BBFC will in time pay 'special regard' to the mounting research evidence that films and television programmes viewed in the home have less impact on the viewer than they would when occupying concentrated attention in the cinema,[22] in which event s 4 could become a basis for applying less rather than more censorship to video. However, the assumption of Parliament at the time the Act was passed was to the contrary, and the BBFC in its early rulings indicated that films suitable for cinema screenings would require cuts in scenes of violence before being regarded as suitable for video classification. Its reasons for this requirement were based on a misunderstanding of the s 4 test.

---

[22] See Jane Root, *Open the Box*, Comedia, 1986, Ch 2.

It states in its guidelines on violence that: 'where horror material is concerned, we have exercised a restraining influence on the explicitness of gory imagery because of our awareness that children and younger teenagers may be particularly tempted to watch such material . . .'. This is a consideration that goes to age-group classification rather than censorship: s 4 does not justify the deletion of 'gory imagery' from 18 or 18R films because of the danger that they will be seen by children. Parliament could (as some MPs wished) have insisted that *all* videos be suitable for children; it provided a classification system based on the notion of parental responsibility. This system is logically undermined by the BBFC whenever it makes cuts in 18 films on the grounds that younger persons may watch.

The sex-shop category
Section 7 of the Act requires video works to be certified as suitable for general viewing and unrestricted supply (i.e., U, UC, or PG), as suitable only for viewing by and supply to persons who have attained a particular age (i.e., 15 or 18); or 'with a statement that no video recording containing that work is to be supplied other than in a licensed sex shop' (18R). The 18R certificate was introduced by the BBFC in relation to cinema clubs that wished to show sexually explicit films of particular merit or heterosexual 'soft porn'. When the loophole that enabled such clubs to avoid local authority licensing was closed, many councils declined either to grant licences for 'sex cinemas' within their areas, or to license 'sex shops'. Those councils that grant sex shops licences do so sparingly. In consequence, the outlets for 18R videos are extremely limited, and are non-existent in many parts of the country where no sex shops are licensed at all. In 1991 there were approximately fifty licensed sex shops in England, and none at all in Scotland, Wales and Northern Ireland. With this limited market, only one distributor bothered to obtain an 18R classification for a video in 1985.

In its reports for 1988, 1989 and 1990 the Board repeatedly drew attention to the limited number of outlets for 18R videos, and to the time-consuming nature of its task of cutting 18R videos down to satisfy an 18 criterion.[23] The Board made clear that its test for granting an 18R certificate is identical to the 'deprave and corrupt' test in the Obscene Publications Act, and it seeks the advice of the DPP and the Crown Prosecution Service in applying the contemporary standards signalled by current jury verdicts and

---

[23] *Annual Report for 1988* (BBFC, 1989), paras 27–8; *Annual Report for 1989* (BBFC, 1990) President's Introduction; *Annual Report for 1990* (BBFC, 1991) paras 31–6.

prosecution practice. However, the commercial interests of distributors dictate that almost all 'adult' films are submitted for 18 rather than 18R certificates, because the outlets for 18R cassettes are minimal. The Board admits to 'quite extensive' and time-consuming cutting to bring 18R videos to the state wherein they can be certified as 18 – i.e., as suitable for viewing by persons over 18. In effect, the BBFC acts like a prudent pornographer, accepting payment for cutting hard-core videos down to a soft-core 18. For an 18 certificate, the Board judges by a much more severe standard than the Obscene Publications Act requires, and since distributors have stopped submitting videos in the 18R category (the only classification to which the obscenity test alone is applied) the BBFC is operating to deny adults access to lawful material. In 1991 the Board was driven to acknowledge that it was imposing censorship under the guise of classification:

> The paucity of licensed sex shops has meant that few customers wishing to find 'sex articles' have any real freedom to do so in practical terms. The resulting regime is stricter than that of any of our continental partners in the EC, especially when 18 videos conform to a decency test more stringent than that of most 'adult' magazines available in high street stores.[24]

After the new European customs and postal arrangements come into effect in 1992, there will be much more hard-core pornography coming into the United Kingdom. Instead of involving criminal sanctions against its distribution, the BBFC recognizes 'a viable, realistic system of licensed sex shops and 18R videos' is the only logical solution.

Offences
The Act establishes two classes of criminal offences, which punish the supply or the possession for supply of unclassified videos (maximum penalty £20,000) and the supply of classified videos to persons outside the classified age-group, or without classification labels or with false labels, or 18R videos outside licensed sex-shop premises (maximum penalty £2,000). The court has no power to imprison, and the defendant has no entitlement to jury trial. The issues for the court will generally be straightforward and un-cluttered by any need for aesthetic judgement, unless a defendant pleads that he or she had reason to believe the work was exempted from classification under s 2. Magistrates may issue warrants for search and seizure if satisfied that there are reasonable grounds for

---

[24] BBFC, *Annual Report for 1990*, note 23 above, para 34.

suspecting offences, and police may arrest persons suspected of offences under the Act if they refuse to give their names and addresses. There is an appeal against conviction and/or sentence to the Crown Court on ordinary principles. The court may, as an additional punishment, order the videos to which the offence relates to be forfeited – an action more likely to be taken where they are unclassified than where they have merely been mislabelled or sold to under-age persons. There is a special provision (s 21(2)) whereby the court cannot order forfeiture without giving an opportunity to any person other than the defendant who claims ownership of the videos to show cause why such an order should not be made. In accord with section 71 of the Criminal Justice Act 1988, the Court can additionally confiscate any profits made from the offence. The police are not primarily responsible for enforcing the Act; this task falls on trading standards officers.

Packaging rules

The Act and the regulations made pursuant to it lay down detailed requirements for packaging and labelling videos with the appropriate classification symbol. Regrettably, there is no duty to mark a video as an exempt work, although failure to do so will be likely to cause confusion among retailers.

The overall purpose of the regulations is to ensure that no prospective purchaser or borrower is misled as to the suitability for various age-groups of the work or works contained in the recording. It follows from this purpose that where a recording contains a number of separate works (e.g., a feature film and trailers for other feature films), the recording must bear the classification of the work that is least suitable for viewing in the home. This purpose is achieved in terms by s 2 (5)(*b*) of the Video Recordings (Labelling) Regulations 1985, which provides 'where a video recording contains more than one video work in respect of which classification certificates which are not equally restrictive have been issued, the video recording shall be taken to contain only the most restrictively classified video work of these works'. Thus, if a feature film classified as 15 is combined with a trailer classified as 18, the cassette package should be labelled 18, the category of the cassette being in such cases determined by the category of the trailer.

The Institute of Trading Standards has objected to this interpretation, on the ground that the labelling of, say, 15 films as 18 because of an 18 trailer is 'a deliberate attempt to mislead', contrary to the Trade Descriptions Act 1968. A prosecution under the Trade Descriptions Act would be unlikely to succeed, because the labelling accurately identifies the fact that there is restricted content in the recording, and such labelling is required by law. A court could not impose a conviction on a distributor for complying with the law; it would have to imply an additional duty, not merely to label the recording as 18, but also to include a clear statement of the sort 'Feature Film 15; trailer 18'. The failure of Parliament to impose such a duty when enacting detailed legislation would be a powerful reason for a court to refuse to imply such a duty, either through the back-door of the Trade Descriptions Act 1968 or by virtue of any prosecution under the Video Recordings Act itself. However, it is clearly undesirable that distributors should be permitted to exploit the law so as to mislead the public about the nature of the main film on the cassette in order to enhance its saleability. The BBFC and the British Videogram Association have attempted to discourage such sharp practice; failure to do so voluntarily may result in amendments to the regulations.

Consequences
The Video Recordings Act has necessitated a censorship system that goes far beyond the initial concern about video-nasties. It would have been possible to deal with this very limited mischief by legislation that permitted the BBFC, on a complaint by the police or a member of the public, to designate a specific video-cassette as prohibited from public sale. Any subsequent breach of a prohibition order could have constituted a criminal offence, pending a right of appeal by the distributor to a jury. Such a reform, which would effectively have banned the video-nasty without exposing much of the industry to a bureaucratic apparatus of censorship, went entirely overlooked. The worst feature of the new system is that it imposes double jeopardy on video distributors because it keeps alive the power of the police, the DPP and private prosecutors to proceed against the suppliers of certified videos for offences against the Obscene Publications Act. Distributors are in breach of one criminal law if they sell uncertified cassettes, and they may still be in breach of another criminal law if they sell certified ones. No censorship system that permits such double jeopardy holds out much hope of rational enforcement.

There may be other unsatisfactory consequences. At the end of the first seven years of the Act's operation, it appeared that the high classification fees were forcing many distributors to delete less profitable videos from their catalogues, thereby reducing viewer choice, especially in relation to vintage movies. The Act has diminished the degree of explicitness of sex and violence, but not the numbers of cassettes dealing with these themes or the prominence given to them. Distributors are discovering the level of 'acceptable' sex and 'acceptable' violence, and their films are full of it. On the other hand, some films of real worth are not being distributed because the profits from art-house audiences do not justify the classification fee. These fees, which pay for the censorship bureaucracy of the BBFC, are necessarily high; foreign film makers may be able to argue that they constitute a non-tariff barrier to imports from the member states of the EEC and are therefore contrary to Common Market rules.

The British Board of Film Classification

Under the impetus of the Video Recordings Act, the BBFC expanded from a family-sized firm of twelve in 1982 to a bureaucratic organization with a staff of sixty including twenty-eight examiners (several with PhDs) by 1990. It is funded by the film and video industries, through fees paid to obtain classification certificates. Its classification categories are the same for film as for video, although, for reasons given above, a film may require cuts before it can secure a video distribution in the same classification as its cinema release.

In relation to films to be shown in cinemas, the BBFC certificate may still be overridden by local councils (see p. 570), who retain statutory powers to permit certified films, ban certified films or alter classification categories. These arcane powers are now rarely used, except in relation to controversial films whose exhibition is opposed by local pressure groups, but the undesirability of regional differences and loss of respect for the voluntary certification process exerts a conservative influence on BBFC decisions.

As they are issued by a non-statutory body, the BBFC film certificates can afford no legal immunity. Although the Board has stressed that it also takes into account 'the moral position of the film maker towards his own material', this is established by asking, in relation to films depicting violence:

- Is the sympathy of the film maker on the side of the victim or the aggressor?
- Is the process of the violence indulged in for its own sake, rather than to tell us anything significant about the motives or state of mind of the persons involved?
- Does the camerawork or editing belie the ostensible moral stance of the film by seeking to enlist or encourage our vicarious enjoyment of the atrocities portrayed?

Like Miss Prism's view of fiction, the BBFC's view of feature films is that the good should end happily and the bad unhappily. But these generalized statements, like the DPP's guidelines, are little more than window-dressing, giving some rational justification for cuts that are made because the violence is of a kind that turns the examiner's stomach. Films that glorify wars and mercenary operations have been passed without deletions; those that depict extremes of violence will be censored, however 'moral' the context. 'Moderation is a useful ideal, and the process of violence can often be toned down by judicious cutting' says the BBFC, ever so pleased at being able to improve on the cinematographer's art, in its guidelines on violence. The kinds of scene that the BBFC will censor in films and videos cannot be stated exhaustively, but some guidance is afforded by BBFC rulings in recent years: the video version may be cut more severely than the film, because of the dangers believed to stem from freeze-frame and reviewing facilities.

Another special problem with the BBFC's video jurisdiction is that as a statutory body in this respect, its policies are amenable to review in the courts. Although the High Court would refuse to act in cases where there was an appeal provided to the Video Appeals Committee, it might intervene if convinced that the BBFC were giving consent as a matter of course to films that were in breach of the law. No licensing body may give consent to that which is unlawful, and the Greater London Council was once upbraided by the Court of Appeal for applying a test that permitted unlawful films to be exhibited.[25] The BBFC's fear that it may be taken to court on this basis by religious vigilantes may explain why it is extraordinarily cautious on the subject of blasphemy.

What will be censored?

Animals
The Cinematograph Films (Animals) Act of 1937 prohibits the infliction of cruelty on animals during film making. The BBFC has ordered cuts in many foreign films where animals are treated inhumanely, especially in Westerns (where horses are brought down by tripping devices) and bullfights, although not in British films showing fox-hunting. It may be doubted whether these deletions serve to improve animal welfare in overseas countries; occasionally they deprive cinema-goers of scenes that are important to the plot. The test is whether the scene has been staged for the benefit of the cameras, or whether it has occurred in real (or wild) life. In 1989 seven films and thirty-three videos were cut to remove scenes in the making of which the Board's examiners felt that animals had suffered, including depictions of fights between snakes. Emotional as well as physical cruelty to animals may not be seen on British screens: a feature film that depicted a non-life-threatening experiment on a rat by dunking it in liquid oxygen was cut

---

[25] *R v GLC ex parte Blackburn* [1967] 3 All ER 184.

because 'for the rat, it was a traumatic return to the condition of the womb'.[26]

Drug-taking
Scenes depicting the administration of hard drugs, or glamorizing or trivializing the consequences of drug-taking in any way, are censored. There are exceptions made for quality films: Woody Allen was allowed to attempt the inhalation of cocaine for comic effect in *Annie Hall*, and *Christianne F* was permitted to shoot up heroin, albeit in shadow and with three minutes of close-ups deleted, because the overall message of the film was aversive. Absurdly, the comic cocaine-sniffing scene in *Crocodile Dundee* was excised before the film was granted a 15 certificate for video release. The Board's 1989 Report welcomes the Reagan presidency and its campaign against drugs but criticizes (and cuts) films that 'by emphasizing the dirt and danger of the drugs scene create an outlaw culture which attracts precisely those to whom the boredom of a safe but sorry existence is no longer enough'. By 1990 the Board had arrogated to itself a parental 'duty of care' in respect of 'older alienated or defeated members of society . . . to such people the risks of drug abuse may offer a kind of challenge, a rite of passage, for which ordeal the easing of pain and the cachet of outlaw status may seem sufficient reward'.[27] The BBFC expresses such opinions throughout its annual reports, often as a justification for censoring scenes that tell it like it is, rather than like the BBFC thinks it should be.

Criminal techniques
Techniques for picking locks, stealing cars or making Molotov cocktails will be censored, especially from videos (where replays may help to instruct). Combat techniques are 'trimmed' where the BBFC fears a danger of imitation – as in neck chops or ear claps. There is great concern about the importation of oriental fighting methods – scenes with rice-flails are 'banned absolutely', even when they are wielded by teenage mutant Ninja turtles. Particular attention is paid to deleting scenes where everyday instruments such as cigarette lighters and garden tools are used to inflict violence, because the BBFC really believes that viewers might not think of such uses without seeing cinematic examples.

In 1988 the BBFC cut pictures of Ninja death devices, kung fu chainsticks, spiked knuckledusters, metal claws, butterfly knives and lighted aerosols, and was particularly concerned to eliminate

---

[26] BBFC, *Annual Report for 1989*, note 23 above, p. 12.
[27] BBFC, *Annual Report for 1990*, note 23 above, para 27.

pictures of crossbows – 'restricted by law but too photogenic for film-makers to resist'. Crossbows were difficult for armies to resist, too, in many historic battles that film makers may now wish to re-enact. In films set in the modern city the Board is particularly anxious to censor weapons so as 'not to whet the appetite of those for whom the carrying of offensive weapons can provide a sense of power or autonomy in a life of relative powerlessness' (several censors employed by the Board have degrees in sociology).

Children

The Protection of Children Act 1978 makes it an offence to have persons under sixteen participate in 'indecent' scenes in films, or to distribute or advertise movies containing such sequences. The BBFC applies a strict interpretation of this measure to all films submitted, and will require evidence of age if a teenager performs in an 'indecent' scene. After the Act was introduced, the BBFC recalled the film *Taxi Driver* and required a cut in one suggestive sequence involving the twelve-year-old Jodie Foster. Films that show violence against children will also be carefully vetted – not for 'indecency' but for any action that may attract emulation.

   The Board spends much of its time deleting expletives on behalf of children, whom it believes should never hear them until they turn twelve, and then only on very rare occasions until they turn fifteen. Thus swear words are absolutely banned from the unresticted PG category, and allowed only very occasionally in films in the 12 category. The latter category does not exist in relation to video classification, and the BBFC's absurd refusal to classify the most innocuous video as PG if it has one swear word on its soundtrack means that a number of cassettes plainly suitable for general viewing are nevertheless classified as 15. In 1990 the BBFC went so far as to 'test screen' films for audiences of schoolchildren, using them as guinea-pigs to identify and remove 'unpleasant' scenes. Such experiments must be ethically question-able.

   The annual report for 1990 notes that 'rules were drawn up to cover the use of schoolgirl attire in sex videos, and distributors of such material were advised accordingly.'

Violence

The BBFC distinguishes between violence 'of a relatively conven-tional and undisturbing nature' in war films and Westerns, and scenes that 'might lead to highly disturbing imagery being planted in vulnerable minds'. This test is particularly applied to videos, where executions and death agonies are cut before they are classi-fied 18. Half the running time of the cuts made by the BBFC in 1985 involved scenes of violence. The BBFC seeks to distinguish between 'video-nasties' and 'conventional thriller or fantasy horror videos'. On the basis of the approach adopted by the Williams Committee the test is whether 'highly explicit depictions of mutilation, savagery, menace and humiliation are presented for entertainment in a way that emphasises the pleasures of sadism'.

These platitudes offer ample scope for busy, nit-picking censorship. The fate of *Rambo III* may serve as an example. It has been screened uncut to adults (and even teenagers) in America and many European countries. The BBFC, however, insisted on many cuts before it could be screened (for adults only) in the cinema or sold as an 18 video. It was feared that Rambo's weapon-wielding would 'encourage anti-social violence on the streets of Britain', notwithstanding that the film was set in Afghanistan and most of Rambo's military arsenal is unavailable at corner stores. The Board required cuts 'in bloodshed and in glamorization of military weaponry', finding it particularly objectionable that Rambo 'killed, on the battlefield though never at home, with a deadly efficiency which seemed increasingly out of place in a world struggling towards new, more reasonable means of settling international disputes.'[28] These sentiments are all very fine, but is it any business of Mr James Ferman to promote international harmony? The notion that *Rambo III* would provoke fighting in the streets if shown uncensored to British adults is comical. All that the Board seems to be achieving by its fussy 'topping and tailing' of violent scenes is the sanitization of violence – and sanitized violence is more attractive than the real thing. *Rambo III* is on many counts an objectionable film, but all the BBFC has achieved by cutting it is to make its objectionable 'message' more acceptable.

The BBFC's emasculation of *Rambo* appears absurd beside the scenes of massive violence that were family television viewing during the Gulf War. The Board has always been prone to make political judgements about the kind of violence it cuts, and confessed as much when in 1989 it censored the new James Bond film, *Licence to Kill*, before it could be certified 15. Bond films had not previously been expurgated, but the Board admitted that 'the key to this change was the [film maker's] decision to present Bond not as an urbane British intelligence man, but as an embittered vigilante seeking personal revenge . . .'.[29] It cut scenes of a woman being whipped and a man being fed to sharks that would, no doubt, have been perfectly acceptable had the urbane 007 loyally taken these actions in the service of British intelligence.

In 1990 the Board refused to reinstate for adult video release

---

[28] BBFC, *Annual Report for 1988*, note 23 above, para 2.
[29] BBFC, *Annual Report for 1989*, para 20.

cinema cuts it had made in *Lethal Weapon II* because 'the hero indulged his vengeful instincts far beyond the needs of narrative' – a judgement the Board believes itself in a better position to make than the writer or director. More disturbing, however was the Board's approach to Asian films, a category where gangster thrillers are traditionally replete with hi-tech but fantasy violence. The Board is appalled that these films have 'no moral dimension in view' (Miss Prism, again) and regards the popularity of their violence as 'a sad comment on the tastes of the occidental audience, or indeed the ethnic communities for whom these untranslated versions are intended'.[30] This approach is both arrogant and ignorant, and appears to reflect Western prejudices.

Sexual violence
The BBFC believes it is amongst the strictest censorship boards in the world in deleting scenes of violence against women, especially in a sexual context.[31] Scenes of torture, threats with weapons, sexual taunting and forcible stripping have been deleted, because of 'the danger in eroticizing such material for the pleasures of a male audience'. Scenes of forcible sex 'must not be trivialized or endorsed by the context in which they are presented'. Scenes of sexual violence leading to rape are usually reduced, and often excised completely. Standards are noticeably stricter for video than for film: scenes that are 'trimmed' on an 18 film may be cut entirely on an 18 video, to remove even the *idea* of the particular form of aggression.

As the BBFC explains in its 1985 report:

> We are very careful with rape scenes, even those which in the cinema were found justifiable by context. On video, with its technological capacity for selective or repeated viewings, such scenes could lend themselves to viewing out of context, perhaps repeatedly by persons whose fantasy life might incline them to act out such images of forcible sex because of the extent to which they have found them arousing in private. The same is true of sadistic material, even where the point of view of the film as a whole is a critical one. We realize the importance here of balancing freedom against responsibility, but the issues must be faced.

---

[30] BBFC, *Annual Report for 1990*, note 23 above, para 18. And see also para 28, where the Third World is blamed for a proliferation of films abusive of women. Salman Rushdie pointed out, in attacking the Board's ban on *International Guerrillas*, that he had more confidence in the common sense of Muslims than did the BBFC.
[31] BBFC, *Guide to the Video Recordings Act 1984*.

The Board to this extent is prepared to abandon the 'taken as a whole' test in the Obscene Publications Act, and go back to the 'purple passages' approach that applied to books prior to 1959. This may mean that even films of great merit will be cut because of the danger apprehended from a few viewers dilating over replayed scenes of sex or violence. The BBFC has always applied a more liberal test to films of recognized social or cinematic merit, by analogy with the public-good provisions of the Obscene Publications Act, although the same largesse is not shown to video works. In 1991 the Board finally brought itself, after thirteen years, to give an 18 certificate for film screening to Oshima's *Empire of the Senses*, a work of recognized cinematic merit, which it has not approved for video distribution. *Straw Dogs* and *The Exorcist* have been refused BBFC certificates for video sale. At the same time, the Board was confused to find itself censoring films of men being humiliated or beaten by women. This was a new experience:

> . . . as the year ended, the Board had begun to consider whether masochism without a convincing display of sadism as its corrupting partner need always be seen as harmful if it satisfies certain needs. Or may it nevertheless draw novices into a world with dangers ahead? Could it attract or arouse the latent sadism in some viewers? The Board began to seek expert advice . . .[32]

Blasphemy

This has become a serious problem for a censorship body so craving of public support as the BBFC. It risks condemnation from fundamentalist Christian groups if it gives 'approval' to films that distort the Bible story, but its application of a controversial and discriminatory law earns it the contempt of the creative community it also purports to serve. The Board launched a massive public relations exercise in support of *The Last Temptation of Christ* (a Hollywood epic that featured Christ fantasizing on the cross about married life with Mary Magdalene), yet it banned a British video about the *Visions of Ecstasy* of Saint Teresa. *The Last Temptation* was a good deal more explicit than *Visions*, but was also a much more substantial work of cinematic art. *Visions* was banned by the BBFC on the grounds that it was likely to be convicted of blasphemy by a jury, although this was entirely a matter of speculation. The DPP would certainly have striven to avoid prosecuting in the wake of the Salman Rushdie affair (which discredited the blasphemy laws in the eyes of all but fundamentalists and the BBFC).

---

[32] BBFC, *Annual Report for 1990*, note 23 above, para 30.

The Board did make clear that it would equally ban a video that gave offence to Muslims or other major religions not protected by the blasphemy law, but this position only underlines the extent to which it is prepared to censor more heavily than the law of the land requires.

The Video Appeals Committee

Section 4 of the Video Recordings Act requires the BBFC to establish a system of appeal 'by any person against a determination that a video work submitted by him' for certification has been either refused or placed in the wrong age-category. This statutory language ensures that only persons who submit videos for classification can activate the appeals procedure, thereby excluding pressure groups and busybodies, but also shutting out producers and directors who may be aggrieved by cuts consented to by the distributors who have submitted their work for classification. The appeals procedure is available only in relation to videos – it is quite anomalous that there should be no provision for appeal by film exhibitors.

The appellate panel is selected by the BBFC itself, and is not therefore truly independent of it. The present ten members represent a reasonable mix of perspectives, but difficult decisions will hinge on whether the more conservative or more liberal members dominate the five-person appeal panel selected for the particular case. This factor was highlighted in the *Visions of Ecstasy* appeal, when the distinguished novelist Fay Weldon, a member of the Committee who had not been invited to sit on the judging panel, turned up none the less to give evidence in favour of the video. The Committee voted 3–2 in favour of the ban – a verdict that would have gone the other way had Ms Weldon (and perhaps other 'uninvited' liberal members such as Professors Richard Hoggart and Laurie Taylor) been asked to sit in judgment. If the BBFC is serious about the 'representativeness' of its Appeals Committee, it should invite the whole panel to sit on controversial appeals.

The Appeals Committee permits legal representation and may sit in public to hear witnesses. It gives a reasoned judgment, upholding the BBFC decision or indicating how it should be varied. Appeal fees will be reimbursed to successful appellants, but there is no provision for awarding them their legal costs, a deterrent to distributors who can usually obtain the classification category they want simply by making the cuts rather than by appealing them. The Appeals Committee will reconsider the matter afresh, and can substitute its own view of the case rather than merely deciding whether the Board's decision was reasonable. It is a measure of how cosy the relationship has become between the

BBFC and the video distributors that an average of only one appeal a year is taken to the Committee, despite the numerous films that suffer cuts and, in a few cases, outright refusals. The Committee has not, in consequence, been able to afford much guidance for film censorship policy. Its first decision was that a video 'consisting largely of women's nude mud wrestling taking place before a mixed audience in a pub in Devon' was 'suitable for viewing in the home' by adults. In a later appeal it upheld a Board decision that called for 'the removal of all crotch masturbation shots and for a reduction in the self-stimulation of breasts' from a video of a woman undressing, before it could be rated 18.[33]

The Appeals Committee's first real test came with *Visions of Ecstasy*, the video that the BBFC had rejected for certification on the grounds of blasphemy. The Committee accepted the Board's submission that it was under a duty to reject any video that infringed the criminal law, but was divided on the question of whether a jury was likely to convict the makers of *Visions of Ecstasy* for blasphemy. The majority took a remarkably literal-minded approach to the video, finding it significant that the actress was younger than the historical personage (St Teresa did not experience her mystical visions until middle age) and looking for historical evidence to support the film maker's imaginative interpretation of a sixteenth-century nun's mystical trance. The Appeals Committee majority judgment did not even mention the expert evidence that was adduced to show that the film was a legitimate artistic exploration of its theme. Three members of the Committee decided that a jury would be likely to convict; while two members decided that a jury would be unlikely to convict.[34] The decision to uphold the ban on this basis is manifestly illogical: if the Appeals Committee was split, the assumption must be that a jury would also be divided. PEN, an organization representing the country's most distinguished authors and playwrights, condemned the ban as 'a serious betrayal of cultural freedom in the United Kingdom'.

The Appeals Committee unanimously adopted a more robust attitude to its other major test case, when it reversed the Board's decision to refuse a certificate to *International Guerillas*, a James Bond-style epic of the Pakistani cinema that portrayed Salman Rushdie as a mass murderer and torturer. The Board, relying on the *Visions of Ecstasy* principle that it was entitled to reject a work that a jury would be likely to convict of a criminal offence,

[33] BBFC, *Report for 1988*, note 23 above, paras 34–9.
[34] *Visions of Ecstacy* Appeal No 0006, 23 December 1989. See BBFC, *Report for 1989*, note 23 above, pp. 17–20.

rationalized its ban on the basis that the film amounted to a criminal libel on Rushdie. It argued, in its usual pseudo-sociological jargon, that the film 'had the emotional weight and symbolic authority that makes the polarization of good and evil a source of moral support and reaffirmation of communal identity'. The Appeals Committee, however, was more inclined to agree with Rushdie himself, who described the film as a piece of trash. It decided the film had as much 'emotional weight and symbolic authority' as an old cowboy-and-Indian movie, and that not even the most gullible viewer of such escapist entertainment would take it seriously. On this occasion it took into account both the unlikelihood that criminal libel proceedings would, in fact, be instituted (a point the *Visions of Ecstasy* majority had ignored) as well as the improbability of a jury convicting.[35] It may be hoped that this decision will discourage the Board from dredging up arcane criminal laws as an excuse to ban videos. It is noteworthy that the film (pirate video copies of which had been selling for £100 while the ban was in force) was not a commercial success after the appeal, and cinema showings in cities with large Muslim populations were so poorly attended that the legitimate video version was never released.

In the realm of the censors

Lord Harewood, President of the BBFC, boasted in his introduction to its 1988 report of its contribution to 'improving the image of the video industry'. The Board's censorship work (which recently extended to removing a scene from the Hitchcock classic *Psycho* before allowing it to be sold on video) is designed to remove images that depict appalling actions, for fear that those actions might be imitated by suggestible viewers. The result is that a great many films and videos have become suggestive rather than explicit, and it may be doubted whether the supposed danger is any the less. Most viewers, of course, receive such scenes as fantasy, and enjoy them as such: the possibility of an appeal to a few unbalanced minds is the basis for curbing the rights of a majority to view as they please. The public, needless to say, are not informed by any message on the video container that the film they are about to hire

---

[35] The BBFC seems incapable of learning anti-censorship lessons, however. In its report for 1990 it alleges that the appeal was decided against it only as a result of Rushdie's intervention; the Appeals Committee judgment makes plain that it was not decided on this basis. James Ferman, the Board's director, is quoted as claiming that 'originally it had been hoped that the Board's rejection of the video might at least deflect some of the [Muslim community's] hatred from Rushdie to the Board itself' – perhaps the most ludicrous justification for a censorship decision ever advanced.

has been censored. The Appeals Committee is rarely activated, and there is no independent evaluation of the BBFC's work beyond its own self-satisfied annual reports.

The massive apparatus of film and video censorship is perceived as a British aberration in Europe, where erotic and violent movies are screened on television and in cinemas and sold on video-cassettes, without the fuss that attends them here. While the BBFC's guidance to parents has always been welcome, its recent reports are full of the fussy, pseudo-scientific jargon that might be expected from a nanny with a doctorate in sociology. It has become, since the 1984 Act, a fully fledged censorship business: it is anxious to increase its turnover (by finding more reasons for cutting films) and to protect its monopoly (it is desperately worried that European unity will render much of its work irrelevant). In 1990 the BBFC required cuts in 42 feature films and 278 videos, although its censorship impact is very much greater than the figures indicate because the film and video trade generally submit work that has already been expurgated to meet BBFC standards.

Film and video censorship has become a comfortable institution in the United Kingdom. The BBFC even offers to advise on film scripts before shooting begins. The film industry distributors, traditionally motivated by profit rather than principle, having willingly cooperated with the system, recognizing that it protects them from the vagaries of prosecution. They have cooperated to such an extent that many submit videos of films that have been so heavily cut before submission that the BBFC has no role other than to approve self-censorship. For the forty-two videos it ordered cut in 1985, not one distributor bothered to appeal. Yet some of those cuts were quite absurd: 5 seconds were solemnly chopped from the Douglas Fairbanks classic *The Thief of Bagdad*, and 6 seconds from a trailer for the Brando classic *On the Waterfront*, while Walt Disney Productions suffered the loss of 4 seconds from *The Biscuit Eater*, 17 seconds from *The Littlest Outlaw*, 16 seconds from *Old Yeller* and 24 seconds from *Nikki, Wild Dog of the North*. The BBFC justify such cuts on the grounds of 'unsuitability due to the emotional power of the scene, and particularly to its potential for producing nightmares . . .'. On this test, it may one day strangle Bambi's cry of 'mother'.

Chapter 15

Broadcasting Law

The recent history of moral and political censorship in Britain has been characterized by a move from criminal law to statutory regulation. The process began visibly in 1954, when the inauguration of commercial television was deemed to require the establishment of a monitoring body, the Independent Broadcasting Authority (IBA), with statutory duties to ensure that political coverage was balanced and that programmes did not contravene the boundaries of good taste. Equivalent obligations were soon voluntarily accepted by the BBC, with the consequence that all radio and television broadcasting is subjected to a regime of institutional censorship, with rules and 'guidelines' that are of powerful effect, although they lack the force of direct law. In 1984 a new regulatory body was established to oversee cable television operators, and in 1988 the Broadcasting Standards Council was set up to monitor the incidence of sex and violence on television. In 1990 a new Broadcasting Act was passed to provide for the 'deregulation' of broadcasting that is planned from 1993. It replaced the IBA with the Independent Television Commission (ITC), which will ostensibly regulate a new broadcasting environment with 'a lighter touch'. However, the ITC has inherited the IBA's existing duties to ensure balance and to eradicate 'offensive' programmes; it will operate not by previewing and precensoring programmes but by invoking a complicated set of reprisal powers, ranging from warnings to fines to the ultimate sanction of loss of licence.

On what basis should broadcasting be accorded a different legal regime to that governing other forms of publishing? Initially, there was a technological justification, in that there was a limit to the number of frequencies, although 'spectrum scarcity' was never a convincing reason for the BBC monopoly of radio and television. The development of fibre-optic cable systems and the advent of direct broadcasting satellites provides viewers with such a multiplicity of choice that it is difficult to find a principle to distinguish broadcasting law from press law. This was the conclusion of the Peacock Committee, which provided the free market philosophy to fuel the Government's moves to deregulate the medium.[1] The

---

[1] *Report of the Committee on Financing the BBC* (chaired by Professor Alan Peacock), Cmnd 9824, 1986.

Government has been careful, however, to limit the logic of Peacock's approach: his call for the removal of paternalistic constraints on broadcasters fell on deaf ears. In contrast, the 1990 Broadcasting legislation erects more censorship controls over the free market than ever burdened the duopoly. By the beginning of 1992 there were seven bodies (the ITC and BBC, the Radio Authority, the BCC and BSC, and – on competition issues – the office of Fair Trading and Oftel) regulating the media through numerous codes on programming and advertising, at an estimated public cost of £21 million (which does not include the executive, legal and research costs incurred by broadcasters in preparing evidence for the regulators). The provision of greater freedom in terms of access to the medium and wider choice was perceived as requiring less freedom in terms of what can be shown. The duties to demonstrate 'good taste' and 'due impartiality', which were understandably imposed on a television service that supplied only four channels to the entire nation, have been reimposed in almost identical terms on services that will carry dozens of channels, many of them to audiences who pay for the privilege of viewing them. There will be much more on display in the market-place, but the products will be standardized and regulated as never before.

The irony that 'deregulation' under the 1990 legislation means 'more regulation' is a tribute to the perceived power of television to influence as well as to reflect ideas and social behaviour. The tabloid newspapers, which most people read, require no statutory controls, although their impact on moral standards must be much greater than late-night television programmes, which play to self-selecting audiences. Much of the debate over the Act was concerned with the problem of maintaining 'quality' in the market-place, an objective that will be achieved, if at all, by empowering licensing bodies to evaluate the prospective programme performance of applicants rather than concentrating on the highest bidder. The regulation of programme contents by codes and disciplinary bodies in the interest of good taste and good politics does not involve a judgement on their quality but on their potential to shock and disturb. In its first report the Broadcasting Standards Council described television as 'a guest in the home', whose conduct might acceptably become 'more relaxed and informal' as the evening wears on.[2] The Council's paternalistic notion that television exists on sufferance, and owes a duty to behave itself according to social norms extrapolated from opinion polls, does not bode well for independence and creative freedom in the new, 'deregulated' environment.

---

[2] Broadcasting Standards Council, *Annual Report 1988–9*, p. 29.

The purpose of this chapter is to examine the restraints on programme making that operate within media industries, and to explore the avenues that do exist for combating interference by regulating bodies. A licensing system is, by definition, a restriction of freedom of expression, although the guarantee of that right in Article 10 of the European Convention is subject to a crucial proviso: 'This article shall not prevent States from requiring the licensing of broadcasting, television and cinema enterprises.' This exemption permits the establishment of licensing systems, but it does not underwrite specific censorship decisions made by regulatory bodies.[3] The European Court emphasized the importance of this distinction in two cases decided in 1990.

> *Groppera Radio* v *Switzerland*:[4] The Swiss government prohibited a Swiss company from retransmitting the pop-music programmes of an Italian radio station that did not use transmitters approved by international communications conventions. The company claimed that this ban on retransmission amounted to a breach of their Article 10 rights to impart information freely and regardless of frontiers. The court held:

- Popular music and commercials could properly be regarded as 'information' and 'ideas', so that the ban was prima facie an interference with Article 10 rights.
- The provision in Article 10 permitting states to licence broadcasting was of very limited scope and did not amount to an exception to the basic right guaranteed by Article 10. It permitted states to control the organization and technology of broadcasting within their territories, but the licensing measures themselves had to be justified as necessary in a democratic society on the grounds set out in Article 10(2).
- That said, the ban was justifiable under Article 10(2) because it had the legitimate aim of preventing the evasion of international law and protecting the rights of others. The ban was not directed at the content of the programmes and had not been applied by use of disproportionate measures (such as jamming transmissions).

> *Autronic A.G.* v *Switzerland*:[5] The Swiss government this time failed to convince the court that its concern for international telecommuni-

---

[3] The 'freedom of expression' guarantee in Article 10 does not, however, imply a positive right to have advertisements or programmes shown on television: *X* v *UK*, 4515/70, European Commission on Human Rights (1986).

[4] Judgment of the European Court of Human Rights, 28 March 1990, Series A No 173.

[5] Judgment of the European Court of Human Rights, 22 May 1990, Series A No 178.

cations law was justified. It had stopped a company specializing in home electronics from demonstrating how its dish aerial equipment could receive Soviet television programmes picked up from a Soviet telecommunications satellite, on the grounds that international law required the consent of the broadcasting state for such interceptions.

The court held that the freedom of expression guarantee in Article 10 was given to corporations as well as to individuals, and applied to restrictions on the means of transmission and reception as well as to restrictions on the content of programmes. It emphasized that interference had to be convincingly established as 'necessary in a democratic society', and was not persuaded that international law required that every interception from a satellite transmission should have the consent of authorities of the country in which the station transmitting to the satellite was situated. It followed that the restriction could not be justified by the exceptions to Article 10(2), and that the Swiss authorities had breached the Convention.

These decisions inject into British broadcasting law the important principle that decisions by the ITC and the Radio Authority, made pursuant to their licensing powers under the 1990 Broadcasting Act, must not amount to an interference with the public's right to receive information and ideas. Regrettably, the Convention is not itself part of British law (see p. 8), so that such decisions may be challenged on this ground only in Strasbourg, or, if they interfere with the freedom to provide and receive services across EEC frontiers, in the EEC Court in Luxembourg.[6] An exception may be an interference based upon the statutory 'due impartiality' requirement, since s 6(6) of the 1990 Act requires that the ITC rules on this subject 'shall not require detachment from fundamental democratic principles'. An English court could, therefore, be invited to strike down any provision in the ITC's due impartiality code that amounted to an interference with the right to receive information.

Other avenues for appeal are limited. ITC decisions can be challenged when they are based on misinterpretations of statutory duties or when they have been taken in breach of procedures laid down by law. There is little that can be done about BBC directives, other than by processes of negotiation within the Corporation. The most effective form of appeal will not be to the courts at all, but to the public through stories leaked to the press. Censorship is news, and some decisions that appear firm when first made within an institution have been rescinded or ameliorated as a result of public criticism. Executives in the higher echelons of broadcasting organizations generally affect liberal sympathies, and dislike the social embarrassment that follows publicity about censorship decisions.

---

[6] *Procureur du Roi* v *Debauve* 1980 ECR 833.

British broadcasting law is in a state of transition. The IBA and the Cable Authority have been replaced by the ITC but the new body will continue to operate relevant provisions of the 1981 Broadcasting Act and the 1984 Cable Act until the new Channel 3 (ITV) licensees begin broadcasting in January 1993. At this point the ITC will cease to have direct legal responsibility for commercial programmes, and will switch to the 'lighter touch' regime of rebuking companies that deviate from its codes rather than pre-censoring their more controversial programmes.

The Broadcasting Act occupied a great deal of parliamentary time during 1990: it emerged as a massive 291-page document with 204 sections and 22 schedules. This chapter will examine those of its provisions that are likely to impact upon creative radio and television programme-making, and that have a potential for enforcement in the courts. Much of the political debate towards the close of the bill's passage focused upon the 'lawyer picnic' that would be enjoyed as learned friends picked over the new requirements for a 'due impartiality' code, which Mrs Thatcher, at the urging of Tory peers, insisted on providing for in the statute at a late stage. Mr Roy Hattersley, speaking for the Labour Opposition, made a solemn promise to repeal this provision in the event of achieving Government.[7] There are many other sections of the Act that will be brought to the attention of future courts, generally by way of 'judicial review' proceedings, which are limited to ensuring that ministers and statutory bodies such as the ITC and the Radio Authority apply the law correctly and reasonably. Although the point may not deter well-heeled litigants seeking to suppress or emasculate programmes critical of their conduct, or organizations committed to reducing a perceived 'anti-establishment' bias in the media, it must be emphasized that the burden of proving that an ITC or BBC decision is 'unreasonable' is a heavy one. The practical effect of the new code requirements may be that fewer contentious programmes will be produced, while those that are made will be subject to interference by executives nervous about contravening vaguely worded code provisions. The 1990 Act ushers in a broadcasting era in which freedom of expression will be bounded not so much by precise laws as by imprecise codes, drafted and interpreted by Government-appointed bodies such as the ITC and the BSC whose decisions cannot be legally attacked on their merits.

---

[7] See Hansard, House of Commons 25 October 1990, Vol 178 No 162, Col 531. Hattersley predicted that 'right-wing loonies' would constantly be taking the broadcasters to court over the impartiality code. Three months later, the Freedom Association announced that it would commence legal action against the ITC if it did not alter sections of its draft impartiality code.

There will, in consequence, be much more scope for behind-the-scenes pressure, whether by way of a wink or a nudge. It is sad and significant that neither the BSC Code, promulgated in 1989, nor the ITC Code, published in 1991, contains any suggestion that their provisions are to be interpreted in the spirit of the freedom of expression guarantee of the European Convention.

Programme Standards

The law of obscenity

The most dramatic change effected by the 1990 legislation is to apply the Obscene Publications Act to radio and television.[8] This means that persons responsible for a transmission deemed to be likely 'to deprave and corrupt' a significant proportion of its likely audience will, on conviction by a jury, be liable for up to three years' imprisonment. Broadcasting had been specifically exempted from the Act when it was passed in 1959, and it is unlikely that any programme transmitted in the succeeding thirty years would have been found obscene by a jury. However, clean-up campaigners convinced the Government that broadcasters should be subject, like other publishers, to the criminal law of the land, in addition to their liability to fines and loss of licence if they breach the statutory prohibitions against transmitting offensive material (see below). The 1990 law has also removed the broadcast media's exemption from prosecution for incitement to racial hatred (see p. 167).

The general law of obscenity, explained in Chapter 3, will henceforth apply to television and sound broadcasting in much the same way as it is applied to books and films, with a public-good defence, which can be advanced by expert witnesses. No prosecution, however, may be brought other than with the consent of the DPP. There is a special provision in the Act that enables a magistrate to require the BBC or the ITC or the Radio Authority to supply a visual or sound recording relating to a programme that police have 'reasonable grounds for suspecting' has constituted an offence.[9] The power extends only to material that has already been broadcast; it does not enable police to obtain advance copies of programmes expected to be controversial. It is unlikely, given the stringent duties not to cause public offence, that programme makers will be prosecuted; if they are, much will depend on the transmission time of the programme and whether children are likely to

---

[8] Broadcasting Act 1990 s 162 and Sched 15.
[9] Broadcasting Act 1990 s 167.

comprise 'a significant proportion' of viewers. There is a useful
defence for presenters and contributors, who may not be convicted
unless they had reason to suspect beforehand that the programme
would contain material justifying a conviction.[10] A particular
danger is that the DPP may chose to proceed by way of forfeiture
proceedings under section 3 of the 1959 Act, which are decided by
magistrates, rather than by a prosecution, which entitles the defendant to a jury trial. During the committee stage of the Broadcasting
Bill, the Government promised that prosecuting authorities would
not favour forfeiture proceedings.[11]

The statutory duties

The duties imposed by statute on independent television, and later
annexed to the licence of the BBC and echoed in the laws relating
to independent radio and to cable television, were formulated in
1954. They reflect the exaggerated fears of that period about the
advent of commercial television.[12] In an atmosphere where Lord
Reith could solemnly liken commercial television to the black death,
it was understandable that ITV should be placed under the close
scrutiny of a licensing body, required to ensure:

(*a*) that nothing is included in the programmes which offends
against good taste or decency or is likely to encourage or
incite to crime or to lead to disorder or to be offensive to
public feeling;

(*b*) that any news given (in whatever form) in its programmes
is presented with due accuracy and impartiality;

(*c*) that due impartiality is preserved on the part of persons
providing the programmes as respects matters of political or
industrial controversy or relating to current public policy.

This was the IBA's duty under s 4 of the 1981 Broadcasting
Act, and it is a duty that has been inherited by the ITC and by the
Radio Authority under s 6 of the 1990 Broadcasting Act.

In 1964 the BBC Board of Governors undertook to comply with
the same standard:

The Board accept that so far as possible the programmes for
which they are responsible should not offend against good
taste or decency, or be likely to encourage crime or disorder,
or be offensive to public feeling. In judging what is suitable

---

[10] ibid., Sched 15(5)(1).
[11] House of Commons, Standing Committee F on Broadcasting Bill, Official Report
Col 1190 (David Mellor).
[12] See p. 29, where the fears at the time of the inception of the IBA are described.

for inclusion in programmes, they will pay special regard to the need to ensure that broadcasts designed to stimulate thought do not so far depart from their intention as to give general offence.[13]

This undertaking is now annexed to the BBC's licence, although (unlike the statutory duties on the ITC) it may not be legally enforceable as against the Corporation.[14] However, the BBC is now subject to the statutory jurisdiction of the Broadcasting Standards Council, and an ingenious litigant may be able to convince a court to injunct a programme that would manifestly breach the BSC code on taste and offensiveness.

The ITC's duties to secure due impartiality go beyond a general supervision of programme output. They are specifically charged to draw up a code 'giving guidance as to the rules to be observed' and must 'do all that they can to secure that the provisions of the code are observed' (s 6(3)). This duty is somewhat complicated by controversial subsections inserted in s 6 after pressure from Tory peers who expressed grave dissatisfaction at the way in which they alleged the IBA had watered down the due-impartiality duty under the previous legislation. Clause 6(5) requires that the code shall in particular have rules that reflect the need to preserve due impartiality on 'major matters' of political or industrial controversy or relating to current public policy. This confusing subsection leaves open the possibility of a legal challenge to the ITC code on the basis that it does not take sufficient account of the need to ensure due impartiality in minor or routine (as distinct from major) matters of controversy. The Government, however, appeared to think that it would mitigate the need to offer another view in response to every contentious comment:

> The purpose of the wording . . . is to make it clear that we do not expect impartiality to be achieved over every nuance of a matter of political or industrial controversy . . . we would expect that treatment of the Gulf issue, for example, should be handled in an impartial way. But that does not mean that every statement or sentiment expressed about the Gulf should receive some kind of equal and opposite rejoinder.[15]

---

[13] Letter from Lord Normanbrook (Chairman, BBC) to Postmaster-General, 19 June 1964. The undertaking was reaffirmed when the BBC licence was renewed in 1969 and 1981, and the contents of the letter are noted in the prescribing memorandum under Clause 13(4) of the BBC Licence and Agreement.
[14] *Lynch* v *BBC* (1963) 6 Northern Ireland Judgments Bulletin, per Hutton J. *McAliskey* v *BBC* [1980] NI 44.
[15] Government spokesperson (Earl Ferrers), House of Lords, 22 October 1990.

On this footing s 6(5) may eventually be interpreted as no more than an indication that the ITC should concentrate its code (and its enforcement of that code) on the need for impartiality in the case of matters that are 'major' both because of their prominence and because of the important consequences of any decision that must be made over them; issues that could affect electoral votes or be the cause of a crippling strike are obviously matters that require a stricter 'balance' in current-affairs programmes than new policy ideas or familiar debates about manners and morals. This is the approach in fact taken by the ITC code on impartiality, which indicates that 'major matters' relates to political or industrial issues of national importance 'such as a nationwide strike or significant legislation passing through Parliament' or for licensees serving a regional audience, issues of comparable importance within their region'. On such questions, licensees must 'ensure that justice is done to the full range of significant views and perspectives'. This approach is supported by the concluding words of s 6(6), which require the rules to 'indicate that due impartiality does not require absolute neutrality on every issue or detachment from fundamental democratic principles'. This permits broadcasters to bias their programmes in favour of life, liberty and the pursuit of happiness; even if (say) the resurgence of racism becomes a 'major matter' of political controversy, impartiality will not be 'due' to the racist side of the argument.

The late amendments to the Act were particularly designed to narrow the exemption from the 'due-impartiality' requirement provided by s 6(2), namely, that in applying the requirement 'a series of programmes may be considered as a whole'. Section 6(5) now requires that the ITC shall make specific rules as to what actually constitutes a 'series'; what time limit shall be imposed before a 'balancing' programme is transmitted (s 6(6)(c)); and as to the publicity that should be given to the balancing programme so as to ensure that it reaches a similar audience (s 6(6)(d)). These subsections are designed to concentrate the minds of the ITC and its licensees, and (while not purporting to interfere with programme content) to send a clear signal that any current-affairs or feature programme that presents a controversial viewpoint should not be made (or, if made, should not be transmitted) unless or until a balancing programme is well under way. These provisions are most likely to affect current-affairs programmes like *World in Action* and *This Week*, which will need to find space in their schedules for a programme to balance any that is deemed to lapse from the standard of due impartiality. It is nonsensical to expect a current-affairs team that has come to a particular conclusion about a subject of political controversy to make another programme supportive of a conclusion they do not believe to be justified by the evidence, yet some politicians undoubtedly believe that the 'series' provision should require another *Death on the Rock* supportive of the Government claims about that incident and another *Who Bombed Birmingham?* (which in 1987 portrayed the 'Birmingham 6' as innocent) portraying the 'Birmingham 6' as guilty. The answer to this dilemma is to confine the 'series' qualification to 'personal view' programmes that have been labelled as such, and to argue that a due degree of impartiality has been provided within the give and take of the current-affairs feature, even if its treatment of the evidence (necessarily, a fair treatment) has favoured a particular side of the controversy. Whether this approach will be sufficient to satisfy the courts remains to be seen.

Enforcement against the IBA/ITC

The statutory duties may be enforced by the Attorney-General, as guardian of the public interest, although no case has occurred in which he has been minded to bring an action in the High Court either to stop the IBA from screening a programme or for a declaration that it was wrong in law for it to have allowed a programme to be shown. However, the courts have permitted two private citizens to bring actions against the IBA, on the somewhat tenuous basis that, as licence-holders, they may be directly affected by screenings in breach of a statutory duty.

The first case, *Attorney-General ex rel McWhirter* v *IBA*,[16] concerned a documentary about the life and work of Andy Warhol.

> Although senior IBA staff had ordered a number of deletions from the programme, it had not been personally vetted by the eighteen members of the authority at the time its scheduled transmission was injuncted by the court on the strength of sensational newspaper publicity. Subsequently, it was viewed and approved by all IBA members and the court declined to hold that their decision was unreasonable, although it sternly reminded them of their duty to ensure that 'nothing' is included in any programme that offends good taste. 'These words', Lord Denning emphasized, 'show that the programme is to be judged, not as a whole, but in its several parts, piece by piece', although the court did concede that each 'piece' could be judged according to the purpose and character of the whole programme. It stressed the personal duty laid on each member by the legislation – a duty that could not be delegated, at least in controversial cases, to members of the IBA staff.

The *McWhirter* case was overlooked by the IBA when its new Director-General and his staff approved transmission of the controversial film *Scum* without referring this decision for Board approval:

---

[16] [1973] 1 QB 629.

Scum was the film of a play that had previously been banned by the BBC because of its explicit scenes of violence in a borstal. The Director-General of the IBA and his staff approved it for transmission on Channel 4 at 11 p.m. with a warning about the violent scenes. They did not, however, refer it to the IBA Board for its approval prior to transmission. The High Court declined to hold that *Scum* was so offensive to public feeling that no reasonable licensing body could allow it to be shown, but it declared, in reliance on *McWhirter*, that the failure to refer the matter to the Board for approval was unlawful. The Court of Appeal, however, took a much more relaxed view of the IBA's approach to its statutory duties. It was entitled to rely on its experienced staff and the system it had established (involving monitoring, audience reaction studies and continuous discussions) to provide sufficient compliance with the statutory duty. The Court of Appeal warned potential applicants for judicial review that the mere fact that one blatantly offensive programme might slip through the IBA's safety-net would not mean that it was in breach of its duty – any such finding would require evidence that the Authority was not maintaining a satisfactory system of safeguards.[17]

Both *McWhirter* and *Whitehouse* emphasize the difficulty of challenging a regulatory body's decision on its merits: once the body has approved a transmission (whether before or after it has taken place) the courts will be hard put to stigmatize the decision as irrational or perverse. Moreover, the approach in *Whitehouse* takes a much more permissive attitude towards the IBA's procedures for complying with the statutory duties, which Lord Donaldson MR described as being:

> none of them precise. All require value judgements . . . Parliament was creating what might be described qualitatively as a 'best endeavours' obligation and was leaving it to the members [of the IBA] to adopt methods of working, or a system, which in their opinion, was best adapted to securing the requirements set out in the section.

In effect, the courts should intervene only when convinced that the system adopted by the regulatory body was so bizarre that no reasonable person could believe it would assist in maintaining programme standards at the general level required by the Act. The Court of Appeal's description of the statutory duties of the IBA may also have put paid to fears that members of the ITC could properly be joined in any prosecution of a television company or programme contractor for assisting breaches of criminal law. A general supervisory duty cannot carry personal liability for aiding and abetting a programme transmitted in breach of the law unless

---

[17] *R v IBA ex parte Whitehouse* (1985) *The Times*, 4 April CA.

there is both knowledge of the illegal content of the programme and a positive encouragement to transmit it. In exceptional cases these elements may be present, but normally the regulatory body can safely leave such questions to the television companies and their legal advisers.

The ITC has inherited the same statutory duties as the IBA, but within a framework that will make the Commission reasonably safe from legal challenge. The IBA's duty, under the 1981 Act, was 'to satisfy themselves that, so far as possible, programmes broadcast by the Authority comply . . . [with the statutory duties]'. Under the 1990 Act, however, the ITC will not itself broadcast programmes – it merely licenses television stations to do so, and enforces the terms of its licence agreements by penalizing them if they fail to observe the statutory duties, which are amongst the terms of the licence. Under s 6 of the 1990 Act, 'The Commission shall do all that they can to secure that every licensed service complies with [the statutory duties] . . .'. This is a somewhat weaker 'best endeavours' clause, and it follows from *Whitehouse* that the ITC will be amenable to judicial review only if it were to turn a blind eye to programmes from a television station that persistently caused public offence. If, for example, it were to do nothing about persistent criticism from the Broadcasting Standards Council directed at a particular station, the Council itself would have the standing to take the ITC to the High Court over its inaction. After *Whitehouse* it is difficult to imagine the courts interfering with the ITC's interpretation of its statutory duties, although they might intervene if the ITC imposed a disproportionate or unjustified punishment (such as a massive fine or revocation of licence) for a trivial breach or failed to produce a code on impartiality that satisfied the requirements of the Broadcasting Act.

The ITC must interpret its duties in respect of programme standards in the context of other general duties imposed upon it by the statute. Thus, it has a duty to provide the public with programmes of 'high quality' and 'wide range' that are 'calculated to appeal to a variety of tastes and interests'.[18] It must additionally encourage 'innovation and experimentation' on Channel 4, and see to it that programmes on this channel 'contain a suitable proportion of matter calculated to appeal to tastes and interests not generally catered for' by other commercial channels. It follows that the Commission may permit greater latitude in taste and potential offensiveness to programmes of obvious merit or those directed at particular minorities, or those that are screened on Channel 4. Although the

---

[18] But compare the Broadcasting Act 1981 s 2 with s 2 of the 1990 Act. The IBA's duty 'to secure a wide showing or hearing for programmes of merit' is not imposed on the ITC.

1981 Act's general provision for public-service television (defined as the dissemination of 'information, education and entertainment') is not repeated in the 1990 legislation, any court would be required to give full force to the ITC's basic duty to provide the public with programmes of diversity and quality. This duty is set out in s 2 of the Act, which is headed 'Function of Commission'. It requires the Commission to discharge its functions 'in the manner which *they consider* [our italics] is best calculated to ensure' programmes that, 'taken as a whole', are of high quality and wide appeal to a variety of tastes and interests. It follows that any legal challenge to the ITC must confront the plain parliamentary intention to make the Commission the judge of what will best serve the public interest, and it will be difficult to convince a court that the ITC has acted perversely in any decision taken in pursuance of its legitimate powers under the Act.

The Broadcasting Standards Council

The Council was established in 1988 as a 'watchdog' body to monitor the levels of sex and violence on television, draw up codes for broadcasters, adjudicate complaints from listeners and viewers and try to devise ways of stopping satellites from transmitting European erotica into British homes. By 1989 it had acquired a Chairman (Lord Rees-Mogg), a Director-General and a staff of 12, and was busy recruiting 2,000 'television monitors' throughout the country who would send reports on sex, violence and bad language to its headquarters at 'The Sanctuary', next door to Westminster Abbey. The establishment of the BSC was greeted with some derision and a certain amount of trepidation. There was hardly any urgent necessity for such a body: the IBA and the BBC had generally erred on the side of caution in maintaining strict rules about transmission of sex and violence, and the BSC was perceived as a political response to the Government's anger over certain current-affairs programmes. It is another external pressure upon broadcasters to bring their professional judgement (about what the public interest requires to be seen) into line with official judgements about what the public does not need to be shown.

The Council is given statutory life by virtue of s 151–161 of the 1990 Broadcasting Act. Its powers to monitor programmes, conduct research into the effects of portrayals of sex and violence on radio and television, and to represent the Government at international conferences concerned with broadcasting standards are unlikely to give any cause for concern. Its codes, however, are another matter. They are to define general standards of taste and decency for television programmes, and to lay down the practices that must be followed in connection with the portrayal of sex and violence. Broadcasting bodies have a statutory duty to reflect the BSC rules in their own codes. This gives the BSC considerable power to influence the content of programmes: the ITC will not only be required to adopt its rules but also expected to punish television services that breach them. The BSC's first Code of Practice was published in 1989 and consisted of well-meaning and somewhat meandering generalities to which few could take exception. However, as it builds up 'case law' from its adjudications of complaints it is likely that some sections of the code will generate hard and fast rules.

The Council is empowered to hear and adjudicate complaints from members of the public who allege lapses in taste or decency in radio or television programmes. Complaints must be made within two months (twenty-one days for radio) of transmission, whereupon it may call for a recording of the programme from the BBC or the licence holder. If it decides to hold a hearing about the complaint, it must invite both the organization that transmitted the programme and 'any person who appears to be responsible for the making or provision of that programme' to make submissions. The 1990 law requires such hearings to be in private unless the Council decides otherwise – a regrettable presumption against the 'open-justice' principle that undermines the purported object of the Council to promote public debate and involvement in media standards. The BSC may require broadcasters about whom the complaint has been made to publish its findings 'in such a manner and within such period' as it may direct. These powers and procedures are virtually identical to those that have applied to the Broadcasting Complaints Commission, and it may be assumed that the Council will direct publication by way of an announcement at a time that will be likely to reach at least some of the audience who watched or heard the offending programme. The power to direct publication is not limited in this way, and the Council might require a broadcaster to take advertising space in a national newspaper to publish the details of its offence. (In 1989 the BCC required a local radio station to advertise its judgment in a newspaper circulating in the locality.) The power to direct publication is not confined to cases where a complaint has been upheld, and it is difficult to understand why broadcasters who have not been found at fault should be obliged to yield valuable air-time to announcements about rejected complaints. Another anomaly results from the Council's power to initiate complaints of its own motion:[19] it will be difficult for broadcasters to believe that they will obtain a fair hearing from a body that acts both as prosecutor and judge.

---

[19] Broadcasting Act 1990, s 154(7).

There can be little doubt that the BSC will exert an important influence over television standards in the future. Its codes must be incorporated into the standards issued by broadcasting bodies, and all licence holders must undertake by contract to comply with them. The sanction for disobedience may initially be no more than a 'mogging' – a criticism issued by Lord Rees-Mogg, which will be given some degree of publicity. The BBC will suffer no further adverse action, but companies holding ITC licences may find themselves liable to further punishment as a result of the ITC's powers to fine them, or to reduce or revoke their licences. How many 'moggings' will it take to earn a fine, or a revocation?

The BSC issues its adjudications on public complaints in regular monthly bulletins. In 1991 its decisions were criticized from all sides, most memorably when it rejected a complaint against the BBC from a Mrs Whitehouse of Essex over the eventual screening of Roy Minton's play *Scum*, thirteen years after it had been made, and between the hours of 11.45 p.m. and 1.20 a.m.[20] It defended the broadcasters over their decisions to show a little of the carnage of the Gulf War in news bulletins, and ironically undermined its own rules about bad language with a survey that showed that the word 'fuck' was fast losing its power to shock and offend viewers.[21] It upheld complaints whenever the broadcaster or the ITC acknowledged a mistake had been made – usually in scheduling the controversial programmes before or shortly after the watershed (which is regarded as permitting a gradually increasing trickle of permissiveness, and not as a flood-gate). However, in a number of respects the BSC displayed both an ignorance of the nature of television and an intention to damage it as a medium for providing education, information and entertainment:

- It condemned as 'unacceptable for showing at any time' scenes from the award-winning and ITC-approved Australian film *Salt Saliva Sperm and Sweat*, shown by Channel 4 between 11.20 p.m. and 12.10 a.m. This philistine adjudication, in respect of a brilliant and provocative television film, demonstrates how 'the shock of the new' can be too shocking for the old at the BSC, despite overwhelming artistic merit.[22]
- Nor will artistic merit save acknowledged writers and directors if they choose to advance their drama with realistic action that the BSC finds violent or erotic, in some cases long after the watershed. The works of Stephen King (*Children of the*

---

[20] *BSC Complaints Bulletin*, October 1991, p. 15.
[21] Andrea Millwood Hargrave, 'A Matter of Manners – The Limits of Broadcasting Language', BSC, 1991.
[22] *BSC Complaints Bulletin*, October 1991, p. 5.

Corn),[23] Catherine Cookson,[24] John Irving (*Hotel New Hampshire*)[25] and David Lynch (*Twin Peaks*)[26] were all condemned on this score.

- The BSC has shown no understanding of the importance of live television. It twice condemned live broadcasts from the Edinburgh Fringe, and its obsession with 'good manners' made it condemn the makers of *After Dark* for not blacking out Oliver Reed's crude and boorish behaviour towards American feminist Kate Millett, when this behaviour was actually proving the point she was making in a discussion of 'men and violence' (as well as amounting to absorbing midnight television, a consideration the BSC never takes into account).[27]

- The BSC rulings have constantly interfered with the examination of censorship decisions. When Channel 4 presented a very late night 'banned' season on this subject, the BSC retrospectively declared that three of its offerings should indeed have been banned: scenes in *Sex and the Censors* (a story of the work of the BBFC) were 'wholly unacceptable', while *Damned in the USA* (an account of American responses to the work of Robert Mapplethorpe) and the feature film about Wilhelm Reich (*WR – Mysteries of the Organism*) 'went beyond acceptable limits'.[28] Although it may be understandable that censors of the world should unite – they have nothing to lose but their jobs – these adjudications failed to recognize that the programmes had an honest rather than a prurient purpose.

Some of the BSC's decisions have been manifestly silly. It solemnly upheld a complaint by the Reptile Protection Trust that Monty Python veteran Michael Palin had been unfair to snakes by selecting a live one to be skinned and eaten in a Canton restaurant while going *Around the World in 80 Days*.[29] In 1992 it condemned a satirical sketch in *Alas Smith and Jones*, quite missing the point of the satire, and condemned *Baywatch*, a series about life on the beaches of California, because 'there appears to be an emphasis on the presence on the beach of young women rather than young men'. More worrying is its evident desire that popular drama and comedy should reflect conventional social and moral attitudes. For example, it upheld a complaint about a repeat of a *Butterflies* episode (first broadcast without complaint eight years before the advent of the BSC) with the following story-line:[30]

Parents returning from a short holiday discover that their adult sons have been smoking marijuana with their friends. The father is

---

[23] ibid., June 1991, p. 3.   [24] ibid., August 1991, p. 2.   [25] ibid., May 1991, p. 5.
[26] ibid., April 1991, p. 6.   [27] ibid., July 1991, p. 2.   [28] ibid., pp. 9–13.
[29] ibid., November 1991, p. 2.   [30] ibid., October 1991, p. 4.

particularly upset by this revelation and challenges the brothers, who seek to justify their behaviour as an escape from the boredom and penury of unemployment. The father points out the hazards of drug-taking and after some amusing exchanges with their mother, the brothers promise that they will not resort to drugs again. The final scene shows the mother, who is facing her own personal crisis, smoking a reefer.

The punch-line particularly distressed Lord Rees-Mogg, because it was thought to 'encourage an attitude of tolerance towards the taking of drugs'. The BSC would feel much happier if popular television ignored social problems entirely, like the soap opera *Neighbours*, one of the few regular programmes against which there has not been a single complaint.

One aspect of the BSC's behaviour that has deservedly attracted serious complaint from programme makers is its failure to give them any opportunity to defend their programme before it is made the subject of censure. This failure arises from the BSC's defective understanding of the requirements of fairness, and from an oversight in the drafting of the Broadcasting Act. Section 155(4) requires that where the BSC holds a hearing, it must invite any person responsible for the making of the programme to attend. However, there is no provision for such a person to be notified, or to make submissions, where the BSC determines to decide the complaint without a hearing. In practice, the BSC usually decides to uphold or reject complaints without a hearing – it has unshakeable confidence in its own opinions – so that the programme maker's defence is never heard. Only the broadcasting body – the BBC or, in the case of commercial television and radio, the ITC/ Radio Authority and the broadcasting company – are notified of the existence of a complaint, and sometimes required to provide a written statement in answer. These statements are not always supportive of the programme – the ITC, in particular sometimes condemns it. After *Sex and the Censors* – made for Channel 4 by a reputable independent production company – was criticized, its director complained:

> The BSC never entered into any discussion with us about the programme and has, it seems, only used as witnesses the most hardened critics of the programme – who were incidentally only a handful of people even though over two million people watched the programme and did not rise up in moral outrage. In the BSC's courtroom there is no defence lawyer. Nor has the BSC thought it appropriate to furnish us with the results of its adjudication. We had to discover our 'sentences' in the newspapers.

The BSC, a statutory body, is amenable to judicial review, and its decisions upholding complaints reflect adversely on the reputation of programme makers. It has a legally enforceable fundamental duty of fairness to 'hear the other side', if only by way of written submissions, so the High Court could be expected to quash any decision adverse to a programme made without inviting such a submission from its maker.

Apart from its complaints function, the BSC busies itself with other duties, notably 'continuing discussions with overseas colleagues' on the threat to British susceptibilities posed by reception of soft-core pornography from European satellites. It will in due course represent Britain in the standing committee that will be established by the European Community to settle disputes that arise under the EC Directive and Convention on coordination of television activities (see p. 641). Sections 153 and 157 of the 1990 Broadcasting Act empower the BSC to commission research into public attitudes to portrayals of sex and violence and to the potential effects of such portrayals on attitudes and behaviour. This power it has used with great relish but little judgement, spending some £200,000 each year on 'research'. This takes such forms as subjecting fifty-two people to interviews about their 'media-based fantasies'; using 'new and innovative computer techniques for analysing the language used in "in depth" discussions with over eighty women, forty of whom will have been subjected to sexual and domestic violence' about their feelings towards television drama; publishing a 'lively debate' between children aged between eleven and thirteen on 'sex-role stereotyping on television and attitudes to marriage, religion, sex and the future'; and commissioning public opinion polls that reveal that 74 per cent of respondents did not subscribe to the view that all television programmes should be suitable for children'.[31] The BSC has clearly been a boon to underemployed sociologists; it must be hoped that their 'research' is less fatuous than it appears from the BSC's annual reports.

The relationship between the BSC, on the one hand, and the ITC and the Radio Authority, on the other, is jurisprudentially curious. Both are statutory bodies, created by the same legislation (the 1990 Broadcasting Act). The ITC has a general duty to secure the exclusion from licensed services of any offence to standards of taste and decency (s 6(1)) and a specific duty to draw up a code giving guidance as to the rules to be observed with respect to depiction of violence (s 7). The Radio Authority has parallel duties (ss 91–2). These bodies, together with the BBC (which has no

---

[31] BSC, *Annual Report 1989–90*, pp. 29–32.

statutory duty to impose codes, but has done so for many years) are amendable to the jurisdiction of the BSC in relation to public complaints about their services, and are required by s 152(3) to reflect in their codes 'the general effect' of codes drawn up by the BSC in relation to the portrayal of violence and sexual conduct, and standards of taste and decency. They are required to cooperate with the BSC in its adjudication of complaints, and to publish its verdicts, but the statute is silent about what (if anything) should follow a breach of the BSC code. Amongst the proliferating codes, it is entirely possible that a programme will be found in breach of a BSC rule but not an ITC/BBC/Radio Authority rule, or vice versa. Indeed, on several occasions broadcasting authorities have supported programmes that have been subsequently condemned by the BSC; in so far as this condemnation involves a question of principle extrapolated from the BSC code, it would appear that s 152(3) would require the broadcasting authority to reflect the 'general effect' of the BSC principle when next reviewing its own code. In the following section the effects of the existing and overlapping codes of practice promulgated by the BSC, ITC, and BBC are summarized: it may not be too much to hope that the present proliferation may ultimately be reduced to 'one big code' that can be adopted by all bodies relevant to broadcasting.

The Codes of Practice

The watershed hour

The statutory duties are elucidated by the Code of Practice issued by the BSC in 1989, covering all television and radio, and by the ITC covering ITV and Channel 4. At the heart of the BSC code is the dilemma of balancing the rights of adult viewers against the social dangers that adult viewing may harm children and those who are 'psychologically frail'. Although the majority of households in Britain do not contain children, over half the children in Britain aged five or over have a television set in their bedroom.[32] This dilemma is resolved by the reference to the 'watershed hour' of 9 p.m. by which time young children are assumed to be both in bed and too tired to operate the remote control switch. This assumption is acknowledged to be somewhat optimistic, especially for Friday and Saturday nights, but the utility of 'the watershed' is that general awareness of this turning point alerts parents to their own responsibilities in exercising discretion as to their children viewing

---

[32] ibid., pp. 24–5.

programmes after this time.[33] Moreover, 9 p.m. is not a turning point so much as a fulcrum, with programmes 'graduating their demands on the audience as the evening progresses and as the expectations of the audience develop'. The BSC endorses a 'family viewing policy', which the IBA has described in the following terms:

> The policy assumes a progressive decline throughout the evening in the proportion of children present in the audience. Within the progression 9 p.m. is fixed as the point up to which the broadcasters will normally regard themselves as responsible for ensuring that nothing is shown that is unsuitable for children. After 9 p.m. progressively less suitable (i.e. more adult) material may be shown, and it may be that a programme will be acceptable for example at 10:30 p.m. that would not be suitable at 9 p.m. But it is assumed that from 9 p.m. onwards parents may reasonably be expected to share responsibility for what their children are permitted to see. Violence is not the only reason why a programme may be unsuitable for family viewing. Other factors include bad language, innuendo, blasphemy, explicit sexual behaviour, and scenes of extreme distress.[34]

This policy must be borne in mind in considering the codes, insofar as they relate to 'good taste' and the need to avoid public offence. The guidance in relation to the specific duties imposed on broadcasters may be summarized as follows.

'Offending against good taste or decency'

Some assistance may be derived from the definition of 'indecency' in the criminal law (see p. 148). The concept relates to what is likely to shock, disgust or revolt ordinary people. It must, however, be remembered that there is a distinction between what shocks and disgusts in real life, and what is likely to have that effect when shown as part of a television programme. The context is all-important, and much material will lose its capacity to turn the stomach if it is incorporated in a programme for the bona fide purpose of illuminating discussion. Thus clips from video-nasties have been permitted in a programme about the desirability of

---

[33] Research undertaken by the Council in 1989 indicates that 80 per cent of parents knew of the 'watershed' policy and 70 per cent would identify 9 p.m. as the significant time (see *Annual Report* note 31 above, p. 16).

[34] This policy is emphasized in the ITC Programme Code (February 1991). 'Progressively less suitable' (i.e. more 'adult') programmes may be shown until 5.30 a.m. when 'family viewing' is assumed to begin.

amending the obscenity law, and racist jokes allowed in a programme about the social consequences of certain forms of comedy. The BBC overlooked this crucial distinction when it refused to allow *The Late Show* to show a picture of the 'foetal earrings,' whose exhibitor's conviction for 'outraging public decency' was the subjet of a panel discussion. It was the actual display of the earrings in a public place that had 'outraged decency', and not a picture of them, which would never have been prosecuted. Newspapers made the BBC look foolish by publishing pictures to illustrate their reports of the court case.

The subjects that the BSC finds the most tasteless are:

Bad language

This gives rise to the most complaints to broadcasting authorities. The BSC regards 'bastard' (a term of affection in Australia) as 'a word whose repeated use generally appears to arouse deep resentment in a majority of people'. Words and phrases with sexual origins should be used only with the greatest discretion: 'The abusive use of any of the synonyms for the genital organs, especially the female organs, or of "fuck" and its derivatives should be permitted only after reference to the most senior levels of management.'[35] The ITC Programme Code requires any use of bad language to be defensible in terms of context and authenticity, while 'the most offensive language should not be used before 9 p.m.'

Sex and nudity

The BSC recognizes that 'nudity, provided that it in no way exploits the nude person by presenting him or her simply as a spectacle, can be a legitimate element' although it warns that nudity 'as a prelude to or aftermath of sexual intercourse' can be justified only by the merit of the individual programme, and that 'half undressed young women' should be used 'sparingly' in light entertainment. In drama 'producers should consider carefully whether the degree of explicitness they plan is justified by the context in which it occurs. Explicitness ought not to be warranted simply by the youth and physical attractiveness of the protagonists, for that can reduce the audience to the status of voyeurs. Actual sexual intercourse between humans should at no time be transmitted.' Actual sexual intercourse between animals, birds and particularly insects is permissible, and probably mandatory in any programme made by David Attenborough. The ITC Programme Code urges that sex and nudity be presented with tact and discretion:

---

[35] Code of Practice, p. 43.

'Representation of sexual intercourse should be reserved until after 9 p.m. Exceptions to this rule may be allowed in the case of nature films, programmes with a serious educational purpose, or where representation is ungraphic.'

Race, religion and disabilities

Racial stereotyping and derogatory racial references should be avoided unless warranted by the context. Religious sensitivities must be borne in mind, and the use of 'Christ' and even 'God' as an expletive should be actively discouraged. Care should be taken in the depiction of people with disabilities, especially to avoid any hint of exploitation in charitable appeals. The ITC Programme Code requires the avoidance of 'patronizing expressions' such as 'handicapped' and 'crippled with', while disabled persons must always 'use' rather than 'be confined to' a wheelchair. The Code urges avoidance of jokes that play upon exploitation or humiliation, and extends this consideration to other minorities, homosexuals and members of minority religious faiths. It portrays no concern about the exploitation or humiliation of women.

'Likely to encourage crime or lead to disorder'

The evidence that portrayal of criminal conduct on television programmes has a 'copycat' effect is not conclusive. However, the BSC is fully in agreement with Oscar Wilde's Miss Prism, whose definition of 'fiction' was that the good should end happily, and the bad, unhappily. Even in factual reporting of violent crime 'programmers should not glamorize the criminal or his actions. The use of nicknames for violent criminals which may soften their image should be discouraged ... defendants should not be presented as heroic figures or the stuff of legends.' Relations and associates of criminals should not 'in general' be paid for retelling their stories.[36] The ITC programme code provides detailed guidelines for television companies on the treatment of crime and anti-social behaviour. The following subjects are discussed.

Interviews with criminals

Interviews with criminals are likely to run the risk of infringing this section of the Act, and there always needs to be careful consideration of whether or not such an interview is justified in the public interest.

---

[36] ibid., p. 26.

Interviews with people who use or advocate violence or other criminal measures

Any plans for a programme item that explores and exposes the views of people who within the British Isles use or advocate violence or other criminal measures for the achievement of political ends must be referred to the licensee's chief executive before any arrangements for filming or videotaping are made. A producer should therefore not plan to interview members of proscribed organizations, for example members of the Provisional IRA or other paramilitary organizations, without previous discussion with his or her company's top management.[37]

Hijacking and kidnapping reports

It would almost invariably be wrong to broadcast any information, whether derived from monitoring of communications or from any other source, that could endanger lives or prejudice the success of attempts to deal with hijacking or kidnapping.

Demonstration of criminal techniques

In programmes dealing with criminal activities, whether in fictional or documentary form, there may be conflict between the demands of accurate realism and the risk of unintentionally assisting the criminally inclined. Careful thought should be given, and, where appropriate, advice taken from the police before items are included that give detailed information about criminal methods and techniques.

Presence of television cameras at demonstrations and scenes of public disturbance

News editors and producers will be conscious of the need to be on guard against attempts to exploit television. Every effort must be made to place what is being seen and heard in context, so that viewers can properly evaluate the significance of activities that have arisen from the hope of television coverage. Incidents known to be 'manufactured' for the cameras should either be excluded or revealed for what they are.

The test of whether a programme or sequence is 'likely to encourage or incite to crime or to lead to disorder' needs little analysis. Anything that 'incites' *a fortiori* 'encourages'. The 'disorder' referred to must have an element of lawlessness. It is not enough for the Authority to be satisfied that a programme would lead

---

[37] This advice must be read in the light of the Home Secretary's ban on broadcasting interviews with members of certain organizations (see pp. 27, 445 and 630). Until the end of 1992 the ITC remains responsible for publishing such programmes, and will insist on approving them in advance.

viewers to take to the streets in protest meetings or demonstrations: that is their lawful right. Nor is it enough to fear that such demonstrations might occasion a 'degree' of disorder by virtue of their size or the angry feelings of their participants. In the context in which it is used in the statute, the 'disorder' to be guarded against seems to be civil lawlessness and mob violence. Thus, a film about a protest movement would not be objectionable if viewers swelled protest rallies, but only if it led them to go further and to join sorties involving civil trespass on, or criminal damage to, the property of others.

There is no guidance in the statute as to how many persons must be encouraged to criminal acts or disorder before the Authority should intervene. Parliament could not have meant the suppression of programmes that might incite one or two mentally unstable persons to crime. It may be that there must be the danger of a general encouragement to reasonable viewers before the prohibition should be invoked. In construing similar legislative language in the Obscene Publications Act (a tendency to deprave and corrupt likely viewers) the Court of Appeal interpolated 'a significant number' of likely viewers.[38] This would be a useful gloss on the s 4(1) duty. 'Significant', of course, may mean much less than 'substantial', but it is none the less a yardstick that excludes reactions from any 'lunatic fringe' of viewers. On this basis, the test is whether, on the balance of probabilities, the programme or sequence in question is likely to encourage a numerically significant number of persons who would view it at the hour of transmission to engage in criminal or lawless conduct.

Quite apart from the BSC and ITC codes, journalists should be aware of criminal law provisions that affect the interviewing of criminals on the run. A prison escapee must not be given any assistance designed to hinder his recapture,[39] while a person known to be guilty of an 'arrestable' (i.e. moderately serious) offence must not have his arrest or prosecution impeded.[40] Except in the case of persons believed to be involved in terrorism,[41] there is no positive duty to provide information or assistance to the police, but any payment of money, provision of a 'safe house' or assistance with travel outside the jurisdiction may amount to an offence. It is also an offence to use a wireless receiver to intercept police messages, or to publish information about messages intercepted without authorization.[42]

---

[38] *R v Calder & Boyars* [1969] 1 QB 151.
[39] Criminal Justice Act 1961 s 22.
[40] Criminal Law Act 1967 s 4(1).
[41] Prevention of Terrorism (Temporary Provisons) Act 1989 s 18; see p. 444.
[42] Wireless Telegraphy Act 1949 s 5.

Violence

The most intractable problem in television scheduling is the possible impact on children of realistic violence. British television averages 2.2 violent incidents in each hour of transmission, predominantly in progrmmes imported from America.[43] Although research is inconclusive, there is some evidence that brutality associated with screen heroes may encourage youthful emulation, and that constant exposure to television violence may weaken moral inhibitions against resorting to force as a means of problem solution.[44] The codes outlaw 'gratuitous' violence and close-up details of assaults and murders, and discourage the depiction of torture techniques capable of easy imitation. They accept the desirabilty of avoiding scenes that might cause viewers unnecessary anxiety or disturbance, a prospect thought more likely if violence occurs in realistic contemporary settings than in historical contexts or stylized settings.[45] Concern about the largely uncontrolled and unpredictable effects of television violence is understandable in relation to glamorized popular serials and movies, but it has less relevance to contemporary features and current-affairs coverage, which may serve to arouse compassion for the injured and anger against the injurer. The BSC is concerned about the possibility that regular exposure to acts of violence (whether real or fictional) may 'desensitize' the audience and make it apathetic towards cruelty and brutality and is worried about the 'copycat' effect. Although neither proposition can be conclusively established, its code strives to minimize the dangers.

Reportage

There should be no concentration or 'lingering' on the casualties of war or crime. Only in the rarest circumstances should broadcasting dwell on the moments of death. There should be no description of methods of suicide. Even historic footage of death or disaster (the street execution of a Vietcong sympathizer, the explosion of *Challenger* over Cape Canaveral) must be used with caution.

Drama

The question is always whether the violence is 'legitimate' or

---

[43] See the *Report of the Committee on the Future of Broadcasting* (chaired by Lord Annan), HMSO, 1977, Cmnd 6753, Ch 16 para 10.
[44] Professor J. D. Halloran, 'Research Findings on Broadcasting', Annan Report, note 43 above, Appendix F. See also *Violence and the Media*, BBC Publications, 1988.
[45] See Anthony Smith, *British Broadcasting*, David & Charles, 1974, pp. 239–45.

'gratuitous'. There must be no confusion between 'violence used in pursuit of a legitimate objective' (which 'can be a badge of courage and leadership') and 'illegitimate violence, the kind perpetrated by villains'. The latter is apparently acceptable in Westerns, because of 'the eventual triumph of the good characters'. There must be no dwelling on any pleasure a villain obtains from inflicting pain, nor on the sexual aspects of any violent incident, and producers are particularly warned to avoid violence that involves animals.[46]

Warnings
The ITC Programme Code requires clear warnings, prior to the screening of violent programmes, that viewers may find some scenes disturbing. Its guidelines are less specific than those issued by the BSC, but it rejects the 'sanitization' approach adopted by the BBFC, pointing out that it may be just as dangerous to conceal or minimize the consequences of violent behaviour as to show them in gruesome detail. It warns against depiction in 'family viewing' time of dangerous behaviour easily imitated by children, while 'ingenious or unfamiliar methods of inflicting pain or injury, which are capable of easy imitation' should not be included in dramatic works.

Drink and drugs

Programmes must not encourage smoking – e.g., by associating it with sophistication – and 'people taking part in discussion programmes should be discouraged from smoking as far as it is reasonable to do so'. (Is it 'reasonable' to refuse to supply ashtrays in television studios?) Drinking must not be portrayed as a badge of adulthood, and nothing should be done to imply tolerance towards the taking of drugs.[47]

Privacy

The media must take particular care not to take advantage of people at a time when they are in deep shock, e.g., in the aftermath of a disaster or at funeral services. The BSC's generalized remarks on the subject of privacy are not as helpful as the ITC's Programme Code, which deals with common problems confronting broadcasters. The ITC rules may be summarized as follows:

● Invasion of privacy must always have a public-interest justification.

---

[46] See generally the Code of Practice, pp. 23–33.
[47] ibid., pp. 48–9.

- Particular care must be taken against intruding upon situations of bereavement and personal distress. Sensationalism and insensitivity must be avoided.
- When recording the words spoken or action taken by individuals in public places, these must be sufficiently in the public domain to justify their being communicated to a radio or television audience without express permission.
- Specific consent should generally be sought for filming in hospitals, factories, schools and other 'closed' institutions. Inmates whose appearance is not 'incidental' should also be asked to give consent.
- When by reason of handicap or infirmity a person is not in a position either to give or to withhold agreement, permission to use the material should be sought from the next of kin or from the person responsible for the individual's care.
- Interviews of conversations conducted by telephone should not normally be recorded for inclusion in a programme unless the interviewer has identified himself and the general purpose of the programme, and the interviewee has consented. The 'rare exception' may be approved by the licensee's senior management if it involves the investigation of criminal or disreputable behaviour.
- The use of hidden cameras and microphones to record individuals secretly is acceptable only where such evidence is essential to establish the credibility and authority of the story, and where the story itself is clearly of public interest.
- Any interviewing of children requires care. Children should not be interrogated to elicit views on private family matters.

'Due accuracy and impartiality'

Section 6 of the 1990 Broadcasting Act requires the ITC to ensure that news is presented with 'due accuracy and impartiality' and that 'due impartiality is preserved' on the part of programme providers 'as respects matters of political or industrial controversy or relating to current public policy'. It was this provision that sparked the most serious attacks on broadcasters during the passage of the new legislation. Many Tory peers and MPs are convinced that the existing statutory duty is regularly breached by anti-Government elements in broadcasting organizations, and must be strengthened by statutory provision for immediate rights of reply, discussion programmes and counterbalancing documentaries transmitted within a short time of any 'partial' programme, and by giving the BSC the power to condemn any lapse from strict objectivity. Some who agree with them, like Lord Chalfont, believe that the solution lies in rigid and detailed codes formulated by the new authorities and backed by the 'strong sharp tooth' of their new punitive powers.[48] During the passage of the legislation the Government strengthened the due-impartiality duty by requiring the ITC to promulgate and enforce a code on the subject, although it did not specify the rules that this code should contain. In February 1991 the ITC produced its Programme Code, which contains special provisions for achieving due impartiality. These provisions will be enforced, like the rest of the Code, by a contractual commitment made by licensees to abide by them, on pain of suffering a range of sanctions that the ITC is empowered to impose.

In its original formulation section 6 required only impartiality in respect of matters of 'current' political or industrial controversy, thereby permitting a degree of partisanship in historical programmes. But elderly peers detected an 'insidious' intention behind the amendment to make the bill 'a charter for revisionist historical programmes' about events they could still remember, and the Government quickly backed down, its spokesman expressing the hope that 'long dead historical political controversies, like the repeal of the Corn Laws' might not, in practice, be subjected to the impartiality rules.[49]

The due-impartiality duty is subject to the important caveat that 'in applying the subsection . . . a series of programmes may be considered as a whole'.[50] This caveat has allowed the IBA to sanction a programme or series of programmes that is 'committed' to a politically controversial subject, so long as other programmes on the same channel at similar times present the other view. Thus a John Pilger documentary that presented the case for unilateral disarmament was allowed to be screened after Central Television had undertaken to make and transmit a documentary presenting the opposing view. The ITC Code defines a 'series' as a sequence of programmes that share the same title or deal with the same issue, and requires licensees who intend to take advantage of the 'series' exemption to link the programmes by an announcement at the time the first is presented and to broadcast a balancing programme within a reasonable time. It emphasizes that the 'series' exemption cannot justify a licensed programme by reference to programmes on other channels, or to publicity in other media, that present the opposite view. The Code narrows the 'series' exemption as a means of presenting minority viewpoints. However, it introduces the concept of 'impartiality over time', whereby a licensee may be able to demonstrate that opposing views have been

---

[48] Hansard (House of Lords) 11 July 1990, col 380.
[49] ibid., col 391, Earl Ferrers.
[50] Broadcasting Act 1990 s 6(2).

sufficiently aired in the course of frequent attention to a controversial issue. This approach is not appropriate for a currently active political controversy, but may be adopted in respect of continuing debates (such as the move towards monetary union in Europe).

'Personal view' programmes

An important exception to the due-impartiality requirement is the 'personal view' programme, which must be clearly labelled as expressing the personal opinion of its presenter. These may take the form of a series, in which a broad range of personal views and perspectives are expressed (not necessarily on the same subject) or by balancing a particular personal-view programme with a right-to-reply programme or a studio discussion. This will at least permit committed, partial and provocative views to be aired, although the ITC insists that licensees ensure that statements of fact are accurate and that opinions expressed, however exaggerated, do not rest upon false evidence.

The term 'due' is significant in the phrase 'due impartiality'. In the past it has allowed the IBA the power to approve one-sided programmes if the side taken is generally acceptable. Thus the ITC will not be required to secure impartiality on matters such as drug-trafficking, cruelty, racial intolerance or other subjects on which 'right-thinking people' are largely unanimous. The BBC, too, claims that there can be no duty to balance the claims of 'basic moral values', defined by Sir Hugh Greene as 'truthfulness, justice, freedom, compassion and tolerance'. In this respect, for once, the present Government has endorsed the broadcaster's approach. As the Home Office minister explained during the debates over the due-impartiality provision in the Bill:

> Due impartiality means that there may be higher considerations which need occasionally to override the requirement of absolute impartiality. Broadcasters should not be expected to be impartial between truth and untruth, justice and injustice, compassion and cruelty, tolerance and intolerance, or even right and wrong. How can one be impartial on such matters? Broadcasters should not be obliged to be morally neutral as well as politically neutral.[51]

This approach is emphasized by the injunction in s 6(6) that the ITC rules 'shall, in particular, indicate that due impartiality does not require absolute neutrality on every issue or detachment from fundamental democratic principles'. One of the most fundamental

---

[51] Hansard (House of Lords) 11 July 1990, col 366.

democratic principles is freedom of expression, and the ITC code emphasizes at the outset that 'broadcasters are free to make programmes about any issue they choose', subject only to the obligation of fairness and respect for the truth.

The ITC code makes special reference to the attainment of 'due impartiality' in the following contexts.

Drama and drama documentary

The measure of impartiality 'due' from plays and films that deal with matters of political and industrial controversy is not the same as must be expected from current-affairs programmes. 'Drama documentaries', however, are more problematic, and any reconstruction of actual and recent events 'must not be allowed to distort the known facts'. The evidence upon which dramatic reconstructions are based 'should be tested with the same rigour required of a factual programme'. Where dramas and documentaries point to a conclusion about current controversies, due impartiality should be secured by providing an opportunity for the airing of conflicting views, e.g., in a subsequent studio discussion programme.

Factual programmes

Due impartiality is secured by 'the fair representation of the main differing views on the matter'. This does not mean that balance is required in a simple mathematical sense, or by giving equal time to each conflicting view, but rather that the programme taken as a whole should avoid giving a biased treatment to any one point of view.

Interviews

Where interviews are conducted on issues that fall within the due-impartiality provisions, they must not be edited to distort or misrepresent the known views of the interviewee. The interviewee must not be taken by surprise in relation to the format of the programme or the use of his or her contribution. The Code provides little assistance in the common situation where spokespersons for one side of an issue decline to accept an invitation to debate it. The ITC says that this 'need not prevent the programme from going ahead', although often it does because 'an impartial account of the subject under discussion' must still be given. There has been some evidence of groups and persons refusing to appear on television to justify their contentious actions, and then decrying the resultant lack of balance; such a situation demands an exception from any rigorous application of the due-impartiality provision.

Enforcing the Codes

Both the BBC and the companies supervised by the ITC and the Radio Authority will be subject to rulings by the BSC (on matters of sex and violence and public offence) and by the BCC (on questions of privacy and fair treatment – the latter concept overlapping with the due-impartiality test). The ITC and the Radio Authority will, in addition, be expected to monitor and enforce compliance with their own codes. Until the end of 1992 the ITC will remain in law responsible for publishing the programmes on ITV and Channel 4; it will therefore insist on being consulted about controversial programmes and on previewing any that are likely to give offence.[52] From January 1993, however, the licensing system will come into operation, and the ITC and the Radio Authority will no longer be legally responsible for programme content. It will thenceforth be the responsibility of the licensed companies to decide whether to transmit programmes that may be accused of breaching code provisions. Although the ITC will be prepared to give general guidance on the interpretation of its code, and will monitor the programmes by licensees, it will not preview programmes or approve specific script proposals.[53] The code will be enforced by a set of sanctions, ranging from a rebuke to a revocation of the licence (see p. 636).

The IBA's methods of securing due impartiality by previewing and 'vetting' controversial programmes were often criticized. Instead of a detached and supervisory role, it at times became deeply involved in the editorial and creative process, casting a blanket of pre-censorship over current-affairs programmes. The Annan Report[54] deplored the fetters on initiative and imagination caused by intermeddling with programmes prior to broadcast. The ITC will have no powers to preview controversial programmes or require script changes, but it has a formidable array of punishments to mete out to programme service providers who fail to ensure due impartiality. It will be interesting to see whether television executives who have complained about IBA interference in the past will

---

[52] Until the end of 1992 the ITC is bound by the provisions of s 4 of the 1981 Broadcasting Act, containing the statutory duties of 'good taste' and 'due impartiality', which it must impose on ITV and Channel 4: see Broadcasting Act 1990, Sched 11, Part II, para 1(3). The ITC Programme Code published in February 1991 will serve as a code in relation to violence (required by s 5(1) of the 1981 Act) and as guidelines in relation to other matters covered by the statutory duties.

[53] See the Broadcasting Act 1990 s 11(2). The licensee must retain a recording of every one of its programmes for up to three months and produce it at the ITC's request.

[54] Annan Report, note 43 above, Ch 12, paras 7 and 10; and also Ch 4 paras 29–31 and Ch 13.

go cap in hand to the ITC for the very same 'advice', which in the IBA days took the form of a directive. The consequences of a mistake may be regarded as sufficiently serious for the ITC's 'advisory role' to become indistinguishable in practice from the IBA's old 'supervisory role'.

The BBC

The BBC has undertaken to comply in general terms with the statutory duties placed upon independent television. This undertaking has no legal force, and no action could be brought by the Attorney-General to oblige it to comply, although the undertaking is given a prominent status by being annexed to the Corporation's licence agreement and it is possible to argue that the undertaking is an 'implied term' of the licence, so that the High Court may supervise the BBC's compliance.[55] Normal BBC censorship operates by a process of 'reference up' the Corporation hierarchy. Any producer who foresees possible offence must alert middle management, which may pass borderline cases to departmental heads, who may in turn consult the Managing Director or even the Director General. The Controller of Programmes has explained:

> The elimination or alteration of material considered unsuitable for public broadcasting is an integral part of a whole system of editorial control ... Reference is obligatory in matters of serious dispute or matters of doubt, and the wrath of the corporation in its varied manifestations is particularly reserved for those who fail 'to refer'.[56]

Internal directives are issued from time to time about programme content, especially in relation to sex, violence and drugs. The 'middle ground' is occupied by avoiding extreme political views and ensuring that controversial opinions are 'balanced' by dispensation of conventional wisdom either in the same programme, or over a series. Censorship is slightly relaxed for Radios Three and Four:

> We assume Third Programme listeners are discerning and intelligent enough to make a conscious choice of what they listen to and, if they find something not to their taste, that they are adult enough to recognize that tastes differ and that the programme has been broadcast because other adult minds believe in its quality.[57]

---

[55] See note 13.
[56] 'Control over the subject-matter of programmes on BBC Television', *Report of Joint Committee on Censorship of the Theatre*, HC 255, 1967, Appendix 3, p. 113.
[57] ibid., Appendix 2, 'Control over the subject-matter of programmes on BBC Radio'.

'Gratuitous' bad language or behaviour is 'eliminated' when not essential to plot or purpose, and four-letter words chanted by football crowds are solemnly edited out of *Match of the Day*, but the Corporation promises to strike the balance in favour of creative freedom where it is exercised for genuine or socially redeeming purposes. Broadcasters, it is said, know honesty and quality when they see it: 'Subjectively most people – and certainly most broadcasters – are well aware when a writer, in trying to convey his perception of the truth and reality, is being honest in conveying sex, violence and blasphemy.' Some BBC censorship decisions have led to doubt about whether these platitudes are any more applicable to television executives than to policemen or judges. *Brimstone and Treacle*, a morality play by a renowned television dramatist about the dilemma of reconciling the existence of both God and evil, was vetoed at the highest level although it contained no single scene that was offensive or in poor taste, and it was subsequently made into a successful feature film. It was not blasphemous at common law, because it lacked any element of indecency or scurrility. But its anti-Christian overtones, and particularly its portrayal of the Devil doing good, upset the Chairman of the BBC, who maintained that 'the whole central theme of the play . . . would outrage viewers in a way that was unjustifiable'.[58] The play was finally screened in 1987, ten years after it was made, without any public complaint.

Political pressure
That the BBC is more vulnerable to political pressures than the IBA/ITC may be seen by comparing the Corporation's behaviour in relation to *Real Lives* in 1985 with the IBA's stand over *Death on the Rock* three years later. Both programmes were condemned, in advance of being screened, by cabinet ministers who believed them to be supportive of terrorism. The IBA permitted *Death on the Rock* to go ahead as scheduled, defended its making and its makers, and set up an independent inquiry, which completely exonerated them from the Government's allegations.[59] The BBC's Board of Governors overrode the views of its top executives and withdrew *Real Lives*, thereby damaging the BBC's reputation for independence from Government. The programme was subsequently screened with a few face-saving deletions, but the damage had been done.

There has been a certain reluctance within the Corporation to devote investigative resources to stories that might directly

---

[58] Letter from Sir Michael Swan (Chairman, BBC) to Ben Whitaker (Chairman, Defence of Literature and the Arts Society), 25 March 1976.
[59] Windlesham/Rampton Report on *Death on the Rock*, Faber, 1989.

undermine Government policies, and which are tackled with more enthusiasm by quality newspapers and independent television. The Corporation's independence from Government, which is so vital to the reputation of its external services as the purveyor of unbiased news, suffered a further blow in 1985, at the same time as the *Real Lives* affair, when it was revealed that a security service official, Brigadier Ronnie Stonham, occupied room 105 in Broadcasting House and was employed to 'vet' staff appointments and promotions. Several distinguished journalists had been blacklisted from Corporation jobs as the result of MI5 influence. It also emerged that for many years political journalists and other senior staff had been obliged to sign the Official Secrets Act, and that all staff at Bush House (Headquarters of the BBC's overseas broadcasting network) had been routinely required to sign the Act. This obligation, which has, in any event, no legal force and has never been imposed on journalists working for the press and independent television, seems to have been a grave error of judgement on the part of BBC management. (The Corporation has now promised to end security service vetting and to put room 105 to a use more consistent with its proclaimed independence.) Ironically, the BBC's tarnished reputation for independence and integrity was partly restored a year later when its offices were raided by the police during the Zircon affair, and the Conservative Party Chairman made a much-publicized accusation of left-wing bias in its coverage of the US bombing of Libya. These accusations were baseless and promptly rebutted by the BBC, but the fact that they were made at least demonstrated to the outside world that the Corporation was not, like many national broadcasters, merely a tool of Government.

Programme rules
The rules for journalists working in BBC news and current-affairs programmes are set out in a published index, which states general principles and emphasizes the importance of 'referring up' difficult ethical or legal questions.[60] The index stresses the need to avoid causing unnecessary distress and anxiety (by withholding names of accident casualties, for example, until the next of kin have been informed) and cautions against the use of concealed recording equipment except in the investigation of activities that 'would be widely regarded as illegal or anti-social'. Chequebook journalism is deplored, unless 'the intended contribution is on a subject of general interest of which the criminal has special knowledge'. The approach to questions of fairness and balance is similar to that in

---

[60] *News and Current Affairs Index*, BBC, 1984.

the ITC Programme Code summarized above. The Corporation accepts that there can be no duty to balance the claims of 'basic moral values'. In race reporting, journalists are urged to consider public interest and relevance: 'Race tags' should not be applied in cases where somebody's race is only incidental to a story and mentioning or dwelling upon it could be provocative. Where a person's race is germane, however, 'the BBC should not flinch from identifying it'.

In showing images of violence the BBC rules require a judgement on whether the purpose of screening is sufficiently important to outweigh audience objections. The balance to be struck, once again in Sir Hugh Greene's felicitous words, is 'between what is true and what is tolerable'. The approach, again shared by the ITC, is set out in the report of a working party headed by Monica Sims.[61] Its recommendations include:

- A story should not be chosen just because violent action film coverage is available.
- Dead bodies should not be shown in close-up, and film should not dwell on close-up pictures of the grief-stricken in the wake of natural disasters and man-made violence.
- In reports of violence on the streets care is needed to ensure that racial tensions and local feuds are not exacerbated.
- The use of cameras should be as inconspicuous as possible so as to avoid inciting violence among partisan groups and exhibitionist hooligans.
- Details of suicides and rape cases should be withheld.
- News coverage should scrupulously avoid the musical and other conventions of fictional violence, horror and crime, and stories should never be sensationalized.

The BBC draws a distinction in its response to police requests for 'news blackouts' on political sieges and hijackings on the one hand, and private kidnappings on the other. The former have a strong claim to news value, and police requests are acceptable only when clearly necessary to avoid risk to life or harm to innocent people. The public's right to know applies with less force to private kidnappings with little political or social significance, and the BBC endorses the 'guidance' on the subject issued by the Home Office in 1976 after consultations between Sir Robert Mark and media representatives. This recognizes that:

- the onus is on the police to justify to the media a request for withholding information;

---

[61] *The Portrayal of Violence in Television Programmes*, BBC, 1979.

- requests should be confined to material whose publication may put human life in jeopardy (the fact that disclosure might impede police operations is recognized as being insufficient justification in itself);
- wherever possible an indication should be given to the media of the nature of the information they are being asked to withhold;
- the period of an agreed blackout should not exceed forty-eight hours at a time, with the police being required to justify each request for an extension;
- reporters should be kept regularly and fully briefed to enable them to report the story in its entirety once the news blackout is lifted; an embargo on reporting should not be regarded as an embargo on journalistic activity.[62]

Government controls

The powers of Government ministers to direct the BBC and independent television and radio to broadcast particular announcements and, conversely, to ban particular programmes or classes of programme are set out in Chapter 1 (pp. 26–8). The power (contained in clause 13(4) of the BBC licence, s 29(3) of the 1981 Act and s 10(3) of the 1990 Act) is all embracing, save for the qualification that it could not be deployed by the Home Secretary so as to require broadcasters to broadcast matter that would involve them in a breach of their statutory duties, or to deny them the right to disclose that such a directive had been given. It follows that these powers cannot be invoked by the Home Secretary for secret censorship or to manipulate the news by prohibiting its presentation with due accuracy and impartiality. The Master of the Rolls has noted that the duty to preserve due impartiality has to be interpreted in a real world in which 'there will always be obstacles to giving every shade of opinion equal air-time', and that 'it is not self-evident that any impartiality is due to those who support or excuse attempts to achieve political change by terrorism'.[63] A Government directive that seriously affected the presentation of news could be challenged by virtue of its unlawful conflict with the statutory duty to present news accurately.

In 1988 the Home Secretary acted directly to ban:

---

[62] *Index*, note 60 above, p. 48. See also Steve Chibnall, *Law and Order News*, Tavistock, 1977, pp. 186–94.
[63] *R v Secretary of State ex parte Brind* [1990] 1 All ER 469, at p. 481, CA.

any words spoken, whether in the course of an interview or discussion or otherwise, by a person who appears or is heard on the programme in which the matter is broadcast where:

(*a*) the person speaking the words represents or purports to represent a specified organization, or

(*b*) the words support or solicit or invite support for such an organization.[64]

The organizations concerned are the IRA, the INLA and other banned organizations, Sinn Fein, Republican Sinn Fein and the Ulster Defence Association. The ban does not apply to coverage of parliamentary proceedings or local, parliamentary and European elections.

The directive creates several anomalies: the words of Gerry Adams cannot be broadcast, but they may be read by a newscaster. His words can be freely broadcast in support of an election candidate, but not the day before the election period officially begins. Old footage of his speeches that had been previously broadcast cannot be repeated. Sinn Fein has dozens of local councillors and on the literal wording of the ban they could not feature in a programme about local affairs, even if it has no connection with republicanism. The Home Office hastily 'reinterpreted' its ban to say that representatives of one of the specified organizations could be broadcast if they were speaking in some other capacity.

The ban was upheld as a reasonable exercise of ministerial powers by the House of Lords in 1991. By this time some broadcasters had acquired the courage to make a nonsense of the ban by dubbing actors' voices that accurately mimicked the voices of the terrorist sympathizers over pictures of them speaking their words. In these circumstances the Law Lords expressed surprise at the minimal scope of the ban.[65] Although the European Commission has rejected a complaint over breach of Article 10 by the much more extensive broadcasting ban in the Republic of Ireland (which precludes all interviews with Sinn Fein members), this decision was based upon a state's 'margin of appreciation' to decide whether particular measures are necessary and effective in the combat of terrorism.[66] The arbitrary and footling nature of the British ban cannot reasonably be described as either necessary or effective to combat the IRA.

A Government directive will require the ITC to direct licence-holders to take the specified action, and their compliance will be

---

[64] Directive by Home Secretary of 19 October 1988 under Broadcasting Act 1981 s 29(3) (now s 10 of the 1990 Act) and Clause 13(4) of the BBC's charter.

[65] *Brind* v *Sec of State for Home Dept* [1991] 1 All ER 720.

[66] *Betty Purcell* v *Ireland*, European Commission of Human Rights, 16 April 1991.

made a condition of their licence. If any were to refuse, on principle, to comply with what they perceived as political censor-ship, the ITC would presumably be expected to revoke their licence. The ITC must also insert a condition into television licences requiring holders to transmit party political broadcasts under whatever conditions the ITC determines.

Appointments

One unnecessary, and indeed unpleasant, power that the Govern-ment has added to the 1990 legislation is its new right to veto an ITC appointment to the board of Channel 4.[67] This channel com-menced as a subsidiary of the IBA, which appointed its board members without Government interference. Under the new arrange-ments Channel 4 will become a statutory corporation, with board members appointed by the ITC subject to Government veto. As it is hardly conceivable that the ITC would seek to appoint a person who is professionally unqualified, it may be assumed that Govern-ments that exercise the veto will do so on political grounds. There is some evidence that political considerations have affected appoint-ments to the BBC's Board of Governors and to membership of the IBA.[68]

Listed events

The Government has reserved to itself the more benign power of listing events of national interest that must not be monopolized by 'pay-as-you-view' channels. Section 182 of the 1990 Act requires the Home Secretary's list to be drawn up after consultation with the BBC, ITC, the authority that will regulate television services for Wales, and the holders of the rights to the event. There is to be no bar on pay-as-you-view screenings that take place at least forty-eight hours after the event. Although sporting events such as Wimbledon and the Grand National are the primary candidates for protection, 'national interest' is defined to include English, Scot-tish, Welsh and Northern Irish interests, and the list is not confined to major sporting fixtures. It may be doubted whether the Home Secretary will condescend to list the Miss World competition, although any attempts to purchase exclusive rights to King Charles's coronation would certainly provoke Government interven-tion.

The Government has also reserved a specific power to order any broadcasting body (including the BBC and the BSC) to 'carry out any function' required to enable the United Kingdom to live up to

---

[67] Broadcasting Act 1990 s 23(4).
[68] See G. Robertson, *Freedom, the Individual and the Law*, Penguin, 1989, pp. 229, 235.

its international obligations.[69] This power is likely to be exercised from time to time in relation to directives emanating from the Council of Europe.

ITC licences

The ITC has a general duty to ensure that a wide range of television programme services is available throughout the United Kingdom, and 'to ensure fair and effective competition in the provision of such services'.[70] To this end, it must allocate licences for Channel 3 (the sixteen ITV stations) and eventually for the new Channel 5 (local television stations) to the highest cash bidder, subject to an exception that permits it to award a licence to a lower-bidding applicant whose proposed quality of service is exceptionally high, or at least substantially higher than the service proposed by the applicant who has put in the highest bid.[71] Every successful applicant must meet a 'quality threshold', judged by a proposed programme schedule that gives sufficient time to high-quality national and international news and current affairs, and other high-quality feature programmes. The programme schedule must offer an appeal to 'a wide variety of tastes and interests', include a sufficient number of religious and children's programmes, and ensure that at least 25 per cent of its programmes are made by independent producers and that a 'proper proportion' is of European origin.[72]

The IBA awarded franchises in darkest secrecy, so that public scrutiny and feedback on its performance was minimal. Section 15(6) of the 1990 Broadcasting Act is an important gain for journalists: it requires the ITC to publish, as soon as reasonably practicable after the closing date for applications, details of the bidders and their proposals and 'such other information connected with the application as the Commission considers appropriate'. It must also issue a notice inviting public comment on the published applications. The only situation in which the Government may directly influence a licence award occurs if the ITC has grounds for suspecting that an applicant's funds may derive from a source that raises public-interest concerns, in which case it must refer this application to the Home Secretary, who may veto it if the source of funds 'is such that it would not be in the public interest for the licence to be so awarded'.[73] If the funds were coming from criminal

---

[69] Broadcasting Act 1990 s 188.
[70] ibid., s 2(2).
[71] ibid., s 17(3) and (4).
[72] ibid., s 16.
[73] ibid., s 17(5) and (6).

sources or from unfriendly foreign countries, or from persons who would otherwise be disqualified or judged unfit to hold a licence, the Home Secretary would presumably be justified in exercising this veto.

Licences are to be awarded for a period of ten years, and may be revoked if there is a change of ownership of the applicant that has not met with the prior approval of the ITC.[74] The ITC shall refuse to give its approval in these circumstances if the suggested new owner would be prejudicial to the programme schedule submitted by the original applicant, or if it considers the change 'inappropriate'. The ITC must not, however, revoke the licence without giving the holder a reasonable opportunity to make representations as to why the change should be permitted. In October 1990, before the 1990 Act came into operation, BSB (which held a DBS – direct broadcasting by satellite – licence) was effectively taken over by Sky Television, in a deal that was not notified to the IBA until after it was completed. The IBA protested, but in the interests of viewers the ITC allowed the licence to continue for two years. The ITC is unlikely to be so forgiving if this situation occurs again. The Act imposes complicated and controversial 'cross-owner-ship' rules, where proprietors of companies bidding for television licences must be EEC nationals or else 'ordinarily resident' in the United Kingdom, and national newspapers must not own more than 20 per cent of the shares in a licence-holder.

In their consideration of licence applications, and in dealings with licences, the ITC and the Radio Authority will be subject to judicial review if they act unfairly. The courts will not superimpose a judicial view of the merits of a decision, but will supervise the procedural steps and ensure that the ITC applies a correct interpretation of the Act. In the 1990 Scottish case of *Clyde Cable-vision* v *The Cable Authority*[75] a local cable company challenged the grant of a licence to a rival on the grounds that it had been denied an opportunity to deal with whatever factors might have persuaded the Cable Authority to turn down its own application. The court accepted that the Cable Authority's decision could be judicially reviewed, but found nothing in the 1984 Cable and Broadcasting Act that placed it under a duty to explain to each applicant the doubts it might have about their potential performance. The 1990 Broadcasting Act makes the award of a Channel 3 licence turn in normal circumstances on the highest cash bid; where the successful applicant has not submitted the highest bid, however, the ITC is placed under a duty to publish its reasons.[76] In many other sections

---

[74] ibid., s 20(1).
[75] (1990) SCLR 28.
[76] Broadcasting Act 1990 s 17 (12).

of the Act it has a duty to afford the licensee an opportunity to make representations before it takes adverse action, and if it fails fully and fairly to provide such an opportunity, or to give sufficient indications of its concerns, any subsequent penalty or revocation would be liable to be quashed.[77]

The first judicial review proceedings against the ITC were brought by Television South West, which had made the highest cash bid for its franchise area (£16 million) but had lost out to West Country Television, which had offered only half that amount. Before granting leave, the Court of Appeal directed the ITC to produce documents explaining its decision, from which it appeared that although both companies had passed the 'quality threshold', the ITC entertained grave doubts as to the highest bidder's business plan, notably its arrangement for bank finance and its advertising revenue projections. The judges found nothing unfair or irrational in the ITC's approach, which had involved a rigorous examination of the 'sustainability' criterion, but were critical of errors in the paper assessing the bid, prepared by ITC staff.

The announcement of the new franchise winners, in October 1991, was an occasion for universal condemnation of the new system, which was introduced by section 17 of the 1990 Broadcasting Act. Even its architect, Mrs Thatcher, expressed her horror at the departure of her favourite television company, TV-am, which was outbid by a consortium that included the *Guardian*, while others saw the demise of Thames as her retribution for *Death on the Rock*. It is wrong to expect judicial review to provide sensible supervision for a crazy system, in which unopposed franchise holders will succeed by offering a pittance while contestants will pawn their programme-making cash in order to win the right to make programmes they then cannot finance.

The courts cannot strike down or re-write legislation because it produces unreasonable results; they can only insist that the ITC does not exceed the wide discretion that the law allows. The economic and industry consequences of the 'highest cash bid' system are beyond the scope of this book; there is little doubt, however, that section 17 will be altered before the next round of franchise applications.

Licence holders will have the ITCs statutory duties incorporated as terms of their contract. Channel 3 licences, as we have seen, must in addition contain undertakings to maintain high-quality news and current-affairs programmes at peak times, ensure that

---

[77] See *R v Gaming Board ex parte Benaim* [1970] 2 QB 417, where Lord Denning indicated that natural justice required the Board 'in every case to be able to give the applicant sufficient indications of the objections raised against them such as to enable them to answer them'.

'sufficient' time is dedicated to religious and children's programmes, maintain a proper proportion of programmes originating from Europe (i.e. at least 50 per cent, including from the United Kingdom, under the Convention of Transfrontier Television) and to fill at least 25 per cent of their air-time with the work of independent producers. Some of these conditions will not be applicable to Channel 5 licences, although these will at least require high-quality news services at peak periods. Channel 4 shall be licensed as a separate corporation, with the duty to maintain a 'distinctive character' by encouraging innovation and experiment and appealing to tastes and interests not catered for by Channel 3. It is, most importantly, specifically enjoined to provide the 'public service' trifecta of 'information, education and entertainment'.[78]

'Fit and proper person'
Section 3(3) of the 1990 Act provides that the ITC 'shall not grant a licence to any person unless they are satisfied that he is a fit and proper person to hold it', and enjoins it to revoke the licence if the holder ceases to merit this description. This statutory wording suggests that the ITC must make a judgement not on the licensee's character as such, but on his fitness to hold a licence: it follows that an old criminal conviction may be overlooked, and that stewardship and quality achieved in other media enterprises should be taken into account.

An ITC determination that an applicant or existing holder is not a fit and proper person is subject to judicial review, and the English courts would be likely to adopt the approach to this question taken by the High Court of Australia in 1990 in the case of *The Australian Broadcasting Tribunal* v *Alan Bond*. That tribunal, like the ITC, is charged to revoke a licence if no longer satisfied that a particular person is fit and proper to hold it. Bond effectively controlled the company that held the licence for a television network, and had demonstrated both unfitness and impropriety by threatening a business opponent with unfavourable coverage on one of his network's current-affairs programmes; by paying a bribe, dressed up as an extravagant settlement for a libel action brought against his television company by the premier of Queensland; and by failing to make full and frank disclosure of the circumstances of the libel payment to the tribunal at an earlier inquiry. The High Court held that these matters were capable of supporting the tribunal's decision to revoke the licence, and that although the actual licence-holder was a company (which was not corporately involved in the improper behaviour), the tribunal was justified in

---

[78] Broadcasting Act 1990 s 25.

'lifting the corporate veil' and imputing unfitness as a result of the character and conduct of a person closely associated with it. Chief Justice Mason remarked:

> Commercial broadcasting is a very important medium in the communication of information and ideas. Moreover, a commercial broadcasting licence is a valuable privilege which confers on the licensee the capacity to influence public opinion and public values. For this reason, if for no other, a licensee has a responsibility to exercise the power conferred by the licence with a due regard to proper standards of conduct and a responsibility not to abuse the privilege which it enjoys. Possession of a licence or the exercise of the privilege which it confers has been described as 'in the nature of a public trust for the benefit of all members of our society . . .'. A licensee which lacks a proper appreciation of these responsibilities or does not discharge them is not, or may be adjudged not to be, a fit and proper person.[79]

The Court accepted that the test involved an assessment of the conduct, character (as an indication of future conduct) and reputation (as an indication of public perception as to future conduct) of the applicant or licensee. The tribunal was entitled to find a licensee unfit if satisfied that the community could not have confidence that he would not abuse the potential for influence provided by a broadcasting licence. Bond's exploitation of his company's licence for political dealings designed to promote his other business interests 'did not exhibit an appreciation of the proper relationship between those with control of media interests and governments'.

Penalties

The ITC is to be given a range of statutory powers to enforce licence conditions.[80] If satisfied that a breach has occurred, it may order the licence holder to:

- broadcast a correction or apology;
- refrain from rebroadcasting an offending programme;
- pay a fine up to a maximum amount calculated by reference to advertising revenue, the ceiling being raised in the case of a second offence;
- accept a reduction of the ten-year licence period by up to two years; or
- rectify a failure within a specified time, or else to suffer revocation of the licence.

---

[79] (1990) 64 ALJR 462, at p. 474.
[80] Broadcasting Act 1990 ss 40–2.

The last three penalties are draconian: the maximum level of the financial penalties for most licence holders will be several million pounds, as would the cost of losing one or two years of licensed operation (at least, if the licence were not renewed). The safeguard, in every case, is merely that the licence holder must be given 'a reasonable opportunity to make representations' before notice of the punishment is served. This would be unfair if the licence-holder's representations were to be directed to a decision the ITC has already taken, rather than to the question of whether it ought to take such a decision in the first place. It is to be hoped that, in practice, the ITC will operate a system of advance warnings of possible licence breaches, and will give licence holders the opportunity to explain themselves before commencing to decided whether to issue a penalty notice.

The ITC's power to revoke a Channel 3 or 5 licence is subject to more stringent procedural safeguards. It must first permit the licensee to make representations about the matters that may end its broadcasts, and then (if dissatisfied) serve a notice indicating the respect in which the licensee is breaking the licence agreement or failing to comply with an ITC directive, and specifying a time period within which the licensee must remedy its behaviour, and any specific steps it must take to do so. If the licensee fails to meet these requirements, the ITC may revoke the licence if satisfied that it is in the public interest to do so. It may revoke a licence without going through these procedures (other than to give an opportunity for an explanation) if satisfied that the licensee provided materially false information in its application or deliberately misled the ITC in the course of the application process.

It remains to be seen how the ITC will correlate its corrective and punitive powers with the much less severe powers of the BCC and BSC to oblige licence holders to publish adverse adjudications. The licence holder is in a position of double jeopardy, in that a BSC decision that it has breached a canon of good taste will also amount to a finding that it has breached a condition of its licence, and render it liable to an ITC penalty – unless the ITC interprets the canon differently to the BSC, in which case there will be complete confusion. It is to be hoped that, in practice, the ITC will regard the BSC/BCC directive to publish an adjudication as a sufficient form of 'correction and apology' for it to refrain from exercising its own punitive powers, unless the licence holder immediately repeats the same offence or else receives a sufficient number of 'moggings' to justify imposition of a more serious penalty. The ITC's exercise of its punishment powers will be subject to judicial review on grounds that it has acted irrationally or disproportionately or has not properly appreciated the evidence.

Editorializing

The BBC licence and its prescribing memoranda requires the Corporation 'to refrain from expressing its own opinion on current affairs or matters of public policy'. The BBC values its reputation for impartiality and insists that all programme intentions be clearly labelled. Specialist correspondents may indulge in personal 'explanations and assessments', and although journalists on current-affairs programmes must normally observe strict objectivity, the BBC recognizes that 'a journalist or broadcaster can rise to a stature where he not only has the right but is expected to express judgement of his own'.[81]

The ITC has a duty to ensure that its licensees do not exploit their privilege to broadcast their own views on politically controversial matters, other than on questions relating directly to broadcasting policy.[82] This means that if directors or executives of a licence-holder do hold forth on contentious subjects, it must be made clear that they are speaking in a personal capacity. The ban on editorializing is limited to 'matters of political or industrial controversy or (which) relate to current public policy' – which is not wide enough to cover the case of a licensee who manipulates his programmes so as to promote his non-broadcast business interests. Behaviour of this kind would probably be regarded by the ITC as evidence that he was not a 'fit and proper person' to hold a licence.

Religion

An important change effected by the 1990 Broadcasting Act is to provide much greater freedom of evangelical broadcasting. There will be no bar to religious groups obtaining licences to run cable or satellite channels or local radio stations, although the ITC will doubtless disqualify cults or religious extremists if it considers them 'inappropriate'. Having obtained a licence, religious groups will be permitted to editorialize by propagating their faith, so long as they do not exploit the susceptibilities of the audience or abuse the religious beliefs of others. The most dramatic change, when the new provisions come into effect in January 1993, will be to permit advertising by religious organizations on mainstream channels. This was absolutely prohibited by the 1981 Act, and its prohibitions will be maintained by the ITC until 1993. Thereafter, religions will be permitted to advertise their services, activities and

---

[81] *Index*, note 60 above, p. 38.
[82] ITC Code of Advertising Standards and Practice, January 1991, Appendix 5.

publications subject to a strict code, which excludes advertisements that play on fear, exploit categories of vulnerable viewers (such as the elderly or bereaved) or proselytize doctrine or denigrate other faiths or philosophies of life. No advertisement may include an appeal for funds (although special dispensation may be given to religious charities that assist humane causes). The object is to avoid the hell-fire preaching, mass emotional appeal and dubious fund-raising motives that have characterized American tele-evangelism.

In respect to mainstream television (i.e., Channels 3 and 4 and direct broadcast satellite services) the ITC has a statutory duty to secure that licensees display 'due responsibility' by ensuring that religious programmes do not involve 'improper exploitation' of audience susceptibilities or 'abusive treatment' of other religions. Its Programme Code contains detailed rules for achieving due responsibility, which will operate as 'guidelines' until 1993, whereafter they will apply as a sanction-enforced code.

This code requires that programmes must clearly identify all religious bodies featured, and should generally reflect the worship and thought of orthodox (mainly, though not exclusively, Christian) religious traditions in the United Kingdom. Programmes must not be designed to recruit viewers into any particular faith, to prey on fears or make claims that living persons have 'special powers or abilities'.[83]

Advertising

Fears of advertising excesses were responsible for the original prohibition on bad taste and offensiveness in commercial broadcasting. The IBA enjoyed wide powers to vet advertising copy and to reject commercials that did not meet its standards.[84] Some of its decisions have been socially objectionable – until 1987, for example, it repeatedly declared that condom advertisements would be offensive to a large section of the British public. This attitude reflected an irresponsible double standard: the media were prepared to promote promiscuity by snigger and insinuation, but refused to help minimize the casualties, and as recently as 1984 the IBA banned advertisements made by LWT for the Family Planning Association. These decisions were entirely ungoverned by rules of law; they reflected the moral prejudices of the IBA's officers and board members as to what constitutes 'good taste'. In 1987 the advent of AIDS made the IBA finally relent in its total ban on

---

[83] ITC Programme Code, February 1991, Section 10.
[84] Broadcasting Act 1981 ss 8–9 and Sched 2.

condom advertisements, although it rejected most that were submitted. Any trace of humour, any attempt to put information about condoms across in ways that might actually appeal to a youthful audience, was rejected as being 'in poor taste'.

In 1990 the IBA employed forty members of staff on the task of vetting some 15,000 scripts and 5,000 completed commercials submitted that year, by applying standards that are more restrictive than those applied to programmes. This task has been inherited by the ITC, and is overseen by the BSC, whose remit to monitor 'good taste and decency' applies both to programmes and to advertisements. This duplication causes the advertising industry great concern, given the high cost of advertising campaigns which might have to be aborted if commercials approved by the ITC are declared unsuitable by the BSC.

Section 8(2) of the 1990 Broadcasting Act sets out the three basic rules for advertising on commercial television:

- There must be no advertising by bodies whose objects are 'wholly or mainly of a political nature' or are 'directed towards any political end'.
- There must be no 'unreasonable discrimination' in acceptance of advertisements, either for or against a particular advertiser.
- Programmes must not, without ITC approval, be sponsored by companies whose products or services cannot be advertised under the ITC code.

The prohibition on advertising of a 'political' nature has caused some confusion in the past. The IBA has refused advertisements for left-wing papers like *Tribune* and *New Socialist* while accepting them for committed Tory newspapers, which make up the majority of the daily press. The ITC claims that the prohibition excludes 'issue campaigning' to influence legislation or Government action. It is doubtful whether its interpretation of the section is correct, or whether it could withstand a challenge under Article 10. So long as an advertisement is not directed towards an issue of current political or industrial controversy (and so in breach of the overriding due-impartiality duty) and is not inserted by or directed towards a party political end, it is difficult to understand why campaigning organizations should not have the same opportunities on television that they have on public billboards.

The prohibition on 'unreasonable discrimination' is valuable, and should be capable of assertion against ITC attempts to ban advertising by newspapers catering for minorities. The IBA had a deplorable record in this respect, banning Channel 4 advertisements for a homosexual newspaper (on the grounds that it would be 'offensive to public feeling' although the ad was unexceptionally worded and photographed) and for a West Indian newspaper (because of its headlines about a controversial inquest). The ITC must specifically approve any sponsorship of a programme by the manufacturer of products that its code deems unacceptable for direct advertisement; these include all tobacco products, guns and pornography (which the ITC defines as 'including "girlie" magazines and the like', but not, apparently, including the *Sun*). The ITC additionally regards as unacceptable all advertisements for gaming and betting services, private detective agencies and commercial services offering advice on personal or consumer problems (other than firms of solicitors).

Section 9 of the Act imposes a duty on the ITC to draw up a code relating to advertising standards, which it is empowered to enforce by giving directives to licensees in respect either of general classes of advertisements that should not be accepted or of particular unacceptable examples. Its directives will also indicate the maximum amount of television time to be given to advertisements in each hourly period, and the spacing of such advertising breaks. In January 1991 the Commission promulgated a detailed Code of Advertising Standards and Practice. Under the Control of Misleading Advertisement Regulations (1988) it has a duty to investigate complaints about misleading advertisements, and it will regard a factual claim as inaccurate (and hence a breach of its rule against misleading advertising) unless adequate evidence to support it can be furnished by the advertiser. In drafting and revising its code and in issuing directives, the ITC must take account of the United Kingdom's international obligations, and its 1991 code incorporates most of the relevant provisions of the European Convention on Transfrontier Television.

The European Convention on Transfrontier Television

The international obligations that have become increasingly important for the British media are contained in the European Convention on Transfrontier Television, adopted by the Committee of Ministers of the Council of Europe on 15 March 1989, and the consequent EC Directive on Broadcasting, which was implemented by all member countries by October 1991. The Convention begins by endorsing the guarantee of freedom of expression in Article 10 of the European Convention on Human Rights as an 'essential condition of a democratic society', and aims to 'enhance Europe's heritage and develop audio-visual creation . . . through efforts to increase the production and circulation of high quality programmes'. It applies to all broadcasting formats, whether cable, terrestrial transmitter or satellite, which can be received (directly or indirectly) in another country that is party to the Convention. The duties upon nations that are parties to the Convention include adherence to Article 10, and ensuring that its laws restrain broadcasters within its jurisdiction from transmitting pornography or incitements to violence or racial hatred, and that they afford a 'right of reply'. Parties must ensure that coverage of events of 'high public interest' across Europe is not restricted by exclusive rights deals so as to deprive a large part of the public in another European country from watching them on television. Broadcasting organizations in each country must reserve at least 50 per cent of transmission time (excluding that taken up by news, sport and advertising) for programmes of European origin.

These Convention objectives are secured in Britain by appropriate provisions in the 1990 legislation. In relation to television advertising, it will be the task of the ITC to reflect them in its code of practice and enforce them through its power to issue directives. Article 11 of the Convention requires all advertisements to be fair and honest and to have regard to the special susceptabilities of children. The amount of advertising shall not exceed 15 per cent of the daily transmission time, or take up more than twelve minutes in any one hour (Article 12). Article 14 causes great anguish to British advertisers and money-minded programme executives: it strikes a notable blow for artistic creativity by providing that advertisements may not be inserted so as to damage 'the integrity and value of the programme'. To this end, advertisements must be transmitted only during natural breaks in sports programmes; films and documentaries must be interrupted only once every forty-five minutes, and other programmes must last at least twenty minutes before an advertising break; religious services must not be interrupted at all, and nor should news and current affairs and religious and children's programmes that last less than thirty minutes. There have been angry complaints that Article 14 'would change the face of British commercial television as we know it[85] – and for most viewers, this will be a change for the better.

The Convention requires bans on tobacco products and on prescription medicines (Article 15). This may in due course require an end to the association of sporting events with their tobacco company sponsors. The rules relating to alcohol advertisements are particularly strict: drinking must not be associated with 'physical performance' or driving or the resolution of personal conflicts. Abstinence or moderation must not be presented in a negative light.

---

[85] 'An Unlawful EEC Convention?' (1988) NLJ 7 October. The argument there advanced, that Article 14 unlawfully interferes with the freedom to impart and receive information under Article 10 of the European Convention on Human Rights, is specious. Article 14 enhances the free flow of information by enabling it to flow coherently and without distraction.

The Convention is astute to prevent advertisers and sponsors from influencing, whether overtly or covertly, the content of programmes or their impact on viewers. Advertisements must be plainly distinguishable as such and there must be no 'product placement' (the frequent device of being paid to use an advertiser's product as a prop in drama programmes). News and current-affairs presenters must not lend their names or their faces to product promotions (Article 13). Sponsored programmes must be clearly identified as such, the sponsor must not be permitted to influence editorial or scheduling judgements (Article 17), and these programmes shall not promote products or services of the sponsor or anyone else (Article 17). There shall be no sponsorship of news and current-affairs programmes, and no programme may be sponsored by the manufacturers of tobacco products, alcoholic drinks or prescription medicines.

The Convention heralds an important European initiative in the standardization of basic broadcasting law, and its provisions relating to advertising are considerably more sophisticated than the rules hitherto applied by the IBA. Advertisers, although restricted in some circumstances by the Convention, do have redress under European law against any EEC member country that tries to discriminate against advertisements broadcast from other member countries. In other words, any legal restrictions on advertising must apply irrespective of the nationality of the advertiser or the country from which the broadcast has originated.[86] In *Bond van Adverteers* v *The Netherlands* the European Court held that a prohibition on advertising broadcasts from other countries directed at citizens of the receiving country was an unlawful restriction on the freedom to provide services and was contrary to Article 59 of the EEC treaty:[87]

> The Dutch government's objective in banning all broadcast advertising directed at its citizens from cable stations in other countries was to ensure that a public foundation in Holland received all the revenue from advertising directed at its nationals. This economic objective was not a satisfactory 'public policy' exemption from compliance with Article 59. It might reasonably require foreign broadcasters directing their promotions to Dutch citizens to comply with local laws relating to the duration of advertisements or banning the touting of certain products, but it could not erect a barrier against all foreign-originated advertising in the economic interests of its own broadcasters.

---

[86] *Procureur du Roi* v *Debauve* (1980) ECR 833.
[87] Case No 352/85, Judgment, 16 April 1988.

The Radio Authority

The IBA's role as regulator of national and local radio has been transferred to a new Radio Authority. Its duties and powers mirror for sound broadcasting the ITC's duties and powers in relation to television. It must do all it can to ensure a diversity of national services, at least one devoted predominantly to the spoken word and one broadcasting 'music other than pop music', together with a range and diversity of local services.[88] Licences are to be granted for eight years to 'fit and proper' people (persons convicted for radio piracy offences in the preceding five years are excluded from this category), and the statutory duties relating to good programme taste and the provision of accurate and impartial news are repeated.[89] Some latitude, however, is provided for partial opinions in current political and industrial controversy – the Radio Authority's duty is merely to ensure that such opinions are not given 'undue prominence' and are not presented as editorials.[90] This less onerous form of the due-impartiality duty may also be applied by the ITC to local television services, which it is permitted to license under s 47 of the Act. The ITC interprets the 'undue prominence' rule as requiring 'a balance of views across the channel as a whole', but within that general balance permitting programmes to 'convey a particular political view or reflect a particular philosophy' without calling for a right of reply or a specific balancing programme. It is likely that the Radio Authority will adopt the same approach, encouraging local radio stations to allow organizations in the area to present programmes that explain their own partisan views. The Authority is enjoined to draw up codes relating to the transmission of 'sounds suggestive of violence' and to exclude political advertising. The Government may issue directives banning particular broadcasts, on the same basis as it may suppress certain television broadcasts.[91] The Radio Authority has parallel enforcement powers to the ITC, although the maximum financial penalty it may exact for non-compliance with a licence condition is limited to £50,000.

It is an offence under s 1 of the Wireless Telegraphy Act of 1949 to make wireless transmissions without a licence, and under the new Act it is an offence to run a radio service that is not licensed by the Radio Authority. The 1990 legislation contains stringent powers to eradicate radio pirates, both on the high seas and on the high streets.[92] It is an offence not merely to produce an illegal

---

[88] Broadcasting Act 1990 s 85.
[89] ibid., ss 86–9.
[90] ibid., s 90.
[91] ibid., s 94.

broadcast, but to own or assist in the control of premises or to supply apparatus used in unlicensed broadcasts. Every conceivable act of assistance is caught by these provisions, and offences may be committed by delivering a 'lecture, address or sermon' on a pirate radio station or by publishing any details of unlicensed broadcasts. Any 'vehicle, vessel or aircraft, or any structure or other object or any apparatus' used in connection with the commission of an offence may be forfeited to the Crown, and inspectors may use reasonable force in the course of their investigations. These provisions are remarkably savage and something of a tribute to the tenacity and popularity of backstreet radio stations in recent years. Whether the incorrigible amateur broadcasters, and their audiences, will be satisfied with the wider range of choice offered by deregulated radio remains to be seen. The provision that makes it an offence to publish 'details of any unauthorized broadcasts' may well be a breach of the 'freedom of expression' guarantee in Article 10 of the European Human Rights Convention, if it is used against publishers of articles or programmes that discuss the social phenomenon of pirate radio.

The popularity of pirate radio ships on the high seas during the 1960s was an important factor in breaking down the BBC's rigid monopoly of the airwaves. In retrospect, the salvos fired by Mr Wedgwood Benn against Radio Caroline appear comical, and many of the original pirates (such as John Peel and Tony Blackburn) are now household names on licensed stations. None the less, the fears that gripped the governments of Europe at the threat to their nationalized broadcasting arrangements produced an early treaty obliging firm action against unauthorized broadcasters, and its terms are embodied in the Marine Broadcasting (Offences) Act of 1967.[93] This Act (the terms of which are revised and extended by Schedule 16 of the 1990 Broadcasting Act) makes it an offence to broadcast from a ship or aircraft within the jurisdiction of the United Kingdom, and an offence for any British citizen to broadcast on or above the high seas. It is an offence to facilitate pirate broadcasts capable of being received in Britain that emanate from beyond territorial waters, and 'facilitation' is widely defined to include provisioning of the radio ship, advertising on the pirate station or publishing any details of its programmes.[94] For many years the London listings magazine *Time Out* published a column

---

[92] ibid., ss 168–74.

[93] European Agreement for the Prevention of Broadcasts transmitted from Stations Outside National Territories (Strasbourg, 22 January 1965) ratified by the United Kingdom Government in 1967.

[94] Lord Wilberforce has severely criticized the extra-territorial impact of these provisions: Hansard (House of Lords) 26 July 1990, cols 1657–1660.

giving programme details for Radio Laser, Radio Caroline and other pirate stations within and without the jurisdiction; a prosecution against it under the 1967 Act failed on a technicality, but the column has not reappeared. In 1990 the Court of Appeal upheld the conviction of a number of British subjects for a conspiracy made in the United Kingdom to breach the 1967 Act by procuring the unlicensed broadcasts of Radio Laser, notwithstanding that these emanated from a Panamanian ship, moored outside territorial waters and manned by Americans.[95]

Cable television

Cable television has been something of a disappointment in the United Kingdom. After a report on the subject by Lord Hunt[96] and an enthusiastic White Paper,[97] the Home Office granted licences to eleven pilot cable operations in different parts of the country, and subsequently passed the Cable and Broadcasting Act 1984 to regulate them and the booming development predicted for this sector of the broadcast media. However, by April 1990 twenty-five cable systems were in operation to service only 92,974 homes. In time, cable television in Britain may emulate its success in America, but its present operations do not require a separate regulatory system. The Cable Authority has been dissolved with the implementation of the 1990 legislation, and its licensing functions have been taken over by the ITC.

In keeping with the market-place philosophy of the 1990 reforms, the ITC cable franchises will henceforth be awarded to the highest cash bidder, rather than on the basis of an evaluation of the quality of the programmes on offer. The relevant provisions are contained in ss 72–82 of the Broadcasting Act, which relate to 'local delivery services', and which parallel the process for awarding Channel 3 and Channel 5 licences. The ITC must publish details of all licence applicants for a particular area, together with their 'technical plan', which must give details of the coverage planned for the service, and the timetable and the technical means proposed to achieve that coverage.[98] In 'exceptional circumstances' the licence may be awarded to an applicant who does not submit the highest bid, and one such circumstance may be where the proposed coverage is substantially greater than that offered by the highest bidder. The ITC shall grant licences to run for fifteen years, renewable for a

---

[95] *R* v *Murray & Ors* (1990) *The Times*, 22 March.
[96] Report of the Inquiry into Cable Expansion and Broadcasting Policy (1982) Cmnd 8679.
[97] The Development of Cable Systems and Services (1983) Cmnd 8866.
[98] Broadcasting Act 1990 s 74(6).

further fifteen years (the Cable Authority licences were limited to twelve and eight years respectively). The due-impartiality duty does not apply, either for news or for general programmes, where a local delivery service relays complete and unchanged satellite programmes of foreign origin, although the licensee will be required to comply with the full rigour of the s 6(1)(*a*) duty to avoid indecency, incitements to crime, or offence to public feeling.[99] The ITC has the same powers to enforce the conditions in a local delivery service licence as it has to enforce a Channel 3 licence (see p. 624).

The powers of the Cable Authority extended only to operators who provide 'sounds' and 'visual images which are such that sequences of them may be seen as moving pictures', and this excluded teletext services such as Oracle and Ceefax. Such services were still subject to general laws, such as obscenity and defamation, but they did not require licences. As the Government spokesman explained in the course of the 1984 Act's parliamentary passage: 'We do not propose to start licensing newspapers printed on paper, which would indeed be Orwellian . . . and for similar reasons we do not propose to start licensing newspapers printed on television screens.'[100]

Six years later, however, the Government was in a more Orwellian mood: the public teletext service that is to replace the IBA's Oracle will be required to conform to the 'good taste' and 'due-impartiality' standards that have yet to be imposed on newspapers.[101]

The Government's White Paper on the Development of Cable Systems and Services promised that:

> once the Cable Authority has granted a franchise, it should use a light regulatory touch and adopt a reactive rather than a proactive style . . . In the ordinary course it should be sufficient . . . for the Cable Authority to operate retrospectively on the basis of complaints or its own selective samplings of programmes as they are transmitted.[102]

The Cable Authority, in its relatively brief life, lived up to these expectations and avoided conflicts over censorship. The ITC will be likely to follow its example, at least in relation to 'local delivery services'.

---

[99] ibid., s 79(2).
[100] Lord Elton, House of Lords 23 January 1984, Hansard Vol 447 No 60, Col 9. See also Telecommunications Act 1984 s 6.
[101] See Broadcasting Act 1990 s 6(8), s 49(2) and Sched 5. Other 'additional services' that are licensed for provision on television broadcasting frequencies will not be required to comply with the s 6 duties.
[102] Note 97 above, paras 143, 146.

The Hunt Report had proposed that cable viewers should be entitled to receive 'adult only' films, screened on a channel that could be specially 'locked' and hence be rendered inaccessible to young children. This prospect was derided in predictable quarters, and the Government hastened to reassure the public of its commitments to family viewing. The inclusion of the 'good taste' requirement ensures that 18R films are not offered by cable companies, and necessitates some editing of movies classified as 18 for the cinema. The meaning of the phrase 'offensive to public feeling' may be more limited in the context of cable television; certainly the Cable Authority found it possible to take no action after the screening to a paying audience of films such as *The Life of Brian* and *The Exorcist*, which the IBA had refused to approve for Channel 4.

Satellite broadcasting

Telstar, the first transatlantic communications satellite, was launched in 1962. It had one black-and-white television channel and was operational for only a few hours of the day. The first legislative provisions for satellite reception in Britain were contained in the Cable and Broadcasting Act 1984, which authorized the IBA to provide direct broadcasting by satellite (DBS) services. It was relieved of the need to ensure due impartiality and a sufficient provision for news on satellite channels, but required to maintain standards of good taste and the elimination of programmes offensive to public feeling.

The era of satellite broadcasting was ushered into Britain by the launch of Sky television in 1988, followed by BSB in 1990. Both proved financially disastrous, and negotiated a merger (without advance approval from the IBA) in November 1990. This was a serious breach of BSB's programme contract, but the ITC decided to permit their licence to continue for a further two years so that their 115,000 viewers could continue to watch programmes provided by the merged company (BSkyB) on BSB 'squarials' rather than switch immediately to Sky dishes capable of receiving Astra-satellite channels. BSkyB is to be granted a 'non-domestic licence' to cover its transmissions from Astra until the year 2001. Satellite television has been a good deal more successful in Europe, where by the end of 1990 seventy-four satellite-delivered services were in operation, reaching 25 million households (mainly via cable links).

The ITC is responsible, under the 1990 Act, for granting licences for 'domestic satellite services' (where programmes are uplinked from and received in the United Kingdom on an allocated frequency – e.g., BSB) and for 'non-domestic satellite services' (where programmes are uplifted from the UK for general reception, on unallocated frequencies – e.g., Sky). Licences for the former service are to be granted on similar conditions to Channel 3 licences;[103] in the latter case, all applications duly made are to be granted unless the ITC considers that the applicant would be likely to transmit programmes causing offence to the British public.[104] Britain has at present been allocated five direct broadcasting-by-satellite channels by the International Frequencies Registration Board, and no newspaper proprietor is permitted to hold more than a 20 per cent interest in them or in any DBS channels allotted to Britain in the future.[105] However, there is no restriction on newspaper proprietors investing in non-DBS channels – hence Mr Rupert Murdoch's ownership of four Sky channels as well as 35 per cent of the national press. The only fetter on the owner of a non-DBS channel is that he or she cannot hold more than a 20 per cent interest in a Channel 3 or 5 licensee. In principle the distinction between owners of DBS and non-DBS services is difficult to justify, since both are able to reach large numbers of viewers in the United Kingdom, and the danger to be averted by cross-ownership rules is concentration of media power.

The British take sex a good deal more seriously than other European nationalities do, and considerable ingenuity has been expended to find ways of stopping the soft-core pornography that is offered in many continental countries from infiltrating via satellite. Domestic satellite operators are subject to the Obscene Publications Act and to the 'good taste and decency' terms of their licences, but material that originates abroad and is transmitted by companies resident outside the jurisdiction cannot be so readily controlled. In 1989 Britons were able to see erotic movies for the first time on television, by courtesy of a Dutch channel that occupied a position on the Astra satellite (which also carries Sky television). The programmes were directed to Holland, but the signals could be picked up in Britain. After official complaints the signals were scrambled, but this expedient will not succeed if decoders become available.

If pornography originates from a country that has signed the European Convention on Transfrontier Television, or that is bound by the EC Directive on television broadcasts, the British Government may be able to require action to be taken, but some European countries are not parties and others may disagree on the definition of the 'pornography' that is discouraged by both instruments.

There is no entirely satisfactory solution to the prospect of pornography from outer space. The broadcasts might be jammed,

---

[103] Broadcasting Act 1990 s 44.
[104] ibid., s 45(2). The enforcement provisions are the same as for Channel 3 licences, except that the maximum financial penalty the ITC can impose is £50,000: s 45(6).
[105] ibid., Sched 2 Part IV.

but the technology is not precise and other channels would suffer interference. Detector vans could be programmed to detect whether television sets inside households are switched to a particular satellite channel, but it is not yet an offence merely to view obscenity. The Government has chosen to rely upon Lord Rees-Mogg, who will have 'a leading role in monitoring the standards of programmes broadcast into the UK from abroad', and upon new powers provided to the Home Secretary to proscribe a foreign satellite service that repeatedly offends against good taste and decency.[106] A 'proscribed' satellite service shall be treated, in law, in the same way as a pirate radio ship: it will be a criminal offence (punishable by up to two years' imprisonment) to supply programmes or equipment to it, or to advertise upon it, or to publish any details of its programmes.[107] These somewhat ludicrous provisions are to be triggered by a report from the ITC that the satellite service is 'unacceptable' because it repeatedly offends public feeling or incites crime or broadcasts indecent material. Although these powers stem from an obsessive concern with pornography, a Home Secretary might also be moved to proscribe a channel for political reasons – e.g., if it were a Libyan propaganda station or a channel that gave air-time to spokespersons from Sinn Fein banned from appearing on British television.

Satellite transmissions are creating complex problems for defamation law. If a cable system picks up the satellite signals and relays them to its subscribers, then the cable operator will be responsible for the libels so transmitted. If the programme originates from England, then the person sending the libel up to the satellite for retransmission will also be liable. There may be a difficulty, however, if the programme originates abroad and is sent up to the satellite from a foreign country by whose law it is not defamatory. For example, the American law of defamation provides a 'public figure' defence – anything said about someone in the public eye will not be actionable unless spoken with malice. So the publication might be excused under American law, but not under English law. Which system of law is applied to determine whether or not the action is successful?

The general rule is that, so long as a tort is committed in England, English law principles will apply. For libel, so long as there is an act of publication in England, only defences known to English law will apply. It has been held that so far as broadcasts are concerned the tort is committed where the broadcast is received, rather than where it is transmitted.[108] Any broadcast received in

---

[106] ibid., s 177.
[107] ibid., s 178.

England would be 'published' in England, and English libel law would apply. If the principle is applied to satellite transmissions, there would be no question of applying foreign law. The only problem for a plaintiff in England trying to sue a foreign defendant in respect of a transmission originating abroad would be in obtaining leave to serve the defendant with a writ out of the jurisdiction. Under the Rules of the Supreme Court leave can be granted to serve a foreign defendant out of the jurisdiction in respect of a libel committed within the jurisdiction.[109] Leave is always at the discretion of the court, and whether an action can be begun will depend on the facts of the case. But if the rule for broadcasts is not followed for satellites (because of the lack of control over the area over which signals can be picked up, and the presumption against applying English rules extra-territorially), then there will be no publication in England – the tort will be committed abroad only, where the signals are transmitted to the satellite. In this case, to sustain an action in England for a tort committed abroad, the tort must be actionable by English law and by the law of the place where the actions took place (i.e., where the signals originated). Only if actionable by both systems of law would a plaintiff succeed in bringing an action.[110]

Many international treaties and conventions proclaim the principle of a free flow of information. However, this principle is generally subject to reservations of national sovereignty, based on the assumption that every state has an exclusive right to regulate its own broadcasting system to prevent transmission of unacceptable programme material and propaganda. Thus, the Soviet Union has in the past insisted that the overriding consideration must be the right of states to pursue political and social development free from outside interference. Some Third World countries argue that the free flow of information principle is contingent upon equal access to the source, and fear cultural domination of developing nations by superpower satellites. The United States and the United Kingdom, the two most constant champions of the free-flow principle, are the two leading exporters of television programmes.

---

[108] *Jenner* v *Sea Oil* [1952] DLR 526; *Gorton* v *ABC* [1974] 22 FLR 181; *Whitlam* v *Victoria Broadcasting* [1979] 37 FLR 15.

[109] Rules of the Supreme Court, Order 11, r 1(1). However, under the Civil Jurisdiction and Judgments Act 1982 an EEC national may be sued in the courts of a state where the harmful act occurred. The rule in *Kroch* v *Russell et cie* [1937] 1 All ER 725, where a foreign plaintiff was not permitted to issue a writ out of the jurisdiction against a foreign newspaper, a few copies of which had circulated in Britain, because he had no reputation to protect in the United Kingdom, requires reconsideration in the case of EEC nationals. See *Handelskwekerij GJ Bier BV* v *Mines de Potasse d'Alsace SA* [1978] QB 708, and *Shevill* v Presse Alliance [1992] 1 All ER 404, CA.

[110] *Chaplin* v *Boys* [1971] AC 356.

The European Court of Human Rights in the *Autronic* case firmly rejected the notion that states were entitled to control the reception of television programmes uplinked from their cities or transmitted by their satellites (see p. 596), and its championship of the right to impart and receive information across national frontiers will prevail in the broadcasting laws of Western Europe and of those countries in Eastern Europe that will follow Czechoslovakia in acceding to the European Convention on Human Rights.

Article 1 of the Outer Space Treaty of 1966 establishes the general principle that 'outer space . . . shall be free for exploration and use by all states without discrimination of any kind'. The United Nations General Assembly set up the Committee on the Peaceful Uses of Outer Space (COPUOS), but its deliberations on satellite broadcasting have been marked by disputes over the need for 'prior consent' by the receiving state, with a majority of the group taking the position that prior consent was necessary. The group has defined unacceptable programme material to include propaganda; incitements to war, racial hatred or enmity between people; or programmes aimed at undermining the foundations of a local culture. If any such material is aimed specifically at a foreign state without its express consent, the transmission should be illegal. The fundamental fear is of overspill propaganda. The only way to combat this is by international agreement, but neither the United States nor the United Kingdom is convinced of the danger of overspill, and the rift between them and the developing countries has precluded any worthwhile international agreement.

The conference that settled the law of the sea continued for nine years before agreement was reached; a satisfactory agreement over the law of the sky may take even longer.

Select Bibliography

Advisory Committee on Drug Dependence: Cannabis, *The Wootton Report*, HMSO, 1969.

Aitken, Jonathan, *Officially Secret*, Weidenfeld & Nicolson, 1971.

Annan Report: *see under* Home Office.

Arlidge, Anthony and Eady, David, *Law of Contempt*, Sweet & Maxwell, 1982.

Aubrey, Crispin, *Who's Watching You?*, Penguin, 1981.

Bailey, Martin, *Oilgate: The Sanctions Scandal*, Coronet, 1979.

Barker, Martin (ed.), *The Video Nasties*, Pluto Press, 1984.

Barker, Martin, *A Haunt of Fears: The History of the British Horror Comics Campaign*, Pluto, 1984.

Bennett, Colin and Hennessy, Peter, *A Consumer's Guide to Open Government: Techniques for Penetrating Whitehall*, Outer Circle Policy Group, n.d.

Birkenshaw, Patrick, *Freedom of Information: the Law, the Practice and the Ideal*, Weidenfeld & Nicolson, 1988.

Birkenshaw, Patrick, *Government and Information*, Butterworths, 1990.

Blackstone, William, *Commentaries on the Laws of England*, 1765.

Blom-Cooper, Louis, *Guns for Antigua*, Duckworth, 1990.

Borrie, Gordon J. and Lowe, Nigel, *The Law of Contempt*, 2nd edn, Butterworths, 1983.

Brittain, Vera, *Radclyffe Hall – A Case of Obscenity*, Femina, 1968.

Calcutt Report: see *Report of the Committee on Privacy and Related Matters*.

Callahan, David and Bok, Sisella (eds.), *Ethics Teaching in Higher Education*, Plenum, 1980.

Callender Smith, Robin, *Press Law*, Sweet & Maxwell, 1978.

Caunt, *An Editor on Trial*, privately published, 1947.

Chapman, Richard A. and Hunt, Michael H. (eds.), *Open Government*, Croom Helm, 1987.

Chesterman, Michael, *Charities, Trusts and Social Welfare*, Weidenfeld & Nicolson, 1979.

Chibnall, Steve, *Law and Order News*, Tavistock, 1977.

Copyright and Designs Law: Committee Report, Cmnd 6732, HMSO, 1977.

Cotterell, Leslie E., *Performance*, John Offord (Publications), 1977.

Cox, Barry, *et al.*, *The Fall of Scotland Yard*, Penguin, 1977.

Cracknall, D. G., *Law Relating to Charities*, Oyez Longman, 1983.

Cretney, Stephen M., *Principles of Family Law*, 5th edn, Sweet & Maxwell, 1990.

Curran, James (ed.), *The British Press: A Manifesto*, Macmillan, 1978.

The Death of Blair Peach: Supplementary Report of the Unofficial Inquiry Chaired by Professor Michael Dummett, NCCL, 1980.

Delbridge, Rosemary and Smith, Martin (eds.), *Consuming Secrets*, National Consumer Council and Burnet Books, 1982.

Denning, Lord, *What Next in the Law?*, Butterworths, 1982.

Department of Trade and Industry, *Intellectual Property and Innovation*, Cmnd. 9712, HMSO, 1986.

Devlin, Lord, *Trial by Jury: The Hamlyn Lecture, 1956*, rev. edn, Stevens, 1966.

Dicey, A. V., *An Introduction to the Study of the Law of the Constitution*, 10th edn, Macmillan, 1985.

Downs, Robert, *The Jungle*, New American Library, 1960.

Duncan, Colin and Neill, B., *Defamation*, 2nd edn, Butterworths, 1983.

Eley, Harold, *Advertising Media*, Butterworths, 1932.

Evans, Harold, *Good Times, Bad Times*, Weidenfeld & Nicolson, 1983.

Findlater, Richard, *Banned!: A Review of Theatrical Censorship in Britain*, MacGibbon & Kee, 1967.

Foot, Paul, *The Helen Smith Story*, Fontana, 1983.

Fox, Sir John Charles, *The History of the Contempt of Court: the form of trial and the mode of punishment*, OUP, 1927, reprinted Professional Books, 1972.

Fraud Trials Committee, *Improving the Presentation of Information to Juries in Fraud Trials,* HMSO, 1986.

Furneaux, Rupert, *Gunther Podola: A Crime Documentary*, Stevens, 1960.

Gatley on Libel and Slander, 8th edn, Sweet & Maxwell, 1981.

Goldstein and Kant, *Pornography and Sexual Deviance*, University of California Press, 1973.

Gower, L. C. B., *et al.*, *Gower's Principles of Modern Company Law*, 4th edn, Stevens, 1981.

Groll, Lennart, *Freedom and Self-discipline of the Swedish Press*, Swedish Institute, 1980.

The Gulf War and Censorship, Article 19, 1991.

Haddon, Tom, *Company Law and Capitalism*, 2nd edn, Weidenfeld & Nicolson, 1977.

Hain, Peter, *Mistaken Identity*, Quartet, 1976.

Hannington, Wal, *Never on Our Knees*, Lawrence & Wishart, 1967.

Harris, Robert, *Gotcha: The Media, the Government and the Falkland Crisis*, Faber, 1983.

Harrison, Tim, *Access to Information in Local Government*, Sweet & Maxwell, 1988.

Hartley, T. C. and Griffith, J. A. G., *Government and the Law: An Introduction to the Working of the Constitution in Britain*, 2nd edn, Weidenfeld & Nicolson, 1981.

Hobson, Harold, *The Pearl of Days: An Intimate Memoir of The Sunday Times 1822–1972*, Hamish Hamilton, 1972.

Home Office, *Future of Broadcasting: Committee Report*, Chmn Lord Annan, Cmnd 6753, HMSO, 1977.

—, *Obscenity and Film Censorship: Committee Report*, Chmn B. Williams, Cmnd 7772, HMSO, 1979.

Hooper, David, *Public Scandal, Odium and Contempt*, Secker & Warburg, 1984.

Hunnings, Neville March, *Film Censors and the Law*, Allen & Unwin, 1967.

Ingrams, Richard, *Goldenballs*, Deutsch, 1979.

Jones, Marjorie, *Justice and Journalism*, Barry Rose, 1974.

Kennedy, Ludovic, *The Trial of Stephen Ward*, Gollancz, 1964.

Knightley, Phillip, *The First Casualty: The War Correspondent as Hero, Propagandist and Myth Maker*, rev. edn, Quartet, 1982.

Knightley, Phillip, *The Vestey Affair*, Macdonald, 1982.

Laddie, H. I. L., *et al.*, *The Modern Law of Copyright*, Butterworths, 1980.

Law Commission, *Criminal Law: Offences Relating to Interference with the Court of Justice*, HMSO, 1979.

—, *Offences Against Religion and Public Worship*, HMSO, 1981.

—, *Report on Conspiracy and Criminal Law Reform*, HMSO, 1976.

Leigh, David, *The Frontiers of Secrecy*, Junction Books, 1980.

Leigh, Leonard, *The Control of Commercial Fraud*, Heinemann, 1982.

Levy, H. Phillip, *The Press Council*, Macmillan, 1967.

Long, Cohn, *Telecommunications Law and Practice*, Sweet & Maxwell, 1988.

May, Sir Thomas Erskine, *Parliamentary Practice*, 21st edn, Butterworths, 1983.

May and Rowan (eds.), *Inside Information: British Government and the Media*, Constable, 1982.

Medawar, Charles, *The Social Audit Consumer Handbook*, Macmillan, 1978.

Michael, James, *The Politics of Secrecy*, Penguin, 1982.

Miller, Christopher John, *Contempt of Court*, 2nd edn, Clarendon Press, 1989.

Munro, Colin, *Television Censorship and the Law*, Saxon House, 1979.

Northey and Leigh, *Introduction to Company Law*, Butterworths, 1981.

Palmer, Tony, *The Trials of Oz*, Blond & Briggs, 1971.

People under Pressure, Press Council, 1980.

Picarda, Hubert, *The Law of Charities*, Butterworths, 1977.

Ponting, Clive, *The Right to Know*, 1985.

The Press and the People, Press Council, 1987.

Press Conduct in the Sutcliffe Case, Press Council, 1983.

Raphael, Adam, *My Learned Friends*, W. H. Allen, 1989.

Reform of the Law Relating to Copyright, Designs and Performers' Protection: A Consultative Document, HMSO, 1981.

Report of the Committee on Privacy and Related Matters, HMSO, 1990, Cmnd 1102.

Report of the Joint Committee on Censorship of the Theatre, HMSO, 1967.

Richardson, P. J., *et al.*, *Archbold Pleading Evidence and Practice in Criminal Cases*, 44th edn, Sweet & Maxwell, 1991.

Roberts and Guelff, *Documents on the Laws of War*, Clarendon Press, 1982.

Robertson, Geoffrey, *People Against the Press*, Quartet Books, 1983.

Robertson, Geoffrey, *Freedom, the Individual and the Law*, Penguin, 1989.

Robertson, Geoffrey, *Obscenity*, Weidenfeld & Nicolson, 1979.

Robertson, K. G., *Public Secrets: A Study of the Development of Government Secrecy*, Macmillan, 1982.

Rolph, C. H., *The Trial of Lady Chatterley*, commem. edn, Penguin, 1990.

Root, Jane, *Open the Box*, Comedia, 1986.

St John Stevas, Norman, *Obscenity and the Law*, Secker & Warburg, 1956.

Schlesinger, Philip, *Putting Reality Together*, Constable, 1978.

Schmid, Alex and de Graff, Jenny, *Violence as Communication: Insurgent Terrorism and the News Media*, Sage, 1982.

Scorer, Catherine and Hewitt, Patricia, *The Prevention of Terrorism Act: The Case for Repeal*, NCCL 1981.

Skone James, E. P., *et al.*, *Copinger and Skone James on Copyright*, Sweet & Maxwell, 1991.

Smith, Anthony, *British Broadcasting*, David Charles, 1974.

Stack, Robert, *Libel, Slander and Related Problems*, Practicing Law Institute, 1980.

Stammers, Neil, *Civil Liberties in Britain during World War Two*, Croom Helm, 1983.

Supperstone, Michael, *Brownlie's Law relating to Public Order and National Security*, 2nd edn, Butterworths, 1981.

Thornton, Peter, *The Civil Liberties of the Zircon Affair*, NCCL, 1987.

Trevelyan, John, *What the Censor Saw*, Michael Joseph, 1973.

Tunstall, Jeremy, *Journalists at Work*, Constable, 1971.

Unfair Publication, Australian Law Reform Commission, 1979.

Violence and the Media, BBC Publications, 1988.

Walker, Sally, *The Law of Journalism in Australia*, Law Book Co., 1989.

Watson, John, *The Juvenile Courts, 1971 Onwards*, Shaw and Sons, 1971.

Whitford Report: see *Copyright and Designs Law*.

Williams, D. G. T., *Not in the Public Interest*, Hutchinson, 1965.

Williams Report: *see under* Home Office.

Wootton Report: *see* Advisory Committee on Drug Dependence.

Young, Hugo, *The Crossman Affair*, Hamish Hamilton and Jonathan Cape, 1976.

Young, Tom, *Incitement to Disaffection*, Cobden Trust, 1976.

Index

adoption proceedings 331
advertising
  broadcasting standards 639–41
  obscene 133
Advertising Standards Authority
  code of decency 559
  function 559
  power of 519
animals
  broadcasting standards 619
  films, in 584–5
Anton Piller orders 255–7, 320
appeals, hearings in camera 320
Attorney-General
  advance vetting 34–5
  contempt prosecutions, injunctions
    and 69–70
  discretion to prosecute in public
    interest cases 33
  injunction applications 13–14
  references; reporting restrictions 338
  stage plays, consent to prosecute 144

blasphemy 160–5
  abolition, proposals for 163–4
  defects in law 161–2
  defence to 161
  films, in 589–90
  literary or artistic value 162
  newspaper prosecutions 161
  offence defined 160
  public-good defence, absence of
    162–3
  religions 162–4
  Satanic Verses, and 163–4
breach of confidence
  civil remedy 173
  'delivery up' orders 178
  injunctions to prevent 13, 20–1, 177–
    8; interim 190–4; plaintiff 190;
    procedure 190–4; rule against prior
    restraint not applicable 69
  public domain 188–9
  public-interest defence 173, 177–8,
    183–7

  security services 188–9, 192–4
British Board of Film Classification
  564–8
  advising local authorities 135
  animals 584–5
  blasphemy 589–90
  censorship powers 13, 32, 64, 106,
    583–93
  child actors 132–3, 586
  criminal techniques 585–6
  drug-taking 585
  jurisdiction 583–4
  sexual violence 588–9
  violence 586–8
  see also films
British Broadcasting Corporation
  appointments to Board of Governors
    28
  Code of Practice 625–9
  editorializing 638
  listed events 631–2
  obscenity, and 105
  political pressures 626–7
  programme rules 627–9
  religion 638–9
broadcasting
  advance notice rule 551
  copyright in 224–6, 233, 249–51
  elections *see* election reporting
  government bans 26–8
  government patronage 28–9
  press conglomerates, and 506–7
  programme schedules 230–2
  public-good defence 121
  qualified privilege, statutory rights
    92–3
  racial hatred, inciting by 168
  regulation 594–9
  right of reply 552
  satellite 648–52
  standards 599–612; enforcement 603–
    6; impartiality 601–2, 620–3;
    obscenity 599–600; statutory duties
    600–606. *see also* Broadcasting
    Standards Council

broadcasting – *cont*
  words in permanent form 101n.
  see also Independent Television
    Commission; television
Broadcasting Complaints Commission
  (BCC) 519–21
  adjudications 31, 558–9
  appointments to 28
  complainants 554–6
  formation of 545–6
  function of 547
  privacy, unwarranted invasion of
    553–4
  procedure 556–8
  structure 546–8
  unjust or unfair treatment 548–53
Broadcasting Standards Council 606–12
  adjudications 608–9
  appointments to 28
  challenging decisions of 610–11
  Code of Practice 612–23; accuracy
    620–3; advertising 639–41; crime
    or disorder, encouragement of 615–
    17; drink and drugs 619; offending
    against good taste or decency 613–
    15; privacy 619–20; violence 618–19;
    watershed hour 612–13
  enforcement powers 605, 624–52;
    British Broadcasting Corporation
    625–9; cable television 646–8;
    editorializing 638; European
    Convention on Transfrontier
    Television 641–3; government
    controls 629–32; ITC
    licences *see* Independent
    Television Commission; Radio
    Authority 644–6; religion 638–9;
    satellite broadcasting 648–52
  functions of 547, 606–7
  good taste, and 106
  procedure on complaints 607, 610
building societies 510
business, reporting
  building societies 510
  co-operatives 509–10
  companies *see* companies
  consumer credit 515
  insolvency 516–18
  investment business 513–14
  financial journalists 514, 542
  nationalized industries 510–11
  partnerships 509
  restrictive practices 515–16

care proceedings, reporting
  restrictions in 331

censorship, growth of 2–3
chambers hearings 320–3
  adjournment to open court 322–3
  exclusion of press 16, 320–3
charities
  accounts 512
  advertising standards 559
  companies as 512
  lack of oversight 512–13
  privileges 511
  registration requirements 511–12
  types of 512
Charter 88 8
children
  actors 132–3, 586
  broadcasting standards, and 599–600
  cinemas, admission to 567–8
  indecent displays 151
  interviewing 620
  obscenity, and 129–33
  photographs: Code of Practice on 534;
    indecent 130–3
  reporting restrictions 331–2
  television viewing hours 612–13
  video standards, and 570–1
  witnesses in sex cases 17, 329, 534
  see also juveniles
Church courts 373–4, 384
cinemas
  limitations on prosecution of 136–7
  see also films
civil servants *see* Whitehall reporting
co-operatives 509–10
committal proceedings
  reporting 16
  reporting restrictions 314, 324–6
  lifting 325–6
communication
  freedom of 1–37
companies
  borrowings 489
  broadcasting and press conglomerates
    506–7
  capital 488
  charitable 512
  Department of Trade and Industry
    (DTI) investigations 507–9
  directors 489; contracts of service 493;
    dealings in own company's shares
    492–3; interests in company con-
    tracts 494; other directorships 494
  economic performance: accounts to be
    published 494–5; auditors 496;
    directors' report 496–7; non-
    compliance penalties 497–8; public
    share issue 497

insolvency 516–18
major shareholdings in other
companies 492
meetings 500–501
ownership and control 489–92;
beneficial 491–2; investigations by
company 491–2; nominee
shareholdings 490; share registers
489–90; 3-per-cent holdings
490–1
press monopolies 502–6
public 488
public documents, inspection of 498–
500
registration 487–8
take-overs 501–2
see also business, reporting
computers
printouts, seizure of 207
see also data protection
confidence
breach of *see* breach of confidence
obligation of 174–6; contractual
relationships 176–9; documents
subject to discovery 183; domestic
relationships 179–81; government
confidences 181–3
original ideas 194–6
see also privacy
conspiracy to injure 46–8
consumer credit 515
contempt of court
active legal proceedings 382
advantages of law 263
for breach of injunction 23
chambers hearings 321–2
change of law 6
courts, relevance of 268–71
defences 281–4; fair and accurate
reports 284; innocent distributors
283–4; public-interest 281–3
deliberate 285–95; ambit of 285–6;
frustrating court orders 293–5;
intent to prejudice 291–2;
intentionally prejudicing potential
trials 286–93; mistake as defence
292
delivery up orders, tampering with
documents 178
examples of 271–8; anticipating course
of trial 272–3; criticizing decision to
prosecute 272; defendants'
convictions and life-style 273–
5; defendants' photographs 275;
payments into court revealed 277;
witnesses' stories 276

free press, and 261–2
gagging writs 284–5
inquests 372
jurors: identifying 277; influencing
268; interviewing 13; publishing
deliberations 299–300; treatment of
266–7
meaning of 265
Mental Health Review Tribunals 376,
385
onus of proof 265
open justice, and 15–16
procedure 302–4
punishment for 262, 302–4
rationale 261–2
scandalizing the court 296–9
silence as 197 and n.
strict liability 264–85; courts,
relevance of 268–71; *see also*
defences
sub judice period 278–81; appeals
280–1; civil proceedings 279–80;
commencement of 278–9;
termination of 280
television coverage 277–8
triable by judge alone 12–13
'trial by media' 263–4
tribunals 386
types of 264–5
contempt of Parliament 395–401
contract
confidences protected by 176–9
copyright
Berne Copyright Convention 225
categories of 214
criminal offences 258–60
defences 215; artistic work, special use
of 249; broadcasts and cable 249–50;
contemporaneous notes of speaker
248; fair dealing 235–9; immorality
241–2; incidental inclusion 247;
judicial proceedings 248; licences
242–50; parliamentary proceedings
248; public administration 248;
public interest 239–40; public
reading 249; scientific or technical
articles, abstracts of 249
effect of law 213
existence of 214–15; artistic works 222;
broadcasts 224–5; cable programmes
224–5; films 223–4; news stories
219–21; original works 216–19;
programme formats 219–21;
published editions 221–2; sound
recordings 223; territorial
connection 225–6

copyright – *cont*
  format rights 221
  infringement of: adaptation 233–4;
    authorizing infringement 234–5;
    broadcast or cable, by 233;
    computer discs 233; derivation 232–
    3; literary, dramatic, musical or
    artistic works 226–8; photography,
    by 233; programme schedules 230–2;
    public performance 234; publication
    234; secondary infringement 235;
    substantial part 228–30; transient
    233
  injunction against breach 13
  moral rights 216, 250–3; categories of
    250–1; derogatory treatment 252–3;
    identification as author or director
    251
  multiple 214
  other rights infringed 215
  ownership of 215
  passing off 216
  performance rights 253–5
  perpetual 214
  photographs, private 208–9
  prior restraint, rule against 173
  remedies for breach 255–8; account of
    profits 258; damages 208, 257–8;
    delivery up of copies 258; disclosure,
    compulsory 255–7; search warrants
    255–7
  symbol 214
  television piracy 194–6
  tribunal 245–7
  Universal Copyright Convention 214,
    225
corrupting public morals 155–7
court reports
  accuracy 341
  anonymity orders 320
  church courts 373–4, 384
  contemporaneous 341
  courts martial 372–3, 384
  dramatic reconstructions 361
  Immigration Appeal Tribunals 374–5
  industrial tribunals 374–5
  information gathering 350–62;
    affidavits 354–5; court record 353–4;
    criminal proceedings, documents in
    358–9; discovered documents 355–8;
    outline of facts 350–1; photographs
    359–60; pleadings 354–5; skeleton
    arguments 352–3; sketches 359–60;
    tape recording 351–2; televising
    360–2; transcripts 352–3; witness
    statements 351; writs 354–5

inquests 368–72
lesser courts 367–8, 382–6; libel 387–
  9; *see also* individual courts and
  tribunals
libel, protection from 362–6
licensing applications 377, 386
media rights 306
Mental Health Review Tribunals
  375–7
open-justice principle 305–8
planning inquiries 377–8
postponement orders 312, 320, 341–5,
  385; challenging 345–50
press bench 306, 310
privilege 307
'proceedings' 344
professional bodies, disciplinary
  hearings of 378
public inquiries 379–80
reporting restrictions: Attorney-
  General's references 338; breach
  triable by magistrates 13; categories
  308; European Convention on
  Human Rights, and 8–9, 307; family
  cases 329–36 indecent evidence 338;
  lifting of 325–6; prosecutions for
  breach 330–1; rape cases 336–7;
  remands and committal hearings
  324–6; requests for anonymity 335;
  serious fraud 326–7; *see also* courts,
  public access to
secrecy orders: appeals 347–50;
  challenging partial 345–50; judicial
  review 346–7; publication in
  defiance of 346; revocation,
  application for 346; section 11 338–
  41
tribunals 367–8, 380
victims of crime, identifying 534–6
courts, public access to 309–22
  appeals 320
  commercial secrets 316
  committal proceedings 314
  court lists, availability of 310
  disorder in court 323
  family cases 316–19
  Haldane exception 311
  'in chambers' hearings 320–3
  indecency of evidence 318
  interlocutory proceedings 310–11
  magistrates' names 309–10
  official secrets proceedings 315–16
  possession actions 319
  principle of 309–10
  private secrets 316
  public interest, exclusion in 310–16

secrecy applications 313
voluntary bills of indictment 314–15
youth courts 318
see also contempt of court; court
   reports
courts martial 372–3, 384
crime
   broadcasting standards 615–17
   victims of 534
   see also witnesses
criminal convictions 77–9
criminal libel 99–102
   alternative proceedings 101
   dead, of 101
   leave for 101
   private prosecutions 99–100
   proposed replacement of 102
   public-benefit defence 100
   requirements for 100
Croham Directive 457–8
customs offences 135, 153–5

D-notices 26, 435–7
damages
   breach of copyright 208, 257–8
   defamation, for 43–6, 96–8
data protection 209
defamation
   apologies 61–5, 94–5; disowning 62;
     failure to give 73; statement in open
     court 63
   attributed quotations 64
   burden of proof 41
   class, of 57
   complexity of law 41–2
   costs 39, 43–6
   court reports: absolute privilege 363–
     5, 387; qualified privilege 365–6
   criminal convictions 77–9
   criminal libel *see* criminal libel
   damages 96–8; aggravated 96; punitive
     97
   damages awards 43–6, 96–8; appeals
     against 44–5; payments into court
     45
   defences: apology 94–5; burden of proof
     70–1; consent 94; contingent on
     findings of fact 42–3; fair comment
     79–85; innocent dissemination 66–7;
     justification 73–9; limitation 95;
     malice, meaning of 71–3, 83–4;
     privilege *see* privilege; 'public figure'
     (USA) 65, 103; truth 40–1
   defendants 61; avoiding responsibility
     61–5; publishers 64; trade unions
     61; unincorporated associations 61

definition: conspiracy to injure
   distinguished 46–8; context,
   importance of 48; defamatory
   innuendo 53; malicious falsehood
   distinguished 46–8; meaning tried
   as preliminary issue 53; 'ordinary
   reader' test 49–53; test of
   defamatory meaning 46
delays 42
discovery of documents 76
essentials of 40
failures of law 103
false statements not necessarily
   libellous 40
foreign publications 65–6
foreigners, English courts used by
   65–6
identity of informants 63
imputation, by 58
jury trial 98–9; inconsistencies of 42–
   3
law reform, proposed 103–4
legal aid, absence of 39–40, 64, 102
libel: reports of proceedings in lesser
   courts 387; slander distinguished
   53–4; waiver of rights on complaint
   to Press Complaints Commission
   527–8; *see also* criminal libel
local government reporting, in
   480–2
opinion *see above* defences, fair
   comment
plaintiffs: companies 56; dead 55–6;
   financial backing for 54–5; groups
   57; identifying 57–8; local
   authorities 56; trade unions 56;
   unintentionally defamed 58–60
press advantages 39–41
press disadvantages 41–6
prior restraint, rule against 24, 67–70
publication: authorization of 63;
   innocent dissemination 66–7; off
   the record remarks 63; printers 67
publishers' indemnities 64
repetition 64, 95
sources, protection of 197–8
uncertainty of law 42–3
unintentional 58–60
see also journalists
Director of Public Prosecutions
   consent to prosecute films 136
   obscenity trials, and 107, 110
   seizure, consent to 119
disaffection, incitement to 448–50
   law reform 450
disorderly house, keeping 159

divorce *see* family cases
drink
    broadcasting standards 619
drugs
    broadcasting standards 619
    films, in 585
    obscenity, as 126–8

ecclesiastical courts 373–4, 384
election reporting
    advertisements 404–5
    broadcasting 405–10; balance 407;
        candidate's veto 406–7; ministerial
        broadcasts 409–10; party political
        broadcasts 407–9
    injunctions 403–4
    meetings, access to 410
    register, access to 410
    returns, access to 410
ESTACODE 458
European Community
    information from 442–3
    television: Convention on
        Transfrontier Television 641–3;
        coordination of 611
European Convention on Human
        Rights
    background to 3
    blasphemy, and 164
    British law, status in 3–4, 7, 8–9
    composition of Court 9
    contempt of court justified under 262
    criticism of public figures 89–90
    delay under 10
    drawbacks 10
    freedom of expression, principle of 4–
        5, 596–7
    journalists, use by 7–8
    judges' attitude 9
    prior restraint, and 21–2
    proportionality 5
    remedies under 3–4
    seizure of obscene material 134
eviction orders, exclusion of press from
        hearings on 16
expression, freedom of
    cases on 6–10
    European Convention on Human
        Rights 4–5
    meaning 1–3

family cases
    adoption proceedings 331
    care proceedings 331
    ouster injunctions 332

private, heard in 316–19
    reporting restrictions 329–36
    wardship proceedings 332–6
films
    censorship 13, 32, 64, 106, 135–7,
        564–6; history 566–9; local council
        licensing 569–72; sex cinema clubs
        571
    classification *see* British Board of Film
        Classification
    copyright in 223–4
    limitations on prosecution 136–7
    local authority licensing 135
    public good defence 120–1, 137
    sex cinemas 106
    target audience 119–20
    see also videos
forfeiture proceedings 105, 125, 134,
        155, 169
free speech
    meaning of 1–2
    restraints on 2–3

government
    confidences, protection of 181–3; *see
        also* Official Secrets Acts
    interference: broadcasting controls
        26–8, 629–32; D-notices 26;
        patronage 28–9; political pressures
        25–6, 629–32; theatre and film
        censorship 32; *see also* Independent
        Television Commission
    reporting *see* Whitehall reporting

homosexuality and corruption of public
        morality 157
horror publications, as obscenity 129

ICSTIS (Independent Committee for
        the Supervision of Standards of
        Telephone Information Services)
        561–3
ideas, protection of 194–6
Immigration Appeal Tribunals 374–5
'in chambers' hearings
    divulging details of 321–2
    pre-trial reviews 322
indecency
    broadcasting standards 613–15
    community standards 149–50
    copyright, and 241–2
    obscenity distinguished 158
    offences 150–5; customs 153–5; public
        display 151–2; telephone messages
        152–3; using the post 150–1

reform of law 165–7
test of 148–50
Independent Broadcasting Authority
  power to stop broadcasts 13
  see also Independent Television
    Commission
Independent Television Commission
    29–52, 594–9
  companies' licences 29
  duties 31, 601, 605
  government appointments 631
  licences 632–7; allocation system 632–
    5; fit and proper persons 635–6;
    penalties 636–7
  listed events 631–2
  obscenity, and 105
  powers over programmes 29–30
industrial tribunals 374
injunctions
  balance of convenience cases 24–5
  binding third parties 23
  breach of confidence, as ground for
    13, 20–1, 190–4; procedure 190–4;
    rule against prior restraint not
    applicable 69, 173; undertaking to
    pay compensation 191
  conspiracy to injure cases 47–8
  copyright, breach of 13, 255–8
  delaying tactics, as 34–5
  disclosures in breach of contract 177–
    8
  exclusion of press from hearings 16
  fair trial, to prevent prejudice to 69–
    70
  interim 13, 21, 190–4; permanence of
    173; privacy protection, for 173–4
  jury's role, courts' reluctance to usurp
    113–14
  libel actions: infringing European
    Convention on Human Rights 24;
    rule against prior restraint
    67–70
  malicious falsehood cases 47–8
  pre-publication *see* prior restraint,
    rule against
  public-interest test 21
  see also prior restraint, rule against
inquests 368–72
  in camera 371–2
  contempt, applicability of 372
  jury verdicts 370–1
insolvency 516–18
intellectual property
  self-incrimination in proceedings
    concerning 204
investment business 513–14

journalists
  chequebook 174, 186, 536–40, 627
  code of conduct 521
  financial *see* business, reporting
  NUJ Code of Conduct 196, 563
  police powers over 415
  political pressure on 626–7
  public interest defence 183–7
  secrecy orders, application for
    revocation 346
  sources, protection of 63, 69, 196–209;
    courts and 198–205; delivery up
    orders, risks of 178; NUJ Code of
    Conduct 196; plaintiffs in libel
    actions 197–8; police and other
    investigations 196–7; police powers
    of search and seizure 205–8; Press
    Complaints Commission Code of
    Practice 542
  special protection 17–18, 207
judicial proceedings, reports not
    copyright 248
judicial review
  secrecy orders, of 346–7
  terrorists' statements, banning of 9
jury trial 10–14
  contempt to cause discharge of jury
    33, 358–9
  interviewing jurors 13
  jury-vetting orders 322
  libel cases 42–3, 98–9
  liberal interpretation of press laws
    12
  media offences not triable by 12–13
  obscenity cases 12
  public-interest defence 11
  qualification for jury service 11
  right to demand 10–11
  usurpation of role 13–14
juveniles
  adult courts, in 328
  anonymity of offenders 16
  murder victims 328–9
  reporting restrictions 318, 327–9
  youth courts 327–8

legal aid
  absence of in libel cases 39–40, 64,
    102
  malicious falsehood, for 47
  undertaking for compensation 192n.
libel *see* criminal libel; defamation;
    seditious libel
licensing applications 377, 386
limitation of actions for defamation 95
lobby system *see* parliamentary reports

local authorities
  cinema licensing 569–72
  indecency, control of 152, 166
  libel of 56
  wardship powers, reporting of 333,
    334
local government, reporting
  admission rights 462–9; agendas 467–
    8; caucuses 463–4; committees and
    subcommittees 463–4; council
    meetings 462–3; limitations on
    464–6; reporting facilities 468–9;
    secrecy motions 464–6
  inspection of documents 469–80;
    accounts 469–71; annual reports
    478–9; audits 471; education 477–8;
    housing 477; land ownership 479–
    80; local ombudsmen 475; local
    parliamentary bills 475–6; minutes
    471–2; planning 474–5; poll tax
    473–4; pollution control 476–7;
    rates 473–4; rating records 471–2;
    register of councillors 471–2;
    reports 471–2; social services 477–8
  leaks 480
  libel 480–2
  media duties 461–2
  sponsored publications 482–4; clause
    28 restrictions 483–4

magistrates' courts
  administrative bodies, as 377, 385
  committal proceedings, ban on
    reporting 16
  family proceedings, press not
    excluded 17
  names of justices 15
  offences triable in 13
malice
  meaning of 71–3, 83–4
malicious falsehood 46–8
marriage secrets 179–81
Mental Health Review Tribunals 375–7,
  385
messages, indecent or offensive 170
ministerial memoirs 438–9
moral rights *see* copyright
mutiny, incitement to 448–50

national security
  breach of confidence cases 188–9,
    192–4
  broadcasting bans 26–7
  disclosure of sources in interests of
    201–2

exclusion of press 16, 18
  prior restraint, rule against 20
National Union of Journalists (NUJ),
  Code of Conduct 196, 563
nationalized industries 510–11
newspapers
  advertisers' pressure 486
  agendas of councils 467
  blasphemy prosecutions 161
  broadcasting and press conglomerates
    506–7
  complaints against *see* Press
    Complaints Commission
  contempt, advice on 267
  information obtained by covert means
    175–6, 178
  press monopolies 502–6
  privacy, self-regulation 175
  public interest defence 183–7
  reporting powers 388
  see also journalists; press; privacy
nuclear secrets 432–3

obscenity
  advertisements 133
  broadcasting standards 599–600
  child involvement 129–33
  common-law offences 155–60;
    exposure to 158–60
  compact discs and 110
  corrupting public morals 155–7
  definition 110–11
  drugs and 126–7
  expert evidence 123–4
  exported 119–20
  forfeiture proceedings 105, 125,
    134
  history of 106–10
  horror publications 129
  indecency distinguished 158
  laws relating to 105–6
  literary merit defence 108–10
  penalties 133–5
  in private 133
  procedures 133–5
  prohibited acts 119–20
  prosecution practice 125–6
  public-good defence 118, 120–3; 'in
    interests of' 121; 'science,
    literature, art or learning' 121–2;
    'other objects of general concern'
    123
  reform of law 165–7
  stage plays *see* theatres, censorship
  test of 107–8, 110–18; aversion
    defence 112–13; contemporary

standards test 118; dominant-effect
principle 115–16; publisher's
intentions 116–17; 'sexually
explicit' distinguished 112, 113;
significant proportion test 115;
target audience 113–14; tendency to
deprave and corrupt 111–12
video-cassettes 136–7
violence, and 128
see also indecency
Official Secrets Acts
1911 Act: penalties for spying 428–30;
purpose of 414–15; s 2 discredited
415–18
1989 Act: insiders' offences 418–23;
outsiders' offences 423–8
civil service disclosures; memoirs
439–40
D-notices 435–7
European Community 442–3
exclusion of public and press from
trials 16, 316
growth of 412–14
military censorship 452–6
ministerial memoirs 438–9
mutiny and disaffection, incitement to
447–50
Northern Ireland 443–6
nuclear 432–3
police powers 430–2; arrest 430–1;
judicial questioning 431–2;
proceedings 432; questioning 431;
search 430–1
public records 440–2
radio eavesdropping 434–5
sedition 447
statutory offences 433–4
telephone tapping 434–5
treason 446–7
war reporting 450–2
open justice
exceptions 16
names of justices 15
principle of 14–15
ouster injunctions 332

Parliament
contempt of 395–401
MPs' conflicts of interest 401–3
privilege *see* privilege
reporting *see* parliamentary reports
televising 395
parliamentary reports
copyright, absence of 248
lobby system 390–9
privilege 391–5

partnerships 509
passing off 216
photographs
court, in 359–60
defendants, of 275
indecent, of children 130–3;
legitimate reason defence 132;
possessing 133
juveniles, of 327–8
private, copyright in 208–9
rape victims 336
right to, in public place 209–10
planning inquiries 377–8
plays *see* theatres
police
Official Secrets Acts powers 430–2
records of spent offences 78
search and seizure powers: excluded
material 205; special procedure
material 205–7; other material 207–
8
Theatres Act 1968, powers under 141
possession actions, private hearings 319
post, indecent material sent through
147, 150–1
postponement orders 312, 320, 341–5,
385
challenging 345–50
lesser courts and tribunals 385–6
Practice Direction limiting 344–5
press
bench 18
exclusion from Official Secrets trials
16, 316
freedom of 1–3, 36
'representing public' 17–18
see also journalists; newspapers
Press Complaints Commission (PCC)
36, 40, 519–21
Code of Conduct: chequebook
journalism 536–40; discrimination
540–1; financial journalism 542;
non-criminal informants 540
Code of Practice 527, 529–42; accuracy
and fairness 529–30; children, as to
534; grief and shock, intrusions into
533–4; harassment 531–2; hospitals
533; misrepresentation 531; privacy
531; right to reply duty 530; victims
of crime 534–6
complaints procedure 528–9
formation 526
ineffectiveness of 542–5
Press Council, history of 521–4;
Calcutt report 524–6; sanctions,
lack of 523–4; wound up 526

Press Council – *cont*
  structure of 527–8
pretrial reviews 322
printers' liability for libel 198 and n.
prior restraint, rule against
  Attorney-General's role and 34
  breach of confidence cases 173
  contemporary position 20–5
  and contractual agreements 24
  copyright cases 173
  historical development 19–20
  libel actions 24, 67–70; affidavit of
    intention to justify 69
  see also injunctions
privacy
  Broadcasting Complaints
    Commission (BCC), and 553–4
  broadcasting standards 619–20
  criminal sanctions for breach,
    recommendation for 211–12
  domestic 179–81
  indirect protection 174
  intrusion and publication
    distinguished 532
  invasion of (proposed tort) 543
  Press Complaints Commission Code
    of Practice on 531–6
  protection of 3
  public interest in disclosure 172
  remedies for breach of 210–12
  right to, absence of 40–1, 173–4, 519–
    21, 526
  stolen information 175
  television camera on private land
    210
  trespass as breach of 210–11
  US law 211–12
  see also confidence
privilege
  absolute 86, 363–5, 387
  parliamentary 391–5
  qualified: Broadcasting Act 1990,
    under 92–3; common interest 87;
    court reports 91, 321, 365–6, 387–8;
    fair information on a matter of
    public interest 88–9; investigative
    journalists, for 87–90; malice
    negating 71–2, 86; parliamentary 91;
    parliamentary reports 394–5; public
    figure doctrine (US) 90, 103; public
    interest 86–7; public occasions 91–
    3; right of reply 90–1, 92–3
professional bodies, disciplinary
  hearings of 378
prosecution policy and public interest
  33–5

public decency, conspiracy to outrage
  157–8
public domain 188–9
public inquiries 379–80
public interest
  defence 183–7
  prosecution policy and 33–5
public morals, corrupting 155–7
public records 440–2

race hatred
  broadcasting, inciting by 168
  counterproductivity of laws 169–70
  defences 169
  forfeiture orders 169
  journalists' code of conduct 540–2
  laws against 167–8
  meaning 168
  messages, indecent or offensive 170
  possessing inflammatory material
    168–9
  prosecutions, paucity of 170
  racial groups, and 168
  stereotyping 615
  theatres, in 168
radio
  censoring 137–8
  eavesdropping 434–5
  pirates 645–6
  see also broadcasting
Radio Authority 644–6
  appointments to 28
rape
  anonymity of victims 17
  reporting restrictions 336–7
registers, public 516
  companies *see* companies
regulatory bodies, pre-censoring
    by 13
religion
  broadcasting standards on 615, 638–9
  see also blasphemy
remand hearings, reporting restrictions
    324–6
restrictive practices 515–16

satellite broadcasting 648–52
search warrants
  police powers 207
  private (*Anton Piller* orders) 255–8,
    320
secrecy
  commercial secrets cases, private
    hearings 316
  orders *see* court reports

seditious libel 170–1
  definition 447
  distributing books 170–1
  violence against state 170
serious fraud, reporting restrictions
  326–7
sex
  broadcasting standards 614–15
  cinemas 106; local authority control
    135, 152, 166; video classification
    579
  offences, press not excluded 17
  shops: local authority control 152,
    166–7; planning applications 474–5;
    video sales 579–80
slander *see* defamation
Society of Authors 108
stage plays *see* theatres

tape recording court proceedings 351–2
telephones
  indecent messages 152–3
  tapping of 175, 434–5
television
  cable 646–8; certified films on 106
  camera on private land as trespass
    210–11
  censoring 137–8
  court proceedings 360–2
  criminal trials, coverage of 277–9
  European 611, 641–3
  Independent Television Commission
    594–9
  obscenity controls 106
  parliamentary proceedings 395
  piracy 194–6
  public-good defence 121
  publishing by 119
  satellite 648–52
  tribunal hearings 381–2
  see also broadcasting; Broadcasting
    Complaints Commission
terrorism
  broadcasting censorship 7, 9, 27, 31,
    445–6, 629–30
  demonstrations, reporting 444
  duty to provide information on 617
  information of use to terrorists 443–4
  prevention of 444–5
  television coverage of trials 277–9
theatres
  censorship 32, 138–47; evidence 143–
    4; plays defined 139–41; police
    powers, limits on 141; prosecution,
    liability for 142–3; public-good

    defence 141; *Romans in Britain*
    prosecution 144–7
  public-good defence 120–1
  racial hatred in 168
trade unions, libel not actionable by 56
treason 446–7
trespass, privacy and 210–11
tribunals
  contempt of court 386
  reporting 367–8, 380
  televising 381–2

United States of America
  First Amendment 1
  Freedom of Information Acts 459–60

videos
  advent of 572–5
  censorship 565–6
  DPP's list 573
  games 571–2
  obscenity, and 569, 572–5
  shops 106, 166
  statutory control 575–83; appeals
    committee 590–2; classification
    576–8; consequences of 582;
    exemptions 577–8; offences 576,
    580–1; packaging rules 581–2;
    sex-shop category 579–80
  see also British Board of Film
    Classification; films
violence
  broadcasting standards 618
  films, in 586–9
  obscenity, as 128
voluntary bills of indictment, heard in
  private 314–15

war reporting 450–6
  military censorship 452–6
  protection of correspondents 450–2
wardship proceedings
  reporting restrictions 332–6
Whitehall reporting
  civil service disclosures 456–8;
    Croham Directive 457–8;
    ESTACODE 458
  see also government; Official Secrets
    Acts
witnesses
  children in sex cases 17, 329, 534
  contempt of court, and 276–7
  payment for interviews 537–40

youth courts *see* juveniles